impasse of the angels

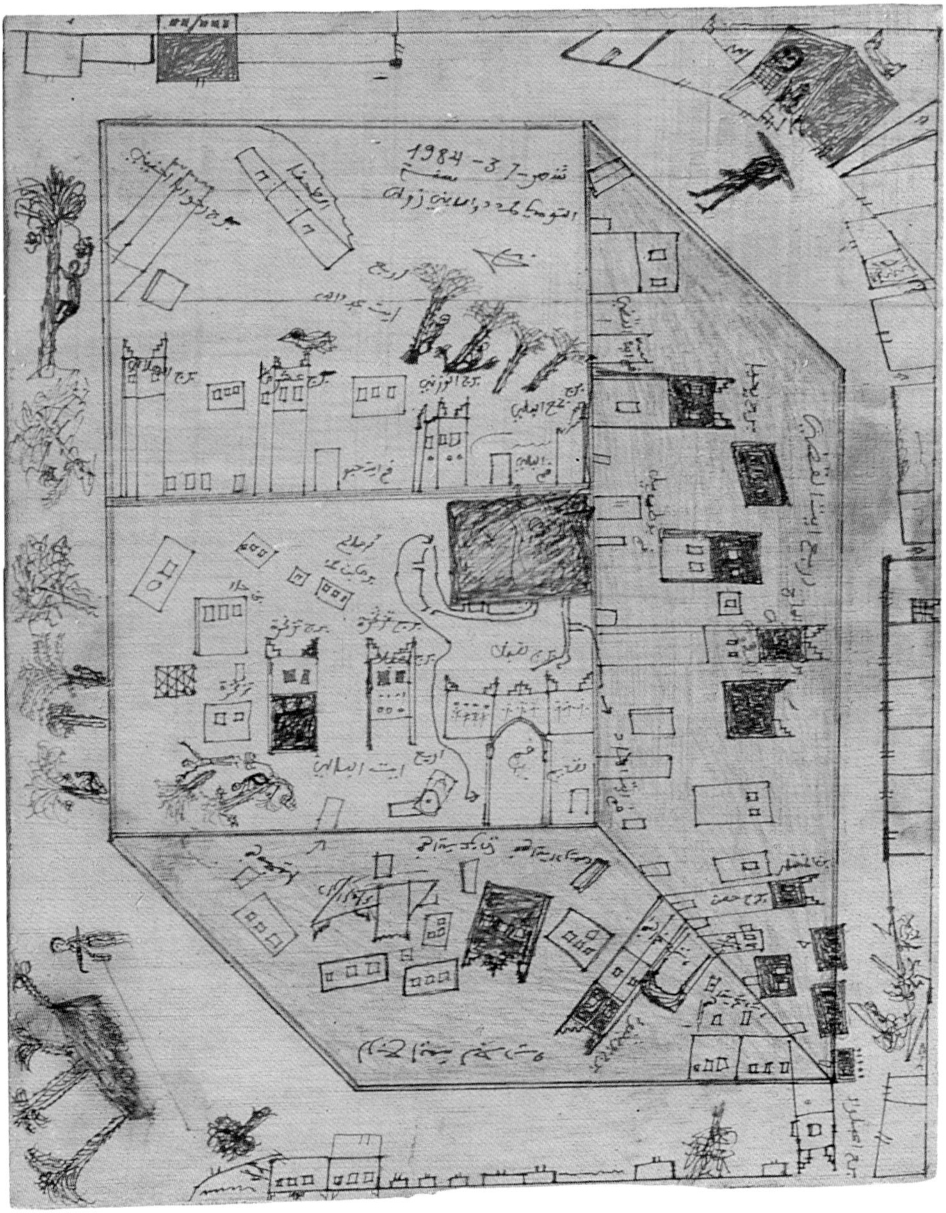
1984-3-7

Impasse of the Angels

Scenes from a Moroccan Space of Memory

stefania pandolfo

The University of Chicago Press
Chicago and London

Stefania Pandolfo is assistant professor of anthropology at the University of California, Berkeley.

The University of Chicago Press, Chicago 60637
The University of Chicago Press, Ltd., London

Printed in the United States of America
06 05 04 03 02 01 00 99 98 97 1 2 3 4 5

ISBN: 0-226-64531-2 (cloth)
ISBN: 0-226-64532-0 (paper)

Library of Congress Cataloging-in-Publication Data

Pandolfo, Stefania.
Impasse of the angels : scenes from a Moroccan space of memory / Stefania Pandolfo.
p. cm.
Includes index.
ISBN 0-226-64531-2 (cloth : alk. paper).—ISBN 0-226-64532-0 (pbk. : alk. paper).
1. Ethnology—Morocco—Dra Wadi. 2. Oral tradition—Morocco—Dra Wadi. 3. Discourse analysis, Narrative—Morocco—Dra Wadi. 4. Ethnopsychology—Morocco—Dra Wadi. 5. Dra Wadi (Morocco)—Social life and customs. I. Title.
GN649.M65P28 1997
305.8'00964—dc21 97-5473
CIP

∞ The paper used in this publication meets the minimum requirements of the American National Standard for Information Sciences—Permanence of Paper for Printed Library Materials, ANSI Z39.48-1984.

TO FOUCH,
and
TO YASSINE,
child of two worlds

The angel, then, brings a handful of earth from that grave yet to be in the cemetery of Tafetchna, and sprinkles that earth over that rotting stuff in the womb, like what you do when you sprinkle spices onto a soup. It is the earth of death. It triggers articulation and shrinking, and from that shrinking and separating out a human being is made.

—Ḥaddya Milûd

contents

part 3. Loss: The sphere of the moon

Note on Transcription

The Draʿ Valley is a multilingual environment. Two distinctive Arabic vernaculars, and Tashelḥit and Tamazight Berber, are currently spoken in a variety of local styles, with French and standard Arabic being introduced through television and schooling. Jewish Arabic and Hebrew were formerly spoken in most centers. Certain settlements are bilingual; in others Arabic, Tashelḥit, or Tamazight Berber are the dominant languages.

Most of the conversations and narratives on which this book is based were recorded in Arabic—often punctuated with Tashekḥit words. In the transcription of speech I have tried to follow as much as possible the actual pronunciation of words, attempting to convey the diversity and distinctive character of the vernacular idioms, while keeping the grammar visible and the syntax understandable. The outcome is necessarily a compromise. For the sake of readability I have chosen not to use a phonetic transcription, but one based on the regular English alphabet.

CONSONANTS

Arabic	Standard Transliteration	
أ	a	
ب	b	
ت	t	
ث	th	(pronounced as "t" in Moroccan Arabic, transcribed as "t" when spoken)
ج	j	
ح	ḥ	

خ	kh	
د	d	
ذ	dh	(pronounced as "ḍ" in Moroccan Arabic, transcribed as "d" when spoken)
ر	r	
ز	z	
س	s	
ش	sh	
ص	ṣ	
ض	ḍ	
ط	ṭ	
ظ	ẓ	(pronounced as "ḍ" in Moroccan Arabic, transcribed as "d" when spoken)
ع	c	
غ	gh	
ف	f	
ق	q	(sometimes pronounced as "g"; transcribed as "g" in these cases, when spoken)
ک	k	
ڭ	g	(this consonant exists only in written Moroccan Arabic)
ل	l	
م	m	
ن	n	
ه	h	
و	w	
ي	y	

VOWELS

Written arabic does not have vowels but only *ḥarakât,* "movements," and *ḥurûf al-madd,* or semivowels. A *ḥaraka,* or vowel movement, is a diacritic mark written above or under a consonant. The vowel movements are pronounced and transcribed as *a, i, u,* and are lengthened in the transcription as â, î, û. *Ḥurûf al-madd,* or semivowels, are ي *y,* and و *w.* They can be used either as lengthened vowel movements or as consonants, which then need a vowel movement to form a syllable. I transcribe semivowels as î and û, when they are treated in the word as lengthened movements, and as *y, w,* when they are treated as consonants. Compared to other Arabic vernaculars, in Moroccan Arabic vowel movements are hardly audible. This is why, to meet the Moroccan pronunciation, I introduced *e* and *o* in the transcription; *e* should be pronounced as a shorter *a,* and *o* as a shorter *u.*

A hyphen signals articulation between nouns and their affixes: articles, prepositions, and so on, which, in Arabic script, would be attached to the word. The most prominent example is the determinative article *al,* which in Moroccan Arabic is pronounced *l.* For example, *al-madîna* in standard Arabic is pronounced as *lmdîna* in Moroccan vernacular, and is transcribed here as *l-mdîna.*

Both in standard and Moroccan Arabic, when the determinative article is attached to consonants requiring the use of the front of the tongue, it is assimilated, doubling the sound of the consonant. In Moroccan Arabic the consonants involved are *t, j, d, r, z, sh, ṣ, ḍ, ṭ, l, n.* I have transcribed them as they are pronounced.

When the determinative article is prefixed to proper names, and pronounced as a part of the name, I have capitalized the first letter of the name in the transcription to highlight the name; thus, *l-Hashmî,* pronounced *Lhashmî.*

 is an Arabic calligraphy that reads *qîla,* "it was said."

INTRODUCTION

A *barzakh* is something that separates two things while never going to one side, as for example the line that separates shadow from sunlight. . . . There is nothing in existence but *barzakhs,* since a *barzakh* is the arrangement of one thing between two things . . . and existence has no edges.
—Ibn al-ʿArabî[1]

April 1984. Walking with a group of men through the village of Bû Zergân, Wâd Draʿ valley, southern Morocco. An official visit. Two engine pumps, the new cement canal, ramparts and towers, the old assembly room of the qbîla; *anodyne talk about different varieties of dates, the illness of* bayud *that kills the palm trees, and the henna prospering on this sandy soil. The group stops in front of a house adjoining the ramparts. A man points to a window with a light blue metalwork; "Qobtân Slimân used to sit in that room," he says. He asked the men of the community about the organization of the* qbîla, *the turns of irrigation, the alliances of the old days.* "Like you are asking us now." *The tone changes; I am directly implicated. Follows the story of Qobtân Slimân.*

It was before the French arrived in this region. A man came, a scholar from the east, a ṭâlib l-ʿilm *like the wandering scholars who journey across the world searching for knowledge. He traveled by foot, wore sandals and a djellaba, spoke eloquent Arabic, and was well learned in the Qur'an and the hadith. An Egyptian perhaps. From village to village he gained the confidence and friendship of all the men who counted. At some point he fell ill; his host, a man from the qṣar of Tanṣita, took care of him as of his own son. One day he said farewell and disappeared. Some time later he reappeared, in a different outfit; "high boots and military uniform." He was an officer in the French army.*

At the head of a convoy of military vehicles, armed men on foot and horseback, Qobtân Slimân led the French army south, on the left side of the riverbank. The convoy made its way through the palm groves. People watched, from the roofs of their homes. Some asked the spirits of the land to halt them, stick their trucks in the sand, and send them back; others said that perhaps the Christians' direct rule would put an end to the violence, the internecine wars, the massacres and murders, fueled by the manipulations of the Christians themselves.

They entered Zagora. It was, then, only a group of qṣûr, and a big open space with that tall pointed rock overlooking the valley. Corvées were called to build the French Bureau. Qobtân Slimân settled in the new headquarters. One day a man was brought to the bureau. He had been arrested for anti-French activities. Qobtân Slimân looked at him, stood up to greet him, and granted him immunity for as long as the French ruled over the land. It was l-Ḥajj from Tansita who had hosted him and saved his life. This is approximately what the men told me.

Qobtân Slimân. A narrative figure of the spirit of colonization, with its practice of *enquête*, its fascinations and deceptions, and its traps of identification and friendship: its betrayals. But also a local retelling of the life and works of Captain Georges Spillmann, a prominent actor in the French military and ethnological history of southern Morocco. In 1931, one year before the French occupation of Zagora, Spillmann (then a lieutenant) published a monograph, *Districts et tribus de la haute vallée du Draᶜ*, his second study dedicated to the social organization of that *région insoumise*.[2] In the preface to that work, he specified that the book was "the fruit of three years of research in the field."

Spillmann's monograph is a detailed ethnological map of the political and social organization of the central Draᶜ valley in terms of its population, ethnic composition, and social hierarchy. It includes what is almost a census of each village: for each qṣar, it specifies the tribal affiliation (*tribu*), and the ethnic origin of the inhabitants (*origine des qsouriens*); it indicates the number of families (*nombre de feux*, "fires"), the nomadic tribe, or tribal fraction, to which each qṣar is subjected by a pact of protection (*debiha*, in Arabic, literally "a pact sealed by a sacrifice"), and its internal form of government (*commandement*): whether the qṣar's political life is administered by a council of notables, and whether the function of sheikh rotates by the year.

Among the surveyed villages in the Commandement du Ternata is the qṣar. Spillmann notes: "*Tribu:* Ahl Telt and Drawa; *Origine des qsouriens:* Ahl Telt; *Debiha:* Aït Ounir; *Nombre de feux:* 350; *Commandement:* Cheikh el ʿam et jmaʿa." Or at least this is what the lieutenant filed in his report in 1930.[3]

Qobtân Sliman's story was addressed to me at the outset of fieldwork as an ironical warning, a challenge. A bait to catch or miss, Ḥadda will say much later. This book is an attempt to meet that challenge by exploring the possibility of an ethnography internally altered by the place and voice of others.

Impasse of the Angels is based on research in the Wâd Draʿ valley during the years 1984–86, 1989, 1990, and all the way to the present. On life, in fact. Speaking, listening, responding, arguing, interpreting, misunderstanding, feeling, remembering, imagining, sharing, reacting against; tape recording, listening again with others, writing, transcribing, writing again(...) The heterogeneous corpus of oral and visual narratives the book stages originates largely from one community and its vicinity, whose stories and histories are also the story of the book. (I generally refer to this locality as the *qṣar*, a style of reference preferred by the people themselves.)[4]

Yet the locality is also an *enunciative space*, a locus from which *acts of speech* originate (a *parole* that says more than what it says, in the sense of Benveniste and Lacan).[5] And even though in this text, made out of others' texts, topographic, toponymic, and historical references are precise and detailed (as often is the case with a local pictorial memory of spaces and names, bodies and landscapes), the place is not a referential entity, the geographical object of a description. Nor is it an objective map of verbal statements—utterances, narratives, or myths—that may as such become objects of knowledge. It is the dialogical space of a locution, at times a conversation, in which subject positions constitute and dissolve themselves in discourse, and in which, between past and future, "words frozen by time" are recycled as voice, once again.[6] The saying overflows the content of its utterances, exceeds fixed territorial boundaries; it migrates and errs. The path of that errancy is the moving space of this text.

> *L'acte de parole a plusieurs têtes, et, petit à petit, plante les éléments d'un peuple à venir comme le discours indirect libre de l'Afrique sur elle-même, sur l'Amérique ou sur Paris.*
>
> —Gilles Deleuze[7]

Impasse of the Angels is composed as a polyphonic dialogue of texts, spoken in voices other than my own. Narratives, conversations, poems, and a drawing, each with a specific personal accent and intonation, each with a slightly different scope.[8] Strung into three main thematic sections as different movements are enchained in a concerto, different scenes in a theatrical production, or independent stanzas in an Arabic poem, through effects of repetition and variation these texts *produce,* in the musical or poetical sense, the thematic and aesthetic unity of the work.

The voices: they are those of Yusef and Ḥadda, Ḥaddya Milûd and Um ʿAṣṣa, Si Lḥussein, Si Thami and l-Ḥajj l-Madanî, Si Lḥassan, Belqasem, and Sheikh Moḥammed the poet; and Kh., who died too soon. They speak, recount, criticize, interpret, theorize, tell stories. They may be called *intercessors,* borrowing a term from Deleuze. Real and nonfictional characters, actively inventing a people, rather than standing for it; inventing it through their act of speech. Real characters, pulling the text in multiple directions, shaping it, and contributing to its creation—which is also their own.[9]

My voice: in many cases one among the voices, that of an interlocutor who is herself a character in a larger play. In places it occupies what might be called an authorial space in the margins (graphically signaled by a change of font or indentation), a space of after-the-fact reflection, translation, or commentary, but one that never attempts to extricate itself from the circumstantial turns of the text. For, as a result of what Deleuze calls a "double becoming"—a becoming related to a certain doubling, that of the author into the characters, and of the characters into the authorial voice—the author is displaced, by the impact of the characters' real life and speech. And through the creative act of telling and interpreting, the characters are also displaced—they are no longer their quotidian selves. For both, there is a becoming other, and an exchange of voices and parts—an exit from oneself that is the glimmering of a beyond.

On the trail of imaginary forms, in the way these come to constitute the present, the book explores what it means to be a subject in the historical and poetic imagination of the qṣar society—in the voice, through the stories and individual reflections, of the men and women who take the floor in the text.

Subject: I use the term in the sense of the always implicated and transactional "I" of psychoanalysis and linguistics, and not as an autonomous and self-mastering subject of consciousness, or as an interiority that would be the private space of individual perception. It is a subject inscribed in a network of symbolic debts, and defined in relation to that Other Scene[10] Freud and Lacan call the unconscious; a subject that speaks through the unmastered realms of dreaming, the *lapsus* or the joke, and manifests itself fugitively—an opening of shutters that immediately close up.[11] There is no analogous Arabic term, although many expressions carry a comparable connotation. Yet this approach to subjectivity can dialogue with conceptual configurations of presence and absence, life and death, which are both colloquially defined in the discourse of the qṣar and elaborated within the larger metaphysical frame of the Islamic philosophical tradition.

On the path of one such conceptual configuration of subjectivity, the text follows the trace of a polymorphous figure of alterity, ever present and elusive, alluded to and never surfacing in full shape, recurring in personal and historical narratives, quotidian speech, and philosophical speculation: the figure of *l-fitna* (classical Arabic, *al-fitna*). *Fitna:* a polysemic concept at the limit of representation and thought, mark of an intractable difference, fracture, rift, schism, disjunction, or separation—separation from oneself—the figure of an exile that is constitutive of the position of subject, as both a possibility and a loss. Ambivalent and paradoxical to the end, in the Qur'an *al-fitna* is the excess, the testing and ordeal that is both the transgression and the foundation of God's law. In its colloquial use, it evokes the other states of madness and love, the cutting force of discord, violence, and war, and speaks of a straying off familiar paths—a straying which is also that of language and which, in the words of Sheikh Moḥammed the poet, is that poetry itself.

Throughout the book, as a circumstantial commentary in the margins, attention is devoted to the concrete way things are said, to a reflection on the specific vocabularies, rhetorical figures, and conceptual configurations, which both resist translation and directly engage notions from a different cultural tradition. The purpose is not to map a territory, nor to unravel the symbolic fabric of a given cultural system—to grasp and circumscribe the other's anthropological difference. It is to travel on the boundary of what Maghribî writers of decolonization have called a *différence intraitable:*[12] a hiatus which destabilizes the assignment of places and parts, which displaces the categories of classical and colonial reason and opens a heterological space of intercultural dialogue—an atopical intermediate region that might be called a *barzakh.* There, in that interstitial mode of identity between languages and cultures, between genders and categorizations, a certain listening becomes possible. And concepts and figures from the qṣar can act as epistemological and aesthetic guides in a hermeneutical journey that, not unlike the journey of an Arabic *riḥla,*[13] is a departure from one's place and oneself.

As in a classical riḥla, a journey made by walking, partiality and incompleteness are both a structural posture and an ethical and aesthetic choice. I think of certain Borges stories where an event, a name, or a person are mentioned with vividness of detail, only to be abandoned in the narrative: narrative holes, floating fragments from a missing context, they bear witness to the vastness of life beyond the grasp and visual field of the narrator, of the writer, and even of the narrative itself.

In its partial and fragmented style, then, this text attempts to listen to the dissonant, often idiosyncratic voices, of an absolutely contemporary society, elaborating in its own ways the fractures, wounds, and contradictions, and a certain intolerable, of the Maghribî postcolonial present. *Speech acts with many heads,* in Deleuze's evocative image, together these utterances plant the elements of a people to come as the "free indirect discourse" of this society about itself, about the world, and about human life in general.

The book opens on its frontispiece: Yusef's map, a visual image, which is both the central piece of part 1 ("Returns"), and an *ouverture* for the entire work. The map—this is what Yusef called it—is a diagrammatic and pictorial representation of the qṣar, a portrait of its spatial and symbolic organization at a moment of radical change. I read it as syncretic topography and a (post)modernist cartographic dream, and as a poetic reckoning of the spatiotemporal universe the reader is about to traverse. It is an image that can never be mine, but that was born in a dialogue with me and what I stood for in Yusef's eyes. A gift, inaugurating a cycle of recollection and exchange.

The "map" takes the introductory place that in ethnographies is conventionally reserved for the setting. Bifocal in its vision and voice, it occupies that place with a difference, and functions allegorically as a prolegomenon to the process of reading a text that like the drawing itself, gently forces the reader to be displaced, to *turn* along with the tracing, setting off on a journey that is also the journey of reading, as was that of writing and doing fieldwork.

Unfamiliarly familiar to his compatriots, Yusef's drawing is the product of a vision in exile. As such, and in its very mode of composition, it bears the mark of a postcolonial subjectivity, a modernist dwelling of the "betweens." Drawn as a syncretic juxtaposition of different representational styles—geometrical and pictorial, perspectival and flat—the map cites and transgresses the perspectival and planimetric codes. It offers itself to the view as a phantasmagoric profusion of signs, yet rests unreadable from the viewer's standpoint. For in this drawing the viewer, the reader, and the draftsman himself are either exiled from the scene, or seized and drawn into the scene. Such is the double bind of its visual modernism.

For the interpreter, or simply the reader, reading Yusef's drawing requires renouncing the viewer's position. It means embracing the posture of a walker, following the path of the tracing. The path is a spatial one through the old qṣar, but also a metaphorical one through memory. For this drawing belongs, if unwittingly, to the Arabic travel genre of the *riḥla*—the migratory journey from which there might be no return.

The map is also a work of mourning. It is the visual elaboration of a break and an exile—in the life of the draftsman, in the body of his community. In its historical contingency (narrated in part 1, "The New Village" and "Splinters at l-Hashmi's Funeral," and evoked throughout the book), it is related to the resettlement of the qṣar community *extramuros,* to the desertion of the old qṣar and the construction of a "New Village" in the surrounding desert—a planned housing project, conceived to meet the spatial, political, and administrative imperatives of the modern state.

As if a part of life had fallen on the other side of a chasm, into an inaccessible past, Yusef's path through memory is a figural stitching of fragments—an imaginal reconstruction from beyond that chasm. It is here that his cartographic dream encounters the modernist sensibility of certain Maghribî postcolonial writers: that of Kateb Yacine's *Nedjma,* oscillating between the ironic celebration of the "inestimable ruins of the present" and the lament for an intractable loss—of the lover, of the nation, of the language, of the self. Or that of Driss Chraïbi's *Le passé simple,* a text written along the edges of the chasm itself, in the interstitial zone of a "thin line" inscribing the border between Orient and Occident, Tradition and Modernity, Arab and French, and in the vision of the fracture which hurled a portion of the subject's history into a grammatical *passé simple*—tense of separation, and of uncanny returns.[14]

Ḥadda is the protagonist of part 2. "Contra-diction: Ḥadda, Son of Ṭamu" is entirely composed around a conversation where he and I are the main interlocutors (alternation of "He says," "I say"), in the contained yet expansive temporal frame of one day and one night; a frame that, somewhat like the multiple frames of the *Thousand and One Nights,* stretches forward and backward (1985, 1989, 1990), following the rhythm of the saying, and mimicking the composite temporality of Ḥadda's recollections.

Our conversation takes for long sections the dialogical tones of a philosophical debate (in the style of a Scholastic *disputatio,* in Arabic *jadal*), a debate where Ḥadda often has the lead. For, in his oral and oratorical way, Ḥadda is an intellectual, a thinker who has a passion for imagining multiple possibilities, exploring the boundaries of his thought, and reflecting about the sources of the powerful drives that animate and shatter his society—power, sexuality, discord, love, envy—in their radically contemporary form.

Our debate revolves around themes of identity and difference: the destabilizing work of the feminine term, a "knot" of alterity, *nasab,* in the genealogical discourse of the *ḥasab,* the discourse of an impossible (masculine) purity; and *l-fitna,* the druglike, carving force of difference (*l-ikhtilâf*): a cleavage, a madness, and a love, which makes life and society possible and undermines it from within. Indirectly, and without ever emerging from the contextual fabric of our conversation, the themes of our debate address a central preoccupation in contemporary Middle Eastern societies—the anxiety of identity, and the paradoxes of the patriarchal and theological idioms coming to terms with the experience of difference, intolerance, fragmentation, and war.[15]

But it is impossible to reduce "Contra-diction" to thematic considerations of content. Identity and difference are not just topical themes in my debate with Ḥadda; they are also inscribed in the flesh of Ḥadda's body and life, in his reckoning of the collective history of the qṣar, and in the contradictory forms of our dialogue. Increasingly, Ḥadda's recitation takes on an autobiographical tone, as if the general themes of our discussion were also metaphors of his personal life—figures of his own "cleavaged" self. The telling shuttles back and forth between our debate on identity and fitna, Ḥadda's flights into the collective saga of his "fatherless land"—land of difference and *métissage,* of the hybridity of people and idioms—and the shattered memory of his fatherless childhood (he who bears his mother's name), to culminate in the long recitation, a monologue that lasted a night, about his ambivalent, joyful, and tragic relationship with his absent father.

Yet to interpret Ḥadda's recitation as a private psychological recollection, or as the voice of a collective memory, a memory accessible and already in place, understood as the archival repository of social identity, would be to miss the poetic and political import of his rhetorical movement between multiple registers. For precisely that movement is the staging of a countermemory. It is the constant exchange between the self and the qṣar, between "my body" and the body of the community, between what I say and the language by which I say it, which makes of Ḥadda's utterances, as of the utterances of other characters in the book, a "speech act with many heads": at once political, personal, and collective.

If part 2 is a climax of face-to-face interlocution within a boundaried, if conventional, temporal frame, part 3 has the character of a chorus, where the voice and the lead are passed on, transferred from one to the other, and where the narrative thread is carried on from one scene to the other, along the expanding and overlapping paths of a spiral temporality.

"Loss: The Sphere of the Moon"[16] explores the subject's relation to the Other Scene of absence in three independent "movements," through the realms of dreaming, historical narratives, and oral poetry of longing and loss. Who, where is the subject of dreaming, of memory, of poetry?

Opening with the account of a dream of my own, staging figures of loss and impasse from the historical imagination of the qṣar, the first section addresses the intersubjectivity of dreaming, transference, and the subject's relation to a fundamental unknowing—a space of forgetting that Freud imaged as the "navel of the dream," and that in Islamic metaphysics, as in the vernacular understanding of dreaming in the qṣar, is reckoned in terms of the configuration of sleep, dreaming, and death, as both an eclipse and an awakening.

Dreams are never one's own. Sendings from elsewhere, from the region of death and the beyond, or at least, as Freud says, from another locality, an Other Scene. Ibn al-ʿArabî calls that Elsewhere a barzakh, an intermediate imaginal realm, an *entre-deux* between absence and presence, spiritual and bodily existence, between self and other, the living and the dead. And in the conversation that forms the core of this section, Si Lḥassan, Qurʾanic scholar and dream interpreter, speaks of an "exit," an otherworldly journey, and an encounter, and of knowledge passed on, between the wandering *rûḥ* of the dreamer and other errant souls, of the living and the dead.

Rather than just presenting an indigenous theory of dreaming, or attempting to interpret that theory in psychoanalytic terms,[17] the hermeneutical strategy of this section (paradigmatic, in this sense, of the entire work) allows Si Lḥassan's interpretations to dialogue with those of Ibn al-ʿArabî, Freud, and Lacan—by setting their theories in counterpoint, as differing ways of formulating a question that is both different and similar. Borrowing Ibn al-ʿArabî's expression, the heterological space of this dialogue could itself be called a barzakh—an intermediate zone of exchanging and doubling, where conceptual configurations are transformed and displaced in their encounter with other hermeneutical traditions.

Resuming a line inaugurated in parts 1 and 2, and returning to figures and themes from the collective history of the qṣar, "Ruins," the second section of part 3, discusses the subject's relation to the scene of alterity in terms of memory. It focuses on historical narratives of fitna: the Great Fitna of the beginning of this century, which "split" the body of the community and turned the region into a theater of terror and warfare; but also the many fitnas of distant and forgotten pasts, readable in watermark through the traces, half effaced, of former settlements, scattered through the physical landscape, and evoking Qurʾanic images of the Apocalypse; and the *fitna* of modern days, a scattering and fragmentation lived as absolutely new, yet as the uncanny return of other scatterings.

The tense of these narratives is a multidimensional and ex-centric present; a crossing point of multiple lines, producing what in terms of the cosmological imagery set forth by l-Ḥajj l-Madanî, I would call the recycling of history. Tilling the ground of "forgotten graveyards," building with the debris of former lives, recycling the inanimate and the inorganic. A folding of multiple layers, this temporal mode expresses at once a cosmological way of reckoning time (with a marked local intonation, imbued of Qur'anic eschatological themes, and resonant of themes in classical Arab historiography—particularly the thought of Ibn Khaldûn) and a specifically modernist one.[18] In this composite present, furrowed by the presencing of a "beyond,"[19] the past is both remote and contemporary, and the postcolonial subject speaks from a space of absence-presence utterances that as was the case with Ḥadda's, are both personal and collective.

As I suggest in different ways throughout the book, this temporal vision is structured by the tropes of ruin, of implication and return. As Si Lḥassan says talking about dreams, as Ḥadda painstakingly repeats in the conversation on *nasab* (itself meaning "implication" and "tie"), and as Azra'il, the angel of death, vividly summarizes with the gesture of sprinkling in the womb of a pregnant woman the earth from the grave where the unborn baby will be buried after death (epilogue), at issue is the ordinary yet marvelous experience of an anterior future: *l-ʿalâqa dyâl l-mâḍî ilâ shedd f l-mustaqbal,* "the legacy of the past when it fastens the future." The here-and-now of a happening is also, necessarily, an elsewhere, inhabited by the visible yet unreadable ruins of an inaccessible past that implicate the future like the legacy of a forgotten loss. This element of ruin, this earth of death, is also the "yeast" that makes life and society possible.

Ḍâqt rûḥî, ḥaj khâṭrî l-blâdî.

Oppressed is my spirit, my mind storms to my land.

The section "Impasse of the Angels" concludes the book. It deals with wounds and words, longing and language, burning passion and unreachable distance, addressing the subject's relation to the Other Scene in terms of poetic inspiration, composition, and *ars poetica.* Written around the stanzas of a frame poem, it is based on conversations with poets about the source of their "saying" and the technical aspects of their art. Two poets have the lead: Belqasem, young and melancholic, and Sheikh Moḥammed, master of rhythm and poetic expression, who "can follow the paths words take, without losing his way."

A paradigm of a poetic tradition and of a vision of life (and a distant kin of a classic *qaṣida* in the genre of *su'âl aṭ-ṭulûl,* "questioning the remains"), the frame poem tells of a man who returns to the campsite of his loved ones to find an empty space, swept by the wind. The only trace is a well, abandoned and dry. The man keeps asking what happened, to the well he addresses his lament: "Tell me Sunken Well." But the answer is only an echo, throwing the speaker into a despair visited by ghosts: "My sleep is light, I wake all night, I can't forget or retreat into oblivion: my demon brings me their ghosts in flesh and blood." Yet from the pain of that loss, from the emptiness of that space, swept by the wind and populated with images, springs the poetical word. For that man is also a poet, the Poet, whose campsite is always already abandoned, whose love always already lost. The Poet who deals in ruins, scattered remains, that is, in words...

"The saying" is born of *l-fraq,* Belqasem says: fracture, separation, and exile; separation from the beloved, exile from oneself. It is born of an impasse, a stricture and constriction, an eclipse of language and thought, for which this poetry has many words and figures. "*Ḍâqt rûḥî, ḥaj khâṭrî l-blâdî*" (oppressed is my spirit, my mind storms to my land), says the song of exile. "*Maksûr mn jnâḥû u bga ʿaḍâmû shḍâyâ / u hua bîh l-hûl, ma-jbar itkellem*" (his wings broken, his bones splintered / fright is in him, unable to speak). Yet that speechlessness, the impasse of that fracturing, is also a passage into another scene. There, like an angel, appears the poetical word.

For Sheikh Moḥammed the Other Scene is rather that of language, and "fracturing" and "joining," a technique of composition. In the style of certain Arab treatises of poetics, our conversations on poetry center on issues of form (word bodies, sound design), on the echoing of structure and sense, on the "masonry of poems" and the technical aspects of that craft. "Melancholic archeologist"[20] and craftsman, Sheikh Moḥammed deals in words and rhythms: he knows that, for a poet, the loss of the object, its disappearance into a distance beyond reach, is the condition of poetical speech. Words, *l-klâm,* which also means poems; poems that themselves can break and need restoring, always at risk of straying into nonsense. Word seeds, which live through the body of the poet for a passing moment, to be "thrown" and to return to their errancy. It is on their path, the path of words, that a poet must voice his "desire to say." For words have a life of their own. And the one who wishes to follow their ways must be ready to depart from himself—from herself. Crossing into another scene, a barzakh of doubles and angels, where the voice that says "I" is no longer one's own...

part one

RETURNS

RETURNS 1

TOPOLOGY OF A CITY

Lâ taltazim ḥâlatan, walâkin
dur bi-llayâly kamâ tadûwru

Don't cling to one state / turn with the Nights, / as they turn.
—Maqâmat al-Ḥamadhâni (tenth century)[1]

Yusef left the map he had drawn in a corner, and moved away. Committed to silence, his drawing is a gift and a debt. For those who can read it, his wooden tablet inscribed with glyphs is a story with images. It is Yusef's story, and the story of the qṣar. It is also the story of the reader. Because as she travels through the roundabout paths of this drawing, the reader's own story gets caught in the tracing. A gift engages the name of the giver, and is for the recipient an obligation to engage her name in turn. This text writes itself around his drawing. It is one of its returns.

The Map

Yusef arrived with the map—for he called it *l-kharîṭa,* "the-map"—one Thursday afternoon, a market day. He was announced by the rumbling of his motorcycle, unlikely noise inside the ramparts of the old qṣar used to the tramping of sandals and to the rhythmed pawing of donkeys. He walked in without knocking, without greeting, and without saying a word handed the map to me. A big plywood board, drawn in bright colors: in its materiality, in its size, it was almost a sculpture.[2] Bodily, dense, irreducibly concrete: yet, at the same time, it conveyed an irresistible sense of dynamism.

Disappointment at the sight of that unfamiliar picture. The map was passed from hand to hand nervously. Masculine hands and looks, talking, laughing, judging. Complicity of the quotidian. No one liked it. A discussion developed into a dispute. Visibly unconcerned, Yusef withdrew into silence.

(What was said is that in the qṣar people didn't draw maps. One knew how to get somewhere, house, garden, village, or tree, or found the way with the help of contextual landmarks. What was said is that the French drew maps during colonial times, and now the Agricultural Office did. But that if a map was required—*and hadn't I asked Yusef to draw a map of the old qṣar?*—it should be drawn in the form of a plan, like the maps of the Bulgarian surveyors who had come to measure the gardens on behalf of the Agricultural Office. What was said is that Yusef's drawing was a confusion of unrecognizable forms, *mkhallaṭ*, a "hybrid product," neither local nor modern; that it was *khayâlî*, "fantastic," and that it didn't belong in the qṣar.)

Yusef paid no attention to their words, and showed me instead the place where he had signed his name with the name of the qṣar and the date: July 3, 1984. He had put his signature inside the Fourth of Ayt ʿAbdallah, he said, where his family had lived for three centuries and where he himself was born. Yusef did not live in the qṣar. He worked as an auto mechanic and electrician in the town nearby. Ever since he had left, he had never wanted to come back, to live there. The map, for him, was a kind of return.

His presence—or was it his map?—made everyone in the room uncomfortable. Si Thami, who had worked with the Bulgarians at the time of the land-tenure survey, got pencil and paper and sketched a map of the old qṣar. It was easy, he said. First you draw the walls, *ṣ-ṣûr* (and he drew a slightly trapezoidal square, rather in the shape of the aerial photograph of the village I had seen at a provincial office); the Gate; the two main arteries of the village, the Alley of Ayt l-Bâlî and the Alley of Ayt j-Jdîd; the mosque; and the various other alleys: the labyrinthine paths of the Ḥarâtîn quarters, Arḥabî (the square), the Alley of Ayt l-Qâḍî, the Alley of Bû Ṭwîl, the Alley of Ayt ʿAbdallah, the Alley of Ayt Aḥmâd, the Alley of Ayt Ḥammu, and the big Avenue of Ayt Driss. You represent (*kat-mettel*) each alley by a line and make the line turn where the alley itself turns—

But still Yusef refused to engage. Finally he said that his drawing was the *only* possible representation of the qṣar. Couldn't they see it? He had made it on wood for it to last. On wood, like the *lûḥa* tablets children used to memorize the Qurʾan, erasing the writing as they committed the word to the body, the *lûḥa* they decorated with colorful calligraphies when, as young adults, they had completed memorizing the Book. And he had drawn it in colors because the village was colorful, the earth walls were of a million tones. Yusef spoke quickly, without looking at anyone, without caring whether they were listening. Then he went.

First Turn: Frame from Afar

I turn the board in my hands, search for a place from which to look and rest my gaze. I find none; my eye wanders through the proliferation of signs. This drawing does not accommodate a spectator's gaze, but it gives itself to the view, an exuberant, baroque panorama. I keep turning the board in my hands. Bright colors of felt-tipped pens: orange, brown, red, green, violet. For the village is colorful, he said.

I see, at the center of the wooden board, as if suspended, a geometrical figure. It is carefully drawn with a ruler, in pencil, underscored by a red pen. At first sight one might call it a cube. I will refer to this figure as the Frame—in all the senses English allows for this term.[3] The Frame is filled with a crowd of graphic images: towers, pieces of buildings and other architectural elements, trees, and fragments of writing. At the center, a dark rectangular spot. The location of this dark area is confusing. Is it located inside the cube, or painted on its surface? In fact, the topology of all these images is ambiguous. It is unclear whether they belong inside the Frame and represent its interior (*l-dâkhel,* "the inside," the interior space of the qṣar) or whether they appear on its surfaces as two-dimensional elements of its outward appearance, its dress or *parure:* like an illustration or a calligraphic motif in the frontispiece of a book. Whether they refer mimetically to an object, an object beyond or inside, or instead they function poetically, and are granted an autonomous status as "images" ("image" in Arabic is *mithal*).

Almost as a commentary in the margin, the Frame is surrounded by a concentric peripheral scene. A sort of circular enclosure, made of buildings, trees, and a few human figures. One building, bigger and colored bright orange, stands out in a corner of the board. It wears a stylized crown (a sort of halo), the emblem of the Moroccan state. Other buildings, on one side of the board, are drawn in conventional planimetric style—a citation from the style of contemporary urbanistic maps. This scene in the margins occupies the remainder of the wooden board, and enframes the Frame. For the limits of the drawing are the limits of the board: in the corners the tracing becomes curvilinear, almost concave, contributing to the impression that the drawing is turning. As a body suspended in space, the Frame populated with images seems to revolve upon itself in a void. It induces an energetic impression of movement, a rotary movement that creates a circular space.

If I stand back without looking at the inscriptions, the Frame appears to me as a solid, tricking my eye into a sense of depth. (The gray pencil shadowing on two lateral sides suggests interpretation as a cube; it is intended to express perspective and volume.) In this mode, the drawing is a picture taken from a distance, from afar or above—like the panorama of a city portrayed from the top of a hill. But there is no vantage point from which to comprehend the whole. However I decide to approach it, some areas of the Frame appear upside down or sideways, as if under someone else's gaze, beyond the range of my eye; or as if they were drawn from different angles, without seeking to produce a global view. When I stand back and look, I see an almost-perspectival construction that offers and then denies itself to the viewer; an elusive view from above, which makes it impossible to dominate the scene; and a cubical figure revolving in a concentric space.

As soon as I focus on the glyphs, my eye is captured and drawn in. The Frame flattens into a composition of multiple frames, planar surfaces filled with inscriptions and images that spill over or push out, oriented in different directions and even upside down in relation to each other. The sense of perspective is lost, the cube disappears, and the eye is cast adrift, transported or seduced by the tracing through a phantasmagoric landscape. In this nonperspectival space I recognize five scenes; four come to compose the Frame, the lines of which form now a flat border, assembled as a composition of borders. (Of these internal scenes, two are shaped as rectangles, vertically aligned with each other; two as trapezoids, forming an angle with each other.) The fifth scene enframes the drawing from the outside, like a corniche or a passe-partout.[4]

Second Turn: The Eye-in-the-Tracing

SCENE 1 (FRONTAL)

The Gate comes to the fore—solemn, pastiche, like a stage prop—and shows the way into the drawing. It is outlined by a double brown-and-red contour, and crowned by a crenelated tryptic. Inside the hollow space formed by its ogival arch, as if hanging in its aperture, an inscription in Arabic reads *fum*, "mouth." A detached fragment of writing to its right, floating adrift in a nongrammatical direction, reads *l-qdîm*, "the old." Joined together to restore the syntax, the two fragments form *fum l-qdîm*,[5] which means "the Old Mouth," and marks the legend of the threshold. Every threshold is inscribed with a legend.

Surrounding the Gate toward the left is an arrangement of sparsely ordered architectural shapes, floating or resting together in a state of levitation: spare parts, with a suggestion of common orientation. They are images suspended, isolated in their graphic contours, brightly colored and represented frontally with no concern for depth, relative size, or any sort of perspectival device. They float like rubble in a nongravitational space. Discrete, discontinuous, they don't fill the flat surface bordered by the rectangular frame—which enframes the scene as a frame does a painting.

A panoply of fragmented images, a scenario in ruins. Crenelated towers: one is hollow, just a contour with orange windows, another is half-filled with brown color; the stylized outline of a well; parts of buildings, which become smaller, more fragmented and adrift, as they seem to distance themselves from the Gate (but not enough to create a sense of depth). Bits of writing, attached loosely to particular buildings, and levitating with the rest of the fragmented materials. And two palm trees with a man climbing upon them, forming what seems to be an emblematic whole. These are some of the elements of the first scene, the vocabulary of its graphic composition. It is a vocabulary found, with a few variations, in each of the four scenes.

To the left of the Gate, in red ink and in bigger letters, an inscription assigns the title of the scene: *Rbaʿ Ayt l-Bâlî,* "Fourth of Ayt l-Bâlî," "Fourth of the Bâlî people."[6]

Directly above the Gate, but at a certain distance, is a large dark rectangular area, densely filled with color. Confused with the dark background, like a graffito or a scratch in the paint, an inscription reads *Arḥabî,* "the courtyard." From this dark area emerge two sets of blue lines; they are drawn with a double trace and suggest direction, alleys. A long single stroke with an arrowhead points to the Gate, as if inviting one to enter, to exit, or to enter again. Another arrow emerging from the dark area points to the outside of the scene, to a small aperture immediately above the dark area, and (through it?) to another space. It is the space of scene 2. There is a narrative path through the dissemination of signs, a *parcours chiffré.*

SCENE 2 (FRONTAL)

The second scene is located directly above the first, and is constructed frontally on a line parallel to it—like the vertical section of a house, or like the setting of an upper pavilion in a Turkish or a Persian miniature painting (where an upper pavilion can refer to a number of different dimensions: spatial, temporal, narrative, gnostic). Inside this scene the arrangement of architectural shapes is frontal and somewhat less scattered. A tower in ruin inaugurates the scene from the right (time reduces towers to rubble, *kharâb*). Suspended above it, and as if following the crumbled outline, the legend reads *burj ajjâmeʿ l-Bâlî,* "tower of the mosque of Bâlî" (in Arabic *bâlî* means ancient, decayed, decrepit; here it is a proper name).[7] Next comes an aperture whose legend reads *fum l-Bâlî,* "mouth of the Bâlî." Continuing to the left, more towers with floating inscriptions. The legends relate them to names, personal or family names, through a possessive attribution: *burj l-Wazzânî,* "Wazzânî's tower," *burj ʿAshirî,* "ʿAshirî's tower." But, like everything else, the names are treated as elements of a graphic composition. And they float—

An oversized pigeon is perched on a crenelation; a group of palms with the same emblematic human figure is resting to one side. A tower looms over the scene, too big and out of place, as if breaking in from the outside. A narrow rectangular box carries the caption, *l-maṭḥana,* "the mill." And there, inscribed in the center in red ink, is the title of the second scene: *Arbaʿ Ayt ʿAbdallah,* "Fourth of Ayt ʿAbdallah," "Fourth of the people of ʿAbdallah."

At the upper right corner of the scene, and aligned with the Gate, is the signature of the draftsman. The giving of gifts engages one's name, and sets it into circulation. Written in brown ink as if to stress a common material fate with the towers, the rubble, and the other images of the composition, the signature floats along with the fragments. A glyph like an old seal, which in Arabic is called *ʿalâma* or *ṭṭâbeʿ;* it is the seal that merchants stamped on their merchandise, judges on their parchments, and that poets grafted onto their poems. Above the signature, the full name of the draftsman, with the inscription of the date and the place: month [*shahr*] 7-3-1984, July 3, 1984. The name is written last name first, in (French) administrative style; the date is given according to the Christian calendar, the current bureaucratic calendar in Morocco; the qṣar is described as *duwwâr,*[8] the official term for village in the modern administrative organization of a province. It is an official inscription offered to the gaze.

SCENE 3 (90-DEGREE TURN)

But there the towers turn, and with them the reader must turn. The direction of the next scene is not just indicated by an arrow (an indexical but still metapragmatic device). It is forced on the reader by the tracing itself. The drawing makes a 90-degree turn, clockwise, and the towers of the third scene present themselves sideways, perpendicular to the orientation of the Gate and of the other two scenes. From where you are looking, facing the Gate, you can see only a proliferation of towers pushing out in a different direction. And if you remain rooted in your place, you will not be in a position to read from the drawing. For in this work reading, writing, and drawing are one and the same movement. As is reiterated in the Arab literary tradition, vision and knowledge are first and foremost a *riḥla,* a moving away from one's place:[9] displacement and travel, dissemination of oneself through space and time. Riḥla is the narrative form of a kind of travel that opens a metaphorical journey, but that is also made by walking: an investment of libidinal energy, an expenditure of the body, and of oneself.

And so the reader, the interpreter who sets out to follow the signs of what appears to be a coded itinerary, *un parcours chiffré,* discovers that the itinerary is also a riḥla, "a moving-away from oneself." And that she, or he, cannot keep reading without surrendering the viewer's position and embracing that of the walker—the position of a *marcheur.*[10] This realization has to do solely with the formal construction of the drawing,[11] prior to any deciphering of the code that contains the key to the reading. Nothing has yet been said about the actual qṣar, the worldly referent of this picture-map. Is the itinerary alluded to by the arrows, and by the turning of the drawing itself, a walking through the picture-map, or a description, real or imaginary, of the qṣar. Or is the encoded itinerary instead, or as well, the itinerary through a life: the life story of the draftsman, or of his village, the community to which he belongs? (The verb for "describing" and "drawing," for "fixing in images," is in Arabic the same verb, *rasama,* in Moroccan vernacular, *rsem; rassâm* is the draftsman or the artist.) All one can know at this point is that there is a narrative development through the deployment of images, a readable story, and that there must be a key to that narrative in its historical and ethnographic context.

But with the automatism of a muscular movement, the reader is drawn into a riḥla before knowing it. She is implicated by the tracing (as one is implicated by a gift),[12] and finds herself captured within the scene. She is "framed." Before determining the referential identity of the figures she follows—towers, buildings, trees, or legends—and before locating the itinerary in history, the path takes her by surprise.

In fact, the capture of the eye by the scene has already taken place, and only at this turn does it become manifest kinesthetically. The eye was caught at the Gate, where images and inscriptions took on a character of *emergence* that was a "showing" rather than a seeing, in the sense in which this showing manifests itself in dreams. At the Gate the reader started walking through a landscape of inscriptions and ruins, inscriptions-in-ruin,[13] and found herself in "another scene," where the laws of perspective no longer applied. Structurally within that scene, the reader's position is already that of a dreamer—as is the position of the draftsman. In a dream "le sujet ne voit pas où ça mène, il suit." Lacan:

> What does this mean if not that, in the so-called waking state, there is an elision of the gaze [*regard*], and an elision of the fact that not only does it look, it also *shows* [*non seulement ça regarde, mais ça montre*]. In the field of the dream, on the other hand, what characterizes the images is that *it shows.* It shows—but here, too, some form of "sliding away" of the subject is apparent. Recall some description of a dream, any dream . . . , place it into its co-ordinates, and you will see that

> this *it shows* comes to the fore [*ce ça montre vient en avant*]. So much it comes to the fore, with the features in which it is co-ordinated—namely, the absence of horizon, the enclosure [*fermeture*], of that which is contemplated in the waking state, and also, the character of emergence, of contrast, of stain [*tache*], of its images, the intensification of their colours—that, in the final resort, our position in the dream is fundamentally that of someone who does not see. The subject does not see where it [*ça*] is leading, he follows."[14]

Since in the Other Scene of the drawing there are no viewing subjects nor objects viewed, no agents and patients, but only a "showing" that comes to the fore, a different voice of the verb should be found to describe the mode of that capture, that being captured or being drawn. The subject of drawing (or that of reading) is not a consciousness exterior or anterior; it is contemporary to the act. Speaking in a "middle voice"[15] of the verb that is neither active nor passive, one could say that the eye *draws with* the scene. Drawing-walking is the performative mode of following a trace which traces itself in the following.

> *In the vocabulary of Islamic ontological thought, the Other Scene is that of* al-ʿâlam al-mithâl, *"the Imaginal World." It is the Imaginal World of Ibn al-ʿArabi's philosophy, a concrete and yet virtual meeting ground, intermediate between the realm of invisible and unknowable essences and that of sensual reality.* Al-ʿâlam al-mithâl *is not a theory of representation as mirror of the object world. It is a real space, a parallel world of "real images," where real events happen, bearing consequences in the concrete lives and destinies of people. It is an angelic space, where bodies are dematerialized and spirits appear in borrowed sensual forms. There, the invisible is translated without being unveiled: it manifests itself in concrete forms.*[16]

Embracing the walker's position means literally displacing one's body around the board, from right to left, to face the other side of the drawing, paralleling the leftward movement of reading-writing in Arabic. In the order of subjectivity, this 90-degree turn signs the end of a project (the project of dominating the scene to discover the keys to the signs), and marks the advent of another "I": an "I-on-the-path," which is also an "eye-in-the-tracing." Neither the reader's nor the draftsman's, it is the eye surprised by the path.

Surprise

> *When the subject is captured, when it finds, when it loses itself in some unexpected place. A fainting or a lapse. Lacan: when something manifests itself fugitively, in a fissure, a crack, a syncopated gap between utterances. A sense of being* sur-pris, *overtaken, in the place in which "it"*

is found. Then and there, something springs out. "Thus the unconscious manifests itself always in that which vacillates in a split of the subject, from which emerges a finding Freud identifies with desire—a desire we will provisionally situate in the denuded metonymy of the discourse in question, where the subject encounters himself in some unexpected place."[17]

*Surprise is discontinuous: a disturbance in the narrative, a punctuation, a scansion, the work of an elsewhere in the here and the now of an utterance. It is new—*tuché, *an inassimilable encounter with the real* [réel]—*yet textual, automatic, machinelike:* automaton, *the return of something old. It has the nature of emergence and the structure of a finding, a sudden discovery, a* trouvaille. *Yet the finding is immediately lost, the* trouvaille *is already* retrouvaille *(a finding again, but also a love reunion after a separation). A reunion with something that is to be lost again and back.* Retrouvailles *are already inscribed within a dimension of loss. In its inassimilable impact, in its particularity, in its newness, surprise is already repetition: a return. The* tuché *is a strike of the automaton.*

"What is repeated, in fact, is always something that occurs—the expression tells us quite a lot about its relation to the tuché*—as if by chance" (Lacan).*[18]

There are literatures of surprise. Hoffmann's and Poe's tales of the uncanny (Freud's material for "Das Unheimliche"),[19] *or the Arabic genre of marvelous travels and uncanny encounters,* al-gharaîb *or* al-ʿajaîb, *a genre of travel narrative, storytelling, and poetry that flourished between the tenth and the fifteenth century in the world of Islam. The corpora of the* Arabian Nights, *and of the Maqamât belong there.*[20] *It is by telling strange and uncanny stories* (gharîb) *that Shahrazad captured the attention of King Shahrayar and suspended her death sentence, saved her fellow women, and educated the king in the art of being human. This genre of the marvelous also permeates the accounts of Arab geographers when it comes to the description of boundaries. It is a genre of finding oneself in unexpected places.*

Surprise can be an effect of its literary inscription. Shahrazad learned her stories from the books of her library, and it is in books, maps, or old tales that in many stories from the Arabian Nights *the characters find direction for encountering the marvelous, and for losing, for finding themselves.*[21] *Surprise, in this drawing, is produced in the reading, at each turn. It is an effect of its re-turns.*

After making the turn around the board, you see that, enclosed within a trapezoidal frame, the third scene is constructed frontally like the others. But because the coordinates have shifted with the turn, the drawing reads now from left to right. Due to the gray pencil shadowing, towers and other glyphs seem to materialize as if through a mist.

A tower in ruin is marked by an arrowhead originating in scene 2, indicating a passage through its hollow body; the legend reads *fum l-Qâḍî,* "mouth of the Judge." A tower half colored in brown follows; suspended on its crenelation is the legend *burj Yaḥyâ,* "Yaḥya's tower." Fragments of buildings are dispersed here and there (one looks almost like a human face), and overarching their tops, displayed like a banner and inscribed in red ink, is the legend of the third scene: *Rbaʿ Ayt l-Qâḍî,* "Fourth of the people of the Judge." An aperture is marked by the inscription *fum Bû Ṭwîl,* "Mouth of the Long," and an arrow originating in the dark area, back in scene 1, directs circulation through it.

At this point the images turn slightly, following the trapezoidal perimeter. They are telescoped, condensed, or conflated into the Frame. As they crowd up in a corner, towers and buildings get smaller and brighter, thickly colored in red. With the force of their visual energetics, some figures push out of the Frame. They break to the outside, or spill into the fourth scene.

SCENE 4: THE RHYME, THE FORCE, AND THE CLOSURE

> *L'oeil, c'est la force. La force n'est jamais rien d'autre que l'énergie qui plie, qui froisse le texte et en fait une oeuvre, une différence, c'est-à-dire une forme. Le tableau n'est pas à lire, comme le disent les semiologues d'aujourd'hui, Klee disait qu'il est à brouter, il fait voir . . . il fait voir ce que c'est voir. Regarder le tableau c'est y tracer des chemins, y co-tracer des chemins.*
>
> —J. F. Lyotard[22]

The eye-in-the-tracing is forced to another turn by the unfolding of the fourth scene. This is an uncanny turn, for at the boundary the drawing seems to develop into its mirror reflection, as if scene 3 quite literally transformed into scene 4. (In classical Arabic geographical descriptions, boundaries are the places of the uncanny, *al-gharîb.*) A tower, which graphically *turns* into its double at the boundary line, leads the path around the board. Redoubling is the other dimension of turning.

At this corner the work of the tracing reaches a climax of autonomous formal elaboration; it disengages itself from the narrative structure of the drawing, from its encoded itinerary, and produces its own showing. The story is surrendered to its pictorial dimension and calligraphic play, and the images gain an autonomous status as *muthul* (images) in an *ʿâlam al-mithâl.*

The cartographic register is transgressed, for its signs operate otherwise—they function poetically. As Michel De Certeau has written of the "alchemic conversion of images" in Bosch's *Garden of Delight,* "This metamorphosis is frequent among the mystics: the criterion of the beautiful replaces that of the true. It carries the sign from one space to another, and it produces the new space. It is by this metamorphosis that the map of a system of knowledge is transformed into a garden of delight."[23]

From scene 3 to scene 4, as in dreams according to Freud, the drawing "allows a rhyme to emerge."[24] The redoubled towers form a poetic couplet, in the way referentially unrelated images can rhyme with each other in dreams. But it is a show for no one. "The productions of the dreamwork," Freud writes, "are not made with the intention of being understood." It is here that most visibly the project disintegrates, the project of dominating the scene to decipher the keys to the signs. For the narrative encoded in the drawing is bent by the energetic force of the eye—of the eye which is a force and a dance. Of the Eye which is an *ʿayn.*

ʿAYN: Vocabulary, in the Colloquial Use

(In none of the uses listed below can the sense of vision as disinterested and disengaged contemplation of an object be found. The eye/ʿayn is a force, a shooting or an outpouring from the inside, an energetic impact or a hollow structure, a void. All these senses are mobilized in the rupturing and paralyzing strike of the gaze—of the ʿayn as evil eye.)

ʿAYN: an eye, the organ of vision; a water source; an origin: *ʿayn shshta,* the eye of the rain, direction where the storm comes from; a hole; a concave structure, a pool, a ring or a circle.

ʿAYN D-DÂR: the eye of the house: a central fissure, hole, and light well, piercing the three levels of the house from top to bottom, around which its body is built, and through which it breathes. Also: interior patio surrounded by pillars, lit through the eye—the core of the house, its center, its source, which is also called *wusṭ d-dâr,* the center of the house, or *raḥba,* the opening, a space around which all activity revolves, the place of exchanges—through the eye—between the inside and the outside, between the human and nonhuman world.

ʿUYÛN L-KÎY: the articulatory junctions of the body in cauterization surgery, where the burning cautery intervenes.

ʿAYN L-ḤBÛB: the tip of a sore, from which pus springs out.

ʿAYN (ع): the name of a letter of the Arabic alphabet with a pharyngeal sound.

> L-ʿAYN: the Eye. Feared and somewhat assumed in the other senses, the evil eye, the other eye, the shot from within. It is called just *l-ʿayn*, the Eye, or *n-neḍra*, the Gaze, or *n-nafs*, which can mean breath, desire, and envy.[25] The Eye is a fascinum, and an energy that breaks. It tells of the disjunctive force of desire. For those who *kayḍarbû b-l-ʿayn*, who "hit with the eye," the eye is the aperture, the place of ejection of something that comes from elsewhere, inside or beyond, in the heart.

A tower breaks out of the Frame, excessive, a shooting into the outside. Severed from it, its legend is already an element of the peripheral scene. Moving inward, a second gate comes to the fore. The legend reads *fum jdîd*, "New Mouth." Through a floating dispersion of fragments with a sense of semicircular movement, the eye is led to meet a hollow ruin by the irregular shape, inscribed with the legend *dâr r-rma*, "the house of the sharpshooters." And the scene becomes a dance. Spread out across its top, like a ribbon, the title in red ink engages in the dancing and closes the circle. It reads *Rbaʿ Ayt j-Jdîd*, "Fourth of Ayt j-Jdîd," "Fourth of the people of the New."

With that closure, the drawing should come to an end, and the tour—the riḥla—to a resting place. But a green arrow discretely shows the way through a small aperture. And before one knows it, as if by chance, one finds oneself back in the first scene. In the circulatory energetics of the eye-in-the-tracing, there is no beginning and no end.

Third Turn: The Gaze outside (*Dwra:* 180-Degree Turn)

Captured by the scene, the eye is also exiled from the scene. If I make a step back I see the cube once again: the Frame cube, with its shading and volume. Its geometrical shape casts me into the position of a spectator—but impotent and estranged from the scene. From outside and above there is no vantage point from which to read the drawing.

Something then becomes visible for the eye exiled from the scene, which could not be seen by the reader following the tracing from the inside—the tracing that can be followed only from the inside, by the eye implicated in the "showing." Within the cubical Frame rotating in the void, the figures undergo a revolution, which determines that the towers in the fourth scene are upside down in relation to those of the first scene, as in the unfolding movement of a fan. The two 90-degree kinesthetic turns of the eye-in-the-tracing appear to the eye-in-exile as stations of a 180-degree turn clockwise of the drawing upon itself, and of the glyphs around an energetic center.[26] The center of that turning can now be identified as the dark rectangular spot marked with the inscription *arḥabî*, "the courtyard." It is the engine, or the heart of the drawing.

What becomes visible for the eye-in-exile is the vertiginous *dwra* of the drawing: the rotation or cycle of the images within the Frame, of the Frame upon itself, and of the peripheral scene around the Frame. (*Dwra: dwr,* the semantic root of turning, rotation, revolution, and cycle; other forms are *dâ'yra,* circle, ring, or circumference, and *dâr,* house or station.) The *dwra,* "180-degree turn," is the complete itinerary of the drawing—as both a realistic and an allegoric topography. It is the design of the riḥla of the reader and of the draftsman—the trace of their moving away.

> PERIPHERAL SCENE, LEFT SIDE, LOWER CORNER. *A cluster of palm trees and a man approaching with a bag of pollen and a bladed tool in his hands. As the eye moves up the man is shown climbing a palm tree; above, two clumsy brown-colored shapes of palms; and a final palm, with the man cutting the dates with his tool. It is a narrative sequence in and of itself, an allegory, in the pictorial sense of the term. It presents the cycle of the palm tree from fertilization-conception, through various stages of transformation, to the final moment of the date harvest, which is at the same time a birth (a pregnancylike cycle) and a sacrificial death (the cutting of the dates). Besides indicating topographically that on that side the qṣar is adjoined by gardens, the palm tree scene is an allegoric allusion to the cycle, the vertiginous dwra of the drawing; it is a cycle of life and death.*

But as a viewer I am unable to read the drawing, half of which unfolds beyond my visual field. When I can see the turning, I can't follow the tracing and I am exiled from the scene; when I follow the tracing, my eye is captured by the scene, drawn into the rotatory movement, and turns blindly with the Frame as an element of the graphic composition. This is the double bind of Yusef's drawing, whose two modes are fated to partial unreadability. Reading it as a whole is a topological aporia: a double movement of implication and estrangement.

As I attempt to follow that movement (paradoxically, between the inside and the outside), I realize that the spectacle of the Frame turning is not intended for me as a viewer. Itself a showing for no one, it is the inanimate reflection of the itinerary of the eye through the drawing. The gaze outside does not see, it has no possible posture for vision, and reflects the meaningless scene of the turning like a mirror. That reflection catches me by surprise, when I am reading the drawing. And with a sense of estrangement at an uncanny turn, I see that "I" is there too. It re-turns as a picture.

Fourth Turn: The Fans

As Yusef rested his drawing on the rusty metal lid of the old well in the courtyard and prepared to leave, I suddenly remembered his fans. I had seen them the day he invited me to his house in town, and we had talked about making the map. In the house the fans were everywhere. They were of all shapes and colors, lonely objects in an empty space by the walls unevenly white, the floors unevenly covered with cement, halfway between the residence of a French legionnaire and a village house in a town that is an outgrown village itself.

That's what he really liked to do—he had said, turning the electricity on and showing me the elliptical shapes formed by the blades fanning at different speeds. He liked to watch them turning, endlessly revolving, like the millstones he played with as a child when his mother didn't watch. He made them from scratch, his fans, with parts he found here and there; sometimes he carved the blades in wood, and painted them in different colors. But the turning itself created colors, he said. I asked whether he made them for selling. He said no. He did sell one or two, if people asked, but mostly he made them for himself. He smiled, "Something like art [*l-fenn*]"—

Later, looking at the drawing deep in concentration, Kh. said that it resembled a magic square, a *jadwal*. (*Jadwal*, chart, table, plan, magic square—the mapping of esoteric geometry.) Kh. had followed the map dispute from the roof, looking down from the edge of the *ʿayn d-dâr*, "the eye of the house." It was so clearly the qṣar! She didn't know how to read and couldn't decipher the writing (I told her they were names), but she could certainly recognize the four fourths. And didn't I see the pigeon perched on the Tower of ʿAshirî? It is always there, just across the street from us.

(I recalled then, even though the fact had nothing to do with her comment, that Kh. had once loved Yusef, and they had even given each other a promise. But this had happened many years before and things had gone otherwise. Kh. had come to like and admire that Laṭifa Ḥassan who had later become Yusef's wife; she and her man had had to fight hard to defend their life together: when his mother told him to divorce her, he refused, and they left the family compound, and the qṣar, and now even the country in voluntary exile.)

Kh. put the drawing in my room. Yusef never asked to see it, and never agreed to discuss it again. Like the staging of a performance, or like a dream at awakening, his work had been consumed.

Fifth Turn: Bi-langue

Jouissance du corps de la langue, inondant ses hantises de mutilation. Ils se caressent maintenant, se rêvant l'un dans l'autre.

—Abdelkebir Khatibi[27]

The perspectival shape of the Frame is the legacy of a Frenchman: a graft onto the text of his life. Yusef mentioned his encounter with him when we first talked about making the map. The map brought the thought of him back, he said. My presence did too. They met before 1970, Yusef was about seventeen. He traveled, landed in Fes.[28] The Frenchman had a car-repair shop, and drew pictures of Moroccan landscapes. Scenes of the old city, buildings and streets, panoramic views of the ramparts. He drew lines with a ruler.[29] This is what Yusef recalled. From him he learned to be the mechanic he is now, and "got" (*khâd*), he said, the technique of geometrical drawing. It was the gift of a foreign language.

Lines drawn with a ruler opened for him a space of imaginary travel; a riḥla, a journeying away from himself that both excluded and made possible the event of a return. Within the lines of his geometrical Frame, altered coordinates of the real, within the borrowed structures of a foreign language, there could be for Yusef a return through dreaming. Dream visions are born of separation and absence: hallucinatory returns of a lack.

Dreams are journeys. In the experience of people in the qṣar, dreams are departures, made possible by a split of the soul from itself and from the world of the living. They are journeys into an intermediate realm of not-life not-death, where absence intersects with presence, and the living encounters the dead.[30] What for Yusef rested beyond reach in the everyday unfolding of life, severed and forever on the other side of a rift, could be encountered through the dream of a map. Within the borrowed lines of the geometrical Frame the map dreamed itself through him. It dreamed itself in the form of a vision articulated through the syntax of his body and forgotten at awakening—

But lines drawn with a ruler also carried the scar of colonial and postcolonial expropriations. They became, in his drawing, the seal of an exile. Geometry is a foreign language that lends Yusef an adoptive place to speak from, a place to dream. But it is also the language that fates him to a solitary imagination, that makes of him a stranger in the eyes of the men of the qṣar. For the gift of a foreign language is always double-edged: "the foreign language gives with one hand and takes away with the other": "Ainsi le texte bilingue—qu'on le veuille ou non—est la trace de l'exil du nom et de sa transformation. Il tombe sur le coup d'une double généalogie, d'une double signature, qui sont tout autant les effets littéraires d'un don perdu, d'une donation scindée en son origine. Un double don, qu'est-ce c'est? La langue étrangère donne d'une main et retire de l'autre."[31]

I look at his name, signed, last name first in French administrative fashion, but in Arabic script, identity-card name, inside the Frame of his drawing. "Comment subvertir son prénom?" asks Abdelkebir Khatibi as he writes around the rift of bilingualism in Maghribî literature of French expression. Effacing it in the act of writing, "confronting it from the outside, by way of a foreign language." The geometrical Frame of his drawing, a way of citing himself, of remembering-forgetting his name through the syntax of another language, bestows on Yusef the possibility of return. Return without returning, to an always other place. "Dream fragmented in its original saying, a dream written through a foreign language": "L'auteur rappelle son enfance. On y entre comme dans un rêve, un rêve fragmenté dans son dire initial, un rêve écrit par une langue étrangère. On ne peut que traduire une mémoire."[32] As I turn the board in my hands, his signature re-turns with the drawing.

Something "speaks in tongues," Khatibi says, through the bilingual text, because the foreign language comes to inhabit and further displace a disjunction, a fissure, already at work in the mother tongue. That disjunction opens a space of ambiguity and doubling in which something (the mother tongue?) returns in fragments, as a hallucinatory production of the text, as the energy that dislocates the text. The laws of this tale that speaks in tongues cannot be extracted or extrapolated from the text, nor can they be applied to the surface of the text, because "elles s'élaborent selon la syntaxe du corps." Reading a bilingual text means following this bodily syntax, listening to the tale of tongues that speak on their own.

Sixth Turn: The Cartographic Dream

> When the whole mass of these dream-thoughts is brought under the pressure of the dream-work, and its elements are turned about, broken into fragments and jammed together—almost like pack-ice—the question arises of what happens to the logical connections which have hitherto formed its framework.
> —Sigmund Freud

When Yusef gave me the drawing, he did not show me the other side of the board. I realized later that his map is double-faced. On the verso of the wooden board there is another map of the qṣar, an earlier draft, a preliminary sketch. The two versions portray the same object and the same space, but in radically different ways. They are the obverse of each other.

Nothing in this earlier draft foretells the Frame cube of the later drawing. There is no attempt at framing the scene, nor at producing a perspectival view. Yet many of its elements will migrate to the other side of the board: towers, sections of the ramparts, the Gate, the well, palm trees, and a peripheral range of buildings surrounding the towers from the outside. The towers

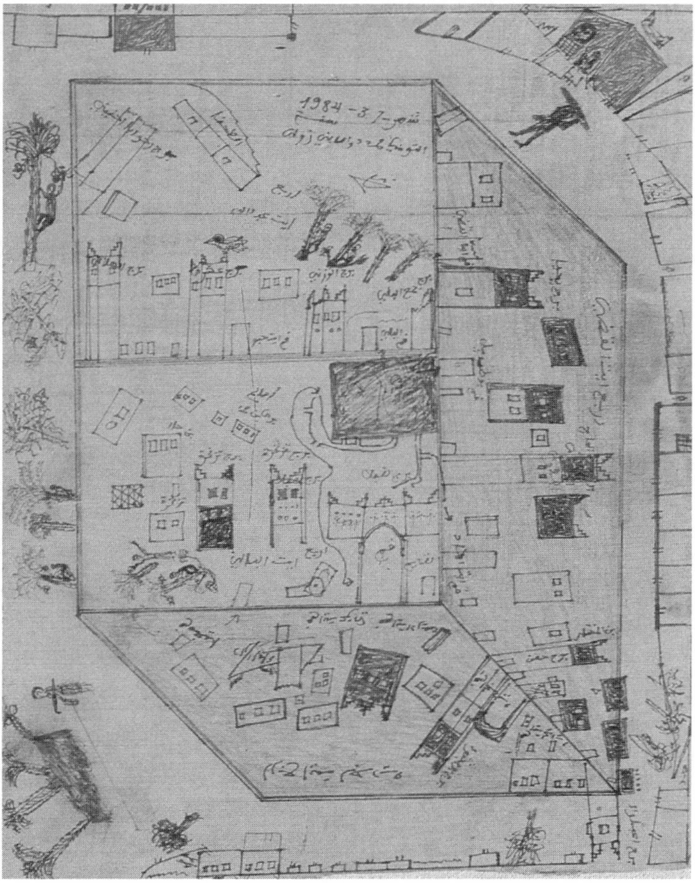

are inscribed with names, but here the labels are used referentially: like toponyms in modern maps. Flat and diagrammatic, halfway between a medieval European map and a contemporary urbanistic plan, the representation is preoccupied with verisimilitude.

A rectangular perimeter bordered by towers, with an indentation at the site of the Gate, refers unambiguously to the perimetric walls of the qṣar. The indentation corresponds to the actual layout, and even the well is in its proper place. The towers are oriented in different directions, but there is no sense of itinerary or turning, and no vertiginous visual effect. Inside the walls the plan of the village alleys: the qṣar's interior. Each alley is named, and Arḥabî is signaled as a small widening in the plan. The peripheral scene is an accurate referential depiction of the new constructions spreading outside the village ramparts.

When I compare the two versions—this sober plan, and the visionary topography on the other side of the board—when I admire the transfiguration of forms, I cannot but think that one drawing is dreaming the other. On the wooden board where Yusef drew his two versions, the two sides can never be seen at the same time. Between them is yet another kind of turn. Not a muscular turn, but a lapse. Suddenly, as if reopening the eyes or turning the page of a book, one awakes in a different world. From one drawing to the other, there is a passage to the Other Scene.

To grasp this transfiguration from one side of the board to the other, I compare features of the two topographies, omissions and additions. In the earlier map there is no coloring of figures; colors are intensified in the second drawing, and make the painted figures stand out as concrete apparitions. Arḥabî is an unmarked element of the layout in the referential plan; it becomes the energetic center of the visionary map, its heart. Omitted from the referential map, the bright orange building with the state halo becomes a pole of the second drawing, where it creates a dynamic sense of space and an uncanny temporal foregrounding. Both Arḥabî and the crowned building have become sites of symbolic condensation (alchemic conversion, in De Certeau's terms), emblematic knots of the visionary topography. Missing in the referential map are also the cycle of the palm tree, a human figure levitating above the Frame, and of course, the signature of the draftsman and the titles of the four scenes.

Had Yusef shown the verso of his wooden board to his compatriots, they would not have contested his work. Approximately drawn to scale, it was an accurate depiction of the old qṣar and its immediate surroundings, something they could recognize as a map. But he chose not to show that first drawing, and opposed their criticism with his silence. Because for him only the second drawing was a true *representation of the qṣar. That was the version he signed. Truth—for Yusef at least—was of a different order than verisimilitude; it could appear in a visionary topography. Rather than a descriptive representation, that topography is a vision, produced by the energetic force of the eye-in-the-tracing. Ibn al-ʿArabî named that imaginal force* al-himma, *"aspiration" or "energetic endeavor"; it is the power of the creative imagination, which dislocates the subject and moves the external world.*[33]

It is so that Yusef's dream of the map is also the inscription of a life, a biographeme.[34] *Not because it narrates a life, even though a life narrates itself in the process, but because it invests and consumes a life in its work. In Islamic metaphysics, as in the experience of people in the qṣar, truth often comes in dreams. It seldom comes in maps. (When it was made to coincide with maps, it became the truth of colonization.) For Yusef's artistic imagination, an unsettled and exiled one, a truth glinted, moonlight on metal, in the visionary dream of a map. In the words of Kateb Yacine, that other visionary writer of modernity's elliptical returns, the map is "un songe hors de mémoire," a vision of forgetting.*[35] *A modernist topography in the ʿâlam al-mithâl.*

In the formal construction of this modernist dream, perspectival optics and solid geometry play a crucial role. They lend a structure of transfiguration, an enclosure, or frame, for the staging of another scene; a scene in which the laws of perspective no longer apply, or where they follow different rules. As with the magic squares Yusef sometimes drew for people (Kh. immediately grasped that resemblance), the tracing of an enclosure can alter the coordinates of the real.

The pivotal transformation between the "referential" and the "visionary" topographies of the qṣar has to do with the geometrical structure of the Frame: its volume, and the whirling rotation of figures. This transformation makes possible all the others. It is within the geometrical Frame that colors are intensified, figures telescoped, and features of the layout emblematically conflated. And it is within the Frame that the four scenes can unfold in a kind of theater, in which each has its independent choreography.

But the Frame is the legacy of the Frenchman; it is the site of a disjunction, a sort of no man's land where the mother tongue dreams into a foreign language, and where the two tongues dream within each other, "chacune fait signe à l'autre, l'appelle à se maintenir comme dehors."[36] Visionary topology of a *bi-langue*. "Ils se caressent maintenant, se rêvant l'un dans l'autre."

On that cube with one face too many or two too few, the trace of the other language is half-effaced yet visible. Watermarked in the construction of the Frame, there is the shadow of a three-dimensional model. It is Yusef's "French" reference: a maquette, or reduced model, used to portray at the same time the plan of a building and its frontal projections, its different external sides as well as its interior.[37] Maquettes are used in the drawing of architectural projects, but are also a standard mode of representation in technical illustrations (such as the diagrams of engine parts in a mechanical handbook). For Yusef, an electrician and a builder of fans, both genres are associated with the Frenchman.

Miniatures and Bird's-Eye Views

In the pictorial vocabulary of early European cartography, maquettes correspond to the kind of representation known as a bird's-eye view.

Bird's-eye views are probably the most common style for the portrayal of European cities, from the twelfth to the seventeenth century. They range from the medieval emblematic, almost ideogrammatic representations of cities within their walls (modeled on a symbolic map of Jerusalem), to the realistic perspectival panoramas of Rome or Venice of the sixteenth century. What bird's-eye views have in common as a genre is that "they show cities as if from a height with at least a few of the most distinctive buildings visible within the walls."[38]

They became popular during the Renaissance, when what was then called perspectiva artificialis *seized the modern European imagination.*[39] *Realistic portraits of cities, they were perspectival panoramas from above, structured by a single fixed viewpoint. The painter stood ideally on a height, and drew the view from that elevated perspective, enjoying from that fixed standpoint "the privilege of presentness."*[40]

Before picture maps and diagrammatic plans parted company in the history of cartography, bird's-eye views were at once plan and picture; they were a pictorial place where perspectival and planimetric registers, referential and allegorical ones, could dialogue with each other at the threshold of reality and dream. The twofold vocation of these depictions as realistic and phantasmagoric topographies becomes apparent in their migration eastward, in a sixteenth-century genre of Turkish miniatures of cities and built landscapes influenced by European perspective and informed by topographical concerns. It is this heteroclite style of paintings that Yusef's map unwittingly most resembles. Because in the syncretic climate of early Ottoman art, the European style of perspectiva artificialis, *with its shading of figures and its receding planes and volumes, was used side by side with other representational strategies, inspired by Persian pictorial techniques and informed by a different spatiotemporal orientation. Overlapping planes, the strategic use of color and calligraphic decoration, the simultaneous depiction of outer walls and interiors, structured multidimensional representations in which "the onlooker is asked to promenade around the pictorial space, to enter the architecture and to climb up and down,"*[41] *and in which "past and future are simultaneously in the present."*[42]

The miniatures by al-Matrâqî and ʿArifî in the manuscripts of the Sulaymânnâma *or of the* Futûhat-i jamîla, *were conceived as illustrations for a new genre of realistic historical accounts, written to narrate the itinerary of the military campaigns of the sultan Suleyman the Magnificent.*[43] *In these works, perspectival depictions of cities and fortified villages, illustrating historical events in real places, are shown side by side with flat scenes, structured by a superimposition of planes and a multiplicity of spaces, because successive times and actions are repre-*

sented on different planes or spaces. As if at the boundaries the representation blurred to indeterminacy, in these miniatures the perimetric walls of cities and the façades of buildings are oriented in different directions, forcing the viewer to move along with the drawing and adjust to shifting frontal projections. Separate and independent spaces are grafted onto the main picture frame, indicating narrative and conceptual multidimensionality (what appears as topological ambiguity). Yet this is found side by side with perspectival scenes, citations from European bird's-eye views. In some cases the technique of perspective is used (with what seems a playful political awareness) to mark differential identities, as in a painting of the siege of Belgrade by ʿArifî, where the dwellings of the Christians are drawn with shading and receding volumes, while the spaces of the Ottomans are painted as overlapping planes.[44] The offspring of this dialogue of genres is a composite style, in which the European code of perspective is cited, and then abandoned to the work of different rules. In many miniatures by ʿArifî, a building or a fortress is shown perspectivally from one side while it flattens into a colorful two-dimensionality from the other, merging into the background like a spot of color on paper; it becomes then the element of another scene, painted on an overlapping plane and according to different aesthetic conventions.

As drawn in the style of contemporary architectural maquettes, a three-dimensional representation of the qṣar from above would show the exterior ramparts and towers and the interior layout of alleys and houses realistically. Hypothetically reconstructed on the base of Yusef's Frame cube, it would be a box formed by the exterior ramparts (the towers in the drawing), hollow inside.

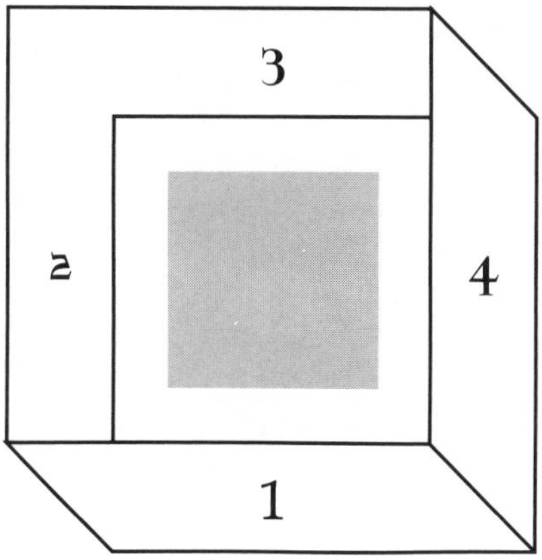

The hollow internal space would be the proper place of the village interior, *l-dâkhel.* (And one would realize that this model is but a three-dimensional rendering of the referential topography Yusef drew on the reverse of his wooden board.) In this hypothetical model the onlooker is situated on a height just above side 1 (in front of the Gate), and sees the ramparts from that fixed perspective. The interior space of the qṣar is visible as a bird's-eye view. But, instead, this is what Yusef drew:

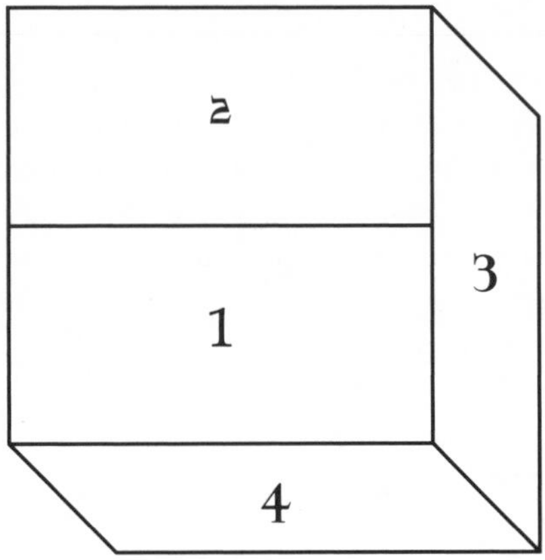

A memory of the three-dimensional maquette is kept in the axonometric construction of the Frame cube (all sides of the cube have the same length; axonometric representations show the plan of a building in elevation and scale).[45] But the model has undergone a transformation, and the container has nothing to contain. Or perhaps it is sealed. The cube has no interior, and only painted surfaces are offered to the view. The axonometric shape of the Frame is just a citation of the perspectival code. It is a citation from the panoramas of the Frenchman, or from the diagrams of engine parts in mechanical handbooks. A reinscription of the code of modernity.

Sides 1 and 2 of the three-dimensional model are conflated on the frontal face of the Frame cube. Compressed by the work of this visionary geometry, the cube itself has only four faces. The three-dimensional bird's-eye view of the interior, with its alleys and houses, is condensed into the composite image of Arḥabî and is superimposed on the frontal surface of the cube. Painted as a dark spot, Arḥabî-the-Interior is assimilated to the background, like an overlapping plane in Turkish miniatures. The maquette of the qṣar has been transformed into a *miniature,* a "reduced model" of a different sort, and is structured by another spatiotemporal orientation. One of the effects of this visionary transformation is that it presents a space that is at once impenetrable and offered to the gaze. A mise-en-scène of the exile of the heart.

Because Arḥabî has become the most charged knot of Yusef's visionary drawing, its *qalb* or "heart."

In Sufi mystical physiology the heart is the locus of a force (*quwwa*)[46] that moves and orients the subject in the cosmos. It is not a fixed place or a static center, but a locus of constant transformation and movement; a center of "fluctuation," Ibn al-ʿArabî writes (and this is why it is called *qalb*, "heart," he adds, from a root meaning "to change" and "to reverse"). In this sense, it is the only human faculty capable of grasping the essential nondelimitation of God, called in many hadiths "the Turner of hearts." As such, Ibn al-ʿArabî writes, "the heart is a faculty [*quwwa*] which is beyond the stage of reason."[47]

In miniatures, the "heart" is the often hidden conceptual center of the pictorial composition.[48] The "heart" of Yusef's drawing is imaged by a specific and concrete location, which becomes a stenographic symbol of the qṣar's interior: Arḥabî.

As a physical place, Arḥabî is a widening in the village alleys, almost a square next to the big mosque.[49] Place of ritual gatherings, talking, dancing, and storytelling, it was, until people started building outside the walls, the innermost communal space of the qṣar—the only uncovered space in the thick network of alleys tightly intertwined with each other. *Arḥabî* is to the physiology of the built body of the qṣar what the "eye" is to that of the house (*ʿayn d-dâr*, "the eye of the house," is also called *raḥba*). The ʿayn/eye is related to the heart.

The Heart and the Kaʿaba

But there is another dimension to Yusef's visionary topography; it is related to the hermeneutics of a mystical ta'wîl.[50] *What "appears" in the drawing at the topographic place of the heart is the Kaʿaba, the sacred "cube" and house of God,*[51] *symbol of the covenant and cardinal orientation of Islam. "Wherever you are, turn your faces in that direction," the Qurʾan says (2:144). The Kaʿaba is imaged by the cube, and within the Frame cube by the dark area inscribed with the legend "Arḥabî"; it is imaged in the sense in which, in Sufi metaphysics, images* (muthul) *are concrete manifestations of the sacred through a borrowed visible form, an "example." (Ibn al-ʿArabî had himself compared the heart to the Kaʿaba, the "noblest house in the man of faith.")*[52] *What is superimposed on the map of the qṣar, and visibly revealed at the place of Arḥabî, is the symbolic diagram of the Masjid al-Ḥarâm in Mecca.*

It is a well-known diagram: a rectangular enclosure, with the cubical Kaʿaba at the center, bordered by a stylized arcade complete with minarets. The Kaʿaba is covered by a black cloth, inscribed in golden letters, and all the important landmarks of that sacred enclosure are in place, including the lamps and the well of Zamzam. From Morocco to Turkey and Iran, this symbolic topography was reproduced until the nineteenth century in miniatures and in manuscript illustrations, in decorated copies of the Qurʾan, prayerbooks, and even on tiles. It can now be found in books, posters, and postcards. The diagram is part of the instructional and orientational apparatus related to the pilgrimage, the ḥajj; it contains a practical template of rituals to perform, and visually represents the cardinal symbolic orientation for a Muslim. Topographic but also allographic, the diagrammatic "view of the Kaʿaba" refers to a theological symbol, and to a journey.

Reference to the Kaʿaba in the map of the qṣar both centers and decenters the representation; it displaces it toward a mystical and geographical elsewhere, grafting the specificity of Yusef's history and that of his community within the universal embrace of the Islamic umma. *In Muslim cartography, no cosmos can ever be self-contained. "Remember we made the House a place of assembly for men and a place of safety; and take the Station of Abraham as a place of prayer; and We covenanted with Abraham and Ismâʿîl, that they should sanctify My House for those who compass it round,* li-l-ṭṭâ'ifyîna" *(Qurʾan 2:125).*

*"Circumambulating"—*ṭawâf*—is what a Muslim is expected to do around the Kaʿaba. Circumambulating, that is turning, is what the towers and other glyphs do around the center of the drawing, and what the draftsman, or the reader, must do around the board.*

If Arḥabî is the "heart" of Yusef's map, its mystical Kaʿaba, and the internal pole around which the representation revolves, the Orange Building in the peripheral scene is the pole of the outside. In the visionary dream of the map, the two sites are symbolically charged, and dialogically opposed to each other.

The Orange Building, which in real life is pink, was for a long time the only cement construction in the area—a big heavy structure, with metal shutters and industrial sliding doors. Harbinger of a change to come, it loomed over the landscape at the edge of the village territory. Only later—after the partition of the communal land out in the desert when people started moving *extramuros*—the pink building became the gravitational center of a new settlement. In July 1984, the date Yusef inscribed on his map, the construction of the New Village had just begun. The map foretold its advent—like a folding of the future onto the past.

Dreams look for pictorial images, capable of becoming scenic material for another stage.[53] The Orange Building in the drawing is a site of condensation, a persona in the theatrical representation of the new world, a compound figure of the desired and terrifying advent of modernity. The crown it wears—that halo—alludes to the new administrative center of the New Village; beyond it, it winks at the modern state, in the organization of which the qṣar is both recognized and effaced. An oversized figure carrying a breadboard—a citation from the everyday world of cities[54]—is shown walking away from the Frame, away from the old qṣar, and in the direction of the Orange Building. It forms a counterpoint to the man climbing the palm tree on the other side of the drawing, suggesting that the new world is turning its back to the gardens and to the labors of tilling the earth, but also that it is "emancipating" itself from the allegorical cycle of the palm tree. The heart of the interior and the pole of the exterior are opposed in the drawing as the Old and the New, in a visual saga of the qṣar's recent history.

Seventh Turn: Remembering from Right to Left

The inscriptions in red ink are explicit. Spread out like banners across each of the four scenes inside the Frame, they make it clear that the Frame cube must be read as a representation of the village interior. The titles of the four scenes are the names of what, with an alliteration familiar to anyone in the qṣar, is called *l-arbaʿ rbaʿ*, the "four fourths": the Fourth of Ayt l-Bâlî (people of the Old), the Fourth of Ayt j-Jdîd (people of the New), the Fourth of Ayt ʿAbdallah (children of ʿAbdallah), and the Fourth of Ayt Driss (children of Driss; in Yusef's estranged reckoning, this becomes the Fourth of Ayt l-Qâḍî). Each fourth is a quarter, in the territorial sense, but also a section of the village body in a symbolic sense; it is a place, but also a group of people, sharing a number of preoccupations and tasks. On the ground, each fourth is a square section of the qṣar, furrowed by three major alleys, and for at least three centuries each has kept its internal organization—its *ḥsâb*, "count"—has sent its representatives to the community council (*qbîla*), and its share of workers to the digging of the irrigation canals. To each fourth is attached a story—a legend—that is a version of the qṣar's history, and each harbors a known group of families and a distinct style of life; each is a storage room of memories. Together, the four fourths compose the articulated body of the qṣar.

But what is visible in each of the four scenes inside the Frame is an emblematic arrangement of architectural shapes drawn from the exterior ramparts of the qṣar. Not the four fourths of the qṣar's interior, but the four faces of its outward appearance, its parure. Inside the village there are no crenelated towers or palm trees, but only a thick network of dark alleys covered by faceless houses that intersect tightly with each other. What shows in the drawing is the qṣar as seen from the outside, or the qṣar reflected in a mirror. (This is one of the first remarks someone made in looking at the drawing: "It is as if *we* were looking at *our* reflection in water." A mirror can also be an impassable barrier.)

Towers and the other architectural motifs are not conventional signs. They are real buildings, each painted with the stress on some telling detail; recognizable fragments, pieces of "a lacunary system."[55] On the Tower of ʿAshirî there is always a pigeon; Yusef faithfully drew it on his map. It is as if a disaster fissured the integrity of a whole that can now be known only through its fragments; as if in the aftermath of that event the use of articulated language was itself partly lost, and only names, displaced and mutilated names, and a few scattered objects were left in Yusef's hands to recount. A suspension of memory, or one of the innumerable wrackings that punctuate the collective memory of his land. Floods, razings, invasions. Just recently, the great flood of 1979, which washed out the entire Fourth of Ayt j-Jdîd in the space of one night, or the slowly disastrous advent of the exodus *extramuros*. As if Yusef was left with the fragments, the towers and the names in his drawing are ruins; not because they are in ruin, even though some towers are portrayed as in ruin, but because they are treated as emblems, concrete remains through which he tells his story. Torn away from their context, they are recycled as images, as the building material for a new construction.

For a reader familiar with the layout of the qṣar, and who can recognize the landmarks inscribed in the drawing,[56] the names attached to the towers indicate that Yusef is (ideally) circumambulating the perimetric walls of the qṣar, in the style of certain ritual events that concern the community as a whole. He is turning around the walls as in the Turning of the Thread (*l-khayṭ*)—that thread of white wool, spun in a state of ritual purity, that women used to tie around the ramparts in times of danger and fear to make *l-ḥjâb ll-qṣar*, a "protective barrier around the qṣar" (for the ominous illness of discord was unraveling the loom of the community, or because the deadly pollen of the *wâqwâq* tree,[57] originating in distant and unknown lands, was spreading an epidemic and killing the children).

Or he is turning around the cubical Frame of the qṣar like a pilgrim performing the rite of *ṭawâf* around the Kaʿaba—or around one of the innumerable shrines that punctuate the familiar landscape. Or simply like someone who has become estranged after a long exile—wanders around the walls without deciding to enter, without finding a way in, since that Gate yet open has become an impassable boundary. And he takes the path around the walls instead, forever captured, forever excluded. Such is the modernist position of the draftsman in this drawing.

And he walks-draws, Yusef, looking at the gate in its faded splendor. He writes *fum l-qdîm,* "the Old Gate." And he sees *burj l-qbîla,* the Tower of the qbîla,[58] where in the old days, and still when he was a child, the *jmaʿa,* the "council of elders," used to meet. He does not cross the threshold, but turns to the left, following the perimetric walls at the limit of the palm trees. There is the well of the qbîla, the communal well of the old days, which he draws just to the left of the Gate. He is walking along the irrigation canal at the edge of the gardens—he draws a man climbing a palm tree—in the direction opposite to that of the *qebla,* "the east," as if he were performing a sort of reverse rite.

Yusef is not turning rightward, to the east, where the sun rises and the river flows, where the white dome of the sanctuary of Sîdî Ṣâfu catches the eye of the traveler and where people orient themselves when they pray. It is rightward (counterclockwise) that pilgrims circumambulate the Kaʿaba, and it is toward the east that the healing rite of the thread was performed around the qṣar. At the gate the procession of women made a right, and kept turning counterclockwise at the chanting of the name of God as the *muqaddema,* the ritual leader of the women, tied at each step the thread of wool to the ramparts with a thorn. In that embrace, the qṣar was symbolically restored. The thread wound its loosened threads, ṭightened its fibers, as in the knotting of the warps of a loom.

But Yusef is turning the other way, as if unwinding the reel of the qṣar, unraveling its fabric. He's turning to the left, *l-gharb,* "the west," where the sun sets and people disappear. The west, the direction of estrangement: *al-ghurba,* the direction of the exile to the cities, the direction of the cemetery of Lâllâ ud Sîdî, the direction of time and forgetting, the direction of writing. It is the direction of the other gaze in his drawing, the gaze of things. Like magic, writing partakes of the inanimate world. *L-ketba,* "writing," is one of the names of magic.

Al-Gharb

For classical Arab geographers, al-gharb, *"the west," is the direction of alterity. Al-Idrîsî (twelfth century) begins the description of each of the seven climates of his world map with an account of the western limit. The edge of the world, in the midst of the Ocean of Darkness. The boundary zone is elusive, "no one knows what exists beyond." On the limit, islands, chance encounters of the traveler astray. Uncanny places—*

gharîb *(from the same root as* gharb, *"west") inhabited by monstrous creatures, "things reason refuses to accept." A statue, sometimes, a raised arm pointing at the boundless space on the other side: it warns the traveler that beyond that point there can be no return.*

From the Kitâb nuzhat al-mushtâq, *by Abû ʿAbd Allâh al-Idrîsî:*

> *And we say that the first section of the second climate begins from the far west* [al-maghrîb al-ʿaqṣa] *where the Sea of Darkness is* [baḥr aẓ-ẓulumât] *and no one knows what exists beyond. In this section*[59] *are found the island of Masfahân, and the island of Laghûs, which are from the six islands called al-Khâlidât, from which Ptolemy began his leveling and measured the length and width of the earth, and where Dhû al-Qarnayn arrived, the man of the two horns, Alexander, and whence he came back.*
>
> *About the island of Masfahân, the author of the Book of Wonders* [Kitâb al-ʿajâib] *recounts that there is a circular mountain at its center, on top of which is found a red statue that was built by Asʿad Abû Karab al-Ḥimyarî. He is the Dhû al-Qarnayn that was cited by Tabuʿ in his poetry; for whoever reaches the edges of the world* [ṭuruf al-arḍ] *is called by the name Dhû al-Qarnayn. Abû Karab al-Ḥimyarî put the statue there to be a warning for everyone who went there from sea, to let him know that there was no way he could take beyond that point, no place at which to arrive. In the island of Laghûs there is another statue, strongly built and impossible to reach. It is said that its builder died in the same island; it is Tabuʿ Dhû al-Marâthid, and his tomb is built of marble and colored glasswork. It is also said by the author of the Book of Wonders that in this island there are enormous animals and things too long to describe and that reason refuses to accept.*[60]

Yusef's landmarks are formulated in the present. Tazgert's tower, *burj Tazgert,* just to the left of the village gate, was only recently bought by that owner. That house and the surrounding neighborhood used to be lived in by the Jews. It had been the Mellaḥ, the Jewish quarter, until 1965, when the last of the Jews left on a red truck to Casablanca, and then to Israel. Tazgert, who up to that time had lived with his family in a tight two rooms in the Alley of Ayt l-Ghandur, bought the house from Khalifa n-Aron, the rich merchant of tea, and moved there.

Yusef knows this, of course. When he was a child and his family was still living in the Alley of Bû Twîl, his father would send him to buy tea and sugar at the shop of the old Jew. Behind that house, at the end of a narrow corridor, still stands the little synagogue with the Well of the Jews, that object of the erotic fantasies of all children like himself: it was there that the young Jewish brides took the ritual bath. But Yusef chooses to ignore all this. Or perhaps he has forgotten. At least at first sight, he chooses to keep himself on the surface of things, opting for a radical presentism. He turns the corner of the walls at *j-jâmeʿ l-Bâlî,* the little mosque of the Fourth of Ayt l-Bâlî, the original nucleus of the qṣar (*l-bâlî,* "the Old"). It is there that the qṣar began, some five hundred years ago. He signals this fact with a tower in ruin.[61]

He continues on, now walking along the cemetery of Lâllâ ud-Sîdî, where the tomb of the Judge is, *l-Qâḍî,* the legendary founder of the qṣar according to the version told by Yusef's lineage. It is he, the Judge, Sîdî Aḥmad u ʿAlî l-Qâḍî, who is said to have surrounded the village with high walls and encircled the walls with a deep moat. Yusef walks by his tomb (that big standing white stone is so imposing), but does not write it in his map. The omissions are as important as the inscriptions. In his visual reckoning of the village, he reserves the right to leave out what he wants.

He marks *fum l-bâlî,* the mouth of the Bâlî quarter, a gate that was just recently opened, the Tower of l-Wazzânî, the Tower of ʿAshirî with the pigeon, and goes on, passing almost without noticing Dyâr l-Makhzen, "the Makhzen Residences," where up to the 1890s a representative of the sultan was stationed with a small garrison of soldiers. It is said that the old makhzen[62] rented that land from the descendants of the Qâḍî; when later a new powerful family arose, it settled there, and during the colonial period ruled over the land in behalf of the new French makhzen. Yusef doesn't write all this on his map—descriptive history doesn't concern him—he limits himself to putting on a tower the insignia of the identity-card name (the choice of a radical present, as opposed to the lineage name commonly used in the qṣar) of a man who is today a judge in the modern world, the last in a chain of powerful and too-powerful rulers.

Yusef is now rounding the corner again: the ramparts have four sides. He walks by the *maṭḥana,* the public mill activated by the engine of a Ford truck, and continues along *fum l-qâḍî,* called in fact *fum l-makhzen,* "the Makhzen's Gate," which was opened in the 1930s by order of a French officer. Another major omission. And he reaches the front of the Gate of Bû Ṭwîl.[63]

Bû Ṭwîl the Long is the alley where his family originally lived. It is the longest and relatively widest alley of the qṣar, residence to some important Ḥarâr lineages: among them Yusef's family. It used to dead-end against the perimetric walls with a sort of enclaved widening that was known as *n-nqob,* "the Hood." The Hood, in front of which Yusef is now standing without allowing himself to step in, used to be a gathering pool for the women of the alley; Yusef's mother used to sit there to mill.

Echoes of the strident sound of the millstones, of the loud voices of women, of laughter, of sexual jokes. Women didn't bother to restrain their tongues in the presence of children. Yusef was too old to sit there, he had to fetch firewood in the gardens, or to learn the Qur'an at the mosque. But he sat there all the same. One day his mother caught him playing with the millstones—flour spilled everywhere. She threatened to separate the stones and make him walk through the path between. Yusef knew what that meant, all children knew. It was the threat of impotence. With a neighbor woman, she pretended to get ready to act, laughing. He'll become as soft as a thread, they said,[64] even softer than the day Ḥammu the blacksmith cut off the tip of his sex. That too happened, after all, in the Alley of Bû Twîl the Long.

He was playing with the children in the alley, barefoot in the dust. She had called from the roof. Smell of bread and smoke. A woman had come in the dark. She had stopped under the narrow spot of light that filtered from the light well of the alley and called his name. He hadn't noticed her in her black veil, until she had spoken to him. She took his hand and told him to follow her, she had something for him. They walked around the corner and she grabbed him, put him on her back, and started running. He was afraid, he screamed. His mother was too faraway to hear. The woman—he couldn't recognize her—climbed the dark narrow staircase of a house several alleys away. Women ululating, the suffocating smell of incense, noise, confusion. Someone grabbed him and held his legs tight apart, till he couldn't move. Then a scream. It took him years to realize that it was a setup; that his mother had known and pretended not to know because in their lineage circumcision was done by kidnapping, kayserqu l-wlâd, *"children were stolen," it was a custom they couldn't break; and that when the woman tied him on her back with his bleeding sex against her skin and ran ululating to his mother's house, and his mother screamed and insulted her, that when his mother threw at her the sifter and the pestle, the pots and pans of the kitchen—that too was a setup. It was the rite a mother had to perform when her "stolen" son was circumcised in a stranger's house and brought back. It was a stage of betrayal.*

Yusef walks on. *Burj l-ḥajj l-Badawî, fum Ayt Aḥmâd,* the "mouth of the Alley of Ayt Aḥmâd," *burj Aḥmâd u l-Mukhtâr,* all the way to the next corner, which in the map is marked by a tower upside down, almost a mirror image. (It is here, on the unstable boundary between the third and the fourth scene, that the autonomous formal play of the images in the drawing is most striking.)

He is now walking along the fourth side of the qṣar. He stops in front of *fum j-jdîd,* "the New Gate." He draws it almost as imposing as the Old Gate, even though it is just an average aperture. For the New Gate is an emblem of freedom. It is the gate young men like him, like him today, fought for in the 1950s at the time of the independence movement, *l-waṭân.* They used to sit there by the walls, discuss and play the lute through the summer nights. Like prisoners planning an escape, every night they dug a bit into the walls. One night they opened a breach; it was an act of open rebellion, against colonial supervision but above all against the old ways of the qṣar, in which they couldn't recognize themselves anymore. The youths were sent to jail, then, but at independence the New Gate was officially opened.

The tour around the walls is almost over, the circle almost complete. Yusef walks faster now, and the drawing is distorted by speed. *Fum Ayt Driss, fum Ayt ʿAzzî,* and then the ruins of *dâr r-rma,* literally "the house of the sharpshooters." It is Yusef's only concession to my interest in the social history of the village or, perhaps, his sole concession to archival history in the name of the one traditional institution that in his view, expressed the dignity and the value of men.

And he is back in front of the Old Mouth, the Gate/Mouth, in its feared yet desired splendor, in its despised yet cherished legacy. The Gate seems impassable, an invisible yet impenetrable wall. Yusef stands impotently at its front. It is as if it were protected by a ritual interdiction. The invisible barrier has a name: *l-ʿatba dyâl Ben ʿAbd l-Mûla,* "Ben ʿAbd l-Mûla's threshold."[65] It is the legend of the threshold. There is a curse inscribed in that threshold of white stone, made smooth by the work of time, which marks the step between the outside and the inside of the qṣar. The curse is one of protection, that the qṣar be shielded and its people live in peace, but is also a sharp saw that excludes those who are not "from us." When the qṣar was first being built—in the mythical times of its gathering—the saint came, buried a saw in the ground where the threshold was to be, and said, "*Ḥa l-manshâr, llî khârj ʿala l-farâʾyd ittenshar*" (this is the Saw; who trespasses the Law will be sawn).

That Saw, an image that became a thing,[66] is also the pact that ties up by sawing apart: "The threshold of Ben Abd l-Mûla is the Saw" (*l-ʿatba dyâl Ben ʿAbd l-Mûla hiyâ l-manshâr*), people say with fear and respect. It is the *ʿatba* that in the past prevented enemies from overpowering the qṣar, that repelled the invasions and shielded the precarious integrity of the land. The threshold protects you if you are "one of us," or if you enter in full confidence and peace, if there, by the *ʿatba,* you "submit" to the masters of the land—alive and dead, of this world and of the other. But if your *niya* is in question,[67] if you have committed a wrong, or feel you have committed a wrong, and you cross the threshold, the consequences of your act will pursue you.

Yusef's *niya* is not in question. But he is caught on both sides of the Saw. In between, *f-l-baînât.* Like the character of Rachid in Kateb Yacine's novel *Nedjma,* Yusef is suspended in midflight, "caught in the wing between ground and target": "Rachid nettoyait la pipe, sur le gouffre nocturne, prenant de la hauteur comme un avion délesté, inoffensif et vulnérable, pris en chasse entre la base et l'objectif."[68] Such is the uncertain place Yusef inhabits in his drawing, which is a map of the exile of the heart. A map his compatriots failed to recognize as theirs. Not unlike the Maghribî writers in the French language, he borrows and subverts a foreign code. He reinvents through it a shared imaginary, which is not the ethnological record of a people that was, but the solitary tracing of a people to come. Personal and collective at once—

Eighth Turn: The Story of the Dough-Boy

Praise to the Prophet, glory and praise to the Prophet, and the devil be cursed. There was a man, yet the only man is the Messenger of God, honor and praise to him, and there was a woman, yet the only woman is Lâllâ Fatima Zoḥra, daughter of the Prophet, praise and honor to her:

There was a mother, and she had a son. It was the son she had shaped with her own hands when her husband threatened to repudiate her if she didn't give birth to a son. She had gone to the kitchen, taken a bit of bread dough, and modeled the dough in the likeness of a boy, subât fîh wâḥed ṣûra dyâl l-wuld. *She wrapped the Dough-boy into a cloth and came down the stairs reciting at each step,* derja b-derja iḥenn mul l-ferja, *"step by step grows pity in the Merciful." When she reached the front door of the house the baby came to life. He sneezed and she said, "Praise be to God, health and happiness my little son." Everybody rejoiced, mother and father. But the Dough-boy grew too fast: children take years to grow, he grew by the hour. Soon he developed into a tall arrogant young man.*

One day the father said to the mother, "That son of yours is constantly making trouble in the streets, getting into fights, no one can have the better of him." The Dough-boy wasn't suited for life in the qṣar. And the father tried to get rid of his son. He sent him to get wood in the forest, in the hope he'd get lost. The ghwâl *will find him and eat him, he thought to himself. But the boy overpowered the ogres. Fourteen came. He killed seven, and put seven to work. At daybreak the muezzin who was calling the faithful to prayer saw the terrifying scene of a forest moving toward the qṣar. He was about to utter "God is the greatest," but in his terror all he could say was "The horror is coming." It was the Dough-boy who had ordered the ogres to carry the trees to the gate of the qṣar.*

The father kept wondering what to do with that son no one could overpower. "If he stays in the qṣar, he will cause disaster and ruin." Finally he thought of a way. He gave him his very best horse, he gave him his mother, and he banished him.

Go away! and never come back...

They went and they went, the Dough-boy and his mother, till they arrived at a place in the desert where was a palace in ruin. The boy went hunting. His mother was approached by a ghûl *who lived in the ruins. He liked her, and proposed marriage to her. She said, "All right, but I have a son, a son no one can overpower." They decided to get rid of him: "We must send him somewhere to die."*

And when the son came back, his mother said: "I am ill, my son. If you love me and care for me, bring me the Water of between-the-Mountains, l-ma dyâl grûn j-jbel. *If I drink it I'll be cured."*

The boy complied, mounted his horse, and went. He was riding too fast and ran over a hut made of leaves. An old woman came out cursing. The Dough-boy promised to build her a new house made of stone. The old woman asked him where he was going. He said, "I have a mother...," and he told her everything, from beginning to end. The old woman said, "She sent you to a dangerous place, she wants you to die." He asked what to do, and she said, "I'll give you a device that will help you come back."

She gave him a bowl and a long rope and she said, "The water you seek springs in the cavity between two mountains. But these mountains hate humans. If they feel your presence, they close up on you and they crush you. You must keep distance. Get close, but not too close to the water, and from there throw the rope and the bowl I gave you. With these tools draw the water, turn your horse back, and run off. The mountains won't close till you are out of their reach."

(And the draftsman was initiated to distance, to measure, and to the art of staying alive.)

The Dough-boy took the bowl and the rope, said goodbye, and went. He went till he approached the place where the magic water was hidden, threw the rope with the bowl, got his water, and ran off. As the mountains closed up they found nothing to seize.

(The story goes on with the boy who keeps coming home alive to his mother, with the mother who sends him out to increasingly dangerous tasks, and with the old woman, whose advice rescues the boy at each turn. The last task—after which only murder is left—takes the boy to an enchanted garden.)

Trees are talking to each other. One tree is saying, "If one of yours died, collect his bones and join them up again. Take one of my branches, beat the bones with it, and that person will come back to life."

Another tree is saying, "If one of yours is murdered (tedbaḥ), *dismember his body piece by piece* (fęṣṣlu ṭerf b-ṭerf), *cut him up, and undo his articulations the way it is done with a butchered animal. Then pound a few of my leaves, assemble his body back together as it was* (jmaʿ), *and when you've gathered those joints and that flesh, stitch them up* (kheyyeṭ) *and smear them with the dust from my leaves. He'll come back to life, God permitting."*

(AND THE DRAFTSMAN LEARNED THE MEDICAL ART OF BEING HUMAN, FOUND HIS ART OF MEMORY AND THE TECHNIQUE OF HIS DRAWING.)

The boy from each of the remedies got a bit, and came back to the house of the old woman. She rejoiced, but warned him that if he went back home, his mother had no choice left but to murder him. "I must go." "She will kill you this time," the old woman told him. "When she does, just before the knife digs into your throat, ask her to cut your body in pieces, put it into a bag, put the bag on your horse and send it off."

The boy went home to his mother. She embraced him and kissed him. One night as he was about to sleep, she approached him and said, "My son, I am the one who nursed you at my breast, confide your secret to me. I know you are stronger than any man on earth; no one can overpower you, but you must have a weak spot; tell your mother which is your weak spot." "If my hair-lock is tied to my foot."[69] *And she had him. With the knife at his throat he screamed, "Betrayal: mother, this is betrayal." She said, "Yes, betrayal."*

The horse brought back his remains. The old woman cried and lamented, he was dead. Really dead. And she mourned him. Then, when she had mourned him, when she was done with her mourning, she got his pieces out of the bag one by one, and, one by one, trekkebhum: *she "rejoined" them bone by bone. She then stitched the flesh with a thread, and smeared it with the powder from the enchanted tree.* Rûḥ, *"life," slowly came back into him, and he started to move. Now he had to rebuild his strength. Slowly she fed him a quarter of an egg, then half an egg, then a whole egg. He started walking around. He was impatient, he couldn't wait; he wanted to go get his revenge. But the old woman held him.*

Still he had to learn patience, s-ṣbâr. *He had to learn how to wait. She said, "Before you get on your horse, throw this rock all the way to the sky. If the stitches don't break, you can go." He did, and the stitches opened up. They had to start over. He waited for long months, till he got his strength back, and the stitches were healed. Then he left to exact his vengeance.*

He arrived at the house of his mother one day at sunset. She wanted to embrace him, but he said, "You are nothing to me." Then he killed that ghûl, *put his mother on his horse, and took her back to the house of his father. He told him, "Here is the gift you gave me, take it back." Then he went back to the old woman's house, married her daughter, and lived with them in peace.*

Ninth Turn: Mullî, the Trope of Re-turn

Crossing without crossing the threshold—of memory, of life, of the qṣar—Yusef throws the rope, like the Dough-boy. His device is that of figuration, the detour by the image, and his strategy that of composition, the stitching together of a whole from fragments, the pieces of a cut-up body.

He—the Dough-boy, Yusef, the qṣar—has to die and allow his body to be dismembered, cut into pieces, and mourned, and then, as a movement of mourning, rejoined, piece by piece, re-membered and stitched up as a new body: one that has known breaking and death and, of that disjunction, has made the imperfect principle of its wholeness. The imagery in the tale is from butchery and ritual sacrifice: "If one of yours is murdered," sings the tree in the enchanted garden, "*fesṣlu ṭerf b-ṭerf,* dismember his body piece by piece." This is what is done to the sacrificial victim, whose body is undone after slaughtering, *mfeṣṣel* by *mfeṣṣel,* "joint by joint," by the butcher. But the imagery is also from medicine, cauterization surgery, and bonesetting—the art of *jabr,* setting back together what is fractured. "Then," continues the tree, "assemble his body back together as it was, and when you've gathered those joints and that flesh, stitch them up and smear them with the dust from my leaves. He'll come back to life, God permitting."

As he walks around the ramparts from the outside—banished, like the Dough-boy, from the community, or excluding himself, as he did when he parted his destiny from that of the qṣar—Yusef is also, at the same time, following a path on the inside. An itinerary is encoded in the movement of his map, a *parcours chiffré*.[70]

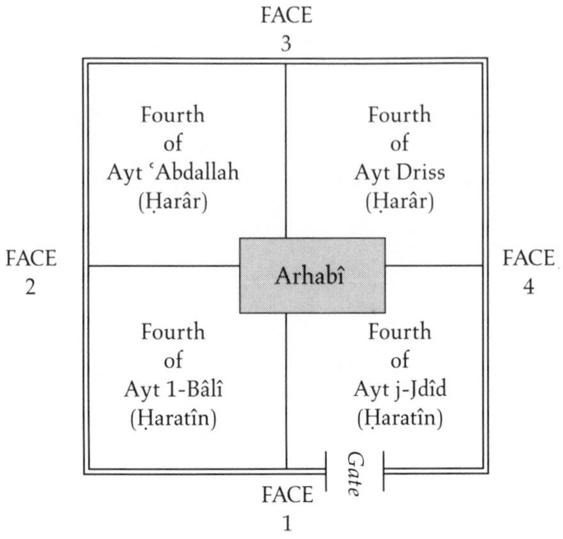

Between the names of the internal fourths Yusef assigned as titles to the scenes, and the imagery from the external faces actually shown in the scenes, there is a discrepancy, the space of a trope. It is Yusef's "rope" ("I'll give you a device that will help you come back," said the old woman to the Doughboy). Suspended with their legends within each of the four scenes, the towers in the drawing act also as dramatis personae; they are masks in a theatrical production. For the path of the eye in the drawing is a known itinerary through the qṣar. Transported from one scene to the next, the eye-in-the-tracing is following a circuit, a central and named image of the qṣar's sociomythical organization. It is the circuit of the four fourths; the circuit people call *mullî*. The map is its dramatic enactment.

L-arbaʿ rbaʿ: Servitude and Excess

The Fourths are four, but always coupled two by two. The couples shift, depending on the context, the ideological connotation, or the activity. The two Fourths of Ayt ʿAbdallah and Ayt Driss (named after two set tlers of the qṣar's mythical past) are composed and inhabited by the Ḥarâr population, landowners for centuries.[71] The Fourths of Ayt l-Bâlî and Ayt j-Jdîd are lived in by the formerly landless Ḥarâtîn.[72] Most Ḥarâtîn used to work for the Ḥarâr landlords as *khmâmes* (sing. *khammâs*), dependent laborers remunerated at "one-fifth" of the crop.[73] Often the entire family worked for the landlord's family, tied by that bond of servitude that was the contract of *khamessat*, "one-fifth"—a spoken contract, sealed by the passing on of the hoe, *l-fâs*, from the landlord's to the worker's hands. The khammâs gave his work, and in a sense his life. The landlord gave the land, the seeds, and tools, and often lent money to the worker for the support of his family throughout the year. It was this indebtedness that reproduced the tie: when the worker got his share at harvest time, he had to pay back the landlord and borrow again. Even though the contract was negotiated between free parties, that debt made it impossible to dissolve the pact.

But not all khmâmes were indebted and powerless. Some had unconditional control over agricultural production, hired seasonal workers, and acted as landlords. And not all khmâmes were Ḥarâtîn. Men from poor Ḥarâr families also worked as sharecroppers, and were almost worse off, for they could not count on the help of the tight-knit black community. Besides, some Ḥarâtîn families had land, wealth, and political influence. In the oral memory of the qṣar, the theme of rich and powerful Ḥarâtîn is recurrent. After independence the land formerly occupied by the French (or by those who ruled locally in their behalf) was expropriated and given in usufruct to the landless. Many Ḥarâtîn started their own business, and today are sometimes better off than their former landlords.

Since the nationalist egalitarian days of independence, the term *Ḥarâtîn* is perceived as a stigma and is replaced with the more neutral *Drâwâ*—from the name of the region, Wâd Draʿ. But sometimes, when used by those who call themselves Ḥarâtîn, it becomes a term of challenge: *ḥna l-Ḥarâtîn, nukni issuqiyin*, "We, the Ḥarâtîn," says l-Ḥajj l-Madanî with a smile of pride. The spatial location of the two Ḥarâtîn fourths, Ayt l-Bâlî and Ayt j-Jdîd, corresponds to the earlier built nucleus of the qṣar. The two quarters stand side by side immediately adjoining the Gate, and next to what formerly was the Mellaḥ of the Jews. In certain ritual events, such as the public sacrifice of the *ʿid l-kebir* or in matter concerning public works, their structural opposition divides the village in half. For the four fourths form two halves, in some contexts splitting the village horizontally, between two Ḥarâtîn and two Ḥarâr halves, in others splitting it vertically, between two Ḥarâr-Ḥarâtîn halves. The configuration of the qṣar is always bifaced. This inscribes a double-edged social dialectic.

Vertical is the axis of servitude, of unequal alliances between Ḥarâr and Ḥarâtîn. Ever since people can remember, the Ḥarâtîn of Ayt l-Bâlî have worked with and for the Ḥarâr of Ayt ʿAbdallah, and those of Ayt j-Jdîd with and for the Ḥarâr of Ayt Driss. They have worked with and for them at the *sâgya,* at the digging of the irrigation canal, and in all public works of the qbîla. At the canal the Ḥarâtîn of Ayt l-Bâlî opened the works, backs naked and hoe in hand, followed by the Ḥarâr of Ayt ʿAbdallah; then came the Ḥarâr of Ayt Driss, and "their" Ḥarâtîn of Ayt j-Jdîd. The work was done with laughter and jokes, metered by the praising of God and the Prophet. But it is the Ḥarâtîn who performed the hardest tasks. A similar hierarchical logic structured, in the household sphere, the relation of dependency between the landowner and his khammâs. After all, this "vertical" system was inscribed in the layout of the qṣar: it was written in the two symmetrical alleys that like two arteries on the left and right side of its body coupled the Fourth of Ayt l-Bâlî with that of Ayt ʿAbdallah, and the Fourth of Ayt j-Jdîd with that of Ayt Driss.

But this vertical logic was disturbed by the play of the horizontal axis—the horizontal split of the qṣar between Ḥarâr and Ḥarâtîn halves. That too was inscribed in the physical space of the qṣar: the alley of the mosque (in Berber, *abrid n jamaʿ*) cut perpendicularly across the other alleys, and marked the boundary between Ḥarâr and Ḥarâtîn quarters. In the horizontal sense, and as opposed to the Ḥarâr fourths, the Ḥarâtîn fourths were said to be *khoṭ,* "siblings" and neighbors, in the physical and social space built into the structure of their houses, as concretely interwoven with each other as their inhabitants were knotted by a thick net of marriage ties. It was the space of a solidarity imaged by the continuing surface of the shared roofs, where voices, laughter, and news could circulate and meet in ways unforeseeable from the ground. If the vertical axis meant complementarity and servitude, the horizontal one implied opposition and insubordination—an element of excess that eluded the possibility of control. In the built space of the qṣar, in its historical being, the two were inseparable. This paradoxical factor, this excessive element, was rehearsed in the circuit of the four fourths—the circuit people called mullî.

Following the path of the tracing: the way into the act is marked by the oversized Gate glossed by the inscription *fum l-qdîm.* The first scene (taken from the outside) is called Fourth of Ayt l-Bâlî, and presents one of the two Ḥarâtîn fourths of the qṣar. An arrowhead directs me to Arḥabî, at the center of the drawing, from which I emerge following an arrow that leads into the scene called Fourth of Ayt ʿAbdallah: a Ḥarâr fourth, which is also that of Yusef's lineage. He signed his name here. But, again, I find myself outside.

From the Ayt ʿAbdallah scene, in the upper left side of the picture, I am directed into the scene called Fourth of Ayt l-Qâḍî (which is in fact the

Fourth of Ayt Driss), the other Ḥarâr quarter and faction.[74] I am not directed by an arrow, but driven by the drawing itself, which at this corner makes a 90-degree turn, forcing me to move along with it. Producing, opening a path each time, rather than covering a path already there, yet moving through a landscape already furrowed by the memories of other passages.

Again I am led into another scene, the fourth. Upside down in relation to the Gate, this is the last scene in the order of the narration, the Fourth of Ayt j-Jdîd, the second Ḥarâtîn fourth of the qṣar. From there, I am led once again into the Mouth, for a new beginning. As indicated by the spinning of the frame, this is an open-ended movement. It is not a circle, but a spiral.

The circuitous itinerary of mullî is the narrative register of the drawing. It determines the order of presentation of the scenes. Ever since the qṣar has existed in its walled form, the Ḥarâtîn Fourth of Ayt l-Bâlî has been associated with the Ḥarâr Fourth of Ayt ʿAbdallah, and the Ḥarâr Fourth of Ayt Driss with the Ḥarâtîn Fourth of Ayt j-Jdîd. For the spatial arrangement of the quarters—the fourths—is the inscription of mullî on the ground.

A bifocal Berber/Arabic expression, the term *mullî* is formed from the Berber verb *illi* and the Arabic verb *wâlyia*. It is a spatiotemporal image, a term of cyclical reversibility. In its local use, it means to pass on, to transfer from one to the other, to be the recipient-giver of something passed on in a chain, to turn in cycles, and to return. In Berber it has the additional connotation of drifting, straying and getting lost.[75] Visually dramatized by the rotary movement of the drawing, *mullî* resonates with other classical terms of rotation, of construction and dissolution: *dwl*, to change periodically, to take turns, to alternate, to circulate, but also denoting, in one of its forms, a sovereign state; *dwr*, to revolve, to turn, to move in a circle or in cycles, to rotate, but also, as a nominal form, a stopping place, a house, a dwelling. Mullî is the 180-degree *dwra* of the drawing: the rotation, or cycle, of the images within the Frame, of the Frame upon itself, and of the peripheral scene around the Frame.

What is passed on might be water, as in the case of mullî of irrigation, where the water of the canal is transferred from obstruction to obstruction, from garden to garden, from the "mouth" of the canal all the way to the end and then back. Or it might be a word, an injunction to work, as in the case of the mullî of the qṣar, the circuit Yusef is following in his map. An image of physical/metaphorical displacement, in the context of the qṣar mullî is the revolving circuit between the four fourths, *l-arbaʿ rbaʿ*, the four scenes in the drawing, themselves a composite metaphor for the village layout, its social organization, and its reckoning of time.

Mullî is the physical yet metaphorical path of the village crier who called people for public works and for any event concerning the community as a whole. From door to door, from the "mouth" of each alley all the way to the "head," and then back on the other side; and from alley to alley, quarter by quarter, fourth by fourth. From the Gate/Mouth of the qṣar and up, through the Ḥarâtîn quarters, all the way to the end of the Ḥarâr quarters, and then back down on the other side, from the Ḥarâr quarters all the way back to the Ḥarâtîn quarters and, again, to the Gate—

If something is proceeding by mullî, it is bound to come back and catch me. ("*Fîn lâḥeg mullî?*" asks the man charged with digging the canal of Tifkert. "Where has mullî reached?" "It reached the Alley of Ayt l-Ghandur," says the village crier, who keeps track of the count. "Next in turn is the *derb* Ayt ʿAzzî, call five working men for dawn.") And so forth...

It is not "I," or my eye, that catches it, but it is "it" that catches me, for mullî is a structure of symbolic implication. This is why—in as much as the drawing is a mise-en-scène of mullî—it cannot but exceed the perspective field of the subject. In the idiom of the qṣar, mullî is a spatial figural representation of the system of exchanges where the subject is caught, by which it is constituted, and where it dissolves, in a cycle.

RETURNS 2

THE NEW VILLAGE

1990

Just outside the ramparts of the old qṣar on the side of the Fourth of Ayt l-Bâlî, adjoining on one side the edge of the cemetery, and on the other facing the gardens and a small bridge on the irrigation canal, lies the oldest informal gathering place for the Ḥarâtîn men of the village. As far back as anybody can remember, old men have spent the afternoon there chatting and telling stories, and younger men have joined them in more organized gatherings if there was a political crisis, or some issue to discuss. The Ford truck of Salem would stop there on its weekly runs from Casablanca, bringing news and packages, and filling the whole space with its huge, roaring presence. As they sit, talk, argue, or tell stories, men lean against the wall of the old cemetery of Lâllâ ud Sîdî—a cemetery where no one is buried anymore but on whose grounds nobody walks without fear.

The little wall is reddened by the last rays of the sun. From that angle those sitting there at *ʿâgub n-nhâr,* at the down slope of the day, can follow the activity of men with their donkeys and carts heading back from the gardens; they can greet and be greeted, ask for a bit of palm-tree pollen in spring or make arrangements for a plowing work party in fall, and watch the sun sink slowly behind the palm trees and the naked hills on the other side of the valley. They sit, and wait for the modulation of the name of God from the roof of the adjoining mosque of Ayt l-Bâlî, calling people for the prayer of sunset.

Yet, since the division of the communal land in 1980, since the New Village has been built out there, on that strip of rocky land in the open desert, only a few old men are left sitting by the old cemetery wall, behind what can be now called *l-kharâb*, the "ruin" of the old village, reflecting on the fecklessness of history, on the precariousness of human fate, waiting, and preparing for the prayer of sunset. Or meditating instead on that enormous change they couldn't have predicted only a few years before, which had transplanted people from their homes like onion or henna plants,[76] the change that came down like a storm and was turning the place into a town, and was looked upon with envy, suspicion, and reproach by the people of the villages nearby—where electricity hadn't yet made its appearance and people hadn't taken the risk of dividing the communal land, where weddings still lasted seven days and the qbîla was not consumed by internecine wars.

"It runs in its blood like a *sûṣa*, like a worm or caries, and is worn from within like a *waswâs*, a whisper in the ear, a devilish insinuation, an anxiety, from the beginning of time," people stated in the neighboring villages, quoting one incident or another from the qṣar's troubled public life. It was that flirtation with the unknown, with the insecurity of novel paths, that taste for dissent, dispute, and hazardous games—*fitna* is the term they used—that inclination to *ketter l-klâm*, "talk too much," speculate and get involved, which had built the qṣar's reputation over the years and the centuries, which had made of it a capital, and which was today the engine behind the transformation that was taking place.

As if by the intervention of a trickster, a heteromorphic gnome of structure and chance (unpredictability of a chance encounter in a familiar place; but every encounter, inasmuch as it happens, has the form of an accident), people perceived in the returns of its history, and in an almost Khaldûnian spirit,[77] a certain automatism in repetition—the same thing kept recurring like the relapse of an old illness—yet, at each turn, the shock of an indigestible encounter with the unknown. The result was an uncanny compulsion to keep changing form—

"We are children of the present, *ḥnâ wlâd liyum*," says Ḥadda, filling his pipe and commenting on the incommensurability of the change as he looks out in the direction of the New Village—the *fillage*,[78] as he jokingly calls it—from the top of the hill where he lives in peace, away from all that noise. There is no point in lingering on what is gone, really, what is gone is gone. He states it coldly, without melancholy. Yesterday it was the qṣar, today it is *berra*, "the outside," tomorrow it will be something else and *berra* too will be gone! The qṣar is gone: with all its presumption, its shouting and bubbling, tumbled down piece by piece. The old mud of its fallen walls accumulates in the alleys, increasingly impassable, and stinking. But then, out there in the New Village people are fixing the alleys, even making a yard with a fountain in the middle of that big space, and they are starting to make money. They'll make money, and then they'll lose it all, and start over.

He smiles. The poet in him can't help thinking about how many times things have started and ended, ended and started—at the indifferent turns of the world.

> O mindless! Look at Dunya, countless generations passed on to the
> Other World and disappeared...
> *yâ l-ghâfel shûf d-dunya shḥal men jîl ddâtu l-akhra u mâbân*
>
> Where is Sheddad who built every palace that his heart desired
> and spent each night with a beautiful eye
> Who raised towers with corals and pearls
> and made them shine with diamonds and gold
> and after that it all returned to nothingness
> *u baʿdha wella l-feniân*

(*Wella, mullî,* the trope of return.)

"It is a bit like that manure business in the qṣar," says Ḥadda only half-mockingly. Once a year, always on a Friday, the qbîla auctioned off the issue of the toilets of the big mosque. They announced, "Gate of God, gate of the Lord,[79] the toilets are for sale [*bab allâh bab n-rebbi, l-maṣaleḥ rant adzunt*]." People gathered by the Gate. The person who bought the shit—and bought it for real money—bought with it the obligation to sweep the public streets of the qṣar once a week, after the Friday prayer. He had to sweep from the Gate through the Alley of Ayt l-Bâlî all the way to Arḥabî, and then on to the alley of the mosque into that of Ayt Driss all the way to where it merges into Ayt Aḥmed and becomes private. When he had swept, and especially at harvest time when there was a lot of straw he gathered along with the dust, he threw all that into the toilets of the mosque, and kept adding to the compost until the *maṣaleḥ* was filled—it's like a big ditch underneath the toilets, where the excrement and dirty water from washing collected. Then he collected the manure with his donkey and laid it on the threshing floors to dry.

Ḥadda's eyes smile. *Dunya,* "the human world," is a matter of recycling.

The center of gravity had switched *berra,* "to the outside," it had moved to the open space around the new marketplace, the medical dispensary, and the administrative center, where Salem, who now had a new truck and who was on the way to becoming wealthy, had opened two shops, a warehouse, and a welding room, and was planning to open more. At the old cemetery's wall people pondered whether they should adjust their sitting place to the new context and move to the industrial gravel outside the new cement mosque of Ighruren: now that no one called the name of God from the roof of the old mosque of Ayt l-Bâlî anymore, now that its old walls were raining down with the rest and instead one could hear from anywhere around, even from the depth of the palmery, the loudspeaker of the mosque of Ighruren calling the faithful to prayer.

But they also reflected—at least those among them who were not carried away by the new acquisitive fever—on how many times the center of gravity had switched (and if one looked at the matter from that angle, could one speak of a center of gravity at all?), on how many times things had changed form from that forgotten age when the qṣar hadn't yet been born and there was but a scattering of hamlets in the palm groves. A scattering like what was happening now. Where did people sit then? Perhaps in that open place that still bears the name of *l-sûq*, "the market," in the middle of the gardens near the property of l-Ḥajj l-Madanî, where the ruins are still visible of a former settlement, of the shops and the rest.

L-Ḥajj l-Madanî laughs, and when he laughs his wrinkled old face takes on the rascally expression he must have had as a boy. He laughs, and without introduction starts telling the story of a Jewish man who landed at the qṣar from somewhere else, was adopted into a big Ḥarâr lineage, converted to Islam taking the name of ʿAbdallah, married a local woman, and shared with her a daughter, Khadija ʿAbdallah. Then one day he disappeared (some said he returned to being a Jew, l-Ḥajj adds, smiling) and the girl started working for a rich Berber sheikh from the mountains, who had property in the qṣar. She helped with the date harvest and at some point—there was a drought and little to eat—he took her to his village and adopted her. Khadija was then turned into Khadda, and from a Jewish girl became a Berber girl, a Shelḥa. She wore their clothes and jewelry, she spoke their language, until one day a man heard about her, asked for her in marriage, and took her back to the qṣar.

L-Ḥajj pauses, looks at the ruin of the old qṣar as if meditating on its successive incarnations, its many turns of face, like the turns of identity of the Jewish-Berber girl. "Look!" he concludes, "people just go adrift like those fragments of bark floating on the water of the canal... carried away by the current they go this way and that way... this is what the world, what life is [*dunya*]."[80]

As if infected by a virus of restlessness and an ancestral dread of being left behind, one by one, in each alley, the families had moved to the New Village outside the walls—leaving their houses in a last migration. They left them empty, it was said, for the jinns to play their music at night. Looking back at the dark alleys of the old qṣar with resentment (toward what they had come to see as a figure of entrapment and a site of illness and malaise), they had carried out their few objects with a sense of defiance ("Space!" they said, *tisaʿ*), but with the sense of an incurable loss.

Yet, on this February afternoon, people are gathered once more around the cemetery wall in animated talk. There is some thought of dividing more communal land, there is dissent among the different factions, and street assemblies have been called to be held in the old qṣar, now almost completely empty, appealing to its spatial organization as a template, and a guarantor, of its social forms. No one in the village understood what had happened. People had built the New Village themselves, according to their very own plan. The government had provided them with the plan of a modular housing project, a *lotissement économique*. They had turned it around, and modified it until it had come to fit their needs, until it bore very faint resemblance to the original plan.

For, they said, the New Village was to be a faithful copy of the old qṣar; unlike the disorderly settlements that had sprawled outside the walls over the years and the centuries, the New Village was to reproduce its internal organization. For the purpose of its construction was precisely to contain that uncanny drive to scattering that people perceived as an ever encumbering threat.

The qṣar itself, the qṣar that was now being abandoned, was said to have been formed in response to a cycle of violent uprisings, a period of dissidence, fitna or *siba*,[81] imaged, in the local narratives, by the theme of a proliferation of independent hamlets at constant war with each other. In the founding act of what was to be the qṣar, the "scattered hamlets" were razed, and their population killed or deported.

The idea of dividing the communal land (*arḍ l-qbîla*) and building the New Village was conceived in response to the most recent occurrence of splitting, the sprouting in the 1970s of a settlement just outside the qṣar's ramparts on the side of the Ḥarâtîn Fourth of Ayt l-Bâlî, only a few steps removed from the old cemetery wall. Those who owned gardens there sold them, and several Ḥarâtîn families started building new houses, which quickly grew into a new quarter, without a pattern, without a rule. Ighruren became a political entity,[82] and like Tighremt two hundred years before, it challenged the existing organization of the qṣar and made the balance of the local scale lean on the side of the black Ḥarâtîn. If the qṣar had four fourths, Ighruren called itself "the fifth," *l-khamsa*, and stirred trouble at the irrigation canal.

At once stressing the spectral recurrence of the event of breaking and emphasizing its novelty and contemporary nature, the Ḥarâr of the qṣar referred polemically to this recent settlement as *l-karyân,*[83] "the bidonville," and its adepts as *ahl l-karyân,* "the shantytowners," and as *ahl Tighremt,* "the people of Tighremt," after the name of a secessionist settlement known as Tighremt, "the Fortress," whose ruins are still visible some few hundred yards from the qṣar.

But the New Village was to be different. It was to be insured against the recurrence of its breaking, against the splitting of the nutshell. It was to be an original copy, a copy with the community council's copyright. "A mirror image," people said, and set off to trace the structure of the old qṣar to reproduce it trace by trace in the outside desert, in an unwitting attempt to apply a geometric notion of point-by-point perspective to the social and physical space of the community.

A man with a notebook in hand was charged by the qbîla to follow the customary circuit through the qṣar—the circuit people called *mullî.* It is ironic that recourse to this cyclical technique was made in order to construct a "plan" that was to become the project of an irreversible space. On the base of that plan's projection on earth, an object was to be constructed that would be protected against the risk of cyclical returns. A sort of *quartier model,* the model of a break-proof society.

From door to door, from alley to alley, from the Gate to the end of the village and then back to the Gate on the other side, the man walked the old path of the village crier and wrote down a long list of the names of all the residents—so that, it was said, the neighbors would remain neighbors in the new place. At the end of that work, people thought, the old qṣar had been captured in the notebook. Now it was just a matter of transcribing it on the ground. A team of men was appointed to do the drawing. They spent weeks out there in the sun, measuring the lots and drawing down the shares. They even planned the space for the alleys, avenues really, that bore the names of the old alleys with the suffix *j-jdîd,* "the new." Those who had a little money set aside started digging wells, and the land was shaken by the trembling blasts of dynamite.

But when the first houses were finally built, and the first families started settling in, people suddenly realized that in the New Village the old neighbors were not neighbors anymore. In the transcription of the qṣar out of its walls something had happened.

There had been a first moment of euphoria. The multilevel mud houses of the old qṣar, intertwined with each other in complex and invisible ways that recalled the ever expanding and encompassing structures of a spiderweb, were seen now as too tight, entangled, dark, and oppressive. In the old qṣar it was impossible to tell where the body of one house ended and that of another began, or even where the house as a private structure merged into the public body of the qṣar. In their complexly articulated form the built space of the house and that of the village were microcosms of each other, and not just metaphorically. In a very technical sense they were part of the same structural system of *ʿaṭabi,* supporting and articulating beams that held each house together and connected houses with each other in the larger structure of the alley. And they were part of the same breathing system, animated by a network of air inspiration, circulation, and ejection, which made the qṣar analogous in many respects to the human body as it was defined in the local medical tradition.

Breathing. The Gate (*fum*) was the mouth (*fum*). In the days when the qṣar had only one gate, air was forced inward through the two main alleys of Ayt l-Bâlî and Ayt j-Jdîd. At each turn it entered a smaller mouth (most streets used to have gates), and then the gate of a yet smaller, private alley. That is when it reached the house, and was pulled up through the opening of the *ʿayn d-dâr,* the eye of the house. It was pulled up, and ejected into the sky—

The body was not only a metaphor.

"My grandmother" says Um ʿAṣṣa Moḥa (we are talking about relationships between people and families, genealogy, and she keeps shifting to houses, walls, alleys, and roofs, to the junctures and entanglements of built space), "my grandmother, then, with Mina ʿAlla, *sharkû s-sṭaḥ,* they shared the roof [of their houses]... if one had a baby, the other gave her the breast, and vice versa. They shared the roof, that is, they shared the breast." For, "had they not shared the breast, they would have had to build a limiting wall [*lû kân ma-sharkû l-bzûla, khaṣṣhum îbnîw s-stâra*]" [84]

Out there in desert, instead, each house was a bounded, independent unit. What had been in the old qṣar a multilayered, standing, dynamic structure, where the social use of space changed according to the season and the time of the day, was flattened in the New Village, spread out, and built on a single plan. Fixed in their places, houses had become objects to be controlled by the eye. Yet, once the new settlement was built, people had difficulty relating to what happened. A trick was played, someone started to say, a trick, some Ḥarâtîn men complained, was played on them by the white Ḥarâr.

"The horseshoe had been opened," some said, rectified. If the old qṣar existed as a circuit and turned, or returned upon itself (so that the beginning and the end, the end and the beginning, would come to join each other like the two ends of a horseshoe), in the New Village the circle was broken, the return stopped, and the two ends were kept apart by over two miles of rocky desert land. The Ḥarâtîn, whose two fourths in the qṣar were adjacent and formed the space of a solidarity that lay outside the white Ḥarâr's subordination and control, found themselves at the opposite ends of the new settlement which now appeared like an open-ended sprawl. The system of the four fourths was shattered, although it had served as a template for the partition of the communal land. The scattering was general, and it affected every aspect of life.

At the cemetery's wall people are talking about mullî.

(A man speaks, drawing on the ground with a stick. Others intervene, a loud debate. My tape recorder is on. I will be asked, halfway through the conversation, to play the tape that is being recorded. The listening triggered a new discussion that went on until the prayer of sunset.)

—*(Drawing on the ground with a stick)* Here is the Fourth of Ayt j-Jdîd, here is the Fourth of Ayt Driss, here is the Fourth of Ayt ʿAbdallah, here is the Fourth of Ayt l-Bâlî... there is plenty of land out there, and the fourths go off on a straight line... The qṣar is round [*ḍayr,* "it turns"], and instead out there, they aligned the fourths on a straight line, they pushed the Ḥarâtîn to the margins, Ayt l-Bâlî way upstream, Ayt j-Jdîd to the Qebla, the East, and stick the Ḥarâr in between them...

—*(I ask,)* Did they make the partition according to mullî or according to the fourths?

—The fourths...

—Mullî...

—There is really nothing to say! A master's stroke... Pushed to the margins and made to shut up! That's what the Yellows [the Ḥarâr] managed to do... a good stroke...

—*(A man, raising his voice to be heard:)* But they did mullî like they used to do in the qṣar. The day they decided to divide up that Amerdûl, that wasteland,[85] they said "get two sticks" [to draw lots], one for the Fourth of Ayt l-Bâlî, the other for the Fourth of Ayt j-Jdîd, this is what was always done. If the lots fall to Ayt l-Bâlî they start mullî on its side, and then follow up Ayt ʿAbdallah and Ayt Driss, and mullî comes back to Ayt j-Jdîd."

—*(Another man, picking up the argument:)* They drew lots with two sticks and then, of course, if it came for Ayt j-Jdîd, they'd go take their land downstream and they'd be followed by Ayt Driss and Ayt ʿAbdallah, and Ayt l-Bâlî would get their land all the way upstream... just like the story here in the qṣar...

—But no! The Ḥarâr are not in the middle here... in the qṣar the Ḥarâr are not between the Ḥarâtîn...

—They are in the middle...

—No they aren't, it is at the digging of the canal that they are in the middle!

—In any case it is mullî that they followed... Listen! where was Lḥassan u Saleḥ, and where were you?

—In the Alley of Bû Ṭwîl...

—And where did he move in the New Village in relation to you?

—He didn't move...

—That's what I mean! They did mullî, what the hell are you all saying?

—But then why aren't Ayt l-Bâlî and Ayt j-Jdîd next to each other as in the old qṣar?

—They didn't do mullî! And anyway, why is it only we who have to draw lots? Why don't the Ḥarâr have to put their stick in?

—This is what our forefathers left us with [*dâk shshî llî khallâw l-luwlîn*].

(A big confusion, no one understands anymore. A man imposes some silence and starts drawing on the ground. He draws a rectangle, long and slim, divided into four sections, roughly square. Then he says:)

Ayt l-Bâlî	Ayt ʿAbdallah	Ayt Driss	Ayt j-Jdîd

—Look! This is the organization of the New Village. From east to west [from right to left], *(raising his voice) along a straight line,* you have the Ḥarâtîn of Ayt j-Jdîd, followed by the Ḥarâr of Ayt Driss and Ayt ʿAbdallah, and finally at the opposite end, the Ḥarâtîn of Ayt l-Bâlî. Right? Now look. *(He lays the stick with which he has been drawing over the rectangle, then bends it until the two ends come to touch each other.)*

You see? if you make the drawing turn upon itself the Ḥarâtîn quarters join up at the bottom... mullî in the qṣar was a circle, and they opened it up, and each came on a separate side... When they allocated the lots in Amerdûl, they didn't tie mullî! This is what happened... It is at the public works of the irrigation canal that they do this kind of organization, with the Ḥarâr in the middle...

—They make the Ḥarâtîn work for them, fight for them if there is war, expose themselves if there is a danger, and stay safely in the middle—

—*(Someone interrupting, in a concluding tone:)* Look! There are two streets and two sticks [for drawing lots]... Right? Before they opened the new gates in the qṣar there was only the Gate and the two main paths of Ayt j-Jdîd with Ayt Driss, and of Ayt l-Bâlî with Ayt ʿAbdallah... What the Ḥarâr managed to do is "Don't load the basket with mud, don't tramp the earth walls, just shuttle back and forth between the real workers; it's more restful!" [*lâ tʿammar lâ tekûn f l-lûḥ, sîr u ʾajî fîh r-raḥa;* this is an image from the work routine of house building, chosen *sur le vif* of the new construction wave].

—Protectorate [*l-ḥimâya*, as in the French Protectorate]...
—It's is the legacy of our forefathers.

"The legacy! the ruse of the first ones... and the trick of the last ones as well [*l-ḥîla dyâl l-luwlîn*]!" Ḥadda shouts when I report this conversation to him.

"It is a trick, a screwed-up stratagem. Say for example that there are two brothers, and they used to help each other in all sorts of things, and a stranger came between them...

"One hand alone can't make applause! Ever since the Ḥarâr came between the Ḥarâtîn they ruled over them. They say, "You work," and sit, watching the spectacle. And this, like what used to happen at the irrigation canal, is what's happening in the New Village today. People didn't understand the trick that was being played on them... they were so happy to have SPACE! that they didn't realized they were being s p a c e d away...

"They are saying it is the same order, there you have a new order... It is because when they divided the communal land they didn't tie mullî! When mullî was done in the old days, it was tied up, knotted [*kay-ḥezmûh*], and the beginning would be adjacent to the end. Mullî turned upon itself like a donkey turns around the pole at the threshing floor."

Something had been lost in the lifting of the qṣar out of its concrete built body and its flesh of mud bricks. It was mullî, say the Ḥarâtîn men sitting by the cemetery wall, it was the movement of re-turn.

The night before, groups of men, flashlights in hand, walked back to the qṣar from their new residences in the outside desert; they unlocked the door of a house that had not been lived in for months, and in that inhospitable space, empty and dark, held one of the twelve alley assemblies the community council had called for. It was the ritual visitation of a sacred site—a site that, now devoid of life, could be invested with the sacredness of emblems. Emptied of its inhabitants and of its living substance, deserted in the space of a few months, the qṣar had taken on the uncanny status of a corpse—a mere resemblance without life or place.

"The cadaverous presence establishes a relation between here and nowhere," Blanchot writes, reflecting on the affinity between images and corpses.[86] The body of the deceased lies lifeless, stuck heavily in its place, but its presence suspends the relationship to place and time, and transforms the here and now of life into an elsewhere, an indeterminate nowhere. For its presence is a presentment of absence, an appearance that, Blanchot says, is the image. "He is, I see this, perfectly like himself: he resembles himself. The cadaver is its own image. It no longer entertains any relation with this world, where it still appears, except that of an image, an obscure possibility, a shadow ever present behind the living form which now, far from separating itself from this form, transforms it entirely into a shadow."[87]

Like certain neighborhoods in cities ravaged by civil wars, which, fled by their inhabitants, take on the status of a no-man's-land and are destroyed by the spreading warfare, the qṣar became a ruin—a *kharâb*. By the sheer fact of having been abandoned, even before raining down concretely, it entered another temporality, the time of ruins, outside of place and time. It then took on the status of an image: a double of the former qṣar, a stage set for the play of virtual lives. (Ruins are "ancient," not just because they carry the memory of an age-old past, but because they exist on lapsed and superimposed time, where incongruous temporal dimensions become contemporary. So is the uncanny temporality of those who have been exposed to living among ruins.)[88] It is only after this crucial turn (a 180-degree turn of estrangement in the visual terms of Yusef's map) that it fell concretely apart, and its being-of-ruin became manifest.

As if haunted by the emptiness of those sites, during the first few months after the desertion people made daily visits to their former homes, for no other reason than a need to go. Later, they started pulling down the beams to complete the construction of their new homes "outside"; deprived of structural support, melted down by the rain, and undermined by increasingly frequent fires, the old houses rapidly collapsed; walls started raining down—houses turned inside out, exposing what had been interiors—and alleys were obstructed by the debris. A year later, centuries had lapsed.

It is thus that, a likeness and a shadow, abandoned and slowly falling apart, the old qṣar became a blueprint for all public endeavors, a standing map and a stage set, that showed how the system of the fourths should work and guaranteed the reality of its reference.[89] Yet the need people felt to physically return "home" to the ghostly nowhere of the qṣar's encircling ramparts, winding alleys, and dark passages, to its smell of earth mixed with manure, meant that in lifting its form out of the walls something was lost.

In itself, the fact that the qṣar had become a ruin was not new: a certain ruin, a certain loss, were felt as irreducible ingredients of life. But unlike the innumerable settlements that had come and gone over the years and the centuries, the planning and building of the New Village was an attempt to exclude that factor of ruin from the newly geometrically mapped space of life. It was an attempt to excise from representation the movement of its own reversal, from the figural lifting, the movement of its sinking, and from the field of the eye (the I) the scene of its annihilation. Mullî, the revolving movement Yusef enacted in his drawing of the qṣar, mullî, the re-turns of the world, where, as poets says, *wella l-feniân*, "everything returns to nothingness."

RETURNS 3

SPLINTERS AT L-HASHMI'S FUNERAL

1986

When l-Hashmi u Ḥammu died suddenly in his blacksmith shop one morning in early June—the heat was starting to beat down and the sun-baked paths of the new settlements outside the walls were deserted by late morning—no one could make up his mind as to who was responsible for his burial. Had he been able to see his own funeral, that shy and gentle man would have despaired at the sight of a scandal he'd never sought in life. For his death had become the emblem of factional conflict, and his funeral a stage for its dramatic production.

According to the calendar of agricultural activities, men should have been busy working at the threshing floors. But on the new threshing floors of the qbîla, those that had been relocated on the communal land out in the desert when the old threshing floors of Sîdî Ṣâfu had been sold by their owners and built upon, there were only sporadic heaps of barley waiting out in the sun. After several years of drought the harvest had been so lean that those who could afford it had disregarded threshing, saying something about waiting for a *makina dyâl drâss*, a mechanical thresher that the Agricultural Office was circulating in the valley, but in fact not really caring that a storm might catch them by surprise and wash those few grains away. Some almost hoped that a storm would come, and sometimes even said it out loud, sitting at night smoking on the dry cement edge of the new irrigation canal, fantasizing a storm like the mythical one that came down as a big wall of water and mud, washing out the land and shaping the territory as it is now.

People threshed words, then, in the long afternoons spent waiting at their customary, and less than customary, gathering places: the old cemetery wall, for the Ḥarâtîn men of Ayt l-Bâlî; the space around the mill machine, for the Ḥarâr of the Fourth of Ayt ʿAbdallah; Arḥabî—the open space at the heart of the old qṣar, where older men gathered before and after praying in the old mosque; the pink side of the new cement mosque, where men from the new settlement of Ighruren chatted the afternoons away, reclining on the industrial gravel soil, until the sunset call to prayer made them rise, shake the dust off their djellaba and gather in the mosque to pray; the bridge over *sâgyât l-makhzen*, the new irrigation canal built by the state in the 1970s, where young men spent the evenings playing the lute. At all these places and innumerable others (for since the division of the communal land the qṣar had entered a new period of scattering, and no one knew where to sit anymore), the news of l-Hashmi's death spread quickly, and brought about a confusion and a scandal that, reserved man that he was, l-Hashmi could never have generated in life.

Si Thami was the first to ascertain his death. He was off to the gardens and (he said a few days later, as we were trying to reconstruct the events together) something made him take the longer way—the path that goes around the qṣar, passing by the shrine of Sîdî Ṣâfu and the Cemetery of the Carrion.

"I found Ḥassan u Driss near Sîdî Ṣâfu. He yelled that l-Hashmi had been struck by something [*dâz ʿalîh shshî*]. I rushed to his house. At the door was Moḥammed u Ydir, he said, 'Come take a look, I can't tell whether he is alive or dead, his son went to get the *fqîh,* they say it's the jinns [ʿ*ashir*].' I checked the mouth of the heart, and it was silence, I checked the vein of the heart, and it was silence, I checked the eyes, and they were fixed and wide open, and I announced: May he rest in peace.

"We broke the news to the women and they started wailing. I went back to the qṣar to look for the shroud. I ran into Bû Sdra u Ḥammû, I told him, and he set off to dig the grave. Then we prepared the water to wash the corpse. They found a ram, slaughtered it, and started dividing the meat among those who were to prepare the funeral meals. And that's when the problem came up and we entered Taqshurîn. Who was going to get the meat? Because you see, according to the customary system, if the dead person is a Ḥartânî, and, for instance, like l-Hashmi, from the Fourth of Ayt j-Jdîd, the people of Ayt l-Bâlî are responsible for the funeral. l-Hashmi was from the Ḥarâtîn. And yet, it is the neighbors who ended up getting the meat, the neighbors who in that new alley are all from the Ḥarâr. They showed up at the house of the dead man as if they were going to the Friday sermon, white turban and immaculate djellaba. It was pure theater. From that moment on every move, every gesture, even the choice of the rock where you sat in the shade, became *ramzî*—'it became a sign.'"

(L-Hashmi was young; the news of his death came unexpectedly. He had come back the day before on the bus from Casablanca—there for a funeral, people said. Some suggested a connection. Others said that the Written should not be discussed. Those sitting by the irrigation canal had seen him coming hastily in his city clothes, a small bag balanced on his right shoulder, walking the few miles through the gardens in city shoes, uneasy, in the passing from one world to the other. He had said *Salâm ʿalikûm* without stopping, without raising his eyes, and had disappeared in the direction of his house. That's the last time he was seen.)

Si Thami: "And the Ḥarâtîn came, his friends, for whom he had made *mnâjel* and *timeskrîn*.[90] How many of them wanted to get the meat! But the new representatives said no... The neighbors had to take the shares of the meat, they said, that's what the Qurʾanic Law prescribes... And what they were enforcing was the law of the Ḥarâr, for only in the funeral of the white Ḥarâr are the shares of the meat divided among the neighbors!

"The leaders of the Ḥarâtîn were watching. They stood by the wall of the sanctuary of Sîdî Ṣâfu and did nothing, didn't even talk among themselves—they just watched and made everyone uneasy. The Drâwâ [Ḥarâtîn] had sworn not to stand up for l-Hashmi, it was to serve as an example for the others... They had sworn that those who left their *khaṭ*, their 'line,' alliance and line of conduct, wouldn't be helped in anything, even in death, until, from that hardship, they'd be forced to come back to the *khaṭ*. But, cunningly, those of the other faction didn't let the hardship strike. Not out of respect for the dead, but for the sake of taqshurîn politics. They took care of everything, the shroud, the meals, the guests! to make sure that those Drâwâ who were with them wouldn't go back to the faction of Ighruren [*Taqshurt dyâl Ighruren*]. People were saying that there was madness in what was happening...

"And we carried the corpse to the cemetery. At the bridge over the new irrigation canal we found them, waiting—the leaders of Taqshurt. We weren't thinking about that mundane stuff, we were thinking about the day when we ourselves will be carried over there... They joined us from behind—couldn't help coming to the burial. Death is stronger! They stood a few feet away, prayed with us the prayer of the dead, until we lowered l-Hashmi's body into its grave, buried it with fresh earth, piled up the stones over it, covered it with thorns and palm leaves so the dogs would not get too close. They stood for all this—then they left. They left from behind, took the side of the desert, and disappeared from sight.

"And we walked back to the qṣar—to the open space outside l-Hashmi's house. We sat there, leaning against the wall of the building. Muffled through the filter of the mud walls, we could hear the women's wailing inside. The voices went up and down, stopped and then resumed, bitter and angry—when a new mourner walked in. 'Allâh ylʿan sh-shayṭân!'[91] yelled a voice from the inside. Women came in from the back door... I imagined the packed hallway, black veils, children crying, I tried to recognize the voices... But all we knew, because l-Hashmi's sister-in-law told us, was that the black women, the Drawyât, didn't abandoned Ḍâwya in her grief and came to the funeral. They didn't play the game of taqshurîn."

A word—*taqshurîn.* Or *taqshurt* in the singular: but its meaning is essentially plural.[92] An image—taqshurîn: the broken shell of a nut, the splinters, the fragments, the shreds, of something that had once been whole—of something that had once been one. *L-qushâr* are fragments, ruins, debris: the ruins of a house, of a village, of a community, of a person, a place of former integrity where little or nothing is left standing (*l-kharâb,* "ruins," has a similar connotation of splitting and fragmenting). But also: the breaking of the *qashra,* "the shell," speaks of the outburst of something from the inside—something that was meant to remain hidden and that, unveiled, unleashes its destructive potential.

Yâm taqshurîn—"the days of fractioning," is the name by which a recent history of fissure is reckoned in the qṣar. The expression refers to the twenty or fifteen years that preceded the arrival of the French army in the valley, a period of great turmoil and intermittent warfare. *Yâm taqshurîn* speaks of that period from the point of view of the internal life of the community—the qbîla. The *qbîla tqashsharat,* "broke up," "disintegrated," and the system of the four fourths was shattered by the emergence of a taqshurt. Not any faction, but "the Faction," "the Splinter," *Taqshurt* proper-named. Soon after its emergence, other factions were formed, and taqshurîn became an almost institutionalized system of internal distribution of power. Written documents from this period concerning the political life of the qbîla amount to long lists of names. They invariably start *Zamâm taqiyid qabîla Banî Sûlî,* "registered survey of the qabîla of Banî Sûlî," or *ḥsâb,* "count," of a lineage, a faction, a fourth. As if, by continuously verifying the count, by accounting for the position of each person in the fluidity of the play of the splinters, it were possible to exorcise the fissure; and as if, by piling up names upon names, it were possible to fill the hole opened by the fracturing of the nutshell.

In the midst of the politics of factions, Taqshurt kept its secessionist connotation: it had its own independent organization and its own public storage room (*ḥanut dyâl qbîla*); it collected its own taxes, counted its own members, and made its own political and military alliances with the powers of the larger world: the neighboring qṣûr, the Ayt ʿAṭṭa Berber nomads, the Awlâd Yaḥya Arab nomads, and the Glâwî.[93] It is Taqshurt that hired Berber mercenaries to murder Baba, the "Father" and legendary sheikh, in that dark alley outside the old mosque one winter evening in 1928. But Taqshurt is also the Splinter of today—*l-khamsa,* the fifth fourth, the contemporary faction of Ighruren.

The new cement mosque of Ighruren is still unfinished. Each day members of Taqshurt add or paint a new wall. New straw mats brought from Casablanca, industrial gravel outside the door, the acrid smell of fresh cement. The building is a gift from l-Ḥajj Lḥassan, who left the qṣar in poverty in the 1940s and then gathered a fortune in Casablanca in the spice trade. L-Ḥajj defiantly describes himself as a Drâwî. The mosque is his gift and his revenge—to a community where for centuries a small group of white landlords ruled over a large community of landless Ḥarâtîn.

Yet Taqshurt is also the story of Tighremt—the secessionist fortress that broke off from the qṣar in a distant past.[94] Ighruren, like Tighremt: and the story of the secessionist Fortress becomes an emblem of uncanny returns.

(Sitting outside the old mosque. Different people gathered at random, caught in the talking as they walk out of praying. Twittering of birds. The thin thread of Moḥammed u Saddiq's voice is almost covered by the birds' insistent song. Yet no one dares to interrupt; there is enchantment in what he says. And for a moment he has the floor—the childless son of a proud white lineage that never granted him respect, he who left the qṣar for a life of wanderings in the inhospitable cities of the north and came back too old. His frail hands, made transparent by the work of time; his gentle, feminine voice; his recitations of the deeds of men he admired, and whom he knew he could never have been.)

The Story of Tighremt
Listen!
Those who went off, moved out to Tighremt, were from Ayt Mḥammad... you know, the lineage of Aḥmed u Brahîm, the one who fixes the water pumps. People recount—some hand it down to others—that at the beginning there were Driss, Mḥammâd, and ʿAbdallah.

Mḥammâd and ʿAbdallah were brothers, Driss was their uncle. The qṣar didn't exist, then, Taghallil was all that there was... It is the people of Taghallil who called in Driss—he was from a faraway tribe in the Atlas Mountains—and made a deal with him. They said, "Weed those weeds, those bugs, from the heart of the land, empty the *blâd,* clean it out, and then, wherever you'd like to have your fourth, your share, we'll give it to you." For in those early days the gardens had become a dangerous place—thefts and daily violence made life impossible. This is what the first people recounted, and we remember. The day they swept that rotten stuff out, the day that stuff was no longer inside the *blâd,* Driss decided to stay over and settle. People were scattered all over the land, and consulted among each other; they said, "Let's come out of the gardens, let's make one country [*blâd waḥda*]!" And the qṣar of Bni Zoli was built. And the people of Ayt ʿAbdallah stayed in the Alley of Ayt ʿAbdallah, Driss was in the Alley of Bû Ṭwîl, and Mḥammâd was in the Alley of Ayt l-Qâḍî—the alley that became of Ayt l-Qâḍî after they moved out to Tighremt. Each would come out of his alley, and they'd walk to the mosque. It was a tiny mosque, and that's were they spent their time. Just three pillars, the prayer area, and a well. It was the mosque of Ayt l-Bâlî—the old village. Ayt j-Jdîd—the New Village—didn't exist in those days...[95]

Listen! All of a sudden the men of Ayt Mḥammâd deviled up, they developed a *niya dyâl fitna,* Mḥammâd started fighting with his brother ʿAbdallah, they argued and fought, and Driss moved to the Alley of Bû Ṭwîl, to be, he said, between the two brothers, so that they wouldn't fight. But the people of Ayt Mḥammâd started moving out—out to Sîdî Aḥmed u Abdelkhâleq, upstream from us. They did like Taqshurt:[96] they split off from this or that house, this or that family, and built houses over there, on the outside... they were building Tighremt. We found the remains [*l-qushâr,* "the splinters"—it is the same word as *taqshurt*], the ruins are still standing, we still find things, tools of all sorts buried inside those mounds of earth. And the people of Bni Zoli said, "Now that our brothers are settled over there, let's leave them alone." But they became our bitter enemies. If the dig of Iflî[97] was announced, we would go work during the day and they'd go at night... They would wait until after the evening prayer—so we have heard—go out to their share of the canal to dig, and undo all the work we had done in the morning. They hated working with us! And if some animal died in their village, a donkey, a cow, a rotting carrion, they threw it in the canal to pollute our waters... They were contrary... everything they did was to oppose...

One day our people got tired, they said, "What shall we do? We can endure this no longer." And they went and told the gatekeeper of Tighremt, "Next time the men go out to the canal, let us know. Don't be afraid, this is a good action in the eyes of God, these men transgress God's boundaries." One night the gatekeeper came and said, "Beware, they are off to the canal." Our men rushed to Tighremt, they took possession of it, drove the women and children out and brought them here. And those families who still recognized their offspring took them into their homes. When the men of Tighremt came back from the canal and knocked at the gate, the gatekeeper said, "Go, your brothers have taken over the village, and they said that who is not willing to give up his house must go and get lost, for he refuses to stay and settle in the land of his fathers." Those who accepted the judgment of God came and settled here, those who refused never came back. Some went to Teyrsut, some to Zawyât Si Moḥammed u Aḥmed, some went to the *gharb* [west, to the cities] and got lost—that's all... Ḥummad u Saddiq stayed in Teyrsut until he died, then his children came back to the qṣar. Those of Ayt l-Qṣibî refused to come back, they said, "We won't come back inside, we'll stay here," and the people of Bni Zoli replied, "He who wants to sit in a no-man's-land, in a no-man's-land may he sit [*llî bgha yga*ʿ*d f l-khala, f l-khala yga*ʿ*d*]!"

Inside the house of the deceased the hallway is packed. Women are sitting in the dark, laughing after crying, making sexual jokes. Ḥaddya is challenging another woman; her vagina is better, she says. Everybody laughs.

"Washed in the morning, washed in the afternoon, washed! What I sit on, thank God, is just cleanness and purity... I bet yours is bent and loose, the lips are worn out and don't close anymore, like the petals of a flower that is past... Mine is round and tasty and tight, no Pestle digs it anymore... When they go in they smash everything." (Ḥaddya is over sixty, and a widow. The other woman is younger and married.)

Then to the other woman: "Come up and see, don't be ashamed, it's dark, no one can see, the eyes that shy away are closed."

The other gets up, makes her way among the crowd, and comes to check the truth of Ḥaddya's words under her skirts: "Little rat hairs!"

Digging inside her drapes, she finds the silver chain that holds Ḥaddya's clothing from within: "Good God! don't you have a donkey to attach with this chain? Is that why you wear it yourself?" Everyone laughs; the allusion to her widowhood is clear.

A chorus of younger voices rises from the back, broken by blasts of laughter. A woman gets up, rolls her veil in the shape of a penis, and swinging back and forth she sings:

> *ʿAndî maʿmûd nâd liyâ*
> *u nester bih kûll d-dâr*
> *Ḥttâ waḥda ma-ḥennat fî-ya*
> *Allâh yʿṭehûm kâmila n-nâr*
>
> I have a Pestle it stands hard / With it I guard the house /
> Not a She who takes pity on me / May they all go to Hell!

A voice, laughing: "May God cool off that on which you sit, hot peppers in your cunts, that's what you need [*Allâh yberd-kûm ʿlesh gʿadtû, Allâh yaʿṭikum l-ḥarûr*]!"

"If you are ashamed of your cunts, go and bury them in the waste pond, and if you don't want to hear, cover your porcupine ears with your hands! Life is too short to be serious all the time, and there's already too much illness and sorrow not to laugh a bit when it comes." Ḥaddya is laughing as she speaks, pretending to be indignant, then suddenly changes tone and says that she was sick, very sick, but when she heard that l-Hashmi had died, she had to come and cry with Ḍâwya, even though it was a long way away from her village and the path was burned by the sun.

A latecomer walks in. Her face covered behind the black veil, she proceeds hesitantly. Such is the persona of mourning. Suddenly, in a theatrical way, she throws herself on the ground before Ḍâwya, the mistress of the house. The two women join their veils as if to form a tent, and wail. Everyone starts crying, once again. Ḥaddya, next to me, is crying too. Myself, I can't cry. (How tears could be at the same time so completely simulated and so completely real was confusing for me at first. Were these real tears? And, if so, how could women slip in and out of despair? It was not the artifice of wailing that was hard for me to understand, but the fact that the artifice was real.)

Her moment of despair past, the newcomer brings news from the outside. A truck unloaded a mound of gray stones in the wasteland. They are the gravestones for the cemetery. For *their* dead, the Ḥarâtîn had said, and had locked the stones in the pink cement house, at the outermost edge of the village. The conversation turns to the fitna of the day.

"Your village is struck by *bû zellûm*," says Ḥaddya, raising her voice, taking the diagnostic tone she has when people consult her for their medical problems (she is an expert midwife, initiated to the arts of cauterization surgery and bonesetting).

"And when a person is affected by *bû zellûm*, her bones are 'open' [*meḥlulîn lîha l-ʿaḍam*], her bones are 'broken' [*maksurîn lîha l-ʿaḍam*], her joints are disjointed... she is disarticulated and can't move anymore. Air [*l-berd*],[98] infiltrates between bone and bone, and the machine stalls, like the engine pumps in the gardens if the pipe is pierced and pressure cannot build anymore. A woman, if she is struck by *bû zellûm,* can't give birth anymore. Take the case of that ʿAysha l-Yazid: she was pregnant and sick, people told her hold your tongue, don't get in trouble, don't get in fights, don't make too much noise [*lâ tketrî ṣḍaʿ, lâ tketrî l-khṣûm*], and instead she went and she talked too much [*kettrat l-klâm*], she got involved in the 'buying and selling of words,' just like this fitna of today at the funeral, and now, there she is about to die, her uterus fell off, her rûḥ came out, they tried to contain it, they tried to tie her up, but there was nothing to do... They had told her not to get involved with the wires of discourse."

"If poor Shṭo Lḥassan were still here, may she rest in peace, she'd turn the Thread around the walls [*ghâdi tḍewwer l-khayṭ ll-qṣar*]...," says a woman.

"Or she'd throw a handful of *sekta* over their heads, over the heads of the men at the village gate, or both." (*Sekta,* the "silencing," is a powder women grind from a wild herb. It induces silence in those who talk too much, and as such is a remedy against fitna.)

They turn to me and explain that in the old days, and until not too long ago, if there was a fitna that was splitting the families and producing a spreading discord, the *muqaddema* of the black women, the ritual leader, collected raw wool from door to door. With a group of women, and during one day of continuous work scanned by ritual ablutions, they spun that wool into a long warp thread; then, starting from the Gate of the qṣar, they pinned the thread into the walls at the chant of *Lâ ilâha illâ Allâh,* until they rejoined the Gate from the other side—embracing the qṣar with a shield of protection. One day—some ten years ago—they were doing the Thread. It was the beginning of the new period of "scattering"; people were fighting over the partition of the communal land, some had been taken to jail, in a climate of fear and distrust. So they decided to collect the wool and do the Thread. But this time it was different. They were almost three-quarters of the way around, had reached the new opening of the Alley of Bû Ṭwîl and were passing the thread across, when the son of Ayt Wardî came by on his mule; he had a *tameskert* in his hands, and with the bladed tool cut the thread of one stroke, accused Shṭo Lḥassan of being a witch, and trod on.

It is at that point that, without any special introduction, Ḥaddya started telling a story. I took it, and so did the other women sitting in the hallway with us, as an implicit commentary on the facts of the day—on the anxieties behind the events at l-Hashmi's funeral. It is a story about men, as viewed from a critical feminine standpoint: about identity and difference, about the "law" and the double, about returns, and about the sensual bodies of words.

The Return of the Double

There was a man and he was sterile, barren were he and his wife, they bore no children, nothing, sat and implored God. Every day that man gathered wood in the forest, brought home his small load, divided it in half, half they cooked with, half he sold for their living. On and on. One day God took compassion on her and she got pregnant; pregnant she got with a child, and she gave birth to a child. On the seventh day he had nothing to sacrifice in the name of his son; he went to fetch wood in the forest [l-ghâba] *and in the wild he found a child—a male child, in addition to the one born of his own blood* [zayd ʿala hâda llî zâd ʿandû]. *He found him, said "bismillâh" and took him, gathered his wood load, and said to his wife, "Our Lord was generous with us, we bore no children, had nothing, and now we have two. Raise these two infants, and we are in the hands of God." And so she gave them her breasts. People take years to grow, the boys grew day and night, they grew, grew, grew, till they became alike* [ḥetta tgâddû], *till he couldn't tell anymore his proper son from the boy he found in the forest. Both courageous and clever, beautiful and tall, what that woman desired they brought to her. They worked for their parents, and the family didn't need a thing.*

One day that man said to his wife, "I found one child in the forest, I engendered the other from my own blood; today I can't tell anymore my own son from the other." She said, "For God's sake, they are both our children, didn't I nurse them both? Didn't I raise them both? Who cares if we don't know which one is which? We don't want anybody's harm, they are both our children, like the one, like the other."

He said, "I must know my proper son from the other."

He sought the advice of a Jew: "I'll tell you what happened to me... I bore no children until the day God took pity on me and I engendered a son. On the seventh day [the day of naming] I found another child in the forest, I brought him home, the woman nursed them both, and now they are grown, they have become men, and I must distinguish my own son from the one I found in the forest." The Jew said, "Go with them to the river, and pretend to fall in the water... your true son will jump at your rescue with his clothes on, the other [wuld n-nâs] *will first undress." So he went to the river, pretended to fall in, and called, "My children, my children!" One jumped in the water with his clothes on, the other took his clothes off. The man said to himself, "Now I know you, my son* [hânî ʿarfek]*!" He embraced the one who jumped in the water with his clothes on, and announced to his wife, "This is our son, that is the son of unknown people." Now when he divided the meat, he privileged "his own son," and gave his entire affection to him. Until the* *other son realized that his father's gaze had turned away from him* [ḥder ʿalih l-ʿayn].

He went to his brother and said, "I have come to tell you goodbye." The brother said "Why?" He said, "Our father discriminates between us [kayʿazelnî mennek]; *before we were one, now he has put a difference on me* [dâr fyia l-ferd]." *"My brother," the other said, "the river that took you away won't leave me here* [l-wâd llî ddak ma-khallanî]; *we nursed at the same breast and today he doesn't want you anymore; let's go away together and leave him alone as he once was."*

They got up and went, the two brothers. God alone empties and fills, God alone empties and fills [mâ yʿammar u ykhlî ghîr Allâh], *till they reached a place where the road split. The one said to the other, "Brother, together we inspire fear in people, take this road, I'll take that road, and we'll plant a tree at this intersection. If you find the tree dead, you'll know I am dead, if I find it dead, I'll know you are dead, and if we find it in good health, we will know that we are both well." So they separated, and each went to seek his fortune in the world...*

He [the "true" son] arrived at the house of a man, and that man had seven sons, he had plenty of animals that he grazed, and he had, with respect to your face, a she-dog that accompanied the herd, and had palm trees, and had his mother and his wife. The boy said, "Guest of God." The other said, "Welcome." "Would you like a man to work for you and be with you in your house?" The landlord said, "I do, but I shall set the conditions of our pact [neshart ʿalik]: *you will graze the animals, and if the she-dog arrives first she'll eat your meal and her meal, if you arrive first you'll eat her meal and your meal; every morning you will catch seven birds for my children, every afternoon you shall carry my mother up to the roof and every morning you shall get her down; and if we have guests you must carry them upstairs so that they don't touch the ground; you must make me a fire without smoke, and water my palm trees up to their hearts, and the one of us who gets mad, shall get his head cut off* [u llî tqallaq iṭqtaʿ lîh r-râs]."

The young man accepted, and the first day he went to catch birds, and when he got the birds the dog ate his meal. At night the landlord inquired, "Yak mâ-tqallaqti, *you are not mad, are you?" and the young man said, "No, no," and carried the old woman up, and carried her down. The next day he went to the gardens to water the palm trees; he opened the water at the canal and gave water, water, and water to the garden for the entire night, but the water didn't come up to the hearts of the palms. The landlord inquired, "You aren't mad, are you?" and the young man said, "Could I be more mad?" And the landlord cut his head off.*

Let us return to his brother, the one who had been repudiated by the father; when he went back to the place between roads [bîn ṭ-ṭerqân], *he found that the sign* [ishâra] *they had chosen was desiccated; he said, "My brother is dead." And he followed the road where his brother had found his death—only God empties and fills, only God empties and fills—till he arrived at the landlord's house. He said, "Salâm ʿalikûm, would you like a person to work for you and live in your house?" The landlord said, "I wouldn't mind," and added, "It is strange* [gharîb], *one who looked just like you* [llî lik shbih] *used to work for me too." The boy said to himself, "This is where my brother found his death." The landlord said, "But you can work for me only if you accept my conditions. Every morning you must catch seven birds for my children, take my herds to graze, and if the dog arrives first she will eat her meal and your meal, if you arrive first you shall eat her meal and your meal; you must make me a fire with no smoke; if we have guests you must carry them upstairs so that they don't touch the ground; every afternoon you must carry my mother to the roof and every morning carry her down; and you must water my palm trees to their hearts... and the one of us who gets mad, the other will cut off his head."*

The boy said, "I accept," and the next morning went to catch the seven birds; he killed the dog with a stone, ate her meal and his meal, took the seven birds and put them in the mouth of a snake. "Tell your children to stick their hand in and catch the birds themselves"; one by one, the children put their hand in the snake's mouth; the snake said, "Tak," the child's mind flew away, and he fell dead. The landlord said, "What happened?" and the young man said, "The bird flew, his mind blew" [ṭâr ṭîrû u ṭâr ʿaqlû], *on and on, till he killed the seven boys, all of them, God have mercy. The guests came; the young man slaughtered the animals one by one, put a sheep on each step until he covered the stairs with dead animals, all the way to the top floor. The guests arrived, said "bismillâh" and went upstairs stepping on sheep skins. When dinner was served there wasn't even a little bit of meat; they said, "The ground is wet with flesh and blood, and they didn't put meat in our dinner!" And the boy took from the guests their guns and with them made a fire with no smoke. In the morning the landlord said, "Carry my mother up the roof, and get her down," and he carried her up, and dropped her down from the roof, her body said, "Hak," and she died. And the landlord said, "You still have the palm trees to do." And the boy got the pick, cut off the trees at their roots, and laid their heart* [qalb] *down on the earth, till he had pulled down all the palm trees; he turned the roots to the sky and opened the water from the canal, until all the leaves were covered. So he watered the palms to their hearts!*

The landlord said, "What's this job you have done?" The young man replied, "You told me to water them up to their heart... I gave them water, would water ever go up to the heart of the tree? I laid the hearts down so that they may drink... you aren't mad, are you?" "Not at all!" the landlord replied. He was afraid his worker would kill him too. For he had killed his mother, had killed his children, had killed his dog, had ruined his gardens.

Thus the landlord said to the boy: "Stick to the door of the house, stick to the foot of the door; the woman wants to go visit her parents." The young man said, "All right." He had killed his mother, his children, destroyed his property—all the landlord could still hope for was to flee. His wife made stuffed bread for the trip and they went.

But the boy took the door off its hinges and carried it on his shoulders, and the place they emptied, he filled, the place they emptied, he filled, until he reached them just as she was saying, "Where can we cut this piece of bread?" And he said, "Here is the door, cut the bread on the door and give me my share." "You followed us all the way to this place and we told you to stay home!" they said. "The door, you told me to stick to the door of the house, and I did, here it is!"

The landlord inquired, "You aren't angry, are you?" "Of course I am not mad!" the boy said. She put the bread on the door, they divided it and ate it.

They were on the seashore. At night the landlord said to his wife, "When we go to sleep, I'll put you in the middle, and him on the sea side. When I tell you to push, push him in the water." But the boy heard and exchanged places. And when the landlord said "Push," she pushed her husband into the ocean. The young man said to her, "He's dead! We finally got rid of him." She repeated, "Finally we got rid of him." But when she realized what she had done she died too. We heard this from some, and repeated it to others.

part two

CONTRA-DICTION

Ḥadda, son of Ṭamu

CONTRA-DICTION 1

DIALOGICS OF FITNA

Moi, Antonin Artaud, je suis mon fils, mon père,
ma mère,
et moi;
niveleur du périple imbécile où s'enferre
l'engendrement,
le périple papa-maman
et l'enfant,
suie du cu de la grand-maman
beaucoup plus que du père-mère
. . . .
Pour nous dégoûter un peu plus de nous,
était ce corps inemployable,
fait de viande et de sperme fou,
ce corps pendu, d'avant les poux,
suant sur l'impossible table
du ciel
son odeur calleuse d'atome,
sa rogomeuse odeur d'abject
DETRITUS
éjecté du somme
de l'Inca mutilé des doigts
qui pour idée avait un bras
mais n'avait de main qu'une paume
morte, d'avoir perdu ses doigts
à force de tuer des rois.
—Antonin Artaud[1]

1985. Ḥadda's house. winter, evening

she might kill you too

"Had he been capable of critical thinking..." Ḥadda stretches his legs on the gray military blanket that serves as a rug and continues, "just think! How could the water ever reach the hearts of the palms? Water doesn't go up to the hearts... On the first day, when the landlord set the rules [*ḥît kayshârṭu*] he should have replied, 'Since when can water rise to the tree hearts?' It is the first day that the cat dies...[2] But the donkey couldn't think [*maʿandu fikra*], he was so afraid of losing, afraid of dying—that thinking he couldn't think cost him his life."

He pauses to smoke the pipe he has meticulously filled (these little pipes are only good for one draw), empties it in the brazier, and says, "The other boy had a sharp mind instead. The landlord said, Do this, Do that, and the boy, while executing his orders, fixed him up for his ruin!"

His eyes gleam and he laughs with complicity. I know Ḥadda identifies with the transgressive boy; we both do. The thought makes me smile. His transgression is embodied by the disheveled hut where he has chosen to live, away from the entanglements, the sophistication and the intrigues of the qṣar. (Mine—detoured travels through countries and languages—by my being here at this time.)

Ḥadda continues, excited: "The clever boy said to himself: 'I'll throw his mother down the stairs, I'll kill her, and if he gets mad I'll cut off his head! Then I'll cut down every single one of his palm trees, and if he gets mad I'll cut off his head!' He caught the landlord in the net of his own words, in his own damn spiderweb! In the end the landlord said, 'Mad, I am not mad, but now that my animals are dead, my children dead, my mother dead, my palm trees dead, no ties are left in this land, I'll move on to somewhere else...' But the boy wouldn't let go so easily, he said, 'I am with you my master [*sîdî*], I'll work for you until the day one of us goes mad, till the day one of us gets his head cut off...'

"You see what I mean, he was sharp. The boy could think. But the part about the good mother, the version that the women told you, doesn't convince me. In the story as I tell it, the woman, who is the mother who is also the sister, is the cause of all the troubles...

"Isn't it so?" he says, addressing the dark space outside the room where his many young daughters are sitting unseen, listening in silence.

In the story as I tell it there is a boy and a girl. Their parents die, they are left orphans and grow up together holding on to each other, living through their hardship, until the girl is old enough to marry, and she marries a man...

(Pause.)

Not a real man: she married a jinn. Jinns transform, they can take any form, and that one took the shape of a man. So she married him and begot a son of him. Now that she had a husband and her own son, she got tired of her brother and plotted to get rid of him. One winter night she said to her husband, "I'll send my brother to fetch wood. Meet him outside and kill him." The man said, "All right," but her son—who was after all the son of a jinn—divined her intentions. So when she asked her brother to fetch the wood, he offered to go in his place. He said aloud, "Lord have mercy on this mother of mine; she waits until late at night to torment her brother by sending him to fetch wood. He's slow and will certainly get hurt."

On and on, several failed attempts. One day she said to her husband, "Hide inside these blankets. I'll send my brother to wash them at the river and I'll keep your son occupied with an errand. Kill my brother. Throw his body in the water and we'll be free of him!" Her jinn-husband took the shape of a snake and hid in the folds of the blankets. She sent her brother to the river and sent her son off with an errand. But the boy disobeyed her orders and went to the river instead, cut two strong sticks from a tree and said to his maternal uncle, "Let's beat the laundry!" "Why?" "Just beat, it's only rags!"

And he knew his own father was hiding inside. "Strike your stick, raise my stick, strike my stick, raise your stick." They shook the blanket and found the snake (that is the father) dead. His son threw the corpse into the water: "Go to hell, may you never come back!"

His mother came. She said, "What are you doing here?" "I came to help my uncle with the laundry." "O me! O me, he murdered my husband!" And the boy said, 'We beat the blankets thoroughly, then we rinsed them in the river. We had no idea there was something in there, but I can assure you, whatever there was is now gone!"

She wailed and then lamented, "I must yet square accounts with that brother of mine..." And when the two young men went out to work in the fields, she bought poison from the spice seller and prepared a bean meal [*l-ʿaṣîda*]. She said to herself, "I'll put my son's share in a bowl, my brother's I'll put in the *ḥallâb* and I'll add poison to it, and my own share I will leave in the pot. I'll go off to mill; when they come from the gardens I'll tell everyone which one is his meal. That bastard will eat the poison and once and for all he'll be dead!"

They came in from the gardens; her brother walked in first. She said to him, "Your meal is in the *ḥallâb*."[3] But the boy stopped him, "Don't eat." The uncle said, "Why?" "Just so, if you are hungry eat the food in the bowl." The uncle ate. Then the boy filled the bowl with the food that was in the pot and ate too. Finally he poured the portion that was in the *ḥallâb* into the pot. When she finished her milling, she said to herself, "By now that cursed one must be dead." She went to the kitchen, ate the meal in the pot, and at the last bite fell stone dead [*ibsât*]. The boy called, "Uncle! this one is dead too. I killed my father to save your life and I killed my mother. Today this land can't accept me anymore—I am off to the world." The uncle said, "Son of my sister, the steps that take you away won't leave me here," and he followed the boy.

They went and went and went, until they arrived at a place in between two roads. The boy said to his uncle, "You take one road, I'll take the other. But one thing I advise you, my uncle: blue-eyeds don't be associated with. Goodbye."[4] The uncle went, he arrived at a village and was hungry, a man stood at the door of his house and addressed him: "Will you work for me?" "I'll work." "But I will set the terms of our contract..."

The uncle noticed his eye [*l-ʿayn*] and said, "No! I cannot work for you! I have a sister's son who warned me, *blue-eyeds don't be associated with.*" The man laughed, "Are you out of your mind? In this country everybody has blue eyes; if you are spared from me you'll find someone else. This whole world is blue-eyed!"

It goes on like your version," concludes Ḥadda turning toward me, "except that the dumb role is plaid by the mother's brother [*khâl*], while the smart boy, who was the foundling in the story the women told you, is, in this case, her own son, the offspring of her union with the jinn. It is he who after having killed his father and his mother goes on to destroy the landlord's possessions and eventually kills him too."

In Ḥadda's version of the story everything seems to contradict some filial or generational norm. I say, "The son kills his father, and then poisons his mother who is planning to murder her own brother... Or *(I hesitate)* is this to say that in some sense the events recounted in the story themselves exemplify the disastrous consequences of what, on many occasions, he has called *the play of words set free?*"

Ḥadda sits up to protest, suddenly refusing to philosophize, as if personally implicated by my comment: "There is nothing absurd or arbitrary in what the son does! From the day that boy was born, his mother repeated to him: Our father left us orphans—orphans, my brother and I. You were alone with that brother of yours, you shared with him hardship and hell. *(As if realizing that his anger betrays his own feelings—is he thinking of Faṭima ʿAlî, who just abandoned him, leaving her many daughters behind, of his own mother, or of a phantasmic chain of feminine figures of deception?—he lowers his voice and withdraws into a more neutral third person):* till one day that bitch [*mujrîma*] grew up and married a man, or a jinn, we don't care, turned against the brother who had shared hardship with her from before she was married, and attempted to kill him! The boy understood from his uncle's experience that his own mother would become his enemy. For did she have a husband, did she have a son when she was alone with her brother? But now that she has a husband and a son, now that she lives in plenty, she wants to get rid of her brother. You will agree with me that God granted the boy the gift of understanding when he said, 'That mother of mine who wants to murder her brother—I must kill her instead!' Because she betrayed his brother. She betrayed! Today she wants to kill her brother, her own blood; tomorrow she might want to kill him too. This is what the boy thought…

"Like Ḥawwa in the Garden of Eden, the mother, the sister of the story, he was guilty of betrayal. Ḥawwa listened to Iblis the devil and got both herself and Adam banished from the Garden, thrown out into the mortal world… Adam followed his wife and forgot about God…"

This is fitna!

"And this woman gets married to a jinn… jinns can take any form, they have no form of their own. And so, in a way, can women. Both jinns and women have a foreign nature, they are *gharîb*. But the young boy, who is an offspring of her union with the jinn, is also *gharîb*, and can fight his mother on her own grounds."

"*Gharîb*," I repeat. (I am thinking of his special relation with his mother, Ṭamu, who raised him and introduced him to many of the feminine arts, and that elusive and legendary father of his whom people described as a kind of jinn himself.)

"So you are like the clever boy of the story," I say.

Ḥadda giggles, "Don't you know that Sîdî Moḥamed u l-Ḥajj *was* a jinn?" Sîdî Moḥamed u l-Ḥajj, his father: a man of many faces and transformations, whose most legendary deed was the establishment of a mint in which he counterfeited money with the help of the jinns at his service. (Forgers, like jinns, operate within a world of simulacra.)

Ḥadda[5] appeared at the house where I lived one day when I was ill (we had never met before), but paid no attention to the fever that made it hard for me to speak. Instead, he challenged me with a riddle in that antagonistic tone that set the terms of so many encounters that followed. In the darkness of the room I could hardly see his face—only his eyes, blinking. He spoke about the difference between *l-ʿaqel* and *l-fikra,* "intelligence" and "critical thought." Without *l-fikra,* he kept saying, without a critical imagination, intelligence was a faculty of no worth. Then his question: Given three men with different levels of understanding and vision—one who has none at all, one who has an average level, and one who can understand and see a great deal—who is most likely to end up in hell? I sensed an Aristotelian point about the virtue of the average man and said, "Are you suggesting that a person with too much understanding is bound to end up in hell?" He smiled. I realized that he was talking about his own hell on earth. And that he was throwing bait for me to catch.

(July 25, 1989)

"I don't expose myself," he says four years later. We are sitting outside of his house on a summer night and I am describing this text to him.

"I can wait—forever if necessary—the occasion perhaps never comes. I throw the bait, if you don't catch it—and you don't catch it because you can't see it—I go my way and keep my reflections to myself. Then I sit with the men outside the walls, chat and entertain them with stories they want to hear, get involved in the endless factional diatribes, and they never suspect. When you came, on the other hand, you took up the challenge and here we are now."

Ḥadda turns to the friend who has accompanied me: "Perhaps it is because she was a stranger, gharîba, *and wasn't caught in the blinding routine of daily life."*

"We accept reality easily, perhaps because we intuit that nothing is real," writes Borges in "The Immortal," a story I have been recounting to Ḥadda and a small group of friends intermittently, intertwined with the tales and commentaries of the others, over the afternoon. Ḥadda is simply a fact of my life. I realize this now more than then, for I have come to recognize the estrangement that makes no one place in the landscape of my life more real, or unreal, than any other. I repeat my reflections aloud. Four years ago I couldn't have said it (the question of what is research, what is literature, and what is life does not preoccupy me anymore). I quote Borges to Ḥadda, "He dicho asombro donde otros dicen solamente costumbre" (I have said astonishment where others say only habit).

"If you lose the capacity to be surprised you might as well be dead," he replies.

His voice. It can reach unpredictably pure crystalline timbres—when he laughs, for instance. Yet his voice is hoarse, like that of an old man (at the different times in these conversations he has been about sixty, sixty-five, and seventy). The hoarseness is perhaps due to the little pipe he empties and fills continuously, but it is also a rhetorical effect (he draws his image from the juxtaposition of contrasts) as is the careful choice of harsh vernacular terms that punctuate and animate his language. His eyes are piercing, his head carefully shaven (he never wears a turban), his legs fragile, weakened by an illness that paralyzed him for many months. His face can take on, as temporary masks, very old or very young expressions. He was once a poet of local renown. Village people remember how, in the days of l-waṭân (the nationalist uprising that led to independence), the young Ḥadda with a handful of tough boys from the black Ḥarâtîn took the word away from the old sheikh of the *ʿamma* and turned the village group of musical-poetic performance into an active nucleus of resistance against the French and the local ruling families.

Then, for reasons inexplicable to many of his fellow villagers, he abruptly withdrew from public life, swearing that no song would be heard from him again, and moved out of the qṣar to a hut in the gardens to dedicate his efforts to the land.

The hut—Ḥadda ironically calls it his tent—is a compound of roughly built mud walls, barely put together and full of holes, with no doors or anything that might stop the winter wind from blowing through. Far from both the walled ramparts of the old qṣar and the new settlements in the outside desert, at the margins of the village territory, Ḥadda's hut rests on top of a mound dominating the major upstream junction of the regional irrigation network. It is the water junction people call Izugla.

Izugla is how Ḥadda sometimes refers to his place.

A place of power and marvel, Izugla is a tripartite articulatory structure, a mouth built of white plaster and stone levigated by the passage of centuries. In passing through it, the waters of the canal of Ifli are channeled into the three canals that from time immemorial bring life and water to the gardens of the qṣar and to some fifteen other qṣûr downstream.[6] They are the veins that run through the body of Ahl Iflî, the "people of Iflî."

Taruga n-Tifkert, Sâgyât n-Ustur, Aghala Ufella. Three veins, carrying water in different directions, furrowing the land of different communities, bonded by that circulatory pact. Three different ways of saying "canal," in gradations of Berber and Arabic. *Taruga* means "canal" in Berber, and *Tifkert* is the name of a region of the gardens where the civilization of the qṣar began, some five centuries ago. *Sâgya* means "canal" in Arabic, for Astur, the canal's final destination, is an Arabic-speaking cluster of villages downstream. Yet, in passing through the land of the qṣar, the name is cast in Berber syntax, *n-Ustur.*

Three names are inscribed in the tripartite articulatory structure of Izugla. They evoke a plurality of histories and the flow of the qṣar's collective memory, from the times of the Judge, who is said to have founded the qṣar and laid out the irrigation canals and before (much before! says Ḥadda), battles were fought at Izugla for the control of water. Shells were aimed at Izugla from the Glâwî fortress at the dawn of the French conquest to break the resistance of the people of Iflî.

For, in Ḥadda's eyes, the canals define the people of the land—against all attempts at colonization. They are the veins that run through his body, too.

(Later)

People were summoned from all over the valley to dig our moat, and the Judge took for himself one-fourth of our village. So now the people of his lineage go around blown up with arrogance, claiming that the qṣar of Bni Zoli is the inheritance the Qâḍî left them! One day I said to one of them, The Judge, you claim, *arma swâgî,* he laid out the irrigation canals. But what do you think came first, the Judge or the canals? Ever since it was created, this land has been furrowed by canals. The people of the canal are related, from Bni Zoli all the way to the villages of Astur, Tignutin, Tinegdid, Ighardain, Aderbaz, Lḥara, and Taghallil. Could you ever believe that they would wait for the Judge to come and "throw" the canals for them? This is theft! *Arma swâgî,* they say, the Judge laid down the irrigation canals! And so the day France came and asked who owned the land in between canals they had the nerve to say, Aḥmed u ʿAlî the Qâḍî![7]

Ḥadda sits in the esplanade outside the ramparts of his hut, at the top of the mound of Izugla, high above, near the hearts of the palm trees. The mound is almost an island, between Taruga n-Tifkert and Sâgyât n-Ustur, an island of mud, formed by the successive excavations of the canals. It is a knot, a layered residue, in the morphological memory of his land. On top of that mound, minimalist and flat, Ḥadda's hut is a contrast to the sophisticated architecture of the three-level mud houses of the qṣar, where he himself spent a large part of his life. Like a gatekeeper, or like an angel, he sits at the threshold of vegetal and social life.

Up to three months earlier (when Faṭima ʿAlî left him, taking away her newborn, Ḥadda's only son), he had been living there with his two wives and eight children, seven girls and the boy, all born of one woman, his older, but still young, wife. He had married her as a young girl when, after the tragic and related deaths of his father and his son, he decided to break his ties with the village, and all ties. He divorced his wife (the wife chosen for him by his mother) and moved out to the gardens where he built his "tent." For years he and his woman lived in chosen isolation, like characters from a Qur'anic parable, restlessly plowing, working, and leveling an arid piece of land until the earth started to bear fruit. Their solitary life had been the unlikely example of a kind of love (made possible by the suspension of social conventions) that people were accustomed to finding only in poetry. He was for her man and woman, husband and wife, father and mother. Scandalizing his compatriots, he helped her during childbirth, and delivered each one of her seven daughters. But for this last pregnancy she chose to be helped by Ḥadda's newly married second wife, and asked him to leave the room—breaking their pact and metaphorically rejoining the society of the qṣar. As she denied him his role as a mother, he denied himself to her as a husband and a father, and refused to name, or even recognize, his own son. They parted over the birth of Ḥadda's only male heir.

Fitna: A Maze of Words to Get Lost In

"What style of narrative is this?" I ask, referring to a classification that Ḥadda had been explaining earlier, a *ḥajayya* or a *ghazawa?*

"A *ghazawa* is a *true* story, it is rooted in reality, like the stories of battles and conquests, like the stories in the Qur'an. It speaks of events that have really happened, or tells a parable that is morally true. This story, instead, is just a *ḥajjâya.*[8] A *ḥajjâya* is like a performance made of words [*l-ḥajjâya bḥal temtîl*]. It's never true [*wâqiʿyia,* "both true and real"]. It is *khayâliyya,* a simulation that springs from the realm of shadows and ghosts [*khayâl*], a theater of words [*temtîl*] in the realm of likeness and image [*mital*].

"When you tell a story you pick up words; by means of words you say that there was this and that. Words act out words [*l-klâm kaymettel l-klâm*], each word prefigures her sister [*kull kelma katmettel ʿala khothâ*], and they go their own way. Illusion induces fitna [*l-khayâlî kayften*]—it draws you in, seduces, confuses you, and loses you in the maze."

FITNA: the danger is the fictional/illusionary play of images and words that don't correspond to an object world but create their own object inside the narrative. And then, with a hyperreal effect, the narrative becomes life. A *mital* [classical *mithal,* pl. *muthûl*] is a likeness, an image, a rhetorical figure. *Al-ʿâlam al-mithâl* is the parallel World of Images, which does not just mirror, but produces realities.[9] A *khayâl* is a shadow, an illusion or a simulacrum. A word, then, as well. *Kankhayyal* means "I am imagining," but also "I am hallucinating."
A representation that feeds upon itself ("false," in Ḥadda's terms) is

a place in which to get lost, for it is a play of images that generates a world instead of referring back to it as its truthful mimesis. In the *khayâl*, the "untrue" image or shadow, the mirror reflection, there is a power of seduction and a sentence to death. And yet *l-wâqiʿ*, "the object world," can be grasped only through images, can be spoken only through words. Thus, as Ḥadda paradoxically phrases it—*aṣl d-dunya men l-klâm:* the world, the material world, itself originates in words.

He says:

"If we want to explicate fitna, it originates in words. Entirely in words: *l-aṣl dyâl fitna kulshî men l-klâm*. History is born of words, marriage is born of words, selling and buying originate in words, everything comes from words. The origin of fitna, the history of fitna, is WORDS! Words are actions... Everybody seems to mind his own business, then, all of a sudden, Qâb Qarqallâb! *l-fitna* breaks out [*naḍt l-fitna*]."

"But there are words and words," I propose. "Or do you mean to suggest that all words generate fitna?"

"No. Good words go with good actions [*l-klâm llî mezyân tabʿu l-ʿamal*]. If you enter in between people to heal discord and restore peace, it is a good action performed in good faith—it has nothing to do with words [*l-klâm*]! Fitna, instead, blows wind in between people [*katdîr l-lju bîn n-nâs*],[10] it ruptures, it makes fissures..."

Ḥadda continues, excited: "How does it develop? Something like a net is woven between person and person, and people are caught in that net [*wâḥed itshebbek mʿa lâkhor*]. It is like wires [*slûka*]: you 'throw' a word, and that word 'works', reproduces [has children], generates new words [*tarmî l-kelma u hyia tekhdem, tûled*]!...

"It works right away! Try! Say one thing to one person and another thing to another person: all of a sudden you'll be in the midst of electric wires, nobody controls the words anymore, everything blows up. A short circuit, you hear a blast...

"And if you get to that point, who can control words anymore? If a word works to the point of reproducing [*tûled*], if the mind starts working on its own and generating images independent of your control [*ilâ mshâ ḥetta wled l-ʿaqel*], there is nothing to do anymore, it is fitna![11] *Al-fitnatu ashaddu min al-qatl*, fitna is more dangerous than murder [Qur'an 2:191], it is more powerful than any art, craft, or calculation [*aktar men ṣinâʿaa u l-qanaʿa*], it does what poison and bombs can't do, it sets forces in motion that not even weapons can stop...

"Take the fitna that developed here in these last few days, look at the scattering [*shtât*], the splitting, the disintegration. I sat by the engine mill and I watched them: running up and down, buying and selling words, organizing assemblies, and plotting beyond the backs of people. And all of a sudden it got out of control, things are falling apart and the whole world is collapsing...

"Or think of the fitna in Palestine! What's happening now in Palestine resembles the big fitna of this valley, the days of *siba,* right before the Christians came...

"It is all from words *(in a concluding tone): asl d-dunya men l-klâm!* words are the origin of everything—the world, the material world, originates in words."

FITNA: semiotic disorder, a mad proliferation of signs, an infectious spreading producing a sort of entropy that fissures the community and may lead to war. An alien force, anonymous and blind, external to the will and the control of individual subjects:[12] "Everybody seems to mind his own business, then, all of a sudden, Qâb Qarqallâb, *l-fitna* breaks out!" Automatic once its machinery is set in motion: "It sets forces to work that not even weapons can stop..."

It is the trope of growth out of control. The medical analogy is cancer: *ila msha l-klâm ḥetta iwlad, kaynuwweḍ l-fitna,* "if words develop to the point of reproducing [literally, having children], they awaken fitna." (In the local vocabulary of the body *l-maraḍ llî kaywled* is an illness that reproduces, that spreads.) It is the straying of language, when representations take on a life of their own and start creating worlds. This is the sense of the double-edged expression *l-biʿ u shshrâ f l-klâm,* "the buying and selling of words," a paradigmatic glossing of fitna in the historical imagination of the qṣar. In the days of (political) fitna, days of instability and intrigue *l-klâm,* "words,"[13] meaning in this context "political influence," the efficacious capacity to control others, could be literally bought and sold for money. Power was the result of monetary speculation. (*L-bîʿ u shshraʾ,* "buying and selling," is an idiom of commerce.)[14] But the "buying and selling of words" is also metaphorical speculation. It is the commerce of words with each other, the speculation of language.[15] At this limit of fitna, the object world dissolves under the tongues of speaking subjects; or this same world is born from the illusory play of language. Worlds—Ḥadda seems to suggest—are born into a theater of words, but become compellingly real.

The image of the wind that blows in between people is important: *l-fitna katdîr l-lju bîn n-nâs. L-ljû,* "air," or *l-berd,* "cold air," is seen as a cause of illness.[16] The image of the outbreak of fitna within the community resonates with this etiology of illness. The bodily infiltration of "wind" (as something that enters in-between, opens the joints, and produces fission) can be of physical or demonic origin. When physical, it causes a loosening up of the body's articulations and thus a leak or loss of vital energy (*rûḥ*), which throws the body into a state of illness. When the "wind" is of demonic origin, it causes a disintegration of the self, which results in a state of confusion and madness. The surgical intervention of cauterization (*l-kîy*)—the cure of fire—attempts to weld the articulations of the body in order to remedy the dissolution of the illness, the fitna, in both a physical and a metaphorical sense.

But one of the classical definitions of *fitna* is itself that of the work of fire upon metals:[17] Ḥadda is aware of this. On the one hand, fire melts metals, it deconstructs them; on the other, it purifies metals, sorting out alloys. Without the fitna of fire, it would be impossible to isolate silver and gold from lead. This is the Qur'anic meaning of *fitna* as "testing" and "trial," the trial of fire. *Fitna,* in this sense, is the inscription of a difference without which life, and society, would be impossible, but a difference that poses a mortal risk.

Like the "air" that lends it an image, the concept of fitna is elusive. Not because its depth is unfathomable, but because it is never there where one would expect to find it. At each turn, it disintegrates and steals itself away. More diffuse and unstable than any occidental representation of evil, harder to integrate, to dialecticize and hence to tame, fitna is a trickster constantly changing shape, mimicking or simulating its referent. It is intractable and untreatable, *intraitable.*[18]

(Without attempting to grasp it, then, I follow its elusive, scattered and labyrinthine path through the curves of texts and contexts, stopping here and there to highlight a turn or comment on a new landscape. This is also the strategy of the commentary on fitna in the fourteenth-century lexicographic dictionary *Lisân al-ʿârab,* which makes of this elusive concept, presented there through the drifting circularity of its figures, both the object of a description and a strategy of interpretation.)

In the sense Ḥadda discusses here, fitna is a theory of the dangerous power of rhetoric, and of language in general, inasmuch as no discourse can do away with its figures. It tells of how, on the one hand, rhetorical operations have pragmatic effects: they produce events, "short circuits," Ḥadda says, disputes, illnesses, wars. And of how, on the other hand, the rhetorical structure of language—the work of the image in the word—undermines worlds and discourses from within.

Fitna, in the end, is the deconstructive strategy of the clever son in the tale with which Ḥadda and I began our conversation. For by executing his orders to the letter the boy causes his master's ruin: by enacting the image in the word, or, as the story itself says, by taking the figure "off of its hinges."

"Thus the landlord said to the boy: "Stick to the door of the house..."

"He had killed his mother, his children, destroyed his property—all the landlord could still hope for was to flee... But the boy took the door off its hinges and carried it on his shoulders, and the place the landlord emptied, the other filled."

It is the uncanny return of the image. One of the most famous Qur'anic condemnations of fitna equates it with the error of following the figural and metaphorical meanings of words (*al-mutashâbihât*); "Those whose heart is consumed by the malaise of straying follow its *mutashâbihât,* seeking fitna" (Qur'an 3:7). It is the danger of infinite regress in chasing the image, the danger of losing the object, and getting lost in an endless chain of allegoric displacements, from image to image, from word to word. It is the first *dédoublement,* Ḥadda goes on to say, the first reflected image, that caused the expulsion from the Garden and the rebirth into the human, mortal world.

Rhetoric of the Expulsion: The Image and the Feces

"Both fitna and dunya, then, originate in words," I suggest, more as a question than as a statement.

"The thing is," Ḥadda says, "that *dunya,* 'the world,' originates in fitna." And continues:

> *In the* jinna, *the Garden of Eden, Iblis the devil presented our mother Ḥawwa with a mirror.*[19] *She saw her reflection, was seized by fitna* [tfetnât], *and got lost. Deceived by the image* [ṣûra], *she believed she saw another woman who was usurping her place with Adam. Iblis confirmed her suspicion: "Adam has replaced you with another woman, and she'll have the same rights as you"* [bghâ ijîb ʿalîk l-mrâ, bḥalek bḥalha]. *Thus following the advice of the devil, she ate from the forbidden tree. For Iblis told her that, if she ate a leaf from that tree, she and Adam would remain the only beings and that the human race would never be born on the face of the Earth* [ʿammar maykhorj benâdem ʿalâ ujeh d-dunya, *or, the human race would never be ejected into the World*]. *She got a leaf from that tree, an apricot or a fig tree, and ate it. As she ate she felt—with respect to your face—the urgent need to shit, and moved by this need to shit she came out to the World to empty her bowels*

[hezz lîha—ḥâsha wajhak—ghobarha, ḥît hezzha ghbârha kharjat l-d-dunya tdirû; dunya, *the material, historical-mortal world]. Once in the World she lost orientation, she lost the direction of the Garden and couldn't find her way back. Adam noticed her absence and came out of the Garden to look for her, he came into the World to find her. He wandered about in one direction, she wandered about in the other. She wanted to return to him but couldn't find the way, and realized she was lost...*

On Earth, Adam walked every day looking for Ḥawwa, and at night he slept. Ḥawwa, instead, walked all day and all night, restlessly looking for her man. To provide for their newly felt need to eat, God gave Ḥawwa a daily allowance of two barley breads, while to Adam he gave only one. She ate one bread and a half, and half she put aside for him; he ate half of his bread, and half he put aside for her. Her wanderings took her one morning to the top of a hill. Looking down, she saw Adam coming from afar. When she saw him coming she didn't call, didn't run in his direction! She sat down, waiting for him to see her. And when he found her he rejoiced, he said, "Oh, Ḥawwa, apart from you I had no peace, I looked for you every day all day." And Ḥawwa, who had looked for him day and night, said, "Myself, I never thought of you, not once did I miss you, Adam! I have been sitting here waiting since I fell on Earth, I didn't move at all." Adam said, "Here is your share of the bread, every day I ate half and left you half." "So did I," she said, and gave him his share of her bread. Adam didn't know, but God was a witness to her deception, and established by Law that her progeny should pay back the part she had taken from him with a lie. This is why, according to the Law [sh-sharîʿa] *a woman's inheritance share is half as much as a man's.*

Then, looking at me: "Surely you women are haughty [*fikum t-takabbur*] and deceptive!"

KHARAJA: Vocabulary

KHARAJA: exit.

KHRAJ MEN J-JENNA: came out of the Garden.

KHRAJ Ṭ-ṬRÎQ: came out of his way, got derouted, lost his way.

KHRAJ L-DUNYA: came out/was expelled/was born into the world.

KHRAJ L-AMSRÎR: left the straight path, strayed on the edge, (literally) wandered about on the riverbank; (of a woman) became a prostitute. (Arabic, *ṭ-ṭerf, aṭrâf,* the margins, frontiers of the land.)

KHARJAT L-ʿARÛSA: the bride was deflowered (evidence a posteriori that she was a virgin).
KHARJU N-NKHAL: the palm trees are budding.
KHRAJT: I was budding, I became an adult.

For fear that her image (the other woman jumped out of herself) might usurp her place with her man, longing to remain unique (so that the human race might never be born on the face of the earth), Ḥawwa, the first woman, opened up the space of repetition and death. Repetition is her work—representation is an effect of the feminine. With her act she engenders dunya, the mortal, temporal, impure world—a world that is born, from her impurity, impure. And at once she produces life and death. As much is expressed in the act of defecating, for "*Pour ne pas faire caca, il lui aurait fallu consentir à ne pas être.*" (Antonin Artaud's "La recherche de la fécalité" is yet another version of this story.[20] Artaud/Ḥadda. They have been forming since I have known Ḥadda, a couple in my reading. It seems only appropriate, in this sense, that they should be allowed to dialogue in this text.)

Artaud/Ḥadda:

Là où ça sent la merde
ça sent l'être.
L'homme aurait très bien pu ne pas chier,
ne pas ouvrir la poche anale,
mais il a choisi de chier
comme il aurait choisi de vivre
au lieu de consentir à vivre mort.

C'est que pour ne pas faire caca,
il lui aurait fallu consentir
à ne pas être,
mais il n'a pas pu se résoudre à perdre
l'être,
c'est-à-dire à mourir vivant.

Il y a dans l'être
quelque chose de particulièrement tentant pour
l'homme
et ce quelque chose est justement
LE CACA.
(Ici rugissements.) . . .[21]

Artaud, like Ḥadda, because of the textualization of their lives. Because Artaud's own biography and body became the private-public field where a drama of identity and otherness, fatherhood and motherhood, interior and exterior, purity and contamination, being and excrement, representation and life, acted itself out, producing the painful, irreducibly personal yet literary forms of his experience. Artaud signs for himself under the name of Van Gogh: "Van Gogh n'est pas mort d'un état de délire propre, mais d'avoir été corporellement le champ d'un problème autour duquel, depuis les origines, se débat l'esprit unique de cette humanité. Celui de la prédominance de la chair sur l'esprit, ou du corps sur la chair, ou de l'esprit sur l'un et l'autre . . . aujourd'hui même, maintenant. . . . c'est la réalité elle-même, le mythe de la réalité elle-même, qui est en train de s'incorporer . . ."[22]

For me, this recalls the textualization of Ḥadda's biography, the uncanny intertwining that I attempt to evoke in this text, in which identity and alterity, singular and plural, masculine and feminine, autobiographical and historical, act themselves out, ironically yet tragically (but with a playfulness foreign to Artaud), in an open field of unresolved contradictions.

(Who is the I of this interpretative act, in writing, but also during the time of these conversations? The I becomes an open field. Contrary to an interpretative position that would depict me as a stable self, prisoner of the categories of my culture, this fragmented field, which is me, is altered, affected, and in a way created anew by Ḥadda's intervention. And vice versa. Together, we open another space, a space that is neither his nor mine. A space in which Artaud's writings also have a place, along with other possible interpretative images. Yet all we do, perhaps, in our interaction, is to make visible an alterity that is, if in a less evident fashion, always at work.)

The mirror image and the feces, paradigmatic figures of separation, speak of the expropriation of some essential interiority, depict a process of becoming other; a becoming other that, we are told in the story, is the labor of becoming human. Artaud:

> *merde, douleur, poème.*
> *. . . or ce que je sors de moi n'est pas moi*
> *et je dois me refaire tout de suite,*
> *pourquoi suis-je fatigué?*
> *Parce que le corps concret dans la vie plus vrai que celle-ci, dans le relatif et le particulier me retiennent de les sortir, se sentant trop heureux*
> *hors de la vie.*
> *Pourquoi sortir et vivre . . .*[23]

Why come out and live?

On Earth, Ḥawwa quickly learns the arts of simulation and disguise—the wrongs she had resisted in the Garden—and endeavors to gain control of her man by pretending indifference: that is, by concealing her desire and postponing its satisfaction. She waits, or she pretends to wait. But pretending is a way of temporizing, it is a kind of waiting: "Myself, I never thought of you... I have been sitting here waiting since I fell on Earth. I didn't move at all!"

Sitting on top of the mountain, it is she who dominates the view at a distance and watches Adam coming. Ḥawwa pretends to do what in fact she has been doing all along, and of which her circuitous peregrinations on Earth are but a figure in space: she waits. And, at the same time, *katmettel*, "she feigns"—like images, like words. The black head veil women wear in this region is called *gunaʿ*, from the verb *qanaʿ*, "to wear a mask."

The Bit and the Bridle of Love

This does not mean, Ḥadda says four years later when I raise this issue again (it is a return, a kind of rewriting, for both of us), that woman by her nature knows how to contain passion. Her patience is only the simulated expression of her incontinence and her impatience. She is always strategically playing on two registers: if she is continent it is because she is incontinent, if she is passionate, she is also simulating passion. Woman is rhetoric—she is the rhetorical hiatus—but man is unable to see this, and in the space of her waiting he is blinded, seduced, and set adrift. He is *maftûn:* drawn into a state of fitna.

Yet that straying is more general than the seduction of women. It implies a certain subject loss, a loss that constitutes the subject; woman is one of its figures. Thus Ḥadda comes to say that life in its entirety—which is, as the story of Ḥawwa shows, the result of an error—entails a certain blinding, and that reason entails a certain unreason. Dunya, he concludes, is made possible by "love."

ʿAQEL: note, in the conversation below, the play on the term *ʿaqel,* which is usually translated as mind, reason or intellect. As a verb, *ʿaqel, ʿaqqal,* means to hold, to tie, to remember. Since the faculty of holding things together, collecting and recollecting, is the mind, *ʿaqel* comes to mean "mind." As a noun, however, *l-ʿaqel* also means string, bridle, tie, and is almost synonymous with the terms *rbṭa, mrbuṭ,* "attached," "tied," as in tying up something, or attaching a donkey to a pole. Like *maftûn* (the passive participle of the verb *fatana,* "a person seized by fitna"], these are terms of bewitchment. Ḥadda says that a person in love *khraj ʿaqlu,* "he is out of his mind," lost in the middle of the sea waves. But then he goes on to compare a person in love to a horse, blindly driven by a bridle. A bridle is a tie, a knot, and a string.

> The tied horse is an image of unreason, the obsession of love, and yet to "bridle" is the fundamental operation of reason, what defines the intellect as a faculty. Ḥadda acknowledges the paradox, as he concludes that *l-ḥubb*, "love"—a certain loss of control—is the force that moves the world. This work in its entirety could be read as a fragmented meditation on different aspects of this paradox as articulated in Ḥadda's world. Would it be fair to interpret that certain loss of control, that subject loss, as a sort of Hegelian *Aufhebung?*

1989

He says:

"The fitna of woman, *fitna gharâmya*, fitna of love, is this: a man's mind is turned inside out, he is confused, he loses his mind [*khraj ʿaqlu*]. When he loses his mind, sometimes he sinks deep into his own thought, sometimes he eats without restraint, sometimes he can't eat at all and he looks beaten up. He is in the deepest trouble, lost in the middle of the sea waves [*dâkhal ghumuqât wasṭ l-amwâj*].

"If we extend this fitna *gharâmya* to phenomena that apparently do not concern love... I mean, if we extend to a whole society what happens to a man if a woman seduces him and sets him ablaze [*fetnâtu maʿana ḥarqâtu*][24] the society is itself on fire! Fitna of riches, fitna of children, fitna of invasion, razing, and war, fitna of blood, fitna of women... It is all fitna, one fitna, and it has no cure! Fitnas come in different forms, but the sovereign fitna, the Sultan of fitna, is the fitna of love. There is no form of colonization [*istiʿamâr*] in the world greater than love! (laughing).

"I'll tell you about *l-ḥubb* with an example [*mital*]. Let's say we bought a horse, and that horse is yet to be trained. We bridle it with a bit and all that. Now the effect of love, when it falls upon a person, is like that bit and that bridle. The horse, that is, the person, can't keep turning on this side and that side, but runs blindly in the direction ordered by the bit. He is driven, and does not see [*kaykûn lîh l-jâm, râh ma-bâqî iqdarsh itrab ʿala hâd jîh u la hâd jîh; ghâdî nîshân l- blâṣa fîn ḥâkem ʿalîh*]! He is *maftûn*. The nature [*aṣl*] of love is exemplified by that horse with the bridle. But this is nothing less than the human condition! It is love that makes things move in the world. Nothing among the things God created can move without love... The pace of Time itself is scanned by love, without love nothing can exist [*ghâdya l-waqt ʿala l-ḥubb*]."

I say:

"This is the root of the contradiction I have been writing about (in the contexts of our conversations about fitna, about *ḥasab* and *nasab*, the masculine and the feminine, the name and the tie [see "Contra-diction 2"]. The bridle is a 'tie!' To have a bridle in one's mouth, you say, is both to be socialized [*mrebbi*] and to be *maftûn,* seized by fitna, obsessed. The horse is 'governed' by the bridle, and this, you say, is love. The horse, the person, *tfetten,* 'lost control over his actions.' And yet, you say, this is the moving force of life. Without fitna there wouldn't be dunya. We are revolving around a *tanâquḍ,* then, a paradox—that to be alive and in control as a subject, a person has to give up control."

He says:

"Exactly! Nothing can succeed without love, no endeavor would ever be undertaken. *N-nâss meblyin,*[25] everyone is obsessed with something, with different things... Some love eating, and even if they die they have no choice but to eat; some love the sky, some love power, some love learning, and if you don't love your garden, nothing would ever grow in it. The world, in its entirety, is a matter of love."

At a different level of discourse, however, there is for Ḥadda a crucial difference between man and woman. It is Ḥawwa who bridles Adam with her strategy of waiting. She ties him with invisible knots. Waiting is the detour of seduction.

Unlike Ḥawwa, who is herself and her reflection at once, Adam operates only on one register. In the story he is blind, she is not. Like the uncle in the tale Ḥadda is commenting on (or the "authentic son" in the version recounted by Ḥaddya, or the Dough-boy without the clairvoyant advice of the old woman), Adam is unable to interpret—to read Ḥawwa's signs—and takes her reactions at face value. Men, Ḥadda says, don't know how to simulate feelings. If through their intrigues and simulations women manage to express their desire in a displaced form, men can only deny it altogether.

"If at some point in his life a man gets stuck in unbearable longings, he still manages to behave with patience and pride. Women, instead, are incontinent and impatient..."

"But earlier you said that it is men who don't know how to contain their passion [*ṣbar*]! That men are like cats, they follow women blindly, while women know how to wait and be patient [*ṣbar*], and with their patience they rule over men..."

"That's because of their haughtiness [*takabbur*]! When a woman desires a man she doesn't show it! So, I was saying, with all that denial and restraint, the ninety-nine passions of that man overflow, till he becomes intoxicated and doesn't make sense anymore... Otherwise, why do women seldom go crazy? It is women who make men crazy!"

Language (like woman), the outcome of a demonic operation, works as the indirect path of seduction: fitna. *L-khayâlî keyfetten,* representation/illusion seduces and leads astray.

So much for the mirror. But excrement, on the other hand, is a figure of the body's materiality, of the asymbolic residue that cannot be put dialectically to work. Shit tells the outside of language. Like a corpse, it blurs into the nameless and the inorganic.

> *Immediately after death a person stops being called by his or her name and enters the realm of the unmarked as a* mûta, *"a corpse." "We don't say, Let's carry Moḥa u Brahîm out of the house; we say, Let's carry the* mûta.*" The word* mûta *is of feminine grammatical gender, just as the "thing"* mûta, *that is, the corpse, is ritually washed with the signs of the feminine (henna, rosewater) to signify its entrance into the unmarked status of death. (Which is a clue into the meaning of the feminine as the unmarked term—like death—rather than vice versa.)*

L-kharâ, "shit," *l-ghobâr,* "manure": many ways of understanding excrement, in an agrarian society such as this—all mobilized, at different levels, in Ḥadda's story of the Fall. One is that shit, *l-kharâ,* is matter that cannot be reworked, that has exhausted its capacity to hold together and have rûḥ (in this context rûḥ is the holding together that technically defines something as an alive body).

"If you pour water on shit, it disintegrates [*tshettet*], it dissolves into dust; you don't notice it here because toilets are dry (from shit we make manure), but you can see it disintegrating on the white porcelain of toilets in Casablanca. (Shit dust on white porcelain: a figure for the disintegration of a world?) If you pour water on flour instead, it becomes dough and you can work it into bread. It develops rûḥ."

The motif of excrement expresses the body at its peak, caught at the point where it becomes a nonbody (doesn't have rûḥ)—where its complicity with the inorganic is exposed, the nonhuman realm of death and the underground. Feces, then, do share something with the bodyless *ṣûra,* the "image" or "form" Iblis steals from Ḥawwa with a mirror—the reflection and original distancing that is seen as the crime at the beginning of both language and life. They share a relationship with death. In "Les deux versions de l'imaginaire" Maurice Blanchot writes about cadaveric resemblance, and what he says illustrates for me the problem of Ḥadda's story.

> Vivre un événement en image, ce n'est pas se dégager de cet événement, s'en désintéresser, comme le voudrait la version esthétique de l'image . . . : c'est s'y laisser prendre, passer de la région du réel, où

nous nous tenons à distance des choses pour mieux en disposer, à cette autre région où la distance nous tient, cette distance qui est alors profondeur non vivante, indisponible, lointain inappréciable devenu comme la puissance souveraine et dernière des choses. . . . La magie tient son pouvoir de cette transformation. Par une technique methodique, il s'agit de ramener les choses à se réveiller comme reflet et la conscience à s'épaissir en chose. . . . "Je" ne "se" reconnaît pas.

L'image, à première vue, ne rassemble pas au cadavre, mais il se pourrait que l'étrangeté cadavérique fût aussi celle de l'image. Ce qu'on appelle dépouille mortelle échappe au catégories communes: quelque chose est là devant nous qui n'est ni le vivant en personne, ni une réalité quelconque, ni le même de celui qui était en vie, ni un autre, ni autre chose. . . . La mort suspend la relation avec le lieu. . . . Le cadavre n'est pas à sa place. Où est-il? Il n'est pas ici et pourtant il n'est pas ailleurs; nulle part? mais c'est qu'alors nulle part est ici. La présence cadavérique établit un rapport entre ici et nulle part. . . . Le cadavre est sa propre image; il "se" rassemble."[26]

1989

I say:

"There is an old dictionary called *Lisân al-ʿârab.* Under the entry of the letter *F [fa]* it lists a long series of definitions of fitna. The first is that fitna is the work of fire upon metals, the process of fission that separates silver and gold from the rest. This is the sense of fitna as trial, ordeal, which also figures in the Qur'an. Then there is the sense of deviation, of leading off the path and losing oneself, and the sense of discord and difference of opinion [*ikhtilâf*]. And then there is the fitna of love and women, the fitna of children and wealth, as it is said in the Qur'an (64:14, 15), 'Your wives and children are enemies for you, beware of them... your wealth and children are fitna.'"

He says:

"Human beings are like the raw material [*maʿaden*] in the mines of Khoribga.[27] All sorts of stuff is mixed up together and in the midst of all that is phosphate. If you leave it at that amorphous state [*ila bqâ ghîr abbud*],[28] if you don't work it, mill it, and paste it again, it's useless. But if fire breaks out and brings ruin [*l-khsâra*], out of that mess emerge [*kharju*, 'come out'] silver and gold! It is like the story of Adam and Ḥawwa in the Garden... *(seen from the opposite moral perspective—but Ḥadda does not care to signal his interpretative switching of sides).* Dunya, the world, is born from that original crime [*danb l-uwwel*], from which difference was spun [*khlaq l-ikhtilâf*]. From that crime, the rûḥ of the loom began..."[29]

Then, excited, raising his voice: "It is that original disaster [*muṣîba*] that at the same time caused life and death, generosity and corruption, cooperation and discord [*l-ikhtilâf*, 'difference'], good faith and betrayal [*l-ghdar u n-niya*]! And from there, my dear, everything was born... The world began, and with it a story of power and oppression! Everything is written. But if Adam hadn't come out of the Garden, the world wouldn't have begun. Instead, God produced a pretext, warned Adam about that tree, created Ḥawwa to tempt him, and induced her to commit a sin, so that he would be punished, and left naked, and hurled into the world, and he would generate progeny from his crime. Had they been faithful to their Lord, there wouldn't have been the world at all! And the warps (of the world/loom) would be left there standing! That original crime is the source of all stories [*men hna l-qiṣṣât kayṭlaʿu*]."

> Al-muṣîba *is disaster, calamity, from the passive form of the verb* aṣâba, *root* ṣwb, *which designates straightness, of a line, of social behavior, of ethics;* aṣâba, *"meeting on a straight line"; its passive form,* usîba, *"to be stricken, afflicted," connotes the interruption of the straight line, its breaking.*[30] L-muṣîba *in colloquial language is a breaking, a misfortune coming from the world external to the subject. In the language of therapy, and in medical texts, the patient is called* al-musâb, *the person "broken" by misfortune. But anyone is liable to be "broken" at any moment:* l-mûmen muṣâb, *states a hadith much cited in daily life: "The believer is subject to misfortune." The place of the subject in the world is essentially uncertain.*

"And what's the cause of disaster? The tongue! It is the tongue... the voice. Words, from which *fitna* germinates, and then carries you away, away, away...

"The voice, your own voice. Like what happened to me when I took up singing, my own voice got me lost. Everything from the tongue... "What's the source of your fire [*fîn jâtek l-ʿafya ya l-ferran*]?" and the answer of the oven, "They put it inside my mouth [*dâru lyia f-fummy*]!"

(Listen!)

"My father, Sîdî Moḥamed u l-Ḥajj, was, everybody knows, a man of knowledge. He had so much knowledge, so much control of the magic squares, that he even managed to issue his own money. He owed nothing to the state! But later, from that work of forgery, he became blind. The crimes he committed struck him back. My father had a friend, Sîdî Aḥmed l-Mubarik. One day, Sîdî Aḥmed visited him to get his blessing. They chatted for a while, had tea, and when the guest was about to leave, my father said: 'Sîdî Aḥmed, join me in an invocation to God [*ṭleb mʿâya waḥd daʿwa*].' 'What are you requesting from God?' 'I am thinking about that son of mine, God gave him a mind more powerful than most, and yet he has been drawn into a corrupted path [*ṭrîq l-fasâd*].'

"And in fact...

"I don't know whether it is time that confused me [*wâsh ḥayr f l-waqt*], or life, or traveling, or the long sleepless nights, or whether I was instead struck by the jinns of the threshold, or of the mosque, or just the demons of Sidna Suliman! God inflicts suffering on whomever he likes.

"This story is also the story of my life. The conflict of learning and poetry, of praying and straying! People listened to my words and were enchanted... It is here that my story comes to merge with the stories of fitna. Estrangement [*l-gharîba*] fell upon me as well: my ruin was my tongue—my singing, my tongue led me astray [*khraj lyia ll-amsrîr*].[31] I turned into a madman or a clown [*majdûb u-la buhâlî*], out there, on the edge [*amsrîr*], I wandered about like a fool. No one did it to me but my tongue, my singing. I used to sit in the mosque and see all sort of strange things, fancies, visions, I saw them in dark corners and then, one day, they pulled me astray [*jerrûnî l-amsrîr*], out there on the riverbank. (You know the saying, 'The edge of the territory is the side of disaster and locusts [*ṭerf l-blâd sehm l-blâ u j-jrâd*]!') I forgot learning, I forgot praying... And I came out as a sheikh, as a poet [*men temma khrajt l-shyâkha*]."

CONTRA-DICTION 2

Ḥasab and Nasab

Since, after a fashion, I am already my ancestors.
—Jorge Luis Borges[32]

Tea and sugar, the masculine and the feminine, the name and the other

1985

"Take the example of tea and sugar."

In his usual style Ḥadda opens the discussion with a paradoxical example, one of those crystalline analytic images that subsequently take hours of talk and effort to unpack.

(The entire session that ensued and, in a way, my own analytic work have been an attempt to unfold Ḥadda's first definition of the problem surrounding a person's identity and name.)

"Ilâ bghît nʿarf shkûn ntiyia khaṣṣnî nʿarf ḥasabk u nasabk" (If I want to know who you are, I need to know your account and your tie).

"It's a contradiction, a *tanâquḍ*. Let me open up the matter," says Ḥadda in an official tone. "*L-ḥasab*, the account, the value..." He pauses, concentrating an instant, idly playing with the burned metal teapot warming on the small brazier next to the blanket upon which he reclines. Then, scanning his words, as for a definition: "Here is the ḥasab: from what you made this tea, that's the account. Considering [*maḥsûb*] that I made it from green tea, it *is* green tea" (raising his voice).

"But! only from sugar it comes alive [*kaytnessem men s-sukâr*]. Green tea leaf and sugar, their junction is tea—as a consequence of this conjunction it releases its flavor and color [*ṭlaq*], only then it becomes drinkable.

"Its ḥasab, its account, value, origin, or name, is Tea, that which we put in the teapot. But its *nasab*, its knot or tie, is sugar: for it to be tied or, better, for it to come alive [*bâsh itnaseb u la itnessem*], it needs sugar. Without sugar it remains undrinkable, it has no efficacy [*madawi*], it is bitter [*marr*], it does not release its flavor [*matferrez*], it cannot be welcome...

"How could it ever be welcome? The tie, the nasab of tea, that which gives it breath, is sugar! But the account, the ḥasab, is another story altogether! If you haven't got tea you haven't got anything. Nothing. How can you call it, just water and air, it doesn't exist. But of course once you add sugar to the tea it's all over, you drink it, then you throw the waste away. You just throw the waste away like rotten grass."

On the one hand something that is, *but is not there; on the other, something that* is there, *but is not. Such is the paradox of the name as Ḥadda poses it. The ḥasab dwells in the potential region of not-yets. The nasab is an afterfact, it exists as a movement of effacement:* "l-haja lli mensûba hyia mûddra, *that which is knotted is lost," says Ḥadda. Consumed—*

ḤASAB: Dictionary
(Standard Arabic)

ḤASABA:[33] to compute, reckon, calculate, count, charge, debit, credit (*ʿala*), to take someone or something into account or into consideration, to reckon with or count on someone, to regard, to consider someone as belonging to.

ḤASUBA, ḤASÂBA: to be of noble origin, to be valued; to settle an account, to get even (with someone), to ask for accounting, to hold responsible, to make answerable, etc.

AL-ḤASB: reckoning, computing, sufficiency.

AL-ḤASAB: measure, extent, degree, value, esteem, noble descent.

ḤASÎB: respected, esteemed, noble, of noble birth.

AL-ḤISÂB: arithmetic, computation, estimation, accounting, bank account, bookkeeping, taking someone into consideration, reckoning with, final accounting; *yaum al-ḥisâb:* Day of Reckoning, Judgment Day.

MAḤSÛB ʿALA: protégé, subservience.

(Moroccan vernacular)

L-ḤASAB: value, esteem, noble descent, origin (equivalent to *aṣl*, origin, blood descent), patrilinear descent.

L-ḤSÂB: calculation, account, count, bank account.

MAḤSÛB ʿALA: responsible for something or someone (reckoned or accounted under one's responsibility and name); protégé accounted to a protector.

In his glossing and his use of the term, Ḥadda is compounding the vernacular (and classical) terms *ḥasab*, origin, value, esteem, patrilinear descent; and *ḥsâb*, count, account, reckoning, sufficiency, estimation, bank account. Subtly playing on their related sense, he exposes the "accounting" that makes the worth of the name. I transcribe the term Ḥadda is discussing as *l-ḥasab*, to emphasize the stress on value, naming, and patrilinear descent (unless specific reference is made to counting, as in the "count" of the community men). But in Ḥadda's argument naming and identity are a matter of accountability; there is a constant play between ḥasab and *ḥsâb*, value and count. This is why rather than translating *l-ḥasab* as "origin" or "descent," I render it literally as "account." In English the word *account* allows a similar play.[34]

Ḥ*asab:* where you are accounted, identified, recorded, registered, and hence fixed, as a recognized person and member of society. To have a ḥasab, and a ḥsâb, is to have a place to be called, to be at one's place. What is your name then, in the sense of *ʿaḍam*, "bone/lineage," the vertical line of transmission of the father's name—the genealogical account that Ḥadda will later call "history."

Ḥasab is abstract value, what remains, the balance. It is the archive of memory, of things recorded, of proper meanings, of fixed reference points. It is the law of vertical relation (*muḥâkamât*, "proper meanings," belong to the order of ḥasab). But *ḥasab/ḥsâb* is used also in the more openly contractual sense of being accounted (counted) within a social community, the qbîla or the Fourth. *L-ḥsâb dyâl qbîla* is the count of adult males capable of working for the community and responsible for paying taxes, digging irrigation canals, fighting in times of war, performing in the village *ʿâmma*.[35]

Nasab: tie, knot, implication, connection, pact, junction, relation, agreement, compromise, comparison, metaphor. *Mutashâbihât*, "resemblances," belong to the order of nasab. Nasab is the implication with the other, the horizontal relation (syntagmatic), the knot of the feminine. What is your nasab, that is, where is your knot, tie, connection. *Nasab* implies betweenness. If the account is a place to be called, the tie doesn't have a place of its own. *Nsîb* is a relative by marriage, *be-nisba* is an adverb of relation. (In general, in the use of the qṣar, relations of the nasab type always presuppose a pact.)[36] But "What is your tie?" also suggests "Where is your bridle?" in terms of Ḥadda's example of the horse blinded by love. And, where is your mirror, your *mitâl,* your likeness, your form, the image that enables me to call you, to speak about you. Therefore, paradoxically, Where is your name? It is in the hands of the Devil.[37] By necessity, *nasab* implies a loss—the loss of the ḥasab, in its actualization.

Ḥasab-u-nasab: opposed yet tied by a likeness of sound, by the palpable knot of a rhyme. Assonance, too, like all poetic ties, belongs to the order of nasab—

"And here I am, once again, interpreting for you allegories and words, *l-maʿna u l-hadra...*" Ḥadda feels comfortable in the role of commentator, as he likes to portray himself. He stresses his words with the rhythmic movement of his hand on the teapot as he concludes: "The account, I said, is like tea [*l-ḥasab huwwa atây*], the tie, I said, is like sugar [*n-nasab huwwa s-sukkâr*]. Without sugar we cannot drink our tea, it sits there bitter (also, in another sense of *marr:* it passes away undrunk, without us being able to consume it).[38] It does not have the breath of life [*nesma*]."

"Let's turn the analogy back to people," I propose.

"All right, let's imagine [*ghâdi nmetlû*] a man, he mentioned to us his ḥasab and his nasab, let's say he is from Bni Zoli, or else from Tuna nAraben... [I seem about to interrupt] Be patient! don't lose the head of the thread I am unwinding!

"Mention your ḥasab and nasab! In the past, when the tents used to meet, you would mention your ḥasab and your nasab, and I'd know who you are. I'd watch out for you, I'd keep in mind that you are an assertive and arrogant man, or a man of thought, a learned man. I'd challenge you: 'Mention your ḥasab and your nasab, then speak!' And you'd say, 'I am Fulân son of Fulân,[39] from a certain history [*men târîkh fulân l-fulânî,* "from the history of so-and-so"].' And I would mention my name and history in turn, and you would put into account [*katermî lyia l-ḥsâb*] what kind of person I am: whether or not I came from a proud and sophisticated land, whether I am a learned or a simple man [*ummî*]. You would ask me questions, I would ask you questions. And you'd say to yourself: 'I have to watch my language and avoid twisted expressions, or he'll ridicule me [*ghâdî ishebbernî*].' Or else: 'Here is a long-eared donkey, he won't even listen to what I say, let alone understand my words!'"

Leaning over the teapot, Ḥadda is speaking. It is his own teapot, from which I am not allowed to pour tea. One of his daughters invariably brings a pot and a glass for me when I appear at the house. Another mark of difference: tea is such a communal drink in other families. Ḥadda's tea is strong and very sweet, like the tea of heavy smokers. Like the tea his father used to drink. Tea, for him, is an emblem—a thing that stands for a name, the name of a dead father. His father, Sîdî Moḥamed u l-Ḥajj, the father, the name: tea is the liquid of fatherhood, a legacy and a curse. His own father died over a teapot, it was a glass of tea that caused his ruin. Like him, Ḥadda is an addicted tea drinker; the space of his life, whether he likes it or not, is spun by a curse of Sîdî Moḥamed u l-Ḥajj. More and more, he discovers in himself the same gestures, the same turns of phrase, the same reactions. More and more, he notices the uncanny return of similar situations: in the way village people react to him, as their fathers did to his father.

Tea is more than an analogical example, and not just in Ḥadda's personal symbolism. It is spoken in terms of seeds: l-ḥubâb taʿ atây, "tea seeds" (but they are leaves), as in wheat seeds (l-ḥubâb), couscous grains, word seeds in poetry (l-ḥabba, "a verse"), or sperm, which, every man knows, impregnates the woman when a seed [ḥabba], as big as a barley seed, is floating inside it. Sugar comes in big conic loaves wrapped in blue paper—a paper used also for magical writing. It is a symbol of agreement—sugar loaves are offered as a ritual gift. By analogy, it represents symbolic circulation—like women or words. Tea is a masculine drink (the sound of pouring tea is the backdrop to any conversation among men), and up to some thirty years ago was reserved for special occasions among the Ḥarâr men. A couple of big landowning families apart, women hardly ever drank tea, nor did the Ḥarâtîn. They had tasabbunt (Berber, f.), their own feminine drink, a sweet and spicy nectar prepared from a dough (ʿajina) of dates and fermented herbs (khmira, "yeast") shaken together in a hollow pumpkin, a paradigmatic image of femininity.[40] Tea making rehearses a process common to many techniques of the household and various crafts, whereby a dry substance (the seed) is soaked to be revived and is, by that act, exhausted. A handful of grains is "thrown" in the teapot, boiling water is added, and the pot is put on the brazier for the tea to "rise" (ṭlaʿ). Sugar is then added, and the teapot is covered with a cloth and left to rest so that the tea may "secrete" (tlaq), may release its flavor and golden color. It is unthinkable to drink this tea without sugar.[41]

Ḥadda is lying on one side, wrapped in his blanket. I can't see his face; taken by our discussion we didn't notice that the sun had long set, and forgot to light the oil lamp. I can feel the silent presence of Roqia and the girls, hiding in the dark a few feet away. Only two months ago Faṭima ʿAlî would have sat with them, and their invisible presence would have been full of giggling commentary. At intervals, Ḥadda fills up his pipe with slow gestures. I can see his face in the blinking light of a match. I am sitting on a mat, in my usual place. He didn't think of offering me a pillow; his indifference puts me at ease. I turn my eyes: a few feet away bunches of henna piled up to dry, a mound of barley, some agricultural tools. A bit farther down, his muddy work clothes. Behind us, in the unfinished mud wall, holes provisionally stopped with old rags. It is a self-conscious rhetoric of poverty and work.

I say rhetoric because, in spite of his normative stand against tropes and the work of the imagination, Ḥadda is the careful metteur en scène *of his own image. (But his normative "realistic" stand may itself be part of a larger rhetorical strategy aimed at constructing his argument—and his life—out of contrasts. My conversations with him, and this very text I am writing, might be an unwitting contribution to a play that eludes me.)*

Ḥadda in the fields: bare chested and barefoot, his bony body tied at the waist by taḥazemt, *the loincloth khmâmes*[42] *used to wear in the old days (he still does). Yet, in his lonesome effort, feet in the mud and hoe in hand, Ḥadda is, at the same time, enacting the character of the "black khammâs." Ironically moving in and out of his act, Ḥadda's life is also—and consciously—a* timtil, *a "mise-en-scène"; so is his discourse. Take our discussions, this particular one, which is constructed as a* timtil *woven out of* amtila. Mital (mithal), *likeness, analogy, metaphor, example, model, image—Ḥadda's favorite phrase,* ghâdi nmetlû, *"let's consider the analogical example" or "here I am, interpreting for you allegories and words."* Amtila, *"allegories and words," belong to the order of nasab.*

We are producing this timtil *together, and my participation is crucial for all the reasons that Ḥadda himself explains. Yet, as I write it, I am increasingly aware of his strategy. Ḥadda is setting the terms, and this is a play in two acts. I thought I had decided to write it in that form in my narrative recollection; I thought I liked the juxtaposition of the two halves of the story. I realize now that the event of our discussion was already structured, it was already a performance, and the twofoldness of its form was Ḥadda's choice. Or, perhaps, in the complexities of the textual structures that preexisted our intervention and were actualized in our encounter, its reason escaped both of us.*

Sitting outside the walls of the old qṣar, in his impeccably kept djellaba, moving slowly, with theatrical gestures, moments before speaking aloud, as if delivering a sermon, whispering moments later, as if confiding a secret, Ḥadda argues factional politics with the other men of the village. Sometimes telling a story, everybody's attention captured for a long while; more often provoking and shouting—how many times has he abandoned the stage in a pompous display of anger? Yet, far from an uncontrolled expression of emotions, his way of arguing is akin to Scholastic debate, disputatio, *in Arabic* jadal, *and to poetry dueling. After all, in spite of his disclaimers to the contrary, he is a poet. His dialectical strategy—in discussions as in the turns of life—is to generate a space of disagreement, a fissure, what in Arabic grammar might be called* sukûn *(°), a gap, a discrepancy, a* vide d'articulation. *Even his rages are theatrical; like the Furore of Italian baroque operas, they act out anger as a rhetorical device.*

"Let's talk about *nasab* in the sense of Woman...

"If we mention the side of women, then, we ask: What is your origin and where is your knot. Your ḥasab and your nasab: Where did you come from and where did you live, where did you come from and where did you marry [*fîn blâd jîtî u fîn ʿashtî, fîn blâd jîtî u fîn juwejtî*]? 'I am a Bû Zerganyia [from the village of Bû Zergân] and I married into the people of Bni Zoli.' That is, her ḥasab is in Bû Zergân and she married a man from Bni Zoli, she is *mensûba* to Bni Zoli. She is 'accounted for' at her father's [*maḥsuba ʾand bbaha*] in Bû Zergân, and she has a knot with the people of Bni Zoli [*nesbat ahl Bni Zoli*].[43]

"Your ḥasab and your nasab, what is your name and where is your life? Always, by necessity, the ḥasab comes before the nasab. Without the ḥasab there can be no nasab; if you are not accounted for you cannot be tied, you are considered to be living in savagery [*aʿisha f l-khala*]..."

—But, in another sense, one can say that without nasab the ḥasab is useless, barren [*makaynefaʿ*]..., I say.

—Take the case of that girl, Salem u Saddiq's daughter...

—Take the case of a man instead, I protest.

—*(Impatiently)* It can be a man, or a woman or a sheep! That woman is unmarried, perhaps she'll never marry. But she is *accounted* as the daughter of a man [*maḥsûba bint flân*]! Even if she never marries, she'll always be mentioned as that man's daughter [*madhkûra bint flân]:* even after her death. But without the ḥasab, without a father, she couldn't be mentioned at all!

(Ḥadda is now shouting, as if personally touched.)

—One who has no father is not accounted for, has no place, cannot be mentioned at all!

The principles of ḥasab and nasab seem to be set in dialectical opposition, at least in the economy of Ḥadda's argument. While the account is vertical and represents the enduring order of the name, the Law, the tie is horizontal and depicts the fugitive order of the event, the concrete happening in its unaccountable particularity. Ḥadda identifies this unaccountability with the feminine. Yet, perhaps despite his own convictions, Ḥadda shows that not only is the name/capital or account menaced by the nasab as something external to it—the destructive work of temporality in the shape of Woman. This could still be controlled with exclusionary measures such as cutting off women, and thus any relative by marriage, from the distribution of inheritance—as in the case of the ḥabûs *(literally the "stopped"), a family trust set on the male line of descent (* ḥasab *and* ḥabûs*, locally pronounced "ḥabas," are composed on the same consonants). It is the account itself that is internally worked by the unaccountable. Vain, then, are attempts to preserve the vertical purity of History and of the ḥasab from the dissolving force of the nasab, the knot of hybridization, the implication with the other. Unadulterated ḥasab is only a logical possibility. Beneath the oppositional ideology of the vertical and linear integrity of the name, an interior claiming to "stand on its own feet," sufficient unto itself and independent from the feminine as its exterior, one finds a texture of ḥasab and nasab that, always imbricated with one another, trace the knotted paths of the name.*

—Tea is reckoned as tea [*teḥsâb atây*], it sits in the teapot without sugar, useless, barren, a poison. You can't drink it: BUT YOU CAN NAME IT! You see, here is the difference, you can call it *tea!*

—It rests as sheer virtuality..., I object.

—Its fruition is secondary in all this, Ḥadda replies coldly. Similarly a woman: if she is not "tied" to a man, without her "knot," she remains barren, she does not give life and doesn't even come to life... But her sterility is accidental from the point of view of her account. Are you following me? Whether she can be mentioned is independent of her nasab, it has nothing to do with her "tie," it exclusively depends on her ḥasab, it has to do with her father! THE ḤASAB STANDS ON ITS OWN FEET! Whereas the tie [*nsîb*], which we modeled on sugar, can never be mentioned alone, alone it can't be mentioned at all [*ilâ kân huwwa buḥdû ma-keytdakar gâʿ*]. Sugar does not have an identity of its own, it borrows it from whatever it leans against! Alone it can only be exchanged or offered as a gift [*itṣerref*]. Dead! Without tea, sugar is dead, and without man, woman is dead! And, in general, the nasab without the ḥasab is dead! Everything comes from the ḥasab: the name, the father, history... without the ḥasab you can't sell, you can't buy. No question about it.

> *The nasab has no form of its own: like a trickster, like women from the perspective of the genealogical discourse, like fitna. It can take any form. The ḥasab stands on its own feet, the nasab is insufficient—a demand, a lack. It borrows, steals, or feigns its identity, it produces identity effects, like the image Iblis the devil stole from Ḥawwa with a mirror (this is why, perhaps, brides are made to carry a mirror,* mrâyat shayṭân, *"the Devil's mirror"). And what can one do with a reflection, other than exchange it and offer it as a gift? Yet the nasab, which has no form of its own, describes also the concrete process of taking a form: the event of* tying. *The abstract value* tea, *the ḥasab, is realized as this particular pot of tea, burned and bent up; we are drinking it, it is quickly getting cold, soon it will be only a bunch of rotten grass. In its nasab, in its "being knotted," imprisoned into a form, the ḥasab becomes mortal. The (logical) purity of the account is a (historical) impossibility: it can only be in its not being. It is a paradox that, in order to be said, the ḥasab has to borrow from a vocabulary of images and words to which it has to be "tied." The ḥasab can manifest itself only vicariously, through its nasab, which stands in its place...*
>
> *(Yet Ḥadda insists on attributing "self-sufficiency" to man and "insufficiency" to woman—)*

—But without the tie the account has nothing to account for, I protest, the seed is barren...

—A *Lâllâ l-ḥasab... (Ḥadda is shouting, exasperated at what he sees as my obtuseness, my incapacity to understand that the account is a concept of a different logical order:)* The ḥasab [ḥsâb], I'll tell you exactly what the account is: you have a big sum of money, say a million reals, even if you don't use it, even if you never touch it and do nothing with it during your lifetime, it is still *mentioned,* it is accounted for under your name. And yet it doesn't exist [*mâkayinsh*], in one sense it doesn't exist! In the end, when you die, it gets mentioned, it is registered [*mqiyyed*], accounted for until the end of time, even after your death, even after the death of your children! On the last day it gets paid (as inheritance), even if that were to be Judgement Day! [*yûm l-ḥisâb,* the Day of Accounting]. What is accounted for [*l-ḥâja llî maḥsûba*], is inscribed in History [*kâyn lîhâ târikh*] and has witnesses! What is just "tied" [*l-ḥâja llî mensûba*] fades away, is forgotten...

—But this is as if you put that million inside a box, dug a hole in the ground, and buried it. You didn't buy gardens with it, or cultivate the land, or produce anything, I object.

—Of course, it does not yield anything [*makaynefa*ʿ], but yielding is another story, it has nothing to do with this. That man can tell himself, "The day I dig out that money I'll conquer the world, I'll wipe it out [*nfettes* ʿ*ala d-dunya, nekhlîha*]!" And he "accounts" it in his own mind, never does anything with it, never profits from it in life, and yet that treasure yields [*nefa*ʿ] in his mind, the benefit is in his head... He says to himself, "I am a big man!" And, look! from that million of reals he hasn't even got one single real to buy a pack of Tide soap to wash his rags! He lives in poverty, never made use of that capital, yet...

Don't you know the proverb? it is actually a rhyme of Sîdî Abderraḥman l-Majdûb:

sûq nnsâ sûq meṭyâr
ya ddâkhallu rad bâlek
iwwerrîwk men r-rbaḥ qunṭâr
wi ddîw lik râs mâlek

(Women's business is dangerous business / If you enter it watch your head / They show you how to profit a pound / And steal your entire capital away.)

(Laughing) Did you get the point?

*The ḥasab/ḥsâb is what is mentioned (*dhkar*, to mention, to remember, to leave traces, to be male). It is what remains. It is a debt that cannot be acquitted. Yet remnants produce uncanny returns: leftovers and remains of the body, detached parts, and, of course, images, are the raw material of sorcery. Protecting the purity of the ḥasab would mean foreclosing the movement of return—the expense, the cycle, in which the ḥasab is effaced.*

"Your wealth and your children are a fitna for you" (Qur'an 64:15).

But this would mean the elimination of the returns of the ḥasab—the yields of the name/capital. For a man is "mentioned" through his returns. I think of the image of mullî as a spatial enactment of the circuit and the cycle in Yusef's drawing of the qṣar. What in the qṣar is called mullî is always the return of something: of a word, of an image, of a name, of a share of water in the canal, of a debt, of a responsibility, of an illness; a thing implicating its recipient in a structure of gifts. This is why Ḥadda says that "from his crime Adam generated progeny," and that without that original crime and related dispossession—the passing on of his error as a legacy—the world would not have begun. But isn't that infectious gift what Ḥadda calls nasab? Elaborating on Ḥadda's un-

derstanding, and somewhat against his own convictions, I take the concept of nasab to express the translation, the coming out of itself of the ḥasab in its returns. Or, as Marcel Mauss would say, in its "traditio." If nasab is translation, or, in terms of the banking metaphor, it is the transfer of funds from one account to the other, then the concept of nasab expresses the paradox that, "the original [the ḥasab] is a priori indebted with the translation" (Derrida). What is original is the knotting—borrowing and "speculation."[44]

The term and the concept of nasab, the knot or tie that implicates one in a (deadly) structure of returns, is analogous to that of nexum *in Roman law, the "tie," "le lien," discussed by Marcel Mauss in the* Essai sur le don.[45] *To be "tied" or "knotted," says Mauss, means to be implicated in the legacy of something as a person can be implicated in the consequences of a crime. For to be implicated by a thing, tied by a contract, is to be* reus *(from the Latin* res, *"thing"): "guilty" and responsible, and therefore condemned,* damnatus. *The pact that is the gift, Mauss writes in his conclusion, is at once present and poison,* don et poison.[46] *Mauss concludes: "Le danger que représente la chose donnée ou transmise n'est sans doute nulle part mieux senti que dans le très ancien droit et les très anciennes langues germaniques. Cela explique le sens double du mot gift dans l'ensemble de ces langues, don d'une part, poison de l'autre. . . ."*[47]

La chose *that makes you* reus, *"criminal and liable," in Ḥadda's story, is the name. But it is also that which makes of you a person. Throughout our debate—and, later, in recollecting his relationship with his father—Ḥadda struggles (and plays) with the paradox of implication and acquittal.*

"You chose the model [*mitâl*] of tea and sugar," I say. "Another model for the concept of ḥasab may be the water in the irrigation canal, I mean, if the water flows away in the canals and nobody obstructs it to irrigate the fields; and if you obstruct, detour, and fragment the water into the fields, then the earth becomes the *nsîb* of the water, the one is knotted to the other [*ghâdi tnâsbu*]."

Ḥadda's answer has the musical form of a fugue. Even the intonation of his voice conveys repetition, a circular, pressing chasing of images.

"Of course if there is no garden, if the water of the canal is not detoured into the fields, it flows away idle, barren [*mâ-ynefa*ʿ]... the yield [*ghalla*] comes from the garden and the palms. But if we have just the garden, if there is no irrigation canal, if the earth is not furrowed by the canals, that earth cannot even be mentioned, it does not exist, it is dead! Earth without water doesn't have a name, belongs to no one, is just called wasteland [*arḍ qâḥila*], dry land. And if there isn't the river [*l-wâd*, m.] that feeds the canal [*sâgya*, f.] with water, the canal has nothing to distribute, it doesn't even exist. It is dead! And if the *sâgya* is not in good working condition [*ṣâlḥa*], the garden can't bloom; but on the other hand, if you don't have a field you can't grow anything, what can you grow on the rocks... Everything is necessary, but, we like to say, the 'foundation' [m.] is the ḥasab, and the 'process of building,' the construction [f.] is the nasab [*l-asâs huwwa l-ḥasab, u l-bnâ hyia n-nasab*]. If we put a blanket on the bare earth we get a very uncomfortable sitting area, dusty and dirty; but if we lay out the straw mat [*ḥaṣira*] first, we can pile on it blankets, and it works perfectly. The account is the man [*l-ḥasab huwwa rrajel*], and it is the foundation of everything...

"If there is ḥasab without nasab, the account is barren; but if instead there is nasab without ḥasab, the tie is false [*nasab mebṭûl*]... false! Like a bastard son [*wuld l-ḥrâm*], yes, my dear, it is false like a bastard son!"

I wonder what Ḥadda has in mind speaking of a Tie without Account, of an attachment without name. Is he thinking of his personal history? In one sense he is: every time he mentions that term, *wuld l-ḥrâm*, "bastard," "illegitimate child," there is tension in his voice. But he insists in repeating it: b a s t a r d. Because while on the one hand he sees himself as the fearless son of Sîdî Moḥamed u l-Ḥajj, the last descendant of a lineage by the long "history" (in his genealogical sense of the term), one of the original lineages of the qṣar, on the other he is called by his mother's name: Ḥadda n-Ṭamu, Ḥadda son of Ṭamu, the legendary Ṭamu of the many crafts, skilled weaver and healer, soothsayer and midwife: Ṭamu, whom women respected and men feared. His father, for whom she was just one among the many women he married and divorced, had refused to recognize him at birth and had "given" him to the qbîla as the community's son. Ḥadda was brought up by Ṭamu alone, from her he learned his feminine skills: he helped her through the operation of setting up the loom, and sat with her behind the warps. He is proud of it. Of course he hates that phrase, *wuld tadgela* (Berber), by which people sometimes characterized him: "Widow's son," son of a woman alone, the insult reserved for someone brought up without a father. But he would not renounce his insider's knowledge of the feminine world: fond of drawing metaphors from weaving while discussing issues from the village political life, Ḥadda can manage childbirth with the competence of a midwife. He owes this to his fatherless upbringing. He knows it.

But, speaking of a nasab that is "false" without ḥasab, along with his personal history Ḥadda is also evoking the social and imaginary history of his village. It is the qṣar itself that "tied up" without ḥasab, without roots, the qṣar itself that formed from the gathering of "foreigners," different people landed from different places with different histories, histories often unknown and forever forgotten. It is the qṣar itself that (with the exception of a few "indigenous" lineages originally settled in the mythical *qṣûr dyâl jnânât,* "the scattered hamlets in the gardens") can claim no origin, no *aṣl,* no account. Unaccountable past, or rather: the unaccountable as the structure of the past.

Ḥadda goes on speaking, suddenly transposing the discussion to a different register, that of the collective history, collective memory, collective forgetting, of the qṣar. The drama of nasab without ḥasab—the wound of his own personal history, bastard son, father forger, forged father; the theory of the principle of "knotting," the danger of fitna—is now expressed in terms of the "origin" myth of this fatherless land, likened to an epic of Babel. From this moment on in our discussion, Ḥadda's recitation will shuttle back and forth between three registers: that of a philosophical disputation about the principles of ḥasab and nasab, the masculine and the feminine, the same and the other; that of Ḥadda's personal life; and that of the collective history of his land. It is as if the general themes of our discussion were also figures of his own "cleavaged" self. But are these really different registers? His story, and the story of his land; his body, and the body of his land; his wound, and the wound of his land—

He says:

"Other villages have history [*târîkh*], and their history is societal [*t-târîkh dyâlhum l-ijtimâʿy*], whereas the people of Bni Zoli—I told you—did not exist at first: there were only those three or four scattered families in the gardens: those of Ighrem u Abdelmalek, Tfu, Ighrem n-Ugjgal. When the Soliyin settled in this land, I mean those who were to become the people of Bni Zoli, the "original" people [*aṣliyin*], who were generous and honorable, they took in any one who came...

"All these foreigners! with them came the Zanagî [Berber nomad], the Ḥammûdî [Arab nomad], the Ktawî [from the southern edge of Ktawa], everyone who landed here was accepted and honored...

"People kept arriving, and from that event every possible species [*jins*] was assembled here in one place, and from the midst of that gathering fitna developed! For it was as if on top of all that were added [*zâdû*] the English and the Italian, the Ḥammuwî and the Drissî [names of local Ḥarâr lineages], the slave [*ʿabd*] and the Ḥartânî, and if you have more add more, all together, all that stuff mixed up together, and fitna was born!

"Look: everybody here is of a different sort [*jins*], some are from Zawyât Takhseit, some are from l-Mansurîa, some from Tudgha,[48] some from some other black hole, till all those species gathered up here [*ḥetta tjemmʿû l-junûs hna*]...

"Each brought something along, and together they made *fitna*! Look at the people of Taghallil:[49] it is composed of only two bones [lineages]! And we have a hundred bones?! The people of Taghallil are either from Ayt Sheikh ʿAlî or from Ayt Ba Sîdî... So, we said, whoever came was taken in by the Ṣoliyin, the 'original' people, till it ended up that everybody got called ORIGINAL! *(laughing)*...

"Everybody got called 'original' and the place itself took the name of Bni Zoli, *Bni Ṣûlî*, 'the children of roots...' The origin of having no origin! Whoever lived in hardship somewhere moved to Bni Zoli and out of hardship he came: from here the reputation of *fitna* built up, from the blending of different sorts."

(Nasab without ḥasab: the nasab of the *blâd*, the land, is false, like that of a bastard son. Like Hadda's, like that of the adopted child/clever boy of his tale. It is their curse, but also their force. A jubilation, barely disguised, shines through his words.)

I say:

"But in terms of your example of tea and sugar, you said that without sugar tea cannot be drunk, that is, without nasab..."

He says:

"Without nasab a woman doesn't exist, she is simply not a woman! As for the ḥasab, yes she is 'accounted for,' but without the 'knot,' if she is not tied to a man, she is wandering about aimlessly in the wide desert." (In addition to the philosophical sense according to which being knotted is the condition for something to be realized, the expression *gaʿ mâ ʿaida mrâ*, "she is simply not a woman," evokes the idiomatic sense according to which "to be a woman" means to have lost virginity. Virginity and the integrity of the name, or ḥasab, share more than a casual symbolic association.)

As if to illustrate his point, Ḥadda continues: "God created the Earth flat and uniform [*mestewya*], but the Earth got tired of swinging aimlessly back and forth and complained, 'I cannot live through the hardship of drifting like this, without a point of attachment, a foundation of some sort.' And God placed on Earth the *uṭâd*, the supports—that is, the mountains. He put a tall mountain on this side, a tall mountain on that side, and valleys were formed in between. This is how difference was introduced on Earth, and how God distinguished different lands [*dâk shshî bâsh fraq Allah l-arâḍî*]."

Consistent with Ḥadda's style, and with the mode of argument of this discussion, which proposes contradictions without attempting to resolve them, a single image summarizes two incompatible ways of thinking.

The couple Earth/Mountain is a figure of contradiction. In one sense, the most obvious, the Earth is woman, the Mountain is man, and their nasab is the mechanism by which they are "tied." It is a possible reading, endorsed by Ḥadda himself at several junctures in this conversation. Feminine is lack of shape and order, masculine is what provides foundation and structure. It is the discourse of the ḥasab qua the order of the law.

Yet in another sense, closer to the practical understanding of the body in daily life, Ḥadda's example emphasizes the intersection, the gap, the valley, opened between mountains. Nasab is the valley of articulation—the empty space of a difference, the forming of form. "This is how God distinguished different lands," he says. What was uniform, flat, and amorphous is inscribed by the mountains, and the gaps, the valleys between mountains [bîn l-jbâl], *are the places where people can live. The mountains, in one sense, are a figure of the ḥasab—they provide a "foundation" (the meaning of the term* uṭâd). *But they function also as articulatory poles, or pegs, that is, in Arabic, as* utâd*—a term drawn from the practical vocabularies of weaving and poetry. Ḥadda's commentary relies on the affinity of sound between these two terms, and moves back and forth between one sense and the other.*

An utâd (classical watîd) *is a stake, a peg, or a lock, as in a tent pole or a vertical beam. Its work is to inscribe the gap of a difference, to rhythm a spacing and a measure. This is why, in the poetic vocabulary, it is the segment of a poetic foot. What Ḥadda is emphasizing in this second sense is the dynamic role of emptiness. This interpretation is foreign to the foundational order of the ḥasab and belongs, rather, to the interstitial order of nasab. Ḥadda's point resonates with the role of the empty space in Chinese painting and thought, where emptiness is seen as the third nonterm between two terms of a binary system.*

"On pourrait dire que, sans l'intervention du Vide, le domaine du Plein que régissent virtuellement les deux pôles que sont le Yin et le Yang reste statique et comme amorphe. Au sein d'un système binaire Yin/Yang, le vide constitue le troisième terme qui signifie à la fois: séparation, transformation et unité. . . . Le Vide n'y apparait pas comme un espace neutre qui servirait seulement à désamorcer le choc sans changer la nature de l'opposition. C'est le point nodal tissé du virtuel et du devenir, où se rencontrent le manque et la plénitude, le même et l'autre."[50]

The Lock and the Loom

The image of the utâd belongs to the technical vocabularies of weaving and of poetry, both dear to Ḥadda and both associated, in different ways, with his mother, Ṭamu. Ṭamu introduced him to the loom and foretold that he would become a poet: "May you be one with the king of bees," she had said, "who sings in the center as the bees dance around him in circle."

The inaugural operation of the loom is called *sdyia,* which means "the closing" or the "knotting." The term refers to the knotting or tying of a bundle of warp threads (*sda*) into an articulated structure. (In this region the loom is called *l-mensed,* "the closed or tied one," from *sedd,* "to close," instead of *l-mansej,* from *nsej,* "to weave.") But the term *sdyia* also evokes the "capturing" of the rûḥ, the alive breath of the loom: its capturing, that is, its "bridling." For in weaving the rûḥ does not preexist its "capturing": it is produced by it. (Capturing, bridling, knotting, tying, implicating: the vocabulary of nasab.)

The sdyia is a ritual performance. Like birth, it takes place in a hazardous zone from which men are excluded (for their sake, women say; a man who witnesses the "closing" of the loom may be harmed). What is generated and delivered by women through a series of ritualized technical steps is the loom as an articulated body, as an alive being: a creature with rûḥ.

The sdyia of the loom is performed on level ground, preferably on the roof of a house. Neighbors and friends are invited—it is an original inscription. What is inscribed is its "form," its *ṣ-ṣûra* or *sh-shakl,* which will later be "lifted up," or "stood up" (*wqaf*) for weaving and framed within the wooden beams of the loom. Three utâd, or metal stakes, are dug into the ground at equidistant intervals. They mark the place of the three vital functions of the standing loom to be: the top, the bottom, and the waist, which is also called the belt (*l-ḥzâm*) or the "place of the rûḥ." Unlike the two external stakes, which are generically referred to as "l-utâd," the median pole is taller and named. It is called Kerkellu, the "lock" (from the Berber *rgel,* "to close or lock," used here as a proper name).

The two lower stakes are opposed to each other: the first marks the place that in the standing loom, will be taken by the upper beam (*afgâg l-fugânî*)—the masculine top, from which the yet unwoven warps are said to be "thrown," or ejaculated like seeds (warps are also called *l-ḥubûb,* "the seeds"). The second stake marks the place of the lower beam (*afgâg l-taḥtâni*) onto which the already woven fabric will be stuck after weaving. (The upper beam is also called "the man," the lower beam "the woman.") Between these two poles of not yet and already happened, the median utâd, the Lock, inscribes the place where the act of weaving will actually take place. It is the region of a fugitive present, which, to borrow Cheng's textile imagery, is "le point nodal tissé du virtuel et du dévenir, où se rencontrent le manque et la plénitude, le même et l'autre" (the woven knot of virtuality and becoming, where lack and plenitude meet, the same and the other).

During the sdyia a woman shuttles back and forth between the two opposed masculine and feminine poles with the head of the warp thread in her hand, turning around the Lock, the median taller stake, as one circumvents an obstacle. This is the job the young boy Ḥadda used to perform for his mother, allowed to trespass into that feminine space because of his fatherless status of *ytim*.

The stake called the Lock serves to detour and articulate the course of the warps. It creates a loop, a hollow space, within which later the loom will be said to be animated or alive. In terms of the image of the Earth and Mountains, that space is the valley where people can live. When, after the birth of the loom, the utâd are removed and the warps are set up on the wooden beams in a vertical position, in the intermediate empty loop are fitted two bamboo sticks that move up and down with the work. They control the intersection of warp and weft, the intersection that is weaving, and are said to operate the rûḥ of the loom (*rûḥ l-mensed*)—its life breath.

1989

I say:

"But when you state, 'Fitna is necessary, difference is the principle of life,' you are speaking in philosophical terms. As in your example of the loom. Wool has no rûḥ, the rûḥ of the loom is born at the moment of 'closing' the warps, when the threads are articulated around Kerkellu, the median pole. That's when *l-ikhtilâf*, 'difference,' is born, and with it rûḥ, the life breath. It's the point you are making when you say, 'Without difference there is no life,' or 'If one doesn't stir things up...' But in your own experience, don't you feel seized when you enter a situation of fitna?"

He says:

"Even this fitna between myself and the village people is a blessing. I am safe now, but if I had stayed there with them... fitna makes you understand, without a fitna that brings things out in the open, 'they' play with you till they set you on fire and reduce you to smoke..."

—If you want fitna, then, you have to enter the field and watch out for your head, I say skeptically.

—*Ilâ ma-dkhaltî l-tirân ma-tʿamel teḍreb l-kûra b r-rjal!* if you don't enter the field you can't kick the ball with your foot, Ḥadda replies, laughing.

—But once you enter the game it's impossible to step out and say, This is a fitna, and fitna is good...

—I withdraw, I withdraw just in time not to be killed in that fitna. I retreat to some peaceful place, out of reach, some "colder" ground, and only then I realize that there was indeed a fitna, I was in it, and I fled just in time not to be destroyed. If that providential fitna that made the hostility visible hadn't broken up, if things had stayed peaceful [*ilâ bqât l-waqt hanyia*], they would have had me! Instead, God created a pretext for me to fight with them and I found an exit, a way out. And today I am on my own and in peace.

1985

I say:

"Are you saying that women have no roots [*aṣl*], that in order for them to come to life [*nessem*], or, as you said, to 'secrete' like tea, they have to leave their ḥasab, renounce their roots?"

He says:

"No... if you say, for instance, Faṭima Ḥadda, Faṭima daughter of Ḥadda, that name, Ḥadda, will never come out of her... But, now, she left the rule of her father [*l-ḥakam dyâl bba*], the authority of the father, her father's education [*tarbyia dyâl bba*], she left the mind of her father [*l-ʿaqel dyâl bba*], she left even her father's vices [*tasafalît dyâl bba*], and she got tied to a man [*tnesbât ʿand r-râjel*]: if she was wasting away [*ilâ kânt katḍiʿ*], caught by the man, she comes alive [*mensûma*]. And yet, she is Faṭima Ḥadda, the name of the father never abandons her, never washes off her name.

"The ḥasab is the ḥasab, the name is the name: bint Fulân,[51] daughter of so-and-so, could never transform into her husband's name, or her husband's family, or their history [*târîkh*]! Take my case. My father, may he rest in peace, is from Ayt l-Ḥajj ʿAbdallah, but my mother, she is from Ayt Mbark u l-Qurshî!... Now, generations go by, grandparents and parents pass away, yet the ḥasab of your mother and the ḥasab of your father, the account, the name, can never become one...

"The ḥasab of my mother [here Ḥadda means her character or style] is from Ayt Mbark u l-Qurshî. She was a bit light [*khfîfa*]... Why do people say 'the father is what counts'? Because the father inherits! [*kay-wuret* in both the active and passive sense]...

"The breast and the beard are different, each goes its own way: we say the breast [*l-bezzûla*] and we say the beard [*l-leḥya*], the beard or the turban: the mother is the breast, and the beard is the father... The import of the mother and that of the father are forever different, forever apart."

There is, Ḥadda seems to suggest, a fundamental split at the core of one's identity—a difference that can never be resolved. But the ḥasab, the principle of the name of the father, which Ḥadda now defines as a sort of "spirit" of the name/lineage, which is passed on from one to the other (as t-târîkh, *"history"), is in his view what determines the style of a person. For better or worse, he is himself the son of Sîdî Moḥammed u l-Ḥajj, and the heir of the "spirit" of his father's lineage, Ayt l-Ḥajj ʿAbdallah; a ghost lives in him too, and of his father he repeats the gestures.*

"One day the people of Bni Zoli gathered their guns and all their weapons and proposed an agreement to the people of Taghallil. They said to their neighbors, 'Let's agree to prevent the explosion of warfare between us...' They figured that the guns of Sîdî Moḥamed u l-Ḥajj—his poetry and his knowledge—would be sufficient to maintain the supremacy of their village! And now it is my turn, I started gunfire [*barûd*] in Bni Zoli again, I declared war on them [*haṭṭit lîhum gaʿ awṭṭu*]! I first moved out to this hut to keep away from their greedy intrigues, and now I am becoming the voice of their conscience. They are starting to listen to me again! Everybody follows his ḥasab, everybody follows his roots. And our *aṣl* ["origin"; in this case it connotes "style," "destiny"] is that wherever we go we stir up trouble [*fîn ma-msha l-waḥed katnuḍ sh-shyâṭen*], I am the same way, it's my turn now...

"After all, as people say, The son of a lion is a lion, the son of a hyena is a hyena, the son of a sheep is a sheep, and the son of a rat is a rat... isn't it laughable that a son-of-rat could wish to become a son-of-lion and arouse fear in the forest?"

Ḥadda breaks into unrestrainable laughter.

Forgetting Names

"At the beginning the Ḥarâtîn filled three fractions of the land [*blâd*], and the Ḥarâr one..."

Again, without warning, Ḥadda is drifting into the collective mode—it is the qṣar itself that was born without a father.

"You know the story of Driss, with Mḥammâd and ʿAbdallah, he was their uncle... *(citing stenographically, assuming I know, and I do).* They *founded* the qṣar! *(laughing)* They usurped the land, strangers with their horses and their weapons. How many times this land was violated! And on top of all that the Romans, and the Portuguese, and the Christians... She [the land] was turned into a real whore, whoever came she had to let in...

"Drawâ [the Ḥarâtîn]... one group came from Sîdî Nûr,[52] from Ighrem n-Ugjgal, the place where we are from [*blâd ʿandna*]. That Sîdî Nûr, we hear of him, we don't know in what sense our aṣl is from him, we don't know his family, just his name, and that we came from there, out of him, we don't know whether we have been rats there, or murabiṭîn, or Shurfa, we don't know whether we descend from his slaves, or he was instead our ancestor! Where the shrine of Sîdî Nûr is now, the people of Ighrem n-Ugjgal once lived[53]—Ayt l-Ḥajj ʿAbdallah [the name of Ḥadda's lineage]—the well is still there, buried [*merdûm*]... there are still traces. Now the earth has been turned over many times, the world has been cultivated all over, *dunya tḥartat*...

"Even the houses, and the village gate. Still there—gone. That is yet another story, the world was scattered, then, *dunya mafṭûsa* [dispersed, fragmented, pulverized], and everybody was on a different side.[54] The day it gathered up [*tjemmʿat*], all these splinters [*khurrâb*][55] assembled, and the pomegranate came together [*tjemmʿat r-rommân*].

"But you know about pomegranates! When you break one, when it falls from the tree, the seeds scatter everywhere... Which is what's happening now! The new houses outside the walls, in that wasteland of Amerdûl... everybody is pushing out, like ants out of their hole, scattering in all directions. And they wanted me to be one of the supervisors of the division of the communal land: I said, No way! Remember that night, at l-Ḥajj's house, at the assembly of Ayt l-Bâlî..."

I remember seeing you arrive, you came late, everyone was already laughing and screaming, men were enveloped in a cloud of smoke, they were making tea and the son of l-Ḥajj, poor fellow, had to buy tea for that whole crowd: black solidarity and all that jazz, but nobody thought of bringing a box of tea! Solidarity was never in fashion here, and, of course, the whole enterprise dissolved like the cloud of smoke in which it was born. You stood at the door, afraid of coming in, rightly so, what in the hell does a woman like you do at a meeting like that? You looked at me—you wanted me to say, Come sit here. Forget it, there you are on your own! They thought they were practicing Ḥarâtîn power! They were fooling themselves! I said no way... No way with my weak legs was I willing to walk every day to that wasteland to make sure they didn't steal during the partition! Who would want to live there anyway, not even the jackals!

"And look at the people of Tighremt! I mean Ighruren, the new settlement... Like the secessionist settlement of Tighremt once upon a time,[56] now the group of Ighruren wants to follow its own ways, and it's going to end up like Tighremt... razed and evacuated... They argue and plot, sitting by the irrigation canal, without realizing that the same story is returning, it's happening all over again, inevitable. As much as they try to elude it. It's the curse [*daʿwa*] of Ben ʿAbd l-Mûla,[57] you might call it the blessing..."

The saint said, "Ya ahl Bni Zoli, Allah idirkum metl rrabûz dyâl l-ḥaddâd, ilâ tenfakh wâḥed, itneffes wâḥed, *People of Bni Zoli, may God make you like the bellows of the blacksmith, if one side inflates, the other deflates.*"

"So, at the beginning, there were the people of Ighrem n-Ugjgal, and those of Iger u Abdelmalek; the two hamlets were in front of each other.[58] And then, toward the lower edge of the gardens, in the direction of the river there was Tfu, where now there is that open space. Tfu was the bigger village; around it was the marketplace. People would go to that sûq from all over. Imagine the activity, the life, the singing—people were born, married and died, had children who married and died—where now there are only palm trees. And the Jews, they were towards the shrine of Sîdî Abderraḥman Bû Yaqûb, in that region of the gardens that is now called Iger Mellaḥ, from the Mellaḥ of the Jews.

"The world fades away, *d-dunyia ghîr katdres,* milled into dust. Our land was splintered into so many small settlements! Slowly, one got knotted [*mensûb*] to the other, some holding on to some [*shî gâbd f shî*], like a net [*shebka*], until the world coagulated [*hetta tsta*], until the bones fused together...

"And some got tied to Ayt l-Ḥajj ʿAbdallah. That Salem from Ayt Thâmi, he too is from us, from Ayt l-Ḥajj ʿAbdallah, and that Abdulghâni is also accounted for under our name [*maḥsûb ʿalina*], the lots used to mention my father to me, the whole bone of ours, we were its watering place, until they all dispersed—each went off in a different direction—and I am the only one left, alone, here...

"Once, during the days of independence [the 1950s] I fought with everybody in the qbîla: I stood on top of the bench at the village gate and I shouted to those bastards, 'God curse your roots and your progeny, both the Ḥarâtîn and the Yellows [*ṣfrîn*],[59] God set you on fire [*Allah iḥraqkum*]! It is my forefathers who carved this Gate!' Because that wooden gate was once the gate of the village of Tfu in the gardens, where my ancestors came from. When the qṣar was created by the oppressors [*mwalîn ssiṭara*] of those days, they razed the villages in the gardens and took the gate of Tfu, and with it they closed the new qṣar of Bni Zoli! I spoke those words, and I left. For those bandits had dared to request that I pay taxes for the garden I held, the garden attached to the position of muezzin in the mosque. When the king came back to rule, the local nationalists came up to me and said, 'You must pay taxes,' and I replied, 'Damn idiots, if today you are nationalists [*waṭaniyin*], it is because I molded you [*derrebtkum*], I am your leader, and if today you are the ʿ*amma,* I am once more your sheikh![60] Damn idiots, who are you to turn against me and say, The king is back?'[61] Standing on top of that bench, the bench where the big men of the old days used to sit, I cursed them: 'God set you on fire, it is my forefathers who carved the door of this village where you are now living, my ancestors! Who do you think I am, the shepherd of your dogs?'"

1989

I say:

"I was invited to lunch in the village of Aghalal during the days of the fitna of the land partition. People were saying all that happens because Bni Zoli is a qbîla of *itâma,* 'orphans'—the children are without a father, dead or alive, and they fight among themselves."

He says:

"Orphans! But that's precisely the source of our power and influence—the qṣar was a capital [*ʿâṣima*] in the old days, don't forget. The other villages had to submit to the word of Bni Zoli! They were forsaken [*medlûlîn*]. They say this is a land of fitna: but fitna is difference [*l-fitna hyia l-ikhtilâf*], without difference there can be no life! Think only of the difference between languages, between nations: if there is no difference there is no movement, nothing, everything is petrified [*jâmed*]...

"A society is like a loom, it must be articulated. If you make the threads go simply straight, there can be no rûḥ, the textile opens up and everything unravels [*ghâdi tḥell kulshî*]. Society is born from disagreement! If I disagree with you, if there is a discrepancy between us [*ilâ tkhalfnâ*], a gap is open and the textile, the society, holds up together. It is like a knot, like the stitching of a bag of flour... Take just the example of those ropes made with palm leaves: if you want to tie something using a whole leaf, it breaks; if instead you split the leaf and knot the two halves by way of a third, it'll never break."

1985

"So, with the input of the foreigners, of all those strangers coming from the outside, people started connecting together, they got 'knotted up' [*tlaṣqû nnâss*], and Bni Zoli was born. There was no qṣar until the people increased, until it got crowded inside the gardens[62] and they said, 'Let's come out into the open land!'[63]

"But if we are interested in telling this story according to history [*târîkh*], most lineages should not be 'mentioned.'"

(I am amazed at Ḥadda's ability to swing back and forth between ḥasab and nasab, between the angry mourning of the lost ḥasab and the joyful celebration of the hybrid origin of his land—and himself.)

"Take Ayt Ḥammu, for instance. Ḥammu was a foreigner, a tribesman from the high plateaux of the Atlas, without tribe; he was brought in as a guardian, came as a shepherd and a mercenary soldier, married in, settled in, and his children multiplied like termites. And, like Ayt Ḥammu, most of the so-called bones in Bni Zoli have no 'history,' they have no ḥasab, people came from somewhere else and settled in...

"And how about that Aḥmed u ʿAlî l-Qâḍî—a stranger, a judge—he came with the traveling army [*ḥarka*] of a sultan, stayed on and took over all this [*siṭr ʿala dâk shshî*]... he ruled from here to l-Mḥâmîd l-Ghozlân, and usurped one-fourth of the village for his own family. He said, 'I shall circle your qṣar with high walls, people of Bni Zoli! I shall dig a moat against the enemy for you!' And his word worked indeed, and with it grew the word of Bni Zoli."

Through the features of the Judge—a "forged," putative father for a fatherless land—those of another "usurper," whose word was authorized not by a seventeenth-century sultan but by the French colonizer, are visible with ghostly resemblance. In his polemic recollection Ḥadda is condensing, superimposing the two. It is Baba (ironically, the familiar term by which a father is called by his children), and not the Judge, who is said to have ruled all the way to l-Mḥâmîd l-Ghozelân, the southern edge of the Draʿ valley. Baba, whose roots are also lost in unspecified foreignness—he is said to have been a converted Jew from the deep south—also took over the qṣar, and, as if to take charge of the returns of history, settled with his family in the Alley of the Judge (what is known as Tagummâ l-Makhzen, the "Houses of the Government"),[64] *married into the lineage of the Judge, and, by way of the newly acquired nasab, managed to share in their landed inheritance. The ghost of the Judge is incarnated by Baba; unwittingly (or, perhaps, consciously manipulating the village imagination), he repeated the gestures of the Judge. The Judge and Baba, the Judge in Baba: two mythical, oversized figures in Bni Zoli's collective memory. The Judge, whose erect, tall, smooth, phallic tombstone stands prominently just outside the village gate, and is visited by women as a shrine. Baba, whose heroic gests are part of the local lore. One of the most traumatic landmarks of the qṣar's historical recollection is his murder in 1927—a sac-*

rifice in many ways, followed by the almost ritual division of his family wealth among his killers—outside of the mosque one cold winter night.

"People were summoned from all over the valley to dig our moat, and the Judge took one-fourth of our qṣar for himself. So now the people of his lineage go around blown up with arrogance, saying that Bni Zoli was the inheritance the Qâḍî left them! One day I said to one of them, 'The Judge, you claim, *arma swâgî,* laid out the irrigation canals [literally 'threw' the canals, like arrows, gunshots, seeds, or semen]. But what do you think came first, the Judge or the canals? Ever since it was created, this land has been furrowed by canals, the people of the canal [*mwalîn swâgî*] are related [*mensûbin*], from Bni Zoli all the way to the villages of Astur, Tignutin, Tinegdid, Ighardain, Aderbaz, and l-Ḥara, and Taghallil. Can you imagine that they would wait for the Judge to come and 'throw' the canals for them!? It is theft! The canals are 'his,' he claims... *arma swâgî,* they say! The day France came and asked who owned the land in between the canals they had the guts to say, Aḥmed u ʿAlî l-Qâḍî!

"So much for the first ones. As for the others, some were brought along by their mothers, some came as foreigners and entered the village through marriage [*tnâsbû*]. Take that Bû Kuwaî who arrived with his mother as a child, she came from somewhere south of here and they 'entered' the account of Ayt l-Qâḍî. They lived in the house of l-Ḥajj Saddîq and were protected [*mḥasubîn*] under the name of his lineage. His mother worked for their women and he grew up like one of their sons until the old man gave him the management of the gardens; he was much more than a khammâs, he had the keys to everything. But he grew tired of being 'accounted for' under the name of a white lineage, of working for the Ḥarâr at the digging of the irrigation canal... So he chose to join up with the black Fourth of Ayt l-Bâlî, married the daughter of Faqîr Baha, became himself a member of the brotherhood of his wife's father, and now he's our doctor and holy man, and due to his blessed status he does not work at the canal anymore! Or take the case of Ayt Ben Ḥafîd; just the other day *l-mʿallem* Ben Ḥafîd the blacksmith arrived from God knows where, he was wearing just a shred of sheepskin and he 'entered' the family of Ayt Abi u l-Madanî, in the Alley of Ayt l-Ghandur. Abi u l-Madanî gave him his daughter, and he settled in. He didn't even have clothes, just a broken up piece of sheepskin! And since Ayt Abi u l-Madanî are from the lineage of Ayt Uman, now the family of the blacksmith claims its descent from that old bone! And everybody says that the blacksmiths of Ayt Ben Ḥafîd descend from Ayt Uman!

"I told you, in this place nasab is all that there is: some came along with their mothers, some 'entered' through marriage!"

But there is still something I should tell you: all these names, Ayt Brahim u Mbark, Ayt l-Ghandur, Ayt Bû Ras, Ayt u Abdelmalek, Ayt Bû Izu [names of families]... these are just names, nicknames [*iknyia u smia*], in them there is neither the Bone nor history [*l-aḍam, târîkh*]. Bû Izu, what is the meaning of Bû Izu, what is the meaning of Buṭ l-Khshâ, Ayt Buṭ l-Khshâ, l-Ghandur... L-Ghandur is even recorded in the name of his alley, Derb Ayt l-Ghandur![65] Now l-Ghandur is a kind of man full of courage and arrogance, a person like that people call l-Ghandur, a bumptious person, full of blown air, this is all that the name [*smia*] tells you! Or, what's the sense of the name Ayt Brahim u Mbark'? There is a name, Brahim, and people got fixated on it and kept using it until it got stuck to this family, and people called it Ayt Brahim u Mbark.'[66] The name is just a nickname! Even the names of the big tribes [*qaba'îl*] like Ayt ʿAṭṭa or, inside Ayt ʿAṭṭa, Ayt Slillu, are nothing but nicknames [*knyia*]...

"People, things, just get some names attached to them almost at random—names are just nicknames! The most fundamental human act is to impute names and to find analogical images. This is the origin of the entire world [*n-nâs ghîr kaykennîw u kaymettlû; hâdâ huwwa l-aṣl dyâl d-dunya kulhâ*]."

I ask Ḥadda whether he means that the Bones [ʿ*aḍâm*] do not exist at all. He seems frustrated that I don't understand.

He says:

"As for the bone, we have been talking about *l-ḥasab*. These names are something else." And explains: "The Bone is the ḥasab, the account, and the name [*knyia*] is the nasab. So for instance Ayt Brahim u Mbark ties, marries [*tnâseb*] that name of his, like a woman... Yes! He marries his name like one marries a woman! And write it down, write down what I say" (scanning his words as if dictating to me).

"Write: We asked about the ḥasab, we discussed the ḥasab, I argued that the foundation is the nasab, Ḥadda argued that the foundation is the ḥasab. Write it down there, then we send that piece of paper to somebody who is better than us in understanding."

(Ḥadda is here citing the style of *fatwa*, "legal opinion," with its questions and answers. Locally the answers of several mufti used to be written on the same long piece of paper that kept traveling from one scholar to the other, in a technically open-ended written disputation.)

Naming is an act of dispossession. Or, to use a vocabulary more familiar to Ḥadda, having a name amounts to attaching to the self some-

thing heterogeneous and external, something other, something borrowed. Ḥadda acknowledges the paradox of the ḥasab and reflects on its consequences. And this brings him to say that names, the stock of names people currently operate with, are only nicknames: manmade, constructed artifacts. While they claim to represent the ḥasab, they belong to the order of nasab: the account can be said only through its figures. Nnâs ghîr kaykennîw u keymettlû, *all people do is to impute names and create new metaphors (examples, representations, images); name giving is the human act by definition. M. Blanchot: "L'horreur—l'honneur—du nom qui risque toujours de devenir sur-nom, vainement repris par le mouvement de l'anonyme: le fait d'être identifié, unifié, fixé, arrêté, dans un présent. . . . La pensée d'écriture, toujours dissuadée, attendue par le désastre, voici qu'elle est rendue visible dans le nom, surnommée, et comme sauvée . . . c'est-à-dire promise à une survie."*[67]

But the essence, the thing that proper names are supposed to refer to, and that in fact they betray, is the Bone: blood and lineage. These are not constructed, they are assumed to be original and natural. The ḥasab is the "true" name: but as the origin becomes discourse, the discourse of the origin, it can only be spoken through a manmade, artificial language, a language that signifies through signs and images, metaphors. Names are metaphors, like l-Ghandur, a figure of arrogance that has come to be attached [tnesbat], *almost by chance, to that particular person and gotten stuck to his lineage (or to what is accounted for as his lineage)—as adjectives are attached to nouns in a process of virtually open-ended substitution. The stories of names are stories of random sets of circumstances, which through unique turns of events have become constricting and have determined people's lives, identities, and fates. Names, Ḥadda is saying, exist in language: they are words. The world originates in words* [asl kulshî ddunya men l-klâm]. *And this is the source of that Babel-like effect called fitna. Dunya is a constructed world. Nasab is the discourse of its construction: the foundation is the ḥasab, the process of building (f.) is the nasab* [l-asâs huwwa l-hasab, l-bnâ hyia nasab]. *And people* kay-tnasbu *their names, they "marry" them, knot them to their lives, in the same way that men marry women.*

I say:

"If so far we have been talking just about names, what is, then, the Bone [*l-ʿaḍâm*]?"

He says:

"Now: the origin [*aṣl*] of humans is blood; the ḥasab, the account is blood, however we chose to call it [*ʿala llî bghîna nkennîw ʿalîh*], but in the bone there is no blood, and yet humans are made out of blood [*bnadem makhlûq men ddem*], and the bone is also made out of blood, but there is no blood in it at all, neither are there veins. Here is our bone! *(Ḥadda now openly plays on the analogy bone of the body/bone patrilineage)* but if you break the bone you won't find blood, and yet it is born from blood [*mûlûd men ddem*]! Its root, its origin is blood [*l-aṣl dyalû dem*], at the beginning it was blood, and slowly it became flesh, and then bone... this is the root of human beings, of everything alive...

"If you go to the cemetery and open a grave, what will you find? Bones! The blood is gone, the flesh is gone, only the bone, the trace of that man who has been, and is no more... The trace of what has passed away. The trace [*l-atâr*], that's the bone [*l-ʿaḍâm*, in both anatomical and genealogical senses]!

Ḥadda is speaking in his combative tone, challenging me by what he sees as a paradox: "But if we find human bones and we don't know their origin [*aṣl*], we say, 'May that person rest in peace' [*Allâh irḥam dâk rûḥ, u lâ dâk nnefs*]. *(Addressing me directly)* Come on, undo this contradiction! We said, nothing is left but the bone, but we don't pray for the bones, we pray for the person [*nefs*], and if we prayed for the bones, it means that the person is dead!"

"It seems," I say, "that we have reached the understanding that the bone (lineage) is something dead and alive, present and absent at the same time [*atâr u ḥader*]... the dead trace in the living..."

Then we enter a contest, which Ḥadda ends, thus getting the last word, with a claim of nonsense: "From the bone to the blood, from the blood to the flesh, from the flesh to *rûḥ* [spirit], from *rûḥ* to the *nefs* [soul, breath], from the *nefs* to the *ʿaqel* [mind], from the *ʿaqel* to *fikr* [critical thinking]... and so we entered an open-ended sea... And the bone [because I protest that I haven't invented the notion, it is theirs, even written down in the documents of the qbîla people have shown to me], the bone is just *l-ftân*, that's the way to fitna, at all times. Bones and blood, engender nothing but confusion, word disorder, factions, and disaster!"

"*Sallîw ʿal nnbî!*" (a whisper in the dark—someone fears that our discussion might degenerate into an argument).

Ḥadda's reply is a plea for dialogue and debate, and a commentary on our relationship: "After all, don't you know that knowledge [*l-ʿilm*], and understanding, and friendship, and relationship, and tie, it is all based on disputation [*l-maʿraka*], battle, if there is no battle nobody learns anything from anybody. If I didn't challenge you, if you didn't challenge me, I wouldn't get honey out of you, you wouldn't get tar from me...[68] If you don't rub the cumin it doesn't release its smell, if you don't rub the porcupine, it doesn't get out its ears and its feet... God knows that if you don't rub it, it only shows you thorns, but if you rub the damn thing, it puts out its ears and feet."

CONTRA-DICTION 3

MY FATHER AND I

I had gone to work and coming home I found a man thrown in a corner... I said to my mother, "How in hell did that disaster land on us?" She said, "That disaster is your father." And I looked at him.

my father and i

Ḥadda begins a long story, which is to capture our full emotional attention for the next several hours, making us forget about dinner, about the night that is fast coming to its end, about the cold wind that comes in through the open door.

This is a story about one man who took off, and another who was left in the desert with his mother. I grew up in the desert, I became a man here. My sisters, I never even knew I had brothers and sisters, till he was on his death bed and said, "I have many children."

Did he have two wives? I ask.

Twenty-two! Twenty-two women he married. He took my aunt, my mother's sister, and she bore him a son. My aunt Talia Aḥmed he took first, Sîdî Moḥamed... When my mother found out that her sister got married to the man who was later to become my father she said to her, "Shame on you! is Sîdî Moḥamed u l-Ḥajj the kind of man that respects the bond of marriage with a woman? Did our father generate you to be the lucky one?" and she insulted and cursed her. She said again, "My dear, everybody knows that when he takes a woman, he spends two or three days with her and leaves her behind. Is God punishing you?" My aunt replied angrily, "Sister, I did what God wrote down for me, it's my fate [*dâk shshî llî ketteb ʿalya allah, hânî dertu*], you have yet to see what God set aside for you..."

As expected, when my aunt was three months pregnant with my brother, he abandoned her with the baby in her womb. That anger [*nefs*], those curses, turned back upon my mother, and when she was herself three months pregnant with me, he abandoned her too.

He divorced them all, and never did break the law. He was a learned man, a scholar! Each time he'd invite two *ṭolba*,[69] he'd write the document, and he'd recite the *fatḥa:* that would be it, he'd marry the woman and enter her [*kaysger l-mra u idkhul ʿaliha*], at that time the *fatḥa* was enough, whenever he found an available woman...

When my aunt had the baby, off he went. Later on he happened to come to the village again, and married my mother. When she was also three months pregnant, off he went again to Zayan country,[70] and I stayed with her... I mean, I stayed in her womb, till she gave birth to me. Again, some business brought him back to the qṣar, he stopped for a glance, and found for himself that pretty ʿAisha, may she rest in peace, who was later to become Ḥassan u Ḥaninî's sweetheart. He took her as a virgin; then, when she was also pregnant with a boy, he left her, and the boy grew up and died.

This was Sîdî Moḥamed u l-Ḥajj's style, may God forgive him! He married a woman in Taghallil, then he took Hera's sister, I can't remember what she was called, the daughter of Ḥammu the blacksmith, Zyna Ḥammu, perhaps... Sîdî Moḥamed u l-Ḥajj, whenever he found an attractive woman, or a divorcée or a widow, he married her, until he reached twenty-two. He divorced them all, didn't leave one on his back [*mâkhallâ waḥda ʿala rqabtû*, "he didn't take responsibility for any of them"], he wrote the document of marriage and he wrote the document of divorce, and off he went.

Always. Simple, too simple: a wife, a divorce paper, a small sum of money as divorcée payment, a real, two reals, half real, or even nothing...! He was the judge, the scholar, and the mufti, he was the ruler, he was everything! He'd get married on his own and divorced on his own! Here is the Qur'an, here is his knowledge, he ruled according to Qur'anic law...

The technical rule to celebrate a marriage is ten Praises to the Prophet. So my father would gather three or four people, recite ten Praises to the Prophet, utter the *fatḥa,* and he'd go straight into his wife... But not everybody would comply with his wishes, of course, maybe someone a bit off the track, unlike just any farmer who gets up in the morning, goes to the fields, comes back, prays in the mosque, and tends his own business!

That was the story... and off he'd go, the woman would find herself pregnant, and she'd say, "There is the father!" and he would say, "I have nothing to do with her!" and that baby would be left in the betweens [*key-bqa had dderri f l-beynat*], and he'd be called, like me, in fact, a bastard [*wuld l-ḥrâm*]...

My father, my own father, not until he was finished, repulsive and blind, not until then did he come to me—because when my father was a man, a presence, he never cared for me, I never saw him... Not until all that was left was the share of the Other World. He left me with my mother, he would show up at the qṣar every once in a while, but never visited us. He married that ʿAisha, I told you, spent the usual couple of days with her, left her, and again, he went off and replaced her with another [*khlafhâ*].

Where in hell did I get to see him? When did he ever give anything to my mother, or even ask how I was? Till he became blind. Wasn't he in Khenifra, people would bring back his news, did Sîdî Moḥamed u l-Ḥajj ever send anything to his son? He was again in Marrakesh, became the prayer leader in a mosque there, and married a local woman. My mother sent for him, she had someone write a letter for her and gave it to a man who was traveling to Marrakesh, she had written, "You have a son in the praise of God, you left him in the womb and now he walks in and out of the house." He got the letter and answered, "That son is all yours. True, the boy is accounted to me [*maḥsûb ʿalyia*] from blood and flesh, but I am old, I have been around too long, and that boy is just born. I give him to the qbîla, I have no use for him [*manfaʿnî*], he does me no good."

You get the sense. *(Ḥadda repeats it in Berber, shouting): Yus n-taqbilt,* that's a son of the qbîla, as for me, he's none of my business! *(Then, in Arabic again):* "I can't profit from him [*ma-ghâdish infaʿnî*], I am old already, and he's just born, the qbîla will benefit from him..."[71] And instead, God lengthened his life until he could profit from my own children! Until I got my own children and they made him smile, calling him "Grandfather, grandfather..."

He came to me as an old man, *shaykhun kabîrun,* an old sheikh... *(This phrase, pronounced by Ḥadda in classical Arabic, is ambiguous: old/respected, old/weak, a sheikh/old man, sheikh/poet, respected yet of uncertain status.)*

An old sheikh like the one in the [Qur'anic] story of Shuʿaib. Our Lord Musa asked one of his daughters: "What is the reason for your affliction, you have plenty of animals and yet... Why don't you associate with the rest of the village people? The rest of the encampment forms a circle, they are all together, they help each other in clearing the rocks so that they may draw water from the wells and give the animals to drink; why don't you exchange help with them? Your animals are thirsty, they lick the mud searching for water!" She said, "Our affliction is that we are despised [*med-lulîn*]." "In what sense?" "We are just girls, women, and our father is a *shaykh*, a very old man, he lies thrown in a corner like a barley bag, and can't even move. And we have a problem with the village people because God was generous with us, he gave us these cows, many, and people envy us because we are women. But they don't dare take the cows away from us by force. So, they envy us and wish us misfortune and the death of our animals. And the animals are dying. Our father is a *shaykhun kabîrun*, and we are despised..."[72]

When I tell you "shaykh," that *mashyakha* derives from age, from learning, from words, and also from poetry... He came back as an old sheikh, how could I ever recognize him! We were at that time in Settat, on that hill of Lâllâ Mimûna, that's where we put our tents.[73] We had carried those tents all the way from Moulay Aḥmed, when the location of Moulay Aḥmed was reached by government planning, and the French said, "This area must be cleaned, and it will be added to the cemetery." They said that the people living there would be moved to that wasteland, to Lâllâ Mimûna, and we had to carry the huts all the way over there, holding them by the poles. The whole night we walked carrying our hut... a disaster, a rotten time: people were dying all over, they died of hunger leaning on the sides of walls. People scavenged in the garbage for the skins of potatoes or beans: if you found something and somebody else came up... if you were stronger than him, you'd hit him with a fist and go home to eat... They [the colonial administration] used to give us a half cup of rice, which was meant to sustain you from eleven o'clock today to eleven o'clock tomorrow, and there is nothing that screws you up like rice, if it falls on an empty stomach!

So we carried those huts, and we started coming to Derb Omar [in Casablanca] as we were older, working in a warehouse [*hrî*], and I was a small boy, actually not so small, I was budding [*meferkesh*], I would seek a livelihood carrying loads around, wherever there was something to do, we would help out those working at the mill machine, we'd turn the mill for them or fill up the bags, and in one way or another were able to scrounge a living. I got together with some other boys, and if we made something we'd divide it. We had a small commerce: each got a knife, and when the people from the countryside came to the market with their donkey loads of wheat or beans, after they sold their wheat or flour, or lentils or beans, we got our knives, cut the stitches on their donkey bags, helped them to put the stuff in smaller bags, carried them and made our little wage, and if that peasant [*ʿarubî*] wasn't paying attention, we emptied out the bottom of the bags, which were still full of wheat or lentils, put it in another bag, put the bag on the pile, and when we went back to the warehouse, after we were finished with our work, we'd go and shake out the contents: people were starving and we managed to be merchants! We'd be selling a measure or two of grain, and people were dying from hunger! *(Laughing)*

When Ben Saddiq found out, the father of that cousin of mine in Aghalal... when he found out that I managed to bring bread on the table, and that my mother, may she rest in peace, was also a good worker [*mderrba*], she had skilled hands, and what hands did she have! Weft and warp, combing, and carding the wool... Every day she went to the ʿArubiât of the town:[74] she combed for one, she spun for another, for one she prepared the weft, with another she entered the loom, she was... we were all skilled and active. Zohra, my sister, may she rest in peace, she worked hard too... [Zohra, Ṭamu's daughter from another man].

So Ben Saddiq saw all this, went to find Sîdî Moḥamed, and discovered that he had become blind and had settled in Taghomart, in the hard core of the land of Zayan, living off his brother, he found him and told him, "Why bother your brother, you've got a son, and God made him smart!" Sîdî Moḥamed asked, "Where is he?" and Ben Saddiq accompanied him to Settat.

I had gone to work, and coming home I found a man thrown in a corner [*rajel f rrokna*]... I said to my mother, "How in hell did this disaster land on us [*fîn jâtna hâd l-khsâra*]?" And she said, "This disaster is your father." And I looked at him... *(Long pause)*

And, may he rest in peace, he knew that I was Aḥmed, he knew everything. My mother told me, "Go kiss his hand," and I went, and I took his hand and I said, "Father," and he said, "Aḥmed, peace on you my little son" [*ʿala slamtek â wlîdî*], and mother called me.

She said, "Aḥmed! May God reward you with plenty and cover you with his blessing, and nurture you and protect you: be good to your father [*dîr l-khayr l-bbak*], and take care of him... Don't ever allow yourself to think that he abandoned you! Now the turns of life brought him back, and he's blind, his fortune reversed [*rhal bîh z-zmân*], Sîdî Moḥamed u l-Ḥajj, the man you are looking at, was punished by God. He spent his life running after his whims and look what God did to him in the end! Now, you be good to him, take care of him, but, as for myself, I don't want to have anything to do with him! I turn my face away from the direction in which he prays [*l-qebla fâsh kayṣallî ana tberrît mennha*], and if this is the ground where he will put his feet, I turn away from it! Even if the Lord himself were to put us back together, I wouldn't accept! I repudiate him [*tteqît mennu*]! I repudiate him, but you... he is your father, be good to him."

She repudiated him, then. They are all dead now. And myself, God gave me the kind of mind that can take care of everything... and all that, the angels take note of for me.[75]

(Lost in his recollection, Ḥadda stops speaking. I don't break the silence. Finally I ask, "Didn't your mother tell you about your father when you were a boy?"

Speaking Ṭamu's words, for a moment, Hadda becomes her. His voice takes the oscillatory rhythm of tales, when a woman is telling, the painful timing of a lament.)

She did tell, she said, "Bitter to me, he fed me only barley bread, he used to bring over some light woman,[76] and make wheat bread for her, and feed her meat, and feed her meat ragout [*dwâz*], and used to give me only bare bread [*l-khubz l-ḥarfî*], and he took me all the way to the Qaṣba of Beni Mellal,[77] my feet were swollen and blistered, and I carried your sister on my back and you in my womb, and by the time he let me climb on top of the camel, my feet were swollen and inflated, dripping blood, and I said, 'This is torture,' and soon we started arguing, and he got in the habit of beating me, and I would cry, 'O Moulay Abdelqader!' and he would say, 'God inflicted me upon you [*allâh sallaṭnî ʿalîk*],' until I was left with no energy or even life, until life came out of me [*ḥatta kherjetnî nnefs*], and he abandoned me there, and kept going along his path over the mountains. I dragged myself till I got to Slillu land, where some Zanaga[78] who knew me as 'his,' took me under their protection and accompanied me back here..."

And she told, and she told, she said, "Torture, an ocean of suffering, your father put me through!"

From there, after he took her up all the way to the Qasba of Beni Mellal, he wanted to take her to Khenifra, and he got tired of her, may God reward her with his peace, and she was as white as a diamond, people took her as an example [*ḍarbu ʿalîha l-mitâl*] and he, he beat her and abandoned her there. From that time she counted that she was three months pregnant and she came back, she never saw him from that moment on, and even back in the qṣar she couldn't stand that people would mention his name to her, because he abandoned her in the wasteland, he left her there to die [*f l-blâṣa fîn tmut*]...

Zanaga brought her back, because the man who divorced her earlier was on friendly terms with some man, and they used to have meals at her house. When she got to that land, people questioned her about her identity, and they said "So you are a Zolotiya... some of our people travel to the Draʿ..."[79] And when they got the news that a woman had been found, they said, "She is our friend's wife," that's why they went to get her, fed her, took care of her, and put her on a mule all the way back to here...

In any case, I said, "Mother," she said, "Yes," I said, "And you? What am I supposed to do with you?" She said, "That's your father, be good to him and look after him." "What am I supposed to look after?" I asked, "is your son the kind of person who gets rented off? So that he can be a disaster for his father and a disaster for you too?... Anyway, now, Mother, he's over there, leave him if you wish, he's over there, take him if you wish..." She said, "No! the place where he is, I shall not be... at all, I don't want to feel his presence [*ma-bghît nesmaʿ ḥessû*], I don't want him to feel my presence, I don't want to speak to him, or him to speak to me..."

But life [*l-aʿmar*] is God's, not hers or mine, and the Lord made her resolution null... I said to her, "Mother," she said, "Yes," I said, "You are in good health, aren't you? You shuttle back and forth from town and bring money back, don't you?" She nodded. "And there is my sister with you, and she works hard, doesn't she?" She nodded. "And Father is thrown there and he's blind, he can't even leave the hut... You go! Get out, you and your daughter, get lost in the wasteland, make your own hut, do whatever you wish, none of my business, I'll stay here with my father! As for you, goodbye! Were you tired or sick, I wouldn't abandon you, but now I can't leave this man who is blind, and you told me "He's your father [*u gultî lyia hâ bbâk*]," how could I follow you and leave him here to die, the ground would collapse on him, and people would laugh at me, they would say: "He let his Father die..." Go! may God provide you with plenty, but I'll stay here, with my father."

She said, "Why should I be banished to the wasteland, while this is my hut?" I said to her, "Forget it, you don't have a hut!" I gave her rags and I had the better of her. Thus I took control of the hut and I stayed there with my father. She went to stay with her sisters. Myself, I went on bringing barley from where I told you I did, and we went on living.

(Ḥadda's tone is conclusive, as if this is to be the whole story. I remain silent. I can't understand how he can throw his mother out so radically (from the hut and from the story), or, at least, how he can tell that part of the story with such detachment, after having identified with his mother so completely a moment before. It is the Law that had made its appearance in the hut—and in the story—in the shape of a blind, ruined old man, thrown in a corner like a bag of wheat. Ḥadda does not attempt to resolve the contradictory quality of his experience: he is the contradiction, he lives it on himself. And he takes contradictory stands, siding first with one and then with the other.)

I spoke with the understanding of a young boy. I told her, "If you are in good health, and capable of earning your way, and my sister is too, and if I can manage to earn my day too... and if we have only one hut..." and she had told me that she didn't want to have anything to do with him, that she couldn't bear his presence... What could I do, not even a criminal would have dared to let that thing die there.

But she had nursed you, raised you, worked for you—your father had abandoned her, and you too...

But a father is a father. She herself had said to me, "May God reward you with plenty, be good to him, he is your father, and don't hold in your mind what I have been telling you, don't listen to my words of hatred, and take from him his learning [*qira'*]... She had given me a sign [*dalîl*]. So, on my own accord, I stayed with my father, to get something from my kin after all [*wâlyia*, lineage, ancestors, blood line]...

Even though I didn't know him: if you know that someone is your father, you must do your best! She showed me the way... And, I thought, that man is now blind, the turns of life brought him back, I won't throw him out and abandon him to a no man's land... I want to look after him... But where can I put him? I can't throw him into the street! So, I said to my mother, "He'll stay in this hut where he found resort, you must get out."

But this is the land of gossip, and she went around complaining, "My son did this and that to me"; talk spread [*kaykettru l-klâm*], and people started telling her, "Your son is right to break your heart and throw you out of the house, don't you know that Hell is welcome for the sake of a loved one [*marḥaba b-jahannama ʿala wjah l-ḥbâb*]? "If you want the boy," people told her, "put up with that bother of Sîdî Moḥamed, contain your anger [*ṣabbrî nefsek*, "renounce your passion, pride"], what do you care about him. Let the old man speak, speak with him if you feel like speaking, keep your mouth shut if you don't." She fought and she fought, but in the end she gave in and had to put up with Sîdî Moḥamed...

One day I said to her, "Sîdî Moḥamed must once again be your husband and you once again his wife... As for your private relations, do what you like among yourselves, everything is apparent to God... But you must take him and he must take you in marriage." We battled for God knows how long, till I had the better of her with God's help, and we invited the ṭolba, we made couscous for them, they recited the fatḥa, may the event be blessed and happy, and I said to my parents, "Now, be enemies or be friends, it's up to you." They managed between themselves, and we all stayed in our house, Ṭamu on one side and Sîdî Moḥamed on the other, till they died. But Sîdî Moḥamed u l-Ḥajj didn't die for many years after he came back, and he stayed with us...

We came back here and we entered the mosque, I became muezzin and he become imam, I called people to prayer and he made them pray...

It is then that I became an adult [*ʿâd bâsh wellît*]: I was a young man, I wandered about. My mother said, "I must build you walls" [*ana kbert u kandûr, gâlt lyia: khâssnî ndîr lîk ṣûr*]. I told her, "I am not ready for marriage," but she said, "You must," and she got me a virgin from Wlâd Ushah, a girl from Ayt l-Ghâli, Zineb. Then, one day, that Zineb complained to me, "Sîdî Moḥamed cursed me," and I said, "Watch out, my father is your father," and she answered, "I will have nothing to do with him,"[80] and I said to her, "You don't know me yet... if you don't know my father, how could you know me! Get out of my way, go away!" She gathered her rags and I divorced her.

In those days my head was still hot, I was ruthless [*mâ ʿandî gharaḍ*]. *(Laughing)* I did not respect anything but my own head, and I had found that young thing... a first-rate woman, not even comparable to that dullard of the *arma*[81] or that waste pond of ʿAlî's daughter [Faṭima ʿAlî, the wife who left him]... To come back to that topic, she is still as she was... she refuses to come back. She's dead, her will is dead, her pride is dead, divorce and marriage are dead for her, everything is dead for her, whether she goes up to the sky or digs herself deep into the ground, she is dead!

As in the saying, *hâk hâdî ʿala hâdi llî dekhkhlhâ matla yaʿraf kîf ikherrejha,* "here is this, over that, who entered her doesn't know how to come out of her anymore." A woman, a woman... she divorced me, what's the sense of a woman with eight children divorcing a man, abandoning her children in the desert?

She did the same as Ṭamu Saleḥ, your mother, she left the hut...

She left the hut, yes... but Ṭamu Saleḥ, when people spoke to her, listened to the voice of reason and came back.

But this is the story of Sîdî Moḥamed u l-Ḥajj, this is the story of my father, my story. One day, people report, l-Ḥajj ʿAbdallah [Ḥadda's paternal grandfather] went on the pilgrimage and climbed the Arafat mountain in Mecca, he stood up, made his ablutions, and uttered his formal request to God, he said, "O God, give me a son, give me a son, who will have memorized the Qur'an at the age of ten." He came back, and gave birth to Sîdî Moḥamed u l-Ḥajj. When my father Sîdî Moḥamed u l-Ḥajj reached the age of ten, he could recite the entire Qur'an in the mosque and had completed his learning; he gathered the Qur'an, and knowledge [*l-ʿilm*], and everything in the invocation of the Prophet [*daʿwa dyâl nnbî*]. And myself, I came from [*khrejt men*] Sîdî Moḥamed u l-Ḥajj, whose father made the request to God, I am included in that invocation! He had said, "What he hears with his ears, may he repeat with his mouth."

But it is not just a matter of listening: he would hear with his ears, see with his eyes, think with his intellect, think with his tongue, everything at once, Sîdî Moḥamed u l-Ḥajj would do, till the magic squares [*jadâwil*] were laid down in front of him, and the jinns started obeying his word. Sîdî Moḥamed u l-Ḥajj had the *jadâwil* of knowledge, and had gained so much control of these magic squares that he started a mint for coining money, silver money, he would make all the money he needed on his own! But the day he was making money, where did we find him! We only found him when nothing was left... He had the knowledge, but never performed sorcery with it [*suḥûr*], he never "wrote" for anyone.[82] Sîdî Moḥamed u l-Ḥajj was a mufti, people would go to him and pose questions, and he would recite answers for them [*kayftîhum*]. Whatever you ask the mufti, he answers you... Just as I am now answering you...

Inscribed within the name of your father, you are included under the umbrella of your grandfather's invocation. Of your father you embody the spirit and the style: a son of a lion is a lion, a son of a rat is a rat. Your words. Everything comes from the ḥasab, you said, account, principle of identification, order of the name of the father. And yet the name you bear is your mother's. She gave you her breast and her name. Her name, or, rather, in terms of what you said before, she marked you with her lack of one. "If there is the nasab without ḥasab," you said, if a person is just "attached" without being "accounted for" under the father's name, "the nasab itself is false, false, like a bastard son." When you were born, Sîdî Moḥamed refused to take responsibility for you.

Another scene and another birth come to my mind. It is night, at the wedding of Faṭima ʿAlî's brother. I am sitting on the roof with the women, waiting for the bride to arrive. Faṭima is bent over the fire, helping to make bread for the guests. She has just given birth, the baby is rolled up at her waist, wrapped in her veil as if still inside her body. It is your only male child, the first son born after a sequence of seven girls. I follow her with my eyes, admiring, as always, the gracefulness of her movements as she works. Suddenly she gets up, unties her belt and pulls out the baby asleep, his eyes blackened with kohl, his head red and scented from the mixture of saffron and rose powder. With a gesture I could not predict she commits the baby to my hands and says, "Take him to Ḥadda, you are his friend, perhaps he will accept him from your hands... since the baby was born a week ago Ḥadda refuses to acknowledge his existence or even look at him."

I looked for you. I found you as you were heading to the room where the male guests were sitting, I presented you with the baby. But you refused to even look at his face, and walked away. Back in the kitchen Faṭima ʿAlî and Roqia explained to me that when Faṭima was in labor you intended to help her through childbirth as you had done with the other children, but she refused and, for the first time ever, asked you to leave the room, as women in the qṣar ask of men during birth. Since you had brought in Roqia a year before, she said, there was another woman in the house, they could manage by themselves: she wanted to be like any other woman in the village, she did not want to be helped by a man during childbirth. You, they said, were hurt by her refusal. You left and did not come back until after the baby was born, and refused to see him, or to have anything to do with him, or with his mother. Faṭima had denied you your role as a mother, thus you denied yourself to her as a man and a father and refused to name the child, abdicating what, in your own view, is, of a father, the fundamental act. As if, by her betrayal, she had decided that your son's destiny be the same as your own. Your depiction of your own father's deeds: "The woman would say, The baby has a father, he would reply, I have nothing to do with her, and the baby would be left in the betweens, and would be called, like me, in fact, a bastard..."

Faṭima ʿAlî named the boy herself, and chose the name of Abdelwâḥad, "slave of the One," the essential appellation of God the Father. And from that day your life became hell till one morning she tied Abdelwâḥad on her back and left the hut forever. You repudiated her as a woman because she repudiated the feminine in you: Ḥadda, son of Ṭamu, who as a child helped with the "closing" of the loom, learned how to weave and sat behind the warps with his mother. Weaving is your favorite source of borrowed imagery: isn't weaving the activity that best rehearses and exemplifies the logic of the ḥasab and the nasab, of life as the fugitive intersection of warp and weft threads?

This is the story of Sîdî Moḥamed u l-Ḥajj. Aḥmed u Baba became sheikh,[83] and people were getting a little better off in Settat, time had opened up its eyes here as well. Aḥmed u Baba was like the king, if he came... A man, like a lion. He came to Settat and asked Sîdî Moḥamed for his blessing.

Aḥmed u Baba asked around until he found him, and said to Sîdî Moḥamed, "Get up, come back to the qṣar, you'll get the mosque of Ayt l-Bâlî and hold the land endowed to the mosque, and your son, praise be to God, is now a man, he'll be muezzin, you'll put together that property, and cultivate it." So we did, we came back to Bni Zoli, cultivated our land, harvested dates, and sowed barley, and we became merchants in the qṣar... Together we gathered the land assigned to the mosque, that of the prayer leader [*ṭaleb*] and of the muezzin, I'd call from the roof, "God is the greatest," he'd recite, "God is the greatest," as he made people pray, I'd call them, he'd make them pray, and we put the gardens together.

It is then that you started learning from your father...

My mother, may she rest in peace, had already struggled with my education. But the hardship we went through ruined me. Before we moved to Settat, she used to prepare soup and sometimes even a chicken, and take it to the ṭolba in the mosque on my behalf. And I bloomed:[84] people could recite two or three *iseddaren*,[85] I recited ten, until I completed one Eighth [*tumun*, of the Qur'an], and when I reached *sabîḥ* I finally had memorized one Fourth... Some people go all the way up to *silka*[86] without being able to recite one Eighth. Myself, instead, from the moment I reached *sabîḥ* they gave me one Fourth of the *ḥizb* to recite.[87] People were amazed and envious,[88] even the jinns couldn't recite as well as I did!

I started my learning as a child, before going to Settat—had I stayed in Bni Zoli with my mother, I would have pursued knowledge, instead hardship ruined me and I went to hell...

When my father came back I turned again to learning, it is then that I started "getting words" from him [*kanftî ʿandu*]. He spoke, and I learned from him "religion," "duty" [*l-ferḍ*], "the Tradition of the Prophet" [*sunna*], "good comportment" [*l-ʾadab*], "the recommended practices" [*l-mustaḥabb*], "the reprehensible things" [*l-makrûh*], "moderation" [*l-ʿitidâl*], "the purity of ablutions" [*ṭahârat l-uḍu*], everything about religion. And having gotten into *Benu ʿAshir* [a book explaining Muslim ritual in verses], we went on explicating [*kanfessru*], and from there again we got into poetry, Sîdî Abdelaziz l-Maghrâwî, Sîdî Abderraḥman l-Mejdûb, Bel Walid...[89]

And I turned into a real questioner, I would stick to him with my questions... only the two of us, and I was learning, I would go off to work in the gardens with my questions in mind, and keep them for when I was back at home with him, or in the mosque. I stuck to him [*lṣaqt fîh*] like a tick. As soon as we sat down I would say, "Let's get on with our stuff!" Just like you now stick to me!... And we'd continue late into the night: like you and me... You stick to me now just like I used to stick to my father then! *(Laughing)* "Sîdî, tell me this! Sîdî, tell me that..." and he used to say, "Hold on, wait until we finish our tea...," and I would say, "No!" on and on till he died, may he rest in peace. Nothing but questions and discussions. Till the fire ate him. I would go to work in the fields with the idea of coming back, so that we could comment and discuss with each other [*ntlaḥḍu*].

But one day, I ended up having to say to him, "You! God will never give you peace, he will torture you, in this world and the other; you shall have no consideration from the Prophet and no compassion from God!" I dared to say these words to the father who generated me... but he had committed a crime [*jarîma*]...

Undoubtedly I am a difficult person, not a nice guy, who would dare to speak like this to a father, my father, to Sîdî Moḥamed u l-Ḥajj... even the bare earth blossomed under his feet, the flowers turned their faces to him!... and people cried for his understanding, for his poetry, for the benefit of his thought... he was an ocean... and then people forgot him, overwhelmed by hardship, and when he died, whoever "got" something from him [*gbaḍ ʿandu shî*] cried, "Sîdî Moḥamed is gone and didn't leave us anything, no traces, no legacy... so much is gone!"

In his day, Sîdî Moḥamed u l-Ḥajj used to answer anybody who asked, like a mufti... people benefited from his learning, both as a scholar and as a poet. He recited poetry for those who invited him. People took all his time, his whole person, he was never at home. But there is more. If you invited him to your house for lunch... before he left you were expected to take sugar, and tea, charcoal, dates, and give them to him. *(Ḥadda whispers, speaking fast, in an agitated tone, troubled by his recollection).*

Soon Sîdî Moḥamed u l-Ḥajj started living in the mosque, with jars full of dates, flour, and lard.[90] He asked people for anything he needed... and so it happened that Sîdî Moḥamed u l-Ḥajj was transformed into a beggar! Say for instance that he had a meal at your house: "Give me a bit of charcoal, sir, may God reward you, a bit of sugar... give, give, give!" *(Ḥadda is excited, angry.)* And so it happened that we, at home, had everything, there was plenty, and he went around begging.

You see, I wasn't a nice person, I was aggressive, bad, all I did was twist and wink [*lwî u shiyyer*], if I had an argument with another boy, we would get down to the ground fighting tooth and nail... and if we played *taqqora,*[91] like nothing we'd start a fight, and if I ran I was faster than the wind, I ran with the ball in between my feet, and that boy... I would lay him down and beat him up... Then his father would come and beat me, skin me like a sheep [*slakhnî*], and my mother, may she rest in peace, she would get *tameskert,*[92] and a battle would break out at the village gate: "My son, my son, they are beating him, they'll beat him till he becomes sterile!" And it was her son who beat up his son...!

People called me widow's son [*wuld tadgela*]. "Look," they'd say to me, "your father goes around begging!" That is, first he abandoned you, and now that he's back, he has become a beggar... I couldn't resign myself to this. I was ashamed. All I could do was hide in some corner and cry or else lock myself inside the house and never come out in the open [*dâkhal ddar*]. Because there was a man *(Ḥadda is switching into the third person,* al-lghâyb *in Arabic grammar, the "absent," as he often does to distance himself when the recollection becomes too painful),* a young man, well aware of his intellect [*ʿârf l-ʿaqel dyâlu*], he was raised in pride and arrogance, and couldn't resign himself to that! And one day I told him. Not just straight words on his face, though: but I explained to him the wrong he was doing...

Myself I have never liked to take gifts from people, not even when I was a poet and I sang at weddings and other public occasions: I want to be free... gifts imprison. Once a man came and offered me presents to go perform at his house, I said, "I don't want anything." He said, "Why? do you think this is illicit wealth [*ḥarâm*]?" "Yes," I said. "You are a fool," he said, "I would understand if you were speaking of those who beg for money or depend on people's charity, or of those poets who first insult the audience in their poems and then dare to say, Give us! But you! If a sheikh comes to sing and people offer him a gift [*l-hedyia*], if he hasn't himself asked for anything, how can you consider it *ḥarâm* to take that gift?" I didn't want to get in an argument with him. So, I put my hand on the ground, gathered a handful of gravel and said to him, "I'll show you how it works. Open your hand! Here, to someone who gives you ten reals, what will you say?" "I would say, *Allâh ya'ṭik l-khayr*," he said.[93] I said, "Here, take this other ten reals, what do you say?" "God bless you," he said. "Here," I said, "you can have the whole handful, how many blessings did you say?" "A lot," he said. "And you," I said, "how many blessings did you put in your pocket? None! The one who takes will never accomplish anything: may God put us among those who give and never take!"

Ḥadda—a word meaning edge, knife, and resembling *hdyia*, gift, offering, sacrifice.[94] Frightening, impossible self-sufficiency, freedom, whiteness of silence, purity, hubris—of a gift, never contracted, a gift forever, for nothing, a gift for the absolute, a gift they can never reciprocate—*Fire!* Annihilation, cleansing, lightness of ashes, flying—Ḥadda out of Their reach. But

liberté, liberté, liberté, liberté.
brûler l'être de la liberté
Il n'y en a pas.
Et je crois que pour être libre
je dois d'abord me déclarer prisonnier[95]

Ḥadda—you want to be the candle, that liquefies, in the light it gives—

(Ḥadda shouts to his daughter to bring a new pot of tea and new charcoal for the brazier. He turns to me.) Since you came I haven't had a drop of tea... just words, words, a torrent of words. *(The teapot is still sitting on the brazier, cold.)* I need tea all the time, I am not like you, you have many things in your life, I lean on this teapot... like he did.

How did I go about reproaching my father for his behavior? I told you that Sîdî Moḥamed u l-Ḥajj was a mufti, he gave opinions on whatever people asked him on the basis of the knowledge in the books. So I appealed to his judgment as a mufti.

The mufti is like a magician [*sâḥir*]*: when you ask the help of a magician, the jinns present an image of what affects you [as-shayaṭîn kayjîbû lîh dâk shshî llî bân fîk ntî*], and, like a mufti, he diagnoses, "You have been stricken in that particular place," and you say, "Yes, Sîdî, it is correct." This is the mechanism of magic: the jinns have a complete knowledge of the human body, and appear in the imagination of that diviner, and say, That's the place where this person is bewitched [*mashûr*]. They come to him as in a dream. Similarly, the mufti is a person of understanding. If you tell him, "I had a dream," he interprets it for you.

Thus I went to the mufti who was my father and I said, "Let us say as an example that a man's mind is deep asleep and finds itself in a market, like our Thursday market; and goes to the butcher shop and finds two sets of animals attached at the meat hooks: one set of animals is fleshy, fat, and beautiful; the other is but skin and bone, full of flies, a repulsive sight. Then the mind of that man notices that in the line for that garbage there is constant activity, while the line for the fat meat is empty, only a few people go to buy. In the morning that thoughtful man remembers that dream [*mûl l-ʿaqel ʿaqal ʿala hâdâk l-mnâm*], and goes to ask the mufti, for the mufti is a professional thinker: it is the faculty of understanding that recites answers.[96]

"The insightful man says to the mufti, 'I can't make sense of this dream.' 'I shall give you an interpretation,' the mufti says. 'There is a perfect woman living lawfully in her husband's house, gentle, poised, beautiful, wearing clean clothes every day, and her husband, instead of spending time with her, goes out to look for a carrion [*jîfa*]... That woman, that meat, is fat and flourishing, and yet forsaken [*mdlûla*].' "

I didn't reproach Sîdî Moḥamed's wrongs directly, may he be covered in God's forgiveness, I approached him with an allegory. I said, "God won't forgive you, watch out, tomorrow, the Judgment Day, the Prophet won't even look at you." He would go to people's houses, entertain them, and ask for charcoal, for sugar, for tea, for lard, for flour, till he set his own place in a room adjoining the mosque, started boiling water [tea water] and making his own fire. He stopped coming home. One day he had to climb out of that room from the window! The fire... people were washing in the mosque, doing their ablutions, they saw the smoke, a dark smoke, and shouted, "What's that smoke, Sîdî Moḥamed u l-Ḥajj?" And I had to climb up to the window, open it, push the door and break the lock; only then was I able to get him out! And another time the ceiling collapsed on him, and there he was, under the debris, in the midst of his possessions, he who was blind. And again I carried him on my back out of that mess. How many times I fought with him, to make him come out of that mosque!

I then said to him, "Sîdî Moḥamed u l-Ḥajj...," he said, "Yes," I said, "God made humans poor and serene; now, let us take the case of a man who has got the soup [*ḥarîra*][97] at home but is not satisfied with it and scavenges around for a fat ragout, bread, meat, and butter, wanders restlessly from house to house, begs, and that soup made in his own house, he despises and doesn't eat... That man lives in servitude!"

He said to me, "God condemns and punishes that man." He said this himself, about himself. Because it was as if somebody had asked him a question, he was answering in his role of mufti. I gave him that example in my speech, and he judged for himself... Of course people pushed me, they would say to me, "Go! What are you waiting for, it's your father, be a man with your father, your father is a beggar!" This is what people used to tell me, and more: "If you have enough pride [*nefs*] to go to battle with people, why don't you have enough pride to clear your father's act?"

From there I came to a realization, and I cried, "I am worse than a woman, I don't even have the face to go out," and my mind would tell me, "You can't go out anymore, be arrogant or proud with anyone, you can't argue or fight anymore..." These and similar thoughts I would ponder inside my mind, and I cried with tears, bitter tears, and I was already a young man [*ʿazri*], already engaged to get married! And I would cry, I couldn't say a word, and there was nothing I could do to make him stop—Till God stopped him! With that idea, he saved me and saved him even more... There is nothing we can do. From when a person is born there is nothing to do. One is a donkey, one is intelligent, one is rich, one is poor. Everything is written. Black and white, lies and truth. All written.

The Fire

My father, then, spoke. He said, "That man, the man who behaves in such a way, God shall punish him! The man who has his own soup and seeks meat elsewhere, that man won't be forgiven!" His nefs had played him a trick. I said, "It is you! Now that you have said so, I must say that you are that man, you challenged God, and tomorrow, the Judgment Day, the Prophet won't consider you and God won't forgive you... But you, you, how could you do this, aren't you a man of knowledge?"

He turned his eyes, may God cover him with forgiveness, he had small, red eyes, the eyes of a blind man; but that gesture he used to make when he could still see. He turned his eyes and said, "There is no trying, no attempt except in God—sit down, a sîdî" [in Berber]. Myself, God only knows, I had not noticed his behavior or thought something critical about it... Only people's words, those words they used to say to me: "Son-of-widow, your father is a beggar! Son of a widow, your father goes around begging. Go home, keep your old man from begging!" It had been people's laughs, the ridicule...

He said, "I am the father of all people, one wants some benefit from me, another one wants to learn about religion." He paused and thought for a moment, then said, "I'll stay home and be saved, and, perhaps, God will forgive me for all my crimes. Today, I promise to renounce everything except for one, that I pose to you as a condition [*sharṭ*], the teapot: I don't ask for bread, I don't ask for meat, I shall accept whatever God presents me with, but tea, I must have it."

So, he put the teapot as a condition between us. I said, "Good, thank you." Then I said, "God, the Qur'an, and the angels are my witnesses that if we have only enough sugar for one teapot, it will be forbidden to me or to my mother or to my children to drink any tea, it'll be all yours... we'll do without it."

But instead we got plenty, and he drank, and I drank. "Bring Khadija the teapot!"[98] and he blew on the fire all by himself, till that very teapot set him ablaze, may God forgive him... Blow, blow, blow, till he started a fire, and fire ate him alive, and in that fire he found death, death and perhaps redemption. Had he been spared to eventually die of some other cause, we, his children and descendants, would have been left in the world to pay for his crimes, the crimes [*dunûb*] he committed, God only knows, the wrongs he committed with women. Instead, God burned him in this world, before the other [*ḥarqu allâh f ddunya qbal l-akhîra*]. Fire is good!

We got up at dawn to go to the gardens, we did our ablutions, and we gave him water for his ablutions before the morning prayer. Nobody was in the house, he was all by himself. The house is adjacent to the village walls, and the upstairs room [*maṣryia*] has windows looking onto the outside. He sat in the room downstairs and the *maṣryia* was filled to the ceiling with provisions, wheat, barley, and beans. The house was full, there was plenty, the world had poured out abundance. Milk, dates, honey, everything you might possibly desire. Fire developed and quickly reached the ceiling and spread upstairs, to the *maṣryia.* Those sitting outside the walls saw the smoke and ran to the door of the house, to every aperture, pushing and screaming, "Ayt Sîdî Moḥamed u l-Ḥajj, family of Sîdî Moḥamed u l-Ḥajj!" Nobody answered but the roar of the fire—we were all in the fields. Screaming broke out at the village gate, and people came running and found him...

He had caught on fire, his body, he screamed, screamed, flames were eating his flesh, he had no escape. If he sought shelter in one corner, fire would catch up with him there, inexorably, his body quickly consumed. Blind, he couldn't find the door to escape, in that room the door is at the center of the wall... Old man, with no clothes on, the fire left him naked, his body all roasted like that of a lamb... Finally they got him out, away from the heat and the fire... People went on throwing water, broke the doors of the house and got him out, then tried to save some of the wheat from destruction, but in vain, everything was gone.

And that house lived on, it lived on till the day it collapsed on us, together, once and for all... rrrrrrrrr... Myself, and Khadija, and Abderraḥman our son... the house split up from wall to wall, one wall rained down from here, the other rained down from there, and the boy lay buried under the debris and he died... The one whose deadline had come, died. That house took the life of my father first, and my son later. Life is in God's hands...

From that fire my father lived on, in agony for fifteen days. Morning after morning I carried him up to the roof, evening after evening I carried him down, for fifteen days. The sixteenth day he died, may he rest in peace. The day the fire ate him up the sheikh came, he said, "Here is the paper, take him to town." I said, "Take Sîdî Moḥamed u l-Ḥajj, my father, to the hospital?! Are you really talking about him? Don't you have fear of God, this man, for your knowledge, should be visited as a saint [*fîh zyiara*], imagine taking him to town to die there, with the Christians, the French, and all that crap! A disaster." He said, "I have notified the Makhzen,[99] the French, that he was burned in a fire, and now he must go to the hospital, and if you don't want to take him you'll be put in jail..."

I said, "I'll go even to hell!" Always, if something seemed unjust to me, it triggered a reaction of pride and arrogance in me. I said, "Sir, I will not take him, it is impossible that at the very end of his life my father be taken to the hospital, and by me, to die there. He's an old man, he has already been killed by the fire! Why should I take him to the hospital, to be passed through the Christian hand and die among Christians?"

He said, "As you like, I'll notify the French captain and you'll be sent to jail." I said, "Notify whomever you wish, as soon as I bury him I'll be happy to go to jail and may God never bring me back to this place!" He died, I buried him, but God protected me and he didn't pursue his threat. My filial duty was to protect my father in his agony of death, wet his lips drop by drop, and make sure he pronounced the testimony of faith.

What did he tell you before he died? Was he conscious?

He was conscious till we parted, but he would only ask me to bring him this or that, and he said, "Go, Aḥmed, the protection of God is with you." But what he wanted to tell me, he said when he was still in good health. I had just come home from the gardens, I was working at the well, the supports at the bottom of the well had collapsed, and the water was rising and making the well fall in. I worked the whole day in the hottest summer days, the henna was almost ready to be harvested, and it was thirsty. You know the crops, only one day of thirst during the heat, and it's all lost. I still had eight days of watering, or even ten, every day a bit until I could water the whole field, and that field had been in need of water for ten days: wounded by thirst, one more day will kill it. I turned into a madman, if I sat down, everything would die. I came home and there he was, may he rest in peace, and my mother was there too. I started telling her about the work when he turned to me and said: "Aḥmed...," I said "Yes..." I wasn't into singing his praise, I was angry. He said, "What are you doing with the watermelons and the other crops?" "You only care about your stomach," I said, "Aḥmed is living through the worst of hardships, and you are here reclining, sipping your tea... leave me alone, Sîdî Moḥamed u l-Ḥajj, I haven't got a thing to give... if only God would turn his eye to me, working all by myself..."

He said, "You mean you are working at the well alone?" "Alone with the jinns," I said, and I was lying, people were helping me. He said, "No, people are working with you... I have been working at making tea, I have eaten dates and not bread..." I said, "Eat dates, eat bread, wait and I'll show you the work at which I am working..."

But he said, "Turn your mind to me [*aʿṭini ʿaqlek*], brush aside your bitterness about past and present hardships, and pay attention to what I do: pay attention to what I do, when I recite the ḥizb, when I pray, when I praise God, when I recite poetry and poetry of praise to the Prophet [*madḥ*]... Pay attention when I pronounce the fatḥa and I say:

Allâhumma ṣlaḥ bihim ma fasad
u neqqî qalbhum men l-ḥiqd u l-ḥasad
u l-ghina men nnefs.

[O God, correct in them what is corrupted / and clean their hearts from envy and jealousy, / wealth is from the spirit!]

And he said, "Here are three words useful anytime, and when I am in my [ritual] function I say them; is this work or is it not?" "This is more than work," I said. "Are they enough," he said, "or shall I tell you more?" "Enough..." "Then you can go, goodbye...!" And I got up and went.

I told you that I used to talk with Sîdî Moḥamed u l-Ḥajj about poetry and spiritual things, and if he found (in his memory) something nice by Sîdî Abdelaziz l-Maghrâwî, I would say, "Praise to those who can think."

One day he said to me, "God gave you a unique mind, but you cannot benefit from it [*ma-nefʿak*]." He saw surprise in my eyes, and repeated, "Nobody has a mind more powerful than yours, but it doesn't do you any good." In those days I had strayed in the direction of dance, singing, and the light life, and I used to go out to Faṭima Salem's house, I came out on the riverbank [*khrajt ll-amsrîr*]...[100] In those days whoever had an event in the house had to invite me to sing.

The day God made me aware of what I was doing I said, "I curse you my head [*allâh ilaʿnak â-râsî*]!" I had gone astray, lost to religion, lost to worship and to learning—I had become a monkey for people to play with [*zaʿṭuṭ n-nâss*]. People sat in their homes in peace, and I'd go around braying. I was forsaken in my father's eyes... The day God took pity on me I went to the gardens of Ba ʿOmar, I got stuck in the sands of Ba ʿOmar for fourteen years.

I only walked through the qṣar after dark, like a bat... Till all that was over and I moved to this garden and found peace! I was saved from the burden of poetry and all those other corrupting things.

But Sîdî Moḥamed u l-Ḥajj didn't die till I settled down, till I cared for the fields and for my work, and I prayed, and I would no longer go out... And then, after he died, I came out here, to this hut... And again I got involved in leveling the ground. This place was high [too high for the water in the irrigation canal], it was a red world, burned by the sun, nothing would grow on it... I worked it till it blossomed and produced, till the words of Sîdî Moḥamed u l-Ḥajj were shown true, "Wealth is from the spirit, O God correct in them what is corrupted, and clean their hearts of envy and jealousy."

And this is true even now, with all my protests and problems with the qbîla I don't want anybody's harm! I shout and yell at someone as I argue, and yet if it were up to me, not even a fly would touch him. All this came true in my father's words, and I became rich [in spirit]. The next morning he said, "Do you want more?" I said, "No, God repay you, this is plenty." I drank my soup, put on my clothes, there was nothing I wanted but wealth of spirit... He who is wealthy in spirit is more wealthy than he who is wealthy in things!

My mother, may she rest in peace, she too said to me that she had a word for me. "What's your word?" I asked, and she said, "May you be one with the king of bees, who sings in the center as the bees dance around him in circle."[101] May you be like a lion, inducing fear in others without being fearful yourself. May you be above all the noise and the bubbles!" "Your word is big too, if God takes it," I said. And I recited poetry, people circling around me, and now some are even afraid of me: "Watch out, Ḥadda, son of Ṭamu, is coming," they whisper when I appear. And I built my house at the mouth of the balance [*fum l-mizân*, the main water junction], above all that crap. I am above everyone in terms of water.

These are the spells of the parents.

The candle

We are sitting in my room, Ḥadda and I, on a dark afternoon before sunset. The somber sky: that slim stream of light that can still make its way through the dirty sheet of plastic over the skylight in my room, that somber sky, reddened by dust, so heavy that I lower my eyes, suggests, unequivocally, a threat of rain. The storm is coming from Bû Zerwal, says Ḥadda without raising his eyes. Storms coming from that side are ruinous. (Bû Zerwal, the Squint-Eyed, is a desolate mountain at the limit of Bni Zoli's visual field. A physical image of the Beyond, a crowded city of jinns is said to sprawl in its caves.) The last time a big storm hit from there, from the desert came a torrent that became a flood.

What is said slides away. Only that sense of heaviness remains, which makes it hard for us to move. Other men in the room, making tea, drinking tea, crisscrossing conversation, someone makes a joke, everybody laughs, without spirit. Boredom and waiting. I say something (is it about poetry?), Ḥadda replies something. Then the rain starts. Almost imperceptibly at first, like sand over the plastic sheet. People pretend not to hear, if you listen too hard the rain stops. If it really comes down you won't get home tonight, someone says to Ḥadda, there'll be mud everywhere. Lost in himself, Ḥadda is sitting in silence. The rain comes down harder, tic tic *on the plastic sheet. I light a candle. Water starts dripping in. The rain comes down stronger and stronger. Awakened by danger everyone suddenly gets up. Frenetic activity. Mud houses don't hold up in the rain. If you are not there to fill the holes that open up with fresh earth, the house melts and collapses on you.*

Ḥadda does not move. From the roof, someone yells to go home while he still can. Between us, on the floor, the candle.

He concentrates on the flame, as bright as the fire of a house, his house, in the darkness of the room. Then, he starts reciting a poem, as if to the candle itself—herself, in Arabic candle *is feminine.*

With pressing insistence a Poet questions a Candle about the source of her pain: Why do you cry when others rejoice? With blind obstinacy he tries to cheer her up, to make her forget her sadness and enjoy the pleasures of this world. If it is a love who turned away from you...

The Candle listens, then speaks. She is Light, and speaks with clairvoyance. Her vision springs from her incurable wound, her awareness of estrangement and death. To be alive is to have one's body fissured by a wick.

Ḥadda the Poet, Ḥadda the Candle.

Tell me
I implore you Candle
Why cry when others rejoice
        tears streaming down on your stick
Consumed by longing[102]
you liquefy
Set ablaze by passion
you give light
Everything is forgiven to the one in love

Yet I find no way around your tears
If it is a love who turned away from you
you must forget him
Remember: those who betray never win
Despise him because of his wrongs

Candle of ours, candle of pleasure
You too lose yourself in the presence of beauty
Surrounded by girls dancing the hadra
Daughters of the best from every tribe
Rejoice, rejoice o Candle! Rejoice in the spectacle of that show of licit beauty
You saw reddened cheeks
Big eyes, blackened with koḥl
You saw young men displaying their pride
each ready to fight a lion
Thus spoke the Poet.

Then, She spoke:
I'll show you, clever one
What has befallen me
And you'll say, "Beware of the wound!"
You did not divine my uncanny story
        in its disguise
I, who sit in the place of honor in celebrations
The craftsman who molded me
to challenge the gas lamp
He hollowed my body with skill
lured me with many a trick
And then planted at the core of my body a wick

"To set her ablaze," says Ḥadda, interrupting his recitation and looking at me for the first time. The roar of the rain covers his words. As if realizing for the first time, he pauses, dismayed for a moment. "God save us!" But the spell of the candle is stronger. Her light is an ecstasy born of pain, it is a movement of dying. Her vision comes from her wick: the inscription of death on her body, the mortal trick, poisonous gift of the craftsman.

They squeezed me and took the honey
        then put me aside and said
"It will serve to put down in front of the guests"
By her, the room is lit
She burns throughout the night

"The Poet keeps pushing the candle," comments Ḥadda, interrupting his recitation again; "he can't understand. He tells her about the advantages of life. The Candle, then, comes down to his level, and ironically proposes to get back to the happy mood."

She said to him:
I have seen it all
and today, it's enough my dear Poet, let's not spoil the party
Let's stick to our rhythms and lutes
    and with our drums dance away this night
This is a word of wisdom
    if you wish to hear
Wise people say, forbearance is rewarded
We thank the present company
And those who challenge us, we ignore[103]

For a long time we sit without saying a word, at a loss for words. Then, suddenly realizing that his family and his house are in danger, he gets up and leaves in the rain. From the threshold I watch him make his way through the torrent of water in the alley. I want to go, but I stay. The others come, hoes in hand with their rubber boots, and loudly take me along.

gerrî lî lillâh yâ shshemʿa
u ʿlâsh ʿlik b-l-bka u nnâss fî l-frâḥ
mâl dmûʿek ghîr sâyla fûg l-ḥeska tsîl

b-ṣṣahd htîra
kunti muluʿâ b l-hwâ
qasḥ men l-ghrâm men zînat îḍwâh

lâzem men laʿshîg ineʿder
sîdî men bkâk mâjberna ḥîla
u illâ maḥbûb fât ʿendek
u lyûm jfâk maṭlaʿ yinfaʿ fîh tenṣâḥ
ma yrbaḥ men nâwî l-ghder
hâdâk jfîh men fʿâylû l-qbîḥa

shemʿatnâ yâ shemʿat l-hnâ
râk tantî tayhâ ghîr f wjûh l-mlâḥ
dâru bîk ʿwâns l-ḥaḍra
ghîr bnât l-khyâr men kull qbîla
aw tnazzahtî yâ shshemʿa

tnazzahtî ʿal lebhâ u-zzîn l-mubâḥ
nḍerti l-khdûd b l-aʿkar
l-ʿaynîn l-kbâr u sswâk w ttekḥîla
û nḍertî shubbân kull wâḥed fîhum men iḥârb sbaʿ
men jihât l-kfaḥ
kul shbâb iṣôl u îfkhar
men qallet l-mrâsem mseggel tesgîla
nḍertî agudât b swâlef

qâlt lu nwerrîk yâ l-fâhem
kîf ṭrâ lî tgûl ʿandâk men l-jrâḥ
ma seqtî l-ghribtî fî khfâh
anâ llî kunt f l-mrâteb l-hfîla

l-mʿallem llî ṣnaʿnî
û fraghnî mn shṭartû
ḍedd ʿala l-meṣbâḥ
u khdaʿnî b-khdâyʿ ktâr
u zraʿ liya fî qalb dâtî l-ftîla

ʿaṣrûnî u ddâw laʿsel u terkûnî
bjîh u qâlu teṣlaḥ
        be l-ḥaṭṭa
guddâm men yiḥdar
bihâ îḍwâ l-bît u tbât shʿîla

jîsh ktîr quwwet leʿsâker
ʿannik l-malîk gultî ll-wzara tslâḥ
l-ḥîla guddam men hdar
. . . .
qalt lû kulshî nḍertû û lyûm khlâṣ shaykh nterqû lmenzah
nqimû b-nghâym û luṭâr
u b-ṭfârejna ngerrḥû had l-lîla

hâda qûl jiyid yâ fâhem
qâlûh l-mâhrîn wa arjah
u-hennî kull men ḥdar wamma men jâhadna njawbûh b tenkhîla

APPENDIX

Fitna

Everyone shall have a taste of death: And We test you through disaster and well being by way of fitna, and to Us must you return.
—Qur'an 21:35

Excerpt from the entry "FTN" in the classical Arabic dictionary *Lisân al-ʿârab* by Ibn al-Manẓûr (fourteenth century):[104]

FTN: al-Azharî and others agree that the general meaning of fitna is temptation through evil, trial and tribulation, affliction and testing, ordeal [*al-ibtilâʿ, al-imtiḥân, al-ikhtibâr*], and that the root of its meaning is grasped when you say, I have subjected to a fitna silver and gold, when I melt them on the fire to distinguish the bad metal from the one of quality [*al-radîʿ min al-jayyid*].

In the Ṣihâh [a dictionary] a metal is called *maftûn* if you have put it in the fire to test the degree of its quality; hence there is also the expression *dînâr maftûn* [a unit of money maftûn]. The *fatn* is the action of burning. In this sense God has said, "It will be a Day when they will be tried (and tested) over the Fire [*yuftanûn*]" [Qur'an 51:13], that is they will be set ablaze by fire. The goldsmith is called *al-fattân,* and also *al-shayṭân,* "the Devil," and this is also why black stones that appear as if they were burned by fire are called *al-fatîn.*

As a commentary to this saying of God it has been said that [in the verse] "There will be a Day when they will be tried over the Fire," *yuftanûn* means *yuqarrarûn,* that is, that the verdict will fall upon them. A paper *fatîn* is burned silver, and according to Ibn al-ʿArabî *al-fitna* is *al-ikhtibâr,* fitna is testing, *al-fitna al-miḥna,* it is the ordeal of affliction and suffering, and fitna is wealth, it is children, it is unbelief, al-fitna is difference of opinions between people [*ikhtilâf bi al-raʾy*], and al-fitna is the *iḥrâq bi al-nâr,* the action of burning by fire. And in the *taʾwîl,* or Interpretation, it has been said that *al-fitna* is *al-ẓulm,* "injustice." And it is said that one is *maftûn* by desire for the things of this world [*maftûn bi-ṭalabi al-dunyâ*]; this means that his desire is excessive.

Ibn Sîdah's opinion is that al-fitna is *al-khibra,* fitna is trial, and the word of God has said, "For we have truly made it [the tree of Zaqqûm] as a trial/ fitna for the wrongdoers" [Qurʾan 37:63],[105] and in this context al-fitna is trial, testing [*khibra*]; and the meaning of it is that the wrongdoers [*ẓâlimîn*] have been tested [*uftinû*] by the tree of Zaqqûm; they denied the existence of this tree, for when they heard that it springs from the bottom of hellfire, they said, This tree burns in fire, and how can a tree grow from fire? And this became a fitna for them. And when the word of God says, "Our Lord! Make us not a fitna for those who practice oppression" [Qurʾan 10:85], this means may they not overwhelm us and think that they are better than us. The fitna in this context is the fact that the unbelievers have delight in their unbelief.

And it is said *futina al-rajul bi al-marʾa,* the man is seduced [put into a fitna, passive verb] by the woman; and it is also said *iftatana,* and the people of the Hijaz say *fatanathu al mar'a,* if she seduces him, fascinates him, and he loves her; and the people of Najd say, *aftanathu.* Aʿshâ Ḥamdân used both idioms in this verse: "If she seduced me today [*fatanatnî*], yesterday she seduced Saʿid [*aftanat*], and from his love for her he took despise on every Muslim." Ibn Barri said that Ibn Jinî claimed that this verse should be attributed to Ibn Qaîs. . . .

And fitna is when you are fascinated by a thing [*iʿjâbuka*]. . . .

Abû Zayd said, "*Futina al-rajul yuftanu futûnah idhâ arâda al-fujûr*" (a man is in a state of fitna when he desires fornication and debauchery). . . .

And a man is maftûn if he is attained by fitna and loses his wealth and his mind [*mâluh wa ʿaqluh*], and also if he is subjected to testing [*ukhtubira*]. God said as well, "We tried you with various trials" [Qurʾan 20:40]. . . .

And *al-maftun* of the fitna is the *maṣdar* on the mode of *mafʿûl,*[106] like *al-maʿqûl,* "the rational," or *al-majlûd,* "the whipped," and the word of God says, "Soon wilt thou see, and they will see, which of you is afflicted by madness [*bi ayyikum al-maftûn*]" [Qur'an 68:5–6].

Abû Isḥâq has said that the meaning of *al-maftûn* [in this Qur'anic verse] is the possessed, the person seized into a demonic state [*futina bi al-junûn*].[107] Abû ʿUbayda has said instead that the *bi* plays no role in the meaning of this Qur'anic passage; [it should be read] as if it said, "Which among you is *al-maftûn*." Abû Isḥâq said instead that in the Arabic language it is not acceptable that the [preposition] *bi* be meaningless, and grammarians are divided between two opinions. . . .

Ibn Barri has said that if the *bi* does not add to the sense, this means that *al-maftûn* is man, the human kind, and hence not a maṣdar.[108] If instead one judges that the "bi" adds to the meaning, *al-maftûn* becomes a maṣdar in the sense of *futûn: iftatana fî ash-shay'*, that is, *futina fîh*. When you are very taken by something, you become a captive [*maftûn*] of that thing.

And *fatana ilâ al-nisâ*, "he practices fitna in relation to women," means that he desires fornicating with them. And al-fitna is also *al-ḍalâl*, "deviance and errancy," and it is *al-ithm*, "error and sin." *Al-fâtin* is the person who makes you deviate from the right path, the *ḥaqq*, "truth," and the *fâtin* is the Devil because he sets the faithful astray, the *ʿabâd*, the "servants of God." And in the Hadith of Qayla [it is said], "The Muslim is the brother of the Muslim; both are content with water and trees and aid each other against the *fattân*." And the *fattân* is the Devil [*shayṭân*], who puts people in a state of fitna [*yaftinu*], deceives them with his illusions, and shows transgression in a good light. If a man advises his brother to avoid this, he helps him against the Devil. It is also said that the *fattân* is the robber who attacks travelers on their path, and they must help each other against him. The plural of *fattân* is *futtân*, and in the hadith it is transmitted with *fa* and with *fu*; the one transmitted with *fa* is singular, and it means the Devil, and the one transmitted with *fu* is plural, and it means that people should help each other against those who make them deviate from the law, and *yaftinûnahum*. *Fattân* is the emphasized form of *fitna*, it is an excess in the fitna. In the hadith there is a wording that says, "As for you, Muʿad, are you a *fattân*?"

Zajjâj reported from the exegesis of the word of God, "You led yourselves into a fitna" [Qur'an 57:14], that this means, You have put your own being at stake in the fitna. And it has also been said [that it means] you have put your beings [*anfusakum*] to sleep [*anamtumûhâ*]. God has also said, "Fatannâka futunan" (We tried you in various ways) [Qur'an 20:40], and this is like saying, We purified you with purification, and he said again, "Among them is many a man who says: Grant me exemption and draw me not into a fitna" [Qur'an 9:49], and this means, Don't put me in a situation where I find myself in error, as when you say, "Go!" and it is not easy for me to go, and thus I find myself in error [*ithm*].

Zajjâj said, It has been said that the Hypocrites had ridiculed the believers in the battle [*ghazwa*] of Tabûk, saying that what they wanted were the *benat al-Aṣfar*, "the daughters of Aṣfar." It is then that the Prophet said, "Do not tempt me [*lâ taftinnî*] with the daughters of Aṣfar." And it is so that he indicated to God the highest that the Muslims had fallen into a fitna, that is, in error [*ithm*].

And the expression *fatana al-rajula*, "he put the man into a fitna," means that he diverted that man from where he was [from his right state]. In this sense God has said, "And their purpose was to tempt you away from that which We had revealed unto you" [Qur'an 17:73], that is, that they will tempt you and set you astray (Ibn al-Anbari).

Fatanat fulâna fulânan, "Fulana has put Fulan in a state of fitna"—some have said that this means "she had diverted him," or set him away from his *qaṣd*, his scope and orientation. And in their saying al-fitna is that which makes a person deviate from the *ḥaqq*, from truth, the right path. And in the words of God, "For, verily, neither you nor those you worship can lead any into temptation concerning God, except such as are themselves going to the blazing Fire!" [Qur'an 37:161–63]. This has been explicated by Thʿalab, who said, "You can only tempt with fitna a person who has already been condemned to Hell." . . .

And it has also been said that al-fitna [in this Qur'anic verse] is *al-iḍlâl*, the action of making a person deviate. That is, you can only make deviate Ahl an-Nâr, "the People of Hell"; and this means that God knows in advance that they are deviants. . . .

And al-fitna is madness [*al-junûn*], and this also as *al-futûn*. The Qur'an says, "Fitna is worse than slaughter" [*al-fitna ashaddu min al-qatl*, Qur'an 2:191]. And *al-fitna* means here *al-kufr*, "unbelief." The same thing has been said by the exegetes. Ibn Sîdah has said, "Al-fitna is unbelief," and in the word of God, "Fight them on until there is no more tumult or oppression [fitna]" [Qur'an 8:39]. And al-fitna is *al-faḍîḥa*, "scandal," and the word of God says, "If anyone's trial [fitna] is intended by God, thou hast no authority in the least for him against God" [Qur'an 5:44]. It has been said that the meaning here is scandal, divulgation, and calumny. And it has also been said that his scandal [fitna] is his unbelief. And Abû Isḥâq has said that this could also mean his *ikhtibâr*, a "trial" for him, because of what becomes manifest in that condition.

And al-fitna is *al-ʿadhâb*, "suffering and torture," in the sense of *taʿdhîb al-kuffâr*, when the unbelievers subjected the poor Muslims to torture to ward them off their faith. Like Bilâl, who was mounted on the Ramḍâʾ as a torture and was later emancipated and saved by Abû Bakr al-Siddiq.[109]

And al-fitna means also the fact of people killing each other, that is, the action of killing [*al-qitâl*]. . . .

And it also says in the sura of Yunus, "Because of the fear of Pharaoh and his chiefs, lest they should persecute them [*yaftinahum*]" [Qur'an 10:83], and this means that he would kill them. As for what the Prophet said, "I see fitna in your homes," it means the action of killing, the wars, and it means *al-ikhtilâf*, difference and discord among groups [*firâq*] of Muslims when they create factions and opposing parties [*idhâ tahazzabû*].

And [fitna] is also that which makes Muslims be tempted/seduced by the beauty of the material world [*zînat ad-dunyâ*], its appetites [*shahawât*], that which makes them forget the Other World, and makes them deviate [*yuftanûna*] from what they should do for the Other World.

And the Prophet said, "I haven't left behind me a more harmful fitna to men than women." He said, "I fear that they will be seduced and led astray by them, and that this will distract them and make them forget the Other World, and what they must do for the Other World."

Al-fitna means also *al-ikhtibâr*, "the action of putting a person to trial." The word of God said, "See you not that they are tried [*yuftanûna*] every year once or twice?" [Qur'an 9:126]. It has been said that this means that they are put to trial by the call to jihad, and it has also been said that *yuftanûna* means that they have been tested by suffering and misfortune [*al-makrûh*].

And *al-fatn* is burning with fire, and *fatana* something with fire means "to burn it." *Al-fatîn min al-ard* is volcanic land, which is covered which black stones as if it were burned. And Shummâr has said that everything that undergoes a change of state, a metamorphosis by the action of fire, is *maftûn*. And it is said that the black woman slave [*al-ama*] is *maftûna*, because she resembles volcanic land in her black color, as if she was burned. . . .

And al-fitna is the action of burning, *fatantu al-raghîf*, I burned the bread. And the fitna of the heart is *al-waswâs*, "obsession and internal delusion" [*wa fitnat al-ṣadr al-waswâs*]. The fitna of life [*al-maḥyâ*] is the fact of losing one's way [*yaʿdil ʿan aṭ-ṭarîq*], and the fitna of death is the fact of being questioned in the grave. And the word of God has said, "Those who persecute (or draw into temptation) [*fatanû*] the believers, men and women, and do not turn to repentance, will have the penalty of Hell: they will have the penalty of burning fire" [Qur'an 85:10]. In this instance it [*fatanû*] means that they [those who persecute the believers] have burned the believers in a fire lit inside a pit, where they hurled them in order to ward them off from their faith.

And in the Hadith of Ḥassan, [concerning] those who have made a fitna for the men and women who are believers, it is said, "They have subjected them to the fitna of fire, that is they have tested [*imtaḥanûhum*] and tortured them." God the highest made an ordeal of hardship for his faithful servants to test their endurance and reward them, and if they refused to endure, he rewarded them with the punishment of fitna.

And God has said, "*Alif lâm mîm.* Do men think that they will be left alone on saying, 'We believe,' and that they will not be tested [*lâ yuftanûn*]? [Qur'an 29:1–2]. And in the Commentary this means that they must be tested [*yubtalûn*] in their deepest being [*anfusihim*] and in their wealth, and through the endurance of calamity and evil [*al-balâ'*] will be possible to distinguish sincere from insincere faith. And it has also been said that *wa-hum lâ yuftanûn* means that they have not yet been tested by that which uncovers [*yabînu bih*] the truth of their faith. For God has also said, "We did test [*fatannâ*] those before them, and God will certainly know those who are true from those who are false" [Qur'an 29:3]. This means, "We have put them to trial and made them suffer [*ibtalaynâ*]."

And God has said about the two angels Hârût and Mârût that they said, "We are only for trial [fitna]; so do not blaspheme" [Qur'an 2:102]. And this means we are an *ibtilâ'* and an *ikhtibâr,* a trial of evil for you. And in the hadith it is said, "The believer was created *mufattanan:* with fitna as a condition of being," that is, by definition on trial, for God puts him to trial with sin, and then he repents, and then he transgresses again, and again he repents. All this comes from the verb *fatana,* in the sense of "putting to trial." It also takes the form *aftantuh,* which is rare. Ibn al-Athîr says that this form was much used in the sense of "the ordeal of misfortune" [*al-makrûḥ*], and later of sin, unbelief [*kufr*], murder [*qitâl*], burning, and the event of annihilation [*al-'zâla, zwl*] and of being diverted from a thing [*aṣ-ṣarf ʿan as-shay'*].

The two *fattân* of the grave are Munkir and Nakîr, and in the Hadith of the Eclipse [*kusûf*] it is said, "You will be interrogated [*tuftanûn*] in the grave." And this means to be interrogated by Munkir and Nakîr [the two angel inquisitors], and derives from the meaning of *fitna* as examination [*imtiḥân*].

He [the Prophet] has many times invoked the protection of God against the fitna of the grave, the fitna of the Antichrist [*dajjâl*], the fitna of life, the fitna of death, and all the others. And in the hadith it is said, "You will be tested by me, and will be interrogated about me." And this means, You will be tried because of me in your graves, and your faith will be revealed when your belief in my prophecy is proven. And in a hadith of ʿUmar it is reported that he heard a man invoking God to be spared from the various fitnas, and ʿUmar said, "Are you asking your God to grant you neither family nor money?" and in saying this he alluded to the word of God, "Your riches and your children are a fitna for you" [Qur'an 64:15]. He did not mention, then, the sense of fitna as murder and as difference [*al-ikhtilâf*].

part three

LOSS

the sphere of the moon

LOSS 1

THE SPHERE OF THE MOON

Libre de la memoria y de la esperanza,
ilimitado, abstracto, casi futuro,
el muerto no es un muerto: es la muerte. . . .
—Jorge Luis Borges[1]

The Dream

Much later, I had a dream.

FIRST SCENE: IMPASSE

In a big house in the aftermath of a death. I have not witnessed the event, no one in the house has mentioned it to me, no one has said a word about it. But I know it is a woman who has died. "The rûḥ of the house," I think in the dream, the life breath of the textile—the woman who held the house together. No one in the house makes any mention of the event, or for that matter of the funeral that must have ensued. I think to myself, Have they forgotten? If the walls of this old building have been shattered by the laments of the women, by the chanting of the ṭolba, by the chatting of the men, by the screaming of the children; if they have been touched by the acrid smells of cooking and incense, no trace is left of all that. It is silence—heavy with waiting—and an empty room with four columns and the central light well, a room like all the rooms of the old houses in this village. Not a rug, not a pillow, not one straw mat on the dirt floor.

There are three people besides me in the house: an old man, a middle-aged woman, and a child. I recognize the man as l-Ḥajj l-Madanî; the house is his house in the qṣar. (But his house is full of life, three generations of children coming and going, while this one is empty and forsaken.) The woman has the face and the tone of voice of one of my aunts in Italy.

I am downstairs, alone. It is dark, even darker than it usually is in these houses, and damp, as if after a rainstorm. From the roof the woman shouts at me to sweep the mud floor. SHEṬṬBI! *(I hear the order in Arabic.* Sheṭṭeb, *"to sweep," is also the term used in the historical narratives of the qṣar for the razing of villages: SHEṬṬBI! RAZE IT![2]) I start sweeping and, as the earth dust gathers up, I see hundreds of dead black bugs. Sense of decay. I am the house being swept/razed. I am the one who is razing it. The woman's voice from the roof warns me to watch my head. I raise my eyes and see the corner of the ceiling falling in. This house, I think, is collapsing.*

"Nelḥag rasmu îṣôt khâli" (I reach its place, the wind blows empty). Remembering the dream, I repeat this verse to myself.[3] In the poetical use a house is a *rasm:* from the verbal root *rsm,* to fix and to settle, to immobilize, to orient, to establish; but also to draw, to describe, to inscribe, to fix in images. (A *rasm* is also the draftsman's drawing.) "Ḥerbet mennu ḥmâmtû / u bga f rasmû ʿrâyâ" (His dove fled from him / abandoned in a naked house); "rasm bgâ khâlî" (The house, the encampment, the self was left in ruins). Poems of loss draw on an imagery of space: houses in ruin, empty settlements, places swept by the wind. The act of "sweeping" is an image of that ruin, of the dissolution of the rasm, of the unsettling of what was settled. *Sheṭṭb,* "to sweep" or "to wipe out," is the opposite of *rsem,* "to fix" or "to draw." Yet, in another sense, it marks the opening of new spaces.

Then the house transforms. It dissolves or expands. It becomes landscape. It turns into the rocky red soil at the edge of the palm groves. I am walking. I am still inside the house, sweeping. The inside becomes the outside. A young man I don't know is telling me, "Watch your step, don't walk, don't sweep here, you are standing on a graveyard [l-mdîna hâdî]. *Everything is disintegrating—the ground is sinking. If you step on it you'll find yourself inside a grave. Corpses are coming out in the open."*

I raise my eyes. I realize that I am walking on the grounds of a cemetery. An old cemetery, unmarked and invisible. One can guess that there are graves only from the shape of the terrain, uneven and full of holes. I think, qbûr mensiya, *a forgotten graveyard.*[4]

L-qber l-mensî, "the forgotten tomb," is a central figure in the discourse and the practice of magic. The tomb of a person whose identity and name have been forgotten, l-qber l-mensî becomes a metaphor for the unknown, that which can never be known or appropriated. A name for what has no name, a place for what has no place. Unmarked, l-qber l-mensî displays the contagious trait of anonymity. But in these cemeteries, expanses of dry ground and stones eroded by wind, there are no inscriptions, names, or dates. Two upright stones at the site of the feet and one at the site of the head indicate that the grave harbors a woman; one stone at each end signifies a man. With time the *shuhûd,* the "witnesses" (this is what the tombstones are called), slowly sink into the ground, and the cemetery turns into a rocky empty space, rippled by the movement of the sand and the emerging tips of the *shuhûd.* If the site is still in use, there is here and there a new grave: a mound of earth and stones covered by a mantle of palm leaves left to dry out in the sun, as the body rots and then dries in its underground dwelling. (Tombs are built and reckoned as homes. Small chambers dug into the earth, sustained and covered by wooden beams; the corpse is laid sideways, the head in the direction of Mecca. Under the rocky landscape is an anonymous buried city of the dead.) Each year on the day of ʿAshûra[5] groups of women visit the cemetery to sprinkle water on the graves: all graves. For if they can sometime divine the site where the remains of their mother, husband, or son are buried, they can never be certain. Graveyards are the writing of oblivion. All tombs share to some extent the anonymous quality of the "forgotten tomb."

Having lost attachment to any memory or identifiable person, l-qber l-mensî carries the atopical and intemporal indifference of death, without name, place, or face—a signifier of disjunction, detachment, and break. Hence the qber mensî is a dangerous physical place, and a zone of avoidance in discourse. A cognitive hole, a fragment of absolute non-sense. As such, detached and arbitrary, it can become a tie in language—an active element in the semiotics of magical operations. Rites of forgetting, untying, and separating, rites of effacing and, in a way, of mourning—all revolve around the ditch, the hollow, of the forgotten tomb. For those bewitched, tied by the knots of *siḥr,* and who, in those knots, have lost themselves and their minds, performing ablutions over a forgotten grave may provide freedom and release. For a person wounded by an incurable loss—or tormented by the memory of an impossible love—a rite involving the forgotten grave can indicate the way out of the impasse.

From *Kitâb al-raḥma fî al-ṭibb wa al-ḥikma* (The book of mercy in medicine and wisdom) by ʿAbd ar-Raḥmân as-Suyûṭî:[6]

> Remedy to get rid of love from the heart of a man [*ʿilâj suluw al-ʿishq min qalb al-rajul*], and to make his heart turn cold toward the woman until he does not think of her or even look at her. Write the formula below on three pieces of paper, and put one inside the heart of some carrion [*jîfa*]; take the second in your hands, rub it against the heart of the man in love and make him drink it; wrap the third in a fragment of a black cape and bury it in a forgotten grave [*qabr mansî*] by the head of the dead, and say: "This is the heart + and + ; may the protection of Allah be with you, o dweller of this grave [*ya ṣâḥib hadha al-qabr*]; this is the heart of Fulân, son of Fulâna, next to your head, until a camel will pass through the eye of a needle. And this is what you must write: "Carrion [*jîfa*], 2, may Fulâna rot [*tjiyif*] in the heart of Fulân as rotted [*tjiyif*] this carrion. May she depart [from his heart], by [the intervention of] the one who says to all things 'be' and they are. . . . 'Henceforth were your hearts hardened: they became like a rock and even worse in hardness' " (Qur'an 2:74).

At once a figure, or a dramatization, of impasse (the hole of the nameless tomb, the blank of memory) and of the way out of impasse, a passage by the forgotten grave can lead to recollection and release. It can untie what is tied, release *l-mtaqqaf, l-marbûṭ*, the person "halted" or "enchained" by the knots of a spell, and by the inscription of a blank, an empty space, make things circulate again. (*Tawqîf*, the "halting," is a diagnosis of bewitchment; from the verb *waqafa*, "to stop." In divination it is a technical term for the impasse in which the person is caught.)

Nsa, nasya: to forget, to obliterate, to fall into oblivion. And *nisâ'*, women.[7] Two different words, phonetically akin to each other. *Nisâ'* is a noun formed from the verb *nasa'*, to postpone, to delay, to give time. But in the local imagination, which is oral and follows the calligraphy of sound, the two words resonate with many echoes. *Nasya,* then, becomes the feminine root of oblivion, as against *dhakara,* the masculine root of memory. *Dhakara,* to remember, to be mentioned, to be male; *dhikra,* commemoration; *dhakar,* the masculine sex. Yet, perhaps (as for the opposition *ḥasab* and *nasab*), any remembrance implies a certain forgetting, anything found, a certain loss.

I see the cracks in the earth.

It is the *mdîna* of Lâllâ ud Sîdî perhaps—the cemetery facing west just outside the walled ramparts, where the big phallic stone of the Judge's tomb dominates the view. *Mdîna,* "city" and, in the local use, "graveyard"—the City of the Dead. My dream plays on that play. Once, when I was sick, I said jokingly that if I died I wanted to be buried there, in the cemetery of Lâllâ ud Sîdî, "my lady daughter of my lord." She was the wife of the Judge, they say, the daughter of the powerful lord of Timsla. He too, the Judge, came as a foreigner. He came along with the army of a sultan, and like all the other foreigners who were woven in the fabric of the land, married a powerful woman from the region, and settled in.

But, I am told, that "city" is full. The mdîna is *ʿâmra*—there is no room for the new dead. That's why people have taken to piling manure up around the old graves. With time the wooden beams inside the graves were consumed and collapsed—just like the beams that support houses do—and the old graves came to expose their hidden side to the sun. (When the "side of the moon" is exposed to the sun, the effect is uncanny; it is "the uncanny.")[8] But the mdîna is also the qṣar. It is the village that today is once again becoming its own ruin—as if the demon of allegory were slowly drawing life out of it—and it is the qṣar that in its peculiar palimpsestic way, imagines itself as always lived in by the remains of alien forms.

Falling in, drawn underground. Cannot move.

(Bni Zoli, March 23, 1986)

Kh. woke me and turned off the oil lamp. It could have started a fire. Again, the thing. A sense of being crushed by an unbearable weight, and an imageless pit in which I fall.

There is a recurrent nightmare I used to have then. I called it "the thing" to emphasize its materiality, its absence of symbolism. (It is Rilke who talks about "the Thing.")[9] Without images, beyond recollection. If there is an event the dream reenacted each time, I never knew.

There is a kind of nightmare that in Morocco is called *bû tellîs.* It is named after the heavy grain bags loaded on a donkey's back. The name emphasizes the sense of being overwhelmed, and the paralysis of the imaginary that characterizes dreams like the one I described. (When I spoke about "the thing," people told me of *bû tellîs.*) Also, *tilles* in Berber means "darkness." To be struck by *tilles* is to be blinded—blindfolded. And *bû tilles,* or *bû sels,* is the name of certain blind narrow alleys in the qṣar. They are sort of bowels one walks through in darkness; shortcuts, connecting alleys parallel to each other and constructed to remain separate; *impasses one passes through.* Sometimes, someone is said to have disappeared in her passing, like that bride who once upon a time was taken to the groom's house in the Alley of Ayt Ḥammu and, still a virgin, vanished with horse and veils into the *bû sels* of Ayt ʿAbdallah. She did not emerge on the other side, was never found again.

SECOND SCENE: THE STAIRCASE

> *The next thing I know I am climbing the exterior stairs of another house, also a mud house, but new, and built in a completely different style. The staircase is exposed, suspended. I can't take my eyes from it. It doesn't look at all like the staircases I know.* (Awaking from the dream, the staircase is what I first remember.) *I notice the smooth, freshly made earth walls. I say to myself, "This is one of the houses* berra, *of the 'outside,' of the New Village. But unlike those houses, which are flat, one-story buildings, this house is elevated—as if suspended in air. I climb the staircase, prominently exposed on the exterior façade. I stop halfway, look up, and see the door of the house, open on a balcony, several meters above. I think, Unlike the staircases I know, this one is exposed, and disengages itself from its base—*

In the houses of the old qṣar staircases are embedded in the internal structure of the building. Invisible, dynamic, and alive, they cannot be seen from the outside, or from inside the downstairs room. Narrow and dark, they withdraw from sight even as one climbs their winding steps; one is carried up by their movement as if blind. A staircase is not just an architectural feature; it is a "work." In their symbolic technology staircases are said to develop from a buried base (like mushrooms out of their mycelia),[10] a zone of opacity bordering on the underground. Masons call this base *aferdu* (Tashelḥit) after the compact wooden base of the mortar and by analogy with the Iferd, a mythical pond of rotting water in communication with the realm of death and the Below. The work of the staircase is a process of displacement of that base of oblivion, which is spun and woven into an elevated, articulated structure. This is why, faithful to an analogy between the craft of poetry and those of building and weaving,[11] poets in this region invoke sometimes the built structure of the staircase as a metaphor for the formal organization of their poems.

Unlike the suspended staircase of my dream, the staircases of the qṣar never disengage themselves completely from the inhuman space in which they are born. Not unlike Giacometti's bronze statues, human flower stems grown from heavy bronze pedestals, these staircases engage in a continuous exchange with their base—heaviness woven into lightness.

I climb up and see a woman with her children playing with a bicycle on the balcony. A man comes, the same man who had warned me not to walk on the graveyard. I recognize him. I say, "Your house is suspended in air..." He says, "Of course! Here everything is sinking; it is a world in ruin. As long as you insist on living in the Ḥajj's house, you won't realize it."

I think to myself that the man is arrogant like those of the younger generation, like those young men who speak in the first person plural to be bold, know all about wells and engine pumps, handle dynamite without fear, light the fuse and climb up in time not to be blown up inside the well (but sometimes they are blown up). Or like those men who one day put on blue jeans and city shoes, reluctantly take the stuffed bread prepared by their mothers or their wives, and get on the bus to Casablanca to seek employment as unskilled laborers on construction sites. Perched on the scaffolding, they feel they have made it—out of the valley, away from the sinking ground, out of the haunting play of memory and forgetting. Sometimes they fall. Like the young man who was found dead on an esplanade of fresh cement one October morning, the day before he was expected back home for the ʿid l-kbîr's festivities.

I look at the man with his children, at the suspended staircase. I wonder whether it is his practice of oblivion, the forgetting of forgetting, that enables them to live on. I decline their invitation to stay, and I go back to l-Ḥajj's house.

(New Haven, Connecticut, November 28, 1989)

Dreams, Heterography, and the Voyages of the Rûh

Pas de folklore donc, ni de littérature coloniale, mais une écriture du Dehors qui accueille le lieu de l'autre dans mon langage, dans mon espace imaginaire. Cette énergie qui se creuse entre lui et moi est offerte à notre relation réelle, à notre distance dissymétrique, incontournable, ouverte vers le Dehors. Je ne peux m'y retrouver.

—Abdelkebir Khatibi[12]

Why begin with a dream—and a dream I, "myself," have dreamed? How can a dream of my own produce ethnographic knowledge, except perhaps to call attention to an unconscious bias, projection, or identification that—as some psychoanalysts might say—can only be seen as a transference, a resistance to the analysis that must be acknowledged and then resolved? Would it suggest that all ethnography is at last autobiography, for in the encounter with others, as Aragon's verse states, "Toi te tournant vers moi tu ne saurais trouver / au mur de mon regard que ton ombre rêvée?"[13] Who, what, is dreaming through the figures, the phantoms, and the historical tropes of the qṣar? What does it mean to speak, to dream, through another's voice, through the vocabulary and grammar of another language, from a place that is not one's own?

This dream (my dream?) is the dialogical effect of an encounter; its mechanisms are comparable to the grammatical works of a bi-langue. Coming to terms with it—as an event, but also as a poetic allusion—means for me to raise the question of the status and the possibility of ethnography, of autobiography, in fact, of writing.

The consequences are not psychological, nor are they simply epistemological. They are ethical, and concern what Lacan calls the intersubjective function of speech: *l'intimation de la parole,* the "summoning force of speech," that implicates me and is effective at the level of the definition of the world in which I live and write. Inasmuch as it is intersubjective, speech "includes the discourse of the other in the secret of its cipher," and transforms the subject to whom it is addressed.[14]

It is in the sense of a transformative, intersubjective writing that I read Khatibi's plea for "une écriture du Dehors": a writing that does not fix the other in place, but is internally altered by the place of the other; that respects the other's difference, the asymmetric distance of the fact that "you never look at me from where I see you,"[15] and makes possible a dialogue that, in its very form—partial and full of holes—eludes the closure of colonial appropriation: the closure of any writing of conquest.

Receiving the "locus of the other inside my language, in the space of my imagination" means that neither "my" language nor "my" imagination will return to me as a piece of belonging; that the *auto-* of the autobiography and the *ethno-* of the ethnography will necessarily be displaced; and that "I will not find myself." It is precisely the distance, the gap, "the energy that furrows the space between us," that makes possible the opening of an heterographic space. Neither ethnographic, nor autobiographic.

(And the reader, the interpreter who sets out to follow the signs of what appears to be a coded itinerary, a *parcours chiffré,* discovers that the itinerary is also a riḥla, a moving away from herself. And that she cannot keep reading without surrendering the viewer's position and embracing that of the walker. Implicated by the tracing—as one is implicated by a gift—she finds herself drawing with the scene; exiled from the scene, for the gift is also an exile, she sees herself revolving with the frame. She is "framed," and re-turns as a picture. Her own story was caught in the tracing.)

I awoke with the sense that this dream was not mine.

ALIEN MOVEMENTS

> Sleep is a state in which the servant passes from the witnessing of the world of sense perception to the world of the barzakh, which is the most perfect world. There is no world more perfect, since it is the root and the origin of the cosmos; it possesses true existence and controlling rule in all affairs. It embodies meanings and changes that which does not subsist in itself, into that which does subsist in itself. It gives form to that which has no form. It turns the impossible into the possible.
>
> —Ibn al-ʿArabî[16]

Dreams are never one's own. Sendings from elsewhere, from the region of death and the beyond, or at least, as Freud says, from another "locality"—*ein anderer Schauplatz,* an Other Scene. Ibn al-ʿArabî calls that Elsewhere a *barzakh,* an intermediate imaginal realm, an *entre-deux* between the living and the dead, a limbo out of which flows dream. Si Lḥassan speaks of an otherworldly journey and an encounter, and of knowledge passed on, between the wandering soul of the dreamer and other errant souls, of the living and the dead—

Even an opponent of phantoms and emanations such as Aristotle, committed to an empiricist explanation of dreaming, understood dreams as, in his words, "alien movements." Delayed energetic impacts, timing devices, affecting the person from without, from a without that is also within, and producing hallucinatory visual effects. (Aristotle calls them demonic effects; and Freud, whose theory of the dream work was much inspired by the Aristotelian argument, makes the term his own.)[17] Aristotle's texts on dreaming are openly aimed at dismantling his contemporaries' belief in the supernatural origin and the prophetic significance of dreams.[18] Yet what the texts propose in their stead is a theory of the alien—which for Aristotle means delayed—temporal scansion of the real, and of the uncanny marriage of contingency and return.

"The affection, which we name dreaming," he says, a kind of illness, really, can be explained in terms of "residuary movements" caused by perceptual impressions that linger in the senses after the disappearance of their cause; because "when we shift the scene of our perceptive activity, the previous affection remains; for instance when we have turned our gaze from sunlight into darkness." Residual impressions produce images that appear during sleep: "The dream proper is an image based on the movement of sense impressions, when it occurs during sleep, insofar as it is asleep." Disconnected from the divine, the "movements lurking in the organs of sense," imaginative movements, have a demonic power. It is the power of deceiving the dreamer into thinking that he or she is presented with the thing itself, while instead it is only an image, a trace, a residuary impression of "absent objects or persons." For the dream is a fresh perception produced by the return of the trace as a hallucinatory object. In their automatic mechanism, timing devices left behind by their departed makers, dreams have a complicity with death.

Demonic is also the fact that those revenants, those returning sensory traces, have, for Aristotle, real effects. This is how he explains the event of oneiric foresight:

> As, when something has caused motion in water and air, this moves another and, though the cause has ceased to operate, such motion propagates itself to a certain point, though the prime mover is not present; just so it may well be that a movement and a consequent sense-perception should reach sleeping souls from the objects from which Democritus represents phantoms and emanations as coming; that such movements, in whatever way they arrive, should be more perceptible at night . . . ; and that they shall be perceived within the body owing to sleep, since persons are more sensitive even to slight internal movements when asleep than when awake. It is these movements then that cause images, as result of which sleepers foresee the future.[19]

"Alien movements," then, happen in the real. But what is the status of the real they contribute to shape, as a woven texture of returning traces? Twisting Aristotle's definition in the direction of Freud and Lacan, but also in the sense of the understanding of dreaming in the qṣar, and in the philosophical tradition of Sufi Islam, I call these "alien movements" *transfers*. Ibn al-ʿArabî named *intiqâl*, "transferal," the kind of sleep in which there are dreams: "I call this state a transferal, because meanings are transferred from their disengagement from substrata into a state of being clothed in substrata, like the manifestation of the Real in the forms of corporeal bodies, or of knowledge in the form of milk, or similar things."[20]

Transfers then: as one can speak of a transfer of funds from one account to another, of a transfer of property from one person to another, of a transfer of water from one irrigation canal to another; of a transfer of sense from a word, or a language, to another; of a transfer of the impossible into the possible, and of the invisible into a concrete form.[21]

It is in terms of energetic *transfers of affect* that Freud spoke of the way Elisabeth von R. loved her brother-in-law without her knowing it, through an acute pain in her upper right leg.[22] And it is as involuntary *transfers into the past*—the fact of being literally carried over into another time—that Breuer described the way Anna O. was "carried over" or "transferred" into the previous year, which she relived day by day, seized by emotions she could not control, reminiscences attached to forgotten scenes she could describe only in her *condition seconde,* when a voice spoke in her stead from the depth of her absences. Involuntary *transfers from the past* haunted instead Frau Cacilie—she called them "old debts"—when an old memory "suddenly broke in upon her clear and tangible, and with all the freshness of a new sensation."[23]

His hysteric patients were affected by "ideogenic disturbances," Freud wrote, temporal disorders that produced somatic symptoms that were painful inscriptions in the flesh. Yet they were also pictorial representations, visual returns of nonrepresented affect. Hermetic hieroglyphics of desire, ruins of a forgotten city. Because for Freud a transfer is the displacement of an affect, a memory, or a thought, which manifests itself elsewhere, in another locality and in a disguised form. "Her mask reveals a hidden sense," he wrote in his notebook upon his first encounter with Elisabeth von R.

Yet as much as he struggled with his hysteric patients to unearth the "buried site," to bring it back to light through a hermeneutical work of "extraction" and "recollection," which he himself compared to an archeological dig,[24] Freud had to recognize that the city was an elusive realm of absence, and that it could surface only as ruins. Because its nature was unknowability, and the modality of its presence was forgetting. Masks—the other voices and somatic symptoms of hysteria, or the displaced hieroglyphics of the dream—did not hide a sense; they were themselves revelations of sense. They were veiled apparitions from the realm of the impossible.

It is in the sense of a forgetting that is foundational and independent of any possible work of recollection, and of a veil, a disguise, that is original—"ce qui se montre, ne se montre que sous une Verkleidung, déguisement, et postiche aussi"[25]—that Lacan speaks of the nonplace of the unconscious through the figure of *les limbes*—Limbo, resting place of the souls of children born dead. "Something that holds itself back, suspended in a waiting area, I would say, of the unborn." It is a limbo of the unborn and unrealized, an intermediate frontier zone[26] populated with larvae, or with sylphs, gnomes, and other "ambiguous mediators" (like those creatures populating the intermediate world in the cosmic constructions of the Gnostics, Lacan says); an intermediate world that shows itself fugitively, as an opening of shutters that immediately close up, and makes itself felt as a dimension of "being surprised," a disturbance, a fissure, an obstacle, a stumbling upon that reveals a beyond, and by which the subject feels overwhelmed: *depassé* and *surpris.* The subjective function is a relationship with this fundamental unknowing.

And Lacan invokes the Freudian figure of the navel, the navel of the dream, "the spot where the dream reaches down into the unknown." It is the place where language and interpretation come to a halt, and where knowledge becomes irrelevant. That *centre d'inconnu,* that "core of unknown," designates for Lacan the scar from which the subject is born from the trauma of loss, the way the scar/hole of the anatomical navel is the physical memory of the place where the umbilical cord was once cut. It is there that the subject is "touched."

> At first, the unconscious is manifest to us like something that holds itself in suspense in a waiting area, I would say, of the unborn. . . . Certainly this dimension should be evoked in a register that has nothing unreal, or de-real, about it, but is rather un-realized. It is never without danger to stir anything in that zone of larvae, and perhaps it is part of the analyst's role, if the analyst is performing it properly, to be besieged—I mean really—by those in whom he has evoked this world of larvae without always being able to bring them to the light of the day. Discourse in this context is not always harmless. . . . It is not without effect that, even in a public speech, subjects are addressed and aimed at, and they are touched at what Freud calls the navel—the navel of dreams—he writes, to designate their ultimate center of unknown, which is simply, like that same anatomic navel that represents it, that gap I am talking about.
>
> . . . I mentioned the function of limbo. I might also have spoken of what, in the constructions of the Gnostics, are called the intermediary beings—sylphs, gnomes, and even higher forms of these ambiguous mediators.[27]

The unconscious, that "limbo," is not a buried city to dig out—an object to unveil and bring to light—but an elusive Other Scene of absence, which manifests itself as hole, fainting, disjunction; or as mask, veil, disguise. Ontically fragile, deceptive, and evanescent, the status of the unconscious is not ontological; it is ethical. What counts is not the hermeneutical question of how to extract the truth of its content (in itself, it has neither truth nor content); but the dialogical dimension of, in Lacan's words, "par qui et pour qui le sujet pose sa question."[28] The reality of the unconscious is intersubjective. Because, Lacan says, the unconscious is both inside and outside: it is "what is inside the subject, but which can be realized only outside, that is to say, in that locus of the Other in which alone it may assume its status."[29] This implies that interpretation is not the decoding of readable texts stored in the hidden archives of the buried city. It is the intersubjective production of "openings," in which the desire of the other plays an active role.

Transference, then—some form of transferring—is foundational; it is constitutive of the position of subject. Transference is not the therapeutic illusion that in theories of psychoanalytic technique, Freud's included, is treated as an instrument to use and to resolve. It is the actualization of the reality of the unconscious: "le transfert est la mise en acte de la réalité de l'inconconscient."[30] Because a transference is the affirmation of the implication and the tie of two desires. Its give and take—to transfer literally means to carry across—defines the space of intersubjectivity: the only space where the subject can speak.

But what sort of relation to the real is actualized in a transference, and what is the status of that transference—that foreign return—that is my dream?

The psychoanalytic discussion of transference is structured by a paradox. A transference is said to be a fiction, a confrontation in absentia or effigy, yet also to happen in the real, as the repetition, and concrete reproduction, of a past traumatic event. On the one hand, Freud writes, "the patient will weave the figure of the physician with one of the *series* already established in his mind"; a father or mother imago, infantile clichés that are reanimated in the analysis through the screen of the physician, and in absentia. On the other hand, the transference manifestations "render the invaluable service of making the patient's buried and forgotten love-emotions actual and manifest; for in the last resort no one can be slain *in absentia* or in effigy."[31] Transference, in other words, says Freud, is a reproduction of a forgotten piece of past life, vicariously summoned to presence through the screen of the physician-medium, who lends voice and face to a set of absent characters on stage.

In his 1915 paper on recollection, Freud reformulates his point in terms of repetition and transference in analysis.[32] Repetition, he says, in itself a resistance to be defeated, should be allowed during the analytic treatment "as to a playground," for it "constitutes a conjuring into existence of a piece of real life," and as such it is a necessary step on the path to recollection and self-knowledge. Freud goes on to define recollection as repetition's dialectical overcoming, and as the scope of analysis as such. For recollection is understood as the process of conscious self-recognition of the subject within his or her biography. Repetition, instead, is a modality of forgetting: Freud describes it as the involuntary return of a traumatic memory as compulsory action, and stresses the need to "divert into the work of recollection any impulse which the patient wants to discharge in action." Repetition is an illness, a memory disorder that produces visual and somatic hallucinatory effects: "hysterics suffer mainly from reminiscences," Freud writes.[33] As such it must be overcome symbolically, that is, for Freud, it must be represented; amnesia as traumatic memory must give way to a recollection of the trauma. Analytic therapy becomes the field of a struggle between the two opposed forces of recollection and forgetting; a struggle to tame repetition, and make it work at the service of recollection, which alone, Freud says, can restore, and restitute, a sense.

In his discussion of "le noyau du réel," the irreducible "core of the real," Lacan questions the terms of the dialectics of repetition/recollection, a dialectics of restitution, as this was formulated in the early Freudian writings on technique. The real is a *rencontre immémorable*, an encounter beyond memory; it is only manifest in the mode of absence, as a missed encounter, and in the sphere of the dream: "Le sujet chez soi, la remémorialisation de la biographie, tout ça ne marche que jusqu'à une certaine limite qui s'appelle le réel. . . . Le réel est ici ce qui revient toujours à la même place—à cette place où le sujet en tant qu'il cogite, où la res cogitans, ne le rencontre pas."[34] Lacan leads the discussion of repetition away from the question of recollection and in the direction of a forgetting without reserve, beyond the scope of any possible restitution of the "alien movement" to its "prime mover." He leads the discussion toward Freud's speculative texts on repetition compulsion and the death drive, where repetition, forgetting, and death are central features of the symbolic.[35]

For Lacan repetition is intractable. It is not the presentment of a forgotten piece of one's life, a lost belonging to reclaim as one's own, but an alien return, a re-turn around a core of unknown, which, for the subject, takes place necessarily *in absentia*, and within an Other Scene of absence. It is related to that fundamental unknowing that designates, Lacan writes, "the complete, total locus of the network of signifiers, that is to say, the subject, where it was, where it has always been, the dream. At this place the ancients recognized all sort of things, including, on occasion, messages from the gods."[36] It is there that the subject is found, and it is that subject who is activated in the transference.[37]

In that Other Scene, which Lacan calls "an *entre-deux* between perception and consciousness," a boundary zone in which the subject is "knocked," a certain beyond makes itself felt. It makes itself felt when the subject is not "at home," when it travels outside, beyond any possible autobiographical reappropriation, to the only place where, paradoxically, it can be "at home," but in the mode of absence: "Here, in the field of the dream, you are at home."[38]

To image the Elsewhere of that return, which is both a return and the shock, always new, of an intractable encounter with the real, Lacan refers to a dream. It is a dream Freud relates in the prologue to the seventh chapter of the *Traumdeutung,* the chapter which develops his topography of the psyche as a dynamic articulation of superimposed localities, and formulates the hypothesis of a fundamental incompatibility between memory and consciousness.[39]

As if following an invisible thread originating in the dream itself, a few pages after its account Freud raises the issue of uninterpretability. He first talks about the "forgetting of dreams." The impression one has upon awakening, of having forgotten part of a dream, or of having distorted it in recollection, is secondary, he says, compared to that fundamental distortion that is the dream-work itself. Because the dream is the veiled presentment of desire, which can only show itself through its figures. Beyond the dream is not a hidden readable text, but an intricate opacity, a scar of unrepresentability. Behind the dream, there is the navel.

Freud:

> There is often a passage in even the most thoroughly interpreted dreams which has to be left obscure; this is because we become aware during the work of interpretation that at that point there is a tangle of dream-thoughts which cannot be unravelled and which moreover adds nothing to our knowledge of the content of the dream. This is the dream's navel, the spot where it reaches down into the unknown. The dream-thoughts to which we are led by interpretation cannot, from the nature of things, have any definite endings; they are bound to branch out in every direction into the intricate network of our world of thought. It is at some point where this meshwork is particularly close that the dream-wish grows up, like a mushroom out of its mycelium.[40]

Beyond the dream, Lacan translates, enveloped in its figures, there is the real: the hole, the phantasm, the loss, which is irreducible to thought. The hole, the scar, the loss, from which the subject is born; because by "showing the impossible," it signifies what is irreducible to sense.[41] This haunting dream is a sudden appearance, a "corporalization," of that real.

Freud:

> A father had been watching beside his child's sick-bed days and nights on end. After the child had died, he went into the next room to lie down, but left the door open so that he could see from his bedroom into the room in which his child's body was laid out, with all the candles standing round it. An old man had been engaged to keep watching over it, and sat beside the body murmuring prayers. After a few hours' sleep, the father had a dream that his son was standing beside his bed, caught him by the arm and whispered to him reproach-

> fully: *"Father, don't you see I am burning?"* He woke up, noticed a bright glare of light from the next room, hurried into it, and found that the old watchman had dropped off to sleep and that the wrappings and one of the arms of his beloved child's dead body had been burned by a lighted candle that had fallen on them.[42]

At the outset, there is an issue of sleep. This anguishing dream seems to be produced just for the sake of prolonging sleep, Freud writes. Under the effect of the flames, which he must have perceived in his sleep through the open door, and *instead of awakening,* the father has a dream. And in that uncertain space "between perception and consciousness," his dream redoubles the scene of the event. While in the "next room" the mortal remains of his child are being consumed by the flames, the father dreams/sees his dead son standing beside his bed, catching him by the arm and saying, "Father, don't you see I am burning?"

The topography of the two rooms doubles the topology of the two scenes: the scene in which the child lies dead, his arm consumed by the flames; and the scene in which the dead child returns, and catches his father by the arm in an uncanny inversion of life and death. Between the two rooms is the frame of an open door, a threshold and a limit: between waking and sleep, between life and death, between this world and the other. For the dream happens *on the limit,* in that ambiguous mode of presence, Lacan says, of the "*I am* before awakening." Who, what, where, is the *I* of the statement "I am asleep?" It shares some of the uncanny temporality of the statement "And thus we all died," in a tale from the *Thousand and One Nights,* the story of the intemporal City of Brass.

> *"And thus we all died" is inscribed on a tablet attached to the deceptively alive body of a beautiful damsel, "we died as thou beholdest, and left what we had built and what we had treasured. This is our story: and after the substance there remaineth not aught save the vestige."*[43] *The damsel herself is a vestige, the former queen of the former city, vicariously addressing her speech to a future audience from the distance of an incommensurable past. "She seemed as though she were looking at people, and observing them to the right and the left." The Amir Musa was deceived by her looks, and he saluted her as a living person, "Peace be on Thee." But his wazir warned him that the damsel was dead. She was an automaton, a mask, a mechanism without soul: "her eyes had been taken out after her death, and quicksilver had been put beneath them... so they gleam." "How can she return your salutation?" he said reproachfully to the Amir Musa. Yet from the infinite distance of her embalmed body there came a return, which was a mortal strike of absence itself, the delayed blow of a* dispositif à retardement. *And when*

the wazir touched the body of the queen to steal her precious attire, the two slave automatons that guarded her sides struck him with their swords and cut his head off. The threshold is impassable and impossible; only a relation at distance, in absentia or effigy, or through the absence of sleep, can be maintained with the dead.[44]

It is with the uncanny temporality of a vestige that the child returns to the father. He addresses him with words forever severed from his living speech, for like the tablet inscription citing the words of the dead queen, a voice from an incommensurable past, the child's speech is automatic. "Father, don't you see I am burning?" a montage, Freud says, of phrases the boy must have pronounced at different moments in his life, during his illness, perhaps: fragments of speech that outlived him, and returned to haunt the father in his sleep, in that house where everyone is either dead or asleep, and only that voice, the voice-off of the child, makes itself heard.

Only during sleep, in that state of absence that resembles death, can the lost child return to the father and catch him by the arm. It happens in a barzakh, the intermediate world of absence-presence whose temporality, Ibn al-ʿArabî writes, is that of a "hereafter"; a hereafter that is opened by sleep and explored by dreaming, and in which things are perceived that one "cannot perceive in any other respect"—

And in a tone reminiscent of certain of Ibn al-ʿArabî's reflections on dreaming and sleep, reflections themselves reminiscent of many a Qurʾanic verse about death as awakening,[45] Lacan asks: Where is the real in this dream? To what reality does the father wake up, from that dream that comes to him *instead of* awakening? Is the dream just a reproduction of the "real" event in the next room, the accident of the child's dead body being consumed by fire? Or is something more "fatal" on stage in the repetition of the accident? For the father is not awakened by the flames: he is awakened by the gesture of his dead son, and by that phrase, which "is itself a firebrand—of itself it brings fire where it falls": "Father, don't you see I am burning?" Like a death sentence, this phrase awakens the father to another reality: the reality of loss, of the incommensurable distance, which is imaged, and concretely appears, as the phantasm of his child: "For it is not that, in the dream, he maintains that the son is still alive. But the dead child taking his father by the arm, an atrocious vision, designates a beyond that makes itself heard in the dream. Desire manifests itself in the dream by the loss expressed in an image at the most cruel point of the object. It is only in a dream that this truly unique encounter can occur. Only a rite, an endlessly repeated act, can commemorate this encounter beyond memory—for no one can say what the death of a child is, except the father qua father, that is to say, no conscious being."[46]

THE JOURNEYS OF THE RÛḤ

> The Real manifest through form is He/not He. He is the limited who is not limited, the seen who is not seen. This situation becomes manifest in the imaginal presence when a person is asleep or absent [*ghaybûba*] from outward sensory things in whatever manner. Imagination in sleep is the most complete and general in existence, since it belongs to both the gnostics and the common people.
>
> Death and sleep share in that into which meanings pass.
> —Ibn al-ʿArabî

When Si Lḥassan u Aḥmed explicates to me the reality of dreaming, the Elsewhere of the dream is expressed through the figure of traveling—*s-sfar.*

But dreaming is not just any journey, even though most traveling shares in its quality of essential displacement to some extent: by the fact of the road, of not being "at home," by being cut off from one's own.[47] Dreaming is a journey away from oneself into another region, a region Si Lḥassan does not name as an abstract locality but as an "exit"—the verb he keeps using is *khraj:* an exit into an Outside. The exiting is that of the soul, the rûḥ, a person's noncorporeal spirit, which leaves the body during the state of absence that is sleep. It leaves the body, drawn by an affliction or a longing, and wanders outside. This "exit" is not a coming out to seek a home elsewhere; it is an exit as such, a state of absolute homelessness of the soul, which wanders on the Outside, suspended, in an *entre-deux* between life and death. In that interim, belonging ceases to exist; and "my soul" is no longer my own.

Outside can be anywhere. The "place" of the journey can be a familiar space, a bridge over the irrigation canal, an alley in the qṣar, a room in the house; or a distant city, a foreign country, Germany or France, emblems of that *gharb* where the sun dies and people disappear; or America, says Si Lḥassan, turning toward me (who in August 1985, the time of our first conversations on dreaming, had just returned from there). Traveling to distant cities has something of the quality of dreaming, he says, for the self displaced is granted a special vision. But in dreaming what counts is not the place of the journey in itself: Outside is a different modality of the real. "As for the place" Ibn al-ʿArabî writes about dreaming, "that is within the sphere of the moon specifically."[48]

(I write in the margin of conversations with Si Lḥassan, fqîh, *Qur'anic scholar, therapist, and dream interpreter, and of one conversation in*

particular, which we had in the fall of 1985. Our entretien *has spanned the space of five years, and the dream itself, that dream which is not-mine, can be read as a return in that exchange.)*

Outside is an atopical domain of the limit, beyond the constraints of space and time, a Hereafter where the living intersect with the dead. In the hereafter of dreaming—a present postponed, suspended—life and death become possible at once. For the Outside is a space of life-death. It is the lieu of an "encounter"—an *ittiṣâl,* Si Lḥassan says, a contact or juncture that makes possible a transference—between the souls of the living and those of the dead. *Dreams are heterographic:* "Dreams come from these encounters of the soul with the other souls [*arwâḥ*]; from those *contacts* or *transfers.*"

Dreaming has the uncanny temporality of vestiges. The composite, superimposed present of the dream is the space of a dialogue between interlocutors from the past and the future, contemporaries *in absentia* across the lapse of an incommensurable time. A dream, says Si Lḥassan, is "the knot of the past when it fastens the future [*l-ʿalâqa dyâl l-mâḍî ilâ shedd f l-mustaqbal*]." For the soul, disengaged from the person during sleep, "enters in contact" with things past and things to come.

Yet dreaming is not a journey of the "living" through the world of the Beyond. The rûḥ of the person asleep, which leaves the body and journeys through the Outside, cannot be called alive; in its "exiting" it has passed through death. *"Ilâ naʿs l-insân kaysemma mât,"* Si Lḥassan says, "when a person is asleep it is considered that he is dead." The life of the soul on the Outside has the ambiguous status of a *survie,* of a virtual life: the soul outlives the person, and wanders like a vestige in an afterlife. Unlike the situation depicted in the tale of the City of Brass, where travelers in flesh and blood engage in an anachronic dialogue with a dead princess, in the Other Scene of the dream all the interlocutors are absent; or rather, they make their appearance as absences-presences. Because sleeping and dreaming are a passage through "my own death"; in them, as Ibn al-ʿArabî writes, "death is made present," and the rûḥ witnesses the world of the barzakh. But can death ever be one's own? ("Celui qui rêve dort," Blanchot writes, "mais celui qui rêve n'est déjà plus celui qui dort, ce n'est pas un autre, une autre personne, c'est le pressentiment de l'autre, ce qui ne peut plus dire moi, ce qui ne se reconnaît ni en soi ni en autrui.")[49] The "sphere of the moon," stage of the otherworldly encounters, has the anonymity and impersonality of death itself. It is in the course of these encounters, says Si Lḥassan, that the intemporal dialogues of dreaming will take place, where "words are uttered that are effective, other words that have no effect, and meanings are expressed metaphorically, calling for symbolic interpretation."

Si Lḥassan

There is a Qur'anic verse that tells us "God takes the souls at death and those who die not, [he takes] during their sleep; he keeps those on whom He has passed the decree of death, and the others he sends back [to their bodies] for a term appointed" [Allâhu yatawaffâ al-nufûsa ḥîna mawtihâ, wa allatî lam tamut fî manâmihâ; fa yumsiku allatî qaḍâ ʿalayhâ al-mawtu, wa yursilu al-ukhrâ ilâ ajalin musammâ, *Qur'an 39:42*].

In other words, the souls God takes from people during their sleep, he sends back to their bodies at awakening; the others he keeps. You see, this verse of the Qur'an gives us a sign [dalîl]: *God takes our souls at death, but he also takes our souls during our sleep, when we dream. Because when a person is asleep it is considered that he is dead* [ilâ nʿass l-insân kaysemma mât]. *The Qur'an says, "And those who die not [he takes] during their sleep/dream"* [w-allatî lam tamut fî manâmihâ]: *if, in other words, you are not dead once and for all, but you are just dreaming, you keep dreaming for a while and then the soul returns to its place, it reenters the body.*

This is why sleep is called *al-maut aṣ-ṣughrâ,* "the small death," in relation to *al-maut al-kubrâ,* "the great death."[50] Sleep, *nûm, l-mnam* (which also means "dream"), is a "state of absence," a *ghîba,* which reduces the body to its silent materiality and frees the rûḥ to journey in the region of the Beyond. If this journey is final, the rûḥ flies to the barzakh, the intermediate resting place of the souls between this world and the other; and there it awaits the Last Judgment. If the journey—and the absence—is temporary, its memory is the dream. But any temporary absence of the rûḥ is always liable to become permanent. This is why, before falling asleep, one should whisper the Shahada, the profession of faith one is to utter at death.

It is this factor of death that determines the truth value, the authority, and the effectiveness of dreams—a *parole* coming from elsewhere; dreams can resolve conflicts, deliver a person from illness, and determine decisions that change the direction of one's life. Their course can be influenced by prophylactic actions and utterances, and in some contexts they can be ritually induced, as when a person who is ill, paralyzed or possessed goes to a saint's tomb to dream, and sleeps there—sometimes for months or years—waiting for the dream that will bring release. The symbolic economy of certain sanctuaries where the sick and possessed go to seek recovery is rhythmed and regulated by the *parole* of dreams, a *parole* that is law. There is often a dream at the origin of the journey to the saint, a dream that "jails" and keeps the person from leaving the sanctuary, and a dream that brings release. Sometimes the vision comes to someone else, a relative or neighbor, and that *parole,* once interpreted, becomes effective in the life of the person concerned.[51] Often the saint himself appears in the dream—*wqafʿlîa,* "he stood in front of me"—and gives instructions as to what needs to be done, sanctions a transgression or grants the path to recovery. When the dream comes, it brings about a decisive turn at the impasse of a person's life. These dreams that have the power to bring about sudden understandings and sea changes in life are visions—"veridical and sound visions" [*ru'yâ ṣâliḥa ṣaḥîḥa*], Si Lḥassan explains; they become nodal junctures in the course of a person's life, and are narrated as foundational events.[52]

If the "message" of a dream is perceived as crucial or dangerous, or if its mode of presentation is allegorical (for some visions, and "veridical visions" in particular, are perceived as self-evident), people go to a dream interpreter such as Si Lḥassan, who has a copy of *Muntakhab al-kalâm fî tafsîr al-aḥlâm* and knows the keys of interpretation. But any layperson has a sense of how to read dreams, and of how to act in response to their injunctions. (For dreams are injunctions, gifts, coming from Elsewhere, and embroil the dreamer in a web of obligations and exchanges. Dreams *do*, and like all that does, they can heal, harm, or even kill.)

The Murderous Dream of Ḥaddya Milûd

Ḥaddya Milûd is older and imposing. Once when I was ill, against my advice she spent the night with me. Early in the morning she spoke of her life. She told me about her first husband, the cousin she didn't like, and about her second husband, the man she loved and who loved her (*bghîtu u bghânî*), and about her divorce, caused by the envious intervention of her mother, and the third marriage with a man she didn't want, into a family that didn't accept her, and the death of her children. It was then, at the point of impasse, that she started reciting a series of dreams. It was a beading of stories in which real-life situations, the circumstances of dreaming, and the dreams themselves were so tightly interwoven as to become inseparable. They were all real. Each dream was a knot in the textile of her existence. The focus was on what the dream had done. With the force of her wounded affect, what the dream had accomplished, each time, was a revenge. One dream is particularly poignant. In Ḥaddya's own interpretation, it did not foresee a disaster to come, but made it happen. In dreaming about it, she said, and in recounting her dream, she had caused her rival's destruction.

(It is found in a hadith of the Prophet: "The visionary dream is the forty-sixth part of prophecy. For the person concerned, it is like a bird; as soon as one speaks about it, it happens." In a different version this tradition reads: "The visionary dream remains for a person like a bird as long as it is not interpreted. As soon as it is interpreted, it becomes real.")[53]

> *The day I told you I fought with my sister-in-law, that Ṭama bint Ḥussein... it was the time when the brothers split up, and each was making his own fire. They used to make me sterile, all the time, the*

wives of the other brothers. They made me sterile and I endured. There was nothing I could do. Until one day she threw a false accusation against me: "Ḥaddya stole my lentils." There was a field of lentils that she and I had watered and taken care of. She got four measures, I got four measures, plus one of my tashghalt, because I went harvesting with the owner. One day I stayed at the house to mill, and when Ṭama and the other women came back from the well she said, "I left the door of my room open. Ḥaddya must have gone in and stolen my lentils." And instead it was she who had stolen from her husband. She stole and sold everything she could. She had no children and didn't trust that he would keep her. I said to the other women, "I didn't take any of her lentils. I have five ʿabrat and she has four." We measured and found that what she had put in her room was still there. I told her "Liar!" and beat her.

One day I went to Aghalal for a visit. I had a sheep, big and in good health, with a kid of just twenty days. While I was gone, she poisoned them. And she was pregnant, then, that Ṭama. I went to a soothsayer, and she said that it was a short woman who had killed my sheep. Ṭama was pregnant and I dried out, I dried out, I had become sterile... Moḥammed stayed dormant in my womb for four years. I had given birth to an Aḥmed and he had died. I had a daughter, Bakka, and she had died...

And I went to sleep the sleep of God. I dreamed that Ṭama gave birth to a boy as big as a goat, and that he fell into a bag and died, and that her husband had a stroke and his mouth was bent to one side, and that, as for her, her tongue was hanging this much. And there was a one-eyed Mina who sold azrûg.[54] This happened in sleep, she said to me, "Come, I'll make peace between you two." And I said, "I am not making peace with her, she accused me falsely and killed my sheep." Then she said, "Don't embitter yourself [la trefdî hemm], she falsely accused you and killed your sheep, but you killed her son. If you want to go on, go on, if you want to stop, stop."

Tatta (my husband's sister) woke me up. She was sleeping next to me. She said, "Ḥaddya, Ḥaddya, why are you shaking like this, what are you saying in your sleep?" I said, "I had a dream, God protect us, may it only turn out to be goodness and peace, khayr wa slâma, this is what I dreamed."

"Mina the one-eyed is right," she said, "what does an enemy do with an enemy? Only revenge pays. Ṭama is about to give birth, ʿAysha is also about to give birth, and you are dried up, you have become sterile, and now you dreamt about it and it's taken care of."

Three or four days later, God have mercy, Ṭama had a baby as huge as a pillow. Before she even reached the next morning, Those People *[the jinns] came and took her. Her tongue was hanging and her mouth was running with blood—this happened in this world* [f d-dunya]*—I came running from my room but I didn't want to see, because when I had the dream I thought it wasn't true. I asked my husband's sister, the one to whom I told the dream, to go see. She went and found that Ṭama had fallen on top of a bag over her baby in a blood bath, her tongue was hanging and the baby was dead. Precisely what I had dreamed had happened. My dream came true. This is why people say, "Don't tell your dreams! Don't tell your dreams at all!"*

Dédoublement

Sleep, says Si Lḥassan, puts a person in contact with the Beyond by producing a cleavage, a split, a *dédoublement,* between the rûḥ and a faculty that he calls *r-ruḥânî.* (Grammatically, *r-ruḥânî* is the nominalization of an adjective formed from the root *rwḥ,* the same root from which the noun *rûḥ* derives; it could be translated "spiritual entity" or "soullike.")

The ruḥânî manifests itself as a separate agency during the state of absence that is sleep, and it is related to the rûḥ as its mundane double. The rûḥ is "fastened" to the ruḥânî, Si Lḥassan explains. The gap of their knotting, a juncture that is also a gulf, opens on the other reality of the dream—

The rûḥ is invisible and unknowable, "incommensurable" ("it bears no similitude," says Si Lḥassan); and as such has no form. It is the ruḥânî that "fixes" it in place, "settles it down" inside a body. For, of itself, the rûḥ has a tendency to migrate and err; it is an elusive nomadic principle. In its intemporal detached state, it cannot be called alive. It remains a virtual possibility in a limbo—it remains "unborn." Its knotting, its fixing, locates it, and brings it to life by lending it a form.

The ruḥânî is manifest in the vital signs of the unconscious body during sleep. It remains rooted in the body, and "connects" with the rûḥ in its journeys. It could be understood as a bodily principle, for Si Lḥassan also describes it as blood, the blood that flows in the veins and fuels the heart and the brain. In fact, it may seem reminiscent of that "rûḥ ḥayawânî jismânî" (animal corporeal spirit) Ibn Khaldûn mentions in his discussion of dreaming, and describes as a "thin vapor" located in the heart, in reference to Galen's anatomy.[55]

But even though Si Lḥassan provides a physiological location for the mundane soul, his theoretical explanation follows a very different track. The ruḥânî cannot be just a bodily vapor, because in his account, rûḥ and ruḥânî are not different principles: "they are both one and two." They are the result of a doubling, by way of which the rûḥ is settled in place and *corporalized,* and can come to existence in a vicarious, visible form. The nature of the ruḥânî is that of a reflection, a "real image," a *mithâl,* Si Lḥassan says: "It is like with a puddle of water when it is hit by sunlight. The light hits the water, and you see a reflection on the wall." The ruḥânî is a trace. In the virtual reality of the dream, it is the semipresent lieutenant of the semi-absent soul.

Barzakh

The Elsewhere of dreaming according to Si Lḥassan is akin to the intermediate world of the barzakh in Ibn al-ʿArabî's cosmological topology: the region of the boundary and domain of the Imagination, in which contraries come together, bodies are spiritualized and spirits become manifest in corporeal forms. Tajassud al-arwâḥ, *"corporalization of the spirits," and* tarawḥun al-ajsâm, *"spiritualization of the bodies," are the two terms by which Ibn al-ʿArabî describes the vicissitudes of the rûḥ in the intermediate imaginal world; they are interpenetrations of* rûḥ/arwâḥ, *"spirit/spirits," and* jism/ajsâm, *"body/bodies," even grammatically. "A barzakh," writes Ibn al-ʿArabî, "is something that separates two other things while never going to one side, as for example, the line that separates shadow from sunlight." Dreaming is journeying on that thin line.*

Barzakh: *a partition, a bar or barrier, an isthmus between two; the intermediate zone between two states or things; intermediate degree of something. The place or state in which the soul waits, after death and before Judgment. A limbo.*

In the Qurʾan (23:100) the term barzakh *is found in the sense of limit or barrier, the line that establishes a difference: "He has let free the two bodies of flowing water; one palatable and sweet, and the other salt and bitter; yet he made a barrier between them* [barzakh], *a partition which is forbidden to be passed." The barrier is also the limit, the bar, between life and death and death and Judgment: "Until, when death comes to one of them, he says: 'O my Lord! send me back [to life] in order that I may work righteousness in the things I neglected.' By no means! It is but a word he says. Before them is a barzakh [partition] till the day they are raised up" (Qurʾan 23:99).*

The concept of barzakh is central in Ibn al-ʿArabî's thought and summarizes the condition of all existence, itself understood as a being-in-between: "There is nothing in existence but barzakhs, since a barzakh *is the arrangement of one thing between two other things . . . and existence has no edges."*[56] *The barzakh is both a limit and an* entre-deux, *the* entre-deux *of the limit: something that stands between two things, both separating and joining them, combining the attributes of both. For Ibn al-ʿArabî it comes to be synonymous with the* ʿâlam al-mithâl,

> *"the intermediate world of real images." In the Moroccan oral imaginary, the barzakh is concretely visualized as a beehive, where the* arwâḥ *of the dead rest waiting for the Final Judgment, after the first "Questioning" by the angel inquisitor, and where each rûḥ has a niche.*

Between the rûḥ in its journey and the ruḥânî asleep there remains a link, a hinge, a connection, which Si Lḥassan compares to the link that ground control maintains with a satellite orbiting in the sky. He calls that link an *iṣîl.* From the same verbal root *wṣl* as *ittiṣâl*—the "encounter " or "contact" of the rûḥ with the souls of the dead—an iṣîl is a conjunction, predicated upon a disjunction, which makes possible a transference. (When, in the brightness of the desert night, a satellite can be seen going by, people notice it with a sense of unfamiliar familiarity; they know satellites transmit images long distance, to and from different parts of the world.)

An iṣîl creates a more or less impermanent relation with an other, an other entity, by way of which something can be passed on. In the qṣar the technical model of the iṣîl is to be found in irrigation; an iṣîl is a hollow palm trunk placed as a bridge between two different canals to allow the transfer of water from one canal to the other. But iṣîl is also reminiscent of *ittiṣâl* in the mystical sense, the "state of contact" with the Beyond in which prophets, having gotten rid of the body and of the conscience, are receptive to revelation and visions.

There is an iṣîl, then, a link made possible by a disjunction, between the rûḥ and the ruḥânî during sleep. It is the channel of a transmission, of the sending of images which is the dream: "It is the rûḥ that sees: the rûḥ sees and sends a vision [*naẓar*] of what it sees to the ruḥânî. A transmission, I told you, they are in contact with each other, the ruḥânî keeps monitoring the rûḥ in its journey."

As a consequence of this doubling a person can be at the same time here and elsewhere, alive and dead, worldly and otherworldly. Dreams are emissions, translations on Earth—in worldly terms—of the experiences of the rûḥ in the regions of the Outside. The narration of a dream often begins, "Last night I met..."; the reality of the encounter is never questioned. But dreams are distorted, incomplete or allegorical, for the mortal ruḥânî cannot bear the extrahuman knowledge of the rûḥ in direct form. Each dream is a sending from the region of death. In dreaming, I am visited by others, and the knowledge I find in myself upon awakening is never only my own. It is the result of a sharing, in the sense in which it is said *ʿaqlû mushtarak,* "his mind is shared," to describe what happens to someone who has been visited by the jinns.

In Si Lḥassan's Words

1985

(At Si Lḥassan's house, a September afternoon, in the interim between the prayers of l-ʿâṣer *and* l-moghreb. *In the middle of our conversation Si Lḥassan will leave, to walk the distance between his house and the new cement mosque, where he leads the prayer of sunset. On a small round table in front of us is a copy of Ibn Sirîn's* Muntakhab al-kalâm fî tafsîr al-aḥlâm *[Elect words in the interpretation of dreams].)*

Si Lḥassan:

Tafsîr al-aḥlâm, "the interpretation of dreams," follows three avenues... the three avenues of the three classes of dreams. There are dreams [*aḥlâm*] we call *l-khayâl,* a product of the imaginary; they are the product of the desire of the individual soul [*nefs*]. A person longs to do something, or his mind is afflicted with something, and when he goes to sleep his rûḥ [soul, spirit] comes out of the body and his ruḥânî stays in. He is preoccupied with something and dreams of it...

And there are *ar-ruʾyât,* dreams which are "veridical and sound visions" [*ruʾyâ ṣaliḥa ṣaḥîḥa*]: like the visions of Sîdna Yusuf, and the dreams in which the Qurʾan descended to the Prophet Muḥammad. Like the visions of prophets. We have in the hadith that the veridical dream is one forty-sixth part of prophecy, and that revelation began for the Messenger of God through veridical dreams...

And there are dreams that are demonic visions [*ruʾyâ shaîṭaniya*], or visions induced by the jinns... these are a cause of confusion in the person. Dreams are always true when they are prophetic visions. But ourselves, we are simple people and not prophets, and our dreams are mixed. Some dreams come to us as true visions [*kayn ruʾyâ lî katjî lîna ṣaḥîḥa*], some dreams pass without even our noticing, and some we forget. And there are dreams that are products of the imagination [*khayâl*], and nightmares, frightening dreams [*ruʾya llî hiya ḥawla*]; you can't speak, you can't move, you feel as if an unbearable weight overwhelms you...

DREAMS—Vocabulary used by Si Lḥassan

L-ḤULM (noun, f. sing.), *l-aḥlâm* (pl.), and *ḥalam* (verb): dream and to dream in the most general sense; becoming, doing something (in the future); to have or gain insight.

AR-RUʾYÂ (noun, f. sing.), *ar-ruʾâ* (pl.): visionary dream, vision (from *raʾâ,* to see).

MANÂMA (noun, f. sing.), *l-manâm* (pl.): both dream vision and sleep, from *nâma,* to sleep, and *nawm,* sleep.

ITTIṢÂL (noun, f. sing.): contact, transmission, dream

(When the rûḥ comes out of the body during sleep, where does it go?)

The rûḥ wanders, she [it] wanders around. Because, I'll explain to you:

The rûḥ is fastened to the ruḥânî [*mshedda ʿala ruḥânî*]. It is tied to it, attached; and as such it dwells inside the human body. It settles there. When the rûḥ comes out, when it vacates the body during sleep, it does not leave completely; for when it leaves completely, it does not return. The ruḥânî remains in its place, and it remains like that iṣîl, that connection, that link, that contact, which is like the connection the ground-control maintains with a satellite [*ṣârûkh*] orbiting in the sky...[57]

Like a radar: this is how the ruḥânî monitors the movements of the rûḥ. Because without that connection, without that iṣîl, the ruḥânî on Earth wouldn't know the whereabouts of the rûḥ in its journey, it would not know what it does and what it sees, and would be unable to bring it back...

Between them is a hinge, a transmission, an iṣîl.

> IṢÎL (noun, vernacular): connection, tie, ligament, isthmus, contact. From the root *wṣl*, to connect, join, interlock, establish a contact, to get in touch (by telephone), and so forth.
>
> WAṢLA (noun, classical): junction, juncture, connection, contact, fastening, tie, link, hinge, line of communication.
>
> TAWṢÎL (noun, classical): uniting, joining, connection, electric contact, feed wire, electric circuit; communication, transmission, transfer, dispatch; *tawṣîl ilâ al-arḍ*, ground connection (radio).
>
> ÎṢÂL (noun): joining, connecting, communication, transmission.
>
> ITTIṢÂL (noun, classical and vernacular): connectedness, juncture, conjuncture, link, contact, liaison, getting in touch, tuning in, telephone connection. (The national telephone company in Morocco is called Ittiṣâlât al-Maghrib.) In the Sufi vocabulary, state of contact with the divine. In Si Lḥassan's use, an *ittiṣâl*, or contact, is the "sending" of the dream; *ittiṣâl* becomes synonymous with dream (*ru'yâ, manâm, aḥlâm*).

(The ruḥânî, then, is the lieutenant of the rûḥ on the ground, its substitute, the sign of the fact that the rûḥ is absent and yet in touch, elsewhere and yet here...)

The ruḥânî... it is like with a puddle of water when it is hit by sunlight. The light hits the water, and you see light on the wall. Or like a mirror when it reflects the sun. It is that [reflected] light that is called ruḥânî. The ruḥânî remains inside the body and fixes the rûḥ in place; and the rûḥ stays alive [*kaystaqarr ḥayy rûḥ*]. If the ruḥânî is no more inside the body, the rûḥ vacates it at once [*matbqash rûḥ*]. For it is the ruḥânî that captures the blood [*kayḥbes ddem*], that keeps the blood from flowing out...

When the rûḥ journeys out of the body, it meets with other arwâḥ [plural of *rûḥ*], and above all with the arwâḥ of the dead. Because it is understood that when a person dies the rûḥ comes out [*katkhrej r-rûḥ*], it disengages itself from the body completely. It departs, but does not die. It goes to the barzakh. But in the barzakh, that rûḥ longs for the things of this world, it desires dunya [*kaytweḥḥem ʿala d-dunya*]. And it exits, it wanders...

And it is so that the rûḥ of the living encounters the rûḥ of the dead [*katlaqa rûḥ l-ḥayya mʿa l-miyta*]. In their journeys... they meet and exchange news; they compare experiences. The rûḥ of the dead person goes back to the barzakh, and the rûḥ of the living person returns into the body [*jasad*]. All it takes is that the person asleep makes a movement [*kaytḥarrek*] or is about to wake up: and the rûḥ comes back into the body...

Who draws her/it back?

The ruḥânî... the ruḥânî is like a radar, it monitors the journey of the rûḥ... it prevents the rûḥ from leaving entirely...

(The ruḥânî is like a reflected light, you said earlier; what does the rûḥ resemble?)

The rûḥ does not resemble anything, it cannot bear any similitude, it is incommensurable [*ma-kat-shebbeh*]. We say that its image [*mithâl*], its visible form, is the ruḥânî, and that the rûḥ herself is never manifest [*ma-kat-ḍhar-sh*]. The ruḥânî is like cold air [*l-berd*], and it is manifest [*kay-ḍhar*]. It is a sort of wind [*rîḥ*, from the same root as *rûḥ*]. But the rûḥ never manifests itself. A group of Jews came to ask the Prophet about the nature of the rûḥ—

(I interrupt—If I understand, you are saying that the ruḥânî is the visible sign of the rûḥ, its "mithâl" you said, that is, its virtual manifestation in the world of senses; and that it is like the mirror reflection of an absent entity that can manifest itself only that way. For the rûḥ is invisible and ghayb, *inaccessible to experience...)*

The ruḥânî... it is the ruḥânî that animates the *nefs*, and the ruḥânî that regulates the blood flow; for the blood is rooted in the ruḥânî [*r-ruḥânî kaytstaqar ʿalih d-dem*]. If the ruḥânî is in the body there is blood, if ruḥânî is in the body, the body has rûḥ and the person is alive; without ruḥânî there is no blood and no rûḥ. The rûḥ vacates, it is the end. And the person dies...

(The ruḥânî dies?)

The ruḥânî dies, the rûḥ does not. When God created Adam, he made him from molded clay, and when he wanted to sow in him rûḥ [*yzraʿ fih r-rûḥ*], he first created the ruḥânî: the rûḥ followed in that place. The ruḥânî comes first, it becomes blood, and the rûḥ settles in it...

A delegation of Jews came to question the Prophet, they asked him about the nature of the rûḥ, what is its similitude and its "form" [*lâsh ka-*

tṣûwwar]: whether it is like a bird, or like this or that. He said that the rûḥ is the life of God, it belongs to the Lord. And that its knowledge is God's knowledge.[58]

But if we consider the matter from a different angle, we can say that the rûḥ and the ruḥânî are one, they are both one and two. We know this from the Science of Spirits [*ʿilm l-arwâḥ*]. Why do we call jinns *l-arwâḥ?* Because they resemble the rûḥ; [in their essence] they are not manifest. If they want to appear they borrow a form, but of themselves they have no form, like the rûḥ. They go through walls and can enter anything, like the rûḥ. And they are also called *ar-ruḥânîyin* [pl. of *ruḥânî*]. Because the rûḥ is invisible, undetectable [*ma-kat-ḍhar-sh*]. When it settles inside a body, it animates it with movement and the person is alive; when it vacates it, it is death.

RÛḤ: Vocabulary

RÛḤ (colloquial f. Classical both m. and f.): breath of life, soul, spirit (in all senses).[59] Immortal spirit; disembodied soul. *Arwâḥ* (pl. vernacular, in Si Lḥassan's use): disembodied souls, spirits of the dead; jinns.

RÛḤ (in the vernacular lexicon of many crafts): the technical principle that holds a body or machinery together, usually by separating-joining. In weaving, *rûḥ dyâl mansej,* the soul of the loom: the knotting of the threads obtained where one thread comes between two; the articulation of warps that enables the thread work, the movement of the loom. In general, movement, animation.

RÛḤÎYA: spirituality, mentality, frame of mind.

RAWÂḤ: departure, going, leaving, return, rest, repose.

RAWḤA: evening journey.

RÛḤÂNÎ (adj.): spiritual, immaterial, sacred.

RUḤÂNÎ (noun, m., vernacular, in Si Lḥassan's use): visible lieutenant of the invisible rûḥ, mortal. Terrestrial double of the rûḥ during the state of absence of sleep/dreaming.

RUḤÂNÎYA (in the mystical literature): vision, transfiguration.

RUḤÂNIYIN (pl., vernacular): the jinns, the spirits.

RÎḤA: smell, odor, perfume.

RÎḤ (vernacular): wind, air, ventilation; *ariâḥ* (pl.): the jinns.

(What happens to the rûḥ when the person is asleep?)

It wanders... it can just wander around the house or it can journey faraway, while the ruḥânî observes it from a distance. It is like when Russia sends a satellite and people monitor it from Earth. The satellite orbits around [*kay-dûr*]... The same is with the rûḥ in its travels; everything it sees with its eyes is transmitted to the ruḥânî on the ground.

(Si Thami, entering the conversation) She/it can travel wherever she fan-

cies, go to France, go to Germany... while that person is snoring, the ruḥânî is asleep...

The ruḥânî makes the nefs go up and down [*kayṭallaʿ nnefs u inezzelha*].[60] And when, for instance, you touch the person asleep, that rûḥ reaches immediately, it reenters its place, and the person wakes up.

(When the rûḥ goes off on its nightly journeys, what happens to the ʿaqel*— the faculty of reason?)*

Si Lḥassan:

The ʿ*aqel* has nowhere to go, it is asleep. It is the rûḥ that animates it [*hiya lî kat-ḥarrkû*]. If the rûḥ is gone, neither the ruḥânî nor the ʿ*aqel* are alive; they are asleep, and that sleep is like death...

(But the dreams, the visions of the person asleep... who receives them?)

It is the rûḥ that sees: the rûḥ sees and sends a vision of what it sees [*naẓar*] to the ruḥânî. A transmission. I told you, they are in contact with each other, the ruḥânî keeps monitoring the rûḥ [*kayrqebha*], it follows its journey, however far she/it goes... There is a Qur'anic verse that says: "God takes the souls at death, and of those who die not, [he takes] during their sleep; He keeps those on whom He has passed the decree of death, and the others he sends back [to their bodies] for a term appointed [*Allâhu yatawaffâ al-nufûsa ḥina mawtihâ, w-allatî lam tamut fî manâmihâ; fa yumsiku allatî qaḍâ ʿalayhâ al-mawtu, wa yursilu al-ukhrâ ilâ ajalin musammâ*]."

That is, the souls God takes from people during their sleep, he sends back to their bodies at awakening; the others he keeps... You see this verse of the Qur'an gives us a sign [*dalîl*]: God takes our souls at death, but he also takes our souls during sleep, when we dream, because if one is asleep it is as if one were dead [*ila nʿas l-insân kaysemma mât*]. The Qur'an says, "and those who die not [he takes] during their sleep/dream [*w allatî lam tamut fî manâmihâ*]": if in other words you are not dead but you are just dreaming, you go on dreaming for a while and then the soul returns to its place, it reenters the body."

In the scene of the dream all the actors are absent or dead. It is in the depth of that silence, when no one is there, that the words and images from Beyond make themselves heard and seen. They are a show for no one, no consciousness is watching: concrete apparitions of that Beyond itself. The ruḥânî is asleep, and its sleep, Si Lḥassan says, is like death. And the ʿaqel *is dead, the faculty of reason; for, like everything else, its life depends on the rûḥ. The rûḥ is like a battery, Si Lḥassan explains, it is the source of energy that brings life and movement to the body: a battery that departs but never runs out, for "God created the rûḥ from the stuff of life* [men l-mâdda dyâl l-ḥayât]*." Yet in itself the rûḥ is un-*

born in the sense of this world; it depends on its "being settled" for the actualization of the life it bears.[61] *It is the ruḥânî that "fixes" it in place and keeps it in the mode of life; through that fixing, that tying, and that capturing, Si Lḥassan says, "the rûḥ stays alive* [kaystaqar ḥayî r-rûḥ]." *The rûḥ is alive only when it is captured in a form, and even though it is the principle and source of life—of light—it can be alive in the mortal world only through its reflection, its mithâl: that ruḥânî, which is both its image and its corporalization. A light reflected on the wall. This is why the rûḥ as such can be conceived only during the temporary death of sleep. Sleep is the absence that makes possible a partial disengagement of the otherworldly rûḥ from its mundane incarnation. They become then thinkable as such, and can communicate with each other as semiseparate entities.*

For when the rûḥ "exits" the body during sleep, when it vacates its temporary home, it returns for the interim of dreaming to its nomadic state—detached, impersonal, and errant—in which it was before its "fixing," and to which it will return when its tie with this world is definitively cut. It returns to an intemporal entre-deux *of life/death, and as such, in such a suspended state, it enters in contact with the other arwâḥ, disengaged and errant spirits like itself. Some souls are still in contact with their mundane doubles (they are "alive" from the point of view of this world), others are disengaged and forever separate, permanently dwelling on the Outside, in that liminal zone Si Lḥassan names the barzakh.*

To understand the implications of this point a conceptual distinction introduced by Ibn al-ʿArabî may be of help. In writing about the ʿâlam al-mithâl, *the intermediate world of real images, Ibn al-ʿArabî distinguishes between what he calls* al-khayâl al-munfaṣil, *"discontiguous imagination," and* al-khayâl al-muttaṣil, *"contiguous imagination." Contiguous imagination is connected to a personal form and, he says, "disappears with the disappearance of the imaginer."*[62] *Discontiguous imagination is instead "an autonomous presence, constantly receptive towards meanings and spirits." It could be said that during the state of absence that is sleep—a temporary disappearance of the imaginer—the rûḥ exits the realm of contiguous imagination and returns to a discontiguous state, where it journeys among other disconnected imaginal entities and is "constantly receptive towards meanings and spirits."*

The rûḥ "sees," Si Lḥassan says, and "transmits" its visions to its mundane double asleep. But in the intemporal space of the Outside there is no consciousness experiencing and seeing, because the rûḥ in its errancy has no agency; and back in the mundane world there is no one to receive the transmission, for the ruḥânî asleep is as if dead. Yet, in that generalized vacancy, images show, and words make themselves heard. "Words are uttered that are effective." The experiences of the rûọh in the region of the Beyond are "inactual real" experiences: less actual and more real than those of waking life. They happen in a realm other than that of the senses, but it is in the world of senses that they manifest their effect.

Si Lḥassan:

In the state of sleep/dream [*manâm*], the rûḥ enters in contact [*kattaṣal*] with another rûḥ, with other arwâḥ—of the living and the dead. In the course of these encounters, words are uttered that are effective [*l-kalîma lî katshedd*], other words that have no effect, and meanings are expressed metaphorically, calling for symbolic interpretation [*l-kalima lî katshebbeh*]. In dreams that come in an allegorical form, the dreamer sees something, and with interpretation the vision he had turns out to be that thing or something else. There are visions that make the distant farther, and dreams that bring it closer. Anything one dreams, its similitude [*mithâl*], can be found in the process of interpretation [*tafsîr*], in the Book of Dreams or in the understanding of a person who knows. Everything you see in your dreams has a meaning in this world [*ʿandha maʿnâ f d-dunya*].

Do dreams always carry omens about the future?

No, they are also signs from the past [*mâḍî*]. But of the past when it fastens the future, when it implicates the future. If for instance there is in your life something past, something you think is gone, and once again it is about to activate itself in the future [*bghat tḥarrek f l-mustaqbâl*]. A dream is the knot of the past when it fastens the future [*l-ʿalâqa dyâl l-mâḍî ilâ shedd f l-mustaqbal*], when it enters in contact with the future [*ila muttaṣel b-l-mustaqbal*].

Because in dreams the rûḥ enters in contact [*kayttaṣal*] with the past and the future... Dreams come from these encounters with the other arwâḥ, from these "contacts" and transfers [*ittiṣâl*]. Their meaning comes from God, but the *ittiṣâl* itself, the sending of the dream, comes from the other arwâḥ...

And how, from the "ittiṣâl," does one get signs about the future?

Say you have a dream... you dream [*rwiti*] that you are in America, in a certain house, or in one of those other distant, foreign countries; and say that your dream is a sound vision, a vision that becomes reality. A few months later it happens: because what you actually saw in your dream was the vision of the rûḥ that had been there, had been there and back, had met with other arwâḥ, and had actually visited those walls and those streets. Over there—

(Si Thami, interrupting) Sometimes you dream of someone who is dead,

you encounter [in the dream] someone you know... and you have a strange awareness, you know that that person is dead...

Yes, you see a man you know is dead, and he tells you, "Go and tell this and that to my children." If he looks well in the dream you know that his rûḥ rests in peace, but if you see him in poor shape, with torn-up and ill appearance, you know that his rûḥ is suffering, it is in torture, and is asking for an offering of alms in his behalf...

And there are situations in which you encounter the dead in your dream, and you can ask them questions. I encountered once Si Siddiq u l-Mokhtâr, may he rest in peace, and Aḥmed u Ṭyeb, you know, Moḥa's father; he wore that red cap of his, while Si Siddiq u l-Mokhtâr wore his green djellaba, with the hood pulled up over the turban. I encountered them on the bridge over the irrigation canal, by the house of Moḥammed u Aḥmed. They said, "Salâm ʿalikûm," and they smiled. "You are aware that we are dead," they said. I said, "Yes, I am; how are you?" Then I added that I would like to ask them some questions. They said to go ahead and ask. And I asked Aḥmed u Ṭyeb whether the peculiar way in which he used to perform his prayers had been accepted as valid, and what was the verdict on him... And he said, "I am still waiting, just like this, suspended, there is no one who said anything to me." And I didn't wake up until I parted with them.

Dreaming Us

Afterward, after my departure, after Kh.'s death, Si Thami and I developed the habit of telling each other our dreams. It was a way to include Kh. in our relationship now that she was gone, and a way to find images for what found no words. He often saw her in his sleep—she was his wife. Listening to his dreams, for me, was a way to soothe my anger at her disappearance. We were in America, a *gharb* that was foreign, in different ways, to both of us. More foreign, for him, than France or Germany—where exile is codified, predictable, inscribed within a genre of immigrant *étrangeté*. More foreign, for me, than Morocco; due to my Sicilian father, perhaps, but also because its foreignness denied itself to me, disguised by a sameness too quickly taken for granted. Dreaming, Si Thami said, made him feel connected. He dreamed a lot, more than he usually did, and in his sleep he journeyed to the qṣar. Some of his dreams were *ru'yât*, "visions," and he recognized them as such. When they concerned other people, he wrote letters to let them know. For he thought that, in his traveling, his rûḥ was granted insight. One day he recounted a dream that concerned me directly. His telling me had a different value. His dream implicated me, "summoned" me, and spoke of the knots of our exchange, the transfers and the debts, the losses, in the voice of the one who was gone. It was a reproachful voice—

He said to me: Last night we were in the qṣar, you and I, on the side of Ayt l-Bâlî. I don't know why or what we wanted to do, we were inside, near the Derb Sîdî Fâteḥ. I went first. We wanted to drink tea there, where the Derb Sîdî Fâteḥ widens a bit, in that darkness. I was waiting, and at some point Kh. came. She was wrapped in her veil, and I didn't know she was dead. She said, "Give me a dirham [a coin]." She said that she wanted to leave the dirham there, as an offering for Sîdî Fâteḥ. She wanted to have a baby, she said, a boy. She seemed to mean that she had given offerings many times and that she had not been granted her wish; she hadn't had the baby she wanted. I told her that I didn't have anything. I didn't even have a dirham to give her. And she said, "Keep wandering around those alleys, and you'll end up marrying an old maid."

Then the wall opened up, a mouth was breached in the dark alley, and we found ourselves outside, outside the walls of the qṣar, but we felt as if we were inside our house, as if in complete privacy, as if no one would ever dare to come and break that privacy. And ʿAlî was playing with his wheel along the irrigation canal, and Kh. was sitting next to me and had opened her veil. After a while some people came. They were from the village of Tinegdid. There was Mbârk u Lḥassan with some young men, and they were carrying a corpse, the body of a child. I asked them who that was, and they said that the corpse was from the side of the notary, the notary's sister had a baby in Bû Zergân, the baby died, and they came to take the corpse. The youths came to sit with us, and the men put the corpse down by the irrigation canal. I said, "What are you doing, do you want to throw the corpse in the canal?" They said, "Mbârk u Lḥassan will carry the corpse with him to Sefrou" [in real life that man is not from Sefrou]. I said to them, "Are you mad? Do you think there isn't God here? Wherever a person dies, there they must be buried." And I woke up.

When he finished telling his dream we remained silent. What could we say? It was about us all, and about that strange voyage that had been our life together in the qṣar. The detail that touched me was the scene of Kh.'s unveiling herself outdoors, under the false certainty of being in a private space, unseen, and instead being surprised by a funeral procession that carried the corpse of a baby born dead. Was that a warning to me, a commentary on our friendship, on my writing? I went on to negate my sentiment—the dream was *his,* and she was only a phantasm of his imagination. I said mechanically, "That detail of Sefrou in the dream must be because yesterday you and I were talking about that town."

He was irritated by my comment (I was denying the dream its reality, and Kh. the right to speak). "There is no relation at all. It is Mbârk u Lḥassan who told me in the dream that he wanted to take the corpse to Sefrou, not me. I didn't say it. Had I said it, it would have come from my mind. But I didn't, it came from outside me, it is new [*dâk shshi ja jdîd*], I didn't know it before."

"But if you went to Mbârk u Lḥassan and asked him, 'Why do you want to take that dead boy to Sefrou?' wouldn't he think that you were out of your mind?"

"But perhaps my dream refers to something to come, which he doesn't know, but is already in his life."

It is so that the dream of the staircase is both mine and not mine. In a similar sense Yusef's drawing of the qṣar, his cartographic dream, was both his and not his.

The coupling *rsm/sheṭṭeb*—settle and raze, build and destroy, inscribe and erase, remember and forget—evokes the themes of the historical narratives of the qṣar, narratives of fitna. The figures of the empty house, of the aftermath of a death, of a sense of mourning detached from the event that produced it; of the "forgotten graveyard," a paradigmatic place of horror and healing, are recurrent tropes. And the staircase is a model of the work of figuration, a poetic-architectonic image of mourning. The imagery of my dream is a transfer, or a borrowing, from the imaginal history of the qṣar—itself a series of mourning dramas: *Trauerspiele,* in Walter Benjamin's phrase. The loss these dramas lament exceeds any of the stories told; it overflows from one story to another, from one event to another, it transforms and is never resolved. It is as if that history were dreaming itself through me by the effect of a transference. Born in the "sphere of the moon," my dream is also someone else's.

Those to whom I recounted it in the qṣar (it was by long-distance telecommunication, like the nightly transmissions of the rûḥ) understood the dream as a moral commentary on the recent events that, within the space of four years, had led to the emptying out of the old village and the resettling in the New Village in the *berra,* burned by the sun and blown by the wind, far from the gardens and the forgotten graveyards, far from the interweaving of memory and forgetting. That was, for them, the disaster acted out in my dream, a disaster experienced as unique, yet as a return of other scatterings—

The Leaving

It was Kh. who, with her resentful, arrogant way of calling attention to a truth, used to say of herself that she was the rûḥ of the house. If she died, she maintained, if They, as she vaguely called the threat that was eventually to get the better of her, managed to fulfill their wishes, the house of Si Lḥussein would collapse—the textile would unravel. When I walked into the hallway of the house three years later—a year after her death—I heard the prophetic resonance of her words. Was it the electricity newly arrived in the village, the compassionless light of that bulb hanging from high at the center of the narrow hallway, shamelessly illuminating a space once impenetrable even at the peak of the morning sun, violently revealing the remotest corners of the uneven earth walls, the imperfections, the darker spots, the holes where some woman had hidden a bit of carved wool or a bundle of hair, the spiderwebs, the dusty old beams of the ceiling—all that which was not meant to be seen.

Or was it the look of ʿAysha Ahmed, now alone to carry on the work, leaning against the door, motionless, unable to stop her child from crying, uncertain whether she'd ever be able to climb the staircase and go up to the roof to make dinner. Or was it the emptiness of the alley of Bû Ṭwîl the Long, once full of activity and noise, where in the space of two years, one by one the families had moved out to the New Village outside the walls and had left their houses in a last raḥîl.

Um ʿAṣṣa Moḥa had been among the first to move out. She moved out at the end of the summer, when only straw was left on the threshing floors and when the fields abandoned after the harvest had turned yellow and dry. That was the time of rest, people said, mût j-jnân, *"the death of the field." Later on in the season the khmâmes would organize groups of workers to turn over the earth before sowing. Men would be seen gathering at dawn at the landlord's house to eat bread stuffed with lard and to drink tea before work, and the gardens would again be animated by the shouts of men plowing in rows with their hoes. But in that interim the yellow burned soil was all that there was.*

Everything happened quickly. Though everyone had known that Yazîd, her husband, was building berra, *no one in Bû Ṭwîl gave it a thought, until, one day, it was done. All of a sudden people in the alley did not hear her soprano voice modulate her greetings as she walked by in the morning or stopped to say a few words through the* ʿayn d-dâr.[63] *Women missed hearing her laugh, when she made fun of their sorrow or their anger and tickled their bellies until they couldn't hold still. They missed her rages. They missed glimpsing her shape behind the loom at Ṭama Lhasmi's house across the street. She hadn't moved very far, less than a kilometer away, but she had moved the distance of another life.*

She hadn't been eager to move. After a first burst of excitement when her son Moḥammed found water at the site where their new house was to be built, she had second thoughts and for a while tried to forget about it all. When she couldn't, and the anxiety of anticipation got hold of her, she said to herself (but it was to minimize the extent of her fear) that she worried about her sons working in the khalâ, *the wasteland burned by the sun, digging the foundations and preparing the earth-dough for the walls. Talia Ṣalîḥ's son had been struck by Something as he was digging the foundations of his new house only a few months before. True, his house was isolated and much farther out in the desert, while theirs was nestled between the still unbuilt plots of their new neighbors. And true, his wife had not wanted to move out there and might have performed some sorcery. But still he had gone to work one morning and did not come back for dinner at night. Later he was found in a ditch, unconscious, and when he finally opened his eyes he was gone; They had got him. He never did come back to his mind, and now spends the days wandering in the* khalâ *like a haunted beast.*

When the house was ready, or as ready as it would be for a while (the construction of these new houses never ends), she kept postponing the move. Each day some small new obstacle emerged, until Ramadan came and everyone said it would be foolish to spend the fasting month out there in the heat. So they deferred it for another month.

Despite the hate she felt for that house when she was first taken there some twenty-five years before, that old house had now grown dear to her—almost like her father's old house in the Alley of Ayt Ujdîg. But her father's house was now empty, and the alley was too. The houses where she had played as a child, where before her first blood ever came women washed her body with henna to send her away as a bride, those houses whose smell she still smelled in her dreams, were slowly becoming ruins. When she went to visit that alley—it was now a zyâra*—at the alley gate she said in between her lips "Bismillâh ar-raḥmân ar-raḥîm."*[64]

After all, she thought as she gathered the few objects of the household, Bû Ṭwîl had never really been her place. She had moved there when Yazîd decided to marry her, after her troubled divorce with Brahîm u Moḥa. But she had never really adapted to living in a white neighborhood, even though Yazîd her husband had lived there all his life. If he had chosen to work for the Ḥarâr, in the gardens and even in the public works at the irrigation canal, she was still the daughter of Moḥa u Aḥmed the butcher, had been born and raised in the black Fourth of Ayt l-Bâlî, and it is there that she felt she belonged. She had never seen the white quarters until one day when her mother sent her to take some koḥl to a woman in the Alley of Bû Ṭwîl. She arrived at the mouth of the alley at Arḥabî, and at the sight of that long street—a boulevard compared to the winding Alley of Ayt Ujdîg where she was born—she was intimidated and wished to head back. It was a trick of destiny that she wound up marrying there! But now she was leaving, and as she made her way from the darkness of the ground floor all the way to the brightness of the roof sprinkling isugar*—the ritual offering of spices for the spirits of the place, a gift to appease her conscience as much as that of the jinns—she recalled the numerous times the village had pulled out of its walls, had been dismantled and rebuilt, had come apart and was joined together again. Now they were moving out, she said, but, God knows, perhaps her grandchildren will move back in again, and their wives will once more give birth in the room where she generated and gave birth to their fathers, and someone will remember to put* jâwî *at the bottom of the staircase to appease the spirits of the house, and the children will scream, climbing up and down the stairs. But she spoke without conviction, appealing to a structure of cyclical return that, she felt, this time would not return.*

I see her eyes during the fire on that Friday afternoon three years later. Lost between an impossible past and an unthinkable future, the fixity of that gaze haunts me. Three years later the Alley of Bû Ṭwîl is empty. Bû Ṭwîl khwa: *it poured out its people to fill the new Bû Ṭwîl out there, in the wasteland behind the enclosure of the Thursday sûq, behind the Bureau of the Sheikh and the adjoining room of the* ʿadl *who writes documents on market days, behind the Sakka that sells tea, sugar, cigarettes, and flour in days of drought, and the adjoining wall where the powerful among the Ḥarâr sit in the shade, behind the big pink cement house. Behind all that—in that open space where up to then only the nomads had dared to set up camp.*

Inside the old alley, only the family of Si Lḥussein was left. All around, houses were slowly raining down. People thought at first of keeping their houses inside the walls for their children—a time will come in which they might need ramparts again. But then they took the wooden beams for their new construction, the way builders in the Renaissance did with the stones of Roman temples. Having lost their support, the old houses started falling apart. And since in the old qṣar houses are tightly interwoven—each fitting alongside the other like the pieces of a puzzle—the danger was that the whole puzzle might go.

A hot Friday afternoon in 1989, July, I sat in Si Lḥussein's house with Ḥadda and other friends, reflecting on the absurdity, or the allegory, of our sitting in that empty qṣar drinking tea, like jinns, or like the survivors of a disaster. I thought of Calvino's Marco Polo, sitting with a melancholic Khan at twilight in the insulated garden of his palace, sipping tea, telling stories of faraway places and debating the causes of the decadence of the empire. We smelled smoke, but were so carried away by our discussion that we paid no attention to that smell, confusing it with the smoke of Ḥadda's pipe.

A man ran in screaming—there was a fire in Um ʿAṣṣa's house next door. The word spread quickly; men came from all over. They came in their holiday clothes, immaculate white, from the Friday prayer at the mosque. For the Friday assembly prayer still took place in the old mosque at Arḥabî, the old mosque, which is still called by the now ironic name of jâmeʿ jdîd, *"the New Mosque."*

The New Mosque was built, people say, after the Judge had come, at the extreme periphery of what was then a small settlement. The other mosque, which took by contrast the name of jâmeʿl-bâlî, *"the mosque of the old side," and simply "the old mosque," could not meet the needs of the growing population, fueled by the arrival of several waves of foreigners. It is then, people say, that the new citadel of Ayt j-Jdîd was built, and the New Mosque, the mosque that is now old, found itself at the center of the qṣar, at the intersection of the four fourths, and has been there for as long as anybody remembers—that their fathers' fathers remembered.*[65]

But as people keep moving out and the qṣar is increasingly empty, when the muezzin calls for Friday prayer men head back to the old-new mosque from their faraway houses in the outside land. They walk past their old house now abandoned, feeling the presences and pretending not to hear, smelling the familiar, slightly suffocating odor of old earth and manure, and perhaps understanding what the elders report the Berber nomads to have said when they came to the qṣar to buy dates; when, with turbans lowered on their faces so as not to breathe the air, they complained that the stuffy odor made their eyes swell.

The Friday assembly had scattered at the news of the fire. People knew that, now that most houses were empty or used for the storage of grain, the whole place could burn down before anything could be done. From well to well the men made a chain of buckets, and even women who would not otherwise open their veils came and helped with the drawing of water. Um ʿAṣṣa arrived in a frenzy. She stared at the flames. She had seen other fires in her life, some more murderous, in which children had died. But now the danger was of a different sort. It had to do with memory. She launched herself into the flames, determined to go in. For no reason. The house was empty; there was nothing to save. Two men held her back. Then, standing outside, in the narrow alley filled with water and smoke, she started calling the names. Of the dead, of those who had lived in that house before her. She called Ḍâwya, her mother-in-law, the woman she had so hated in her life. Then she screamed. And everything stopped. For that cry summarized for everyone the pain of abandonment and the trauma of the loss. She fainted. We put her down in the hall of Ṭama Lhasmi's house, across the street. Um ʿAṣṣa and Ṭama used to set the loom together, in that hall. Ṭama died of fever before she even started to build her house in the berra. Um ʿAṣṣa lay in her house, waking up to the smell of smoke and mud. All around her women cried, each for herself.

LOSS 2

RUINS

"And the Last Is Left Empty-Handed": Scenes from Si Lḥussein's History of Fall

tisilt temsilt
l-qurtas tnaqartas
ameggaru tqarmshas

Horseshoe and sandals / Gun shooting / The last blow is empty

When the day starts declining and shadows grow longer—it is the time people call *ʿagub n-nhâr,* the "slope of the day," between the calls to prayer of *l-ʿâṣr* and *l-moghreb*—the roof of the house, usually swarming with activity and voices, remains silent. A sense of emptiness surrounds the mud walls, the uneven earth floor, the fireplace, where moments before women were busily at work. Before leaving for their afternoon chores, they have sprinkled water and swept the floor; the smell of wet soil combines with that of ashes in the fireplace and produces an olfactory memory, the melancholic smell of an absence. Moments later, the woman whose turn it is to prepare dinner will come up. The kitchen will be smoky again, lightened by the short-lived palm-leaf fire that will draw long shadows on the already dark wall. Then, the sunset call to prayer, and at dusk the uncanny ululations of the children paying their tribute to the night.

Soon the rest of the family will come, and the roof

will again be filled by the noisy routine of life that covers the breathing of the walls. In the meantime this is a space of waiting, suspended. A sense of emptiness seizes those who sit on the roof at this time, as if, for an instant, they could see the wreckages of time. The empty roof becomes, at such moments, a stage for the production of those images that in Benjamin's terms, are "loomed for us by forgetting."[66]

In that interim, the voice of Si Lḥussein can be heard.

Si Lḥussein has the color of old age. He is blind, almost completely deaf, and spends his days on the roof, immobile like a tree in a white tunic, keeping the flies off of his face with a whisk, calling, sometimes, as if from another world. He became blind as a consequence of a curse—a curse that fell on him from the side of his lineage, back at the zâwya in the mountains where he is from. (Every day he invoked death, but death never came. Then, when no one expected it anymore, he silently went.)[67]

He speaks to Si Thami, his son, and to me indirectly (he touches my hair from time to time to make sure it is me), spinning the invisible threads of forgetting into a story that weaves images of loss from his own life with images of ruin from the larger horizon of the qṣar. At times, however, his speech eludes any address—it becomes visionary, the remembering voice of forgetting. The rhythm of his recitation—addressed to no one if not, perhaps, the demons that disturb his sleep at night and that he furiously fights with his stick—is monotonous. As he speaks, Si Lḥussein , who is blind, sees his words one by one. And, as he speaks, Si Lḥussein, who is deaf, hears the clashing of the images he summons up from the dead. He speaks in the present tense, and sees.

Si Lḥussein's recollection is at the same time a moral assessment of the recent history of the qṣar that adopted him—what I call a history of Fall—and an autobiographical account of the circumstances that caused him to lead the life of an exile. He tells the story of the last of the great fitnas of the valley, of how it developed, of the horrors and the violence that haunted much of his life and the life of his generation. He tells *l-khûf,* "the fear," which is the first word to come to the minds of people when they speak of those years, a fear that caught people in their entrails, and made social life impossible. In the words of l-Ḥajj l-Madanî: "For eight months we guarded the locked gate of the qṣar, sleepless, holding guns, we couldn't go out, and those who were out couldn't come in. And if a man was killed in an ambush, he had to be left there, at the mercy of the dogs. We couldn't grow barley in our gardens; we couldn't grow anything at all; we could not farm and we had plenty of water; the river flowed away full."

Or, in the imagination of a younger man, who did not live through that time of war but reenacts it now in his dreams, as a way, perhaps, to lend face to other fears:

I dreamed that I was coming back home from my garden at Tamda,[68] *and I heard gunfire from the direction of Tiqoyya. I reached Tamdet n-Igjgalen and I saw l-Ḥajj Lḥabib and Aḥmed u Lḥassan. They were resting in the shade of clustered palm trees and told me that the road was clear, but I had to be careful at Tiqoyya. They—the Enemy—were hiding by the canal of Astur. After a while I ran into some people from Tafrawt; I asked, "Are you out of your minds to walk around the gardens without weapons, and the road is dangerous, haunted* [fiya shi]*?"*[69] *They decided to join me, and to walk with me all the way to the qṣar. We arrived at Adghar and we saw them. They were wearing military clothes, and some had camouflage suits. They started shooting at us from the other side of the canal of Astur. I took up my gun; I shot back. I killed one, I killed two, I killed three... As I shot I was thinking, "Those who say that killing is like trance* [jedba][70] *are right, you never have enough."*

This oneiric geography of fear is borrowed from the narratives about the fitna of the 1920s (the Great Fitna), when the gardens surrounding the qṣar had become a site of terror. Behind each palm tree one's death might be lurking, each irrigation canal was where one's corpse might be thrown. Still now, for many older men, the gardens are marked as a map of violent deaths. Their physical landscape functions in discourse as an aide-mémoire—a space of bodily orientation, of marking and remembering. Yet, for the people of the qṣar, the gardens are also a figure of the unknown buried under their grounds. As such, they become a narrative theater of horror and fear, a fear that exceeds any given event or particular history—the fitna of the 1920s, the horrors of war, the arrival of the French army—and of which each remembered event is a provisional and insufficient figure, a way to lend a face and a concrete body[71] to something that eludes the possibility of telling.

Even though the historical chronology is not respected, and mystical connections are established between events that seem unrelated from the point of view of archival history, Si Lḥussein's recitation is an interpretation of the period that immediately preceded the French occupation of the Draᶜ valley[72] ("la pacification du Draᶜ," in the words of Captain Spillmann).[73] It is a period of great confusion and turmoil, of sudden changes in the political alliances between the different forces on the local scene, a time of political murders and massacres, related in part, but not exclusively, to the French penetration into this area and the control the French sought to obtain by manipulating old antagonisms and fueling the animosity between different local factions.[74]

But Si Lḥussein's story also speaks of a generalized sense of insecurity, and a fear more elusive, more terrifying than the fear of warfare. It is the fear sensed in the stories about men traveling back from a village or a marketplace, robbed and then killed for a bag of onions. It is that sense of generalized insecurity that, in written documents from the turn of the century, is officially called *al-khûf,* "fear." (Because of the times of *khûf,* it is said in many written agreements, Fulân engages himself to look after the children of Fulân, provide food and shelter, and so forth, for as long as the state of fear continues.)

Si Lḥussein's narrative is colored by a sense of ineluctability. The telling springs from a wound, in the life of the teller as in that of his community, an original loss that, like an illness, infiltrates the whole body and brings about dissolution and death. "And the last is left empty-handed" is the melancholic conclusion, drawn from the prophecy of a holy fool who traveled from village to village across the valley, announcing the forthcoming end of the world.

Through poetical gaps and esoteric connections, in Si Lḥussein's recitation all the elements conjure up a disaster: a famous murder, a sacrifice and an omen; the body of the victim is left dismembered in the gardens, cut into a hundred pieces—like the *blâd,* the homeland itself.

The killer, a man who wished no harm but was forced to kill by a trick of chance (inscribed despite himself into a larger fate whose logic escaped him), finds sanctuary at a zâwya nearby. After a year, the *murabiṭin* of the zâwya send a procession of children, along with a calf to be slaughtered on the threshold of the house of the victim, so that Khalifa u Abdelmumen (that is the killer's name) might be accepted back inside the qṣar. But the sister of the victim sets the sacrifice on fire. "And that fire she ignited put the whole world ablaze [*u hâdîk l-ʿafiya lly shaʿalât shaʿlât d-dunya kullha*]."

One night when Khalifa is on the roof of the zâwya, bathing his sorrow in the indifferent sky, he sees a ribbon of fire moving up along the riverbed and descending over the walls of the qṣar of Teyrsut. It is an *ʿalâma,* a "sign," foreteller of destruction and ruin. Gunfire breaks out. It is a massacre. Bodies of slain children and women pile up in a public well, the Berber invaders divide the spoils, a baby nurses from the breast of his dead mother; and then Baba, the sheikh of Bni Zoli, is murdered in an ambush after the evening prayer; and on, and on... and the Christians come. It has the musical rhythm of a fugue and the narrative vertigo of a fall.

But Si Lḥussein is not just telling a story about ruin and loss. His recitation produces a narrative loss. The images he makes appear in his telling take on a life of their own and rupture the narrative sequence. The characters make their entry as if on stage. (Si Lḥussein uses the verb *nad,* "he got up," to indicate the beginning of a relevant action, every time an actor makes an entry: "nad Moḥamed u Saʿid, u nâdû l-ghaziân" [Moḥamed u Saʿid got up, and the invasion began]. He "got up"; that is, he appeared in the scene.)

The narrative is discontinuous, born from the juxtaposition of images, a montage of independent scenes. As in the petrified landscapes of allegory described by Benjamin, Si Lḥussein's images are fixed, mummified in the shock of an immemorial present that celebrates the catastrophe of time.[75] The narrative sequence is fissured by the violence of the visual. His depiction of the razing of Teyrsut, a neighboring qṣar "swept" by the Ayt ʿAṭṭa Berbers in 1927 (in an act of resistance against a group of local notables compromised with l-Glâwî and with the French, but also of violence against a sedentary and agricultural population forever doomed), is almost obscene in its painting of death. The focus on the imagery of corpses (details such as the swelling of the smallpox marks on the face of a dead man), on the rhetoric of fracture (the breaking of the village along with that of the bodies of people), is not just descriptive of violence; it produces violence as a narrative effect. It belongs to a style that may be called baroque, aimed at producing a shock through rhetoric, at the level of both the imagery and the syntax. For Si Lḥussein, breaking the narrative is a way of enacting the disaster he can't find the words to describe. "The Horrors," he repeats, almost as a refrain, "the Horrors cannot be recollected, they cannot be said."

In a short text with the subtitle "Il racconto che non si fará mai" (the story that will never be told), Pier Paolo Pasolini attempts to evoke the pain of everyday life during the Algerian war through the lenses of Paris immigrant experience and Algiers street violence. He fails, as he knows he would, in his effort to represent it through language. His description of the language of Brahim, "as an auditive fact," becomes emblematic of his entire aesthetic project of telling through the gaps: seeing the words, bending the syntax, rupturing the grammar, exposing the holes, the silences, between word and word, "in the trembling"; the holes that expose other lives, and make one dizzy: "Le sue parole si vedono ad una ad una" (his words "show" one by one by one). "Naturally the language, of Brahim, as an auditive fact, cannot be reproduced: it is true that like spears it is fully frontal and linear, but between word and word, in the trembling, there are holes, and you look into those holes you get dizzy, because they open onto chasms..."[76]

THE BIRDS

(The first scene—almost as a matter of course—is that of the death of his father. It is Si Lḥussein's recollection of the first dismembering, and an invocation to the Angel of Death: Siwâl, the angel inquisitor, who questions the dead about their deeds on the first night after burial.)[77]

And I held him, like this, on my lap. His mind drifted at times, and he faded away. He kept praising God with his beads. With a whisk I kept the flies off his face. Slowly Death came to break him. I was outside. Mother called, "Get up, come to your father's side, this is Death." He poured the eye into the eye, and his eyes were running with tears, God give him peace in his compassion. And it seemed as if he were asked [*tsewwel*] before even being buried. The birds came, the birds. Could he speak, he would tell you that three birds came in the middle of the night, kajjj kajjj kajjj, in the middle of the night, and we knew that he was being asked by the angel, about his deeds in this world...

Not any thought of giving us a bit of bread, not even a handful of dried figs. We walked from morning to morning, and we came back empty-handed...

> "It is from that turn that he can't stand the people of the zâwya."[78] Si Thami, his son, is filling the gaps later: "This is the story of when my father took his father's body back to his homeland for burial. Forty kilometers in the desert mountains! It is about the madness of his mother, my grandmother. So what if his father left a legacy! A child, by himself, and his shoulders didn't reach the donkey's back. They hired a man, and that man sealed the turban on his face not to smell the odor of death. He wouldn't walk with them at all, and when the corpse threatened to fall, the boy had to hold it by himself. His mother didn't go, she was 'tied up' in mourning [*rbṭat ḥaqq allâh*]. That was my grandfather, l-Madanî ben Aḥmed. It is from that day that my father can't stand his zâwya. He was in shock, had lost his father, was sent to Zâwya hungry. They didn't give him anything to eat—spent the night hungry and came back hungry."

(That journey, from which he came back empty-handed, reminds him of another journey years before, which, he knows today, also left him empty-handed.)

So we came to the Draʿ from Zâwya, but we didn't come till we had lived through eight days of hell. Nothing to eat, God overpowered us, nothing! Some people brought dates from Ktawa, and the murabiṭin released them on credit, my uncle bought a little bit and Lâllâ Iṭṭo, may she rest in peace, used to steal from her father, and not just a bit. She'd give it to my mother, saying, "Take this, give it to that child to revive him a bit..."

Father, may he rest in peace, knew how to make saddles and leather buckets, and came all the way down here. He came first and settled, ate plenty of dates and couscous. Then he brought us along. Mother didn't want to leave Zâwya, even though Zâwya was a hardship. She went on crying, "Oh my, oh my! I am separated from the family of my father, oh my, I am separated from the family of my mother!" My father told her, "What in the world does your family give you? Get up, move to where you can get something for yourself." And we came, and the valley was well off. People were harvesting and they'd give us a sheaf of barley, they'd say "Here, make couscous for your children..."

But my mother cried, "I am a stranger, I am a stranger in a strange land." The people of Ayt l-Ḥajj ʿAlî never let Father rest. He was always on the move, there he was making buckets for them, there he was making saddles... He stayed on with them and was well off... Slowly, till he died. We lost him and our hand was cut, our life was shattered...

(Si Lḥussein is lost in recollection. His voice is drained, breaks for a moment into a glottal stop that is almost a cry, and runs out. When he resumes his recitation, painfully, in a declamatory voice, he is talking about the shattering of his land.)

THE BUYING AND SELLING OF WORDS

I witnessed the dissolution of this world in the days of fitna and taqshurîn, the razing, the killing, the invasions...

The one who came first in the story of fitna is Moḥamed u Saʿid. He was the leader of Taqshurt [the secessionist faction in the qṣar].[79] Moḥamed u Saʿid "got up" [*nad*], and the troubles broke out, and the invasions began. Soon everything was ruined. *Tshettet dunya,* the whole world was shattered.

It all started with the buying and selling of words, *l-bîʿ u shra f l-klâm.* It is always from words that fitna starts...

Moḥamed u Saʿid told the Makhzen,[80] "How much taxes [*ʿashar*] do they gather for you? I'll collect much more." And l-Glâwî said, "How much would you bring me?" "Thirteen thousand real Hassanî," he said. Baba and his friends said to l-Glâwî, "From the entire valley you couldn't squeeze even two thousand reals!"[81] But l-Glâwî said, "That man claims he can, and if you don't let him I'll send you to jail." "Put us in jail then," said Baba. But l-Glâwî changed his mind and freed them. Instead he got those of Taqshurt—the secessionist faction—Moḥamed u Saʿid and his people, and threw them in the underground jails of the palace.

So the pasha [l-Glâwî] called Baba and his friends, gave them weapons, and said, "Go! you will rule in the Draʿ," and kept Moḥamed u Saʿid and his people in jail. The qbîla auctioned off the property of those who were in jail. All the gardens of Moḥamed u Saʿid were sold in that auction, and his enemies bought them. So much money, so much wealth was gone! His house was full of dried dates, and the qbîla sold it all and kept selling his stuff. They sold his dates, they sold his gardens, they sold everything he had...

After l-Glâwî gave the weapons to Baba and l-Ḥajj Thami, they had the word. Baba ruled from here all the way to Mḥamîd just with his purse [*shkara*], without a gun, without a dagger, and nobody dared to speak [*makân llî qdar itkellem*]. The world was quiet, quiet was the world... And the villages [*qaba'îl*] gave him the money...

And also this went by...

DISMEMBERING

On top of all this [*zâd ʿala ma zâd*], the disaster of Ayt Khalifa. God inflicted Moḥamed u Saʿid upon them. When their fighting was over, the henna field was threshed. They turned the earth over in the struggle...

Because Moḥamed u Saʿid had betrayed, he had made a deal with the enemy; he had called them in. He had hired forty gunmen, who were to wait until the market warmed up...

It was Fitna...

On Monday he met with the enemy, he hired them to "sweep" [*sheṭṭeb*] the village out. He said, "Next Thursday, market day, wait at the entrance of the sûq, wait for the market to warm up, then go in. The gate will be open. Enter the village, take over the towers, and wipe everything out with your guns."

But Destiny was written otherwise...

Ayt Khalifa got up. It was Tuesday. Water was running out in the irrigation canal and they had the Tuesday turn... Moḥamed u Saʿid was at home, and his khammâs came and complained that Ayt Khalifa had taken the water by force [the two families share the water turn]. But it wasn't true...

Moḥamed u Saʿid came out of his house. We were sitting at the entrance of the alley. We saw him passing. His dagger spoke his intentions [*dalîlu jenwi*]. It was noon, the sun was hot. He reached the others at the canal. "Bastards, infidels, you stole my water!"

They fought over water. Moḥamed u Saʿid said, "I count myself on one side, and the qbîla on the other. And so come up, if you dare, herd of sheep! You are worth nothing to me!" And Khalifa said to Moḥa his son, "Moḥa, what in the world are you waiting for? Grab *tameskert!*"[82] He said to Moḥamed u Saʿid, "Taakk...," from this shoulder, from this shoulder... all the way to the ground! He hit Moḥamed u Saʿid till his heart came out.

The human heart is small, like this *(Si Lḥussein makes sign with his hands)*, and the liver is small too. Khalifa bent over the body of Moḥamed u Saʿid and he could see his entrails. He saw the shit in his intestines. Death came. Moḥamed u Saʿid died, and, God only knows, people say that someone else came and cut his body in pieces. The news spread. We ran to the place of the killing and we found the blood already dry. I looked at the corpse; I saw the heart. They hadn't left even a bit intact. They dismembered everything, everything they butchered and cut into pieces. As though he were a sacrificial victim, they opened his joints [*mafaṣil*] and entered the knife in between...

Ayt Khalifa, they fled. Khalifa sent his khammâs: "Go tell our family to stay together and lock the door. We are off to the sanctuary... To the zâwya of Ben ʿAbd l-Mûla.[83] They escaped to the zâwya. The gardens were deserted. The khammâs brought the shouts to the village, he said, "*Lah lah l-qbîla!* People of the qbîla, get up, Moḥamed u Saʿid was murdered!" They brought the litter for the dead [*nʿash*], gathered up his remains, and took his bones to the sanctuary of Sîdî Ṣâfu[84] just outside the walls. They washed them, and buried them there. He was all broken in pieces.

Khalifa and his son went to the zâwya, and the murabiṭin granted them sanctuary [*zugûhum*]. After a year had passed, they sent the children of the Qurʾanic school in a procession to the qṣar, to ask forgiveness. They brought a calf and slaughtered it on the threshold. They offered it in sacrifice for the family of the dead man [*debḥû ʿalîhum*].[85] But his sister, the dead man's sister, came out of the house in a frenzy, grabbed a burning palm leaf, and set the victim on fire. Um ʿAṣṣa ut Saʿid was her name.

AND THE FIRE SHE IGNITED SET THE WHOLE WORLD ABLAZE!

And there they are, I see them, they assemble!

Even the spirits of the land helped them, even the saints [*sâdât*] helped Ayt Unir![86] They slaughtered a ram for Si Moḥamed u Saʿid [*debḥû l-kebsh ʿala Si Moḥamed u Saʿid*], they slaughtered a ram for Si Moḥamed u Brahim of Aghalal, they slaughtered a ram for Sîdî Aḥmed ben Naser...[87]

And Khalifa, Khalifa u Abdelmumen, was there. He was still in his refuge at the zâwya, and he saw... He waited till the middle of the night and went up to the roof. He looked this way and that way, and he saw a ribbon of fire... He saw a ribbon of fire moving up along the river. It moved up, up, rrrrr... till he saw it landing on the village of Teyrsut. It was the *ʿalâma,* the sign, the fire. And a little while later he heard gunfire, the voice of guns, whistling there. Ayt Unir invaded Teyrsut [*dakhlu lîha*], they entered her with the help of Ayt Isful...

Ḥammu of Mama Saleḥ, with Ḥammu of Usha, with Ḥammu of Bû Ykemez: they are the ones who raped her...[88]

THE BREAKING OF TEYRSUT

Guns push against her gate, guns break it open... There they are... they enter... they occupy the assembly room... the screaming... the blood...

The news [*l-ghwât,* "screaming"] reached Tinnerden. An armed group came from Tinnerden to help the invaders. Because it was close. They were almost driven back by the people of Teyrsut... It is there that they killed Sheikh Lḥassan of Teyrsut!

People dug a hole, and got out the women and whomever dared. And the men from Bni Zoli who had come to help the victims climbed the walls with a rope. Seven of them were shot climbing on that rope; seven of them were killed in Teyrsut...

The day Teyrsut broke up [*ṯhersat Teyrsut*], Salem u l-Hashmi was broken there for life. Salem u l-Ḥajj died there, Aḥmed u l-Ḥajj died in the storeroom of a house—he fell, the roof collapsed on his head, there he died. And Driss of ʿAmmî Sâlem was left unburied, overnight. He rotted. As he rotted and swelled, the marks of smallpox on his face disappeared. As I was looking around for the wounded, I said, "Where is Driss of ʿAmmî Sâlem?" And that bastard of Mâma Saleḥ's son said to me, and perhaps he had killed him himself, he said, "My dear Murabiṭ, that's the son of ʿAmmî Sâlem," and he was there, in front of me, dead, swollen, so transformed in putrescence that I hadn't recognized him...

We carried out the dead, all day long, I grabbed the corpse until its hand became one with my leg... I felt the hand of the dead grabbing my legs as if to take me away...

Look at the invaders! They carry out wheat, they carry out barley, they carry out dates, so many dried dates, so many dried figs, so many dried carrots... to the threshing floors; they drive out the cows, they drive out the sheep, they evaluate all that, they divide up the spoils. And we carry out all those butchered dead bodies...

And the public well outside the gate became a communal grave, bodies thrown in and piled up in there to rot. And on the threshing floors, how many dead bodies! among them a baby nursing from the breast of his dead mother... Until the dogs came and ate them, until the crows came and ate them, until all the animals ate their share and dogs were wandering freely over the land. There, on the threshing floors... The horrors of Teyrsut cannot be recollected, they cannot be said...

L-gharayb, l-gharayb! The horrors, incredible things happened there. I never went back.

There was still Baba, then. He and l-Ḥajj Thami were still coming and going, and the Berbers didn't dare to approach our qṣar. But the day Lḥassan of Teyrsut died, and Baba Ḥadda of Taghallil was assassinated... [89]

GO!...

THE MURDER

Ḥassan u Saʿid[90] hired two Berber mercenaries, introduced them into the qṣar, and showed them a dark corner in the alley near the main mosque where they could ambush Baba: "It's here that you are going to murder him." Baba had prayed the prayer of sunset. He walked out of the mosque with l-Ḥajj Thami. L-Ḥajj Thami said, "I sense danger, let's take the other way home. Come and have dinner at our house..." But Baba said, "No, let me go home. If it's written that I die..." He let him go. L-Ḥajj Thami hadn't even reached the mouth of the next alley when he heard gunfire. "Takk,

takk," spoke the gun, and Baba fell in front of the mosque. Those Berbers had murdered him, and Ḥassan u Saʿid who had hired them hid them inside his house. The people of the qṣar said, "Let's break into his house with our hoes [*naʿṭiw l-fas l-dârû*]. We'll destroy and empty it [*nekhliwha u nrîbuha*], and we'll get hold of the assassins and kill them."

But Baba's brother came out, his own brother, and spoke: "People of Bni Zoli," he said, "my brother won't come back to me from death, and our children must not say that Bni Zoli fell because of my thirst for vengeance! Don't kill them, and let's try to come to a pact with the Berbers..."

And they let them be. The Gate was closed. People couldn't come in or go out from the qṣar. Baba's body had to be buried inside.[91] They put him in Dyâr l-Makhzen. It is there that they buried him...

These are incredible events... The horrors... Ayt Unir, the jackals, got hold of the best villages...

They seized Zawyât l-Qâḍî, a couple of days after Teyrsut. They entered it, entered the palace of Si Moḥamed al-Saghir. They found him in the open courtyard where he sat. They killed him and destroyed everything they found. The whole place was full of papers, registers, manuscripts, documents, letters of the sultans.[92] There were the records of the whole world [*knanesh taʿ d-dunya kullha*]. They dispersed everything [*fettsu*], made a big mound of papers, and set them on fire. Then they took some rams from the stables, and slaughtered them, and went on roasting the meat on the fire saying, "Burn, burn, roast, roast [*shawat, shawt*]!" And they took Zawyât l-Qâḍî, and took Teyrsut. Before, whoever wanted to buy dates went to Zawyât l-Qâḍî and brought dates back, they had the best dates; whoever wanted barley went to Teyrsut... and now they don't have enough to eat for their own children.

The Horrors... So much passed, and passed, and will still have to pass [*mâdâ fât u mâ fât u bâqi bgha ifut*]...

Even the palm trees were bleeding. In Taznaqt, there was a palm forest. People used to go cut the dates. There was a bounty: until l-Glâwî came, the fortress of Taznaqt was built, the Khalifa settled there and decided to have new palm trees brought in from the orchards of the French, where palm trees were of types imported from the east, and they were planted in rows. One by one, he had the trees of that palm grove cut down, one by one, until a big empty space was left; a white space. But when the *fâs* hit the stems what came out was not water: it was blood...

Again Ayt Unir overpowered l-Glâwî, again blasted gunfire, again there was shouting and crying. From Taznaqt l-Glâwî shot over Iflî with his cannon to cut off our water and make our gardens die of thirst,[93] and the people of Bni Zoli shot at his fortress from Izugla to push him out. We built in one night, one night only, a watchtower by the mouth of the canal of Iflî. I was there too. As we were building, people called me "aya Agurram," "ahi l-murabiṭ," and I shouted at them, "Shut up, you expose me by calling my name!" All the masterbuilders of the village where there working. Some were building, others were struggling with the water trying to make a dam to obstruct Iflî [*kayrabṭu Iflî*]. And the whole thing under l-Glâwî's fire! And Si Lʿarabi n-Ṭalb [the imam of the mosque at the time] stood there crying: "Where is Bni Zoli, Bni Zoli is dead, may she rest in peace [*fîn Bni Zoli, Bni Zoli mâtet, Allâh irḥamha*]..."

People gathered by the walls, until we heard the water arriving, rumbling in the canal. The women came out, ululating, rejoicing... L-Glâwî had become the enemy [*wella laʿdu*], and Ayt Unir became one with Drâwâ...

Incredible things, uncanny things happened in the Draʿ...

We never rested, gun forever in hand. I used to go pick up *l-blaḥ,* the early dates, and they would ambush [now it is Ayt ʿAṭṭa again], and if they got hold of a Drâwî they'd kidnap him to get money in exchange... I saw them, and I was picking up dates from the ground... we were in that Ajgal of Ṭahar, where I had come to pick up dates. They surrounded me in a ring, they wanted to take me. Ḥammu of Mâma Saleḥ told me, "Watch out, *agurram,* you'll get yourself killed, you'll fall in some ambush..." I said, "If you want to kill me, I am just picking up some dates for my mother." He said to his friends, "Don't touch him, he has the *baraka,* the blessing, he's the murabiṭ of Si Moḥamed u Saʿid..."

I brought up the gifts [*l-hadiya*] from Mḥamîd all the way to Bni Zoli to the beat of the drums, and my mule was loaded with wheat, with a ram on top of it. The villages of the lower river sent the offering up to Baba, when Baba had the wedding for his sons. All of our people, our murabiṭin and the men of my lineage at the zâwya, told me not to go, "The Berbers will kill you, what do you care, those are not people of your blood..." And I said to them, "How could I not go? The people of Bni Zoli have been good with me and my family, I settled in their land and cut grass in their gardens [*ḥashshît f bladhum*], I take care of those who die, and when someone is wounded in some place, I go get him. I never said, "I want to go back to the land of my fathers," like my father said!

(Then, addressing Si Thami, his son, and me,) I don't want to be buried back in the homeland...!

Ayt Unir, the jackals, didn't make peace with us until they cut up Bni Zoli like a butchered animal, bone by bone, and divided it among themselves home by home. Each Berber got his own house, the family he controlled;

Ayt Bujuj had their house, Ayt Taʿbulut had theirs. They would sit in Teyrsut till they were starved, then they'd come with their guns, they'd say "Get up, make us a meal, we are hungry." They cut up the whole of Bni Zoli, house by house, like a butchered ram...

In those days there was a murabiṭ, a holy fool,[94] who traveled from village to village and lived off people's alms. Sheykh ʿAbdullah was his name. He was a Berber from the Sous and wandered up and down the valley announcing the forthcoming end of the world. Wherever he went, he repeated his mysterious warning:

dîru l-qnaṭer
fîn idûzû l-kyader
bab Allah f znaṭer

(Build the bridges / For the horses to pass / The big heads are auctioned away)

(And then in Berber)

tisilt temsilt
l-qurtas tnaqartas
ameggaru tqarmshas

(Horseshoe and sandals / Gun shooting / The last blow is empty / The last is left empty-handed)[95]

And so it was. The big heads were auctioned away. Baba Hadda was murdered in Taghallil, Sheikh Lḥassan was murdered in Teyrsut, and Baba of ʿAmmi ʿAmar was murdered here. They came, the Berbers, they came like a wind of destruction. They swept and razed where they passed, they took over Teyrsut. It became theirs. They threw out the people they didn't slay, and the survivors were left crying, "O our people, where shall we go? Where shall we find refuge [*fîn ndekhlû*]? Where will we spend our nights?" They cried and cried, and whoever had some relatives somewhere went to them, whoever didn't have any went up the river, to the *gharb*, and disappeared...

And the dates, the dates sat thrown there, scattered, on the ground, in front of the village gate. Dogs ate them, donkeys ate them, they sat there until they rotted, until they developed worms, and nobody dared to touch them. They were the dates of Ayt Baba.

Baba was dead, his family was in hiding at the zâwya of Ben ʿAbd l-Mûla.

Their bone was broken (*maksur*)!

m-a-k-s-u-r

Everyone from Ayt Baba had fled: even their women and children, even their khammâs. They had to abandon their houses, they had to abandon their gardens. Their enemies divided the spoils in an auction. The wheat, the barley, the rugs, and the silver trays, the doors they took off their hinges and carried like trophies.

People cut their dates and left them there in a mound; nobody dared to bring them inside the village, nobody dared to take them.[96] They stayed there, menacing. Dogs ate from them, donkeys ate from the piles...

When the time of fertilization came, those who were still their friends went to fertilize the palms of Ayt Baba. They went at night, like thieves, they put the male pollen into the flower without chanting the song, without observing the ritual prescriptions...

And the last was left empty-handed...

Trauerspiel and the *Disiecta Membra* of Allegory

It all started with the "buying and selling of words." According to Si Lḥussein's history of fall, fitna is a speculative process of symbolic give-and-take that produces disastrous effects and, in the end, leaves the last empty-handed. In Si Lḥussein's melancholic view, history is a slope, a process of sliding issued of a first dispossession, which, as in the passing on of a curse, keeps producing further dispossessions.

This is the sense of his swinging between the autobiographical and the collective registers:[97] a first exile, the exile from the ancestral land; a first loss, the death of his father; a first betrayal (a betrayal taken as original in his narrative), that of the man who sold the qṣar to the enemy. Each exile caused further exiles, each loss further losses, each dismembering further dismemberings.

In Si Lḥussein's recollection the imagery of betrayal, breaking, dismembering, decomposing, disappearing, both evokes a particular history, that of the valley at the beginning of the twentieth century, and depicts the work of history: the destructive force of time. At once a victim of that work—the disaster is also that of his personal life—and a spectator to it, Si Lḥussein is in the position of the dreamer in the local understanding of dreams. Because of his *ghîba,* his state of absence and exile, because of his essential nonbelonging, he is granted special vision. Where others see a succession of events, he sees a collection of scenes related to one another like the debris of a wreckage: "His eyes are staring, his mouth is open, his wings are spread. This is how one pictures the angel of history. His face is turned towards the past. Where we perceive a chain of events, he sees one single catastrophe which keeps piling wreckage upon wreckage and hurls it in front of his feet."[98]

I think of the *Trauerspiele* of the baroque age, which Walter Benjamin, in a study that laid the foundations of all his later thought, called "the mourning dramas."[99] They are *Trauer-spiele,* mourning drama, because they stage, he writes, "a being impregnated with death," because in them, "the corpse becomes the supreme emblematic element," and because their "deep awareness of the caducity of things derives from a vision which cannot be obliterated." This vision, the revenant that haunts its imagery, its plots and scenarios, is the trace of an (original) disaster, a disaster that happened offstage and can never be represented as such. (In fact, it is precisely the event that, according to Benjamin, liberates the materials for representation, just as, he says, the debris piled up from the collapse of Roman temples was used in the construction of Renaissance palaces.)

In one sense, this disaster is epitomized for Benjamin by the dissolution of the ancient world, from the ruins of which a new civilization was born and whose mythical forms, emptied of their life—as dead as corpses—populated baroque stages, paintings, and statues in the guise of allegories/ruins. Those allegories, compositions of fragmented and decontextualized images, are, for Benjamin, like a dance of ghosts: they exist only in a space of death, "they signify precisely the non-being of what they represent. . . . They are not real and can assume the quality of what they are made to stand for only under the subjective gaze of melancholy; they are this gaze, which is annihilated by its own products, for these only signify its own blindness. . . . *The allegory flows into the void.*"[100]

In a more radical sense, then, the "vision which cannot be obliterated" is oblivion itself. It is "forgetting" (a notion Benjamin will keep pondering, coming close in places to Freudian ideas on the unconscious and the dream work) that opens the possibility of knowledge as allegoric "remembrance." The meaning of the world has been forgotten, and always already so: it must be constantly produced anew, and every construction can only be an allegory. But also knowing, remembering, is itself a work of forgetting, as it happens in dreams and in involuntary recollection: "Is not the involuntary recollection . . . much closer to forgetting than what we usually call memory? And is not this work of spontaneous recollection, in which remembrance is the woof and forgetting is the warp, a counterpart to Penelope's work rather than its likeness? For here the day unravels what in the night was woven. When we awake each morning, we hold in our hands, usually weakly and loosely, but a few fringes of the tapestry of lived life, as loomed for us by forgetting."[101]

Trauerspiel, in sum, is mourning drama because it stages allegories, corpses in funeral display, but also because it originates in an always-lost transparent knowledge of the world and its signs. It chants the obsequies of presence, of sense as located in the object of knowledge or in the language of knowing, and celebrates the ruins, the debris, the fragments, the dust (the recurrence of these terms in Benjamin's texts and in the theater plays he quotes is insistent), of a dead world in which things are emblems and language is forever emblematic, in which sense can only be allegoric—fugitively constructed through a piecemeal work of recollection.

It is in the wake of such baroque drama that Benjamin developed his neobaroque vision of history as catastrophe and his theory of allegory (as opposed to the romantic symbol) as the mode of representation of the space of death. If the work of the (Romantic) symbol, from the Greek *sym-bolon,* is to unify and infuse life into things, if the symbol belongs to the universe of organic life, the allegory, in contrast, fragments and draws life out of things: it deals in corpses and pertains to the universe of the inorganic and petrified, the realm of the dead and the demonic. From the Greek *allos,* "other," its work is to divide. Benjamin speaks of "the disintegrating and dissociating principle of the allegorical vision." Opposed to the *sym-bolon,* allegory is a *dia-bolon.*[102] "Allegories grow old because decadence and corruption are inherent in their very essence. Under the gaze of melancholy the object becomes allegoric: if life flows out of it, if it is left there petrified like a dead object and yet guaranteed for eternity, then it is available for the work of allegory. This means that from this moment on it is forever incapable of irradiating a sense; its only meaning is that which the allegorist can assign to it. . . . Under the work of allegory a thing becomes another, it speaks of something other . . . of which it is taken as the emblem."[103]

In one sense, then, for Benjamin, allegory is the emblematic writing of a world reduced to powder, which builds from the dead remains, the *disiecta membra* of other worlds. In another sense, allegory is the condition of all knowing. Mourning is the work of language, the silence that hollows it from within: "The language of the Baroque age is constantly shattered by the rebellions of its elements."[104]

Mourning, then, describes the condition of the subject drawn out of himself—seized by the unknowable.

> In all mourning is contained the tendency to the absence of language, which is infinitely more than the simple incapacity, or reluctance, to communicate. The subject of mourning feels himself totally known by the unknowable. To be "nominated"—even if he who gives the name is a semi-god or a saint: this is perhaps considered one of the feelings of mourning. But how much more it is: *not being nominated, but only read, uncertainly* read by someone who knows how to interpret allegories, and becoming meaningful only thanks to him! . . . Things steal away from their simple being to present themselves as a network of enigmatic allegoric deferments, and, above all, as dust.[105]

The Inestimable Ruins of the Present

Il bourra la pipe et reprit lentement, distinctement, le regard fixé au pied du Rocher: "Pas les restes des Romains. Pas ce genre de ruine où l'âme des multitudes n'a eu que le temps de se morfondre, en gravant leur adieu dans le roc, mais les ruines en filigrane de tous les temps, celles que baigne le sang dans nos veines, celles que nous portons en secret sans jamais trouver le lieu ni l'instant qui conviendrait pour les voir: les inestimables décombres du présent."
—Kateb Yacine[106]

With relief, with humiliation, with terror, he understood that he too was a mere appearance, dreamt by another.
—Jorge Luis Borges[107]

L-Ḥajj l-Madanî

One day my father, may he rest in peace, went to water the gardens by the dam of Teyrft nRibaṭ, right where there is the graveyard of domestic animals [*ist-l-jifat*], the Cemetery of the Carrion of Si Hassein. There, in that big open space of the Carrion, he saw a woman. The woman addressed him: "O man, do you remember the qṣar that stood here?"

My father was dismayed, he never knew that there had been a village in that place. She said again, "Noise, lives, voices, laughter, dancing!"

She started clapping her hands, as if she were following the rhythm of dancing: "How much *aqallâl* was scanned by the clapping of these hands!"[108]

She spoke these words and disappeared. No trace was left of her. It was only the Cemetery of the Carrion [*roda ta*ʿ *l-beheim*], and the stench, the stench of manure people lay down in that place to dry. It must have been the rûḥ of some dead woman who had lived in that vanished qṣar.

In its historical consciousness, the qṣar of Bni Zoli was born from the ruins of a former civilization, made of the debris of another world. A world erased by the work of time, or destroyed in a disaster of unimaginable proportions? A flood, a war, a famine, a violent invasion? Stories referring to that nebulous past invoke a state of fitna—that sovereign figure of alterity: the figure of what has no figure, in which language comes to a halt.

The *qṣûr dyâl jnânât,* "the scattered hamlets in the gardens," were razed, emptied, and violently destroyed. Their inhabitants, original settlers, were killed or deported. As if materialized from its dust, from that disaster the qṣar of Bni Zoli was born. The deported became the flesh of its people.

Tfu—out there, in the middle of the palm groves—a few remains, shreds of mud walls, and a big empty open space. One of the rare uncultivated spots, burned by the sun and blown by the wind, Tfu is an inexplicable blank in the intensely cultivated landscape, tightly packed with palm trees—a marketplace from that time before time that stands for the essence of time itself. The biggest hamlet from that Age (the capital letter of allegories), Tfu is said to have had high walls, a cemetery, and a mosque. Where the mosque and the cemetery used to be, there is now a garden that belongs to the *ḥabus dyâl j-jâmaʿ*, the entrusted property of the mosque. L-Ḥajj l-Madanî and his sons rent it, and have made it into a big henna field. The land can be rented, but it cannot be bought and sold—a legacy from another world. According to Islamic Law, l-Ḥajj says, one can cultivate a cemetery forty years after the last burial.

Carved out of heavy palm wood made smooth by the passing of time, Tfu's Gate (this is what people call it) stands now as a relic at the entrance of the "new" qṣar of Bni Zoli—it has, people say, ever since the village was built, over five hundred years ago. (Lit candles and benzoin in the hole of its hinge, where the wooden lock enters the mud wall: women keep putting offerings.) The mark of a foreign inscription, of another name in the name, the door hangs there as an emblem of the returning paths of time. Or take Taurirt, or Tabḥert, or Ighrem n-Ugjgal, Ighrem ʿAwn, l-Mansuria.[109] The whole landscape is punctuated by traces—names—of former settlements.

L-Ḥajj l-Madanî:

> There was Tighremt of Ayt Ḥammu downstream, and Tighremt of Sîdî Abdelkhâleq upstream, and there was Sîdî Abderraḥman Bû Yaqûb. Now there is only that grave, that shrine, but then there was a qṣar, and right next to it there was Iger Mellaḥ, the Mellaḥ of the Jews, and where the shrine of Sîdî Nûr is now, there also used to be a qṣar; at Tabḥert n-Ḥizb, there was a qṣar, at Ighrem ʿAwn, there was a qṣar, at Ighrem nʿAsha, there was a qṣar, and of course at Tfu, there was a qṣar—it is there that the marketplace was... we still call it "the sûq"; and in that *tabḥert*, that little garden of l-Hashmi u Ḥnini, there was the mosque. It was the mosque of Tfu.

In some cases nothing but the name is left, a ruin that in everyday speech has come to designate a garden or an area of the gardens, but whose legacy of unknown is felt nonetheless—

> *Punctuated by names of others, traces of an experience that cannot be erased nor retrieved, forgotten nor remembered: the condition of this*

writing is akin to that of these gardens, of these narratives, lived in by countless ruins of vanished settlements. I think of the way Borges cites in his stories dates, names of people and places, genealogies, with extreme detail but without providing the context of his references, which stand in his texts like ruins, remains of a discourse mutilated at its inaugural speech. Fragmented references, the use of determinative articles to introduce characters who haven't yet been mentioned and will not be mentioned again, passing presences rooted in a missing context, function in Borges's stories like symptoms, glimpses of a reality beyond the visual field of the observer—a reality that eludes any totalizing description.

Contrasting versions seek causes, impute responsibilities. Yet all versions agree to see in the past of the qṣar an (original) crime or act of violence, bloodshed or natural catastrophe; an "event" invoked in the different versions, each attempting to give it a form and a name. Forgotten or repressed, the disaster is passed on and keeps happening. Is it the fitna of that distant past before the village was formed, or that of the recent past, leading to the arrival of the French army? The destruction of the Scattered Hamlets in what was perhaps the fifteenth or sixteenth century, or that of Tighremt, the secessionist fortress of the nineteenth century? Or is it instead Ighruren, the factional settlement of today? Are the stories a political statement about a renewed need for destruction, or a melancholic recognition of the new reality of scattering? Is it the physical space of the gardens, the concrete walls of the villages, the mud of the ruins, and the stench of the corpses that are being talked about, or the metaphorical space of language and memory? Is the disaster something that really happened, are the ruins actual remains, or is it an allegory of the disastrous work of repetition (in the sense talked about by Ḥadda), stressing the fact that, "when a name becomes audible" (Benjamin), it already has the structure of a ruin? No one reading can do justice to the polyvalent quality of those images. They should be left free to intertwine and resonate with each other, for the mode of representation of these narratives is scenic, simultaneous and visual—

To read the melancholic attitude of these narratives solely as a consequence of colonial trauma would amount to a dismissal of their sense of temporality, as if this culture did not have its own ways of reckoning, or not; of mourning, or not; or simply accepting disastrous events coming from the external world. Colonized twice over, it would be denied the right of reinscription: that of viewing the French army like one of the many ḥarkas that landed in this region over the centuries, each foreign and ruinous in its own way, and even to view the French invasion (as many do) as less bloody, and actually more restful, than the *siba* of the earlier days. It would be as if the impact of the west could only be understood in western terms, as the only singular event in an otherwise returning tissue of repetitions, the only "fact" that may not be reinscribed into an already existing palimpsest.

There is a local oral poem, a love poem, that says:

kwatni b lughtha ʿajamyia
ya mwaliya mûhi lught l-ʿarab

(She burned me with her foreign tongue / O fathers! It's not the tongue of the Arabs.) The poet describes the beautiful girl he saw in the fields; she turned her gaze to him, he was on fire. He praised her, she teased him in a language he could not understand. Back home he burned with passion, composed verses for her. The old women of the qṣar, twisted tongues, reproached him. In love with a foreigner, dared composing poetry for her! And, revealing the identity of the stranger "How dare you praise a Berber woman in the Arab tongue [*wash sh-shelḥa kattshker b l-ʿarabiya*]?" The "other" in the poem is a Shelḥa, one of the Ayt ʿAṭṭa girls who wandered bareheaded through the gardens (Ayt ʿAṭṭa didn't wear a veil), arrogantly provoking the men and stealing from the crops in the days of *siba*. But she can also be a French woman. (One day, these verses were addressed to me.)

Or take many a poem of war and fitna, which were recast to condemn the French invasion and are sung today in the context of modern-day emigration to Casablanca or France. Here is a poem decrying the fitna that blasted the brothers, caused the scattering of the family, and made possible the invasion and the violent takeover by a group of "others." The last verses say:

We have fallen under the rule of a Stranger
With his Strangers
Spun of a different warp
Shall not colonize us!
Children of best roots!
We are tied by an oath
And by the ultimate limit of death
Son of the Bone, come back to the land of your fathers,
and be your children buried side by side with your body[110]

"Strangers spun of a different warp [*l-ʿajam b sdâhum maghzûl*]" are once again the Ayt ʿAṭṭa Berber nomads. Yet they are also the French, and this poem, along with many others, is also a cry of anger against the Christians, the *ʿajam* of modern times, and the weakness of the brothers that made possible the spread of their control. At the same time, it is a sad assessment of the situation that has led to modern-day emigration to Europe, as another verse says: "I saw the brothers giving up their land for a land rich with pastures for their camels."

But between reinscription, repetition, and ruin there is a play that must be reflected upon. For what is repeated is the occurrence of a break. Each break is catastrophic: new, final, intractable. It has the radical nature of fitna, cannot be integrated into an already existing vision of life, and changes the world beyond the possibility of return. SHEṬṬEB: it "sweeps" everything away.[111]

Yet each break is also the return of other breaks, each occurrence conjures up the ruins, the names, and the marks by which memory—and life—are lived in and inscribed. (A specter, says Blanchot, is the return of that which cannot return, the return of an absence.) In its irreducible novelty, each rupture is already a repetition. The event of *sheṭṭeb,* "sweeping," erasing and wiping out, is also a reinscription, a rasm, a fixing, a drawing, a representing.

It is repetition that causes the falling into ruin, but it is also repetition that makes possible, each time, the reconstruction of new worlds from ruins. Repetition, that is, redoubling and reinscription; the process of dismembering, the break, and that of re-membrance, the re-joining together of broken parts. The first verse of the poem on the fitna of the brothers says:

Nʿajna ulla ʿala nʿajtayn
âsh men hemma bânt lîk
nta llî jârî f frâgu?
Shuf wîn tḥellu bibayn
Ha ḥna hnâ wusṭ l-bḥûr
seddhum mâ ighrâgû

(Our house split into two-houses / What did you envisage, seeking after this rift? / Look! there opened two gates / we are shunted between seas, / close them or we shall drown.)

According to one version, in the early days of fitna the people of the scattered hamlets, elusive and ungraspable like jinns, haunted the territory and spread terror in the valley. Their settlements were upstream, and they aggressively polluted the waters of the canals (a recurrent theme from all times in this region), raided the other villages, stole their animals, cut their dates, broke into their houses, and raped their women. People were not free to travel or to trade. Activity was paralyzed by fear. Again, *l-khûf.*

This version, which in its general lines is shared by the white Ḥarâr of the qṣar and claims that the inhabitants of the scattered hamlets were black Ḥarâtîn, stresses the illegitimacy of their status and their moral "excess"; the term used is *ṭghaw* (root *ṭghw*), "they exceeded and overstepped all boundaries." (In this sense could be read a nineteenth-century *fatwa* [legal opinion] from the family archives of the qṣar, blaming the state of fear [*al-*

khûf] caused by the "evil" and the "plague" of the Ḥarâtîn, their "excess and overstepping of all boundaries" [*ṭaghâ*], the "ruptures" [*taqaṭʿ*] and hatred they induced, and their inhuman practices of "murdering their children and women.") Yet the fitna of those early days is also modeled on the raids of the Ayt ʿAṭṭa nomads at the turn of this century, when the Berbers set up camp in the gardens and imposed their "protection" by force.

L-blâd wellât khaṭîra, "the land had become dangerous." One day, this version goes, the people of Taghallil called for help from a Berber tribe in the Atlas Mountains. They slaughtered a sheep (*debḥû ʿalihum*), as a ritual request for protection. The mountain warriors sent a ḥarka of armed men to *sheṭṭeb l-blâd,* "sweep the territory," and clean out that "rotten stuff." They wiped out the settlements in the gardens, destroyed the houses, and subdued the Ḥarâtîn, who were later deported into the newly founded qṣar of Bni Zoli, where they became the bulk of its working population. (For, in this version, the warriors did their work and went back, but a man, Driss, with his two nephews, Mḥammâd and ʿAbdallah, were left as tokens of the relationship of protection, and the people of Taghallil granted him one-fourth of the territory, which he could claim wherever he wished, on which to build his own place, etc.)

In another version, the *qṣayb,* "hamlets," in the gardens were scattered—the houses had no walls and the men had no arms for protection—and became easy prey for the Arab and Berber nomads who raided the territory during a time of uncertainty and danger. The black Ḥarâtîn of the Scattered Hamlets, who lived off agriculture and were not warriors, called for the protection of Berber mercenaries, who eventually settled in by force, subjugating the Ḥarâtîn and appropriating their land... (etc.).

It may have been Aḥmed u ʿAlî l-Qâḍî, the Judge, who came with the ḥarka of a sultan and decided to stay, and with the authority of his word—a word that was, by definition, law—mandated the settlers of the fragmented hamlets out of their scattered existence and "gathered them" into one village, surrounded that village with fortified walls, encircled the walls with a deep moat, and took the best alley of the new qṣar for his family. He married (according to some) the daughter of a holy and landed family upriver, that Lâllâ ud Sîdî after whom the old cemetery is named, who brought him blessings and wealth; or married (according to others) the daughter of a powerful family of a village nearby, managed by some manipulation of the law of inheritance to get control over his wife's family wealth, and with that wealth established a *ḥabus,* a trust to his male descendants, a *ḥabus* that became the charter of his lineage and the written foundation of the new qṣar... (etc.).

Each lineage, each person, has a different version, and the versions coexist in a polyphony no one attempts to resolve into a single voice. It is as if it were clear that your story could never be consistent with mine, just as the remedy that Faqîr Moḥammed (the cauterization surgeon of the qṣar) prescribes for my illness is never the same as the one he prescribes for yours, even though our ailments have similar symptoms and might be treated in the same way at the hospital in town. ("To each person her ailment," Faqîr Moḥammed maintains, "to each her remedy, to each her body [*kulla u nṣâfû, kulla u dwâh, kulla u dâtu*].")

Yet what all versions have in common is an uncanny resemblance with the Qur'anic parable of Yajûj and Mâjûj (Gog and Magog): their excess, overstepping all boundaries, their violence and raids, and the iron wall built by Ẓul-qarnain to keep their threat at bay (Qur'an 18:83–100).

It is a story retold many times. The Maghribî geographer al-Idrîsî even inscribed it on his map of the world. On the eastern limit, end of space and of time, region of the apocalypse, the last section of the map reads, "Bilâd Yajûj wa Mâjûj" (land of Gog and Magog); slightly to the right, a high wall is visible with an emblematic tower and a gate; the legend reads, "shadd Ẓul-qarnain" (barrier or wall of the Two-Horned). Ẓul-qarnain: the man who reached the two ends of the world, and is sometimes identified with Iskander, Alexander the Great.

The iron wall built by Ẓul-qarnain is inexpugnable, and its gate is well guarded, and locked by many locks. But, the Qur'an says, it will be turned into dust on the Last Day. On that day, the forces of destruction will be unleashed again, the unsubdued tribes of Yajûj and Mâjûj will pour into the world, and the Earth will be pounded to powder.

The story of Ẓul-qarnain, voyager of the limit, is narrated in the Qur'an as a parable of mundane authority for the establishment of God's law: from one end of the world to the other, Ẓul-qarnain travels to restore justice and social law, like the Judge, in some of the hagiographic narratives from the qṣar. Yet, stressing the impermanent and provisional nature of the endeavor, the Qur'anic parable leads to the theme of Judgment Day—of the End as always awaiting behind an iron wall.

> They asked you concerning Ẓul-qarnain. Say, I will rehearse you something of his story. We established his power on earth, and we gave him the ways and the means to all ends. One [such] way he followed, until, when he reached the setting of the sun, he found it set in a spring of murky water. . . . Then followed he another way, until, when he reached a tract in between two mountains, he found beneath them a people who scarcely understood a word. They said, "O Ẓul-qarnain! The Gog and Magog [people] do great mischief on earth: shall we then

> render you tribute in order that you might erect a barrier between us and them?" He said: "The power in which my Lord has established me is better: help me therefore with strength: I will erect a strong barrier in between you and them: bring me blocks of iron." At length, when he had filled up the space between the two steep mountain-sides, he said, "Blow"; then, when he had made it [red] as fire, he said, "Bring me molten lead, that I may pour over it." Thus were they made powerless to scale it or to dig through it. He said: "This is a mercy from my Lord: but when the promise of my Lord comes to pass, He will make it into dust; and the promise of my Lord is true. On that day We shall leave them to surge like waves on one an other: the trumpet will be blown, and will shall collect them all together." (Qur'an 18:83–86, 92–99)

The impermanent character of the wall is made apparent in al-Idrîsî's map, which is constructed as if around this parable. The map follows Ẓul-qarnain's returning shuttle between the western and the eastern limits. On that path, time becomes space, and ruin infiltrates the present—

> *When in 1154 Abû ʿAbd Allâh ibn Muḥammad ibn Idrîs, the Andalusian scholar and Maghribî expatriate known as Sharîf al-Idrisî, presented his map of the world to Ruggero II, the Norman count and ruler of Sicily,*[112] *the map was a representation of the human world carved in a disk of pure silver. The term used was* dâyra, *"a circle," "a body of circular shape" (but also a rotation, and a stopping place in the turns and returns). In the preface to* Kitab nuzhat al-mushtâq, *the text he wrote to narrate his map,*[113] *al-Idrîsî tells of how skillful craftsmen carved in the* dâyra *"the configuration of the seven climates, with that of the regions, the countries, the shores that were distant, or close to the sea."*
>
> *According to a style drawn from Ptolemy, the "disk" was divided into seven regions or climates,* iqlîm, *which corresponded on a cosmological level to seven combinations of the four elements, fire, air, water, and earth. The first climate is situated at the extreme south, beyond the equator and at the top of the disk, and the seventh at the extreme north, at the very bottom of the disk.*[114] *Oriented south-north, the disk was divided into ten sections, "traveling" from the occidental to the oriental limit. The structure of* Kitab nuzhat *makes it clear that the map must be read from west to east and from south to north, in a movement of displacement from right to left and from top to bottom. The description of each climate begins at the occidental limit—the lands of the setting sun (*maghrîb*). Himself a writer of the Two Horns, al-Idrîsî moves from one end to other, and back, to begin a new journey and a new description.*

As he travels eastward in his narrative, he tells the story of peoples and cities, of their rise and their fall, of the alternation of plenty and ruin, desertification and cultivation, construction and destruction. In the tenth section of the fifth climate, at the leftmost edge of his map, he describes the Land of Gog and Magog.

The peoples of the land of Gog are issued from Sam, son of Noah, and are designated [in the Qurʾan] as corrupted populations, plaguing the face of the earth. As for the people of Magog . . . they are entirely covered with a sort of down, and have huge ears, hanging and round. . . . Their language resembles a whistling . . . their temperament is fiery and their race prolific. These people are fundamentally evil, of bad faith, and practice great mischiefs. . . . Before the time when Alexander [the Two Horned] traveled to their land and had a barrier constructed at the gateway of their mountains, they used to come out and raid the land of their neighbors; they caused such destruction and ruin in their territories, that they emptied them almost completely of any human settlement. The entire region had become deserted, uncultivated, uninhabited. Snakes had made it their home, waters had furrowed the course of new torrents, and the land itself had become sterile.[115]

As if staging the Qurʾanic warning in act, and simultaneously showing a wall standing, and one reduced to dust, in the movement of al-Idrîsî's map the process of falling to ruin is made present. The Last Day becomes everyday—

And the different versions blend with the afternoon shadows on the thin reddish dust outside the village walls, where men tell stories leaning against the enclosure of the old cemetery of Lâllâ ud Sîdî, measuring the sun going down on the long thin trunk of the closest palm trees, *wagfa* after *wagfa* (the length of one standing man after another), watching the water flowing slowly in the canal of Aghala Ufella, listening to the distant crackling of the engine pumps, to the shouts of the Ḥarâtîn girls washing clothes in the silver reflection of the afternoon sun on the water, responding to the greetings of the men coming back from a day of work in the gardens and crossing the bridge over the irrigation canal with their donkeys. Or instead contemplating the streambed of the canal, gone dry in the heat, wondering whether the water will ever come back, citing other times of drought when all the palm trees died, when even the richest wells ran dry, when everyone who could migrated north to the *gharb*, and watching a child pulling a bunch of dry palm leaves in a cloud of dust—for firewood is all that the gardens have to give.

The men sit there and tell stories, waiting for the sunset call to prayer from the old mosque of Ayt l-Bâlî, where now only a few old men go to pray, and sometimes don't even make the effort to go, but pray right there by the wall, kneeling on their djellaba, turning their backs to the cemetery, one side to the irrigation canal, and looking toward the mosque, toward the distant white dome of the sanctuary of Sîdî Ṣâfu, and, beyond all that toward Mecca.

Their stories are fragments of stories, and I can only rewrite them as such. Stories of ruins, they are themselves made of ruins. Like the towers in the scenes of Yusef's drawing, like the painted details in Si Lḥussein's recollection, they are ideogrammatic, fragmented, and atopical; a bit like those proverbs—ideograms of a story—which Benjamin likens to the ivy that grows on the broken walls of old ruins.[116]

"It was in a time of drought like this," says old Moḥammed u Saddiq, breaking the silence between two gusts of hot wind, "that the village of Bni Zoli was born."

(It is the peak of five years of drought and people despair that the river will ever reappear. The world has become more unpredictable than it has ever been, they say, because now men wish to control it without respecting the arbitrariness of its laws, because the dynamite the "boys" bring back from their trips breaks the resistance of the soil, because the engine pumps pull water up from too far inside the earth and cause the palm trees to dry at their roots, because the canal of Iflî is now wrapped up in cement and the blood of the sacrifice performed at its mouth by the procession of barefoot women and children asking God to send water does not filter into the earth, but dries out to form a black stain on the pristine cement esplanade of the new dam, which now stands in place of the old gate of Iflî.)

And Moḥammed u Saddiq goes on to tell the story of how the qṣar was born of an original "sweeping," and its primitive accumulation of land realized through the speculative sale of waste materials—*tiskert,* an image of waste and recycling.

> When the people of Taghallil offered one-fourth of the territory to those who will become the people of Bni Zoli in exchange for the cleaning job these had done, they asked, "Where do you want your land?" and the others said, "Give us the land upstream." The Taghallilyin said, "The land upstream is deserted and dry, you deserve better." They meant that the hill of Teyrft l-Arbaʿ over there was too high in relation to the water level, and that a great deal of that land belonged to the mosque—the old cemeteries were there, and in those days they couldn't yet be farmed. But they insisted upon their request and

got their fourth upstream. A year went by and there was a severe drought. The palms didn't blossom in the spring and gave no dates in the fall; on the trees there was only *tiskert*, the poor empty trace of the miscarried fruits. The people of Taghallil didn't bother to harvest the *tiskert* on their palms. They told the people of the qṣar, "We don't want that aborted stuff. If you feel like cutting it, it's yours." And so the people of Bni Zoli got up, and measured the *tiskert* by donkey loads, while the people of Taghallil went on slaughtering their animals, for they had nothing else to eat. Another year went by, and the water didn't come. There was still a drought. But now there was nothing to eat, for the people of Taghallil had run out of animals to roast. And so it happened that the people of Bni Zoli, who had all that *tiskert* stored away, started selling it to the people of Taghallil, a bag of *tiskert* against a whole garden! And Bni Zoli bought up the gardens of Taghallil, until they were forced to draw the boundary between the two places...

For there were Driss, Mḥammâd, and ʿAbdallah. Mḥammâd and ʿAbdallah were brothers; Driss was their uncle. When the people of Taghallil called them in, and made their deal with them, they offered them one-fourth of the territory. They said, "Weed those weeds, sweep out those insects from the heart of the territory, empty the land from the scattered hamlets, clean it out, and then, wherever you like to get your fourth, we'll give it to you."

This is what the first people recounted, and we remember [*dak shshi llî ʿawdu lîna l-awlîn, u ḥnâ ʿaqalna*]. Driss and his friends were from Ayt Ḥaddiddu.[117] The people of Taghallil had called them to break the population of the hamlets in the gardens [*bâsh iherrsuhum; hrs* is to break, disintegrate, reduce to powder],[118] for those bandits harassed them and made their life impossible. Those of the hamlets surrounded it from every direction, the Taghallilyin feared to come out of their houses. If they did, the others attacked them with stones. They lived in fear. So they called Ayt Ḥaddiddu, and swore that if their armed men were able to "sweep" all that stuff out and clean up the region, they would all emerge from the gardens and build a new village outside, out there in the wasteland, where the air was clean and the water was sweet.

And the army of Driss destroyed [*khlâw*, "emptied"] the settlements in the gardens—six qṣûr they destroyed! The day they swept that rotten stuff out, the day that stuff was no longer inside [inside the heart of the land and, like an illness, inside the body], Driss and his nephews decided to stay on. People were scattered, and consulted with each other. They said, "Let us come out of the gardens. Let us move out to the desert, and we'll make one country [*blâd waḥeda*], and we'll fix [*nressmu*] all the people in one place." And they made this place, and the family of ʿAbdallah stayed in the Alley of Ayt ʿAbdallah, Driss was in the Alley of Bû Ṭwîl, and Mḥammâd was in the Alley of Ayt l-Qâḍî, that is, in the alley where the people of Ayt l-Qâḍî are today. When they went to the mosque they used to come out at Arḥabî,[119] and then the first would enter the Alley of Ayt l-Qâḍî, the second that of Bû Ṭwîl, and the third that of Ayt ʿAbdallah... [120] The mosque was the little mosque of Ayt l-Bâlî, just those three columns. The whole quarter of Ayt j-Jdîd did not exist then. The whole village in those days was formed by the three alleys and the little mosque of Ayt l-Bâlî. It is there that people spent their time.

Listen!

All of a sudden the men of Ayt Mḥammâd deviled up, they developed a will to fitna [*n-niya dyâl l-fitna*]. Mḥammâd started fighting with his brother ʿAbdallah. They argued and fought, and Driss moved to the Alley of Bû Ṭwîl, to be, he said, between the two brothers, so that they wouldn't fight. But the people of Ayt Mḥammâd started moving out—out to Sîdî Aḥmed u Abdelkhâleq, upstream from us. They did like Taqshurt: they split off from this or that house, this or that family, and built houses over there, on the outside... they were building Tighremt...

And then there is the story of Ḥammu. The day the people of Bni Zoli decided to gather into one village and assemble the country [*nhâr llî bghâw ijemmʿu l-blâd*], the children of Ḥammu were still in their hamlet in the gardens [*tighremt n-Ayt Ḥammu*]. The people of Bni Zoli said, "Those Ayt Ḥammu, we can't afford leaving them outside, they'll make trouble for us, we'll bring them in whether they like it or not." And they chose a house, a big house in the Alley of Ayt ʿAbdallah, and summoned the children of Ḥammu and said, "If you choose to stay with us, we'll give you a house inside the walls. If you resist, we'll cut your heads off. And that house became a slaughterhouse [*megzara*]... blood running everywhere. Those who chose to stay and live were divided into twelve different houses, scattered all over the qṣar to prevent them from creating a faction, and inducing fitna, destruction, and ruin [*bash ma-ifettnu*].

Everything Returns to Being Earth

"This land was formed from the debris of a ruinous flood." L-Ḥajj l-Madanî is speaking as we walk to one of his gardens in the area of the canal of Tifkert, where his sons are turning over the earth before the beginning of the new sowing season. Leaning on his cane, he laboriously climbs the winding path under the palm trees.

The path goes up and down following the uneven ground, drops deep in the depression between two hills by the banks of naked earth, and then climbs on top of a third hill, where we rest for a moment contemplating the tormented landscape. Each of us finds a lump of clay to sit on, a *ṭobba.* From that vantage point, the small cultivated plots, bright green with peppers and henna, resemble craters dug into the side of a volcano. There is something disquieting about this region of the gardens, something that is conveyed by the terrain itself, by the cracks in the clayish soil burned by the summer heat—even if you don't know that according to the story this is the area of the gardens Driss and his people requested from the village of Taghallil in exchange for their "sweeping" job; that this is the area upstream, "too high" in relation to the canal of Tifkert; that the old qṣar of Tfu, the bigger of the ancient settlements, used to stand on these grounds; and so forth.

L-Ḥajj is old, and his long hands are reduced to skin and bone, the dark skin made lighter, at places, by the work of time on the body. (It is he who told me once that the skin of black people gets lighter with old age, and when death is approaching it develops a grayish patina as if dusted with chalk. And it was his house in the village I was sweeping at the beginning of my dream, which then transformed into a forgotten graveyard in which I sank, and it is to that house that I returned at the end of the dream.)

L-Ḥajj looks up, and with his arm indicates a small mound nearby, where a fig tree, bent by the wind and by time, stands alone like a torn flag after a battle. "The figs from that tree over there cost the life of Ṭayab u Ḥammu, the grandfather of the man who sells salt in the sûq. It was in the days of *siba,* and the gardens were infested—enemies hiding everywhere. He was determined to get his figs. People told him not to go. The enemies were hiding, planning to ambush someone else, and they shot him instead. We couldn't come out of the qṣar to bury him, and his dead body was left there for two days. When we finally found him, he was swollen, he was rotting, and was covered by a thick coat of ants and flies, attracted by the figs and by the odor of death. We dug a hole and buried him right there, under the fig tree; no one was willing to carry the corpse all the way to the shrine of Sîdî Ṣâfu."

L-Ḥajj smiles, then laughs, for he sees the grotesque. For some reason, he says, this story reminds him of when he was a child, and his mother baked bread on market day and sent him to sell her small flat breads at the entrance of the sûq. He was always hungry. People were always hungry in those days—perhaps they just worked more and ate more. And he and ʿAyyed his brother, who later died in the Ayt ʿAṭṭa warfare not far from this area of the gardens, were orphans, and they were hungry, and so they ate all the crumbs inside the breads. One day their mother woke up to their trick (some angry customer must have told her), and as a punishment she locked them inside the walls of a garden behind the sûq, right where the butchers washed the intestines of the slaughtered animals in the canal. He can still remember the stench.

"Burying the dead was a gamble in those days. You risked ending up dead yourself. That's why people started using the graveyard of Sîdî Maḥmud [one of the shrines, right outside the walls]. The *roda* of Si ʿAlî u Mseʿud [the main cemetery of the qṣar] is too far, out there in the desert. Many times we went to take the dead in a procession and then were forced to abandon the corpse and *nʿash* on the path, to find refuge back inside the walls!"

(I am left to visualize the scene. The rocky desert in the oblique afternoon light that outlines the contours of the stones one by one on the reddish ground, and the corpse, abandoned like a bright white spot, wrapped up in white cotton tied at the head and feet with newly spun wool, threatening to slide off the wooden litter that in normal times sits by the gate of the qṣar ready for the next to go. And the men running back to the village under enemy fire.)

Earth, in all its dimensions, is l-Ḥajj's central concern. He is, after all, an old khammâs. (But a khammâs who throughout his life managed never to be under the rule of one master. His playful independence is legendary. He worked for several landlords at once and made a strategy of quitting after a year, not to develop a pattern of dependency. Then he went to the northern plains, *l-gharb,* worked for a French colon, made some money, came back, and bought his own gardens.) He indicates the lump of dirt on which I am sitting.

"You see," he says, "in the qṣar what counts above all is the earth, *trâb.* It is earth that marks the passages of life and of death. Women give birth sitting on a lump of earth, a *ṭobba* that is passed on from mother to daughter, and when they are postpartum [*tanzoght*] they lay in a bed of earth and sand. On the seventh day, the baby is wrapped in bands and put down on the bare earth; and before washing a corpse, a lump of earth is put on the navel of the dead person...

"The nomads, like the Ayt ʿAṭṭa or the Arabs of the 'outside,' are concerned with bones and blood descent, for they don't have the earth, and view themselves as alone, as wandering in the wide world. We, instead, have the earth. You won't understand anything about this place if you try to figure out the blood lines and the different families. You must understand the [spatial] organization of the village [*khassek tefhem n-niḍâm taʿ l-qṣar*], its houses, its alleys, its *ḥyût,* its earth walls, and that of the gardens, their paths and their canals, the shrines, the cemeteries. The qṣar is its mud walls, *l-ḥyût.* Those who come to live in Bni Zoli, like all these foreigners who came from somewhere else in the early days, swept out their past, washed it away, and came to settle inside these earth walls."

L-Ḥajj gets up, shakes the dust off his djellaba, and we resume our walk. "I was telling you about the flood."

"Do you know why this land is so tormented in its shape and so high in relation to the canal? All the gardens you see have been dug in, and earlier, before the arrival of the engine pumps, they used to have *bû ʿanfer,* those well holes from which people pulled up the water with mules... The ground is all pierced with dried up well holes...

"The earth on which we are walking now was thrown here by the river, a flood, a ruinous flood: the region of Tifkert was "thrown," regurgitated by the river [*blâd Tifkert llî rmât l-wâd*]. Before that event the land was flat. Then one day came a storm, which became a flood. The river came. Its front was like a mountain. Where it passed, it brought destruction and death. It came from the direction of the area of Ayt ʿAlî u Nuḥ. There were many villages there in those days, and a mosque to which students came from all over to study, a mosque with a library full of books. The river washed away everything, and carried the debris along with the flood. There was an open place in the middle of the gardens: it is there that the mud piled up, and became the plateau of Teyrft l-Arbaʿ. And the flood came down this way, Iger Igenna and on, all the way to the canal of Tifkert... Still today the ground is uneven, with mounds everywhere... All this was the debris brought down by the river. For the flood swept out everything that was built or planted [*l-bni kullu*], from the settlements of Ayt ʿAlî u Nuḥ to Teyrsut. How many houses, how many families were gone that way, became mud in the river... Houses, dead bodies, animals, trees, everything was washed out and the debris gathered in this place."

We arrive at his garden. L-Ḥajj says, "Bismillâh," and walks through the small door made of palm wood and colorful tin cans (like houses, these gardens are surrounded by high mud walls), and we go sit in the shade, watching his two sons plowing with their hoes, naked in their loincloths, buried to their knees in the ground they are digging. (If you don't dig that deep the water does not penetrate the earth enough for the barley to stand the thirst between two water turns, l-Ḥajj says.)

"It is women who dismember and cause the families to fall into ruin," l-Ḥajj says suddenly.

"Salem... *(he indicates his son),* his wife left last year. Now she is at the house of a man in Tanagamt, but she won't last. When a woman starts doing fitna in the house, when she starts the buying and selling of words, it's like an illness that spreads quickly and mines the house from the inside. She left a first time and went back to her parents. I went and got her, for her father is a cousin on my mother's side. But then she left again. I wasn't here; I was away on a trip. When I came back, I found that the women of her family had come, they had emptied out the bridal room [*l-ḥanût*] of everything, they had taken her stuff and swept the floor, they swept everything [*sheṭṭbu*] until the space was completely clear. Then they pulled out the utâd from the walls [*gellʿu l-utâd*], uprooted the 'poles.' so that our house might be ruined.[121] Before they left, they urinated in the middle of the empty swept floor; or so we were told."

"That flood was like the big fitna that razed the hamlets in the gardens," he says a while later. "This place where we are sitting now used to be the ground of the qṣar of Tfu.

"This land," he continues after a pause (as if reluctant to use the term), "is but a huge *qbûr mensiya,* a forgotten graveyard..." He goes on reciting, almost as a lament:

The remains of the old market I found in this garden
I found the shops
Still there, gone,
leaning against the wall of my property
I found the oven of the potters
I found the oven of the whitewash
Still there, gone
Look at the pots, the twajin, *the water jugs*
And there was a mosque
There, in the middle of the barley patch
There where is now the garden of Ayt Lḥassan u Ḥummadi
And the graveyard
of course the graveyard...

"We were plowing, turning the earth over. As we worked, our hoes uncovered our fellow men of the early times [*kullshi l-mrafeg taʿ bekri*]. Dismembered limbs, the arms, the skulls, of the dead people. All that, God spare us, you just touch it and it turns into dust, it dissolves, except for the teeth. *(He smiles.)*... The teeth don't deteriorate. But the rest, everything else, everything returns to being earth [*kullshi kayʿud l-trâb*], once more."

I look at l-Ḥajj's sons half buried in the ground, piling up the earth on the side of where they are digging. I remember that, when I first came, women predicted that I would turn the color of earth, for no one can resist the erosion of dust. I recall the funeral of Um ʿAṣṣa Moḥa's father a few weeks earlier, when I sat alone by the side of the corpse watching that lump of earth over the white sheet, at the height of the navel, until women came and took me away. And I think of l-Ḥajj's fascinating link between the mud that came from the melting of villages in the flood by which this land was formed, the *trâb* that the Bni Zoli people cultivate today, and the decomposition of dead bodies into the earth of the old graveyards, the ruins of that former world beyond memory that provide the materials for the construction of the present.

I see him giving instruction to his sons; the new henna plants should not be watered before sunset, and the plastic bags should be tied over the branches of the two valuable palm trees—a windstorm could come and scatter the young dates. With his pragmatic sense of the *bricoleur,* he knows that, besides being places to dream, ruins are places to live in.

He comes to get me, and we head back to the qṣar. As we walk back on the winding path, l-Ḥajj is again in a playful mood. His little eyes—the eyes he has passed on to each of his five sons and his daughter—are laughing like those of the rascal who used to steal bread in the sûq, when he thinks of a story he wants to tell me about the recycling of ruins. It is a story not unlike that of the village's primitive accumulation from the speculative sale of *tiskert.* But, in tune with his taste for the grotesque, it tells of the birth of one of the big Ḥarâr lineages from a broken water jug filled up with shit.

"Now they reproduce like locusts, and their children are spreading all over, a disaster considering their unpleasant nature, but there was a time when their bone had truly run out of steam. One woman was left, and she was sterile. She went to see a Jewish curer. In those days there were still the Jews in the Mellaḥ. And the curer told her, 'Go out into the desert, and find a piece of dry feces of unknown origin, collect it and bring it home. Then find a *gerruj,* and if you don't have one make one by breaking off the head of a *gulla.*[122] For seven days, when you feel like defecating, collect your shit in the *gerruj,* until it is half full. Then fill the other half with water, and put it in the sun, on the roof of the house, for seven more days. Wait until the liquid rots [*hattâ ikhmar*], until you cannot stand the smell. Then, drink from it a cup a day for seven days, and you shall be, God willing, able to conceive.' "

"This is why," l-Ḥajj concludes laughing, "the people of Ayt . . . are called still today the family of the broken jug."

The Topography of Forgetting

Sometimes the ruin, the trace, is a shrine, and the place is inscribed in the mystical map of ṣaliḥîn dyâl l-blâd, *"the Protectors of the land." Sîdî Abderraḥman Bû Yaqûb, for instance: a built-up tomb on a mound, the remains of a small graveyard, and a well. It lies between two of those former settlements, now completely disappeared—only the names are left—of whose lives the shrine is, people say, the crystallized and sedimented form. The gardens are punctuated by these sites, and their distribution on the territory forms a mystical map of undercurrents of which these points are, so to speak, the knots. One site is visited to get rid of fever, another to cure diseases of the eye, yet another to heal mental disturbances.* Ṣaliḥîn *are the concern of women, who alone know the healing virtue and the appropriate offering for each—*

But apart from the tales narrating the disaster of the scattered hamlets (a catastrophic philosophy of history implicating the present as much as the past, interlaced, and superimposed on a single plan), little or nothing is said about these shrines, sunken into forgetting—that zone of unknowing out of which flows dream. In some rare cases, legends are told about the ʿalâma, *the "sign," that made manifest their location. In one place a big* qasriya *of couscous descended from the sky. In another, a light is said to shine in the darkness of the palm grove at night. In some cases,* mujahiddîn, *"martyrs in a holy war," are said to have died there, but who were they and what were they fighting for?*

In a land so fond of storytelling, where an abstract point is always imaged in the particular form of a story, it is puzzling how few stories are told about these sites, which are so important in the lives of people. Collectively, they are referred to as rodat, *the "graves," making explicit their relationship with death. There is something unspeakable about these graves. In discourse they are treated like symbolic blind spots. No one knows, no one tries to imagine (by capturing the unknown into a figure, or by spinning it out into a story). Not because their stories are a secret, but because there are no stories to tell. For that unknowing is the source of their force.*

Istinzâl: The Broom and the Ladder of Rhetorics

> In certi momenti mi sembrava che il mondo stesse diventando tutto di pietra . . . era come se nessuno potesse sfuggire allo sguardo inesorabile della Medusa. L'unico eroe capace di tagliare la testa alla Medusa e' Perseo, che vola coi sandali alati, Perseo che non rivolge il suo sguardo sul volto della Gorgone ma solo sulla sua immagine riflessa nello scudo di bronzo.
>
> —Italo Calvino[123]

When we are walking in a procession to take a dead person to the cemetery [it is only men who attend the burial while women mourn at home], slowly our thoughts withdraw from their mundane paths. When we arrive at the site of burial and put the corpse down in the direction of

Mecca to pray the ṣalât l-gnâza *in front of it, the prayer of the dead, as we contemplate the corpse, the gaze of death slowly takes hold of each one of us. There is a moment of silence, when sitting on the ground we see Death, and we are colonized by its overwhelming thought... We forget our families, then, our children, our property, the work in the fields, and we lose ourselves in the infinity of that vision, where everything becomes indifferent. Dunya, then, the world and its affairs, disappears for us. Left to itself that sentiment would produce the destruction of social life. We would sit there forever...*

But the angel comes...

An angel comes, flies over us and sprinkles a handful of earth over our heads. It is the earth of forgetting and makes us blind, once again, to the paralyzing vision of Death. Again we can see the world, set back into its boundaries by our blindness, and again we find ourselves caught in daily affairs. The thought comes back of our children, of the henna that needs to be watered, of the money we lent to a neighbor, of the house we are planning to build, of the approaching elections of the Agricultural Council. We look around for our allies and our enemies. By the time we get up, we have forgotten all about Death, and the funeral has become a social occasion... Someone invariably makes a joke, and everybody laughs. It is a signal, people gather in little groups, each with his friends... and we walk back to the qṣar as if we had never seen Death... as if nothing had happened. Of course it's a delusion, but without that delusion dunya, and society, could not exist. (Si Thami, after the burial of Moḥa u Ḥammu.)

A resigned story, ironical in a way (for those who tell it draw the outline of a frame by which they claim to be framed), it tells of an encounter, direct and intractable, with an absolute other. Men's experience of death in the cemetery is that of the petrifying sight of Medusa. Under her gaze they lose themselves, and for a moment, they glimpse the face of what has no face, no reality, no history—and are turned into stone.[124] At the cemetery the experience of alterity is not tamed by figuration—by the appearance, even threatening, of a face. The men sit on the ground with their heads reclined, and, transformed into statues, they would sit there forever, were it not for the angel who comes to break the spell.

Is it possible to speak in the vision of death? to recount from within a space of forgetting? to look at Medusa without being turned into stone by her gaze? In the Greek myth, Perseus, who conquers the Gorgon and turns her deadly powers to his ends, does not look at her directly, but at her image reflected on his copper shield. (When he cuts her head off, from her blood a flying horse is born—heaviness transformed into lightness—and the head of Medusa, hidden inside a bag, becomes Perseus's secret weapon—)[125]

When Si Lḥassan u Aḥmed performs a rite to heal a person stricken by the jinns, he never addresses the jinns directly.

"If you can see the jinn," he says, "it is because you are already caught." The rite he performs—*l-istinzâl*—is a rite of figuration. It is aimed at deflecting direct vision by way of reflected images. It centers on the imaginary setting of a stage for the jinns to manifest themselves, and on a rigorous strategy of avoiding a face-to-face encounter.

The exchange is mediated by the intermediary of a child, who acts as *tarjamân*, "translator," between the diviner and the jinn. The child—who sees the jinn on the mirrorlike surface of his right hand, previously shined with oil—translates the speech of the diviner to the third person: *qâl l-fqîh*, "the fqîh said." It is *al-ghayb*, the "absent person" in Arabic grammar. Short of this mediation, this detour through the absent, Si Lḥassan says, the diviner himself would be caught in the field of *fascinum* and be struck.[126]

> Between us and the jinns there is a screen of avoidance, a curtain [*l-ḥjâb*]. We can see them only as reflections. Only the sick can see them. Myself, when I am reciting an exorcism [*ʿazîma*], I can only guess their shape in smoke, or in the shadows, or reflected in water or mirrors. There must always be a *wasiṭa*, an intermediary, a link, a term between: for if the jinns appeared right in front of me, they'd put me in a state of fitna, I would be seized by madness [*ghâdî yfetnûnî*], and I'd be lost.

Fitna: ghâdî yfetnûnî, he says, they will make me lose myself, and I shall be seized. Seized, he will find himself on the other side—the side of the sick. That danger, he knows, is always waiting. This is why it is so important that he observe the ritual rules of purity, and that he lead a balanced life. More than one fqîh doing what he does has become mad or has died. His own brother, a few years older, who had been his teacher and had introduced him to the magic squares, died of *aders*, a gangrene whose origin was not just physical.[127]

When he invests himself in the struggle and utters the *ʿazîma*, the recitation by which he fights the jinns, Si Lḥassan feels, he says, a tightening inside his body and a cold current going up his spine. The words he pronounces come back to strike him. He is afraid of being seized, but he knows that if he gives way to fear he'll become easy prey for the jinns. During that time, and the waiting that follows, not even a glass of tea makes it down his throat. Yet he knows that if he is not seized somewhat, if he does not manage to enter the space of fitna and operate on it from within, he cannot help the person in crisis. The problem is how to stand on that edge without staggering, entering fitna without being maftûn—

The istinzâl is a strategy of regulated implication. Unlike the men's response in the cemetery, Si Lḥassan's approach is oblique. It is precisely his indirect strategy that enables him to perform a direct intervention. His interpretive work is not one of decoding; rather, it is akin to the strategy of myth, which elaborates one image into another without ever breaking the code. His healing strategy is one of figuration, it amounts to providing a narrative and a set of characters that lend face to that experience of alterity that manifests itself as illness. Yet the demons he makes appear are not just interpretative figures: they are dangerous apparitions from the region of the unknown.

Istinzâl is one of the forms of the verbal root *nazala*. It means to bring down, make descend, or cause to be revealed. With his intervention and his privileged access to a hermetic language, the diviner "makes descend," "brings down" into the world, that is, channels into a manageable and reduced form, the otherwise unmanageable reality of the Beyond. Without his reduction to form, the direct descent—or manifestation—of that Beyond is destructive and overwhelming. It is a theatrical stage for the mise-en-scène of the illness.

Only if the istinzâl is performed are the powerful among the jinns willing to make an appearance. I bring in a child of about seven, for he or she must be before puberty yet with an already formed mind; with puberty comes the need for avoidance [l-ḥjâb]. *I write on the forehead and the hand of the child who serves as a medium* [nadur] *a magic square with the secret letters* [l-ḥarf llî fîha serr]. *Then I rub his hand with oil until it shines like a mirror. I tell him to keep looking at the writing until he can see the face of a man or a woman. And all of a sudden that seed of writing on his hand opens up, like a seed popping, and shows a face with eyes and mouth. I ask the child what he sees. If he says, "I see a black face," that's good, because it is the slave who came first to work for us and set up the place. I say to the child, "Tell him to sweep the room* [sheṭṭeb]*." The child repeats, "The diviner said to sweep the room." When the jinn is done with sweeping, I say to the child, "Tell him to bring the rugs." And I ask the child what kind of rugs did he bring—because I myself can't see anything. Then I say, "Tell him to bring the chairs." If there are seven chairs, I tell the child, "Tell him to invite the king of the day." And when the king comes with his minis-*

ters, I say to the child, "Ask them whether they wish to eat..." After they have eaten I can finally address them and I ask, "Why did you harm that person?" And the negotiation begins...

Through a kind of writing that lends face (literally so, the letters pop up to show a face), and through speech, with a description that is a prescription, which produces a world instead of referring back to it, Si Lḥassan manages to open an imaginary world that is at once born from within the illness and removed from it. This world exists only in discourse, yet it exceeds discourse; it produces a reality of its own, and it makes possible the manifestation—the istinzâl—of a Beyond. The act of sweeping the room is a central image of this process: it is the clearing, the opening of a stage—an Other Scene—upon which the characters may appear. The right context is created with rugs, chairs, the offering of a meal. By the end of the process a place has been created, a house, a rasm—an imaginary reference.

Putting the rugs down—*l-frâsh*—means to materialize for a moment the space of a house, to create a fugitive permanence. Before meaning "house," *rasm* means "tent." When guests are expected to come, *kanfrashû lihûm,* "we set the place up for them" with rugs and pillows. What was until a moment before an empty corridor with a dusty dirt floor, a place no one would know how to use, becomes a comfortable sitting room, where tea can be prepared and conversation can start. And for certain ritual events that take place outdoors, such as the henna ceremony at weddings, a place is materialized by putting down a straw mat. On that mat—a symbolic rasm—a whole world can be made to appear.

In that new space, another space in which uncanny events can unfold, Si Lḥassan reads and writes, and the letters that he writes pop up and transform into faces. They are the masks with which Si Lḥassan, fqîh and *metteur en scène,* will stage his demonic representation.

He will summon the faces one by one, the jinns, and to each he will ask their name; once it gives its name, a jinn is obliged to work for him. The jinns will resist. Si Lḥassan will recite charms and sections from the Qur'an, burn perfumes, and do everything in his power to lower their resistance. He may have to give up, and try again at a different time, in a different place, with a different supporting crowd. The jinns may vanish and never come back—and the person will remain ill. But if a jinn surrenders and lets its name go, the fqîh has it on a leash. They can negotiate, and eventually make a pact.

And yet, as Si Lḥassan is aware, the images that lend face are an ambivalent and dangerous remedy. They deface by the work of lending face. If you are not careful, he says (*kay-fettnûk*), they "draw you in," and claim your life—

IN SI LḤASSAN'S WORDS

(Now, about the istinzâl, from what I understand the fqîh provides a diagnosis, an interpretation of the illness... he explains to the patient the reason why he fell sick.)

The istinzâl is a kind of X ray. You are sick and go to see the doctor, and he looks at what you have inside. But, unlike what happens with X rays, we cannot see the jinns directly... Even people like me, who are not sick, but recite incantations against Them, don't see them face to face, but only, at times, guess their shapes. Myself, for instance, when I am reciting an exorcism, I can only guess their shape in smoke, or in the shadows [*khayâl*], or reflected in water or mirrors. There must always be a *wasiṭa*, an intermediary, a link, a term between: for if the jinns appeared right in front of me, they'd put me in a state of fitna: I would be seized by madness [*ghâdî yfetnûnî*] and I'd be lost...

We do the istinzâl when the patient is conscious and can talk, but is paralyzed in a limb or a half of the body, or when he is subjected to intermittent fainting fits or the like...

Only if the istinzâl is performed are the powerful among the jinns willing to make an appearance. We bring in a child of about seven, for it is said in the texts, "Write on the palm of the hand of a child before puberty [*tuktabu ʿala keff sabî dûna al-bulûgh*]."[128] That child must be in possession of his or her faculties and yet prepubescent. Because after puberty a screen [*ḥjâb*] is erected between humans and jinns. We can't see Them without losing our minds...

And we have to choose the girl or the boy among those who are *zuhariyin*, who have on the palm of their hand the line that is a mark of vision. If we find that the child has that line, that *khaṭ*, we write the magic square on his hand, with *samagh* ink, and we write it on his forehead, between the eyes. We write it on the forehead of the medium, not on that of the patient: the patient sits back and watches.

That child who serves as a medium is called *naḍur* [literally "the viewer" or "the lens"], and becomes the translator [*tarjamân*], the translator between us and the jinns. For the jinns avoid us [*kay-ḥeshmû menna*]. There is no way to have a direct hold on them. Because, as I told you earlier, if you get to see them it means that you are captured, maftûn, they caught you and pushed you to the other side.

We target the names of the Seven Sultans in the magic square, for the powerful among the jinns, the sultans of the jinns, make an appearance only if the istinzâl is performed. Otherwise they never show up...

And when we write the magic square on the hand of the medium, we put the diacritic dots [*nuqat*] on the secret letter [*l-ḥarf llî fîha serr*], the "powerful letter," and we write the Ayat al-Kashf from the Qur'an [*kashf*, "uncovering," "revelation"]. Then we rewrite it on a bit of paper and we tie it around the neck of the child as a talisman. In the meantime we keep shining the palm of his hand with oil, to make it translucent, and keep putting on oil until it shines like a glass or a mirror, until it becomes luminous like a television screen. We tell the child to keep looking at the dots on the letters and to look at the edge of the hand, where the magic square is...

Until that writing, that seed of writing on his hand, opens up, like a seed popping, and transforms into a face with eyes and mouth [*Ḥettâ dîk l-ketba, dîk l-ḥabba llî ktebna, katterteg, katwellî katdîr l-ʿaynîn u l-fum*]:... and to the child becomes apparent the face of a man or that of a woman...

It is the child who tells me what he sees: myself, I don't see anything. At that point *kanʿazzem*, I invest myself in the recitation, and recite the Ayat al-Kashf. The child keeps looking at the palm of his hand and his feet tremble, and when the jinn makes his appearance, when he sees the apparition, the image in the margin, I ask: "Did you see anything?"

If he answers that he has seen a black face I am comforted, for it is the Slave, the Worker, who has come first to work for us. I say to the child: "Tell the Worker to get up and sweep the room [*sheṭṭeb l-maḥal*]."

The boy repeats the order to the jinn, he says, "The fqîh said to sweep the room..."

If the jinn gets up and moves around the hand, it's done, we have him. If the jinn doesn't move and refuses to work, we send him away and call in another one. When the boy tells me, "There he is, he's moving around," even a glass of tea if they give it to me doesn't pass through my throat: for that spell I am reciting strikes back upon me with an effect of recoil [*katrjaʿliyâ dîk l-ʿazîma*]...

When the Worker has finished sweeping, I say to the child, "Tell him to bring in the furnishing [*l-frâsh*]..."

The boy repeats, "The ṭaleb said to bring in the furnishings."

The jinn brings in the furnishings, and sets up the place. I ask the child, "What kind of rugs has he brought in? Are they red, green or white?"

The child tells me whether it is this color or that color, and again I tell him, "Tell him to bring in the chairs."

The child repeats, "The fqîh said to bring in the chairs."

And I ask him, "How many chairs did he bring in?"

If he says "Three," I tell him: "Tell him to bring in the others until he reaches seven..."

When the child says that the jinn has brought in seven chairs, I tell him, "Tell the jinn to invite the sultan of the day, the ministers, and their scribes..."

And the child repeats, "The fqîh said to invite the sultan of the day, the ministers, and their scribes..."

And I keep an eye on the child, to make sure he's not cheating, and watch out for the jinns of the house [*jnûn l-ʿammâr*]. Because when you start the istinzâl the jinns who inhabit the house are the first to appear, they rush to the child's hand and lie... they lie, and seek to distract your attention and to make the istinzâl fail. The jinns who have attacked the patient, those who really harm people only come later... So I must be careful to detour the jinns of the house with my recitation, to make them go away...

Then I ask the child, "Who is sitting on the big chair?"

And if today is Friday I know that it is *sultân l-byaḍ*, "the White Sultan," that is supposed to appear; if the child says instead the Black Sultan, I say, "Let's try again at another time," for it is either the child who is lying, or else the jinns of the house are disturbing the event. If instead the child says that there is the White Sultan sitting on the chair, I know he is telling the truth, and that we are in the presence of the sultan, and not a jinn of the house in disguise.

Then I say to the child, "Welcome them, tell them Salâm ʿalikûm!"

And the child repeats, "The fqîh said, 'Salâm ʿalikûm.'"

I ask the child, "Did they reply to your greeting?"

If the child says yes, I say to him, "Ask them whether they would like a meal..."

The child asks them, and if they say yes, I tell him to ask them whether they like it cooked or raw...

What's the Raw? The Worker brings a sheep in front of them, and they get it, they slaughter it and take the skin off and eat it raw, or else cook it. And there are instead those who tell you they want a normal meal. In this case I tell the child, "Tell the Worker to bring them the meal they desire..."

And when they are eating I ask the child what meal did the Worker bring: is it a ragout or a couscous?

Then I say to the child to tell them, "Eat, you are welcome!"

And when they are finished I tell the child to tell them, "Those who want to drink coffee can drink it, and who would like to smoke can smoke..."

Only then! Only then I address them with regard to the patient. I say to the child, "Tell them that I say 'Salâm ʿalikûm.'"

The child repeats, "The fqîh said 'Salâm ʿalikûm.'"

I say, "Ask the sultan, 'Your Highness, we want you to tell us whether it is one of your people who has injured this person...'"

The child repeats the question to the sultan, and if the sultan says no, I call in the sultan of another tribe and check upon the answer, I ask him whether it was in fact someone from the first tribe or not. If the second sultan says yes, I ask him to produce the responsible ones, I ask him, in other words, to act as a guarantor between them... And he goes to fetch them wherever they are; if they are female jinns he brings them, if they are males he brings them, and makes them stand before the sultan of the day.

I ask the child, "Who have they brought in?"

He says, "They brought in two men," or two women, or three, or four, or one...

I ask, "What color are they, black or white?"

I say to the child, "Ask them whether it is they who have attacked this person..."

The child repeats, "The fqîh wants to know whether it is you who have attacked this person..."

If they say yes, I say to the child, "Ask them what the sick person has done."

The child repeats, "The fqîh said, 'What has that person done to you?'"

And they say that they just felt like it, or else the person is bewitched or that he or she stepped on a jinn in the street, and so forth...

If they say he's bewitched [*mesḥûr*], I say to the child to order them to reveal that witchcraft [*siḥr*]: is it buried or tied up somewhere? They say what sort of witchcraft it is, and I tell the child to order them to produce it right there. But the child can bring in only a simulacrum [*timtil*], not the real thing. I ask the child, "What is it, a hidden bundle [*serra*], or an amulet [*ḥerz*]?"

If it is a hidden bundle I tell the child to order them to open it. I ask, "Is it written in black, white, or green?"

But it is only an image. Then if the patient says, "God's mercy on you, free me from that witchcraft"—for during the istinzâl the patient is awake and listens to everything—I answer, "If you want to get rid of the witchcraft, it has its price..."

When we agree on the terms, I tell the child to ask the jinns, "What do you want, a visit, a sacrifice, or an offering [*zyâra, dbiḥa,* or *nashara*]?" They say what they want to free the patient, and finally we take a bowl where we write the incantation, and free the patient from the witchcraft.

LOSS 3

IMPASSE OF THE ANGELS

Time, which despoils castles, enriches verses.
—Jorge Luis Borges[129]

Tell Me Sunken Well

The voice of the poet rises and falls—it grows like a lament, painting the desolate landscape of his poem in the spellbinding opacity of the late night, when cold and fatigue have taken hold of the bodies, and the embers in the braziers have turned to ashes. The men circling around the poet or reclining half asleep along the walls of the room carry on the refrain like a dissolving, increasingly distant echo, after this is sung first by the poet alone.

Tell me Sunken Well
Where are they who drank from you
  on summer days
Tell me Sunken Well

The song is one of loss and sorrow, a mourning monument to the transience of things—the world, dunya, and its annihilation.

The voices of the refrain, spreading into the room, postpone its conclusion as if reluctant to end. They resonate like a chorus of ghosts, between night and day, in that "other night," which is not the sleep of reason, but the wake of unreason.[130]

This poet is young, little more than a boy, but when he covers his face with his left hand (the canonic pose of singing) and sings, he seems old, for he is infused with the authority of what is spoken through him. As with the storyteller in Benjamin's reckoning, the poem, the story, lives through the body of the poet for a passing moment, only to come out of it again; for the telling "sinks the thing into the life of the storyteller, in order to bring it out of him again."[131] This is independent of whether the composition is old or created anew, for the stuff of stories is always old, and always produced anew.

Ygḍa lyûm u ghedda b rrkha u shshedda
hâda ḥâl l-yâm ma-tdûm ad-dunya

In good times and hard times today and tomorrow
   are spent,
This is the state of days, the world doesn't last

he will intone moments later, almost playfully in the lightness of the drum beat, ironic and disengaged, a sort of dance rhythm in counterpoint with the severity of the words. But now he's singing with grief and regret, almost anger, and the beat of his drum, slightly off rhythm, "adds," as his poem says, "sorrow to the heart." For this poem opens on the scene of a shock for which there is no explanation, no remedy.

As the only survivor of a catastrophe, or a witness from another time, a man returns to the site where there was once a settlement full of life and there is now only a well, a hollow, ineffaceable emblem of the absence of what it signifies. His friends, a community, and a whole world have vanished, without his knowing how or why. A sense of estrangement colors the opening verses of the song. The coordinates of time and space are suspended, and the man finds himself outside (where the boundaries of sense and self dissolve), in a nowhere that is opened by the radical unreality of death.

And to the well the man keeps asking what happened; to the ruins he addresses his lament. "Tell me Sunken Well..." But the well is only a vestige, the trace of a vanished world that can be only uncertainly remembered through its emblems, evoked for the space of a telling. In this world where houses are made of mud and literally dissolved by the work of time, wells are what remains, the trace never effaced yet forgotten, a measure of what can never be had or known, yet, somehow, was and is there.

Wells

In houses divided and divided over the decades and the centuries by the splitting off of children, by the partitioning of the inheritance, by the fractioning of one generation after another,[132] by the sales in times of need and famine, the places of the well and that of the staircase remain fixed, ineffaceable marks. Take one of the many small houses in the Alley of Bû Ṭwîl, or in the Alley of Ayt Ḥammu. The well—*l-ḥassî, l-bîr, tânût* (Tashelḥit)—used to sit at the center of the central patio.

You can still find the well at its place in some of the noble mansions that have been left intact: because there was enough wealth to buy new houses elsewhere, because in a time of drought the family left for l-gharb and disappeared, or because at the father's death one of the brothers took everything while the others were pushed into the place of servants—

The well used to be located in the space created by the four, six, eight, or twelve columns around which the entire house was built. For a house in the old qṣar is reckoned by the number of pillars (*swârî*, sing. *sârya*): a twelve-pillar house is a mansion, a two-pillar one is a modest abode. In that space the well stood in correspondence with the *ʿayn d-dâr,* the "eye of the house," and of that ʿayn/eye onto the sky it was the ʿayn/source into the world of the Below. The house's navel.

The well is not there anymore, not because it was moved but because the house was split and rebuilt many times over, and now where you enter is a small room with just two columns or even no columns, for the columns have been incorporated into the dividing wall. You turn the corner into a dark corridor and then a passage into another small room (these, you are told, are the houses of the owner's two children who fought after their father died and divided the estate, and that little room with an independent door to the alley is their sister's share).

You find yourself following the winding paths of memory, turning the corners of family history many times over, and finally you find it, the well. Hidden on the side of a narrow corridor—which is a passage between the different shares of property, as a path between the different histories—only half of it is visible. This well that once stood at the center of the open patio, around which women must have sat working and laughing and pushing away the flies that gathered on the puddles of water, in which over the decades children have perhaps fallen and died, is now in the corridor between two small houses, its mouth split in two halves by the dividing wall.

People have a drilling archeological eye. Looking at the house that is now his own, Si Thami reads the shape of an earlier space in watermark: "The courtyard was big, perhaps eight or twelve columns, and the house must have extended to the other side of the alley; that's why the alley is covered now. The *tʿalalut,*[133] the private alley we share with our neighbors, must have been contained within that former house." (Like the well inside the house, the tʿalalut is a trace, a vestige in the living economy of the street; it inscribes the cipher of another temporality. Technically a tʿalalut is a private blind alley off the main street whose entrance is marked by a heavy door—the door of the house that was—which now serves as a gateway to several family houses, each with its own entrance. The qṣar itself is but a reticulate of alleys and tʿalalutîn.) "It was a twelve-column house with a huge courtyard, the house of a rich landlord, and had a completely different shape." And the house, the qṣar—becomes a space of reverie. People live inside its moving space, and there, just beyond one's reach, is felt the presence of other, vanished lives.

Wells are uncanny entities. Sometimes they overflow. They *feiḍ* and *taqallaq*, "overflow" and "get mad," and become agents of destruction. It is because their being—the presences that inhabit them, but also their being of absence, is insurgent and rebellious. They are maddened when by chance they steal a life. Like the day the daughter of ʿAbdallah u Brâhim of Ayt Mûsh fell as she was drawing water from the well of the mosque in Tinegdid. She stood too close to the edge, balancing her legs on the narrow brink, hauling the pulley with a secure movement of her raised arms, laughing with the other girls and splashing water from the bucket of black rubber made from recycled truck tires. They were teasing her, the girls, to dispel the sadness that lingered in the courtyard of the mosque, for that morning her mother had told her that she had been promised in marriage, and that the wedding would take place in the fall, and even though she had heard that the man was young and was attractive and good-natured, his family lived in a village faraway. Soon she would not play with her girlfriends anymore, she would draw water from other, unknown wells. But that morning the girls didn't talk about any of that, they splashed water and laughed. Then, as she turned to pass the bucket to the girl who was filling the water jugs just below—her body stretched by the tension of that movement—she staggered and fell.

A woman came running from Tinegdid. She said that the daughter of ʿAbdallah u Brâhim had fallen in and had died, that her head opened up and there was blood all over, that the guardian of the mosque had gone in to try to rescue her or at least retrieve her corpse for a Muslim burial, but that the well had gone mad and had overflown, *fâḍ l-ḥassî*, the water had risen from the bottom all the way to the top, and the man was left trapped at the bottom with the dead girl. When the well claims one life, it often claims another. She said that women brought oil, henna, and milk, and threw all that over the bubbling waters, to appease the well, making it subside, and that a man slaughtered a cock at its base, and they waited, and asked God for forgiveness.

Wells partake of the sacred. So many wells, now abandoned and dry, punctuate the gardens and the desert surrounding the qṣar. Sometimes a shrine is found in their vicinity, and they become a place of visitation; the land is tattooed with such ritual sites—*atâr,* traces from an irretrievable past. At once figures of memory and oblivion, some of these wells are, people say, vestiges of the hamlets of the gardens (*qṣûr dyâl jnânât*) where the original people are said to have once lived. At these sites there is often a *bîr mardûm,* a "sunken well," a well whose water has become inaccessible, and almost always a tomb, a long and narrow mound of earth limited by two standing stones, the *shuhûd.* Oversized, as if housing a giant, it depicts the size of the unknowable buried there: "Men of the past were so tall!"

ʿawd l-akhbâr yâ l-menhel	Tell me Sunken Well
wyn l-ʿarâb yworduk yêm ṣyf	Where are they who drank from you on summer days
ʿawd l-akhbâr yâ l-menhel	Tell me Sunken Well
wyn ʿarâbyn ya l-ḥâyr	Where are those who lived here tell me maddened one
fûq s-sedsât kân hua nggar l-kûf	Riding his horse he was beating the drums of war
u mnîn tjihum ndâʾyr	When the news of war arrived
u lthem glâmha trkeb kḥel shûf	He covered the desert riding his dark-eyed
shâmû b n-niûg u d-dkheʾyr	They left with their camels and women
khâleg yûm lṭâm mayrahajhum khûf	No fear in the day of the strike
wa ḥlâl b ṭbûla tzelzel	*Trembling rumble of drums*
u ḥess aqarîan nsmeʿû lih tzilîf u zghârîd n-nsaʾ îfuwuḷ u fgârishu mgabila rîf hdâ rîf	Noise of gunfire, listen to its whistling. Women shouting ululations, young men arrayed side by side
ʿawd l-akhbâr yâ l-menhel	Tell me Sunken Well
wyn l-ʿarâb yworduk yêm ṣyf	Where are they who drank from you on summer days
ʿawd l-akhbâr yâ l-menhel	Tell me Sunken Well
u suwultek radd ly swâly	I questioned you, answer my question
win lfa hêj mn hnâ najaʿ nanât	Where is it gone, vanished from here, with its women and tents

u nelḥag rasmu îsôt khâly	I reached its place, the wind blows empty
u lly maksûr mayṭyr blâ janḥât	The broken can't fly without wings
u l-Gwasem shaṭnyn bâly	The departed maddened my mind
ʿazethûm zâyda lil dellâly mḥnât	Longing for them adds sorrow to my heart
kîf nwâsy kîf nʿamel	*How to heal the wound, what to do?*
u hada ly shḥal nûmy ʿâd khfîf	My sleep is light, I wake all night,
mansahâ mangedd neghfel	I can't forget or retreat into
shiṭany jâb khbarhum ṣîfa wa kîf	oblivion: my demon brings me their ghosts in flesh and blood
ʿawd l-akhbâr yâ l-menhel	Tell me Sunken Well
wyn l-ʿarâb yworduk yêm ṣyf	Where are they who drank from you on summer days
ʿawd l-akhbâr yâ l-menhel	Tell me Sunken Well
wyn l-masruḥ b lmshâṭi	Where is the untied, combed hair
wyin l-maṭlûg b-slûk ila l-gdâm	Where the hair loose in silk threads down to the feet
wyn l-ḥazemât u l-fâṭy	Where the belts and the veils
wyin s-sbêni msiḥât ʿala l-riâm	Where the scarves flapping loose on the girls' heads
wyn l-mjâdîl b rḥâti	Where the hair braided and rolled up
wyin aburi maʿ l-melûḥ u agjdâm	Where the different qualities of cloth
wyin l-bugi maʿ l-maḥrbel	*Where are the different qualities of cloth?*
wyn dlalât f-l-fujûj mnin thîf taʿmel	Where is the breeze at the shadows of dawn
kuma nujûʿ tarḥal	Lifting the tents as if they were departing
naʿnîha jand jâybâ naṣara ll sharîf	Like an army approaching, bringing support to the king
ʿawd l-akhbâr yâ l-menhel	Tell me Sunken Well
wyn l-ʿarâb yworduk yêm ṣyf	Where are they who drank from you on summer days
ʿawd l-akhbâr yâ l-menhel	Tell me Sunken Well
u bâgî maḥjûb b jḥajaḥ	The Well was wrapped by its camels,
u ḍall mgûra ʿalîh jbâḥ jbâḥ	They sat around it group by group
u dulât maʿ wtâ tfajaḥ	And the herds ran freely on the hillsides

tʿamel regba mn zzgâ u lokhrâ siyâḥ	One neck crying, the other screaming out
yṣgel lekhlâg kâseb nâjaḥ	It shined the herdsmen's hearts
u ʿabyid îkefftu ʿala ḥeddu sarrâḥ	as the shepherds drove the herd back in the corral
u mulâna bâsh râd yfʿal	*Our Lord makes of our lives what he wants*
Ghabet l-akhbâr mâ jbrna liha kîf	The story of what happened has forever vanished we'll never find it or join it back together
nshkû lillah b kûl mfṣâl	We implore God with every joint of our bodies
ghâbû ʿannâ ʿarîb huma yâlaṭîf	Our loved ones have disappeared, God have mercy
ʿawd l-akhbâr yâ l-menhel	Tell me Sunken Well
wyn l-ʿarâb yworduk yêm ṣyf	Where are they who drank from you on summer days
ʿawd l-akhbâr yâ l-menhel	Tell me Sunken Well
ya mzîn shuftû b-shâra	It was beautiful, its beauty showed,
u tnânatu ilalshû fûg l-hadbân	shining curves on the desert hills
u jayy mn serḥatu ʿarâra	He used to come back tired from herding
u benât ʿashâr yhadrû fatrâ l-ḥarrân	Girls played friendly games like unripe young camels
fi ârd âymmyim u shgâra	And this happened in the land of rosemary
ṭlîla wa llyim u l-ghumri u l-gḥauân	of oregano, thyme, and chamomile . . .
mâ mn maʿshûg fîh khawwûn	*How many loves are stolen away*

Is it a He, or a She, or a They, or perhaps an I, that the man is mourning? The event happened offstage, and cannot be retrieved as such. One won't understand from the poem whether this event was a battle in which the friends and family of the narrator perished, or a natural calamity that effaced their village and mode of life; or whether the images of death and warfare are an allegory for a story of unfortunate love, or the catastrophe itself is but a figure of the shattering of self in the condition of being in love. Or whether what the man laments is the impossibility of retrieving experience through words—

But the man is perhaps a traveler from another time, facing the chasm of interpreting the meaning of a world forever gone for him (impossibility of acceding to the speech of the Other[134]). Or possibly he (she?) is simply a poet, the Poet, and does what all poets are expected to do in this poetic tradition, since the early days of classical Arab poetry. "Melancholic archaeologist"[135] and *bricoleur,* traveler on a route marked by the traces, half-erased, of other passages, his word is born of a loss, a distancing, an exile from experience, and his craft from the manipulation of the debris of other worlds. Alone by the water hole, he, the poet and the man, contemplates the scattered vestiges of former settlements. He (she) deals in ruins, remains, that is, in words.

In its opacity this event is the point of origin of the narration. At the outset there is the positing of something uninterpretable—a forgetting previous to the possibility of any remembrance. With it the man in the poem (through the poem) attempts to cope, by remembering the debris and reading the traces, as one might read the stone markers on the graves of the cemetery of Lâllâ ud Sîdî: mute *shuhûd,* "witnesses," of a happening that due to its very structure, can be known only vicariously.

Libre de la Memoria

In the mdîna, *the city of the dead, there are no inscriptions, only anonymous stone markers—the shuhûd. One standing stone at the place of the head and one at the place of the feet for a man, two stones by the feet and one by the head for a woman. On the day of burial the grave is covered with a mound of stones; each family member or close friend throws a stone on his way out (only men attend the burial on that day), and the mound is in turn covered with a thorny sheaf of palm leaves to keep the dogs at bay during the time of stench and putrefaction. It is a dangerous time, when the rûḥ of the dead person is still struggling with its attachments, names, and faces of this world, and wanders in the vicinity of the house. Then, when a year has passed and the corpse is dry, there is the rite of forgetting.*

We set off for the cemetery at noon—one has to go when the sun is highest in the sky and the heat is at its peak, Kh. said. I had not wanted to go; Kh. had asked me to take her place. I recalled Faṭima Saleḥ's funeral a year earlier. Kh.'s aunt comes to meet us with a hoe, a broom (sheṭaba, *from* shṭeb, *"to sweep"), and a bucket of lime. A few of her friends join along the way. At the grave, she removes the palm leaves, then the stones, and "sweeps" the space of the tomb. She puts lime on it to make it white, and we quickly leave, without turning back. The grave becomes a grave among many.* Libre de la memoria, *in Borges's phrase, "free of memory." Soon, even the closest relatives will not recognize its location.*

As the song folds upon itself to come back to its *mugef,* its refrain, its "stopping place" or pivot, after each detour—after each new painted scene of sorrow—the phrase returns like an obsessional theme: Tell, Tell, Tell, Tell me Sunken Well, *ʿawd l-akhbâr yâ l-menhel!*

ʿAwd l-akhbâr means both "tell the news"—the referential truth of a happening—and "recount a story," in the sense of a possible reading, what people say and narrate. The poem swings between these two senses and finally seems to move from the first to the second, from the searching for truth to the telling of stories, mimicking the development of a work of mourning. In the end the man has not succeeded in discovering the truth of what happened, the listener/reader is left suspended between the uncertainty of many versions and the beginning of a reverie: "He used to come back tired from herding / Girls played friendly games like unripe young camels."

From having been the presences that haunted his sleepless nights, the ghosts that kept returning, painfully present in their absence beyond reach, the loved ones are turned into a story; there is recovery in the telling. Yet, at another level of reading, a reading suggested by the performance of the poem, by its formal structure and by the play of form and content, mourning is never resolved. Loss consumes the mourner, and the poem, like a fire. The well is a sunken hole of silence, and its reply is only an echo.

Disoriented at the first realization of his loss, "How to heal the wound, what to do?" the man wants to know and keeps asking, "What happened?" "Where is...?" But he gets only possible versions in reply. Fragmented images, debris of memory, and perhaps, the ingredients of a story: "Riding his horse he was / Beating the drums of war"; "when the news of war arrived...," "*Trembling rumble of drums.*" Again the theme of breaking and fitna.

"Noise of gunfire, listen to its whistling.!" For a moment the imagery creates the illusion of drawing the listener into the scene. Called in to share the experience of destruction, a participant in and through the narration, the man seems at last allowed to die with the beloved. But the scene was only an illusion, a story among many possible stories. What was lost in the event (and what but this loss is the disaster itself?) is the possibility of retrieving the truth: "The story of what happened has forever vanished / We'll never find it or join it back together [*ghabet l-akhbâr mâ jbrna liha kîf*]."

From this moment on, knowledge, severed from its object, can only be allegory: a montage of dead traces, scattered fragments—readings without truth. And from this moment on, telling *l-akhbâr* can only be storytelling. Tell tell tell, as if there could ever be enough telling to fill the emptiness of that space ("through which blows the wind") left by the event he cannot know or explain. The event that "emptied" (*khala*) a world, and made it disappear. What has happened? Where have they, or he, or it, or she, gone?

And at last, the deception of genre. Questioning the well can only be a rhetorical act, a citation from a poetical code. *Su'âl al-ṭulûl,* "the questioning of vestiges," is a well-known motif in classical Arab poetry. Interrogating the ruins is a theme, and raises an issue of genre. In his discussion of the craft of poetry Ibn Khaldûn describes genre as a "mold" or a "model" (*uslûb*), and takes the theme of "questioning the ruins" as an example of the functioning of the poetical mold itself.

> Each branch of poetical speech has methods peculiar to it and existing in it in different ways. Thus, in poetry the subject of inquiring after the traces of abandoned camps is treated in the form of direct address. For instance:
>
> O house of Mayyah on the height, and the cliff.
>
> Or, it is treated in the form of inviting one's traveling companions to stop and inquire. For instance:
>
> Stop you two, and let us inquire about the house whose inhabitants left so suddenly.
>
> Or, it is treated in the form of asking one's traveling companions to weep for the abandoned camp. For instance:
>
> Stop you two, and let us weep in remembrance of a beloved and an encampment.
>
> Or, it is treated in the form of asking about the answer given to an unspecified addressee. For instance:
>
> Did you not ask, and the traces informed you?[136]

Robbed of his suffering, of the uniqueness and reality of his pain, the man at the sunken well is himself but a shadow—the return of a trope. "I question you, answer my question!..." *Rdd ly swâly,* "return my question to me." A specular, endlessly deferring echo, the answer can only be the reformulation of one's question.

u hua bîh l-hûl ma-jbar itkellem...
He is in fright, unable to speak...

And there, in that space of forgetting emblematically imaged by the well, the man drowns.[137] Hanging from the thought of the departed, like a person in love (his condition could describe both states), he finds himself in an existential nowhere: *"The departed maddened my mind / Longing for them adds sorrow to my heart / How to heal the wound, what to do?"*

Shaṭnyn bâly: "they obsess, colonize my mind" (from a verb meaning "to fasten" and "to tie," and from which Shiṭân, "the Devil," is derived). It is the vocabulary of a maftûn, a person drawn into a state of fitna. Sucked in by the void he experiences—*"I reached its place, the wind blows empty"*—the man is paralyzed, his imagination halted. His wings are broken. And, *"llî maksûr ma-iṭîr bla jnâḥ,"* "the broken can't fly without wings."

In that space—through which blows the wind—the boundary between this world and the other is blurred, and the man's ability to discriminate between the real and the imaginary is lost. He does not reflect or fantasize: he hallucinates, becoming the theater of a play of simulacra so lifelike as to be confused with the lost object. He is in a state between night and day, sleep and waking consciousness: *"My sleep is light, I wake all night, I can't forget or retreat into oblivion: my demon brings me their ghosts in flesh and blood..."*

What he sees are apparitions, images that have transgressed the guarded field of representations and claim their due as reality "in flesh and blood." It is the return of the dead who have come back as images to seize the living and steal their life from them. *Shiṭany jâb khbarhum ṣifa wa kîf:* what I translated as "my demon" (*shiṭany*), means in this context "my imagination." In their bottomless illusory quality these images belong to the demonic.[138]

Another image of broken wings, among many, a story of unfortunate love, or perhaps, a story of falling in love:[139]

shewwshnî wuld l-ḥamâm bât ybergem	I was upset by baby-pigeon, cooing all night
maksûr mn jnâḥû u bga ʿaḍâmû shḍâyâ	His wings broken, his bones splintered
u hua bîh l-hûl ma-jbar itkellem	Fright [*l-hûl*] is in him, unable to speak
herbet mennu ḥmâmtû u bga f rasmû ʿarâyâ	His love left him, abandoned in a naked house
u yâ sîdî biya deggêt l-maʿlûm	O Lord, I am love-struck![140]
u ila mshît ya wuld umma imshîw mʿâyâ	And if I go the spell goes with me
âya—hâj l-khâṭer bîk ma-bga methennî	The heart is in flames for you, has lost its peace

Aysha u Fâṭna u Zohra mâleḥ l-ulâyâ	ʿAysha and Fatna and Zohra, beautiful among the women
hâj l-khaṭer bîk ma-bga methennî	The heart is in flames for you, has lost its peace.

L-hûl, fright, terror, panic, confusion. L-hûl resists description and interpretation, it is intractable.[141] I am in it and cannot speak about it. L-hûl is an experience of extreme insecurity, where all the points of attachment have temporarily been suspended and the constraints of sense lifted from things: a crisis of mourning that could also be a crisis of love. By the end of the poem one does not know anymore whether the imagery of abandonment and paralysis describes the shock of separation from a lover, or the shock of being in love. "The heart is in flames for you, has lost its peace."

Abandoned by his love, alone in an empty house (*ʿarâyâ* literally means "naked"—a naked house); disintegrated, reduced to the pieces of a dismembered body, his wings are broken, his bones splintered. *ʿAḍâmû shḍâyâ*, "his bones are shredded," reduced to dust by the trauma of separation. In the words of another poem,

Anâ ḍrebnî l-ḥabîb degga mtniya	My lover struck me with a double strike
Ana ḍerbnî shettet l-ʿaḍâm u l-mukh jelah	He struck me, scattered my bones, dispersed my brains (the marrow)

And the space is opened of an asymbolic death, a death irreducible (at least for the eternity of a moment) to symbolic elaboration and dialectical overcoming. Abandoned by his dove, baby-pigeon does not try to master her absence symbolically by a game of hide-and-seek.[142] The loss cannot be invested symbolically, at least not at the moment captured by the poem. Work of all sorts is arrested. The experience of pain cannot be displaced: "u hua bîh l-hûl ma-jbar itkellem" (fright is in him, unable to speak). And pain burns, consuming the self like fire: "The heart is in flames for you." A vocabulary of sacrifice.

The poetic vocabulary of confusion is large. *Shewwesh* ("shewweshni wuld l-ḥamâm"), from a root *shwsh*, to be confused, to be ill, to be at a loss, to become absent minded; *hâj l-khaṭer*, which I translated as "My heart is in flames," from a root *hyj*, to be upset, agitated, stirred up, to be furious, to be in a rage, to disquiet, to inflame, to set ablaze; *jaḥ* (*dâwînî qabl njîḥ*, "heal me before I go mad," says another poem), from *jwh*, to annihilate, destroy, ruin, flood, sweep away, and, colloquially, to be mad; *ḥâyr* (*ya l-ḥayr*, is how the man addresses the well, finding in it an analogy for his own flooding), from the classical root *ḥyr*, to be confused, helpless, to be at a loss, to be baffled, and which in vernacular takes on a stronger connotation of being bewildered, speaking incoherently, and being in a trance. And then the imagery of broken wings, dismembered bodies, fragmentation, paralysis, speechlessness. *Hua bîh l-hûl ma-jbar itkellem,* "L-hûl is in him, unable to speak"; *hezznî w-ana la-waʿyan,* "He collected me, and I was unconscious." Yet, poets say, it is from that speechlessness, from that unconsciousness, that the "saying" is born.

L-ghîḍ, l-hîḍ, and the poetry of exile

> Have poets left anything to say? And—did you recognize at last the site where the beloved once lived?
> —Muʿallaqat

"*L-gûl* is always the result of a flooding," says Belqasem, interrupting a bitter personal account and suddenly displacing the conversation onto the level of theory. (*L-gûl,* the "saying," is what poetry is currently called; *ʿandû l-gûl,* "he has the saying," means that he is a poet.) "Poems are like tears," he explains, "they spring from the affliction of the heart..."

We are walking early in the morning on the desert path between his village and the qṣar[143]—a path that almost blurs into the sandy ground and is marked, at regular intervals, by the small pyramidal mounds of stones that a madman from Belqasem's village builds and dismantles each day. We are both tired after a sleepless night spent at a poetical session. Not a wedding or a formal occasion, but just *l-hawa dyâl l-laʿb* was what had gathered the young men of his village, a "desire to sing," jammed in a room with a gas lamp, a teapot, and a large metal basin, which serves as a drum. The echo of the singing is still on us, and even if our throats are dry and our eyes are red, we are talking with a strange restlessness.

Belqasem has reached the end of his story: "And then she married, too, and left for another village, and had her children, and I had my children, and when she came to visit her family, she could never see me, she found my children and held them, and kissed them, so I was told, as if they were hers, and now she has gotten prematurely old, I am told, her face is furrowed by wrinkles, her body is heavy and weak, and someone said that she is growing an illness... And now even if I wanted to find her—we used to say that one day we'd be reunited—it would be like finding a lost past, she's gone, she can only exist in the poetry I sing for her. Still today when I walk home at night on this path, my mind drifts to her, here is where we used to sit, there is where we use to eat the melons. She inhabits me..."

Belqasem is dreamy, *hawâwî* people say, and has been so ever since he was little and his mother recognized his nature and treated him differently from the other children, penciled his eyes with koḥl and kept his original hair, the hair of the womb, in a lock on the back of his head, long and woven with shells and amulets. He is moved by *l-hawa*, which can be glossed as "passion" or "desire" but also means "air" and "wind"—like the leaves of the palm trees in the afternoon breeze—and despite his seven small children and a life of hard work, in the fields or on the overnight trucks that carry vegetables to distant markets, he is ageless and always somewhat *gharîb:* he's never fully there. He oscillates between a saturnine sadness and moments of almost ecstatic transport: when he sings with his friends, when he scans the rhythm with the drum and moves his head in counterpoint with the beat of the hands—

This is not the first time he tells me the story of his love. The story, in fact, has been a sort of bond between us, ever since he recounted it to me one night, in the interim of a long wake. A kind of gift. For a long time, carried by the rhythm of his speech, we were both half asleep, half awake. The thread of his words was at last interrupted by the coming of dawn. But that story we shared was a place where we kept coming back, the place from which his singing and our talking sprung. Belqasem sees it as the archetypal loss at the origin of his *gûl*—his "saying." Yet it is not a story of disaster the way stories of impossible loves are usually told. It has to do with his own failure—his own renunciation. (Somewhat as in the classical tale of Qays and Layla, he had her and could not take her, and chose not to have her, to lose-find her on the detoured paths of poetry.)

For it is not just that Ḥaddya his mother had sworn he wouldn't marry Henia of all girls, precisely because he loved her, because he had wanted her since they were children and had shared with her the imaginary world of his adolescence. "Love creates factions in the house and breaks the solidarity of the brothers," had been Ḥaddya's cold verdict as she set out to break her son's life the way her own life had been broken some thirty years before. "A woman, if you'd die for her and she'd die for you, is dangerous for the family; she brings fitna and ruin! A good wife instead is cold, you wouldn't die for her and she wouldn't die for you, she respects your parents, works hard and is afraid, and if the family divorces her, you bring in a new wife and that's all!"

At first Belqasem had resisted. He was Ḥaddya's favorite son, and he knew it, had always believed he could have anything he wanted. And he wanted Henia. He couldn't renounce their evening meetings when hiding in the dark she passed him a bit of meat she had put away for him, or he offered her a melon or a pomegranate he had brought for her from the gardens, and they sat unseen and talked about all things without shame, for until she had started budding and covering her hair they had played together every day at the well.

When she had become too grown up to play, she began coming to the well at the time of the prayer of sunset, to avoid finding Belqasem's father. "Father used to drive the camel home, and I would stay on to close the irrigation ditch, gather up the tools, or with some other pretext. She used to come, then, and we sat there by the well until we heard the distant voice of the muezzin calling people for the evening prayer... We lived in a world of our own, and we said to ourselves that this would never end... we didn't partake of the world of other people."

"When she grew up *(and he indicates the body blooming like a flower)*, she wasn't allowed to leave the house anymore. We had our signs, then, to set our secret meetings. I would take a walk every night, by her house. The room where she slept had a window on the alley, and if she could see me she threw a stone, and I waited for her by the door. Those moments we spent together every night made us endure the days."

Belqasem is lost in his recollection, in the other world of his love. Then he recalls when he fled to Casablanca because his family wanted to marry him away, and they found him, and brought him back with a trick, and he learned that he was already engaged to a woman he didn't know or want to know, and that soon she was to become his wife. It was Henia herself who told him. They could have fled together; "If you go up to the sky I'll go with you, if you sink into the ground I'll follow you," she had said. But he couldn't. And he became the passive instrument of their will.

"And the day of the wedding they put that woman in front of me, I never knew her or wanted her, what was I supposed to do? I shed her blood. They had presented her to me like a sacrificial victim, poor woman, and after a week, a week of prison, I could finally run off to Henia. Every moment I could escape I went to visit her. People said I was bewitched, that she had bewitched me. They can only understand it as witchcraft! The fact that a person could love another person and die for her is unintelligible to them, it doesn't exist in their world."

Henia had told him she'd wait. But he couldn't make up his mind: "She is more courageous than I am." He was torn between his love and his brothers. Finally they had the better of him, and Henia, too, was given to a man, transplanted to a faraway village.

The day of her wedding she sent for him, "she was bathed in henna and wrapped in a white drape. She said, and as she spoke she cried—she who didn't like to cry—'I am being sent away, this is the end, God wrote for us separation, *l-frâg,* separation and loss, but don't forget me, I won't forget you until I die.' I cried with her. Had I had what I wanted, had I had her courage, she would have been my wife, and now instead both of our lives are ruined. I felt like a cow, heavy with all the unbearable weight of life. She left, and my mind was shattered. Only when I sang the words of poetry could I find some peace. With my wife I had children, she sat with them and

I sat alone. Until I realized that she was the mother of my children, that I had to respect her and care for her. And I began to care for her..."

Yet (as in the legend of Qays and Layla) not just the constraints of the world, his mother, his family, the moral imperatives of his society, are responsible for his loss. In their reality they are also figures of another sort of loss, previous to any possible finding. The truth is, Belqasem concludes, that "the object of love does not exist in this world."

"Love [*l-ḥubb*], its object, its *maqṣûd* is not of this world, and its fulfillment doesn't exist in this world. It belongs to the dreams of people, and finds breath and release in the words of poetry, like the poetry I sing. The object of love, you'll never grasp it, you can only attain it through poetry..."

> *It is a circular logic, a circular exchange between person and poem, life and literature. The encampment, the village, the house, is always already abandoned, the beloved has always already left. Belqasem's word springs from the loss of Henia, but that loss is itself already inscribed into a hundred poems, half-readable in the palimpsest of his life. For, as he himself says, the object of love can only be attained through poetry, or in the shadows of dream, or in the distant voice, the distorted echo of a sunken well. Like dreaming, poetry is the record of the "voyages of the rûh," it happens in a space of absence populated with images. And so it is that both Belqasem and Henia, in their concrete, insubstitutable reality, in the singularity of their experience, are also, themselves, literary characters: images of a dream "dreamt by another."*[144]

"So many times in the Words[145] of poetry I find my own story, and I sing them, and the pain that burns inside me [*l-ḥarr llî f- galbî*], finds voice and release...

"You see, when I start singing a poem, when I 'throw' it, I find my voice, and my whole being is wrapped in it [*kayttekhsha bih d-dmâgh dyalî*]. Because when you sing a poem you enter it with your senses and soul [*nefsek*], you find yourself in the situation of that 'saying,' and all your longings [*shwâq dyalek*], all your being [*jwareḥ dyalek*], make your voice vibrate and are expressed in the performance [*laʿb*]. Myself, when the others perform a Word [*kelma*, "a poem"] to which I am insensible, that doesn't touch me, that does not bring me back to a situation of my own life, that poem is cold in my mind, and the voice doesn't come. Instead a poem that speaks to me, or that comes to my mind without my knowing it, brings out of me the strongest voice..."

Belqasem bathes in poetry, but strictly speaking is not a poet. The Words he sings belong to a poetical genre called *rekba*, at the margin of the great tradition of the local oral poetry yet indissolubly related to it, in terms of inspiration, *ars poetica,* and formal structure. *Rekba* means "knee" and connotes a sense of beating something down with one's feet. But *rkâbi,* "knees," are also men, and rekba is the poetry performed by a multitude of young men like Belqasem, at night, in the open space around the gate of their village, or at weddings (the big stage for these poetic encounters), or simply during pauses between work in the fields. There is no Poet, no Sheikh: everyone who has something to say can throw in his own Word. Poems are often improvised, assembled from a stock of floating memorized fragments, stored in the back of one's mind and in the corners of one's body.

This is why Sheikh Moḥammed, the great poet of the day, can say, with the awareness of his own paradox, that the words of rekba are like "weeds": *dîs,* a weed that resembles an ear of wheat and disguises itself in the midst of wheat fields. Anonymous fragments without authors, they are carried by the wind, the "wind of singing," and disseminate without control, infesting the garden of true poetry and falsifying its coins. Yet the Words of rekba—anonymous flying seeds—show something about the nature of this poetry in general: the relation between creation and repetition, inspiration and montage, singularity and plurality of the voice, which shapes the paradoxical notion of authorship in this poetic tradition. For rekba is a code of emotional expression, a repertory of images available to anyone whose senses are "flooded" by longing, to gain access to that other world of absence-presence, which, Belqasem says, can only be visited through poetry and dream.

But, to gain access to that Other World one must follow precise rules. And Belqasem takes on the practical tone and the technical precision of a craftsman, as he explains about the *shurûṭ l-kelma,* "rules of the Word." They concern its *jerr,* which I provisionally translate as its "mode," its meaning (*maʿna*), its rhyme (*ḥarf,* literally "letter"), its appropriateness to a certain situation, and what I understand as its harmony: the reciprocal relation between these terms.

Jerr is a noun formed from a verb, *jarra,* meaning "to pull" or "to drive"; it has to do with rhythm, in both the metrical and the musical sense, and, according to Belqasem, it functions as a *qaleb,* "a mold." Each poem is composed and sung in a specific jerr, and is built on a delicate balance between its *mizân,* the "weight" of the words, and the pattern of modulation in singing. Jerr is this pattern of modulation, an empty form that could, he says, theoretically be rehearsed as "la la la," but that only exists through its marriage with particular bodies of words. Somewhat as in the modes of ancient music[146] the number of jerrs is limited to a few (*mtellet,* "the tripartite"; *mserraʿ,* "the quick": *dhanî,* "the milling one"; *jerr l-wâd,* the jerr of the river—to cite the most common among Belqasem's peers). Different jerrs are appropriate at different times: while the tripartite and the quick are passionate and belong to the night (the quick, Belqasem says, *kay-shaʿl,* "it burns"), the jerr of the river is appropriate at dawn, to celebrate the coming of the day. There is a general correlation between jerr and *maʿna,* "the meaning," sometimes transgressed to produce effects of counterpoint: some modes are more suited than others to express strong emotional states, so that, for instance, poems of love and anger are preferably composed in the "quick" jerr, Belqasem's favorite mode: "The quick jerr conveys the burning [*shaʿl*]," the *semm,* "poison," of the wound.

What counts is harmony in arrangement. A composition of rekba, a Word, or a *ḥabba,* a "seed," is always made of three verses, often structured by the crisscrossing of two-letter endings, and by a concluding long verse. It is possible to mount together three independent fragments, originally from different poems, if they make new sense and form together: if they have the same jerr and the same rhyme, evoke the same theme and emotional state. But poems are almost never new. They are appropriated for the space of a telling, borrowed by a person to give voice to a cry. In that space, and for a time that dramatizes the parable of a whole life, the singer is author.

There is a complex relation between the emotional charge of a poem, the event of its tailoring to the specific circumstances of a person's life, its form, and its public performance. For the Words of rekba live an intense, ephemeral life in the public space of a performance, in which the poem is "thrown" [*zraʿ*], like a seed or a gunshot, is "picked up" [*rfed*], and then dies, "buried" or "destroyed" [*rdem*] in the course of a dance. In this space the poem is alive and active: you "throw" it and it works, like an incantation, charged with the force of your affective investment in it, when, as Belqasem says, "Your whole being is wrapped in that word."

For almost every Word Belqasem has a story, a sort of fictional founding myth, describing the event of the "flooding" that gave way to the utterance. A story of impossible love, of betrayal, of revenge, of unsayable truths, which systematically ends: "That night there happened to be singing [*laʿb*] in the village, and in the middle of the performance that man 'threw' his word..."

Sometimes the story concerns himself, the event of his own appropriation, and emphasizes what the "saying" did. Like the time he had fought with his uncle's wife, and the two families had not spoken for a long time, until one night at a wedding he felt an urge to "throw" a poem that emerged compellingly from his lips, and he "threw" it, and as he was singing he realized he was shaking, and that his body was running with sweat. He said:

yâ l-bellâl rfîgî ma-bgâ mʿâyâ	O people my companion is no more with me

nker khîrî berrmûh d-dûwâyâ	rejected me, slanderers turned him away
ya l-bellâl ḥâlû binnâ tnâya	O people there are mountains between us
jbâl mgeṭṭfîn u-lokhrîn ʿarâyâ	pointed tops and naked hills
ya l-bellâl frâgu jâ blâ hwâyâ	O people I didn't want this separation
bkît ṭûl ssnîn u ʿaynî jerrâyâ	years of crying and my eyes still running

He had no idea that she was there with the women, wrapped in a black veil on the roof of the house. Until she "threw" an answer, sent for him, and after many years, they talked. For Words make ties—

"L-gûl is born of a *feyḍ*," he says, an "overflowing."

L-fayaḍan is a flood. And it is with the dream of a flood that Sheikh Moḥammed (a living myth for young men like Belqasem) was granted the gift of the poetical word. It is from Belqasem that I first heard Sheikh Moḥammed's story. Sheikh Moḥammed was injured and very ill; a gun had exploded in his hands as he was cleaning it, his right hand had been cut off. He had a fever, was in pain, and lay at a loss. For he had been a proud man of action, and was now mutilated. Then, in that state between sleeping and waking, he had a dream. He dreamed that the river had come down in a flood, that its front was like a mountain, and he was standing right there, in the dry riverbed, and could see it coming, carrying trees and carrion, carrying everything it encountered on its path. He dreamed that he opened his mouth and swallowed the muddy waters, with the debris, the wood, and the carrion. Upon awakening he recounted the dream to his mother: "The river in flood entered my mouth and I swallowed it"; and she told him that he had become a poet. He who had never recited a verse or cared for poetry, he who had even ridiculed poets in his previous life, began to "speak" (*bda igûl*), to utter poetical "words."

The telling springs from an overflowing, then, but also from a loss that in this story is described as a symbolic castration. Sheikh Moḥammed is at a loss, after a gunshot he can blame no one for left him mutilated for life. Almost literally castrated, for in Arabic the hand is a masculine attribute; symbolically castrated, for he used to be a fierce "man of action" and now he is reduced to helplessness. Poets are known to partake of the feminine, in spite of the logic of challenge that structures poetic performances, and of the public demonstration of masculinity that poetry duels can often be. For the feminine is the sign of the unmarked, the rhetorical figure by which loss and absence are reckoned: the fountainhead of poetry.

"You tell because you hurt, and your words are a cry. Without a wound that doesn't heal, a wound that mills inside you [*l-jarḥ llî kayḍḥan fîk*], an obsession that works you from within, no poem would ever be sung." Words come despite yourself, and even if what you say is never new—words are ancient and carry the memories of forgotten worlds—when you sing you don't think, cannot think. Singing rises in you like a fury [*l-gûl kayṭla‘ ‘ala j-jahd*], an irresistible anger. It is like gun shooting, one shot follows the other.

"L-gûl kayṭla‘ ‘ala l-ghîḍ u ‘ala l-ḥîḍ," poetry springs from l-ghîḍ and l-hîḍ. *Keytla‘*—that is, it "rises" in you, like milk in a pot when it boils, or like tea when it comes up to the surface under the effect of the fire.

L-ghîḍ is anger, fury, exasperation, or an erotic passion that cannot be contained.[147] Poems of l-ghîḍ are "hot"—violent. Even though their expression is mediated through words, they exceed the economy of representation. According to Belqasem they don't represent the pain, they are a precipitate of pain; they come out of you compulsively, like gunshots. They hurt, and can touch and hurt those to whom they are addressed. Their preferred imagery is drawn from illness, and from the surgery of cauterization, *l-kîy*, fire and burning skewers that leave scars that never heal and are never forgotten.

anâ llî tekwît kîy maho khâfî	I was burned I don't hide the burn
fâtû lekhrîn gublî râhum tekwâw	Others have been burned before me
dak llî kâwînî ya‘raf bâsh ydâwî	The one who burned me knows how to heal
khâlla mḥâwrû fî jûfî rshâw	He left his cautery dug into my heart
dâk l-bâhû llî bân zînu ṣâfî	That beautiful one, his beauty is so pure
weṣṭ ḍḍlâm râh khdûdû ḍwâw	His cheeks are radiant light in the dark

Poems of l-ghîḍ are often love poems, they speak of the fire of an unfulfilled desire. But in their compulsive inspiration they are unreflexive: in their violence they are not melancholic. They have the intensity and sometimes the pragmatic effectiveness of a curse, rather akin to the poem a sheikh is said to have composed in the last century under the effect of anger—a fury that seized him like a trance—against his village that had betrayed him. Shortly after his recitation, the village was abandoned and fell in ruin, and to this day has not been rebuilt.

Half-voice, Belqasem recites:

men neḍra wâsh llî bîh leghrâm ibrâ	How can the sick with passion recover with a look

ibrâ yâ ṣḥâb lehwâ men ṣifâtû	Recover, people of desire, from his state
u shaʿla fîh mḥâwer u maysîb ibrâ	How can he recover with the cautery burning inside him
baʿden ibrâ ifeggdûh kiyyâtû	Even if he recovers, his scars remind him
wâsh mâ fîkum ya wî bû ftîl nuqra	Is she not among you, O friends, the one with silver filigree,
mejdûl ḥrîr ʿallgu b-nunâtû	with braids of silk bound up like *n* letters[148]
bel ghzel Rqîya ʿashegha kwâtû *fâzet fûg ar-riâm u zzîn ddâtu*	Rqîya of the gazelles, his passion for her set him ablaze, she towers above the girls, her beauty carried him away.

*

nlâga râmî f l-mdig wâjd lyia	I found a gunman ready for me at a narrow passage
f jûf qâsny rewweḥnî maʿtwb	He struck the heart, sent me back wounded
yâ dukhkhân ʿamârtû kmaha fyia	Smoke of the shot he discharged in me
mazâl demmhâ f jûfî mekbûb	Blood is still pouring inside my heart
mansḥâb lî ʿazîz ighder fyia	I couldn't know a lover would betray me
u mnîn dârha neṣbar l-mektûb	Now that he has, I endure my fate

L-hîḍ, instead, he continues, "*huwwa l-gûl dyâl l-ghurba u l-frâg,* it is the poetry of estrangement and separation—the poetry of exile. It is like a bird with broken wings. I am faraway, I miss my land and those I care for: I miss *l-ulîf,* those I am accustomed to. I can't reach... And I start singing, even if I am alone in a naked room in Casablanca, and there is no one to pick up the refrain with me."

L-hîḍ is the singing of exile.

ḍâqt rûḥî û hâj khâṭrî l-blâdî	Oppressed is my soul, my spirit storms to my land
u ila bkît yâ ʿaynî mantlâm	And if I cry, O eyes, I am not to blame
wâsh nhyiâ ya wnzâht l-berrânî	What joy is there for a stranger?
llî khṭâ blâdû may lîh shân	If you leave your land you give up your worth
u llî nebghî baʿdû yâ dellâlî	O Mind! Those I love get farther and farther

hemm l-ulîf zâd l-ʿâsheg tekhmâm	Concern for the loved increases the affliction of the lover

*

dâk llî nebghî dergûh tnaya	The one I love is hidden behind the pass[149]
jbel khâlî ya meshyet kâm men yûm	Deserted mountains and so many days of march
û ṣghîr iweṣlû mayjîb nhâya	The young who reach him don't bring any news
khaff men l-bârûd mnîn igûm	Faster than a bullet when it's shot
bîh nzûr l-khyâm bâhû nzâya	I would visit the campsite of the beautiful face
jâḥat lʿqel qbel ijîh ṣûm	Reason was flooded before fasting age[150]
sâher ṭul l-lîl demʿâtû jerrâya	Waking all night, tears running
lâ men igûl ihasen ʿawanû l-mefṭûm	No one who says, God help the weaned![151]

*

râsem ḥbîbî bgâ ʿârî yâ	The house of my love is empty
u ṭṭyûr tḥûm fîh	Birds flying in it
wa khlâgî raghba tshûfû	My whole being yearns to see him,
u anâ meḥtâj bih	I cry of need for him
netmenna targî lewwel	I wish to return to the beginning
neʿnî metwelleʿ bîh	I burn of love for him
lîshîra iyâk ma-ṭṭuwlî l-ghîba	My babe, don't stay away too long
u beʿʿed shshîn yâ	Harm be kept at bay

Ḍâqt rûḥî û hâj khâṭrî l-blâdî, says the song of exile, "oppressed is my soul, my spirit storms to my land." That is, as one traveled with his donkey load of henna to Marrakesh in the nineteenth century, across the snows and the narrow paths of the Atlas Mountains, or as one worked the obligatory corvée for the French colon in the 1930s, in those snows and on those paths, to open the road across the Atlas that would allow the French army to pass; as one slept on the threshing floors of the western plains of Chaouia as a temporary worker at harvest time; or as one lived a life of hardship in the exile of l-gharb, land of exile, during the famines that forced entire families to move, some never to come back; or as one lies in bed in an apartment project in Casablanca today, or sits at the window of a room in a French *banlieue,* listening to the Arab-Berber children playing in the street and yelling at each other in French—one's spirit is oppressed, and one's mind storms away to one's land.

Ḍâqt rûḥî, my spirit, my soul is oppressed, it chokes in its place. *Ḍâqt,* I feel oppressed, confined, anguished, exasperated. A *ḍîq* (or *mḍîq*) is a narrow passage, a stricture; in colloquial Arabic *ḍḍîqa* is a lack of breath, a crisis of asthma, but it is also a difficult situation, a moment of despair, an impasse. At the moment of impasse, then, an overflowing, and a passage to another scene: *hâj khâṭrî,* my mind, thoughts, and desires rise and overflow, like water is moved by the wind. They spill out and depart from my body, from my narrow and confining present, and journey away. They migrate back to my *blâd,* the land from which I am separated, for the intemporal and atopical journey of a "saying." The *kelma,* the poem, is an impossible return. However much I cry I can't reach: my wings are broken. *L-hîḍ,* from the root *hyḍ,* means "to be powerless, broken," "to have broken wings": *maksûr men jnâḥû u bga ʿaḍâmû shḍâyâ,* "His wings are broken, his bones crushed and fragmented."

Yet the broken wings of the body, the powerlessness in the real world, liberate the wings of the imaginary. The semantic structure is clear, and it summarizes the fundamental inspiration of this poetry: *ḍâqt rûḥî, hâj khâṭrî,* the spirit confined and anguished overflows its boundaries and flies away, it moves to an Other Scene opened by the stricture of impasse. The telling is born of a gap, a separation, a *frâg* (*l-frâg* or *firâq* is a split, a fracture, a separation) between the subject of speech and his or her "own": her own world, land, language, belonging, but also her own name and most intimate identity; between desire and its object, between the word and its referent. *Dâk llî nebghî dergûh tnâya,* "The one I love is hidden behind the (mountain) pass": he (she) is hidden behind a wall, I cannot see him (her). And deserted mountains separate us—I cannot hear his (her) voice.

All I can do is imagine, and describe (*rsem*) what I don't have by the intermediary of words and images. Words are the messenger that, however fast and light, by its nature can never reach. There is always a gap, a delay, between the sending and the reaching. Only *l-bârûd mnîn igûm,* "the bullet when it's shot," might be capable of minimizing the gap. The melancholic awareness of the gap, that the messenger "doesn't bring back news," is the true exile and the source of longing and despair. Ultimately *l-gûl dyâl l-ghurba,* the "poetry of exile," is born of the exile of the speaker from herself and her language, a *ghurba* and a *ghîba,* a state of absence, akin to the one from which dreams originate. Of that ontological absence-presence, of that distance, geographical exile is only a figure in space. But if going to l-gharb (the geographical northwest and the symbolic Occident, land of exile) to seek work is a concrete figure of another *ghurba,* that of being human, physical displacement can in some cases induce an acute awareness of that other exile, and bestow on a person clairvoyance—the melancholic vision of poetry.

Belqasem is implicitly opposing l-ghîḍ and l-hîḍ to each other as direct versus indirect, bodily versus allegorical expressions: the first, a precipitate of passion and anger, the second, the melancholic song of broken wings. L-ghîḍ is compulsive, unreflexive, illocutionary, violent, and, in a way, direct. It exceeds, or breaks, the order of representation. Its figures are the gunshot, *l-barûd,* that reaches almost simultaneously and wounds or kills where it strikes; fire; and the burning wound of the cautery, *l-kiyya* (pl. *l-kiyyât*), which can be an open sore or an ineffaceable scar. The cautery, *l-mḥâwer,* is an incandescent metal point used in cauterization surgery;[152] it penetrates and marks the flesh, producing a pestilential stench and leaving a physical scar for life. Sometimes sulfur is applied to the wound, and the sore keeps burning inside the flesh; it is a wound that doesn't heal—

The condition of l-ghîḍ is described as blinding bewitchment, the paradigmatic unreflexive state: "O God I am bewitched!" says the speaker in one of the poems above whose inspiration is definitely l-ghîḍ, "where I go the spell goes with me."

L-hîḍ, instead, as *l-gûl dyâl l-ghurba u l-frâg,* "the poetry of exile and separation," is born of a gap. Its poetical strategy is one of detour—the detour around the mountain pass that prevents me from seeing or hearing the object of my longing, along a path, which is that of the imaginary, riding a horse, which is that of language.

Yet l-ghîḍ and l-hîḍ are more related than Belqasem is willing to admit. Their motifs intertwine in each poem. The wound that doesn't heal is produced by the passion for an object I don't have. The desired object *ghâb,* it is "absent," and I am *gharîb,* "exiled" from myself by its loss. From that exile the poem spurts out like a gunshot, or like blood from a wound. The inspiration of l-ghîḍ is a pain that cannot be displaced; it has the form of a burning and a sacrifice. L-hîḍ, instead, its strategy, is rhetorical displacement itself. Its song is born of distance, and operates through distancing. Through the telling the distance only increases: "O Mind! Those I love get farther and farther!"

Belqasem does recognize the complicity between the two drives—l-ghîḍ and l-hîḍ—when he stresses that all "telling" is the result of an overflowing, a flooding that leaves you speechless, yet that the wound can be reckoned only through words. As happens with the double-faced nature of l-fitna, which depicts at the same time the outside of language and the work of language (the trauma that leaves you speechless and hurls you into an impasse without image, and the danger of losing yourself in a labyrinth of signs and a demonic play of mirrors), l-ghîḍ and l-hîḍ are two sides of one movement. The one slowly consumes by burning; the other disappears into the distance of its figures. Both aspects, tightly interwoven, are played out in the poem of the well.

Black words

> And the Poets—it is those straying in Evil, who follow them: Seest thou not that they wonder distracted in every Valley?
>
> —Qurʾan 26:224–25

In the disaster the speaker at the well lost access to the possibility of unmediated knowledge—of the event, of any event. The event is therefore also a fall and an exile, as a consequence of which all direct experience of reality is foreclosed, condemned to be mediated by language and stylistic convention. *Suʾâl al-ṭulûl,* "questioning the remains."

Language itself is in ruins. Shreds of images, concrete fragments of scenes, spare parts, emblems by which the man attempts to evoke and recollect his vanished world, for a moment conjuring it back from its nonexistence. Take the third stanza, a series of isolated synecdoches scanned by the anxious, pressing repetition of the *wheres:* "Where is the untied, combed hair / Where the hair loose in silk threads down to the feet / Where the belts and the veils / Where the scarves flapping loose on the girls' heads."

Where are the girls, the brides, the mothers, metonymically represented by details of their coiffure? Where is a whole mode of life, alluded to through the feminine imagery? The allegoric montage of trace memories is all that the man has left. But like the photograms of a film, like the "spare parts" of a dream, and like the concrete and decontextualized images from which local historical narratives are woven, these traces are born in a region of death.

Is it a He, then, or a She, or a They, or even an I, that the man is mourning? Perhaps all of those at different levels of reading. For in this poetry different situations are used as the emblems of each other in a multiple game of cross-references. A description of warfare can be taken as itself, and as an allegory of the intensity of erotic passion and the shattering of the self this entails; the praise of a chief walking through his encampment is often also the metaphorical praise of a loved woman. The lament over male friends dead or departed is often also a song for a lost love. The feminine is systematically disguised in the masculine, and grammatical agreement rarely exposes the feminine gender at all. For the feminine is a figure of the secret. Here, for instance, is a displaced description of the confusion of a man upon seeing the woman he longs for.

î wella deʿdû dâz bîn khyâmû	Oh—the Awesome walking among his tents
mennû jâḥ l-ʿaqal u-l-ʿayn fâhet	The mind is lost, the eye stares in wonder

î wella hâd shsherîf jâb ʿalâmû	Oh—the sultan approaching with his flag
râkeb ʿla khaḍer tebʿûh l-gâdât	Riding his black horse followed by the girls
yâ khûyâ l-ʿabâd kâmla f ḥkâmû	Brother, all servants are under his rule
ressâ mḥâllû qiyâdû u l-bâshât	He has his army of officers and pashas
Gâʿ llî mâ-mât yâ l-maʿanâwiyâ	People of understanding! those who are not dead,
llî mâ-fnâ itmennâ	who have not passed away, can still hope,
issyeb ad-dellal mel-menḥâ	that the heart be freed from its torment

Or, with a subtler ambiguity:

wulfî shettû shâf fîya u rjaʿ zerbân yâ	My love, I looked at him, he looked at me, and ran back in a rush
wulfî allah lâ irebbaḥ z-zmân llî beddâl yâ	My love, cursed be Time that betrays
wulfî meskîn mâ-jber wîn yṣedd nrâh yâ	My love, he finds no way to go where I can see him
—ʿend Roḥyiât lâsh jît ʿeshyia	—To the Rohyiât this afternoon I went
yâ fâhem l-lghâ zâdûnî kiyât	Understand this language, they added to my burns
ʿend Roḥyiât lâsh jît ʿeshyia	To the Rohyiât this afternoon I went

The poetical word must be hermetic. For poetry, poets say, is the domain of *l-klâm l-kḥel*, "black words" or "black speech":[153] veiled words, words aimed at concealing the object of desire, but also at showing desire in the drapes.

The language of poetry—*l-gûl*, "the saying"—eludes everyday reference. Things are not called by their mundane names, but by an alternative lexicon of *smiyât*, "names," images and formulas that poets master to different degrees and that are opaque for the uninitiated ear. In poetry duels one of the criteria for judging the winner is the degree to which the poem protects its secret, at the limit of intelligibility. A composition that makes use of words from everyday language—that speaks *byaḍ*, "white"—is not a poem.

Black words are also called *ḥajbîn*, the "disguised" or the "veiled," from a verb meaning to veil, cover, screen, shelter, to seclude and hide, to mask, to eclipse and to disappear from sight. *L-ḥjâb* is a screen, a curtain, and the rule of avoidance between entities belonging to different worlds, or different dimensions of the real: it is the curtain between men and women, between humans and jinns.

Or they are called *l-muʿjam,* the obscure, foreign, or unintelligible, from a root *ʿjm,* to be obscure, ambiguous, ungrammatical and foreign. *Aʿjamî* means foreigner, alien or non-Arab.

"Kankhḥellîw l-klâm u kanʿajmû," explains Sheikh Moḥammed, "we blacken words, we conceal meanings, and make them obscure, foreign."

Not unlike magic and divination (the words *shiʿr,* "poetry," and *siḥr,* "magic," have an equivalent semantic spectrum and almost blur into each other in matters concerning the effectiveness of words), poetry is a problem of initiation to a vocabulary of restricted access and to a set of technical operations on language. The poetical lexicon (*ʿandu smyiât,* "he has the names," is said of a good poet) is composed of a repertory of formulaic, metonymical images, metaphors, and similes: types of guns for types of men, types of hairdos for types of women. Different "names" are appropriate in different situations. In some cases it is the sheer foreignness of a word that makes it suitable for poetic appropriation. Black words are the way desire protects its object—or at least this is how poets view things. They are a way of passing on the secret without breaking its seal, of transferring its "burning" without translating it into discourse.

Note the play of form and content in the poem of the well. The stanzas (*byût*) revolve around the refrain, the sunken well, as if around a pivot, while the content of the poem revolves around the event of the loss as if around a hole. One might "circumambulate" it, as the stanzas of the poem do the refrain of the sunken well or as women do the forgotten tombs during their ritual visitations.[154] But questioning it, as the man in the poem insists on doing, can only be a rhetorical act. *Suʾâl al-ṭulûl,* "questioning the remains."

Yet the poem also suggests that passing on the secret in poetry is a dangerous operation. Black words, the rhetorical strategy of disguise, lead to a paradox, from which derive melancholy and a sense of despair. Protected by the black veils of rhetoric, the object of desire is also lost in those veils. To protect its secret, the poem sets it in circulation, committing it to a play of displacements that, once begun, can no longer be stopped. We can't know whether it is a She, a He, a They, or an I that the man is mourning, because, on the one hand, the object has vanished in the disaster that gave rise to the story; on the other, it vanishes again and again in the process of figuration and telling.

The poetical word, then, according to the poets themselves, springs from and returns to despair. Through the work of the poem it rebuilds a *rasm,* a house, where only an empty space was left. But the rasm it builds is undermined by the process of building, and the place is left once again empty—swept by the wind. As in the prophecy of the madman in Si Lḥussein's history of Fall, in this process "the last is left empty-handed." The double bind of the oral poet resonates with that of the European allegorist in Walter Benjamin's view: rhetoric, which protects the secret of the object, is also a void in which the object gets lost.

About this double bind of figuration, about the risk of the image (which he views as an angel), Benjamin wrote one of his most beautiful and hermetic texts.

> In no way is this name an enrichment of the one it names. On the contrary, much of his image falls away when that name becomes audible. He loses above all the gift of becoming anthropomorphous. In the room I occupied in Berlin the latter, before he stepped out of my name, armored and encased, into the light, put up his picture on the wall: New Angel. The *kabbalah* relates that in every instant God creates an immense number of new angels, all of whom only have the purpose, before they dissolve into naught, of singing the praise of God before His throne for a moment. The new angel passed himself off as one of these before he was prepared to name himself. I only fear that I took him away from his hymn unduly long. As for the rest, he made me pay for that. For in taking advantage of the circumstance that I came into the world under the sign of Saturn—the star of the slowest revolution, the planet of detours and delays—he sent his feminine form after the masculine one reproduced in the picture by way of the longest, most fatal detour, even though both happened to be—only they did not know each other—most intimately adjacent to each other. . . .
>
> The Angel, however, resembles all from which I have had to part: persons and above all things. In the things I no longer have, he resides. He makes them transparent, and behind all of them there appears to me the one for whom they are intended. That is why nobody can surpass me in giving gifts. Indeed, perhaps the angel was attracted by a gift giver who goes away empty-handed. For he himself, too, who has claws and pointed, knife-sharp wings, does not look as though he would pounce on the one who was sighted. He fixes his eyes on him firmly—a long time, then yields by fits and starts but incessantly. Why? In order to pull him along with himself on that way into the future from which he came and which he knows so well that he traverses it without turning around and letting the one he has chosen out of view. He wants happiness: the conflict in which lies the ecstasy of the unique—"once only"—new, as yet unlived, with that bliss of the "once more," the having again, the lived. That is why he can cope for the new in no way except on the way of the return home, when he

takes a new human being along with him. Just as I, no sooner than I had seen you, journeyed back with you, from whence I came.[155]

inhabiting the vanishing

Motionless with his broken wings, unable to imagine, to speak, or to think, the man becomes impermeable to the work of time. And like the well in the story, like the refrain in the poem, his body becomes a pivot, a *rasm*, a fixed point in the aimless movement of the world. For a moment he can suspend time—the displacement, and restless migration, which is the cause of the loss he laments.

The experience of mourning in the poem makes temporality visible as the mortal principle of dunya. Dunya, this world, life, time, or however one decides to translate this elusive notion of marked feminine gender. Dunya is experienced here as the realm of the perishable, insecure, and essentially transient. A dunya was lost in the event reckoned with in the poem; but loss is the principle of dunya itself.

And singing springs from this experience of generalized insecurity. A voice and a rhythm are born from the awareness of "inhabiting the Vanishing [*l-fâniya*]," as another poem goes, from dwelling in that uncertain space between life and death, that death suspended (*arrêt de mort*, in Blanchot's double sense of death sentence and suspension of death).[156] The man's lament by the sunken well, like all such poems in this tradition, comes to terms with and celebrates that transience. Just before dawn, and before singing "Tell me Sunken Well," the young poet scanned the ironically light rhythms of "Dunya doesn't last": "*ygḍa lyûm u ghedda b rrkha u shshedda / hâdak ḥâl l-yâm ma-tdûm d-dunya.*" Celebrating the vanishing...

> In good times and hard times today and tomorrow
>   are spent,
> This is the state of days, the world doesn't last
>
> Dunya doesn't last I remind you don't hold hopes
> Its pleasures are fugitive, O dupe!
> When you say life is generous, beware
> She betrays you at once, take my advice
> She seduces your mind away from your prayers and duties
> Sell this world and buy the other, O buyer!
> *And if you think I am lying, don't take my word*
> Inhabiting the vanishing is like those tents whose dwellers
>   broke camp and scattered one day, and of their life
>   together only traces were left

In good times and hard times today and tomorrow are spent,
This is the state of days, the world doesn't last

Dunya doesn't last, I am dazed at all that is gone
Where are the generals, the rulers, the kings
Where the palaces built by Sheddâd in their splendor
Where the Prophet, advocate of all nations
Life's impermanence is like a guest, stopped in for the night,
Moved on at dawn, traveling from land to land, carrying his load
Such is the nature of things, we are all stepping out of this world
Time provides for a man until he holds the flag, then ruins him, and of his possessions and glory nothing is left;
She betrays even the saints, she betrayed our father Adam

In good times and hard times today and tomorrow are spent,
This is the state of days, the world doesn't last

Dunya doesn't last she betrays, her drug is illusion
[*ma tdûm ad-dunya tghadar u mʿadenha l-gharr*]
I looked at her in a good moment
There was such a plenty he was filled,
Then his fate was reversed, and all that disappeared
Where is the community that surrounded him with its arms
Where the young men of the tribe in lasting covenant
Where is our Lord ʿAlî bearer of goodness
Where is he with his spear defeating the unbelievers, where is Ghilân, where the Arabs Hilâlî, and where even is the hardship they endured before coming to rule, Dunya doesn't last

In good times and hard times today and tomorrow are spent,
This is the state of days, the world doesn't last

Dunya, this world, life, time, is feminine. A capricious mistress, an irresponsible mother. Seductive and deceiving, she fetters and then abandons you. Mother or lover, she seduces (*gharra*), entices and betrays (*teghdar*), and then vanishes. *Maʿadenha l-gharr:* her true nature, the material out of which she is made, is seduction and deception. Born of separation, separation is the curse she casts on those who choose to follow her ways. *Aṣl sh-shiʿr huwwa l-frag:* separation is the root of poetry.

In this vision, life and death keep exchanging places. Dunya as life is the real world, where one is born, works, has children; it is the realm of attachments. But life works by leading astray, enticing into a world of illusions—she knots and then betrays you. Dunya reveals itself as a realm in which presence manifests itself in vanishing.

And then one day the man emerges from speechlessness, and starts singing his grief. L-hûl becomes "l-hûl," l-fitna becomes "l-fitna," and the result is the poem, the poem of the man at the well. The narrating function is restored—again the bird can fly. Born of death and destruction, the poem is a rite of mourning; it recollects, restores the fragments through a series of images.

But the poetic dialectic of mourning rests unresolved. L-hûl, l-fitna and all the figures of the intractable—speechlessness, broken wings, sores that never heal—asymbolic states of paralysis, are not just stages of a dialectical movement leading to acquittal and symbolic mastery. In this poetic tradition loss can be sung, but never mastered.

Were one to borrow the vocabulary of Freud's essay on mourning, where mourning's reaction to loss is opposed to melancholia's, the inspiration of this poetry would rather lean on the side of melancholia.[157] "Profound mourning," writes Freud, "the reaction to the loss of a loved person, contains the same feeling of pain, loss of interest in the outside world—insofar as it does not recall the dead one—the same loss of the capacity to adopt any new object of love, which would mean a replacing of the one mourned, the same turning away from every active effort that is not connected with thoughts of the dead [as melancholia]." Yet, Freud says, in spite of this initial resemblance, mourning and melancholia perform different "works." Mourning is a process of substitution and detachment from the lost object, at the end of which, "when the work of mourning is completed, the ego becomes free and uninhibited again." Melancholia instead is an "inner labor" that "consumes the ego," and from which there is no acquittal. For, while mourning is the reaction to a known loss, melancholia is the elusive affection of an "unknown loss"; a melancholic person "cannot consciously perceive what it is that he has lost." And the scar keeps burning like fire: "The complex of melancholia behaves like an open wound."

That the poetic dialectic of mourning is unresolved becomes apparent at the levels of the performance and of the formal metrical structure of the composition. For what is emphasized in both cases is not the moment of mourning as symbolic mastery, but the moment of mourning as intractable loss.

Independent of its particular genre, a poem is treated as a coming to life, which lasts for the space of a performance. Within that space, a Word is made to appear and disappear. The performance culminates with a staging of death—a sacrifice.

The concluding section of a poem is called *redma,* which from the verb *redem,* to bury, to make sink, to destroy, means burial—and is technically equivalent to a funeral.

I'll take the example of those shorter poems from the genre of rekba—Belqasem's songs. The performance of one such poem develops in three stages (not three verses or stanzas, but three phases of the action) called "the throwing" (*zraʿ*) (of the seed, the poetical phrase), "the gathering" (*rfûd*), and "the destruction or burial" (*redma*). It summarizes and stages in the space of a telling the drama of recollection and loss.

The spatial disposition of bodies is important. At the beginning of the performance it is dispersion—people are scattered, each person on a different side. From that dispersion a voice is "thrown," piercing that confusion like a gunshot. It is the *ḥabba,* the seed. Someone *zraʿ,* "threw or sowed," the first word. This throwing produces the first gathering. Two men, or two couples, engage in a dialogue in which the second man, or couple, replies with another verse. It is the stage called *rfud,* "gathering," collection, or impregnation—*refdât* is said of a woman becoming pregnant.

When a whole poem has been brought to existence this way, people prepare for the conclusion—its destruction or burial. At this point no one can be a spectator anymore, and the crowd of men coagulates in two groups for the redma, the final stage. This is also what happens at funerals, when the entire community is mobilized, and all the men gather in a procession to take the corpse to the cemetery. No one is left to watch.

The redma takes place like a ritual sacrifice. It is the sacrifice of the sense and the word matter that were generated in the space of the telling. The original concluding verse of the poem—a line such as "The heart is in flames for you, has lost its peace"—is first divided in half between the two groups, which start to play with it, back and forth, as if with a ball. During this process, which can go on for a long time, to the physical exhaustion of the participants (and much longer than the assembling of the poem itself), the poetical phrase is endlessly divided and repeated, splintered into smaller and smaller units that come to lose any referent and dissolve into pure sound material.

Slowly, words become syllables, then letters, then just sounds that fuse with the beating of the drum, while the performers enter an almost ecstatic state and the poem is annihilated, transformed into erotic energy. Words are turned into dust, and as dust are beaten down by the men with their feet, as a visual, dramatic enactment of destruction and burial. The poem becomes the dust raised by their dancing. The dust of dancing, people say, is polluting, because of its erotic force. It is the erotic power of death.

On the Paths That Words Take

L-KLÂM, WORDS[158]

Sheikh Moḥammed's house is new, but unlike most new houses it is built in the old style. When we talk, sitting on the colorful rugs that cover the cement floor, our voices resonate against the light-blue walls of the empty reception room. His accent is soft, in the distinctive pronunciation of Roḥâ Arabic, where "qaf" becomes "gef" and words flow in waves. His intonation is artfully modulated, due to his sensibility to rhythm, sound, and voice—to the metrical weight of a person's speech. His voice is gentle, made thinner by age, but when he sings or simply cites from the repertory of his poems, it rises assured, vibrates energetic. For the voice of a sheikh who understands the words is never hesitant: "A good poet knows how to follow the path that words take without losing his way." His words.

Words, l-klâm. The words that flow in the space between us, and bounce against the wall creating a strange echo; the echo that later, much later, as I listen once again to the recordings of our conversations, will appear as a solidification, a kind of phonetic crystallization, of distance. These words, our words, were spoken in December 1985, in March and April 1986, at his house, in the qṣar Awlâd Hrîz. Sheikh Moḥammed died in the summer of 1993. I am left with the tapes of our discussions and a few recordings of his public performances; an uncanny remain, words always are—they live on—and an unspoken request, never formulated as such, to respect l-klâm: the Words. His words, his poetry, but also language, poetry, speech, and the practice of interpretation—

Sheikh Moḥammed

> *L-klâm,* ila ma-kaytfesser, *words, if they are not interpreted, even if you listen to them, if they are not interpreted, you cannot know or understand their* maʿna *[their meaning, their enunciation]. We must enter the*

> *meaning, explicate the words, and reconstruct its source, the cause from which that poem sprung, till the "word" is fulfilled* [khaṣṣna nedkhlû l-maʿna, u nsherûḥ l-klâm, u ndirû l-ibtidâ u s-sbâb ʿlâsh bdâ, u ndirû s-sbâb ṭaʿu ʿlâsh khrej, ḥettâ tekamel l-kalîma].

L-klâm: the words of his poems, the *wording,* the choice of expressions, the arrangement of sounds and shapes, which Sheikh Moḥammed is so careful to select.

> *You see, in the realm of Words, l-klâm, three ingredients are necessary: measure* [l-mizân, *"meter"*], *letter* [l-ḥarf, *that is, "wording and rhyme"*], *and meaning* [l-maʿna]. *If one of these ingredients is missing or faulty, then the Word is broken* [maksûra], *it doesn't work. The realm of Words is like a basket full of dates: there are dates of countless colors and kinds, and in the basket they are mixed together. A man comes and starts eating indiscriminately from the edge of the basket, he eats everything he finds, ripe or unripe. Another instead chooses the good dates from here and there, he selects and rearranges. This man is like the poet, who looks for good meanings. A good poet can follow the paths that words take* [kayʿref l-klâm wîn kaytmeshsha]. (For words—the physical shape of the letters and the vibrating design of the sounds—have a sensual life of their own.)
>
> L-klâm l-meḍlûl *instead, words adrift, words that have gone astray* [ḍalla, *"to go astray"*], *happen when a sheikh is not firmly in control of style* [ma-mebḥâr meziân], *and gets lost, comes to some place between two words, two* ḥarûf *that resemble each other, and the path steals him away* [katserqu ṭ-ṭarîq]. *And he's lost. A good poet knows how to follow the path that words take without losing his way.*

Thinking poetically is following the path that words take, deploying oneself on the ways of language: a foreign way, which is not one's "own," a way that was there before I came, and will be there after I am gone. Thinking poetically, Sheikh Moḥammed suggests, is not expressing a thought, conveying a meaning, that can exist independent of words. Words: concrete, moving agents, resisting subjection. The poet: a *nawâya,* a "desire to say" (from *nîyâ,* "volition"), something that seeks to come out, but on their path, the path of words. Inhabiting the words. Being a poet is knowing, recognizing, where the words are leading; it is leading *with* them, in that "middle voice" of the verb which is neither active nor passive. Who is the subject of poetry?

L-klâm, words, la parole: in the general sense of poetry, poetics; a work on the substance of words and an art of saying. Poetry as a praxis (a *poiesis*), an art of making, a *ṣinâʿa,* that is, a "craft," as Ibn Khaldûn wrote in the fourteenth century. And poetry—l-klâm—as an art of saying, of expressing a "parole" that is more than what it says (l-klâm as *énonciation,* in Benveniste's and Lacan's sense). In Sheikh Moḥammed's vocabulary, as in that of every poet from this poetic tradition, a *kelma,* or *kalîma,* a Word, is a poetic composition.[159] It is an artifact and a saying, an act of speech that *katmess,* "touches," or *katḍreb,* "strikes," those to whom it is addressed. The weapon of poets is *l-hijâ',* the throwing of effective speech,[160] a *parole efficace* that mortally wounds its recipient. "Like a poisonous spear [*ḥerb mesqiya*]," Sheikh Moḥammed says.

L-klâm, words, are also remains—vestiges. Like buildings (and for Sheikh Moḥammed, as for many classical scholars of poetics, masonry is a model for poetry), poems *kaytksru,* they "break," they rain down and fall apart as ruins. Breaking is a hazard of transmission, the double-edged drug of repetition. Then, whenever possible at all, the task of the poet becomes that of restoring. And the sheikh-poet becomes a *jebbâr,* a "restorer" of broken word bodies, like the sheikh-physician who heals the fractures of human bodies (*jibâra* is the art of bonesetting). Through a creative work of deciphering, interpreting, and rebuilding from the traces, half-effaced, of broken words, he attempts to restore the meaning, repair the meter, reconstruct the body of the poem.

But l-klâm are not just any words. Only certain utterances deserve the name of poetry. Poetics is both a theory of structure, of inner relations; Sheikh Moḥammed calls it *naḥû,* "grammar," and a theory of poetic imagery, what he calls "black words," *l-klâm l-kḥâl:* a theory of the way utterances are metaphorically shaped, and withdraw from the gaze.[161]

Yet, in a more general sense, *naḥû,* in Sheikh Moḥammed's specific use, encompasses both aspects. Words are "black and beautiful," he says, if they are "permeated by grammar"; if, in other words, they are built on a harmonious balance of expression, structure, and direction. Expression must be "hermetic and foreign," and it must be "well structured." For poetic discourse is not the information it conveys, nor the communication it makes possible; it is not based on an everyday perception of the real—what Sheikh Moḥammed calls "white words." It is a transfiguration of the real; the foreign design of an Elsewhere in the here and now of an utterance. Poetry "blackens words, conceals meanings, and makes them obscure." Because, as wrote an eleventh-century scholar of poetics, "if we prefer one line of poetry to another because of its meaning, we will not be preferring it as poetry and expression."[162]

Sheikh Moḥammed

Words... if they are well structured and grammatical, they become black and beautiful, and I call them good words [l-klâm ila dekhlû n-naḥû,

> kḥâl u zyân, itsemma mezyân]. *White words... even a child can understand them, I don't even call them Words! Good words are well structured and concealed* [mgâdd u mkhabbî]. *For instance, if you want to indicate the mouth you don't say* l-fum *[the mouth], you say* tghûr *[the aperture]! The expression* tghûr[163] *is hermetic and foreign* [maʿjûm]. *Listen: would you ever say* l-meḍaḥek *[the laughing one] to describe the mouth? No! it is white, it has no [metaphorical] meaning* [maʿndha maʿna], *you should say instead* l-mbessem *[the smiling], which is black. Is the expression* l-menâkher *[the nostrils] ever comparable to* n-nîf *["the nose," literally "the high"]? And if one says* l-ʿâneg, *is that the same as saying* r-rgba*? [Both are terms for the neck.] This is why we blacken words, we conceal meanings, and make them obscure.*[164]

Even though Sheikh Moḥammed calls the concealed expressions *smyiât*, "names," it is not just a question of lexicon.[165] Words are black and beautiful, if they are obscure and well structured—grammatical, in his sense of the term (*naḥû*, "grammar," means direction and likeness, purpose and method). On the one hand he emphasizes construction, the fact that an expression is poetic within a harmonic configuration of form and content. On the other, he stresses the importance of the wording, the opacity, or necessary displacement, which distances the everyday reference, and any direct reference—the "white" sense—and makes a poetic reality appear in that vacant place. In the folds of the darkened expression, something manifests itself *as veil;* not to hide a desire, but to display it in the work of the drapes. Poetic speech says more than anything it says; that *more* is concretely expressed by the veil. The poetic imperative of black words is a theory of the irreducibility of metaphor. Metaphors express in other words and other images something that does not yet have a language of its own.

1986

Outside—in the spacious patio with whitewashed columns and almond trees—Sheikh Moḥammed's two sons are talking after their return from the fields. They run a prosperous melon farm and, involved in the practical preoccupations of life, look upon their father's poetry with seeming condescension. Yet this attitude covers another story that exceeds the new house, the cement columns, and the tractor sitting outside the door. It is said—but never publicly mentioned out loud—that one of the sons had wanted to be a poet, that he had composed poems that were inspired, and that for some time he had actually sung in public, at weddings or simply among friends. But the father had vetoed his son's desire, and with the force of his will had prevented the young man from ever singing again. (It is also said that Ḥadda's father cursed his son never to become a successful poet. "Your word won't be fertile [*maghadîsh infaʿ*]," he had said.) Sheikh Moḥammed's reason was that the life of a poet is difficult and uncertain; poets must stand without staggering on the narrow edge between respect and disrespect, between admiration, envy, and contempt.

"Poets: don't you see that they wander distracted in every valley?" he cites to me from the Qur'an. But there is another reason: he could not stand the thought of his own son becoming a poet like himself. He's aware of the paradox ("If words were not repeated, they would disappear," says a treatise of Arabic poetics);[166] it is the anxiety of the dissemination of the spoken word.

I think of this story as we sit together in the light-blue room listening to the tape recording of a poetic performance. Sheikh Moḥammed is explicating its formal features to me, its meter and tune, and the meaning of the different figures: what he calls *s-smiyât,* "the names." The song spreads through the room, distorted by its echo against the cement walls, "Tell me Sunken Well..." It is an old Word, he says, handed down for generations, passed on from poet to poet, first composed by l-Ḥajj Ḥammû Kerrûm, some say, the legendary sheikh from the Maḥmîd remembered for his unfortunate love for ʿAgîda, and considered by many the patron saint of poets (*ṣaliḥ dyâl shuʿarâ*). It is to her that he addressed the famous verses *ṭalaʿ l-helâl fîha men l-qadem ʿAgîda baʿd ḍlâm ḍwât darna yâ uddî,* "the moon rises with her, after darkness, at the sound of ʿAgîda's steps our house is luminous again." (She walked in as he was dying; healed for a moment, he spoke.) "These stories [*qaṣaîs*] are important—the stories at the origin of poems," Sheikh Moḥammed concludes, "they are not always true, but tell us about the source of poetic inspiration."

Sheikh Moḥammed has himself sung "Tell me Sunken Well" on many occasions. "Old Words"—the poems received by a sheikh in a chain of transmission—fully belong in the repertory of poets who compose their own.

The version on tape is slightly different from the one he "has." His reaction to the recording is critical. He finds places where the composition is *maksûra,* "broken" or "cracked," here and there, the *ḥurûf,* "letters/rhyme," are not woven together as they should be. The voice on tape is young, angelic even, but Sheikh Moḥammed suffers as he listens to the poem being sung. There are errors, he says, the singer is unfaithful to the integrity of the text, and, in places, the Word goes astray.

Sheikh Moḥammed

> *Those who "got" that Word* [gabdû l-kelma], *that "acquired" it and passed it on, they ruined it! When one "gets" a Word in its authenticity, without wasting anything in it, it can still be understood after a long time. But if they transformed it, its sense and purpose can't be understood anymore... The expression* l-ṭem, *"the clash," may become* tlemm, *"they gather..." just because the two phrases have a similar sound.*

Irritation turns into sadness. Sheikh Moḥammed is thinking of the fate of his own compositions, after he is gone, and of the fate of this poetic tradition, "oceans of words and knowledge," when the generations to come will understand it less and less. And he addresses me directly, the interlocutor who has received, from him, his words; the interlocutor who, herself, is not a poet.

> *I told you, Duktura, search this entire region for someone who can give you the interpretation and commentary of poetry I gave you. We explicated every word, every image, every similitude... we didn't leave the different names of* l-ʿaqel, *"the mind," sentiments, the heart, and those of* l-khayl, *"horses," and* j-jmel, *"the camel,"* n-naga, *the "she-camel," and didn't forget the well,* l-bîr, *the gazelle, did not leave out* smiyât l-ʿayelât, *the "names" of women, and* smiyât r-rijâl, *the "names" of men, and we didn't forget the names of* n-njûm, *"the stars." But this knowledge is a gift of God. We weren't arrogant nor were we haughty and pretentious, we didn't claim that our poetry is issued from reasoning or just intelligence and skill: it is from a gift of God* [muḥḥib men allâh] *that we speak our poetry. Big oceans of words and knowledge, but all this, people understand its importance less and less; there will be another age when even if you search the entire world, no one will know any of this anymore...*

Part of him wishes that his poems could remain inside him, stored in the archive of his heart; that they would die with him (he says this smiling). But he knows that a poem lives only in its being told and retold. And he chooses to tell. In the poems that "he cuts," *kayqtaʿ*, "he spins," *kayghzel*, or "he strings," *kayneḍḍem*—these are the local figures of composing—he weaves his *ṭabʿ* into the last verse, the "seal" of his poetic inspiration. Every singer who ever repeats his verses will have to pay dues to his name—

I look at him listening to the recording as we talk. I move the tape forward, searching for a certain stanza, I find it, I play it twice to understand the words. We are analyzing the poem on an editing machine. Poets, I reflect—especially younger poets like Belqasem who practice the *gûl* of *rekba*, a genre very popular among the youths—are at ease with the tape recorder. They often record their poetry among themselves, like to perform in front of the machine, and use it as an aide-mémoire. They tape their compositions as a way of writing down the words; most of them don't know how to write. Played again and again to refine the construction of a poem, to find a better word or add a verse, the tape recorder becomes a tool in the art of poetic writing.

Despite its oral and performative quality, this poetry is based on an *art of writing*. This is why it lends itself to reproduction—even "mechanical reproduction."[167] The automatism of the tape recorder, paradigmatic figure of modernity, mimics a certain automatic quality of the poetic voice-off itself. For these poems are made of fragments that are woven together, assembled in a construction, and then undone. They are composed from a repertory of materials, memorized and forgotten, that come together and rise, like tea in a pot, under the pressure of intense emotion.

In *L'auteur et ses doubles* Abdelfattah Kilito writes of "the metempsychosis of the poem," reborn, at each turn, from the debris of former incarnations; each time new, each time inhabited by the echoes and shapes of former utterances. He tells the story of Abû Nuwâs's initiation to poetry, an Arab poet from the eighth century whose experience is so distant yet surprisingly close to that of oral poets such as Sheikh Moḥammed.

> When Abû Nuwâs asked his teacher Khalaf-al-Aḥmar to authorize him to compose his own verses, Khalaf answered: "I shall not authorize you until you will have learned by heart a thousand old poems." Abû Nuwâs disappeared for some time; then he returned and announced to his master that he had memorized the required number of verses. And in fact he went on reciting them for several days. Then he reiterated his original request. Khalaf hinted to his pupil that he would not authorize him to compose verses until he had completely forgotten all the poems he had just learned. "This is too hard," said Abû Nuwâs, "I put so much effort in memorizing them." But the master was firm on his point. And Abû Nuwâs had no choice but to retire for a certain time in a monastery, where he occupied himself with everything except poetry. When he felt that he had forgotten all the poems, he returned to his master, who finally authorized him to begin his poetic career.[168]

What does it mean, asks Kilito, for poets like Abû Nuwâs to make one's voice heard "in the concert of ancient voices?" One's voice: a voice that "is a reflection, an echo, but that has also its own character, its own texture; a voice that frees itself by that same gesture that renders it dependent. Have the poets left anything to say? Yes, it replies." Who, where is the subject of poetic speech? Memorizing a thousand ancient poems, and then committing them to forgetting is the path toward becoming a poet. After a lapse of time, a break, a discontinuity: "The thousand ancient poems have been displaced, have become like an abandoned encampment that offers only scattered remains to the gaze. Forgetting is a disaster that dismantles the structure, disjoins the blocks, and pulverizes the stone; the thousand poems have turned into a chaos without name, an amorphous magma with no recognizable form. Poetic creation will be, then, a reorganization of the scattered materials—a new *mise en forme.*"[169]

Even when poems spring from an overflowing of passion and are spoken in that feverish state Belqasem describes as "being wrapped" in the words; even when they originate in that mark of "true inspiration" classical poets called *at-ṭbaʿ*[170] (a revelatory moment that in the hagiography of Sheikh Moḥammed's art, is imaged by the dream of the river in flood entering his open mouth), compositions are never simply new. Each poetic creation is the product of a painstaking work on language, and bears the trace of countless other poems half audible in watermark.[171]

Following this double movement of repetition and creation in the palimpsest of the poem (always created anew, always reborn from the reinvention of old materials, within the coded constraints of a genre) one comes to understand the apparent contradiction between an ideal of impromptu creation, of unmediated poetic revelation, and a practical ethics of skillful craftsmanship, diffused authorship, borrowing and adoption of poems, construction and reconstruction of Words. Perhaps the tape recorder is most foreign to the "other" automatism of the poetic voice-off, in that it preserves the integrity of the original transcript, interfering with that practice of remembering and forgetting, constructing and dismantling, which is the breath and the method of this poetic tradition.

Consistent with the inspiration of his poetry, and with the practical lesson of Abû Nuwâs, Sheikh Moḥammed's request to respect l-klâm, his words, is an invitation to poetic reinvention "on the paths that words take." For l-klâm must be understood in the double sense of *parole poétique,* "living poetic speech," and *écriture poétique,* the reinscription and reinvention of words, remains scattered in abandoned landscapes.

Sheikh Moḥammed curses the poets who repeat and reassemble bits of other poems without worrying about the integrity of the text and the faithfulness of the repetition. "Their words are like weeds [*dak shshi bḥâl ddis*]," he says.

They proliferate in the fields and endanger the harvest, their seeds are carried by the wind and you can't know anymore where a word you hear came from. "This is a cause of breaking." The *ḥabba,* the "seed," which is what poems are also called—is scattered. *Guwwâla* who are not *shuʿara,* "true poets," he says, repeat, rearrange and eventually break the poems. (*Guwwâla* from *gûl, qâla,* "to speak," but also "to sing poetry"; *shuʿarâ* from *shiʿr,* "poetry," and *shâʿîr,* "poet." But the current way of referring to a poet is "sheikh." Because a desire to sing is not enough to make a poet. Poetic speech must be authorized. In poetry as in medicine and in the Sufi sciences, a sheikh is someone who was initiated and authorized, and who, in turn, can initiate others. It is a poet with a *ṭbaʿ.*)

And yet he—who lost his arm before becoming a poet—knows. He knows that fragmentation and repetition, dismembering, are also the formal ingredients of his own poetry, the yeast of all (symbolic) articulation, just as a certain fissure of the heart, and a certain exile of the subject, are the wound from which the telling is born. They are the structural principles according to which the rasm, the "house," and the poem are built—

(Rather than a title of property, then, the *ṭbaʿ* by which Sheikh Moḥammed signs his compositions is like the notes, initials of his family name, that J. S. Bach disseminated throughout *The Art of the Fugue,* and on the spelling of which he died. The forgetting of the name, forgetting in general, is woven into the work of the poem.)[172]

RASMA: THE CONSTRUCTION OF POEMS

Our conversations turned increasingly to the technique of *n-naẓm,* "construction," and to the question of *tarâkîb,* "structure." It was impossible, Sheikh Moḥammed kept saying, to speak of poetry independent of its craft. Because poetry is like a source, which remains pure only if water is drawn from it every day. It is based on an attitude that must be cultivated and refined—somewhat in the sense in which Ibn Khaldûn spoke of the poetic sensibility as a *malaka,* an "acquired permanent disposition," formed and reproduced through practice. And because if words come to the poet, the poet "goes to them." And only if the poet proceeds according to certain rules, following a precise "path" or "line," a *khaṭ,* which is not just that of immediate inspiration, he (or she) can "find" the poem he is composing; the poem that is composing itself *with* him.

Sheikh Moḥammed

If you hear a kelma, *a "word," that is, a poem, and you don't understand its* tarâkîb, *the way it is formally put together, you don't understand anything. A* kelma *is like a house. If you are not a craftsman, and don't know about house building, if you don't know about construction, you walk into the room on the second floor and say, I want a column in this place. And you don't know that the column must be built over a column on the first floor, and at the juncture of a beam, or else the whole house falls apart. It is the same with a poem.*

The poems Sheikh Moḥammed sings and recites (old poems he "acquired," like "Tell me Sunken Well" or "Dunya doesn't last," or new poems he composes) belong to a genre called *rasma*, from the great tradition of oral poetry in the Draʿ valley. Taken as a verb, *rsem* can be translated as the fixing, the describing, the imaging, the drawing; taken as a noun, *rasma* is the description or depiction, the settlement, the house, the place. (See part 1, "Topology of a City.") The metaphor of rasma is spatial, territorial. In the context of poetry, *kan-rassem*, "I describe or fix in place," comes to mean "I compose."

A distant relative of the classic qaṣida,[173] a poem in the genre of rasma can have any number of stanzas, each a complete body on its own right. In Arabic a stanza is a *bît* (classical *al-bait*), a term that means "house," "building," and in vernacular "room," and that carries in both classical and vernacular the poetic meaning of "verse." The poetic vocabulary is spatial. Each *bît* is structured by the crisscrossing alternation of two consonants. They are *l-ḥurûf* that constitute the *qâfiya*, the "rhyme."

Ḥarf (pl. *ḥurûf*) means sharp edge, rim, brink; by extension it means letter of the alphabet (in Arabic always a consonant) and profile of the face. When poets say *l-ḥarf* in the technical context of prosody, they mean the letter that carries on the rhyme—the sharp edge of the verse. Different stanzas are structured by different consonants, and each stanza, in this sense, is a world of its own. But *l-ḥarf* is also the wording, "the letter," the selection of expressions and figures, the choice between two "names," as Sheikh Moḥammed calls them, of a well or a dove, two different ways of saying "I hurt." *L-ḥarf*, then, "the letter," corresponds to what in classical poetics was called *l-lafẓ*, "the expression or wording." It is the concrete way in which things are said—

The stanzas return to a refrain, called *l-mugef*, "the fixed point" or pivot, and the entire composition, stanzas and refrain, is "oriented," Sheikh Moḥammed says, by a tune, which he calls the *rîḥ*—the "wind" in which the poem is composed.[174] (Rasma has some ten named riyâḥ, "winds," each rîḥ with its specific features.) Playing on a phonetic and semantic resemblance between the kin terms of rîḥ-wind and rûḥ-spirit, one could say that the rîḥ of the poem is the "wind" that moves it, and the "spirit" that holds its body alive.

The rîḥ is the "mold" of the poem—its *qâleb,* Sheikh Moḥammed says, an empty form, which can be sung as a tune without words. But it is impossible to conceive of a poem independent of its "wind." Because the rîḥ is not an air added to the poem as an ornament; it is the mold within which the words are composed. It is the *khaṭ,* the "line" or "track" of the words.

Sheikh Moḥammed:

"The qâleb [sing. *qaleb*], the 'molds' or 'forms' (we mentioned them earlier), are the riyâḥ. If we follow its track, the track of the rîḥ, and proceed in its direction, we find that the poem is in place, and well built. If we abandon its track [*khaṭ*], we lose direction—and the Word itself is lost. It is that 'track' or line that we call rîḥ or qaleb—'wind' or 'mold.'

"Also... each Word [*kelma*] should be given the rhythm that suits it best: one requires acceleration, another quickness, a third slowness; each Word and her needs. But the Poet who knows their ways, the ways of Words, goes to them [*kaymeshihum*]; he comes to meet them. Because the practice of poetry is like a source: if you draw from it everyday, its water springs pure; if you let it stagnate, it is wasted to all use..."

—I ask, Can a poem be converted from one "wind" into another? You said that "Tell me Sunken Well" is composed in the rîḥ called Wuḍef; could it be converted into the rîḥ of Bû Rda?

—No! Were a poet to convert a poem into another rîḥ, how many changes in the wording and the rhyme would he be forced to make! He would transform that Word so much, that it'd become a different Word... The wind in which a poem was first composed is given, once and for all...

—Is the rîḥ built into the words?

—Of course! And the rîḥ itself is built on the "desire" of the poem, it is chosen to express its intention [*nuâya*]. And the mugef, the "pivot" [refrain], is built around that wind, and so are the other components of the poem: they are all constructed around that rîḥ, and around that desire. Once composed, a Word should not be transformed. Only if it is broken [*maksûra*], and needs to be restored [*tjebbar*]. If its measure [*mizân*] requires restoration, it is easy to do; if its meaning [*maʿna*] needs to be restored, it is not an impossible task for a poet who understands the principles of his art. But reversing that Word in a completely different direction? No! A poem is unconvertible, it dies for its faith [*miyta ʿala dîn-ha*]!

—The rîḥ, then, is a sort of qebla of the poem [fundamental orientation, direction of the Kaʿaba and of Muslim prayer]. When you are composing a poem—a new poem—do you already know the rîḥ? When you have a thought you want to express in a poem, what comes first, the rîḥ or the words?

—It is the rîḥ that determines the meter [*l-mizân*]... *(Sheikh Moḥammed starts singing. He intones one rîḥ after the other, a* le-le-le *without words:)* You see, the rîḥ is in my head! I intone the wind, and enter the Word. Bring me the rîḥ and the Word can begin. Then, if the wind that you brought in suits the thought [*maʿna*] that you want to express, you compose on it [*katnḍḍam ʿalih*]. This is why the rîḥ is a mold. If you see that it does not agree with the Word you have in mind, you then try another wind, which is more appropriate for what you want to say...

We must come in from the front door. If we don't enter from the door, we can't reach the interior room where we are sitting. The door is the rîḥ; it is the wind you chose. You choose the wind and then you fix the mugef, the refrain, consistently with that rîḥ... and you can express what you want, the *maʿna* you desire: praise, or curse, or passion. And if you find that the words don't agree, bring in another rîḥ. Until you find what works. But the mugef, the "fixed point," is the heart of the poem: it shows you the way [*huwwa llî kaywurrîk ṭarîq fîn temshî*].

In a composition of rasma each stanza is an independent construction—a "house," or "depiction," painted in different colors and evoking a different scene. Scenes are loosely related from the point of view of content, except that the auditive dimension of rhythm plays a scenic role. It is the design of the *ḥurûf*.[175]

But the poem has also a vertical structure, which cuts across stanzas and articulates the independent units into a whole. A warp of two consonants, always the same two, runs through the composition from beginning to end and ties its body together. They are the median and ending letters of the mugef around which the poem revolves. *Mugef:* from the root *wqf*, here pronounced "wugef," meaning to stop and to stand up, to fix in place or to dig down, as one digs a stake into the ground. L-mugef is the refrain, with which the poem begins (it begins by citing a return and inscribing its cyclical development: it does not start, it recommences) and to which it returns at the end of each stanza.

But it is not just the mugef that weaves the composition together. If the cyclical reiteration of its two consonants and, of course, of the content of the refrain (as in "Tell me Sunken Well") constitutes a pivot around which the composition turns, the same two letters also form the structure of the concluding two verses of each stanza. These are the verses that introduce the refrain. A poem, then, is made of diachronic and synchronic elements or, to use an image from weaving more familiar to poets like Sheikh Moḥammed, of vertical and horizontal threads.

Sheikh Moḥammed is analyzing with me the structure of "Tell me Sunken Well." We take the example of the first stanza, with its structures of support. First comes the mugef, the return, which contains the two consonants of the vertical structure, *L* and *F:*

ʿawd l-akhbâr yâ l-menhel
wyn l-ʿârab yworduk yêm ṣyf
ʿawd l-akhbâr yâ l-menhel

(Tell me Sunken Well / Where are they who drank from you on summer days / Tell me Sunken Well).

The refrain introduces the opening stanza of the poem. First is a series of three verses, or six half verses, stitched together by the crisscrossing alternation of two letter endings (the median and ending rhymes), in this case *R* and *F,* which are different from the letters of the refrain. These verses are called *ḥrishât* (sing. *ḥrîsh*), which could be translated as the "sharp ones," and are sung by the poet alone, without drums. The canonic number of ḥrishât is three, but, as Sheikh Moḥammed goes on to explain, there is room for improvisation.

wyn ʿarâbyn ya lḥâyr	(Where are those who lived here tell me maddened one
fûq ssedsât kân hua nggar lkûf	Riding his horse he was beating the drums of war
u mnîn tjihum ndâʾyr	When the news of war arrived
u lthem glâmha trkeb kḥel shûf	He covered the desert riding his dark-eyed
shâmû b nniûg u ddkheʾyr	They left with their camels and women
khâleg yûm lṭâm mayrahajhum khûf	No fear in the day of the strike)

Sheikh Moḥammed: "If you have sung the three ḥrishât, the 'sharp verses,' and you feel you didn't complete the thought [*l-maʿna*] you wanted to express in the stanza, you can add *t-tdrâj* to the poem. You add it when you feel an urge to say *more.*"

Tdrâj: from the root *drj,* "to advance in steps," it could be translated as "gradation," the addition to the stanza of a flight of steps. A sort of verbal fugue. Sheikh Moḥammed explains that it is made of three groups of decreasing verses, each structured by a different rhyme, and proportionally shorter than the preceding one. Gradation is the mark of a virtuoso: "It enhances the elegance of the poem, and adds to its expressive force; a sheikh gets pleasure from composing it [*kaybaghî ylaḥnû*]." He pauses. "It has an artful language [*fih l-lghayâ*]."

Without interruption from the last of the ḥrishât, but with a dramatic metrical break, the poet introduces a short phrase, half the weight of the others, and repeats it twice, accompanied by his supporting cast: "*wa ḥlâl b ṭbûla tzelzel*" (trembling rumble of drums). It is at this point that, for the first time, he uses the drum, which will beat the rhythm of the poem until the beginning of the new stanza. This short, dramatic verse is called *neggâr,* "beat" (as in drumbeat). The name refers to the fact that it introduces the drum, but also that it beats the poem like a drum.

Neggara are usually the most hermetic and aphoristic verses, where the expressive force of the stanza is condensed in a nutshell (or gun shell—*neggâr* is also gunfire). Sheikh Moḥammed describes it as a "lock" that ties up the threads of the stanza. The letter ending of the neggâr is the same as the median consonant of the mugef-refrain (*L*). This verse, like the long verse that follows it, has the same letter structure and shares the vertical quality of the refrain—a fact that is emphasized by the beating of the drums. The poem has entered in the gravitational zone of the mugef: these are its support structures.

Sheikh Moḥammed: "When you have three ḥrishât, three 'sharp verses' then, end the stanza [*bît*] and start the neggâr. There you go, you 'locked' the stanza with the neggâr..." (*Raḥ nti sedditi bih,* "you knotted it with it," is from the vocabulary of weaving: at the end of each horizontal input the weaving is "knotted" by pulling down a cane that separates the warps—and is said to hold the rûḥ/spirit/breath of the loom—to make the threads intersect tightly and "close up." Without this closing the fabric would technically and symbolically unravel, as would the poem without the neggâr.)

From the structure, Sheikh Moḥammed turns to the performance; it is always a matter of weaving, of joining together that which is, by its nature, separate—or which had to be separated in order to be joined. The structure of the poem, as that of the performance, is an articulated *disiecta membra.*

"The neggâr is then picked up by those who sing with you. Wait until it is almost over, but leave a little bit of flow, as you do with water in the irrigation canal. While they are still repeating the last words of the neggâr start with *tifelwinât,* so that the flow, the voice, keeps going, is not cut. Sing tifelwinât, and when you are finished sing the 'head' of the refrain. At this point the chorus picks it up and repeats."

From the neggâr one moves to the last, and longer, verse of the stanza, called *tifelwinât,* probably, Sheikh Moḥammed says, from the Berber word for gate, *tiflût:* it is the gate out of the stanza and into the mugef, which is also the passage to another house/stanza. (The logic is spatial, architectural, urbanistic even. The poet walks inside a house, explores its space, comes out of the gate, into the alley, onto a widening where all the alleys return, and then into another house, etc.)

The two structuring letters of the gate verse (tifelwinât) are, again, *L* and *F*, the two letters of the refrain. This final verse, sung in a long breath without interruption, ends with a citation of the last segment of the mugef—what Sheikh Moḥammed calls *ras l-mugef*, "the head of the refrain"—"Tell me Sunken Well."

"*U ḥess aqarîan nsmeʿû lih tzilîf u zghârîd nnsaʾ îfuwuḷ u fgârishu mgabila rîf hdâ rîf / ʿawd lkhobâr yâ lmenheḷ*" (Noise of gunfire, listen to its whistling. Women shouting ululations, young men arrayed side by side / Tell me Sunken Well).

Which leads straight back into the mugef: "*ʿawd l-akhbâr yâ l-menhel / wyn l-ʿârab yworduk yêm ṣyf / ʿawd l-akhbâr yâ l-menhel.*"

Sheikh Moḥammed: "This is how Words get built [*dak shey bâsh iṭlaʿ l-klâm*], how they grow and build up, layer upon layer! And the 'letter' that you already used should not be repeated. You should use his brother or one that resembles it [*shebihû*]. Only the mugef is repeated, the refrain. It keeps returning, it is like a pillar [*sârî*], like the pillar around which is built a staircase, or like an *uṭâd*, fixed in its place. The mugef is also like the road: everyone goes through it, everyone eventually comes to pass by it. It is like that *dwra*, that circular turn by the municipal court in Zagora—the round point. Who arrives there must turn around it, and get back on the other side... again and again...

"But listen to what I say! In the last resort it is the tongue, l-lisân, it is the tongue that gives you the just measure of the verses. If you start singing something and you find that it flows easily and is well balanced for the tongue, you know that you have the right *mizân;* if you find it heavy and full of obstacles for the tongue, you know that the poem doesn't work."[176]

(Ultimately it is the tongue, that is, the body of the poet, that can determine the right meter for the poem.)

"Let me explain to you about the structure of the mugef. Let's take the example of this stanza..."

Sheikh Moḥammed doesn't pause, and starts reciting a poem. But not any poem. He doesn't change his expression, doesn't introduce it or comment upon it afterward. He just sings it. It is a poem of fitna and war, of *meḥna*, "affliction" and suffering. It is a mourning song about a splitting that fractured the drums of singing, a lament for a lost cause, lost friends, violence, and a betrayal that left incurable wounds.

ba'd l-ghamrâ yâ Zâhra	After the deluge, O Zâhra,
f-Timtîg bâhra ma gâlû	so much was said in Timtig,
u-jarît ṣabrî	I went beyond my endurance
jârit ṣabrî mâ-dâ men meḥnât	Beyond my endurance so much sorrow and suffering
u llî linâ ṣdîg 'âd 'adâwâ	Our friends became our enemies
ba'd l-fitna ma' l-qbâil hayhât	After the fitna with the tribes alas
mâ rinâ men ishûf shuft khâwâ	We saw no soul looking with fraternal gaze
jabûnâ lîl-mhân keshfû l-'arabyiât	They brought us affliction, unveiled our women
l-âmân glîl ma-bgâ f-Drâwâ	Not a bit of trust is left in the Drâwâ[177]
u gddât jwârḥî u lâ-ṣâbû ṣbar yâ Zâhra	Broken is my heart, can't find endurance, O Zâhra
'aynyia men fgâdhum dem inhâlû	My eyes from their loss drip blood
shshbâl fî shugghum ṭbel ksarâ yâ Zâhra	Young lions, from their splitting drums are fractured, O Zâhra
û ghâb lâ ṭla' ibân khyâlû	He disappeared, his shadow no longer visible,
u-jarît ṣabrî	I went beyond my endurance
Ba'd l-ghamrâ yâ Zâhra	After the deluge, O Zâhra,
f-Timtîg bâhra ma-gâlû	so much was said in Timtig,
u-jarît ṣabrî	I went beyond my endurance

"You see, that letter *û* which we find in *inhâlû,* in the "gate verse," *'aynyia men fgâdhum dem inhâlû,* is the same *û* of *ma-gâlû* in the refrain: *f-Timtîg bâhra ma-gâlû.* Because the verse of the Gate [*tifelwinât*] announces the structure of the refrain, and hints at its meaning by the recurrence of the same rhyme. That rhyme introduces the head of the mugef."

Sheikh Moḥammed does not seem to pay any attention to the painful content of the poem and goes straight to the form, its *tarâkîb.* The work of the form is itself a work of mourning. Form and content, his explanation and his recitation, are in counterpoint; the effect is dramatic. It is as if the metrical structure, the crossing of the rhymes, and the recurrence of the refrain were a way to contain the loss lamented in the poem, and the madness, the rupture that ensued. Yet the work of formal articulation of the poem is itself comparable to that "splitting," that "fracturing" of which the poem speaks.

Sheikh Moḥammed: "The verse of the gate [*tifelwinât*] is where a poet shows his craft, or his weakness, if the letters in the last account don't match, in their measure and balance [*mizân u l-ʿabar*]: it must be precise by the millimeter!

"The content [*maʿna*] of the gate verse [*tifelwinât*] hints at the content of the mugef. So in this case the gate says, 'My eyes from their loss drip blood,' while the mugef says, 'After the deluge, O Zâhra, so much was said in Timtig.' Similarly the form: one letter rhyme of the gate is the same as the central rhyme of the mugef, in this case *û*, the other letter is that of the 'head' of the mugef, in this case *î*.

"What is called the head of the mugef [*ras l-mugef*] is the last section of the refrain. It is recited first, as an introduction, like a circle that closes upon itself. The head of the mugef here is *jarît ṣabrî*, "I went beyond my endurance." The letter *î* of *jarît ṣabrî* is reinscribed in the conclusion of tifelwinât, which then ties up with the beginning of the refrain. The gate verse, in other words, belongs to the order of the mugef; it is tied to its head and to its ending, and has the same structure."

THE STAIRCASE

The work of the form is a work of mourning. Its figure in space is the staircase. Sheikh Moḥammed likens the structure of these poems—their *tarâkîb*, the way they are joined together—to the winding staircases of the earth houses people build in this region. These develop one flight in one direction and turn, returning to the pivot, the ideal empty center of the structure. The pivot is generated by the turning, and is called *s-sârî*, "the pillar," or *r-rajel s-sallûm*, "the man of the staircase."

> *You see, the composition of rasma resembles a* sallûm, *a winding staircase. You go up and down the steps with the telling. A staircase winds out of its base,* l-merdûm—*the "buried" or the "pit." In Berber they call it* aferdu, *the "mortar." The mugef is the* sârî (sarya, *"column"), the central pivot, you know, but it is usually called* rajel sallûm, *"the man of the staircase." The stairs go up turning around it, turn after turn, all the way up. The* ʿatabi, *the horizontal beams of the staircase, are the various neggara of the poem (the "beating" verses); the tkiyât of the staircase are tifelwinât (the gate verse) in the poem, and* d-duruj, *the steps of the staircase, are the ḥrishât (the "sharp" verses) of the poem. Three steps and a turn, three verses and re-turn, a flight is a stanza, you see!*

Si Thami is a mason, a *bennay*. At Sheikh Moḥammed's house (we were there together) he perfectly understood the poet's point. I realized later that I had missed the most important implication. We take the staircase of the old house in the alley of Bû Ṭwîl. Si Thami explains to me the internal workings of the sallûm ("staircase," from a root *slm,* to be safe and sound, to preserve from danger, to hand over, to surrender).

As he often does, Si Thami emphasizes details that are meaningful only within a framework that remains implicit. I cannot understand what he is saying because I see the staircase as static rather than dynamic object: the sallûm is so much an alive thing, in its building and in its being experienced, that its *tashbîh,* its "similitude," is with the work of the mortar and pestle: *aferdu* and *l-maʿmûd.* In the work of the staircase, the pestle encounters the mortar—the "above" the "below"—in a constant movement of up and down.

Si Thami

If you want to understand how the sallûm works, imagine aferdu, the wooden mortar women use to grind spices. The body of a mortar is carved out from one piece of wood, but it is not carved, that is, hollowed, all the way down. Its base is "buried" [*merdûm*], that is, it is made of "full," solid material. Without its "buried" base, the mortar could not do its work. It is there, on that base, that the pestle works. Now the bottom of the staircase, its base, is also called *aferdu,* the "mortar," or *l-merdûm,* "the buried."

(It is out of that buried, amorphous base, that the work of the staircase develops—for the sallûm is not a thing, but a work. And it is to that buried base that the staircase returns.)

When you want to build a staircase—the site is always one of the four structural corners of the house—you must perform a sacrifice. This is because the sallûm, like the well, is in direct communication with the underground, and because, like the bearing columns and unlike the walls and the organization of the rooms, the staircase will be there as long as the house exists, whatever its shape. It is one of the house's fixed points. One digs a hole, then, and starts building aferdu: the mortar, the buried base.

(Blood has to be shed, and right there, because symbolically the staircase develops from the underground, realm of the inhuman. Its winding movement out of its buried base becomes a figure of the work of symbolization. This is why these staircases have metaphorical and conceptual possibilities, and why, in more than a technical sense, they have, as Sheikh Moḥammed says, an affinity with poems.)

We dig the base of the mortar in a corner of the house where we shed the blood, down where the well is, where *tamdet*[178]—the pond of waste waters of the house—is, at the place of the animals. We first build the side wall, then the edge of the mortar, that is, its *ḥarf*, its "letter," with earth bricks. We mark the threshold of the first step with a piece of wood. We bring in dry earth and we fill that space until it is completely solid and thick. Then we go on building several other steps with earth dough, reinforced at the edge with wood, until the space of one step is left to reach the corner of the wall.

There we begin the first turn. We make that last step oblique. It is at this point that we start building the wall of the pivot of the staircase [*l-ʿaks dyâl sallûm*], where the solid thick body of the mortar, the base, "dies" and starts growing into the "man of the staircase" [*rajel sallûm*]. It is here that the pestle [*l-maʿmud*], that is, the "man," encounters the mortar...

Now we bring wood—four or five long boards—and we build the first leaning board [*tkiya*, from *ttekka*, to lean, to provide support, to provide a ground]. We place it in climbing position; it is here that we lean the steps going up. This is a very delicate moment, when the staircase is severed from the ground and starts growing on its own, like an airplane taking off.

The tkiya is the first "artificial" base; it is the first of a series of *sqayf*, by way of which the construction articulates and grows. It is, in the sense of the analogy with the poem, the first image, or rasm. *Sqayf* means "covering," "roofing," but also means "to provide a suspended, artificial ground," over which other things can be built, as the second floor of a house.

This first tkiya, at the intersection of the two realms, is the place where jinns dwell—Um ʿAṣṣa Moḥa says—be careful: "The haunted place of the staircase is right above the mortar, on the first leaning board, that's where people throw *jâwî* [benzoin] to appease the spirits... The dangerous place is at the turn of the last step of the mortar, that's the limit. Above it grows the airy staircase, below one sinks into the "buried" part [*l-merdûm*]. That's where it is dangerous, lived-in."

From this point on, the staircase grows on its own. Its main points of articulation are the *ʿatabi* (sing. *ʿatba*), horizontal wooden beams that support the *tkiyât*, the oblique leaning boards over which, with wood and earth dough, are built the steps. There are three steps for each tkiya, which amounts to a flight of stairs and a turn, and every tkiya is placed between two *ʿatabi* or supporting beams. (Sheikh Moḥammed: "The ʿatabi are the neggara of the poem, the tkiyât are tifelwinât, and *d-drûj*, the steps of the staircase, are the ḥrishât. The mugef, place of return, is the central column.")

Like the neggara in the poem, the ʿatabi in the staircase are the joints of articulation. They provide the support on which the boards can be leaned, and create the possibility of that displaced, artificial space that is the staircase. But they are also the knots, the places of crossing and break, which constitute the staircase as a living body.

"You tied the composition with it [*hâ nti seddîtî bîh*]," says Sheikh Moḥammed, explaining the role of the neggâr, the "beating" verse. Like the beams in the staircase, the neggara knot the poem up by breaking it, by inscribing a difference, which holds the work together and allows it to turn, to re-turn to its refrain.

This ambivalence is reckoned through the relationship of the staircase and its base—of the dynamic, airy, and alive, and the static, fossilized, and dead. The crossing of the ʿatabi, its sedimentation, is what comes to form the central pivot, the "fixed point" and imaginary center around which the staircase revolves.

Si Thami: "*Rajel s-sallûm,* to be precise, is *khayâlî,* imaginary. It is not a thing, but just a point where the staircase goes back upon itself. It is the mizân, the balance, the gravitational center of the staircase, like the mugef in poetry. It is the *rujûʿ*, the point of return and refrain of the staircase, where it comes back after each turn [*dwra*], made of three steps.

"There is a reason if we call that pivot man [*rajel*], and not simply pillar [*sarya*]. We call it man because it does not go up by itself [*makayṭlaʿ buḥdu*], and the staircase rotates around it; it meets with the ʿatabi and goes up. He, the man of the staircase, is always a hybrid [*dayiman huwwa mkhallaṭ*], for it is formed by the encounter of the ʿatabi."

Thus, in one sense, the man of the staircase is the pestle, which dynamically enters the mortar—the base—with a rhythmical movement that scans the life of the staircase. Yet in another sense *rajel sallûm,* the "man," the "pillar," the pestle, is born from the mortar, the buried base, and goes back into it. It is the sedimented trace of its work.

Perhaps the best image to evoke the inspiration of this poems-staircase—ascending from, made possible by, and existing in a continuous exchange with its base sinking in an inaccessible Beyond—are certain bronze statues of Alberto Giacometti, growing like flower stems, progressively weightless, out of the solid impenetrability of their heavy pedestals. In Jean Genet's words:

> Toutes les statues de Giacometti ont les pieds comme pris dans un seul bloc incliné, très épais, qui rassemble plutôt à un piédestal. Parti de là, le corps supporte très loin, très haut, une tête minuscule. Cette énorme—proportionellement à la tête—masse de plâtre ou de bronze pourrait laisser croire que ces pieds sont chargés de toute la matérialité

> dont se debarasse la tête . . . pas du tout; de ces pieds massifs à la tête un exchange ininterrompu a lieu. Ces dames ne s'arrachent pas d'une boue pesante: au crepuscule elles vont descendre en glissant une côté noyée d'ombre. . . . Les statues (ces femmes) de Giacometti veillent un mort.[179]

(All Giacometti's statues have their feet somehow caught in a single, sloping, rather thick block that looks something like a pedestal. From there, the body supports, at great distance, high above, a tiny head. This enormous—in proportion to the head—mass of plaster or of bronze might suggest that these feet are loaded with all the materiality of which the head frees itself . . . not at all; an uninterrupted exchange occurs between these massive feet and this tiny head. These ladies are not pulling themselves out of an oppressive mud: at twilight they will come sliding down a slope drowned in shadows. . . . Giacometti's statues [these women] hold a wake for the dead.)[180]

Epilogue

The funeral is over. The wailing and the laughing, the sleeping in the same room, the dirty jokes, and the sudden unbearable sadness that falls upon you like a heavy load, like a frozen silence that cries out its rage and then melts into tears, then dissolves like dew in the sun—

The chanting and the singing are over, the beat of the *ḥaḍra*—one long strike between two short ones, and the deep sound of the drum that gives you a trembling inside; and the voice of the *muqaddema* screaming her songs of *ṣṣalat ʿala nnbî* (prayer to the Prophet), and the trancing, yes the trancing, because Atti Thela was an old woman, and when an old woman dies it is fair to perform the trance dance.

It is not fair when a young woman dies, or a young man, like that Lḥassan u Brahim who fell from the scaffolding in Casablanca where he went to work, or that young woman from Tanagamt whose funeral was crowded by waves of women in mourning coming from the villages downstream, arms raised and weeping loudly, pulling their hair out in despair, because her death came bitter, unexpected, painful. She had come to the qṣar only a year earlier as a bride and she was beautiful—her eyes always blackened with koḥl, her cheeks always reddened with *l-aqar*—and she was kind, always available to help, a joke ready for everyone. She had been about to give birth: her first child. Her husband left on a trip. When he came back, she had given birth, and she had died.

No, for that woman no one thought of performing the *ḥaḍra,* no one even thought of organizing the funeral. The pain was too bitter. But when Atti Thela died her gentle death four days earlier, just before dawn on that Friday morning before there was even enough light to distinguish a black thread from a white, when her niece came out screaming to break the news and water was put to heat for the washing, when a man was sent to awake l-Ḥajja Ṭama who was to prepare the body for burial, people were thinking that Atti Thela had lived her good share, and if they wept, it was because they were thinking about their own deaths, about Death, and about the bitter fate of that only niece, divorced and with no one left in the world except for her grandmother's chickens rummaging about in the house.

Kh. had liked Atti Thela's gentle smile and had chosen to take her under her covering in death. The funeral was performed in our house. Women had come, from the Ḥarâr and the Ḥarâtîn; Atti Thela had been a white woman, but with a leaning toward the Ḥarâtîn. The *muqaddema* had announced she'd perform the trance dance. Death was going to be life, she said, and life was going to be death. For when she beats the drum, chanting with her eyes open as if she could see, it is like an inkling of the Last Day.

We were to celebrate a life-death, she said, a laughing-crying. For three days it had been an alternation of laughter and despair—the despair of the *muqaddema* herself, who cried over her lonely woman's life, childless, and blind, "Cry with me women of Bni Zoli"—

That too had passed. The women had washed their hands in the bucket filled with henna put at the entrance of the house as is the custom, and were ready to move on with their lives. The henna cools off *l-ḥarâra dyâl l-mût*—says Kh.—the heat of mourning, the burning of death. The women came back from the cemetery at sunset, walking on the cement edge of the new irrigation canal like a flock of black birds—black veils fluttering in the afternoon breeze. The men sitting on the new bridge over the canal, or by the shop of the blacksmith, had looked at them coming with suspicion and curiosity; they always do. They had tried to guess the different women from their feet, and commented among themselves that it is *ḥarâm*, "illicit," to sit on the graves and eat.

At the cemetery women sat on Atti Thela's grave, where the palm leaves were still green and the earth was still fresh. They had talked about her and her niece, about the fragility of their own health undermined by the summer heat and the drought that showed no signs of respite, and they kept silent and listened to the whistling of the wind. Then a woman had opened the basket with the stuffed breads—hot peppers to cool off the heat of death—had cut them in pieces, and had distributed them among children and the women. Like the couscous eaten in the sanctuary tomb of Sîdî Ṣâfu, the *khubza*, "bread," is a ritual meal and a *zyâra* of the dead, a visitation.

Coming back from the cemetery, women had washed their hands with henna, had said "*Allah irzeq lîkum ṣṣbar,*"[1] and had left. Ḥaddya Milûd had decided to stay. She had found a pretext for the neighbor woman who had asked her to walk back to their village together—her foot was swollen, she needed to rest. She was a distant relative by marriage, but that's not why she liked to visit the house. She liked to sit in the enveloped space of the hallway downstairs, or in the protected zone of the roof enclosure, halfway between the earth and the sky; to sit, and let words flow on their own. (Later, when Kh. died and I left, she seldom came anymore, and if a funeral or a birth brought her to the qṣar, she stopped by for a minute or two and moved on.)

We climbed the narrow staircase of the house in the darkness, and we went up to the roof. The sky was dark, it was the new moon. We sat on a mat on a corner, the walls were still warm from the heat of the day. Ḥaddya spoke. She had been there when death had first struck Atti Thela. The old woman had asked to be held, to make a last tour of the house. *Bghat tsâmeḥ mʿa d-dar*—she wanted to depart from the house, from everything.

Ḥaddya:

When Death comes, it first comes to the feet. The feet die. When the feet have died, the joints [*mafâṣil*] come open, they break...

and it's like wind when it comes from somewhere and stirs up a place where it hasn't yet reached. A premonition...

and the one who's dying repeats the Shahada and keeps looking ahead, ahead and high up, without moving her eyes, without withdrawing her gaze, and lost in that vision her eyes become opaque, as if a veil had descended on them. She is looking at the one who has come, the one who is about to take her rûḥ. You who are at the bedside of the dying can't see anything, only the dying can see the angel. She's fascinated, can't withdraw her gaze from that vision...

My grandmother, may she rest in peace, or my husband, my husband's brothers, my children... all of those I have seen dying. It's always like this: death enters by the feet, when it reaches the small intestines you can hear it moving up, you can hear its voice, like a rumbling, goes up step by step, opens its way, breaks where it passes...

My grandmother, God give her peace, she kept calling: ʿAysha, Moḥammed, Faṭna, help me through the flood [*ʿawnûnî f shshaʿba*]. That is what she said. When Death enters the small intestines, it's like a windstorm when it reaches...

There she is, Death reaches the navel...

There she is, Death reaches the mouth of the heart...

When Death reached the mouth of the heart my grandmother opened her eyes, wide open, she looked at the angel, the angel sent by the Just. It was Azraʾil, the Angel of Death. And the angel kept going up and down, up and down, like a shuttle, and she kept looking... The one who's dying keeps looking at that angel sent to claim the rûḥ, and if the rûḥ of that person is blessed in the eyes of God, the angel collects it in a white cloth...

The rûḥ comes out of the body. The nefs stays in for a while, khi, khi, khi... Death keeps rising, it reaches the chest, and the dying cannot speak anymore, only the eyes are left, and the nefs also comes out, it comes out like a bit of foam, a bit of white foam, like those drops of milk that gush back from a baby's mouth...

And the angel takes the rûḥ and puts it in a bag...

And if the life and works of that person have been good, takes the rûḥ to God. There is, up there, a place like a beehive, each bee has its hole, each rûḥ fits in a hole, like a box...

But if the life of that man has been bad in the eyes of God, if he stole and committed crimes, the rûḥ resists, doesn't want to be caught, it escapes and flies up to the sky, and then falls back on earth like a stone, sinks in the water and disappears in the mud. It keeps screaming, "You torture me, you'll be tortured!" That is what the man says who committed crimes in life, and his rûḥ doesn't leave the body until the angel is himself exhausted, and the witnesses at the bedside of the dying say, "Ikhhh!" disgusted at the sight of that person...

For the signs of a good and a bad life are apparent in death, everything becomes visible...

When Atti Thela died (we invoke God to accept her among the blessed), Death also entered her by the feet. And when Death entered her feet, she asked us to hold her as she walked through the house for the last time. It was her farewell. Death had entered her, and we held her, and it was like holding a tree that was cut from its roots.

Ḥaddya pauses. Tinkling of bracelets, then silence. Smell of couscous mixed with smoke, dinner cooking on every roof, children's shrieks, a rare engine pump still at work in the gardens and the distant noise of the neighbor's television set. Kh.'s little daughter has fallen asleep on Ḥaddya's lap; the old woman whispers "Bismillâh" and covers her with a piece of her veil.

When she resumes speaking, the rûḥ that she has in mind is a yet unborn one. She speaks fast and she whispers. Kh. moves closer. It is the parable of the manufacture of life out of death. Kh. is familiar with it, of course, but it is new for her to hear it from Ḥaddya Milûd's lips—younger women are shy in the presence of older ones. (Only as children they can listen without feeling uneasy: "From my grandmother's lips to my ears, and I was small on her lap [*men fum ḥennatî l-udniya u anâ taḥt mennha ṣghîra*]," Ḥaddya said once.)

Women share this story among themselves; men are not familiar with it. They don't ask in most cases and, if they heard something in childhood, have now bracketed it away, along with many a vision from the women's world, and the memory of when as small children they rushed into the mosque with their mothers and grandmothers in festive clothes—women never enter the mosque in this region—after having closed the gate of the qṣar and locked the men outside. Men have their own version for what concerns conception, and when women talk with their men, they don't attempt to deny it. The story men recount is the story of the seed. There is a seed, as big as a barley grain, that sometimes, but not always, a man ejects with his sperm. When the seed enters the woman, and she is in a condition to receive, the woman collects it and is impregnated.

But this story is different, a tale of spiral temporality. It is the story of an angel, and of a handful of earth. It tells of the sending from a future already past, a future in ruins, which turns upon itself and creates the present, the present of presence, as a fugitive intersection of threads.

It is Azraʾil that comes to the woman at the beginning of the fourth month of pregnancy, Azraʾil, the Angel of Death.

It is when rûḥ develops in it that the thing in your womb starts moving. At the beginning it's nothing, it is like *l-ḥarîra,* the soup we prepare in the morning. A formless liquid amalgam, like putrescent water from a pond, like *amalûs.* That's all you can smell when you are pregnant, the odor of *amalûs.* Putrid water. Inside your body that stuff is rotting, it is decomposing, stinking and black, like the mud of a swamp or the black sewage from the washing rooms of the mosque,[2] or like the rotting water of *tamdet,* the waste pond at the bottom of the house. This is what human beings are like in the beginning!

In the beginning human beings are like putrid water.

Imagine those pools left stagnant in the canal, after the flow has stopped. Water gets mixed up with the mud and the leaves; it stagnates and ferments [*kaykhmer*]; it stinks [*kaykhnâz*], it slowly becomes black [*kaykḥâl*]. After a while you notice little bugs swimming in the black waters of that rotting stuff. They weren't there before. This is what happens in the womb. The man releases his water, and slowly that water turns black and ferments, it ferments and rots, it rots and smells like shit...

In the Water of Man [*l-mâ dyâl r-rajel*], there is nothing. It is sterile like egg white. When the man releases his sperm, his water, inside the woman, is just that: clean water. Pure, pure like silver! *Ṣâfî kîf n-nuqra.* The water gets caught inside the woman's womb, and it rots...

It is that rotting water in her womb that causes in a woman the cravings [*l-wuḥâm*], that's what gives her compulsive desires. Her heart darkens up, she is filled with stench. *Kân lîha l-khnez f gelbha.* She herself smells bad, and whatever she smells, she dislikes. She spits, she vomits, and she flees the company of her fellow humans. You find her sleeping in the place of the animals, or in some dark corner, at the bottom of the staircase.

The water released by the man rots and keeps rotting. Then slowly starts shrinking, like stew boiling down in a pot or cheese curdling out of milk. A form starts separating out from that amorphous amalgam. Slowly it shrinks into a lump, then it forms something like a chick, it keeps shrinking, it gathers up and keeps gathering, and slowly, very slowly, a form develops from that black water, from that stench, from that rotting, and one day what is left is a human shape. When she is cured from that black mud in her womb, she is cured from her cravings. And there you go! You are back among your fellow humans, back to the family, back to the qṣar, you eat with them again, you drink with them again...

But this process of shrinking and separating out doesn't happen alone. It is God that gives form to that stuff rotting in the womb...

One day an angel comes—Azraʾil, the Angel of Death, the angel that collects the rûḥ of the person when she dies—and brings a handful of earth from the grave where that person yet to be will be buried after death...

Say that woman, or that man, will die in old age, or in young age, say that it is written that she will fall into a well and die as a young girl, or that she will die during childbirth, or that she'll live up to very old age and see her children's children grow old and have children, and say that woman will be buried in Tafetchna. The angel, then, brings a handful of earth from that grave yet to be in the cemetery of Tafetchna, and sprinkles it over that rotting stuff in the womb, like what you do when you sprinkle spices onto the soup. That bit of earth reacts with that water, it triggers fermentation and shrinking...

It is the Earth of Death.

(The earth thrown by the angel inscribes on the fetus its own death. That inscription is the ambivalent remedy that triggers articulation, and with it movement. The image Ḥaddya uses is that of the hand of the fetus, that splits up into five fingers and starts moving. The thing in the womb suddenly *kaytḥarrek*—it starts moving and breathing. It has developed rûḥ. It has come to life as a human body.)

The angel throws the earth of Death like a throwing of yeast on flour—yeast [*l-khamira*]. From that throwing, a form is separated out from the rest: like butter from milk, like gold from the other metals under the effect of fire. From that shrinking and separating out a human being is made [*tbaʿna l-adami*].

When the body of the baby is built, she expels all that rotten stuff, that blood and pus and filthy water, all that decayed and dead substance, and she gives birth to the creature in her womb. She opens up, she breaks, her bones are splintered, her joints are shattered, you can hear them cracking, they say, "Tak, tak," everything opens, everything comes undone! And she has to lie in bed until the bones are set, set back together, until the womb is stitched. And you, the qebla who assisted her during birth, you push her body hard to set her joints back in place, for everything is dismembered, everything is cracked, *mṭerṭeg*—

Ḥaddya paused. Hesitant, authoritative voice, Kh. interrupted the train of our thoughts.

There were once two brothers, Sîdî Ḥamam and Sîdî Imam. Their father was a ghûl, *their mother was a* ghûla. *They lived with their parents on the other side of a forest, on top of a desert mountain. They lived in the land of the* ghwâl.

Then they transformed into birds, and flew away.

They flew to the sea shore; they built a house and settled there. A woman slave worked for them. She cooked their meals and served them on two plates. One plate was made of silver, the other was made of gold. One day Sîdî Ḥamam married ʿAysha bent Solṭân.

He was a bird; she was a woman like all women.

She came to live in the house. They lived in peace until Sîdî Ḥamam told her, "My father is a ghûl, my mother is a ghûla. You cannot come with me to my parents' land." But she said, "I must visit your parents' land, I must." "No!" he said, "you can't. We are going to live here and we'll be safe. Don't ask to see them. Makateqadarsh ʿalîhum, *you are not strong enough to face them."*

One day as she was combing her hair, a lock of hair came off her comb. A bird came and stole it. The bird stole the lock and flew away. As the bird flew away with the lock, it flew away with her mind. She lost herself... she went mad...

As she lost herself, she went to her father's house and she laid there. She laid like a statue carved in stone. Words were dry in her throat. She had lost her speech. Doctors came, they tried their art on her, they tried their remedies on her. No one succeeded.

She wasn't alive, nor was she dead.

One day an old old woman wanted to set up a loom. She went to wash the wool on the shore of the ocean where Sîdî Ḥamam had his house. It was night, but she thought it daylight. There was a full moon and she walked in her sleep. She awoke and she saw a house on the shore. She went and sat by the door waiting for dawn. It was the house of Sîdî Ḥamam and Sîdî Imam.

They came, they sat down to eat dinner, the slave brought the water to wash their hands, she brought the meal, they ate until they reached the moment of dividing the meat, they divided the meat and they said, "Hâ ḥaqq Sîdî Ḥamâm, Hâ ḥaqq Sîdî Imâm, Ha ḥaqq ʿAysha bent Soltan, l-ḥadara f l-qulûb, l-ghâyba bîn l-ʿayûn, bki yâ shjâr, bki yâ l-ḥjâr, bki yâ l-ḥût f l-bḥar" *[This is the share of Sîdî Ḥamam, this is the share of Sîdî Imam, this is the share of ʿAysha bent Solṭân. What is Present in the heart, is Absent between the eyes. Cry O trees, cry O stones, cry O fish in the ocean].*

And all the plants in the house would die, their color would fade, their flowers would drop, as if a burning wind had come and had blown everything away. The world would cry, each time... Soon every living thing in that house fell ill, because she was ill...

The old woman waited until the brothers left for work; she went in and took a cup of water from the jug. The jug said, "Stop! wait for the slave to give you some." She went to the tajin that was cooking on the fire; the pot said, "Stop! wait for the slave to give you some." And so said all the objects of the house.

She went out in the street. The town crier was calling: "There is no god but God and Muḥammad is his prophet, O people of good faith, if you heard something or you dreamt something, come and report it to ʿAysha bent Solṭân."

People came in crowds. She was the king's daughter, and everyone had a dream to recount, everyone had a story to tell. But to no one did she give a sign of life. Sunken in her state, she lay there like stone. The old woman came to report what she had heard. People laughed at her, they said, "If cocks did not awake Lâllâ ʿAysha, how could fishbones awake her!?" They insulted and made fun of her. But she finally made her way to ʿAysha's bedside. She said, "My daughter, I found myself in a house on the seashore, I heard Sîdî Ḥamam, I heard Sîdî Imâm, they divided the meat and they said, 'Cry O trees, cry O stones, cry O fish in the ocean!'" When she heard this, ʿAysha screamed "What!" and her mind came back to her. She asked the old woman to take her to that house. They went, they sat outside the door, until the brothers came home, until they sat down to have dinner, until the old slave brought the food and they divided the meat and they said, "This is the share of

Sîdî Ḥamam, this is the share of Sîdî Imam, this is the share of ʿAysha bent Solṭân. What is Present in the heart, is Absent between the eyes. Cry O trees, cry O stones, cry O fish in the ocean."

But the trees didn't cry, the leaves didn't fade, the flowers didn't drop. Everything was alive and green. The brothers were amazed. They said, "Today we are not alone in the house, Something is here with us." They searched the house and they found her. He said, "Where were you, ʿAysha-ruined-her-happiness-with-her-own-hands [fîn kunti, ʿAysha khassrât saʿdhâ b-iddhâ]?"

She said, "I was ill," and told him everything.

He said, "Come, ʿAysha-ruined-her-happiness-with-her-own-hands! I try to make the loom of life beautiful for you, and each time you unravel it with your own hands!"

And again he told her, "My parents are ghwâl, they live in a world that is forbidden to you." She said, "No way! at the risk of death I must go!" He said, "You will have to walk on thorns and scorpions, and in the desert mountains there are wild beasts and monsters..." "I will walk in the fire..." He said, "Let's go, then, ʿAysha-ruined-her-life-with-her-own-hands." And they went.

They entered the region of the desert mountains. Each time a thorn wounded her, he told her, "Keep going, ʿAysha-ruined-her-life-with-her-own-hands."

They went and went, until they reached the tree that marked the boundary. He told her, "Enter, and as you enter you'll find my mother, she has seven breasts, and you'll find my father. Fill up your mouth with honey and almonds, empty it on my mother's right breast and say to her: I am under your protection [hânî f ḥurmtek], *like that Sîdî Ḥamam who nursed at this breast." So she did, and she nursed from the breast of the ghûla, and the ghûla said, "If it wasn't that my son's well-being comes before my own, I would eat you up in one bite." Lâllâ ʿAysha went back to Sîdî Ḥamam in tears. "Shut up," he said, "whatever they say to you, for God's sake shut up. Don't spend with them more than the two minutes I allow you, and return to me..." She went, and came back.*

The ghwâl put her through an endless number of trials, and each time she came back to him for help, each time he helped her. In the end they put a candle in her hair—like the candle that is put on the head of the bride during the henna ceremony...

They told her, "Don't move! Don't move your head this way or that way, if you move your head we'll eat you." Sîdî Ḥamam was watching from the top of a tree. She staggered, and fire broke out in her hair. He told her, "Kill the fire with your hands, your hair is burning!" And she said, "My heart is ablaze, imagine my hair..." "Kill the fire, kill the fire..." "My heart is on fire, just imagine my hair..." At the last moment he rescued her. But did he rescue her? He lifted her up, she dissolved into air, and disappeared into the sky.

...

Notes

INTRODUCTION

1. Ibn al-ʿArabî, *Al-Futûḥât al-makkiyya* (The Mekkan openings), cited in W. C. Chittick, *The Sufi Path of Knowledge: Ibn al-ʿArabî's Metaphysics of Imagination* (Albany: State University of New York Press, 1989), 14.

2. G. Spillmann, *Districts et tribus de la haute vallée du Draa: Documents et reinseignements de la direction générale des affaires indigènes (section sociologique): Villes et tribus du Maroc,* vol. 9 (Paris: Champion, 1931). Spillmann's first study was an interpretative reading of aerial photographs, a view from afar (Capitaine Pennés and Lieutenant Spillmann, "Les pays inaccessibles du Haut Draa: Un essai d'exploration aérienne en collaboration avec le service des affaires indigènes du Maroc," *Revue de Géographie Marocaine,* 1929).

For a description of the occupation of Zagora in January 1932, see G. Spillmann, *Souvenirs d'un colonialiste* (Paris: Presses de la Cité, 1968), 71–128.

3. In 1931 Spillmann built a French post on a strategic height in the region of Mezguita, in the northern Draʿ valley. In January 1932, as he later recalled in his memoir, "the Groupe Mobile gathered in Rebat, under the command of the lieutenant-colonel Chardon, and moved towards the region of Ternata. On January 8th, it crossed this palmery, and reached Zagora, with no incidents, two days later" (*Souvenirs d'un colonialiste,* 101).

4. *Qṣar,* "palace" or "fortification" in Arabic, here means simply the settlement surrounded by ramparts that is specific to this region. I have chosen to avoid directly naming the place, unless its name is cited in a conversation or a narrative. Yet I have resisted changing its name, because its vicissitudes are not fictional, and I am bound by their reality. I did change the names of people throughout the book, including those of the main characters. I made a few exceptions, for those who prefer (or I believe would have preferred) being mentioned by their own name: in particular, Ḥadda and Sheikh Moḥammed the poet (who was locally a public figure).

In 1984 the qṣar had approximately 2,500 inhabitants, and its old walled settlement comprised some 400 houses. According to the 1994 official census, the "commune rurale" of which the qṣar is the largest settlement and administrative center (including some fifteen neighboring villages, or *qṣûr*) today has 17,175 inhabitants, divided into 1,712 households. The number of inhabitants of the qṣar community itself, now relocated to a new site, is yet unpublished. The closest large urban center is the town of Zagora, which according to the same census has 26,174 inhabitants, divided into 3,452 households. The provincial capital for the entire region is the city of Ouarzazat, situated some two hundred kilometers northwest of the qṣar, at the gateway of the Wâd Draʿ valley.

Factual ethnographic information about the qṣar and the region (social, historical, geographical, bibliographic) is scattered throughout the book, when needed as a contextualization. In most cases, I have chosen to put it in the notes, not to disturb the flow of the narrative.

5. See E. Benveniste's distinction between *énoncé* and *énonciation,* the statement (*énoncé*) and the enunciative act (*énonciation*), or act of speech—*parole.* According to Benveniste a subject position, or the lieu of an "I," can only emerge in relation to an act of speech, which he views as necessarily processual, relational, and intersubjective (*Problèmes de linguistique générale* [Paris: Gallimard, 1966]). "Je ne peut être definit que en termes de 'locution,' non en termes d'objets, comme l'est un signe nominal" ("La nature des pronoms," 252; see in general "De la subjectivité dans le langage"). See also the uses and elaboration of the concept of *parole* by J. Lacan, "Fonction et champ de la parole et du langage," in *Écrits* (Paris: Seuil, 1966).

6. "Les mots que le temps a gelés, vont-ils redevenir des voix (adressées par qui et à qui?)" (M. De Certeau, *La fable mystique* [Paris: Gallimard, 1982], 224). On the topic of enunciation as fugitive locus of subjectivity, see "Le conversar" and the chapter "La scène de l'énonciation" in *La fable mystique,* 216–45.

7. G. Deleuze, *L'image-temps: Cinéma 2* (Paris: Les Éditions de Minuit, 1985). "The speech-act has many heads, and, little by little, plants the elements of a people to come as the free indirect discourse of Africa about itself, about America, or about Paris" (*Cinema 2: The Time-Image,* trans. H. Tomlinson and R. Galeta [Minneapolis: University of Minnesota Press, 1989], 223).

8. The language of these texts is the local version of vernacular Arabic, with the exception of a few conversations in Tashelḥit Berber. A center of multiple civilizations, which since pre-Roman times have settled, passed, blended, and alternated each other in this irrigated region, the Draʿ valley is an ethnically mixed and plurilingual environment, and has been such over several centuries. The qṣar dwellers are for the most part bilingual—between vernacular Arabic and Tashelḥit Berber (only the modern-educated younger generation speaks some French), and often express themselves in a mixture of the two. Concerning pronunciation, intonation, syntactical structures, vocabulary, and idiomatic expressions, both the Arabic and Berber that people speak have a distinctively southern regional character, different but fully intelligible for speakers from other areas of Morocco. There are also in the area a number of only-Arabic-speaking and only-Berber-speaking settlements, inhabited by populations that define themselves as "Arabs" and "Shleuḥ" (Berbers)—from formerly nomadic or seminomadic tribes. Their Arabic and Berber speech is viewed as significantly different from that of the people of the qṣar, even though they are reciprocally, and almost completely, intelligible—with the exception of poetic expressions.

9. "The author must not make himself into the ethnologist of his people, nor invent a fiction which would be one more private story: for every personal fiction, like every impersonal myth, is on the side of the 'masters.' There remains for the author the possibility of finding 'intercessors,' that is of taking real and not fictional

characters, but putting them in the position of 'making fiction,' 'making legends,' 'fabulating.' The author takes a step towards his characters, but the characters take a step towards the author: double becoming. Story-telling [*la fabulation*] is not an impersonal myth, but neither it is a personal fiction: it is a parole en acte, a speech-act through which the character keeps crossing the boundary which would separate his private business from politics, and himself produces collective utterances" (Deleuze, *Cinema 2*, 222, translation modified).

10. The spatial trope of the Other Scene or Other Stage—*ein anderer Schauplatz*—as *lieu* of alterity, was first used by Freud in *The Interpretation of Dreams* (1900, trans. J. Strachey [New York: Avon Books, 1965], 81: "The scene of action of dreams is different from that of waking ideational life"). Freud borrowed the concept from G. T. Fechner.

11. The image is J. Lacan's (*The Four Fundamental Concepts of Psychoanalysis*, trans. A. Sheridan [New York: Norton, 1978], originally published as *Les quatre concepts fondamentaux de la psychanalyse* [Paris: Seuil, 1973]).

12. For a definition of the concept of *différence intraitable*, see A. Khatibi, *Maghreb pluriel* (Paris: Denoel, 1983); for a narrative dramatization of it, see A. Khatibi, *Le livre du sang* (Paris: Gallimard, 1979); A. Khatibi, *La blessure du nom propre* (Paris: Denoel, 1974); A. Khatibi, *Amour bilingue* (Paris: Fata Morgana, 1982). Cf. also the collective work *Imaginaires de l'autre* (Paris: L'Harmattan, 1987), and in particular the contributions of A. Diouri, "Traiter de l'intraitable," and of C. Buci-Glucksmann, "Fitna, ou la différence intraitable de l'amour." For a discussion of the Eden Babelien, and the foundational place of difference as multiplicity of languages and idioms in classical Arabic literature and Qur'anic commentaries, see A. Kilito, *La langue d'Adam* (Casablanca: Tubkal, 1996).

13. On the notion of *riḥla* see part 1, note 8.

14. Kateb Yacine, *Nedjma* (1956), trans. R. Howard (Charlottesville: University of Virginia Press, 1961); D. Chraïbi, *Le passé simple* (Paris: Denoel, 1954). The French grammatical *passé simple* is usually translated as the English preterit, or historic tense. Yet, while the preterit is mostly used as a literary past tense and conveys a fictionalized sense of fracture, the French *passé simple* denotes a radical separation of the action from the subject who accomplished it. For this reason, it is almost never used in the first person.

15. This is a preoccupation discussed in different ways in other recent ethnographic works on the Middle East, with which this book dialogues indirectly, often through the notes: A. Hammoudi, *La victime et ses masques: Essai sur le sacrifice et la mascarade au Maghreb* (Paris: Seuil, 1988); M. Fischer and M. Abedi, *Debating Muslims: Cultural Dialogues in Postmodernity and Tradition* (Madison: University of Wisconsin Press, 1990); B. Messick, *The Calligraphic State* (Berkeley: University of California Press, 1993); V. Crapanzano, *Tuhami: Portrait of a Moroccan* (Chicago: University of Chicago Press, 1980); M. Meeker, *Literature and Violence in North Arabia* (Cambridge: Cambridge University Press, 1979); L. Abu-Lughod, *Veiled Sentiments* (Berkeley: University of California Press, 1987). In a larger sense, and beyond the specifically ethnographic genre, there are M. Arkoun, *Pour une critique de la raison islamique* (Paris: Maisonneuve et Larose, 1984), and J. Genet, *Un captif amoureux* (Paris: Gallimard, 1986).

16. The title is a quote from Ibn al-ʿArabî about the other region and specific place of dreaming.

17. In the style of psychological anthropology or ethnopsychiatry.

18. In her book *Blindness and Autobiography* (Princeton: Princeton University Press, 1988), on the textual structures of Tâhâ Husayn's *Al-Ayyâm*, Fedwa Malti-Douglas discusses the complex temporality, and "the dialectic between temporal modes," in the autobiography of the Egyptian modernist thinker. In terms of G. Genette's notions of "prolepses" and "analepses"—jumps forward and backward, or "temporal intrusions" in a narrative, referring to events that haven't yet been mentioned, or are instead superseded in the chronological sequence—she describes Tâhâ Husayn's "mixed temporality," synchronic and diachronic at once, as a specific feature of his modernist sensibility and style. Another example of "historical recycling" as a modernist and specifically postcolonial temporal mode is found in the spiral narrative structures of Kateb Yacine's novel *Nedjma.*

19. On the notion of "presencing of a beyond" on the boundary, see H. Bhabha, *The Location of Culture* (New York: Routledge, 1994, 4): "'Beyond' signifies spatial distance, marks progress, promises the future; but our intimations of exceeding the barrier or boundary—the very act of going *beyond*—are unknowable, unrepresentable, without a return to the 'present' which, in the process of repetition, becomes disjunct and displaced."

20. The term is A. Kilito's, in *L'auteur et ses doubles: Essai sur la culture arabe classique* (Paris: Seuil, 1985).

PART 1. RETURNS

1. Maqâmat Badî az-Zamân al-Ḥamadhâni (Beirut: al-Hilâl, 1993), 21.

2. See frontispiece. Drawn on an approximately square piece of plywood, the map measures fifteen by eighteen inches. I borrow the title of this section, "Topology of a City," from A. Robbe-Grillet's novel *Topologie d'une cité fantôme* (Paris: Les Éditions de Minuit, 1976). The English term *city* does not render the connotation of the French *cité.* While *city* immediately conveys the sense of a large urban settlement, *cité* carries a stronger metaphorical connotation, of moral community, spatial sociopolitical entity, and it does not necessarily indicate a large urban settlement. The qṣar in this sense would be more appropriately called a *cité* rather than a *city.*

3. "*Frame, n.:* 1 a: something composed of parts fitted together and united b: the physical make up of an animal and especially a human body: PHYSIQUE, FIGURE 2 a: the constructional system that gives shape or strength (as to a building); *also:* a frame dwelling b: such as a skeleton not filled in or covered 3 a: an open case or structure made for admitting, enclosing or supporting something b: a machine built upon or within a framework [a spinning machine] . . . 5: a particular state or disposition (as of the mind): MOOD 6 a: an enclosing border b: the matter or area enclosed in such a border" (*Webster's Ninth New Collegiate Dictionary*).

4. "Le trait alors se divise en ce lieu où il a lieu. L'emblème de ce *topos* paraît introuvable, je l'emprunte à la nomenclature de l'encadrement: c'est le *passe-partout.* . . . J'écris à même le passe-partout bien connu des encadreurs. Et pour l'entamer, à même cette surface dite vierge, généralement découpée dans un carré de carton et ouverte en son 'milieu' pour y laisser paraître l'oeuvre" (J. Derrida, "Passe-Partout," in *La vérité en peinture* [Paris: Flammarion, 1978], 17).

5. The correct Arabic syntax would be *l-fum l-qdîm,* "the old mouth," or *fum*

qdîm, in the indeterminate form. Beside the fact that the draftsman is not fully literate, the syntax points at a certain oral quality of the writing. The inscriptions in the map are internally carved by a diglossia that in Arabic inhabits the relationship of speech and writing: between the spoken vernacular (which, in the case of this region, is intermingled with a Berber vocabulary) and a written classical language. Inscriptions in the map are between written and oral expression, between Arabic and Berber, and in that bilingual zone they float.

6. *Ayt* is a Tashelḥit and Tamazight (Berber) term, equivalent to the Moroccan Arabic *bni,* or *bânî,* "children of," "descendants of," and identifies people as attached to a lineage, family, or some other affiliation. (In Moroccan Arabic *bni* and *bânî* are more commonly found than *awlâd,* "children of," to indicate community or tribal affiliation.) *Ayt* is in the first place a genealogical term, but it can be extended to fictionally genealogical or simply nongenealogical phenomena, to address or indicate a group of people belonging to an institution, or doing something together (*ayt l-ʿaza,* "the funeral party"; *ayt l-ʿars,* "the family who is having a wedding"; *ayt l-benian,* "the workers who are building a house"; etc.). In this case the affiliation is with a fourth of the village (*rbaʿ*), a "quarter," quite literally, in the territorial and symbolic sense.

7. Here again is visible the diglossic work of the oral expression in the written: *burj j-jâmeʿ l-bâlî,* "tower of the mosque of the Bâlî," is missing the determinative article (it is actually written *burj jâmeʿ l-bâlî*). This is because in Moroccan vernacular, unlike standard written Arabic, *j* is a "sun letter" (like *s, sh, r, d, t*) and in words beginning with *j* the determinative article *al* (*l-*) is assimilated to it and becomes *j-*. Yusef abolishes it altogether, thus altering in the inscription the syntactical form of the *iḍâfa* (attributive genitive construction).

8. The official Moroccan transcription of *duwwâr* in French is *douar.*

9. From the verbal root *raḥla,* to set out, to depart, to move away, to emigrate, to be constantly on the go, to wander, to lead a nomadic life, the noun *ar-riḥla* means "travel," "journey," and is also the technical Arabic term for "travelogue." *Ar-riḥla* is the name of a classical literary genre of travel writing, which blossomed in Dâr al-Islam, "the land of Islam," from the eleventh to the fifteenth century and lasted in different forms all the way to the nineteenth century.

As a genre, the riḥla was related to the ḥajj—the Muslim pilgrimage to Mecca—but also to the Muslim practice of *ṭalab al-ʿilm,* traveling for "seeking knowledge." As mentioned in a hadith, "He who follows the road seeking knowledge, God will make the path to heaven easy for him. And the angels will place their wings as to aid the seeker of knowledge" (cited in S. Gellens, "The Search for Knowledge in Medieval Muslim Societies: A Comparative Approach," in *Muslim Travellers: Pilgrimage, Migration, and the Religious Imagination,* ed. D. Eickelman and J. Piscatory [Berkeley: University of California Press, 1990], 54). The riḥla as physical journey and existential displacement was the style and condition of possibility of learning. Across the Islamic world, from one center of learning to another, a constant flow of scholars moved on endless peregrinations: from teacher to teacher, and from text to text, for texts were embodied in the scholars who had memorized them and could comment upon them, and were by and large orally transmitted. (Cf. G. Makdisi, *The Rise of Colleges* [Edinburgh: Edinburgh University Press, 1981]; B. Messick, *The Calligraphic State* [Berkeley: University of California Press, 1993].) The imperative of traveling for seeking knowledge determined the cosmopolitan character of the centers of learning, where everyone was a foreigner and everyone belonged.

As travelogues of the pilgrimage, *riḥlat,* or riḥla texts, are pilgrims' memoirs, narrating the circuitous and dangerous journeys that led pilgrims by foot or horseback from their region of origin to the land of the Hijaz (where Mecca is). The path was circuitous because on their two-year journey to and from Mecca (if from the Maghreb) pilgrims made detours to visit the important shrines and holy places on the way, and at each station stopped and spent time. Sometimes, as in the case of the famous fourteenth-century traveler Ibn Battuta, they spent years or never came back. The journey was a life experience; it had become life itself.

At the opening of his *Riḥla* (1355, in *Travels in Asia and Africa,* trans. H. A. Gibb [1929; reprint, New York: Routledge, 1983], 43), Ibn Battuta writes: "I left Tangiers, my birthplace, on Thursday, 2d Rajab, 725 [14 June 1325], being at that time twenty two years of age, with the intention of making the Pilgrimage to the Holy House [at Mecca] and the Tomb of the Prophet [at Madîna]. I set out alone, finding no companion to cheer the way with friendly intercourse, and no party of travellers with whom to associate myself. Swayed by an overmastering impulse within me, and a long cherished desire to visit those glorious sanctuaries, I resolved to quit all my friends and tear myself away from home. As my parents were still alive, it weighed grievously upon me to part from them, and both they and I were afflicted with sorrow."

As a journey and as a travel narrative, the riḥla to Mecca had a twofold character (cf. A. El Moudden, "The Ambivalence of *Riḥla:* Community Integration and Self-Definition in Moroccan Travel Accounts, 1300–1800," in *Muslim Travellers,* ed. D. Eickelman and J. Piscatory [Berkeley: University of California Press, 1990]). On the one hand it was a journey through Dâr al-Islam, the *umma,* the land of Islam, which, as a movement of gathering, constituted the community of Muslims. On the other hand it was a movement, a displacement, through unfamiliar lands and populations, each with its specific customs and languages, singularity and alterity—strangeness. The theme of the *bilâd Bâni Kelbûn,* for instance, the "land of the dog's children," where people have a human body and dog's head, or of the *bilâd Bâni ʿArra,* where everyone walks around naked, are recurrent in oral narratives of the riḥla style telling the marvels and horrors of the journey to Mecca. Ibn Battuta himself, who started his world travels as a journey to Mecca, tells in the *Riḥla* of his homesickness and sense of exile, and of his amazement before the strange customs of many of the populations he encountered.

The riḥla is also a philosophical genre of narratives of displacement. It is a genre that might be called "cynical." As in the case of the *Maqâmât* discussed by Kilito (*Les séances: Récits et codes culturels ches Hamadhanî et Harîrî* [Paris: Sindbad, 1983], 30), it is a narrative genre of reflections about the journeylike character of life, the instability of fate and of the world, the irony of human existence and what Kilito names "l'identité fugitive," in the context of a "celebration of instability."

10. For a discussion of the figure of the *marcheur,* "walker," and its philosophical implications in classical Arabic literature, as a sort of *être en route,* "being on the path," see Kilito, *Les séances.* For a discussion of the hermeneutics of following a path—*parcours*—as uncertainly deciphering a landscape of writing, see A. Kilito, "La cité des morts," in *L'oeil et l'aiguille: Essai sur Les Mille et une Nuits* (Paris: La Découverte, 1992).

The work of Michel De Certeau is a crucial reference point here. Concerning the particular issues of displacement, orientation-disorientation, and travel raised by a reading of this drawing, see *The Mystic Fable,* trans. M. B. Smith (Chicago: University of Chicago Press, 1992), originally published as *La fable mystique* (Paris: Gallimard, 1982), part 1, "Un lieu pour se perdre"; *Heterologies: Discourse on the Other* (Minneapolis: University of Minnesota Press, 1986), for instance, "Montaigne's 'Of Cannibals': The Savage 'I.'"

In what is rather a promenade than a reading through Hieronymus Bosch's famous painting ("Le jardin: Délire et délices de Jerôme Bosch," in *La fable mystique*), De Certeau discusses the way Bosch's fifteenth-century painting "se cache en se montrant" (hides in its showing itself), and provokes in the viewer a proliferation of interpretive discourses, all the while resisting the possibility of deciphering. Because, De Certeau says, a "this-means-that" approach to decoding, which would make each signifier "confess" its signified, is for this painting out of the question. *The Garden* does not hide a sense. Like a dream, it is a "production" of sense. The internal alchemy of the multiple elements of the composition is productive. As an "éclat de rêve" (a dream blast) the representation functions poetically rather than referentially. Reading/seeing Bosch's *Garden* is not attempting to discover a referential context; it is following the energetic deployment of figures, and analyzing the formal principles of its construction.

Behind the selection of figures, De Certeau says, there is a classificatory logic, drawn from the vocabularies of zoology, botany, astronomy, astrology, and the natural sciences of the period. In this sense *The Garden* is a modernist product of the European Quattrocento; but, "taking up the signs that accommodate all the scientific curiosities of his time in his painting, Bosch makes them function *differently,* just as he does the different various fragments of the world that he brings together in the non-place of his painting. He makes them into a garden" (*Mystic Fable,* 57).

11. Writing around a very different picture, Michel Foucault makes a similar comment. In his masterful description of Velázquez's *Las Meninas,* the first reading of the painting has to do with the formal composition and the place assigned to the various figures. In that first reading it is unnecessary to know that the two figures outside the visual field and being looked at by all the characters are King Philip IV and his wife, or that the girl in the foreground is the Infanta Margherita with her court, etc. Only later will Foucault bring in that information, which he calls anecdotal (*Les mots et les choses* [Paris: Gallimard, 1966]).

12. I speak of implication in the sense in which Marcel Mauss says that receiving a gift means to be implicated by it, and engaging in a contract in which one mortgages oneself. Explaining his point with an example from ancient Roman law, Mauss says that receiving a thing makes the recipient *reus* of that thing, that is, both its "owner" and the subject "incriminated" by it. The phrase Mauss uses is poignant: having the thing (gift) is to be condemned by the thing, under accusation by it: *damnatus* (*Essai sur le don* [1923], in *Sociologie et anthropologie* (Paris: Presses Universitaires de France, 1950).

13. For Derrida, dreaming is "marcher dans un paysage d'écriture" (walking through a landscape of writing; "Freud et la scène de l'écriture," in *L'écriture et la différence* [Paris: Seuil, 1967]).

14. J. Lacan, *The Four Fundamental Concepts of Psychoanalysis,* trans. A. Sheridan (New York: Norton, 1978), 75, (translation slightly modified), originally published as *Les quatre concepts fondamentaux de la psychanalyse* (Paris: Seuil, 1973).

15. E. Benveniste, "Actif et moyen dans le verbe," *Problèmes de linguistique générale,* vol. 1 (Paris: Gallimard, 1966). See also H. White, "Writing in the Middle Voice," *Stanford Literary Review* 9 (fall 1992): 179–87; R. Barthes, "To Write: An Intransitive Verb?" in *The Languages of Criticism and the Sciences of Man: The Structuralist Controversy,* ed. R. Macksey and E. Donato (Baltimore: Johns Hopkins University Press, 1970). Without referring to the grammatical notion of the "middle voice," but in the context of a discussion of subjectivity in painting and drawing, Derrida raises the issue of intransitivity between the active and the passive in the form *nous fascinons:* "Je propose d'user de ce mot intransitivement, comme on dirait 'nous hallucinons,' 'je salive,' 'tu expire'. . . ou le bateau mouille" (*La vérité en peinture,* 16).

16. On Ibn al-ʿArabî's notion of *ʿâlam al-mithâl,* see H. Corbin, *L'imagination créatrice dans le soufisme d'Ibn ʿArabî* (Paris: Flammarion, 1958); W. C. Chittick, *The Sufi Path of Knowledge: Ibn al-ʿArabî's Metaphysics of Imagination* (Albany: State University of New York Press, 1989); M. Chodkiewicz, *Le sceau des saints: Prophétie et sainteté dans la doctrine d'Ibn Arabî* (Paris: Gallimard, 1986).

17. *Four Fundamental Concepts,* 28, translation modified. "Ainsi l'inconscient se manifeste toujours comme ce qui vacille dans une coupure du sujet—d'où resurgit une trouvaille, que Freud assimile au désir—désir que nous situerons provisoirement dans la métonimie dénudée du discours en cause, où le sujet se saisit en quelque point inattendu" (Lacan, *Les quatres concepts,* 29).

18. J. Lacan, "Tuché and Automaton," in *Les quatre concepts,* 54. *Tuché* and *automaton* are terms Aristotle discusses in the *Physics.* Lacan borrows the Aristotelian terminology to develop a paradoxical argument about the double play of repetition (in the symbolic order) and the "event" of surprise, which happens in the order of what he calls "le réel."

19. S. Freud, "The Uncanny" ("Das Unheimliche," 1919), in *Standard Edition of the Complete Psychological Works,* trans. J. Strachey, vol. 17 (London: Hogarth Press, 1955).

20. Kilito, *Les séances.*

21. Kilito, *L'oeil et l'aiguille; The Arabian Nights,* trans. H. Haddawy, based on the text of the fourteenth-century Syrian manuscript edited by M. Mahdi (New York: Norton, 1990); *The Thousand and One Nights,* trans. E. Lane (London: Knight, 1938).

22. J. F. Lyotard, *Discours/figure* (Paris: Klincksieck, 1971), 14. "The eye is a force. . . . And force is never anything but the energy that pleats, that crumples the text and turns it into a work, a difference, that is, a form. A painting is not to read, as claim the semiologists today, Klee used to say that it should be *grazed,* that it makes one see, it makes one see what seeing is. Looking at a painting means tracing paths through it, cotracing paths with it."

23. De Certeau, *Mystic Fable,* 58, translation slightly modified. "Cette métamorphose est fréquente chez les mystiques. . . . Elle transporte le signe d'un espace à un autre, et produit le nouvel espace. C'est par elle que la carte d'un savoir se mue en un jardin de délices" (*La fable mystique,* 83).

24. S. Freud, *The Interpretation of Dreams,* trans. J. Strachey (New York: Avon

Books, 1965), 376. The autonomization of the tracing from the narrative and from the referential description of the map that I am discussing here cannot be fully appreciated without a knowledge of the itinerary, of the narrative, and of the actual plan of the qṣar itself. It will become apparent later. At this point I am attempting to follow the drawing without introducing its referential dimension, and without deciphering the narrative. Concerning the couplet of towers that rhyme with each other, however, it is important to know that the rhyme has nothing to do with the place or the function these towers occupy in the actual plan of the village. It is a rhyme that springs solely from the play of forms for their own sake.

25. Cf. E. Doutté, *Magie et religion dans l'Afrique du Nord* (1908; reprint, Paris: Geuthner, 1984), 317–30. In his discussion of the split between the eye and the gaze ("l'oeil et le regard"), J. Lacan makes a direct reference to the notion of the gaze as developed in cultures of the (evil) eye, and by certain uses of the image in magic. "It is striking, when one thinks of the universality of the function of the evil eye, that there is no trace anywhere of a good eye, of an eye that blesses. What can this mean, except that the eye carries with it the fatal function of being itself endowed—if you will allow me to play on several registers at once—with a power to separate" (*Four Fundamental Concepts*, 115).

26. In Arabic the term for station is *dâr* (pl. *diâr*), which also means "house," and, in the astrological vocabulary, refers to a position (station) of the stars in the turning of the heavenly sphere, represented as a circular diagram divided into sections. Each section is called a *dâr.*

27. A. Khatibi, *Amour bilingue* (Paris: Fata Morgana, 1983), 23. "Pleasure in languages' body, inundating his obsessive fears of mutilation. They were caressing each other now, each one dreaming each other's dream" (*Love in Two Languages*, trans. R. Howard [Minneapolis: University of Minnesota Press, 1990], 16).

28. Fes is an unlikely and unfamiliar destination from the point of view of the Draʿ valley. The familiar route has since the time of the caravan trade been to Marrakesh, and now is to Casablanca. Fes is outside the gravitational area of travel from the region and, because of its peculiar cultural style, its self-conscious urban tradition, and the specificity of its Arabic vernacular, is perceived as a distant and unfamiliar place.

29. There is a whole genre of orientalist sketches made by French colons or colonial administrators. Some of them illustrate colonial ethnological compendiums, like the series *Villes et tribus du Maroc;* many of them are architectural in style.

30. For a discussion of dreaming, see part 3, "Dreams, Heterography, and the Voyages of the Rûḥ."

31. A. Khatibi, "Bilinguisme et littérature," in *Maghreb pluriel* (Paris: Denoel, 1983), 186. "It is so that the bilingual text—that one likes it or not—is marked by the exile of the name and its transformations. It falls under the strike of a double genealogy, a double signature, which are both the literary effects of a lost gift, of a donation fissured at its origin. A double gift, what does this mean? The foreign language gives with one hand and takes away with the other" (my translation).

32. Ibid., 196. "The author recalls his childhood. It is like entering a dream, a dream fragmented in its original saying, a dream written through a foreign language. Memories can only be translated."

33. H. Corbin, *Creative Imagination in the Sûfism of Ibn ʿArabî,* trans. R. Manheim (Princeton: Princeton University Press, 1969), originally published as *L'ima-*

gination créatrice dans le soufisme d'Ibn Arabî. See particularly "Imagination théophanique et creativité du coeur," 167–89. William Chittick translated *al-himma* as "aspiration" (*The Sufi Path of Knowledge,* 218).

34. The expression is Derrida's, in *La vérité en peinture.* Derrida uses it in his discussion of "le trait" (the tracing) in Valerio Adami's drawings.

35. Kateb Yacine, *Nedjma* (Paris: Seuil, 1956).

36. Khatibi, "Bilinguisme et littérature," 186. "Each language winking at the other, calling it to remain as if outside."

37. I thank Mohammed Hamdouni Alami, who disagreed with my interpretation of the drawing in an earlier article, made visible for me the transformation of the maquette into the Frame cube, and caused me to extensively rewrite parts of this chapter. I owe to him the visual formal understanding of Yusef's modernism.

38. J. B. Harley, "Local and Regional Cartography in Medieval Europe," in *The History of Cartography,* vol. 1, ed. J. B. Harley and D. Woodward (Chicago: University of Chicago Press, 1987), 477.

39. Cf. E. Panofsky, *Perspective as Symbolic Form,* trans. C. S. Wood (New York: Zone Books, 1991); H. Damish, *L'origine de la perspective* (Paris: Flammarion, 1987).

40. Corbin, *Creative Imagination.* Corbin discusses *perspectiva artificialis* contrastively, in relation to a different kind of spatial orientation found in Persian miniatures and "imaginal" representations, where the viewer (who is not a viewer in the Western sense) "is not meant to immobilize himself at a particular point, enjoying the privilege of 'presentness' and to raise his eyes from this fixed point; he must *raise himself* towards each of the elements represented. Contemplation of the image becomes a mental itinerary, an inner accomplishment" (91).

41. R. Milstein, *Miniature Painting in Ottoman Baghdad* (Costa Mesa, CA: Mazda Publications, 1990), 58. For a discussion of perspective in Chinese painting, which addresses some of the same issues discussed here ("a double perspective," according to which the viewer moves through a dynamic space, immersed in it yet seeing it, simultaneously from the inside and the outside), see F. Cheng, *Vide et plein: Le langage pictural chinois* (Paris: Seuil, 1979).

42. Corbin, *Creative Imagination,* 91n. I thank Jalal Toufic, who oriented me in the direction of miniatures to understand the representational specificity of Yusef's drawing, and who shared with me an interest in the theories of *'âlam al-mithâl* and the question of modernism and visual representation in an Arab context.

43. Cf. N. Atasoy and F. Çagman, *Turkish Miniature Painting* (Istanbul: R.C.D. Cultural Institute, 1974); S. Blair and J. Bloom, *The Art and Architecture of Islam, 1250–1800* (New Haven: Yale University Press, 1994); Milstein, *Miniature Painting in Ottoman Baghdad.*

44. *The Siege of Belgrade* from 'Arifi's *Sulaymânnâma,* Istanbul, 1558, is reproduced in Blair and Bloom, *Art and Architecture of Islam;* see also E. Atil, *Suleymanname: The Illustrated History of Suleyman the Magnificent* (Washington, DC, 1986).

45. Axonometry is a technique of representation used in technical handbooks and in architectural three dimensional drawings. Unlike a normal perspective projection, in which the dimensions of the object are systematically distorted to accommodate vision (so that two lines that are actually parallel will be drawn as convergent), ax-

onometric projection is faithful to the real dimensions in scale, and represents parallel lines as parallel. Its method of parallel projection onto an oblique plan produces an all-seeing effect of overview—a global view of the object from above. This is what in French manuals of perspective is called *perspective cavalière.* Cf. R. Vitali and U. Ghianda, *Traité de dessin du bâtiment* (Paris: Dunod, 1972); W. Ware, *Modern Perspective* (Boston: Osgood, 1882).

46. Cf. Corbin, *Creative Imagination.*

47. Cited in Chittick, *Sufi Path of Knowledge,* 111. The faculty-force of the "heart" is discussed at length in the chapter "The Heart." "Surely in the constant change in the cosmos there is a reminder of the constant change of the Root, 'for him who has a heart' (Qur'an 50:37), since the heart possesses fluctuation (*taqlîb*) from one state to another. This is why it is called 'heart' (*qalb*). . . . We know that one of the attributes of Time (*al-dahr*) is transmutation and fluctuation (*qalb*) and that "God is Time." . . . If man examines his heart, he will see that it does not remain in a single state" (Ibn al-ʿArabî, *Al-Futûḥât al-makkiyya,* cited and translated in Chittick, *Sufi Path of Knowledge,* 107).

48. Milstein, *Miniature Painting in Ottoman Baghdad,* 58.

49. In standard Arabic the term is *raḥba* (root *rḥb*), "a public square surrounded by buildings" (*Hans Wehr Dictionary of Modern Written Arabic*).

50. "The tawîl is essentially symbolic understanding, the transmutation of everything visible into symbols, the intuition of an essence or person in an Image which partakes neither of universal logic nor of sense perception, and which is the only means of signifying what is to be signified" (Corbin, *Creative Imagination,* 13).

51. In Arabic *al-kaʿba* means "cube," or "cubical structure." For a discussion of the privileged ontological status of the Kaʿaba as reference point in the organization of space of Moroccan houses, villages, and cities, see M. Boughali, *La representation de l'espace chez le marocain illettré* (Casablanca: Afrique-Orient, 1974), especially chapter 7. Verse 144 of sura 2 in the Qur'an reads in its entirety: "We see the turning of your face to the heavens: now shall We turn you to a Qibla that shall please you. Turn then your face in the direction of the sacred Mosque: Wherever you are, turn your faces in that direction."

52. Cited in Chittick, *Sufi Path of Knowledge,* 107.

53. "The direction taken by the displacement usually results in a colourless and abstract expression in the dream-thought being exchanged for a pictorial and concrete one. The advantage, and accordingly the purpose, of such a change jumps to the eyes. A thing that is pictorial is, from the point of view of a dream, a thing that is capable of being represented: it can be introduced in a situation in which abstract expressions offer the same kind of difficulties to representation in dreams as a political leading article in a newspaper would offer to an illustrator" (Freud, *Interpretation of Dreams,* 375).

54. In the qṣar, as usual in rural areas, bread is made at home, and there is no public oven. The public oven, where the bread is sent to bake, and the public bath (*ḥammâm*) are paradigmatic traits of city life. From the point of view of the qṣar, they are signs of urbanization and modernity.

55. De Certeau, "The Garden," 56.

56. Being able to read the names not only implies decoding the blend of Arabic and Berber in which Yusef writes—he never went to school, except for the two years

he spent at the mosque when he was a child. It also means being familiar with the actual topography and social history of the qṣar, and with that of Yusef's personal landscape. Unlike the names of the Four Fourths, which are public and even institutional, the names attached to the towers are references expressed in Yusef's subjective terms, though they are fully intelligible to the local audience. The device of naming particular towers after their owners is itself a sign of the outlook of Yusef's generation, for up to the 1970s the towers along the village walls were a public space, under the jurisdiction of the community council.

57. What in the oral tradition of the qṣar is known as the deadly pollen or smell (*rîḥa*, "smell" or "perfume") of the wâqwâq tree, brought by the wind from distant and unknown lands, in the classical Arabic literature of *al-ʿajâib* is a well-known geographical figure of the marvelous and the uncanny. *Bilâd al-Wâqwâq*, the "land, or islands, of al-Wâqwâq," is an elusive and uncanny location in the geographical descriptions of medieval Arab geographers and compilers. According to Ibn al-Wardî (*Kharidat al-ʿAjâʾib wa-Farîdat al-Gharâʾib*, fifteenth century), the islands of al-Wâqwâq are inhabited by an exclusively feminine population, and among their wonders is a kind of tree that bears womanlike fruits: "fruits like women, with shapes, bodies, eyes, hand, feet, hair, breasts and vulvas like the vulvas of women. . . . They are the most beautiful of face and hang by their hair. When they feel the wind and sun, they yell, 'Wâq Wâq,' until their hair tears apart" (cited and translated in F. Malti-Douglas, *Woman's Body, Woman's Word* [Princeton: Princeton University Press, 1991], 88). In al-Idrîsî's twelfth-century map of the world and related geographical description, the land of al-Wâqwâq is situated south of the equator (al-Idrîsî, *Nuzhat al-mushtâq*). On the figure of Bilâd al-Wâqwâq, see also F. Malti-Douglas, "Sexual Geography, Asexual Philosophy," in *Woman's Body, Woman's Word*, 85–110; A. Miquel, *La géographie humaine du monde musulman;* M. Arkoun, J. Le Goff, T. Fahd, and M. Rodinson, *L'étrange et le merveilleux dans l'Islam médiéval* (Paris: Éditions J.A., 1978).

58. The term *qbîla* (classical *al-qabîla*) is usually translated as "tribe" and has been an important descriptive and analytical theme in French colonial and Moroccan postcolonial ethnological and historical accounts. See, among others, R. Montagne, *Les Berbères et le Makhzen dans le sud du Maroc: Essai sur la transformation politique des Berbères sédentaires: Groupe Chleuh* (Paris: Alcan, 1930); J. Berque, *Structures sociales du Haut Atlas* (Paris: Presses Universitaires de France, 1956); J. Berque, "Qu'est-ce qu'une 'tribu' nord-africaine?" in *Hommage à Lucien Febvre* (Paris: Éventail de l'Histoire Vivante, 1953); P. Pascon, *Le Haouz de Marrakech* (Rabat: Institut Agronomique et Vétérinaire Hassan II and Centre Universitaire de la Recherche Scientifique; Paris: Centre Nationale de la Recherche Scientifique, 1977); A. Toufiq, *Al-mujtamaʿ al-maghribî fî al-qarn al-tâsiʿ ʿashar: Inûltân, 1850–1912* (Rabat: Publications de la Faculté des Lettres et des Science Humaines, 1983); L. Mezzine, *Le Tafilalt: Contribution à l'histoire du Maroc aux 17 et 18 siècles* (Rabat: Publications de la Faculté des Lettres et des Sciences Humaines, 1987); R. Jamous, *Honneur et Baraka: Les structures sociales traditionnelles dans le Rif* (Paris: Maison des Sciences de l'Homme, 1981); and studies inspired by British structural functionalism, or related critically to that approach, e.g., E. Gellner, *Saints of the Atlas* (London: Weidenfeld and Nicholson, 1969); A. Hammoudi, "Segmentarité, stratification sociale, pouvoir politique, et sainteté: Réflexions sur les thèses de Gellner," *Hespéris-Tamuda* 15 (1974): 147–79.

Without engaging in a debate on the appropriatedness, or not, of the "tribe" translation in general terms, it must be specified that in the qṣar the term *l-qbîla* does not carry the sense of social group based on descent and blood ties. The qbîla is the political and symbolic institution that gathers the community of the *ahl l-qṣar,* "people of the qṣar," and their mechanism of social identification. When used in general terms, as for instance in an invocation to God to bring well-being to *kâmil l-qbîla,* "the entire community," it simply refers to the group of people who recognize themselves as people of the qṣar. (For a social-historical discussion rich in archival documentary evidence of the institution of the qbîla in a region neighboring the Draʿ, and comparable to it for its village-based sociopolitical organization, see Mezzine, *Le Tafilalt.*) When used in specific political terms, it refers to the community council, the assembly that in the past was called *j-jmaʿa* and was composed of elders or notables from each important family of the Four Fourths, and which is now still called *j-jmaʿa,* but refers to the elected administrative council of the "commune rurale," located within the administrative organization of the province. On the political reorganization of the postcolonial Moroccan state in rural areas, see R. Leveau, *Le fellah marocain défenseur du thrône* (Paris: Presses de la Fondation Nationale des Sciences Politiques, 1976); Y. Hamdouni Alami, *De l'ordre tribal au développement local: La commune dans la region de El-Hajeb (Maroc central),* doctoral thesis, Université de Montpellier, 1989.

59. Literally, "in this section of the islands is found the island of." For al-Idrîsî, as for many compilers of early maps, islands belong to the limit.

60. Al-Idrîsî, *Kitâb nuzhat al-mushtâq fî ikhtirâq al-âfâq* (1154), in *Opus Geographicum* (Naples: Istituto Universitario Orientale per il Medio ed Estremo Oriente, Brill, n.d.), 103–4. Thanks to Mohamed Hamdouni Alami for help with the translation from Arabic.

61. To follow Yusef's path around the walls as he represents it in the drawing, the two standing scenes must be read from right to left, and the two oblique ones from left to right, in the order indicated here below.

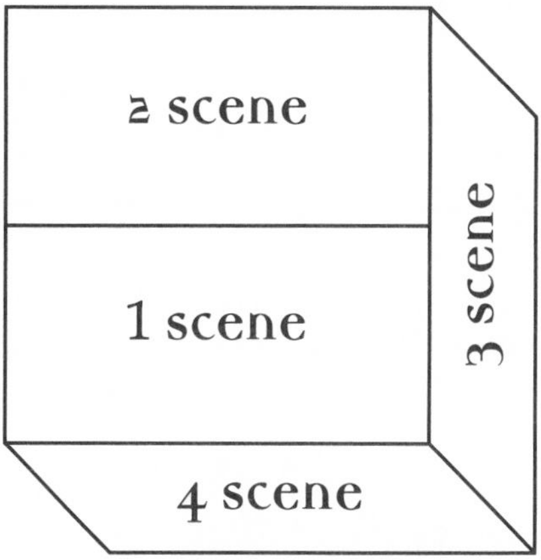

62. The term *l-makhzen* (standard Arabic *al-makhzan*) could be translated as "state" or "government," or not translated at all—as a number of Moroccan

historians have chosen to do, inasmuch as neither translation renders the specificity of the precolonial Moroccan institution. The term is formed from the verbal root *khazana,* "to store, stock, or accumulate," and it literally means "warehouse."

In oral recollection, people distinguish between *l-makhzen l-qadîm,* the Old Makhzen, which ended in this reckoning with the death of the sultan Moulay Lhassan I (1892), at the dawn of the French protectorate, and *l-makhzen,* "the state" or "the government," that was established after independence, in 1956. The French colonial administration was also referred to as *l-makhzen.*

63. Apart from the Makhzen's Gate and a gate called *fum jdîd,* "the new gate," the other secondary gates were opened in the 1970s in the context of a project of restoration of the qṣûr settlements and in general the earth architecture of the region, sponsored by the United Nations.

64. For the sexual magic associated with the millstones (*r-raḥa*), see M. A. El Khaznaji, *Rites magico-sexuels, le rbat et le tasfih,* Cahiers des Arts et Traditions Populaires, no. 6, (Tunis, 1977); F. Skhiri, "Le mariage au Sahel: Le rite du Tasfih"; S. Pandolfo, "Detours of Life: Space and Bodies in a Moroccan Village," *American Ethnologist* 16, no. 1 (1989): 3–23; Doutté, *Magie et religion dans l'Afrique du Nord;* E. Westermark, *Ritual and Belief in Morocco,* 2 vols. (London: Macmillan, 1926).

65. Ben ʿAbd l-Mûla is the name of a local saint who plays an important role in the symbolic and social life of the qṣar and surrounding villages. His tomb is within walking distance of the qṣar.

66. By a process of literalization of a metaphor. *Nashara* as a verb means to open, to emit, to proclaim. *Al-manshûr* is a decree, an edict, but also something sawn apart; *al-manshâr* is a saw.

67. *Niya, an-niya,* a noun formed from from the verbal root *nawa,* "to intend, purpose, or resolve," is a term with strong ethical and energetic connotation. It can mean intention, volition, will, resolution, good faith, or simply faith. In this context, it refers to the intention of the person who submits to the rule and invests himself or herself in a social pact, or in a pact with God or otherworldly beings. "Submitting" is the rite of *taslîm* (from the same root as *Islam*). For a discussion of *niya* and *taslîm* in a therapeutic and symbolic context, see A. Diouri, "La résistance du nom," *Bulletin Économique et Sociale du Maroc* 153–54 (1984): 25–31.

68. Kateb Yacine, *Nedjma,* 190. "Rachid cleaned his pipe, leaning over the dark abyss, gaining altitude like a balloon unballasted, harmless and vulnerable, caught on the wing between ground and target" (Kateb Yacine, *Nedjma,* trans. Howard, 254).

69. The hair-lock, *taqyot* (Berber), is a relic of prenatal times; it is what is left of the hair the baby had in the womb (children's heads used to be ritually shaved on the fortieth day after birth).

70. This schematic plan shows the four external "faces" of the ramparts, and the internal partition of the qṣar into the four fourths (*arbaʿ rbaʿ*). The faces are called *wjûh* (sing. *wajh*), which also means "human face." The dark spot near the center is Arḥabî.

71. As I mentioned earlier (note 5), the Tashelḥit term *ayt* is equivalent to the Arabic *bânî* or *bni,* and could be translated "children of." It is, however, also used in nongenealogical contexts, where it simply indicates affiliation with an institution or an action. In the case of the Four Fourths, the names of the Ḥarâr fourths are fictionally genealogical (children of ʿAbdallah, of Driss), while those of the Ḥarâtîn fourths

elude the genealogical register altogether: Ayt l-Bâlî (the people of the old side) and Ayt j-Jdîd (the people of the new side).

Ḥarâr is Arabic, sing. *ḥurr,* "free person." The term *ḥurr* has a connotation of freedom—the condition of being autonomous, independent, and untied (as in English), but also one of purity and authenticity. A product in its "free" state is authentic, nonmixed, natural, wild, as opposed to something artificial, synthetic, or cultivated (e.g., *zaʿafrân l-ḥurr* is real saffron, *l-meska l-ḥurra* is natural chewing gum, *l-ʿasel l-ḥurr* is wild honey, *l-ḥarîr l-ḥurr* is real silk, as opposed to fake silk, etc.).

Ḥurr is also a legal category: every Muslim adult, man or woman, who can be considered responsible for his or her actions is "free," that is, is submitted to the Law for his or her rights and duties. Slaves (*ʿabîd*) were not part of this category until the abolition of slavery, but they could be "freed" and legally granted the status of free Muslims. In Berber the term *amazigh* (pl. *imazighen*) has the same range of meaning as *ḥurr* (*ḥarar*). In the qṣar both terms are used.

The term *ḥarâr* as a social and ethnic denomination is specific to the Wâd Draʿ region and to a few other areas and oases of southern Morocco, such as the Tafilelt, whose social organization resembles that of the Wâd Draʿ in many respects. (In Fes, Rabat, and the plains of central Morocco, the term *ḥarâr* would not be understood in its social specificity.) *Ḥarâr* as a term and as a social category is historically constituted in a dialogical opposition to the category of *ḥarâtîn,* to which it is opposed as free to dependent, white to black, etc. Yet both *ḥarâr* and *ḥarâtîn* convey the sense of a sedentary lifestyle, of the agricultural and "urban" mode of life of the qṣûr, centers of craftsmanship and often of learning. Together, they are therefore set in opposition to the category of "nomad" (*raḥḥala;* in this region currently referred to as *Shleuḥ* or *Znaga,* locally understood as Ayt ʿAṭṭa, Tamazight (Berber)–speaking tribe members, and *l-ʿarab,* referring to the Awlâd Yaḥya Arabic-speaking tribe members. Even though these former seminomadic groups are today sedentary for the most part, and have been in some cases sedentary for a long time, they are categorically nomad in the perception of the (categorically) sedentary inhabitants of the qṣûr.

In their conceptual, and formerly political and sometimes armed, opposition to the "nomadic" (Berber or Arab) groups, the qṣûr dwellers—Ḥarâr and Ḥarâtîn—are associated by their common interests, their sedentary "urban" lifestyle, and their larger identification with the qṣar community, the qbîla. For while the term *qbîla* in the context of the formerly nomadic Arabic- and Berber-speaking groups is usually understood as meaning "tribal" association, structured by a genealogical ideology, in the context of the sedentary organization of the qṣûr it simply indicates the qṣar community as a whole (*ahl l-qṣar,* "the people of the qṣar"), defined territorially.

For a comparative historical account of the social organization of the qṣûr society in another area of southern Morocco, see Mezzine, *Le Tafilalt.*

72. *Ḥarâtîn* (sing. *ḥartânî*) is a word of disputed filiation and meaning. Even the language within which it is supposed to have a sense is in question. By some, *ḥartânî* is interpreted as an Arabic word, a vernacular version of *ḥurr-thânî,* "second-free," that is, semifree, hierarchically inferior (the term of reference is, of course, "free," *ḥurr*). By others it is treated as a Tashelḥit word, related to the adjective *aḥrḍan,* which means "dark brown."

The dispute is not just philological. In manuscript documents from the eighteenth and the nineteenth centuries I was shown from local family archives (texts often colored with racist overtones when treating of the black Ḥarâtîn population), the word *ḥarâtîn* is spelled *Ḥarâthîn,* invoking the Arabic interpretation "second-free." In other locally written documents (the internal "count" of the Ḥarâtîn fourths of the qṣar, for instance, concerning men's participation in digging the irrigation canal), the word is spelled *ḥarâṭîn,* invoking the Berber interpretation "dark brown." In conversation the Ḥarâtîn revindicate the Berber spelling and the reading "dark brown," which they consider less marked in hierarchical and racist terms.

But whatever its spelling, the term *ḥarâtîn* carries the stigma of a long history of marginalization and exclusion. In postindependence days the more neutral term *Drâwâ* (from the name of the region, Wâd Draʿ) has become locally preferred, especially in a public context or in the presence of outsiders to the Ḥarâtîn community (especially Ḥarâr). Yet among themselves the Ḥarâtîn still use the term, and sometimes reclaim it with pride. Another term that carries an ambivalent stigma if mentioned in public, but that remains a current term within the black community, is *Issuqiyn* (sing. *Assoqî*), a Tashelḥit word formed from the Arabic term for "marketplace," *ṣûq.* Throughout the book all three terms will be used—Ḥarâtîn, Drâwâ, Issuqiyn—depending on the context and on the conversation cited.

Despite a history of subordination (which had its insubordinate and even insurrectional moments) and despite the exclusionary practices vis-à-vis the *Ḥarâtîn,* these were technically "free" (*ḥurr*) in terms of Islamic law, and their legal and social status had nothing to do with that of slaves (*ʿabîd*). In the qṣar and in general in the Wâd Draʿ region there were slaves (with the ʿabid status) until the 1930s. They were found particularly in zawyât as workers in big landed estates; yet also in the qṣar several Ḥarâr families had two or more slaves. In locally written documents from the eighteenth century the practice of giving a *khâdem,* "woman slave," to a daughter as a dowry is mentioned. Today there is a large community of descendants of former slaves still based in the region. They are of course free Moroccan subjects, but still keep the (now cultural) denomination of *ʿabîd,* maintain close ties with each other, and perform the rituals characteristic of their community. During the Muslim month of Mawlûd a big ʿabid festival is held in the valley, gathering members of the community upriver from village to village, and slowly forming a big itinerant procession which for a month travels across the region, stopping to hold festivals in a number of qṣûr. The rituals and songs of the ʿabîd are performed in what is called *l-lugha l-gnâwiya,* a language partly unintelligible for its users that is a legacy of the sub-Saharan languages (among them Bambara) spoken by their forefathers brought to Morocco through the slave trade.

On the history of the status of the slave community in Morocco, see M. Ennaji, *Soldats, domestiques, et concubines: L'esclavage au Maroc au 19 siècle* (Rabat: Eddif, 1994). On the social hierarchy in the Wâd Draʿ region, between Ḥarâr and Ḥarâtîn (in the French colonial ethnological literature), see D. Jacques-Meunié, "Les oasis des Lektaoua et des Mehammid," *Hespéris* 27 (1947): 399–429; D. Jacques-Meunié, "Hierarchie sociale au Maroc présaharien," *Hespéris* 9 (1958): 29–43; F. De La Chapelle, "Une cité de l'Oued Draʿ sous le protéctorat des nomades: Nesrat," *Hespéris* 9 (1929): 29–43; G. Spillmann, *Districts et tribus de la haute vallée du Draa* (Paris: Champion, 1931). On the social and the ritual role of the Ḥarâtîn in another oasis, see D. Champault, *Une oasis du Sahara nord-occidental: Tabelbala* (Paris: Éditions du Centre National de la Recherche Scientifique, 1969). For a contemporary critical historical approach to the question of social hierarchy in the region, see Mezzine, *Le Tafilalt;* and, concerning a different area, A. Hammoudi, *La victime et ses masques: Essai sur le sacrifice et la mascarade au Maghreb* (Paris: Seuil, 1988).

73. On the institution of *khamessat* in Morocco and the role of the *khammâs,* see J. Berque, *Études d'histoire rurale marocaine* (Tangier: Éditions Internationales, 1938).

74. The lineage of the Qâḍî (the Judge) is another important Ḥarâr lineage in the qṣar. But none of the fourths takes its name from it. In Yusef's drawing the confusion arises from representing the inside by way of the outside. The families of Ayt l-Qâḍî reside in the Alley of l-Qâḍî, which belongs to the Fourth of Ayt ʿAbdallah. But in taking the picture from the outside, Yusef ends up representing the exterior face that is shared by the houses of Ayt l-Qâḍî and those of the Fourth of Ayt Driss.

75. I thank Ahmed Toufiq for pointing this out to me in the debate that followed a lecture I gave on this subject at the Institut des études africaines, Université Mohamed V, Rabat, in April 1992.

76. Onion and henna plants are first grown in a nursery, then transplanted into their plots. They are here figures of transplanting.

77. In the first and second volumes of the *Muqaddima,* Ibn Khaldûn, the fourteenth-century Maghribî philosopher of history, develops a theory of history's returns, and a view of change as both a catastrophic break and the cyclical return of the same structure (*The Muqaddima: An Introduction to History,* 3 vols., trans. F. Rosenthal [Princeton: Princeton University Press, 1981]).

With a subtle mastery of paradoxical argumentation, and against the possibility of any reductive understanding of the dialectics of Bedouin-nomadic versus urban-sedentary life (*Muqaddima,* vol. 1) and their cyclical alternation in the destiny of human society, Ibn Khaldûn emphasizes how the possibility of human society as such—what he calls *al-ʿumran,* the filling, the occupation, the human settlement of the world—is based on an element of ruin and dissolution that is at the same time what makes human life possible and human (as opposed to animal or divine), and what determines its impermanence and mortal fate. All the while mourning the loss of an original Bedouin "independence" and "purity" (structurally equivalent, on the theological register, to the end of the period of prophecy and direct revelation, and the need for a religious law and for scriptural mediation), Ibn Khaldûn shows how independence, purity, and immediacy are but logical (im)possibilities, destined to turn into their opposites as soon as they are realized. In his work he stands rather on the side of urbanity, of the development through learning of human skills—the side of *ṣinâʿât,* "crafts," a recurring theme in the *Muqaddima.* It is the side of that element of ruin that is both the strength and the weakness of human life.

78. *Fillage* (from the French *village*—Arabic doesn't have the letter *v*) is the colloquial name given all over rural Morocco to the administrative urban center around which their villages gravitate today. Often these centers are former French posts, and have grown around a nucleus of buildings from the colonial period. In a *fillage* there is a main street with shops, a bank, several cafés, a local office of the Ministry of Agriculture, a police station, a *qiyâda* (the office of the district representative of the state), and possibly an army post, a local court, a secondary school, a hospital, etc. In

the context above, however, the use of the term is ironic. Ḥadda is the protagonist of part 2.

79. *Bab allâh* is the formula by which auctions (*dlâlât*) always begin. The phrase is in Tashelḥit. *Masaleḥ* is an Arabic word, a polite term for toilet.

80. "Ḥâ n-nass ghîr katmeshi bḥal dik l-kernafa llî kayna fûq l-mâ; hâ hiya mshât l-hak, ḥâ hiya mshât l-hak, dak shshî llî ʿâdet d-dunya."

81. *Siba,* from the Arabic root *sby* (*sabâ*), to take prisoner, to capture, to fascinate, in the Maghreb has the specific connotation of dissent, insurrection, sedition, and rebellion, and is synonymous with the more classical term *al-fitna,* used colloquially in this region in its full spectrum of senses.

The concept of *siba* plays an important role in the French colonial ethnological literature on the Maghreb (e.g., Montagne, *Les Berbères et le Makhzen.* In that literature, *siba* was systematically translated as anarchy, disorder, and conflict, and was opposed to the notion of *makhzen,* understood somewhat inappropriately as the central state. The dialectical opposition *siba/makhzen,* anarchy/state, periphery/center, was then seen as the paradigmatic structure of the precolonial Moroccan political system, where the *blâd siba,* "land of dissidence," was generally identified with the Berber-speaking populations of the Atlas Mountains and of pre-Saharan Morocco. This understanding informed an entire generation of colonial scholarship, and was subjected to a radical critique by the historians and sociologists of decolonization (cf. A. Laroui, *L' histoire du Maghreb: Essai de synthèse* [Paris: Maspero, 1970]; A. Laroui, *Les origines sociales et culturelles du nationalisme marocain, 1830–1912* [Paris: Maspero, 1980]) who questioned simultaneously the notions of anarchy and of central state, along with the rhetoric of their opposition, as these had been strategically articulated by colonial historians and ethnologists.

82. *Ighruren,* used in this sense as a proper name, is the plural of the term *aghrûr* (Tashelḥit), designating a well operated by animal power. This area of the gardens at the limit of the palm groves used to be watered by *aghrûr,* from which it gets its name. It is the area of first expansion of the village *extramuros.*

83. The colloquial Moroccan term *karyân* likely results from a metamorphosis of the French *carrière,* "quarry"; the first shantytowns were located in open quarries.

84. *Stâra* means literally "a screen or veil," a protection to shield and conceal—from the gaze of strangers.

85. *Amerdûl* has become the proper name of the area in the desert steppe where the New Village is being built, and in conversation it is simply used to refer to the new settlement. But in the local Tashelḥit Berber it is a term designating an uncultivated uninhabited area at the margins of a cultivated or inhabited one. It is conceptually intermediate between *l-khalâ* (from a verbal root *khlw,* to empty, to destroy, or to be desert), the wasteland, beyond the reach of human intervention, and the space inhabited and transformed by human settlements. Unlike *l-khalâ,* an amerdûl could conceivably be exploited one day. But the difference is conceptual and relative, rather than descriptive (in this case amerdûl is as deserted as the wasteland). What today is khalâ can tomorrow become amerdûl, etc. In this case Amerdûl and the surrounding khalâ are within the territorial boundaries of the qṣar and under its jurisdiction. They administratively represent what is called its *berra,* its "outside," somewhat like the territorial waters of a nation in the ocean. This "outside" is collective

land that belongs to the qbîla and cannot be sold. But if the qbîla decides to partition it, and does so with the approval of the provincial administration, once divided it effectively becomes a sort of private property, even though its legal status remains disputed.

86. M. Blanchot, "The Two Versions of the Imaginary," in *The Space of Literature,* trans. A. Smock (Lincoln: University of Nebraska Press, 1982), 256, 258, originally published as *L'espace littéraire* (Paris: Seuil, 1955).

87. Ibid., 258.

88. "Though still, years-wise, a youth, one has become the contemporary of what is much older than one. Another tradition, one that has not to do with memory, but with amnesia" (J. Toufic, *Vampires* [New York: Station Hill, 1993], 35). Drawing examples from the transformation of landscape in civil war Beirut, Jalal Toufic discusses the idiosyncratic and lapsed temporality of war ruins, which is only indirectly related to the actual event of falling into ruin, and has instead to do, he says, with the fact of having been deserted, severed from living presence, and with the related transformation of objects and places into their image—virtual space, as in the set of a film: "It is because these houses have become ruins by being deserted that the war gets extended until they begin to turn explicitly into ruins, to manifest their being already ruins" (32); "Except in ruined areas, the placards with street names and building numbers imply a virtual road rather than the adjacent road on which the cars and the pedestrians pass, this giving the impression that the area is a set, with the 'offscreen' to these placards being at variance with the surrounding streets on the 'set.' . . . Though still, years-wise, a youth, one has become the contemporary of what is much older than one. Another tradition, one that has not to do with memory, but with amnesia" (35).

89. In the old qṣar when a person died, the neighbors of the alley were charged with taking care of the funeral, cooking food for the guests, etc. At a funeral in the New Village, if one tried to understand what the logic was behind a certain woman's preparing the bread or another's cooking the meat, one had to go back to the layout of the old qṣar. The two women lived far apart, and were not the actual neighbors of the woman who died. Yet, without hesitation, they were referred to as *ahl d-derb,* the "alley neighbors."

90. Agricultural tools: l-Hashmi was a blacksmith.

91. They actually say *Allâh ynʿal sh-shayṭân,* which is a local distortion of *Allâh ylʿan sh-shayṭân,* "God curse the devil," a formula aimed at calming a person who has entered a maddened state of mourning and risks losing her mind.

92. *Taqshurt* is the Tashelḥit rendering of an Arabic word. *L-qshara* is the shell (of a nut, an almond for instance), the bark, the envelope of something. A *taqshurt* (f., denoting smallness as the grammatical feminine often does in Tashelḥit), is the fragment of a broken shell, the debris of what had been an envelope—or something that falls off, like dandruff from the scalp or scales from the skin of a snake. To speak of a *taqshurt,* then, implies two things: something is broken and can't be put back together, and the breaking has shelled, revealed something inside, unveiled in its bareness—or possibly in its threat. Both senses are mobilized in the idiom of *taqshurîn* as the outburst of political factions and fitna in the qṣar.

93. Al-Glâwî is the name of a powerful clan that sought to impose its rule over

the Moroccan south with the investiture of the French protectorate administration. See part 3.

94. *Tighremt,* the feminine (diminutive) form of *Ighrem,* is the Tashelḥit equivalent of *qṣîba,* and means "small, fortified village," "little fortress." The ruins of Tighremt—which is here also a proper name—are about a mile from the qṣar, upstream in relation to the flow of water in the canal. The episode of Tighremt is historical. Written documents and property deeds situate it at the beginning of the nineteenth century.

95. As I indicated earlier, *l-bâlî* means "the old, ruined, or rundown," here the old section or the old village; *j-jdîd* means "the new," here the new section or village, as Moḥammed u Saddiq specifies. Old property deeds from the qṣar speak of *al-qaṣba al-qadîma,* "the old citadel," and *al-qaṣba al-jadîda,* "the new citadel." Both the old and the new sections are old, and can be dated back to the sixteenth or seventeenth century.

96. "Like Taqshurt": he should say, they formed a "taqshurt," but he is thinking in terms of the *taqshurt* of today, Taqshurt proper-named.

97. Ifli is the master canal of this irrigated region, which brings the water from the river to be redistributed into smaller canals. Since the building of a dam upriver in the 1970s (Barrage Mansour Eddahbi, Ouarzazat), Ifli has become a modern cement canal, but it used to be an earth ditch about fifteen meters deep, in periodic need of repair. Its maintenance was (and in a way still is) the joint responsibility of the Ahl Iflî, the "people of Iflî," the village communities that "drank" from its waters. Each year an *ʿamil dyâl mâ,* a superintendent for the water and the maintenance of the canal, was chosen from a different village with the endorsement of a holy lineage from a nearby zâwya (the Zâwya Naṣiriya of Si Lḥassein). Ḥafîr Iflî, the "dig of Ifli," was the most important public and ritual enterprise in the social life of the villages of the canal.

98. I translate *l-berd* as "air" or "wind," rather than "cold air," which it literally means, because the term is used interchangeably with *l-jû,* "air," in a configuration in which the wind is associated with a certain demonic power. Jinns are also described as *l-berd,* and infiltrate the body, taking hold of the *rûḥ* (breath or life principle) of the person. L-berd, l-jû, and rûḥ are figures connected with the development of fitna within the community, or within the mind/body of the person.

PART 2. CONTRA-DICTION

1. A. Artaud, "Ci-Gît," in *Oeuvres complètes* (Paris: Gallimard, 1956), 12:77–78.

> I, Antonin Artaud, am my son, my father, my mother,
> and myself;
> leveler of the idiotic periplus on which procreation is
> impaled,
> the periplus papa-mama
> and child,
> soot of grandma's ass,
> much more than of father-mother's.
> . . . .

to make us
a little more disgusted with ourselves,
being this unusable body
made out of meat and crazy sperm,
this body hung, from before the lice,
sweating the impossible table
of heaven
its callous odor of atoms,
its alcoholic smell of abject
detritus
ejected from the snooze
of the fingerless Inca
who for idea had an arm
but for hand had only a dead
palm, having lost his fingers
killing kings.

"Here Lies," in A. Artaud, *Selected Writings,* ed. S. Sontag, trans. H. Weaver (Berkeley: University of California Press, 1988), 540–41.

2. *N-nhâr l-lewwel kaymût l-mush,* proverb referring to the importance of getting the conditions of a pact straight at the outset.

3. *Ḥallâb* is a large bowl used for preparing food.

4. Blue eyes are often associated with the evil eye, *l-ʿayn.* The evil eye is clearly at issue when a bit later the uncle notices *l-ʿayn* of the landlord and attempts to leave. In the story (as in life), *l-ʿayn* is a figure of harm and danger, here an omen of the deadly pact that will tie the two parties together and eventually lead them to reciprocal destruction.

5. Ḥadda is a local diminutive of Aḥmed. Although the name Ḥadda may resemble a feminine name also found in Morocco, the two names are distinct. While Ḥadda (pronounced Ḥ'dda) is a common southern diminutive of Aḥmed, the feminine name is pronounced Ḥâdda or Ḥaddya.

6. *Izugla* is the plural of the Tashelḥit (Berber) word *azaglu,* which can mean "articulatory junction" or "obstruction," and in the local vocabulary of irrigation is used to refer to a place where the water of a canal is partially halted to be distributed into two or more smaller canals. In the qṣar's surrounding territory, Izugla propernamed is the place where the water of the master canal of Ifli (*sâgya Ifli*)—the large canal that brings inland a portion of the Wâd Draʿ waters—is articulated into the three main canals that bring water into the palm groves of the qṣar and carry it on to some ten villages downstream. It is also known as *mizan l-mâ,* "the water's balance." In the history of the qṣar and of the region in general, Izugla is a strategic place. For controlling the water means controlling life. Battles have been fought at Izugla, alliances sealed, sacrifices offered, miracles performed.

7. For the context of this citation see below.

8. A *ḥajjâya,* from *hajw,* "to state an opinion" or "to speak in riddles." In the colloquial use of this region, a *ḥajjâya* is a fantastic tale, a made-up story, approximately what in literary Arabic is known as *rwia.* (*Ar-râwî* is the storyteller.) Elsewhere in Morocco this kind of story is called *khurâfa.* *Ḥajjâyât* are considered a

feminine genre, preferred space of women's recitations. A *ghazawa* instead (from the classical term *ghazwa,* "a campaign of conquest," "a raid or expedition") is a legendary or epic narrative based on a historical event, often modeled on the campaigns of the Prophet and his companions against the infidels in the early days of Islam, and almost invariably recounted by men about men.

9. For the notion of *ʿâlam al-mithâl* see part 1, "Topology of a City," and part 3, "Dreams, Heterography, and the Voyages of the Rûḥ." See also F. Rahman, "Dream, Imagination, and *ʿAlam al-Mithâl,*" in *The Dream and Human Society,* ed. G. E. Von Grunebaum and R. Caillois (Berkeley: University of California Press, 1966).

10. *L-fitna katdîr l-lju bîn n-nâs:* the expression is double sense. In colloquial Moroccan it can mean both "it blows wind in between people," if one takes *lju* to mean "air" or "wind" (*al-jaww* in standard Arabic), and "fitna causes disjunction between people," that is, it unscrews, works relationships loose. *Lju* in this sense is taken to mean "play," as the play of a screw, in the colloquial Moroccan use of the French *jeu,* "play." The two senses resonate with each other.

11. *L-ʿaqel* is the faculty of control. As a verb, *kanaʿqal* means to hold, to have a hold with one's hand, to tie. Now Ḥadda is suggesting that, in addition to the play of words escaping the control of the mind/ʿaqel, the ʿaqel itself might start working on its own. If the faculty of control, which is supposed to supervise the production of images, starts reproducing on its own...

12. In an article on the concept of fitna in the Qur'an and in pre-Islamic tradition ("Quelques Remarques sur la racine FTN dans le Coran et la plus ancienne littérature musulmane," *Revue des Études Islamiques* 37, no. 1 [1969], 86), C. Vadet writes: "Il n'ya pas de *fitna* sans une atmosphère de panique démoniaque. . . . la *fitna* couvre alors tout l'horizon des hommes de son ombre menaçante: elle est l'événement monstrueux par excellence. . . . Ainsi, quatre événements majeurs, violations successives de ce que l'Islam primitif a de plus sacré, le califat, la Communauté, les cités saintes, la suprématie arabe, font apparaître comme inéluctable la *fitna,* c'est-à-dire la présence et la domination du mal sur la terre et même à l'intérieur de la Communauté, et peut-être des consciences. La *fitna* est voulue par des puissances inconnues, auxquelles n'ose pas trop donner de nom. . . . Ce quî concerne la Communauté et, à l'intérieur de celle-ci, la vie de chacun, dépend de facteurs que l'on ignore."

Vadet draws his description of fitna from the Qur'an and from the article "Fitna" in the fourteenth-century philological dictionary *Lisân al-ʿârab,* by Ibn al-Manẓûr (Beirut: Dâr Sâdir, 1968). In an appendix at the end of part 2 I provide a partial translation of Ibn al-Manẓûr's text on fitna, as a literary reference related to the theme of this work.

But unlike the text of *Lisân al-ʿârab,* unlike, in a way, the array of different meanings and condemnations of *fitna* found in the Qur'an, and unlike Ḥadda's paradoxical glossing of the concept, Vadet's orientalist reading does away with the essential ambivalence of fitna, which is at once the illness and its remedy, a blessing and a curse—the perverse drive and the rhetorical strategy by which its condemnation is advocated, the ordeal of fire that distinguishes the good from the bad, and the crime that is punished by "burning" in Hell, . . . the condition of possibility of life and society, and the destructive force which undermines them from within. Instead, Vadet sets the discussion of fitna within the familiar frame of the classical European philosophical opposition of order and chaos. Clifford Geertz's discussion of the ever incumbent threat of fitna in the marketplace, in his essay "Sûq: The Bazaar Economy in Sefrou" (in *Meaning and Order in Moroccan Society* [Cambridge: Cambridge University Press, 1979]), is informed by a similar presupposition as to the "chaotic" nature of fitna.

For a work that instead explores the ambivalence of the concept of fitna (among other ambivalences), in the context of a discussion of speech, writing, revelation, and dialogue in Qur'anic tradition, coming therefore much closer to the inspiration of Ḥadda's dialogue on fitna, see M. Fischer and M. Abedi, *Debating Muslims: Cultural Dialogues in Postmodernity and Tradition* (Madison: University of Wisconsin Press, 1990). The chapter "Quranic Dialogics" discusses the ambivalent rhetorical strategy of a famous Qur'anic condemnation of fitna (Qur'an 3:7), argued in terms of fitna's metaphorical straying and of the unstable opposition *muḥâkamât* (proper meanings)/*mutashâbihât* (resemblances or allegorical meanings). I would like to thank Michael Fischer and Mehdi Abedi for the thoughts and comments they shared with me in Houston in 1990.

13. The expression is commonly used in the plural, *l-klâm,* which in Arabic also means "discourse." The use of the plural connotes, perhaps, the plural quality of the process of proliferation and destabilization of signs this entails. In other areas of Morocco, and in general in Arabic, *l-kelma,* "the word," in the sense of political and social influence, is used in the singular. To say that a man *ʿandu l-kelma,* "has the word," means that his word is influential/powerful, and that his power is a power to do. For a discussion of the rhetoric of the "buying and selling of words" in the historical imagination of the qṣar, see part 3.

14. Commerce is referred to as *l-bîʿ u shrâ,* "selling and buying."

15. Cf. R. Barthes, "L'ancienne rhétorique," in *L'aventure sémiologique* (Paris: Seuil, 1985), 91: "Il est savoureux de constater que l'art de la parole est lié originairement à une revendication de propriété, comme si le langage, en tant que l'objet d'une transformation, condition d'une pratique, s'était déterminé non point à partir d'une subtile médiation idéologique (comme il pu arriver à tant de formes d'art), mais à partir de la socialité la plus nue, affirmée dans sa brutalité fondamentale, celle de la possession terrienne: on a commencé—chez nous—à réfléchir sur le langage pour défendre son bien. C'est au niveau du conflit social qu'est née une première ébauche théorique de la *parole feinte* [simulated speech]."

16. Cf. part 1, "Splinters at l-Hashmi's Funeral," for a comparison between the illness of *bu zellûm,* that "opens up" and breaks the bodily articulations, and the recent fitna in the qṣar.

17. See at the end of this section the entry "Fitna," from the classical Arabic dictionary *Lisân al-ʿârab.*

18. "Ce qu'on ne peut traiter d'aucune manière, l'intraitable, est proprement ce qui se dérobe à chaque fois, et de manière à la fois imperceptible et radicale, à toute action d'être trait, d'être manié; ce qui, de par sou essence, échappe à l'entreprise de toute soumission; ce qui, en quelque sens, demeure hors l'atteinte de l'homme et aussi, en définitive, de la pensée" (A. Diouri, "Traiter de l'intraitable," in *Imaginaires de l'autre* [Paris: L'Harmattan, 1987], 50).

19. This local version of the story of the Fall does not correspond to the Qur'anic text. An important difference is that in the Qur'an (unlike in the Bible) it is Adam

who is first tempted by Iblis. At least for one of its elements (the theme of defecation), the tale also departs from other Moroccan versions of the Fall, which focus exclusively on the theme of the mirror. In the Qur'an the account of the Fall is narrated three times: Qur'an 2:30–34, 7:19–25, 20:120–21. The focus is on the forgetting of the covenant, and on the "nakedness" and shame "made apparent" by the transgression. In the popular version these themes are expressed through the image of the mirror, which is both deceptive and truthful.

"Thus have We sent this Down—an Arabic Qur'an—and explained therein in detail some of the warnings, in order that they may fear God, or that it may cause their remembrance [*dhikra*]. We had already, beforehand, taken the covenant of Adam, but he forgot [*fa-nasiya*]: and We found on his part no firm resolve. When We said to the Angels, 'prostrate yourselves to Adam,' They prostrated themselves, but not Iblis: he refused. Then we said: 'O Adam! Verily, this is an enemy to Thee and thy wife: So let him not get you both out of the Garden, so that thou art landed in misery. There is therein (enough provision) for thee not to go hungry nor to go naked, nor to suffer from thirst, nor from the sun's heat.' But Satan whispered evil to him: he said, 'O Adam! Shall I lead thee to the Tree of Eternity and to a kingdom that never decays?' In the end, they both ate from the tree, and so their nakedness appeared to them: they began to sew together, for their covering, leaves from the Garden: thus did Adam disobey his Lord, and allow himself to be seduced" (Qur'an 20:113–21).

"He said: 'Get ye down, with enmity between yourselves. On earth will be your dwelling-place and your means of livelihood, for a time.' Then Satan made them slip from the Garden, and got them out [*fa-akhrajahumâ*]" (Qur'an 7:24).

20. A. Artaud, "La recherche de la fécalité," in *Oeuvres complètes,* vol. 13 (Paris: Gallimard, 1956). "Because in order not to make caca, he would have had to consent not to be."

21. Artaud, "The Pursuit of Fecality," in *Selected Writings,* 559:

> There where it smells of shit
> it smells of being.
> Man could just as well not have shat,
> not have opened the anal pouch,
> but he chose to shit
> as he would have chosen to live
> instead of consenting to live dead.
>
> Because in order not to make caca,
> he would have had to consent
> not to be,
> but he could not make up his mind to lose
> being,
> that is, to die alive.
>
> There is in being
> something particularly tempting for
> man
> and this something is none other than
> CACA.
> (Roaring here.)

22. A. Artaud, "Van Gogh le suicidé de la societé," in *Oeuvres complètes,* 13:20, 30, translated as "Van Gogh, the Man Suicided by Society" (1947) in ibid., 487, 491:

> Van Gogh did not die of a state of delirium properly speaking,
> but of having been bodily the battlefield of a problem around which the evil spirit of humanity has been struggling from the beginning.
> The problem of the predominance of flesh over spirit, or of body over flesh, or of spirit over both . . .
> [T]oday, in fact, right now,
> in this month of February 1947,
> reality itself,
> the myth of reality itself, mythic reality itself, is in the process of becoming flesh.

23. A. Artaud, "Dossier d'Artaud le Mômo," in *Oeuvres complètes,* 12:173. My translation:

> Shit, pain, poem
> . . . now, that which comes out of me is not me
> and I have to make up immediately
> why am I tired?
> Because the concrete body in a life more true than this one, in the relative and particular, keeps me from dropping them out, feeling too content outside of life.
> Why come out and live . . .

24. Literally, "She put him into a state of fitna, that is, she set him ablaze." The list of fitnas below evokes the various definitions of *fitna* in the Qur'an.

25. *N-nâss meblyin,* from the verbal root *bala:* it means in this colloquial sense "to be obsessed," "to be mindlessly following something." In *Lisân al-ʿârab* fitna is equated, among other things, to *al-ibtilâ* (one of the forms of *bala*)—in the sense of temptation and affliction.

26. M. Blanchot, *L'espace littéraire* (Paris: Gallimard, 1955), 352, 353, 344.

> To live an event as a image is not to remain uninvolved, to regard the event disinterestedly in the way of the esthetic version of the image and the serene ideal of classical art propose. But neither is to take part freely and decisively. It is to be taken: to pass from the region of the real where we hold ourselves at a distance from things the better to order and use them, into that other region where the distance holds us—the distance which then is the lifeless deep, an unmanageable, inappreciable remoteness which has become something like the sovereign power behind all things. . . . Magic takes its power from this transformation. Its aim, through a methodic technique, is to arouse things as reflections and to thicken consciousness into a thing.
>
> . . . The image does not, at first glance, resemble the corpse, but the cadaver's strangeness is perhaps also that of the image. What we call mortal remains escapes common categories. Something is there before us which is not really the living person, nor is it any reality at all. It is neither the same as the person who was alive, nor is it another person, nor is it anything else. . . . Death

> suspends the relation to place, even though the deceased rests heavily in his spot as if upon the only basis that is left him. To be precise, this basis lacks, the place is missing, the corpse is not in its place. Where is it? It is not here, and yet it is not anywhere else. Nowhere? But then nowhere is here. The cadaverous presence establishes a relation between here and nowhere. . . . He resembles *himself*. The cadaver is its own image.

The Space of Literature, trans. A. Smock (Lincoln: University of Nebraska Press, 1982), 261–62, 257–58.

27. The area around the town of Khoribga is where phosphate is found most abundantly in Morocco.

28. *Abbud* (Berber) is a local image for something mixed up and undifferentiated. In its literal sense, it is a pastry made with a paste of mixed dates.

29. The loom is a model of life and the world—and not just for Ḥadda. The rûḥ, or life breath, of the loom derives from the inscription of a difference, of an articulation between thread and thread, which makes weaving possible. Weaving—the horizontal insertion and knotting of the weft threads between vertical (standing) warp threads—is the realization of the potentiality of the warps. The warps are seen as masculine, and overtly symbolize masculinity, while the woofs are feminine (*ṭaʿma*, from the same root as *ṭaʿam*, "food"). What is called a loom (*mansej* or *msedd*, the "tied" or "locked" one) is not its wooden frame—an object—but a "work," the process of weaving. (The wooden frame is called *l-muʿwin dyâl msedd*, "the loom's utensils.") In the vertical looms Ḥadda is referring to, the rûḥ is the articulation of two warp threads, knotted by a weft thread: it is what holds the textile together. See below.

30. Cf. *Hans Wehr Dictionary of Modern Written Arabic*. For the patient as *al-musâb* see any popular manual of magic and therapy, such as *Shumûs al-anwâr* by Ibn al-ḥajj Tlemsânî al-Maghribî.

31. *Khraj ll-amsrîr* is a conflation of Berber and Arabic that literally means "to come out, wander along the riverbank." *Amsrîr* is the place where the sand touches the water, the gravel bed. *Kharj ll-amsrîr* is the common local way of expressing the condition of losing orientation, leaving the right path, etc. It is a concrete image of the margin, the edge. A woman who becomes a prostitute is said to "have come out to the riverbank." The riverbank, the actual bank of the river, threshold of the water, is a no man's land, outside of the jurisdiction of village communities. The Arabic equivalent of it is *ṭerf* (pl. *l-aṭrâf*, standard Arabic *al-aṭrâf*), which indicates the margin, the frontier, the limit. The margin is a dangerous non-place, as in the local saying "Ṭerf l-blâd sehm l-blâ u j-jrâd" (the edge of the territory is the side of disaster and locusts).

32. Jorge Luis Borges, "Deutsches Requiem," trans. J. Palley, in *Labyrinths* (New York: New Directions, 1962), 141.

33. *Hans Wehr Dictionary of Modern Written Arabic*. For a discussion of *ḥasab*, of *nasab*, and in general of the genealogical rhetoric and its contradictions in the Maghreb in a number of different contexts, see *Hasab wa nasab: Parenté, alliance, et patrimoine en Tunisie*, ed. S. Ferchiou (Paris: Éditions du CNRS, 1992); P. Bonté, E. Conte, C. Hamés, and A. Ould Cheikh, *Al-Ansâb: La Quête des Origines: Anthropologie historique de la société tribale arabe* (Paris: Éditions de la Maison des Sciences de l'Homme, 1991); J. Dakhlia, *L'oubli de la cité: Récits du lignage et mémoire*

collective dans le Sud tunisien (Paris: La Découverte, 1990); M. Kilani, *La construction de la mémoire* (Geneva: Labor et Fides, 1992); A. Sebti, *Aristocratie citadine, pouvoir et discours savant au Maroc précolonial: Contribution à une relecture de la littérature généalogique fassie, 15–20me siècles*, thesis, Université de Paris, 1984.

34. "*Account:* Reckoning, computation; a record of debit and credit to cover transactions involving a particular item or a particular person or concern; value, importance; esteem; consideration (to take something or someone into account). *Accountable:* subject to giving an account: answerable; capable of being accounted for: explainable; responsible for someone or something" (*Webster's Ninth New Collegiate Dictionary*).

35. The sense in which Ḥadda is using the term *l-ḥsâb dyâl qbîla* is consistent with the local idiom for identifying a man as belonging to the village community or, in a different context, to some of its forms: *maḥsûb f l-qbîla*, "he is accounted for as a member of the qbîla" (local political community), or *dkhal l-ḥsâb dyâl l-qbîla*, "he entered the count of the qbîla" (for a boy who just reached puberty), or *maḥsûb f rbaʿ Ayt l-Bâlî*, "he is accounted for within the Fourth of Ayt l-Bâlî." Here, however, what is called an Account is the name of a descent line, what is locally called a Bone (*ʿaḍam*). While in the first and more general sense *maḥsub ʿala, ʿand*, or *maḥsûb fi* (accounted to, with, or within) indicates belonging to a community of some sort, the qbîla or the fourth, in the second sense it indicates belonging to a patrilineage—where belonging is coded in terms of blood and direct transmission of the name.

36. In setting the opposition of *ḥasab* and *nasab* the way he does, Ḥadda is following the local usage of these terms, where *nasab* is the connection, the relation through marriage, the mother's side, the side of women in general, the "tie" through the pact. In the classical use (e.g., *The Encyclopedia of Islam*, ed. B. Lewis et al. [London, 1979], s.v. "nasab") it is rather the other way around, inasmuch as *nasab* carries primarily the sense of genealogy and descent, and only adjointly that of in-law relationship, tie, and the like. This is *never* the case in Ḥadda's use of the term in this discussion, or even in the local use of the qṣar, where *nasab* is unquestionably an in-law, contractual relation, and never one coded in genealogical terms.

37. "Being accounted under the name of" is the way names are composed. For instance, Moḥammed u Ḥassan n-Ayt Ḥammu Sûlî: the person is placed under the father's name, then under the bone's name, and finally under the name of the qbîla, which in this case means the village. Or Faṭima Aḥmed u l-Faṭmi: the woman is under her father's name, himself identified as a subset of his own father's name. Sometimes in the case of women the nasab (in the sense of marriage tie) is also mentioned, as in Ṭaṭṭa Aḥmed taʿt Ayt Lḥassan u l-ʿAdnanî, where the older woman is identified by the intimate Ṭaṭṭa, a respectful short name for Faṭima, her father's name, Aḥmed, and the preposition *of* (*taʿt*) syntactically attaching her name to her husband's lineage, identified by the union of her husband's and his father's names within the linguistic structure of a lineage (in Berber, *ayt*). Yet her case is unusual because her father died when she was just born and she is *maḥsûba itîma*, "accounted as an orphan."

Finally, the expression *maḥsubîn ʿand ayt* so-and-so refers to people who live in a protected subordinate status, working for the lineage that lends them an account, a place to be called, and enjoying some indirect privileges as protégés. So, for instance, the families who enjoyed protected status under the account of the lineage of the Judge were exonerated from performing the annual corvée for the Makhzen (i.e., for the *qaid* of the sultan, intermittently stationed in the qṣar until the end of the nineteenth century), but in turn they had to dig the irrigation canal in behalf of their name-giving masters. The Ḥarâr of lineages who have such Ḥarâtîn protégés speak of them as "our Drawâ."

38. In the local colloquial use the verbs *marr,* to pass, to flow away, to run by, and *marr,* to be bitter, which in the dictionary are two different words, each with its semantic constellation, are treated as connotations of the same word. Hence the term *marrâra,* "gallbladder" (which should have to do with the *marr* because of its bitter secretion), is understood as the organ that regulates the circulation (*murûr,* "flowing through") of liquids in the body, working like a gauge.

39. *Fulân* is the Arabic equivalent of "so-and-so."

40. The *gar'a,* "pumpkin" or "squash," has a strong feminine connotation. It plays an important role as double of the bride during the wedding ceremony, it appears as a substitute for a woman in tales, and it is protected by ritual interdictions in agriculture (if a woman walks across a pumpkin field, people say, the pumpkins split open, due to the collision of the two feminine energy fields).

41. Both tea and sugar have relatively recent histories in Morocco as elsewhere in the Mediterranean. This fact, however, has nothing to do with Ḥadda's argument or with my reading of it. Tea did not make an appearance until the eighteenth century through international trade (and later in this southern region), and sugar made an even later appearance in this area where dates and honey were the customary sweeteners. Tea was, and still is, a luxury item, an expression of value—and this is indeed consistent with Ḥadda's use of the image of tea as a metaphor for the ḥasab. It was made available through the caravan trade, brought back from Marrakesh with cloth and other luxury goods in exchange for the locally exported dates and henna, and its commerce was for a long time monopolized by the local Jewish community. The consumption of tea was reserved to the local elite and, for the most part, only to men. Sugar came with the colonial period, and, again, Jews had a monopoly on it. Ḥadda is speaking of sugar as of today, and in his argument sugar stands for anything that reacts and sweetens, bringing tea (as abstract substance) to concrete realization.

For a social and cultural history of the use and connotation of tea in Morocco, and the popular and legal discussions concerning its social and medicinal uses, see A. Lakhsassi and A. Sebti, *Kitâb al-atây (The Book of Tea): A Cultural History of Tea in Morocco* (Rabat: Publications de la Faculté des Lettres at des Sciences Humaines, forthcoming).

42. *Khmâmes* (pl. of *khammâs*), literally "one-fifther," land laborer at the remuneration of one-fifth of the crop. In principle a *khammâs* was landless, and in his contract with the landlord didn't put anything of his own except his work and that of his children. (In other sharecropping arrangements the sharecropper put in his tools, or part of the capital seeds, etc.) The contract of *khamessat,* which in this region is called *l-khumus,* was formally abolished during the French protectorate, but survives in this region in some form, even though *l-khammâs,* without losing this name, is increasingly becoming a wage laborer.

43. Of course, when the analogy is brought from tea back to people, *nasab, tenseb,* and all the adjectival and verbal forms of this word could be translated as "to be related." So, for instance, "she is accounted at her father's in Bû Zergân, and she is related to Bni Zoli [by marriage]."

An extended discussion of *nasab/nisba* (and a related term, *qarâba,* from the root "to be close" or "to be neighbor") in the sense of relation is found in the work of H. Geertz, C. Geertz, and L. Rosen (*Meaning and Order in Moroccan Society* [Cambridge: Cambridge University Press, 1979]) and D. Eickelman (*Moroccan Islam: Tradition and Pilgrimage in a Pilgrimage Center* [Austin: University of Texas Press, 1976]), where the symbolic configuration of nasab (in Eickelman, *qarâba*) is seen as a pragmatic way in which social relations are constructed in Moroccan culture (as against a view that emphasizes the importance of lineages and segmentarity; cf. E. Gellner, *Saints of the Atlas* [London: Weidenfeld and Nicholson, 1969]). Significantly, Rosen's contribution to that volume focuses on "points of attachment," a term that is a dialogical negotiation between the Moroccan notion of nasab and Western sociological pragmatism (see also L. Rosen, *Bargaining for Reality* [Chicago: University of Chicago Press, 1984]).

That approach, however, overlooks the importance of the genealogical idiom in Morocco altogether (while instead the logic of *nasab*, and even the discourse of *nasab*, could be seen as a deconstruction, in practice, of the lineage ideology of descent). That paradox at the heart of the genealogical discourse, and the melancholic attitude that ensued, is discussed by M. Meeker in a poetic and narrative context (*Literature and Violence in North Arabia* [Cambridge: Cambridge University Press, 1979]), and, in a different sense, by L. Abu-Lughod (*Veiled Sentiments* [Berkeley: University of California Press, 1987] and *Writing Women Worlds* [Berkeley: University of California Press, 1993]).

The Victim and Its Mask by A. Hammoudi, trans. P. Wissing (Chicago: University of Chicago Press, 1993; originally published as *La victime et ses masques* [Paris: Seuil, 1988]), is one of the rare attempts in the ethnography of the Maghreb to explore the essential ambivalence and irreducible paradox of the idiom of paternity and patriarchy, which at the same time excludes the feminine and depends on it. Hammoudi does this through an analysis of the double play of sacrifice and masquerade, law and outlaw, masculine and feminine, fathers and sons, human and inhuman, at the ʿid l-kbîr festival in a valley of the High Atlas Mountains. In many ways his conclusions meet Ḥadda's paradoxical considerations on paternity, naming, and descent, and in general the analytical orientation of this work. The work of V. Crapanzano on the ambivalence of gender categories (*The Hamadsha* [Berkeley: University of California Press, 1973], and *Tuhami: Portrait of a Moroccan* [Chicago: University of Chicago Press, 1980]), and the early ethnography of E. Westermark on ritual gender reversals in Morocco (*Ritual and Belief in Morocco* [London: Macmillan, 1926]) are, if in different ways, important earlier attempts. On the ambivalence of gender categories, see also S. Pandolfo, "Detours of Life: Space and Bodies in a Moroccan Village," *American Ethnologist* 16, no. 1 (1989): 3–23.

I am translating *nasab* here as "knot" or "tie"—a translation that is at the same time more literal and precise in Arabic and less commonsensical in English—because this is the analytical sense emphasized by Hadda, and because I believe that it should be situated theoretically within the larger idiom of "articulation" taken as epistemological guide. I read the discourse of nasab as a possibility and a necessity already contained in the ambivalence of the genealogical discourse (the discourse of the ḥasab-nasab), and the concept of nasab itself as a figure (among other figures, the most elaborated of which is fitna) of the preoccupation with what may be called the inevitability of structural loss.

44. "L'original n'est pas un plein qui en viendrait par accident a être traduit. La

situation de l'original est la situation d'une demande, c'est-a-dire d'un manque, d'un exil, et l'original est à priori endetté à l'égard de la traduction. Sa survie est une demande de traduction, un désir de traduction, un peu comme Babel demande: traduisez moi. Babel est un homme, enfin est un Dieu male" (J. Derrida, *L'oreille de l'autre: Otobiographies, transferts, traductions* [Montreal: VLB, 1982], 201). (The original is not a fullness that would accidentally be translated. The situation of the original is the situation of a demand, that is a lack, an exile, and the original is a priori indebted with regards to the translation. Its survival is a demand of translation, a desire of translation, somewhat as Babel demands: translate me. Babel is a man, in the end, it is a male God; my translation.)

45. *La dette symbolique,* "symbolic indebtedness" or "symbolic exchange," is a central concern in the writings of Lacan ("Séminaire sur la lettre volée," in *Écrits* [Paris: Seuil, 1966]). It is addressed by Derrida in *La carte postale: De Socrate à Freud et au-delà* (Paris: Flammarion, 1980; *The Post Card: From Socrates to Freud and Beyond,* trans. A. Bass [Chicago: University of Chicago Press, 1987]), a reading of *Beyond the Pleasure Principle* (1920), one of Freud's texts on gifts and returns and in *Donner le temps* (Paris: Galilée, 1991). The issue of whether it is possible to break a chain of symbolic implication and "withdraw one's stakes from the game" is the contested core of the discussion, from Nietzsche to Freud, Mauss, Bataille, Baudrillard, Lacan, and Derrida. According to Bataille, and in a lesser sense to Mauss, a chain of implication can be broken by an expenditure *à fond perdu,* a radical loss, the elimination of all *restes,* the annihilation of the self and its representations exemplified by the potlatch. (Cf. G. Bataille, *Visions of Excess: Selected Writings, 1927–39* [Minneapolis: University of Minnesota Press, 1985]).

The themes of implication and acquittal are recurrent in the conversation on ḥasab and nasab, and represent a central preoccupation in Ḥadda's life. Ḥadda's interpretation of the disastrous fire in which his father found death is a poignant example of his attitude: "Had he been spared to eventually die of some other cause, we, his children and descendants, would have been left in this world to pay for his crimes. . . . Fire is good!" (Cf. Contra-diction 2, "The Fire.")

46. "Le contractant d'abord est *reus* [guilty, responsible]; c'est avant tout l'homme qui a reçu la *res* (chose) d'autrui, et devient à ce titre son *reus,* c'est-à-dire l'individu qui lui est lié par la chose elle-même, c'est-à-dire par son esprit." And in a note Mauss specifies:

> *Reus* appartient d'abord a la langue de la religion. . . . L'equivalent de *reus* est *voli damnatus,* et ceci est bien symptomatique puisque *damnatus = nexus.* L'individu qui a fait un voeu est exactement dans la position de celui qui a promis ou reçu une chose. *Il est damnatus jusq'à ce qu'il se soit acquitte.*
>
> . . . *Reus* c'est l'homme qui est possede par la chose . . . impliqué dans le proces.
>
> . . . Nous dirions: 1. l'individu possédé par la chose; 2. l'individu impliqué dans l'affaire causée par la *traditio* de la chose; 3. enfin, le coupable et le responsable. De ce point de vue, toutes les théories du "quasi-délit," origine du contrat, du *nexum* et de l'*actio,* sont un peu plus éclaircies. Le seul fait d'avoir la chose met l'accipiens dans un état incertain de quasi-culpabilité (*damnatus,*

nexus, aere oberatus), d'infériorité spirituelle, d'inégalité morale vis-à-vis du livrer (*tradens*).

Essai sur le don, in *Sociologie et anthropologie* (Paris: Presses Universitaires de France, 1950), 235–36.

47. "The danger represented by the thing given or legated is nowhere better felt than in the old German law, and in German languages. This explains the double sense of the word *gift* in the ensemble of these languages: gift (*don*) from one side, poison from the other" (Mauss, *Essai sur le don*, 255, my translation).

48. Names of nearby and faraway places from which local families are said to have originated.

49. Taghallil is the qṣar's familiar other—historically the customary enemy and customary friend. The qṣar of Taghallil is located not more than a half mile from the walled ramparts of Bni Zoli, and the two qṣûr look at each other's backs. They seem almost identical, their past is tightly interwoven, their gardens are watered from the same canals. Yet, while Taghallil is viewed (from Bni Zoli's standpoint) as a land of agreement and cooperation, Bni Zoli sees itself, and is viewed by others, as a land of disagreement and fitna.

50. F. Cheng, *Vide et plein: Le langage pictural chinois* (Paris: Seuil, 1979), 33. This text influenced a generation of contemporary Moroccan writers and artists. Thanks to Abdelhaï Diouri for directing my attention to it.

"One could say that, without the intervention of Emptiness, the realm of Fullness virtually governed by the two poles which are the Yin and the Yang, remains static and almost amorphous. Within a binary system Yin/Yang, emptiness constitutes the third term that at once means separation, transformation, and unity. . . . Emptiness [*le Vide*] does not just play the role of a neutral space, which would only serve to defuse the shock without changing the nature of the opposition. It is the woven knot of virtuality and becoming, where lack and plenitude meet, the same and the other" (my translation).

51. Personal names are composed from the father and possibly the grandfather's name, and this applies to women as much as to men. The only difference is that, while a man's name is attached to his father's and grandfather's name by the word *ben* (*ibn*) or in Berber *u*, "son of" (Moḥammed ben ʿAbdallah or Moḥammed u ʿAbdallah), women's names when used informally (that is, not in document or in magical writing) are directly followed by the father's name (e.g., Faṭima Aḥmed, or Faṭima Aḥmed u l-Madanî: Faṭima Aḥmed son of l-Madanî). Women don't change their name at marriage, and this emphasizes the heterogeneity of a woman's presence in her husband's household.

Family names in the Western sense of the term did not exist in Morocco until after independence (1956) with the institution of a unified national identity card, and their use is still not evenly spread, especially in the rural, mountain, or southern areas. With the institution of the national identity card people were asked to choose a family name that would remain unchanged. In this southern region some selected the nickname (*knyia*) informally attached to their lineage and turned it into a surname. Others followed the inspiration of the moment, or the name of their profession, or what they saw as an auspicious or distinctive denomination, or finally transformed Berber lineage names (preceeded by the word *ayt*) into French-type surnames where *ayt* became *De* or *D*. In the qṣar, however, people are still known by their customary names, be those the genealogical ones (e.g., Moḥammed ben Aḥmed ben ʿAbdallah) or the local nicknames (which can be different in different contexts). The identity-card name is used for administrative purposes, or at the post office.

52. Sîdî Nûr is a shrine in the palm groves, place of visitation (*zyara*) and site of an annual ritual sacrifice. The gardens are punctuated by shrines diversely marked, sometimes just a mound of stones (*rjem*) or a tombstone semihidden in the sand, sometimes a complex of ruins with a long narrow tomb, marked by two standing headstones. Sîdî Nûr is the most developed of these sites: the ruins of a former settlement surround the shrine, which is said to stand at the place of the old mosque. But of the mosque, only a well is left. The shrines—people call them *aṣ-ṣalḥîn dyâl l-blâd,* "the saints of the land" (by the "presences" of which they are the mark)—are said to be the trace (*ʿalâma*) of the former settlements in the gardens, *l-qṣûr dyâl jnânât,* the "scattered hamlets" of the legendary past. See part 3.

53. *Ighrem* in Berber means "village," *qṣar* in Arabic. Agjgal is a region in the gardens (*Ugjgal* is the genitive), traversed by an irrigation canal called Aghala Ugjgal.

54. *Kull waḥd f jîh,* sense of centrifugal movement, inevitability, fission. The term *maftus/a,* "scattered," is locally used (both in Arabic and Berber) instead of *mshettet/a,* from the verb *shatta,* "to scatter, fragment, disperse."

55. *Khurrâb,* "splinters," from *khrb,* the semantic root of falling in ruin. *Kharraba,* to fall in ruin, to fragment, to destroy; *l-kharâb* (classical *al-kharâb*) means "ruins."

56. For the story of the secessionist settlement of Tighremt, founded by the rebel lineage of Ayt Mḥammâd, and later razed by the people of the qṣar, see part 1, "Splinters at l-Hashmis Funeral." Ighruren is a new settlement, sprawling in the late 1970s just outside the walls of Bni Zoli (the first wave of pushing out), whose inhabitants—mostly Ḥarâtîn—sought to attain autonomy from the father village in matters concerning public works, maintenance of the irrigation canals, etc. In the idiom of today, both Ighruren and Tighremt become figures of fitna.

57. Ben ʿAbd l-Mûla is a *walî* from a remote past, a saint, and the qṣar's local protector. His hagiography is rich with miracles and tales concerning the qṣar's public life and its protagonists. He is said to have settled in mystical ways critical social and political situations, including disputes over water distribution. It is this saint who marked his blessing of protection and exclusion at the threshold of the gate of Bni Zoli, still known as "Ben ʿAbd l-Mûla's threshold" (cf. part 1, "Topology of a City"). The zâwya of Ben ʿAbd l-Mûla, the saint's sanctuary, is located in the palm groves, a few miles from the *qṣar,* and is a local pilgrimage place. This powerful holy lineage is still much involved in the political and ritual life of Bni Zoli, and even today his descendants are called in to arbitrate in case of serious internal discord.

58. *Iger* means "garden" in Berber.

59. *Ṣfrîn,* the "Yellows," is the colloquial (and disdainful) way by which the Ḥarâtîn refer among themselves to the white Ḥarâr. It connotes illness, a thinness of blood, and in general, a lack of life (as in *bû ṣfîr,* "hepatitis").

60. The *ʿâmma* is the organized village performance group. This local use of the term is related to the classical sense of *al-ʿâmma* as "the common people" (opposed to the *al-khâṣṣa,* "the aristocracy").

Ḥadda had been for many years the head poet, sheikh of the qṣar's ʿâmma. In the 1940s he organized a group of youths who performed nationalist anticolonial poetry. One event is particularly impressed in the local memory. A French officer and his entourage, stationed in Zagora, used to visit the qṣar and have meals at the houses of some local notables. They came in their cars, people recall, sometimes accompanied by their "blond wives" dressed in European clothes. On these occasions the sheikh of the ʿâmma would be summoned and ordered to gather his people for a performance—to sing for the French guests. One day, it was the ʿid l-kbir, the feast of sacrifice, when traditionally the ʿâmma performs at the village gate. The French "guests" arrived, and the the sheikh of the qṣar, the local authority, summoned Ḥadda, who was then the sheikh of the ʿâmma, and ordered him to gather his men for a show: not at the village gate (*fum l-qṣar*), as was the custom, but by the new gate called *fum l-makhzen,* the "mouth of the government," where the local authorities resided and where the French officers felt more comfortable. They gathered, but not one man opened his mouth to sing. For a long time there was a tense silence, until a former sheikh of the ʿâmma, respectful or fearful of the colonial authorities, got up and started to sing, forcing the ʿâmma to perform. People were singing and dancing, people recall—and they were crying. On that day Ḥadda resigned as sheikh of the ʿâmma.

61. That is, the French rule is gone, now everybody is equal, and you no longer have a right to the garden you cultivated as an employee of the mosque.

62. The gardens with the palm groves are called *dâkhel l-blâd,* "the inside the land," while the surrounding desert is called *berra,* "the outside." The rhetoric of inside/outside in this story is a precise replica of the new concern with pushing "out," into the *berra.*

63. *Ghâdi nkharju ʿala berra* is also the formula people use today to describe their move out of the walled qṣar and into the open desert.

64. Tagummâ l-Makhzen is from the Tashelḥit Berber *tigemmi* (pl. *tagumma*), "house." Also called Dyâr l-Makhzen.

65. Ḥadda here literally says, "Kayn ʿalîh târîkh," it is recorded in history, or there is a history for it, meaning the trace of this lineage is left in the name of the alley. Therefore, as he is now starting to do for the notion of ḥasab itself, Ḥadda is subverting his use of the concept of târîkh. A name can be recorded in history, yet it is a "false" name, a name only "attached," a nasab, which does not correspond to the truth of the bone/lineage to which it claims to refer.

66. In other words, not only the surnames by which a lineage is identified (like Ayt l-Ghandur, as Ḥadda just explained), but even the names of lineages themselves such as the Lineage of Brahim son of Mbark, share the same quality of nicknames; they are just attached, somewhat randomly, to the people who identify themselves by them. This is the philosophical core of Ḥadda's paradoxical argument.

67. M. Blanchot, *L'écriture du désastre* (Paris: Gallimard, 1980), 17. "The horror—the honor—of the name, which always threatens to be become a title [*sur-nom,* "nickname"]. In vain the movement of anonymity remonstrates with this supernumerary appellation—this fact of being identified, unified, fixed, arrested in the present. . . . And thus the thought of writing—the ever-dissuaded thought which disaster awaits—is made explicit in the name; it receives a title and is ennobled thereby; indeed, it is as if saved—and yet, given up. It is surrendered to praise or to criticism (these amount to the same): it is, in other words, promised to a life surpass-

ing death, survival. Boneyard of names, heads never empty" (*The Writing of the Disaster,* trans. A. Smock [Lincoln: University of Nebraska Press, 1986], 7).

68. *L-aʿsel* and *l-qaṭrân,* "honey" and "tar," are commonly associated in discourse.

69. *Ṭolba* (sing. *ṭaleb*), "Qur'anic scholars," men who have memorized the Qur'an.

The *fatiḥa* (or *fatḥa*), literally "opening," is the opening chapter of the Qur'an, which is recited at the end of important ritual occasions of a religious nature, such as a wedding, circumcision, festival, or public sacrifice. It is the performative formula of marriage, and its performance alone used to be sufficient to ratify the marriage contract. Ḥadda had mentioned this before (possibly with the story of his father in mind), and in both cases he stresses that the *fatḥa* ought to be accompanied by the writing of the marriage contract—which until well into the colonial period (the 1940s) used to be written by the *ṭaleb* himself, the local scholar and Qur'anic teacher. In earlier days, however, it was common not to write the contract at all, for the one-week-long celebration of the wedding, involving the whole community or a large part of it, was itself the biggest of social engagements.

70. The Zayan country is a Tamazight Berber–speaking area in the Middle Atlas region, northeast and very far from this Saharan region. It was not common for people of the Draʿ valley to travel to the Middle Atlas (with the exception of people from Tamazight Berber–speaking villages of former nomadic tradition, such as the Ayt ʿAṭṭa people, as Ḥadda will mention below). Ḥadda's father, like Ḥadda and everybody in this village, spoke both Arabic and Tashelḥit Berber, and a mixture of the two specific to this region. Because Sîdî Moḥamed u l-Ḥajj was a Qur'anic scholar, it was easy for him to become the prayer leader in a mosque and be granted the privileges attached to the position. He could make a living wherever he wished.

71. *ʿAṭa wuldû ll-qbîla,* "he gave his son to the community," has also another, more technical sense. The *khedma dyâll qbîla,* "public works," is mostly the work of maintenance at the irrigation canal, which is considered an obligatory civil responsibility. In earlier days older men still required to work their share at the canal would sometimes "offer" their newborn to the qbîla and, by that gesture, step out of the obligation to serve the community. This meant that the child would enter the "count" of the qbîla in his father's place, and independent of his having reached the canonic age, he would symbolically stand in his father's place. As a child and incapable of working, he would be sent to the canal to represent his father. Other men used to dislike this practice because it meant one hand less in the work, and a child in the way.

72. Ḥadda's reference to the Qur'anic story of Shuʿaib is a creative adaptation to the theme of our discussion rather than a faithful citation. In the Qur'an (7:85–93, 11:84–95) Shuʿaib is a prophet sent to preach justice and the word of God among the Madyan people, corrupted merchants who do not respect the ethics of commerce. He is mistreated by the local leaders, who threaten to stone him and drive him out of the city. "They said: 'O Shuʿaib! Much of what you say we do not understand! In fact among us we see that you have no strength! Were it not for your family, we should certainly have stoned you! For you have among us no great position!" (11:91). But an earthquake struck the town, bringing ruin to the homes of the wealthy merchants.

In both chapters of the Qur'an the story of Shuʿaib immediately follows that of the prophet Lûṭ (Lot), associated with the destruction of the corrupted cities of Sodom and Gomorrah. The story of Lot resembles that of Shuʿaib; Lot and his family are also driven out of their city. Unlike Shuʿaib, Lot has two daughters; like Shuʿaib, he is old and frail. Possibly Ḥadda borrows these traits from the story of Lot, and collapses them into that of Shuʿaib.

73. Settat is a town on the plains of the Chaouia, in central Morocco. Today a boomtown on the industrial axis of Casablanca and at the edge of a fertile agricultural region, in the 1930s it was a large village, with just a train station and a marketplace. It was a junction on the road between Marrakesh and Casablanca, and a marketplace for a number of big colonial agricultural estates in the surrounding countryside.

In the mid-1930s a drought struck the Draʿ valley and other areas of Morocco. Hundreds of people died of hunger; the palm groves died. Many villages saw a massive exodus of all those who could work toward the northern plains of Morocco. The landless Ḥarâtîn, who in normal times worked as *khmames* for the Ḥarâr landlords, had no choice but to migrate north.

Growing under colonial rule, the rural center of Settat became a gathering place for the refugees from the Draʿ. Over a period of almost ten years entire villages found themselves displaced in temporary huts in the wasteland surrounding that town. The deserted hill of Lâllâ Mimûna, mentioned in Ḥadda's story, is today near the center of town, and the sanctuary of Lâllâ Mimûna is visited by people from the south. Most of the residents in the neighborhood are originally from the Draʿ valley. They are those who didn't go back. The drought over, most people returned to their villages and fields. Those who had no property or family chose not to return; some moved to the bidonvilles of Casablanca and found work in the city. Sometimes they built fortunes, in some cases commercial empires.

The famine, which closely followed (significantly so in the eyes of people from the Draʿ) the arrival of the French army in this Saharan region (1932), is locally reckoned as *ʿâm r-rûz,* "the rice years," after the food subsidy of rice provided by the colonial administration. Unlike other areas of the Middle East, in Morocco rice had been quite unknown and never was considered real food. Today in the Draʿ valley the memory of the famine and the colonial connotation of rice are so strong that rice is largely disliked. (For a history of the town of Settat and the region of Chaouia, see *Casablanca et les Chaouia,* in *Villes et tribus du Maroc* [Paris: Publications de la Mission Scientifique du Maroc, 1915]; E. Burke III, "La grande siba de la Chaouia," *Hespéris-Tamuda* [1976–77]; E. Burke III, *Prelude to Protectorate in Morocco: Pre-Colonial Protest and Resistance, 1860–1912* [Chicago: University of Chicago Press, 1976].)

74. *ʿArobya* means "countryside." Here, however, it is used as the proper name of a region, from the point of view of the Drawâ, the people of the pre-Saharan oases. It designates the plains of the Chaouia, south of and around Casablanca, where extensive wheat farms are the main agricultural style. People from the Draʿ used to work there as seasonal labor at harvest time—many still do—and are acquainted with the customs of that (only) Arabic-speaking region, which they view as uncultured and unsophisticated. From the point of view of the Draʿ, the attribute *ʿarubî* means "peasant" and carries a disparaging connotation—a rude, simple, unsophisticated person. The views of people from this region about the Drawâ are also preju-

diced; *Drawî* becomes an insult. In the context of this particular passage, however, the ʿArubiât are simply the women from this region.

75. This is a reference to the two guardian angels, appointed by God to stand by the person and note down her good and bad actions. The two angels are mentioned in the Qur'an (50:17–18, 23):

> Behold, two (guardian angels)
> Appointed to learn (his doings)
> Learn (and note them)
> One sitting on the right
> And the other on the left.

76. *Sharqia,* literally "easterner," a woman from across the mountains. A prostitute or a *sheikha.*

77. In the Zayan region, in the Middle Atlas.

78. Ayt ʿAṭṭa Berber tribesmen.

79. *Zolotiya* is a woman from the village of Bni Zoli.

The men who found Ṭamu were Berber nomads from one of the Ayt ʿAṭṭa groups. Although she was days away from her village, the name of the qṣar was known to them because some people travel to the Draʿ valley with their herds. There are settlements of the same Ayt ʿAṭṭa group in the area surrounding the qṣar. Men also knew each other from the caravan trade, and among those who traveled to the Draʿ valley was a "friend" of her former husband. Ḥadda says, "Shrek mʿa shî waḥd l-khayr," a term of reciprocity that in the context of sedentary/nomad relations may mean that Ṭamu's former husband acted as a "protector" (*zeṭṭat*) of the Ayt ʿAṭṭa man, when the latter visited the qṣar, for instance to buy dates; or vice versa, depending on the particular historical contingency in the relations of the Ayt ʿAṭṭa tribes with the sedentary people of the qṣûr.

80. *Rabbî bînî u bînu,* literally "God between me and him."

81. *Arma,* "thrown thing," like a bag.

82. *Kteb,* he never "wrote," here means never did he engage in sorcery. Magic is also called *l-ketba.*

83. A member of Bni Zoli's most powerful family during the days of the French protectorate, Aḥmed u Baba was the son of the sheikh murdered in 1928 (see part 3). He held the position of sheikh of the village from the early 1930s to his death, in the late 1940s, when the position was taken over by one of his brothers, who ruled until independence (1956).

84. *Khrajt,* like a palm tree.

85. *Iseddaren* (Berber) literally means "beams," as in the beams in a house. Here is the equivalent of the *ḥizb* in Arabic, a chapter of the Qur'an that is recited whole.

86. *Silka* is the serial group recitation of the entire Qur'an, where the different sections are recited simultaneously. The term means "to wire" something together, *selk* means "wire" or "thread." *Silka* is recited at weddings, circumcisions, funerals, and in general as an offering to God.

87. *Ḥizb* is the sixtieth part of the Qur'an; *sabîḥ* is the Muslim rosary.

88. *Kaytʿajjbu,* both "marvel" and "envy"; *l-ʿjeb* is the astonishment of the envious (evil) eye.

89. Inventory of the central elements of the teaching of Islam as Ḥadda reckons them. The categories correspond approximately to those of Malekite Islamic Law. But for Ḥadda, who cannot write anymore, these references are traces from a former landscape. Ibn ʿAshir is a short manual in rhyme (with the rules of ablutions) for the use of beginning students. Bel Walid, Sîdî Abderraḥman al-Mejdûb, and al-Maghrâwî are poets of renown in this region and elsewhere in Morocco (see A. al-Jarârî, *Al-qaṣîda: Zajâl fi al-Maghrib* [Rabat: Maktaba at-talâb, 1969]; for the quatrains of the fifteenth-century mystic Sîdî Abderraḥman al-Mejdûb, see *La tradition orale du Mejdûb,* bilingual edition, 2 vols., ed. A. de Prémare [Aix-en-Provence: Édisud, 1986]).

Finally, notice the idiom of "entering" by which Ḥadda is reckoning his path of learning: entering a *bâb,* "gate," "passage," as in going through the *bîbân* of a text, or the *bîbân* of a divinatory session.

90. Ḥadda specifies *l-ḥlaleb,* "full of dates," *l-gurarej,* "full of flour and lard." These are names of pottery containers: the first (sing. *ḥallâb*) is wide and bowl-shaped, and is used in mixing soup or couscous condiment. The second is the name of the water amphora (*gulla*) when its "mouth" and "hand" are cut off, a mutilated *gulla,* used to store wheat or dates.

91. A local game with a ball and long wooden sticks, similar to hockey, that young men used to play in teams.

92. *Tameskert* (Tashelḥit), *as-shfra* (Arabic), a long bladed tool that people use to cut palm leaves, and the main traditional weapon.

93. *Allâh yaʿṭik l-khayr,* "may God give you goodness," "God bless you."

94. The two words are from different roots (one has an *ḥ,* the other an *h*).

95. Artaud, "Dossier d'Artaud le Mômo," 12:152. My translation:

Freedom, freedom, freedom, freedom.
burning freedom's being
there isn't any
And I believe that to be free
I must first declare myself a prisoner

96. *L-fikr huwwa llî kayftî.* The noun *mufti* and the verb *kay-fti* are different articulations of the same word, to recite answers, to dictate, to understand.

97. The *ḥarîra* (or *ḥsa,* Tashelḥit *askif*) is one of the basics of the local diet. Made from barley semolina and spices, it is the traditional morning meal, and in general is used as an image of what is simple, basic, and good in terms of food.

98. Khadija was Ḥadda's wife at the time. All told Ḥadda had four wives: the first he divorced as a young man; the second he left after his father died; with the third he moved to the garden, and after many years she left him; and now he lives with the fourth.

99. *Makhzen,* the "state." Here simply the authorities, who in this case are the local French adminstrators.

100. Faṭima Salem was a *sheikha,* a woman singer who lived in the qṣar in the 1940s and 1950s. She was originally from an Arab village and did not speak Berber, but she was respected by most as a mistress of words, a skilled poet.

In this context Ḥadda's reference to her means many things. Considering that he is talking about his father's criticism (one might even call it a curse: and in fact people in the qṣar say that Ḥadda was cursed by his father never to be a successful poet), it means that he had gone astray and spent his time in the brothel—however metaphorical this might be. Faṭima Salem, the singer and the prostitute, becomes an image of his own prostitution, of the alienation of his father's name. A moment before it was his father, Sîdî Moḥamed u l-Ḥajj, who had taken a corrupted path. At the same time, reference to Faṭima Salem indicates that Ḥadda had surrendered to the feminine side of himself, the poetical one, as hinted at by the wording of his mother's invocation below. The singer and Ḥadda remained good friends until her death, a few years ago.

101. It is an image from the Qur'anic legend of Joseph, told in oral tales as the story of Sidna Yusuf.

102. *B-ṣṣahd htîra,* literally "consumed by utter heat."

103. The poem of the candle is not Ḥadda's composition, but a well-known poem in Morocco, and almost a genre on itself. Ḥadda's version is, however, different from most published or recorded versions. Yet the general thrust of the composition is consistent with the others: a man questions a candle about the cause of her tears, tells her his own story of suffering, and she replies with her story. (Cf. the commercial recording (Titcka-phone) of *qaṣîda ash-shma*ʿ in the poetic genre of *malḥun,* by al-Ḥajj Lḥussein Tulâlî.)

*Qaṣida as-shma*ʿ, "the poem of the candle," belongs to a genre of popular oral poetry in colloquial Arabic called *l-malḥûn* (from the verbal root *laḥna,* to compose, to set to music). It has also been adapted to other styles, and was performed by the Moroccan pop band Jîl Jilâla. The poetic genre of l-malḥûn is related to other genres of oral poetry in colloquial language, such as that of *rasma,* specific to the poetic tradition of the Draʿ valley (see part 3). Like rasma, a poem of malḥûn is composed to be sung, within a metrical mold that is first given as a tune for the voice. The wording of malḥûn poems, however, tends to be less hermetic than in rasma compositions, and hence more accessible to a large audience. Poems often make use of everyday language and celebrate or mourn events from daily life. This is why, with the spread of the media and the commercialization of audiotapes, l-malḥun has become something close to Morocco's national poetry in colloquial Arabic. The scholarly and mediatic attention dedicated to it during the nationalist period and after independence contributed to its reputation. (The other poetic and musical genre associated with the national image and mediatically spread nationwide is al-Andalusîa, also known as *al-âla,* a genre of *taqsîm* instrumental music and sung poetry in classical Arabic, and originally from Muslim Andalusia. Both l-malḥûn and al-âla remain, however, mainly urban genres.)

According to Ḥadda, and in general in the view of people from the Draʿ valley, the style of l-malḥûn—which blossomed in the traditional urban environment of cities such as Marrakesh and Meknes—is an urban refinement and instrumental adaptation of compositions that originated elsewhere, namely in the south. A genre known in the Draʿ valley as *aqallâl* (from *qâla,* "to speak or recite") is viewed as the ancestor of l-malḥûn. The poem of *sh-shma*ʿ, "the candle," used to be sung by Ḥadda in this style.

For a history of l-malḥûn in Morocco, see al-Jarârî, *Al-qaṣîda,* and the influential work of M. al-Fâsî, *Maʿlamat al-malḥûn,* 3 vols. (Rabat: Publications de l'Académie du Royaume du Maroc, n.d.).

104. *Lisân al-ʿârab,* by Ibn al-Manẓûr, A.H. 630–711 (circa 1311). *Lisân al-ʿârab* is an analytic dictionary in 15 volumes, for the use of poets. Its first print edition dates from 1892. The entry "FTN" is found in volume 13, under section "F" (*al-fâ*).

I thank Abdelahad Sebti, Abdesalam Bahi, and Mustapha Kamal for help with the translation from Arabic and the interpretation of this text at various steps. There are a few passages we decided to skip for the sake of readability.

We tried to leave in Arabic the term *fitna* and its cognates as much as possible in the translation, to convey the spiral textual play between interpreting and interpreted language that characterizes both Ibn al-Manẓûr's commentary on fitna and the concept of fitna itself.

105. The tree of Zaqqûm is a bitter and pungent tree described as growing at the bottom of Hell. "For it is a tree that springs out of the bottom of Hell-fire: the shoots of its fruit stalks are like the head of devils" (Qur'an 37:64–65).

106. A *masdar* is a verbal noun. "The nomina verbi are abstract substantives which express the action, passion, or state indicated by the corresponding verbs, without any reference to object, subject or time. The nomen verbi is also called *masdar* (lit. the place whence anything goes forth, where it originates), because most Arabic grammarians derive the compound idea of the finite verb from the simple idea of this substantive" (W. Wright, *A Grammar of the Arabic Language* [1859; reprint, Cambridge: Cambridge University Press, 1971], 110).

107. That is, in this case, *al-maftûn* would be a passive participle. *Futina* is the passive of *fatana.*

108. *Al-maftûn* would be a passive participle, a person striken by fitna.

109. Bilâl was the muezzin of the Prophet. The Ramḍâ' is an unbearably hot part of the desert. Tortured by the unbelievers, Bilâl was laid down on the sand with a huge stone on his chest. Abû Bakr al-Siddiq bought him back from his master and freed him.

PART 3: LOSS: THE SPHERE OF THE MOON

1. J. L. Borges, "Remordimiento por cualquier muerte," in *Obras completas* (Buenos Aires: Emecé Editores, 1974), 1:33.

> Free of memory and hope
> without limit, abstract, almost future,
> a corpse is not a dead man: it is death. . . .

2. In Moroccan vernacular *sheṭṭeb* means "to sweep"—as in sweeping the floor, but also as in sweeping off something. In classical Arabic *shaṭaba* (root *shṭb*) means to cut into slices or strips, to strike out, to cross out, to scratch out, write off, to erase or efface, to cancel (*Hans Wehr Dictionary of Modern Written Arabic*). In the local use of the qṣar, in the oral historical narratives in particular, both sets of meanings are mobilized. The vernacular *sheṭṭbî* is an imperative in the feminine form of the verb, for in the dream it is addressed to me.

3. These poems are discussed below, in "Tell Me Sunken Well."

4. *Qbûr mensiya,* literally "forgotten tombs" (sing. *qber mensî,* "a forgotten tomb," or *l-qber l-mensî,* "the forgotten tomb"), a technical term in the magical-medical texts and in current discourse. In classical Arabic *qabr mansî,* or *al-qabr al-mansî,* "the forgotten tomb," from the verbal root *nsy,* "to forget, efface, or obliterate."

5. *ʿAshûra* is the tenth day of the month of Muḥarram in the Muslim calendar. It is a day of mourning sacred to the Shiites (for it commemorates the martyrdom of Ḥusayn at Karbala), and in the local culture of this region is treated as the day of the dead. All over Morocco ʿAshurâ is also the time in which a variety of transgressive rituals are performed.

6. A. Suyûṭi (1445–1505), *Kitâb al-raḥma fi al-ṭibb wa al-ḥikma* (Beirut: Dâr al-Qalâm, n.d.), 134. This text is one of the reference texts used by Si Lḥassan, the *fqîh* of the qṣar, for his magical-medical prescriptions. The chapter on the remedies of love immediately follows the medical chapters on the different types of fever, as if the illness of love were a fever of the heart. In each of the magical remedies described the crucial element for release is the *qber mensî,* the forgotten tomb. This chapter of Suyûṭî is discussed by E. Doutté in *Magie et religion dans l'Afrique du Nord* (1908; reprint, Paris: Geuthner 1984), 225, 301.

About the magic of death and of the "tombe oubliée," Doutté writes: "Le cadavre joue en effet un role capitale dans la magie noire. Le mort ne pouvant plus ni parler ni voir ni entendre, doit transmettre son impuissance. . . . La mort etant d'ailleurs une chose contagieuse doit pouvoir se transmettre aux vivants et les faire mourir. Par example les aliments preparés avec la main d'un cadavre doivent avoir de terribles propriétés. . . . La terre du tombeau participe aux vertus du cadavre lui-même et est souvent employée par la sorcellerie. Elle a surtout la propriété de faire oublier les peines et, par suite, de consoler. Cette propriété, de provoquer l'oubli, appartient sûrtout au tombeau dans lequel est un mort dont on ne connait plus le nom. Le *qbor mensi* (*qabr mansi*) ou 'tombe oubliée' est fameux dans la magie musulmane. Nous en avons déjà vu plusieurs fois l'emploi au cours de ce chapitre: il est surtout classique dans les recettes destinées à faire oublier un grand amour" (302–3).

In an article entitled "Al qbor al mensi, la tombe oubliée," by M. Djeribi (in *Psychanalystes,* "L'islam au singulier," no. 40 [1992], 44), an interpretation is proposed in terms of the Freudian notions of the forgetting of the name and of the work of mourning. The author's conclusion addresses directly the themes of loss I discuss here: "Pour que quelque chose commence, il faut que quelque chose tombe, dans l'ordre du langage comme dans l'ordre des choses magiques, que se constitue un trou sans nom, une chute dans l'innommable, afin que s'élabore, par un rapport latéral, superficiel, vocalique, l'errance toujours bénéfique dans la chaîne des associations, que passe le courant 'sympathique' comme on l'appelle dans la théorie de la magie, et qui n'est autre que ce courant de pensées épinglant des signifiants-choses et permettant au sujet de prendre le large pour sortir du face-à-face muet avec la mort. Cette mouvance ne se met en branle qu'a partir d'un trou de mémoire sur un nom propre, d'une trace effacée d'une voix qui se tait et qui, comme une tombe oubliée, fait, par l'appel du vide, circuler le sens." (For something to begin, something else needs to fall, in the order of language as in that of magical things; a nameless hole must take shape, a fall into the unnameable, so that it might develop, by way of a lateral relationship, superficial and vocalic, that always beneficial *errance* in the chain of association. [That errance] makes a "sympathetic" current flow (as this is called in the theory of magic), which is but the flow of thoughts pinned on signifiers-things, allowing the subject to clear off and withdraw from the speechless face-to-face with death. This movement can be set in motion only from a blank of memory, from the loss of a proper name: from the trace yet effaced of a voice lapsing into silence, which, like a forgotten grave, makes meaning circulate by the call of the void [*vide*] [my translation].)

7. The verb *nsa,* "to forget," and the noun *nsâ,* "women" (which only exists in the plural, or in some derivative forms, e.g., the adjective *niswy,* "feminine"), do not have grammatical kinship, in as much as "to forget" comes from a root *nasya,* and "women" from a root *nas'a.* In the colloquial use, however (and over 60 percent of the population is illiterate—or, to be more precise, is "orally literate"), they are unquestionably associated. *Nsa* becomes the feminine root of oblivion.

8. S. Freud, "The Uncanny" ("Das Unheimliche"), 1919, in *Standard Edition of the Complete Psychological Works,* trans. J. Strachey, vol. 17 (London: Hogarth Press, 1955). In his circular search for a definition of the concept of the *Unheimlich,* which literally means "unhomely," Freud cites Schelling, "Unheimlich is the name for everything that ought to have remained . . . secret and hidden but has come to light."

The phrase "the side of the moon" is from Ibn al-ʿArabî. See below.

9. R. M. Rilke, *The Notebooks of Malte Laurids Brigge,* trans. M. D. Herter Norton (New York: Norton, 1964).

10. The image is Freud's.

11. Cf., for instance, Ibn Khaldûn, *The Muqaddima: An Introduction to History,* vol. 3, trans. F. Rosenthal (Princeton: Princeton University Press, 1967); J. E. Bencheikh, *Poétique arabe* (Paris: Gallimard, [1975] 1989).

12. A. Khatibi, *Figures de l'étranger* (Paris: Denoel, 1987). "Not folklore, then, nor some kind of colonial literature, but a writing of the Outside that welcomes the locus of the other inside my language, in the space of my imagination. This energy that furrows the space between us is offered to our real relationship, to our asymmetric distance, unbound, open to the Outside. I cannot find myself in it" (my translation).

13. L. Aragon, *Le fou d'Elsa,* cited by Lacan in *Les quatre concepts fondamentaux de la psychanalyse* (Paris: Seuil, 1973), 21. "Turning towards me, you will encounter/on the wall of my gaze only your dreamt-of shadow" (*The Four Fundamental Concepts of Psychoanalysis,* trans. A. Sheridan [New York: Norton, 1978], 17, translation modified).

14. J. Lacan, "Fonction et champ de la parole et du langage," in *Écrits* (Paris: Seuil, 1966), 1:160, 177–78 ("c'est une parole en plein exercice, car elle inclut le discours de l'autre dans le secret de son chiffre"), my translation.

15. Lacan, *Les quatre concepts,* 1:85, "Jamais tu ne me regarde là où je te vois."

16. Ibn al-ʿArabî, *Al-futûḥât al-makkiyya,* translated and cited by W. C. Chittick, *The Sufi Path of Knowledge: Ibn al-ʿArabî's Metaphysics of the Imagination* (Albany: State University of New York Press, 1989), 124.

17. S. Freud, *The Interpretation of Dreams,* trans. J. Strachey [New York: Avon Books, 1965], 37, and note 1. On dreams and the "daemonic" see also page 652. "In

the two works of Aristotle which deal with dreams, they have already become a subject for psychological study. We are told that dreams are not sent by the gods and are not of a divine character, but that they are 'daemonic,' since nature is 'daemonic' and not divine." This text was revised in 1914; in a note the old version does not speak of nature, but of a difficulty of translation: "Aristotle declares that dreams are of a 'daemonic' but not of a 'divine' nature; no doubt this distinction has some great significance if we knew how to translate it correctly."

18. Aristotle, "On Dreams" and "On Divination in Sleep," in *The Complete Works of Aristotle*, vol. 1, ed. J. Barnes (Princeton: Princeton University Press, 1984), 738.

19. Aristotle, "On Divination in Sleep," 738. Aristotle adds that this explains why those who can best foresee the future are usually simple people, "for the mind of such persons is not given to thinking, but as it were, derelict or totally vacant, and, when once set moving, is borne passively in the direction taken by that which moves it. With regard to the fact that some persons who are liable to derangement have foresight, its explanation is that their normal mental movements do not impede the alien movements, but are beaten off by them. This is why they have an especially keen perception of the alien movements."

20. Ibn al-ʿArabî, *Al-futûḥât al-makkiyya*, cited in Chittick, *Sufi Path of Knowledge*, 120.

21. Under the voice "transfert" in the *Vocabulaire de la psychanalyse* (by J. Laplanche and J. B. Pontalis [Paris: PUF, 1973], 492), one reads: "The French term *transfert* does not properly belong to the psychoanalytic vocabulary. It has in fact a very general sense, close to that of *transport* [carrying over, transporting, moving, emotional transport towards another person], but that entails a displacement of values, of rights, of entities, rather than a material displacement of objects (e.g., transfer of funds, transfer of property, etc.)" (my translation). In French there is only one term, *transfert*, that includes both the English *transfer* and *transference*.

22. J. Breuer and S. Freud, *Studies on Hysteria* (1895), trans. and ed. J. Strachey (New York: Basic Books, 1987).

23. Ibid., 70n.

24. "This procedure was one of clearing away the pathogenic psychical material layer by layer, and we liked to compare it with the technique of excavating a buried city" (ibid., 139).

25. Lacan, *Les quatres concepts*, 36. "What shows itself, shows itself only under a *Verkleidung*, a disguise, and fake as well" (*Four Fundamental Concepts*, 35, translation modified).

26. Like *barzakh*, a Persian word that means "barrier" or "limit," taken in by Arabic and used as such in the Qur'an, the word *limbo* or *limb*, from the Latin *limbus*, means literally "border" or "barrier." In Roman Catholic theology Limbo is a resting place of souls barred from Heaven for having died without sin, but without having been baptized. It is traditionally known as the suspended abode of the souls of children born dead. For a discussion of the barzakh both in the Maghribî oral imagination and in the Qur'anic use, see below.

27. *Four Fundamental Concepts*, 23, 30, translation modified.

> L'inconscient, d'abord, se manifeste à nous comme quelque chose qui se tient en attente dans l'aire, dirai-je, du non-né. . . . Cette dimension est assurement à evoquer dans un registre qui n'est rien d'irréel, ni de deréel, mais de non-réalisé. Ce n'est jamais sans danger qu'on fait remuer quelque chose dans cette zone de larves. . . . Tout discours n'est pas ici inoffensif . . . ce n'est pas en vain que, même dans un discours public, on vise les sujets, et qu'on les touche à ce que Freud appelle le nombril—nombril des rêves—écrit-il pour en désigner, au dernier terme, le centre d'inconnu—qui n'est point autre chose, comme le nombril anatomique même qui le représente, que cette béance dont nous parlons.
>
> . . . J'ai évoqué la fonction des limbes, j'aurais pu aussi bien parler de ce que, dans les constructions de la Gnose, on appelle les êtres intermédiaires—sylphes, gnomes, voire formes plus élevées de ces médiateurs ambigus.

Lacan, *Les quatre concepts,* 26, 32.

28. Lacan, "Fonction et champ" (Paris: Seuil, Points), 1:186. "Through what and for whom the subject is posing its question" (my translation).

29. Lacan, *Four Fundamental Concepts,* 147. "L'inconscient, que je vous représent à la fois comme ce qui est de l'intérieur du sujet, mais qui ne se réalise qu'au-dehors, c'est-à-dire dans ce lieu de l'Autre où seulement il peut prendre son statut" (*Les quatre concepts,* 134).

30. Lacan, *Les quatre concepts,* 134, 133.

31. These early considerations on the question of transference in analysis are to be found in Freud's writings on technique ("The Dynamics of Transference" [1912] and "Observations on Transference-Love" [1915], in *Therapy and Technique* [New York: Macmillan, 1963]). The quotations are from "Dynamics of Transference," 109, 115.

32. S. Freud, "Further Recommendations in the Technique of Psychoanalysis: Recollection, Repetition, and Working Through" (1914), in *Therapy and Technique* (New York: Macmillan, 1963), 157–66.

33. J. Breuer and S. Freud, "On the Psychical Mechanism of Hysterical Phenomena" (1883), in *Studies on Hysteria,* 7.

The opposition recollection/repetition, already central in *Studies on Hysteria* in the form of reminiscence/rememoration, is indeed a classic one, and can be traced back to Aristotle's "De memoria et reminiscentia"; cf. Aristotle, "On Memory."

The expression *les maladies de la mémoire,* "memory disorders," among which "amnesia" was of course central, was current at the end of the nineteenth century, in the medical and philosophical climate that led, for Breuer and Freud, to the redaction of *Studies on Hysteria.* See M. S. Roth, "Remembering Forgetting: *Maladies de la mémoire* in Nineteenth-Century France," *Representations* 26 (spring 1989): 49–68.

34. Lacan, *Les quatre concepts,* 49. "The subject in himself [*chez soi*], the recollection of his biography, all this goes only to a certain limit, which is known as the real. . . . Here the real is that which always comes back to the same place—the place where the subject in so far as he thinks, where the *res cogitans,* does not meet with it" (*Four Fundamental Concepts,* 49).

35. Freud, "The Uncanny" (1917) and *Beyond the Pleasure Principle* (1921), trans. J. Strachey (New York: Norton, 1961).

36. Lacan, *Four Fundamental Concepts,* 54, slightly modified. "Le lieu complet, total, du réseau des signifiants, c'est-à-dire le sujet, là où c'était depuis toujours le rêve. A cette place, les anciens reconnaissaient toutes sortes de choses, et à l'occasion des messages des dieux" (*Les quatre concepts,* 45).

37. It is in this direction that I understand the theses of Jeanne Favret-Saada on the intersubjective entanglements and the fundamental "unknowledge" that characterize the effectiveness of both the psychoanalytic and the ethnographic encounter (J. Favret-Saada, *Les mots, la mort, les sort* [Paris: Gallimard, 1979]; J. Favret-Saada and J. Contreras, "L'embrayeur de violence," in J. Contreras, J. Favret-Saada, and J. Hochmann, *Le moi et l'autre* [Paris: Denoel, 1985], and especially "La thérapie sans le savoir," *Nouvelle Revue de Psychanalyse* [1985], "Les Actes").

38. "Ici, dans le champ du rêve, tu es chez toi" (Lacan, *Les quatre concepts,* 45).

39. Unlike most of the dreams in the book, it is not Freud's own dream. It was repeated it to him by a patient who had heard it at a lecture, was impressed, and went on to "redream" it: "to repeat some of its elements in a dream of her own." There is a gift, at the origin of this dream about returns (Freud, *Interpretation of Dreams,* 547–50; the text of the dream follows on the same page).

40. Ibid., 564.

41. G. Comolli, "Padre, non vedi che brucio? Dall'alienazione del soggetto al campo delle trasformazioni oggettive," in *Aut Aut,* May–August 1980, 3–27. My reading of this dream owes much to that essay.

42. Freud, *Interpretation of Dreams,* 547–48.

43. "The City of Brass," in *Stories from the Thousand and One Nights,* trans. W. Lane (New York: Collier, 1909), 16:321. A. Kilito proposes a suggestive reading of this story as "La cité des morts," in *L'oeil et l'aiguille: Essai sur Les Milles et une Nuits* (Paris: La Découverte, 1992). See also A. Hamori, "An Allegory from the Arabian Nights: The City of Brass," in *The Art of Medieval Arabic Literature* (Princeton: Princeton University Press, 1974).

44. Kilito, "La cité des morts," 96.

45. "God says [to the soul at death], 'We have now unveiled from you your covering and your sight today is piercing' " (Qur'an 50:22).

46. Lacan, *Four Fundamental Concepts,* 59, translation slightly modified. "Car ce n'est pas que, dans le rêve, il soutienne que le fils vit encore. Mais l'enfant mort prenant son père par le bras, vision atroce, désigne un au-délà qui se fait entendre dans le rêve. Le désir se présentifie de la perte imagée au point le plus cruel de l'objet. C'est dans le rêve seulement que peut se faire cette rencontre vraiment unique. Seul un rite, un acte toujours répété, peut commémorer cette rencontre immémorable—puisque personne ne peut dire ce que c'est la mort d'un enfant—sinon le père en tant que père—c'est-à-dire nul être conscient" (*Les quatres concepts,* 58).

47. In an essay on the work of Segalen entitled "Celebration de l'exote" (in *Figures de l'étranger*), A. Khatibi speaks of traveling as the "exiting" that makes possible writing and that is, he says, a "rencontre avec l'inassimilable," an encounter with that which cannot possibly be made one's own. This, of course, touches at the core of that kind of "exiting" which is ethnography—at least ethnography as is in-

tended in the present work. But "exiting" is not just traveling. Segalen, warns Khatibi, distinguishes three modes of traveling: that of the "tourist" ("even a great artist can be one"), that of the "folklorist" (as a writer or an *ethnologue*), and a way that he names with a neologism as the Exote. While the tourist never leaves home, and the ethnologist looks at the other with a gaze he or she trusts to be "impersonal and neutral," a gaze that looks back at home while seizing and encompassing the other's difference (this is how Khatibi defines "l'ethnologie coloniale"), only the exote practices "l'inassimilable": the encounter based on an *égalité dissymétrique,* with a nonsymmetric equal, which is the "practice of this difference, and of this dignity." Only the Exote exits the home, looks elsewhere, and is displaced and destabilized by that look, where "I cannot find myself," at least not in the same place. Only the exote recognizes that "I can never *possess* the other, reduce him in his reality, and even less in his imaginary."

> Voyager, Écrire? Pourquoi doit-on voyager pour écrire? Qu'est-ce que l'Exote? . . .
>
> Pas de folklore donc, ni de littérature coloniale, mais une écriture du Dehors qui acueille le lieu de l'autre dans mon langage, dans mon espace imaginaire. Différence distante: c'est lorsque l'autre est maintenu, respecté dans sa singularité que je peux être reçu peut-être par lui. . . . Cette énergie qui se creuse entre lui et moi est offerte à notre relation réelle, à notre distance dissymétrique, incontournable, ouverte vers le Dehors. Je ne peux pas m'y retrouver. . . . Je ne peux jamais posséder l'autre, le réduire dans son réel, encore moins dans son imaginaire. L'Exote ne m'assimile pas: "Partons de cet aveu d'impénétrabilité. . . ."
>
> En tant qu'exote, je m'initie à la rencontre avec l'autre. Rencontre en tant que quête initiatique, car aussi bien l'autre que moi sommes des étrangers dans la vie, la mort et la survie. C'est pourquoi je voyage sur cette terre, et il n'y en a pas d'autre pour Segalen. (24, 28, 29)

48. Ibn al-ʿArabî, *Al-futûḥât al-makkiyya,* cited in Chittick, *Sufi Path of Knowledge,* 121.

49. M. Blanchot, *L'espace littéraire* (Paris: Gallimard, 1955), 361. "He who dreams sleeps, but already he who dreams is he who sleeps no longer. He is not another, some other person, but the premonition of the other, of that which cannot say "I" any more, which recognizes itself neither in itself nor in others" (*The Space of Literature,* trans. A. Smock [Lincoln: University of Nebraska Press, 1982], 267).

50. The figure of the "small death" is commonly found in the colloquial understanding of sleep and dreaming, but is also rooted in the Sufi philosophical tradition, and, indirectly, in the Qurʾan. While Ibn al-ʿArabî repeatedly cites the Qurʾanic verse (50:22) on death as unveiling and equates death and sleep in as much as both give access, in different degrees, to witnessing the object of belief, al-Ghazâlî compares life to sleeping and death to awakening. In this paradoxical sense sleep itself (as a temporary death) is a form of awakening, for it makes possible dreaming, which puts a person in contact with the "unseen": "God most high . . . has favored His creatures by giving them something analogous to the special faculty of prophecy, namely dreams. In the dream-state a man apprehends what is to be in the future, which is

something of the unseen" (al-Ghazâlî, *Munqidh min ad-ḍalâl,* trans. W. Montgomery Watt, *The Faith and Practice of al-Ghazâlî* [Oxford: Oneworld, 1953], 68).

In the classical dictionary *Lisân al-ʿârab* (Ibn al-Manẓûr [Beirut: Dâr Sâdir, 1968]), both sleep and dreaming, along with other "states of absence" of a gnostic type, are discussed under the entry *al-mawt,* "death," as death's closest associates. Sleep and death are defined reciprocally as a "light death," and a "heavy sleep." For a discussion of the "states of absence" (*ghîba*) that resemble death, among them sleep and dreaming, see also Ibn Khaldûn, *Muqaddima,* vol. 1.

51. In her study of the sanctuary of Bouya Omar, an important center for the traditional cure of the possessed and mentally ill in Morocco, Khadija Naamouni describes in some detail the effective and "judicial" economy of dreaming, and gives examples of dreams that once interpreted—by a *mul al-idn,* an "authorized" bearer of the *baraka* of the saint, or simply by the community of patients—have brought changes to the patient's symbolic status, and eventually release from seclusion within the territory of the saint. For the couple patient-jinn is "imprisoned" by the saint, and on his premises, for long months and often years until the dream that will bring release. Cf. K. Naamouni, *Le Culte de Bouya Omar* (Casablanca: Éditions Eddif, 1993).

52. In an article on Moroccan dreaming Vincent Crapanzano discusses the structuring function of dreams in the text of a person's life, and reports among others a dream that could be called "foundational," both in terms of the role it plays in the dreamer's life and of the imagery it mobilizes. Moḥammed was a man from Marrakesh, who lived in Meknes with his family but had decided, somewhat despite himself, to move back to his hometown. The night before departure he dreamed that he was in the esplanade of the sanctuary of Sheikh al-Kâmel in Meknes: "There was a place there that was very well swept. It was washed. There was a pole in the center. . . . I sat down and suddenly I saw someone come out of the window next to the door to [the sanctuary of] Sheikh al-Kamal. The man was tall, he was in a white chemise, he had a hammer in his hand. He came up to the pole and looked at me. 'Are you not ashamed to want to leave?' he asked. He hammered the pole all the way into the ground. When the pole was hammered in, he said, 'You can stay or leave.' The man disappeared. . . . Then I told my wife to unpack everything" (V. Crapanzano, "Saints, Jnun, and Dreams: An Essay in Moroccan Ethnopsychology," *Psychiatry* 38, no. 2 [1975], reprinted in *Hermes' Dilemma and Hamlet's Desire* [Cambridge: Harvard University Press, 1991]). Through the imagery of the "swept space" and the "pole," which the saint hammers in, the dream *provides a ground.* In this "swept space"—a blank of meaning—the word of the saint can be heard, a sending from Elsewhere, which, like the hammering of the pole (literalization of a metaphor) authorizes the man to settle in Meknes. In the context of my discussion, I view this dream as containing a metanarrative about dreaming: dreams hammer in poles, they create points of orientation. (Hammering poles, settling, fixing: *rasm,* a recurring term in this text; *uted,* "poles, *rasm/shtb,* "fixing/sweeping" are structuring images in the discourse of the qṣar.)

53. "De quelques hadiths relatifs au rêve," in Ibn Sirîn, *L'interprétation des rêves dans la tradition islamique* (Lyon: Alif Éditions, 1992), 223–24.

54. *Azrûg* is a cosmetic black substance.

55. Ibn Khaldûn, *Muqaddima,* vol. 1, chap. 1, sec. 6.

56. Ibn al-ʿArabî, cited in Chittick, *Sufi Path of Knowledge,* 14.

57. The term *ṣârûkh* technically means "rocket," as can be found in the standard Arabic dictionary. But thoughout Morocco it is also the vernacular term for "satellite" (metonymically, rockets carry satellites), for there is no specific term.

58. "They ask thee concerning the Spirit (of inspiration) [*ar-rûḥ*]. Say: The Spirit [comes] by command of my Lord: of knowledge it is only a little that it is communicated to you, (O men!)" (Qur'an, 17:85).

59. See *Hans Wehr Dictionary of Modern Written Arabic* for standard Arabic dictionary glosses below.

60. "The *ruḥânî* makes the *nefs* go up and down": here it means that it makes the person keep breathing during sleep, while the rûḥ has vacated the body. In this context *nefs* should be understood as "breath," "respiration." When instead, earlier in the conversation, Si Lḥassan spoke of nefs as the individual soul, locus of the desire from which the dream is triggered, the nefs is understood as the locus of imagination and desire in the person, the "self" (also in the modern psychological sense). For Ibn al-ʿArabî the *nefs* (classical *nafs*) is the imaginative faculty, which corresponds in the microcosm of the person to the cosmic realm of the Imaginal World, the *ʿâlam al-mithâl*. Many of Si Lḥassan's considerations about the couple *rûḥ/ruḥânî* during sleep and dreaming resemble considerations formulated in terms of the nafs in the writings of Ibn al-ʿArabî and in the Qur'an. For instance, in the Qur'anic verse cited by Si Lḥassan, "God takes the souls at death, and of those who die not, during their sleep," the term translated as "soul" is *nufûs* (pl. of *nafs*). It is the nafs that, according to the Qur'an, undergoes temporary death during sleep, while Si Lhassan talks of the "exit" of the rûḥ during sleep. Yet it would be wrong to say that Si Lḥassan uses the concept of rûḥ/soul in the place of that of nafs/soul. Because the rûḥ, in this context, is the metaphysical concept of the soul as immortal spirit, which is "settled" or "attached" (as Si Lhassan says) to a body for the space of a life, but is essentially disengaged, and does not belong in the person. The nefs instead is mortal, irreducibly attached to the person, in fact it is the person herself. Hence, while a person's nefs is "taken by God" during sleep, the rûḥ "exits" the body, returns for the interval of sleeping to its disengaged, untied, impersonal, immortal, but also virtual form.

61. In the technical use of the concept of rûḥ in weaving, the first operation in the "closing" of a loom is the "capturing" of the rûḥ.

62. Cited in Chittick, *Sufi Path of Knowledge*, 117.

63. *ʿAyn d-dâr*, "the eye of the house," internal light well. Cf. part 1.

64. *Bismillâh ar-raḥmân ar-raḥîm*, "in the name of God, the Most Merciful, the Most Compassionate" is the opening formula of each sura of the Qur'an (except the ninth), and is repeated at the beginning of every act that one wants to dedicate to God. It is also a formula of protection, and in this context it is a protection from the jinns that haunt the abandoned alley.

65. In property deeds concerning houses located within the ramparts of the qṣar (*fî ḥawz Banî Ṣûlî*), and dating from the eighteenth century, there is mention of two territorial sections that are called *al-qaṣba al-qadîma* and *al-qaṣba al-jadîda*, "the old citadel" and "the new citadel." The location of the "new citadel" corresponds approximately to the current section of the village called Fourth of Ayt Driss, including, perhaps—if one were to follow the architectural style—the Alley of the New Mosque, at the edge of the Fourth of Ayt j-Jdîd, and the Alley of Bû Ṭwîl, in the Fourth of Ayt ʿAbdallah. From the written records it can be inferred that the "new citadel" was built as an addition to an already existing settlement, before the con-

struction of the fortified ramparts and the moat surrounding the qṣar. It is therefore possible that, consistently with the oral accounts, it was built to house a settlement of "foreigners," perhaps families related to a military garrison—the *ḥarka* mentioned in the narratives. The architecture of the two sections of the qṣar is quite different. While in the "old" section, houses are significantly smaller and alleys are winding and narrow, in the "new" section, especially in the upper Ḥarâr quarters, houses are much larger and alleys are wider and relatively straight.

66. W. Benjamin, "The Image of Proust," in *Illuminations*, ed. H. Arendt, trans. H. Zohn (New York: Schocken Books, 1969).

67. Si Lḥussein died in the winter of 1989. I wish to thank his children, Si Brahim, Mina Lḥussein, Lḥassan, ʿAbdallah, Si Moḥ, Khadija Lḥussein, and Lâllâ Shto, for permitting me to publish a translation of part of their father's conversations with me. Like me, they find the text of Si Lḥussein's recitation poetic and moving. ʿAbdallah made a first Arabic transcription of the tape on which this text is based. Si Brahim and Mina Lḥussein participated in the conversations with their father over a period of several months. Mina had a way of making herself heard by speaking in Si Lḥussein's ear, and transmitted to him my questions, or Si Brahim's questions. But for the most part our "listening sessions" were a way for Si Lḥussein to narrate the painful memories that disturbed his nights; and the tape recorder became a vehicle of poetic release. I believe he also intended his narratives, and especially this particular one, as a moral warning for us—people of a younger generation—who had no direct memory of the horrors he had witnessed.

Even though Si Lḥussein's language of choice was Berber (like everyone in the qṣar he was bilingual), in these conversations he spoke Arabic for my benefit. Si Lḥussein had a fairly good sense of who I was, culturally and psychologically, and made this known to me on several occasions. For fifteen years of his life—partly as a consequence of his disillusion with his adoptive land and the horrors he describes in this narrative—he had lived as an immigrant in Larache, a coastal town in the Spanish colony of northern Morocco, and had worked in the agricultural firm of a Spanish colon—who was a Republican and a writer. Si Lḥussein was still fond of the memory of José Maria, the Spaniard who became his friend and proposed that he become his associate, and in several of our conversations (which I could not include in this text) he narrates life in Larache and his relationship with the Spanish colon. In the 1950s, just before independence, he eventually decided to take his family back to the qṣar and live off the few gardens he had acquired with his savings. At the time of our conversations, Si Lḥussein was in his nineties, while his children were still relatively young (Mina, the youngest, was in her twenties), because after a first disappointing marriage with a cousin from the zâwya, he had not remarried until he was in his fifties.

68. All the names of places in this dream are names of areas in the gardens (*jnânât*) surrounding the qṣar. The gardens belong for the most part to residents of the village, and are considered under its jurisdiction (for public matters concerning the irrigation network, for instance). Tiqoyya is the second major junction of the irrigation system, and it is located in the middle of the gardens; Sâgyât Astur is the "alien" canal in the village territory, because it carries water that goes to the other villages downstream; and Tamdet nIgjgalen is an "impasse," a depression that becomes a swamp in the rain. *Tamdet*, in Berber, means "swamp" or "pond." The whole dream is about fear and impasse: then, the surprising ending about discovering

the same violence within oneself. There is an erotic resonance in the man's last words, and an almost explicit association between sexuality and violence. *Jedba,* "trance," is also a way to talk about orgasm.

69. *Fiya shi* (something is in it) is an expression used for an illness whose suspected cause is the spirits. It is also used for a haunted place.

70. The old word for trance was *fitna,* and the dreamer knows it.

71. In her discussion of the role of the Second World War in Céline's narratives, Julia Kristeva writes that for Céline the war is a "crying out theme": a theme at the edge of the possibility of theme, a figure at the limit of the absence of figuration ("Suffering and Horror," in *Powers of Horror,* trans. L. Roudiez [New York: Columbia University Press, 1982]).

72. Only in 1932 was the French army able to occupy what was to become the military post of Zagora. Partly due to its physical inaccessibility for a motorized army—behind the barrier of the Atlas Mountains—the Draʿ valley remained for a long time among the *zones insoumises,* one of the last to be "pacified" and directly submitted to the colonial administration. (The French officially called the military occupation of new territories *pacification.*)

Yet, during the ten or fifteen years preceding its annexation to the protectorate, the French administration had sought to gain indirect control of the pre-Saharan region through the hand of local leaders—and the active promotion of what the colonial establishment called "le caïdalisme": the concentration of tyrannical power and wealth in the hands of a few big lords, or *caïds* (Arabic *qayḍ*), related in part to their prerogative of extracting taxes from the tribal populations under their armed control. Among the *grands caïds,* the big warlords of southern Morocco, the most powerful by far was the French-invested Glâwî clan. From the dawn of the protectorate at the beginning of this century all the way to the 1950s, the Glâwî clan played a crucial role in internal and international affairs. Named pasha of Marrakesh in 1909 with the indirect support of the French, Thami al-Glâwî officially became a French protégé after 1912; he quickly rose to the role of crucial ally and *homme de main* of the colonial administration, and to that of tyrannical ruler of the Moroccan south. (For a comprehensive discussion of the role of the Glâwî clan in the history of southern Morocco and in the process of capitalist transformation of the region of Marrakesh, see P. Pascon, *Le Haouz de Marrakech,* 2 vols. [Rabat and Paris: Centre Universitaire de la Recherche Scientifique, 1983]; for an analytic discussion of the period of the *grands caïds* and the "anarchy" that preceeded the landing of the French in Casablanca, see A. Laroui, *Les origines sociales et culturelles du nationalisme marocain, 1830–1912* [Paris: Maspero, 1980]).

Since the 1870s the Glâwî family had been established in power in Telwet (in the district of the Glawa tribe), a strategic High Atlas location on a mountain pass used by the caravan trade, and near important salt mines. The first member of the family to receive recognition from the Makhzen and the title of *qayḍ* (*caïd*) from the sultan Moulay Lhassan I is Moḥammed Ibibat, who established himself as a warlord against other lords in the region, started the construction of a big fortress in Telwet, gained the monopoly of the salt trade, instituted a tax on the crossing of the Glawa mountain pass, and started a market where he also collected a tax. Ibibat's two sons, al-Madani and Thami, built the Glâwî empire with the support of the Makhzen first, and of the French admistration later. The use of modern weapons was crucial at first: al-Madani al-Glâwî received or took from the army of Moulay Lhassan I a cannon and modern guns, with which the clan was able to impose its military supremacy on the region (cf. Pascon, *Le Haouz de Marrakech;* G. Maxwell, *Lords of the Atlas: The Rise and Fall of the House of Glawa* [London: Century, 1966]; R. Montagne, *Les Berbères et le Makhzen dans le sud du Maroc: Essai sur la transformation politique des Berbères sédentaires: Groupe Chleuh* [Paris: Alcan 1930]). Then with political intrigue, with the forceful occupation of agricultural land in the region of Marrakesh, and with the imposition of a tax over the different populations of the Atlas Mountains and the pre-Saharan oases, Thami al-Glâwî, al-Madani's younger brother, gained control of the political game in Marrakesh during the period of instability that followed the death of Moulay Lhassan I. Thami was eventually named pasha of Marrakesh by the sultan Moulay Hafid in 1909. His brother-in-law Ḥammou al-Glâwî was named qayḍ of the pre-Saharan region, from Tineghir all the way to Zagora, and made his headquarters in the fortress of Taurirt, near Ouarzazat. The general headquarters of the clan remained in the palace of Telwet. From there the family ruled over the south.

Preparing their landing in Zagora, and using the hand of the Glâwî family, the French maneuvered the chessboard of the local political landscape in the Draʿ valley, fueling animosities between the different Arab and Berber groups, and between those groups and the sedentary populations of the oases. At the same time, they worked at opening a road across the Atlas Mountains, all the way to the southern tip of the Draʿ. The construction of that road (*shanṭi,* from the French *chantier,* "construction site"), connecting Marrakesh to Ouarzazat, and crossing the Atlas Mountains not far from the Glâwî palace of Telwet—is an ineffaceable memory for the people of the Draʿ, who were forced by the Glâwî to work corvées in the winter snows. Yet, partly due to Thami al-Glâwî's ambivalence toward the road project—which meant the end of the clan's absolute arbitrary control over its pre-Saharan empire, and the transferring of that empire to the protectorate administration—the road across the mountains was not completed until 1930.

73. For the French perception of the Draʿ valley in the period immediately preceding military occupation, see Capitaine Pennés and Lieutenant Spillmann, "Les pays inaccessibles du haut Draa: Un essai d'exploration aérienne en collaboration avec le service des affaires indigènes du Maroc," *Revue de Géographie Marocaine,* 1929.

For a history of the conquest through its various steps, written by one of its protagonists shortly before the complete annexion of the Draʿ and the establishment of the French headquarters in Zagora, see G. Spillmann, *Districts et tribus de la haute vallée du Draa* (Paris: Champion, 1931). G. Spillmann, *Les Ait Atta du Sahara et la pacification du Haut Draa* (Paris: Champion, 1933). (For a general discussion of the preprotectorate years, see E. Burke III, *Prelude to Protectorate in Morocco: Precolonial Protest and Resistance, 1860–1912* [Chicago: University of Chicago Press, 1976].)

74. Besides the people of Bni Zoli and the murabiṭîn of the Zâwya of Si Moḥammed u Saʿid (village of Tafetchna, Si Lḥussein's original homeland), the actors mentioned in Si Lḥussein's narrative are al-Glâwî (*l-basha*) the pasha of Marrakesh and "lord" of southern Morocco under French investiture, and various groups from the Ayt ʿAṭṭa Berber nomadic tribal confederation.

Though presented as an individual in people's recollection (l-Glâwî), the Glâwî were a clan. The members of the Glâwî family most concerned in Si Lḥussein's narrative are Thami al-Glâwî, pasha of Marrakesh and lord of Telwet, the qayḍ Ḥammou, stationed in Ouarzazat and lieutenant for the pre-Saharan region, and l-Khalifa

Amzdû, stationed in the fortress of Taznaqt, just outside the qṣar of Bni Zoli. In people's recollection "l-Glâwî" grows to phantasmic dimensions of fear, horror, abuse, and, rarely, respect. In Si Lḥussein's story it is from the palace of Telwet that "he," the Glâwî, extracted heavy taxes and imposed work corvées on the Drawâ. And it is to that castle—a traditionalist-modernist dreamscape full of European gadgets and oriental decoration, with a central heating system and a big parking area for the Glâwî's American cars—that the local notables of the Draʿ traveled for their appeals. And it is in the jails of this palace—an underground horror in people's recollection—that those who fell into "his" disgrace were thrown.

In its rule the Glâwî family deployed all the signs of "traditional" power and authority: violence, generosity, a battery of slaves, conspicuous consumption, mobilization of masses of people, etc. Yet in its practice and inspiration, its style of government was a new, rationalizing sort. Certainly many French administrators at the local level, who saw their action as a "mission for progress," had difficulties accepting the fact that the atrocities committed by the Glâwî clan and their lieutenants—the systematic exploitation of masses of people, the murders, the thefts, the imposition of arbitrary taxes and corvées that reduced to poverty entire communities and destroyed local political and social institutions—were in fact functional and even in harmony with the project of the French protectorate. But the important policy-makers of the French administration were well aware of this fact, and supported the Glâwî family almost until the end. In his social historical study of the region of Marrakesh (*Le Haouz de Marrakech*), P. Pascon cites correspondence of the *maréchal* Lyautey, governor general of Morocco, who, in response to the increasing number of reports of French officers stationed in the south about the atrocities committed by Pasha Thami and his nephew Si Ḥammou against the local populations and their increasingly arbitrary rule, reiterates the strategic need to temporize and to rely on "la politique des grands Caïds." Already in 1912 Lyautey had written (cited in Pascon, *Le Haouz de Marrakech,* 1:325 n. 82): "La question des grands caïds est ici prédominante. Leur rivalités, leur luttes, leur passages constant d'un camp à l'autre, ont été à la base de tous les troubles de cette région. Le problème le plus délicat sera donc de les utiliser en maintenat entre eux la juste mesure." And when in 1918, at the death of al-Madani al-Glâwî, General de Lamothe suggested taking the opportunity to reduce the power of the clan, Lyautey answered: "La situation en Europe et dans le Sud du Maroc actuellement très troublée nous oblige à faire fond sur des gens influents, intelligents, énergiques et surs. Thami est de ceux-la, c'est le seul Glaoui qui réunisse toutes ces conditions. . . . nous avons plus que jamais besoin des Glaoua, en l'espece de Thami" (1:324).

The "feudal" rule of the Glâwî was also stategically functional to the capitalist transformation of the region of Marrakesh, and made possible the colonial *lotissement* and the settlement of French colons. Pascon mentions how Thami al-Glâwî operated a sort of "original accumulation" of agricultural land, by expropriating or simply appropriating by force the agricultural land belonging to the different communities and *qabaʾîl* of the Haouz. He then deported populations from the south, particularly black Ḥarâtîn from the Draʿ valley and surrounding areas, to undertake an ambitious project of *defrichement* (land clearing), as the French called it, and modern irrigation of the agricultural plain, which prepared the region for industrial exploitation.

South of the Atlas the situation was somewhat different, due to the absence of the

French administration and to the armed resistance of the powerful Ayt ʿAṭṭa and Awlâd Yaḥya nomadic groups, which, until the landing of the French army in Zagora, prevented the Glâwî from gaining total control of the region. (Significantly, upon the French landing and the final defeat of the Ayt ʿAṭṭa resistance by the air force [battle of Bû Gafer, Saghru Mountains, 1933], the colonial administration in Zagora sought to gain the sympathies of the local Ayt ʿAṭṭa groups, and protected their interests against the sedentary populations of the qṣûr. Hence all the villages and gardens the Ayt ʿAṭṭa had violently conquered in their struggle against the Glâwî and their allies [which were in fact exploited populations subjected to an imposed servitude], were legitimately granted to them by the protectorate.)

Wherever the Glâwî clan was able to reach, it built a *qṣîba (qaṣba)*, "a fortified castle," in a style that recalls, in the mode of parody, the local earth architecture of the qṣûr. In each qṣîba was stationed a distant member of the family as a *khalifa*, or "lieutenant," and sometimes a garrison of Makhaznyia (from *makhzen*, "state" and "state authority"), in a style mimetic, or perhaps parodic, of the style of the Old Makhzen, the old sultanate, which had come to an end in the 1890s with the death of Moulay Lhassan I. There is documentary evidence that Bni Zoli had been a *guish* village, one of the many settlements all over Morocco that were "touched" in the past by the passage of a *ḥarka*, a traveling army of the sultan, and had kept special ties with the central government. To legitimize his presence within that older tradition, the Glâwî set up a base in Bni Zoli and assigned a khalifa to that post.

Representatives of the Old Makhzen had been intermittently stationed in Bni Zoli for at least two centuries, until 1892, when the last qayḍ was made to leave after the death of the sultan and was later put to death in Marrakesh. He had resided in the Dyâr l-Makhzen, "the Houses of the Makhzen," in the Alley of Ayt l-Qâḍî, and had never interfered with the internal political affairs of the qbîla. When the people of the Glâwî arrived in 1919, invited by one of the powerful factions of the qbîla, they were symbolically offered the Dyâr l-Makhzen for their headquarters. Later, they built a large fortified qṣîba in the desert, a few miles from the qṣar (but within its field of its vision), and attempted to impose their rule on the villages of the region.

Yet because of the interference of the Ayt ʿAṭṭa Berber nomads and of the Awlâd Yaḥya Arab nomads, and because of the complex games played by the various factions in the sedentary villages of the region, which kept switching sides to play out their internal rivalries, the Glâwî never fully succeeded in establishing supremacy in the region of Bni Zoli.

75. *Petrified, mummified,* and *shock* are Benjamin's terms. Cf. *The Origin of the German Tragic Drama* (London: NLB, 1977) and the "Theses on the Philosophy of History," in *Illuminations*, ed. H. Arendt, trans. H. Zohn (New York: Schocken Books, 1969). See also C. Buci-Glucksmann, *La raison baroque: De Baudelaire à Benjamin* (Paris: Galilée, 1984) and S. Buck-Morss, *Walter Benjamin and the Arcades Project* (Boston: MIT Press, 1989).

76. "Le sue parole si 'vedono' a una a una. . . . Naturalmente la lingua, come fatto auditivo, di Brahim, non si puó riprodurre: é vero che come le aste é tutta frontale e lineare, ma tra parola e parola nel tremito, ci sono dei buchi, e a mettere l'occhio in quei buchi viene il capogiro, perché danno su dei baratri" (P. P. Pasolini, "Rital et raton," in *Ali dagli occhi Azzurri* [Milan: Garzanti, 1965], 512).

77. In the scriptural Islamic tradition the two angel inquisitors who question the

soul after death are called Munkir and Nakîr. The questioning itself is known as *ʿadhâb al-qabr,* "the torment of the grave." (See the commentary of al-Ghazâlî, *The Faith and Practice of al-Ghazâlî.*)

In the oral reckoning of the qṣar the two angels are "condensed" into one, referred to as Siwâl, the Questioner, who questions the dead on the first night after burial. The terror of this first night at the threshold of the afterlife is rooted in people's imagination, and in the qṣar a meal is offered to Siwâl in the mosque, to distract the angel from his pitiless job. It is a couscous with wild figs (*qorran*), which are full of seeds. It is said that, occupied counting the seeds, Siwâl will forget to count the sins of the soul. The "birds," in Si Lḥussein's recollection, indicate both the coming of death (death and the birds is a recurrent poetic theme) and the questioning by the angel.

78. Si Lḥussein's original homeland, which he calls Zâwya (Zawyât of Si Moḥamed u Saʿid, located in the village of Tafetchna), is a village of murabiṭin in the mountains, some thirty miles from the qṣar. It is one of the main gravitational zawyât for the people of Bni Zoli; in turn, the qṣar is their marketplace in the valley.

79. *Taqshurt,* "the Faction," literally the "fragment of a broken nutshell." See part 1, "Splinters at l-Hashmi's Funeral," for a discussion of this term.

80. The term *al-makhzen* could be translated as the state, the state authorities, the government; yet neither the concept of makhzen nor its historical practice corresponds to the practice and concept of the modern nation-state (even though, of course, the term *makhzen* in the contemporary Moroccan usage has come to mean the state, the state apparatus such as the police and the authorities in general, including judicial institutions. In the narratives of this book, the term is in some cases used by the speaker to refer to the French colonial administration or to the Glâwî's rule. In future references, I will leave *l-makhzen* untranslated, letting the context clarify its sense.

In this particular case *l-makhzen* is used in an almost phantasmic sense, and refers to the Glâwî. The story beads together and elaborates into a narrative disastrous events from the local history of the village (situated in the larger context of the Wâd Draʿ region), which took place between approximately 1910 and 1930. In the history of Morocco, and in the local history of this region, this is a period of great turmoil, upheavals, and violence, directly and indirectly related to the French establishment of the protectorate in the north (1912) and to the French penetration in the south, through the indirect rule of the Glâwî.

81. Baba is the same Baba mentioned earlier, the sheikh of Bni Zoli during this period, up to his murder in 1928.

At the time the qbîla of Bni Zoli was split between two factions. The split was official, recorded in written documents from the period, and the two factions were named Tulut and Tletayn, literally "the One-Third" and "the Two-Thirds," according to an old system of taxation based on the number of palm trees owned by each independent head of household. Tulut was overall favorable to the Glâwî rule and not opposed to the French; Tletayn was opposed to the Glâwî and on better terms with the Ayt ʿAṭṭa Berber nomads, who were fiercely opposed to the French and the Glâwî.

This is, however, a rough simplification, for the play of alliances inside and outside the qṣar (which included other villages, and another powerful actor, the Awlâd Yaḥya Arab nomads, led by the charismatic Qayḍ L-ʿarabî) was fluid, slippery, and rather unaccountable. Within the qṣar Baba was the leader of the pro-Glâwî faction (although he himself did not favor the Glâwî rule and was murdered before the arrival of the French); the man by the name of Moḥamed u Saʿid mentioned in Si Lḥussein's account was until Baba's death the leader of the anti-Baba faction, a faction that sought the support of Ayt ʿAṭṭa. Inside the qṣar these factions mostly concerned the white Ḥarâr, charged by the black Ḥarâtîn of having a *n-niya dyâl l-fitna,* a "will to fitna." Yet with the institutionalization of the Tulut and Tletayn factions something changed (or at least this is how the matter is reckoned in the light of today's fitna). For the first time the Ḥarâtîn were split, drawn by the Ḥarâr into opposed factions; having lost the unanimity of their word, they lost (it is said today) their word altogether.

82. "Grabbing tameskert" is the most poignant expression of the intention to kill.

83. Finding sanctuary at a zâwya is what was customarily done in case of murder, the sacred territory belonging to a lineage of holy descent. It could not be any zâwya: each village or group of villages in the Draʿ was related to a particular zâwya, according to the local configuration of political alliances. If the victim was a man, the killer and the close male members of his descent group (the inheritance group) had to retreat within the inviolable boundaries of a zâwya and could not leave for a year, or risk becoming a target of revenge. If the victim was a woman or a child, the period of retreat was six months. At the end of this seclusion (a means of protection as well as of purification), the members of the holy lineage, who had taken the killer under their protection, would send an envoy—often accompanied by a procession of children—to the village of the victim (in this case it is a *maḥdra,* a group of children learning the Qurʿan). The envoy would first slaughter a cow at the gate of the village—an offering for the whole community—then another at the threshold of the house of the victim. The relatives of the dead man could choose not to accept the offer and perpetuate the state of war. The setting of the *dbîḥa,* "sacrificial victim," on fire is the most aggressive response possible.

84. The sanctuary of Sîdî Ṣâfu—a tomb with a dome—is outside the ramparts, at the center of the threshing floors. Once a person has died outside the village walls, the body cannot be carried through the village gate into the qṣar. Only the living can enter. This is why the remains of Moḥammed u Saʿid (like the bodies of all those who died in the gardens) were taken to Sîdî Ṣâfu to be washed and prepared for burial. This practice is still observed, when someone dies in the gardens. If, although wounded, a person is still alive, he or she is brought back to the house. The symbolism of the village gate—and of every gate—is such that the dead can only go out and should never come in.

85. *Debḥu ʿalîhum* implies the sense of making an appeal, a request for forgivenness, paying back, etc.

86. Ayt Unir is the name of one of the groups of the Berber tribal confederation of Ayt ʿAṭṭa. Names of other Ayt ʿAṭṭa groups mentioned in Si Lḥussein's account are Ayt Isful and Ayt Mskûr. (See Spillman, *Les Ait Atta du Sahara;* D. Hart, *Dadda ʿAtta and His Forty Grandsons* [Cambridge: Middle East and North African Studies Press, 1981].)

The events Si Lḥussein is reporting are related to an Ayt ʿAṭṭa offensive in the Draʿ (against the Glâwî and the villages that had fallen under their influence) for a final partition of the territory before the arrival of the French army. Within the space of two years the Ayt ʿAṭṭa groups and their allies managed to eliminate every "big man" in the region, to invade and occupy some ten important villages, and to impose their protectorate over many others. Among the traumatic events were the razing of Teyrsut in 1927, the murder of Baba in Bni Zoli, and the invasion of Zawyât al-Qâḍî in 1928, with the symbolic execution of the Qâḍî (judge) and the burning of all the written records kept at his house.

After the murder of Baba, sheikh of Bni Zoli, the pro–ʿAyt ʿAṭṭa faction took over internally, and the Ayt ʿAṭṭa imposed their rule over the qṣar. The protectorate was reckoned a "pact of brotherhood," *tata* in Berber; according to this pact two Ayt ʿAṭṭa groups, Ayt Isful and Ayt Mskûr, divided the people of Bni Zoli among themselves. For this partition, they followed the traditional split of the qṣar into four fourths (*arbaʿ rbaʿ*). Ayt Isful took the Fourths of Ayt Driss and Ayt j-Jdîd, while Ayt Mskûr took the Fourths of Ayt ʿAbdallah and Ayt l-Bâlî. The Berbers did not live in the qṣar; they settled in the village of Teyrsut (which they had occupied a year earlier but had the right to request work corvées and a meal any time they asked. The rule of *tata* was such that each man from Ayt ʿAṭṭa was assigned an individual household in Bni Zoli. The pact did entail some reciprocity; if the "protected" family was indigent, the protector had an obligation to provide, as happened in a few cases. For a discussion of comparable situations of "protection" in nearby areas, see F. De La Chapelle, "Une cité de l'Oued Draʿ sous le protéctorat des nomades: Nesrat," *Hespéris* 9 (1929): 29–43. In his social historical study of the region of Tafilelt, Larbi Mezzine (*Le Tafilalt: Contribution à l'histoire du Maroc aux 17 et 18 siècles* [Rabat: Publications de la Faculté des Lettres et Sciences Humaines, 1987]) discusses extensively the role of the Ayt ʿAṭṭa in that southern oasis, and the sociopolitical and juridical internal organization of the qṣûr in that region. His work is of crucial comparative interest from the point of view of the Wâd Draʿ. See also A. al-Bû Zîdî, *Al-târîkh al-ijtimâʿî li-Darʿa, qarn 17–20* (Casablanca: Afâq Mutawassitiyya, 1994).

At their arrival in 1932 the French froze the situation they found, thus legitimizing Ayt ʿAṭṭa rule over the qṣûr they had taken by force. Ironically, the proud anti-French Ayt ʿAṭṭa found themselves under the protection of the colonial administration. In 1930 the so-called *dahir berbère* (Berber edict) had instituted separate jurisdictions for the different ethnic groups, and for the first time in the history of the Maghreb an Arab-Berber divide was applied to judicial matters. Berber-speaking populations were referred to newly created *tribunaux coutumiers,* "customary courts," while Arabic-speaking ones were referred to Islamic Law courts. A *tribunal coutumier* was opened in Zagora, where disputes among Ayt ʿAṭṭa were settled in Berber and French, according to the *ʿurf,* "custom," while all the other disputes concerning the local sedentary populations were assigned to an Islamic Law court. What the French did, in fact, was to invent and establish a local tradition. Up to that moment everyone in the Draʿ valley, whether Berber, Arab, Ḥarâr, or Ḥarâtîn, followed the custom of the qbîla for criminal matters, and went to the Islamic Law judge for civil matters (disputes over property, inheritance, marriage and divorce, etc.).

As for the villages occupied by the Ayt ʿAṭṭa in the 1920s, a lawsuit is pending (put forward by the descendants of those who lost their houses and land) to establish who has the right to settle there.

87. These are names of sanctuaries/saints in the region surrounding the qṣar. Si Moḥammed u Saʿid is a saint whose zâwya is located in the village of Tafetchna (Si

Lḥussein's homeland). Si Moḥamed u Brahim of Aghalal is a sanctuary located in the qṣar of Aghalal, a few miles from Bni Zoli. Sîdî Aḥmed Ben Naser is the well-known Zâwya Naṣiriya, located in Tamgrout, thirty miles south of the qṣar.

88. It is a vocabulary of rape: Teyrsut, beside being feminine in the grammatical form of its Berber name, is also treated as feminine in this context.

89. Lḥassan of Teyrsut and Baba Ḥadda of Taghallil were the sheikhs of the two neighboring villages allied with Bni Zoli.

90. The brother of the man who had been killed in the water fight.

91. The same problem discussed earlier, but in the reverse form. The dead have to be carried out of the village gate as soon as possible after dying, or the village could be contaminated. In this case the gate was closed, and the qṣar was in a state of siege. Baba's body is buried in a little mosque located in the Dyâr l-Makhzen, which symbolically did not belong to the territory of the qṣar.

92. Si Moḥamed al-Saghir was the last descendant of a scholarly family that for generations had represented Islamic Law (*ash-shra*ʿ) in the Draʿ. Until the razing of the village and the murder of the last qâḍî, the judge held court at his house.

93. Ifli is the main canal that brings water in from the river. The course of the river is punctuated by *uggug* (Berber), dams that detour the water into big canals like Ifli which, in turn, carry the water inland and feed the irrigation networks of each village or groups of villages. Each big irrigation canal serves a group of villages that share all the privileges and obligations related to the use of its water. *Izugla* is where the water of Ifli is divided into the three canals that bring the water inside the gardens. Since the control of the water was (and is) strategic for the survival of the villages, warfare used to gravitate to the points of access to water: *fum Ifli,* "the mouth of Ifli" at the river, and Izugla. There were two ways of cutting the water of a village or a region: the first was to break the *uggug,* the dam in the river. The second was to obstruct the "mouth" of Ifli, or to make it change its course and waste its waters in the desert without reaching Izugla.

94. Here the term *murabiṭ* is used in the literal sense of tied, *majdûb,* madman and visionary with mystical foresight.

95. *Ameggaru tqarmshas* (Tashelḥit; *tlâni khwat lih* in Arabic), the last blow is empty, the last blows empty, the last is empty-handed. The phrase has a sexual connotation of impotence, an empty ejaculation. In the interpretation of most people, it is a prophecy about the "last" of the great people, who lost the word and became "impotent."

96. Nobody dared to take the dates because, like the blood of sacrifice, they were ritually dangerous. They partook of the violence of the murder of Baba. As an event, this potlatch of Ayt ʿAmmi ʿAmar's dates—which is paralleled by the (ritual) destruction of their houses, even the doors, and by the cold, systematic distribution of the spoils, down to the smallest objects, among the various chiefs of Ayt ʿAṭṭa—sheds light on the meaning of Baba's murder for the people of the qṣar, and explains the place of this traumatic memory in local recollection. (A manuscript I found in a family archive of the qṣar supports the oral recollection in every sense. It is a record of the division of the spoils between the chiefs of the Ayt ʿAṭṭa groups, written in their presence, and signed by a local notary. It lists all the items of the house's wealth: rugs, silver and copper trays, glasses, the doors, wheat and barley reserves, dried onions and carrots, and finally the animals in the stables.)

In Si Lḥussein's recollection the murder of Baba is experienced as a sacrifice: similarly, if in a different sense, the killing of Moḥamed u Saʿid. Only sacrificial murders are remembered in the history of Bni Zoli's fitna. This explains the sense of pollution attached to Ayt Baba's things. Piled up in a mound by the village gate, no one dared to touch their dates. This is more than just a way of shaming Ayt Baba. The power of those dates has to do with the sacrifice of Baba—of him as father (*baba* is what children call their father in the qṣar). Cf. R. Girard, *La violence et le sacré* (Paris: Seuil, 1969).

97. The switching of registers is even more pronounced in the unedited version of Si Lḥussein's recitation, which I have cut for the sake of readability. His recollection is at the same time a moral assessment of the recent history of the village that adopted him, and an autobiographical account of the circumstances that caused him to lead the life of an exile. The story does not end where I cut it, but returns to the personal register. Si Lḥussein goes back to the death of his father, when the "hand of the family had been cut" and he lived with his mother and his sister a stranger in a foreign land. Still a young boy, he was sent to work in Bû Zergân, a neigboring village inhabited by Roḥâ Arabs, who did not understand his Berber tongue and did not give him enough to eat. His recollection then turns to a story of betrayal of the ancestral land itself, when he was tricked by his paternal uncle into marrying his first cousin, who then refused to be a wife for him and forced her father to take her back home.

98. W. Benjamin, *Theses on the Philosophy of History*, in *Illuminations*, trans. H. Zohn (New York: Schocken Books, 1969), 257.

99. W. Benjamin, *Ursprung des deutschen Trauerspiels* (1928; Frankfurt: Suhrkamp Verlag, 1963). I use the Italian translation, *Il dramma barocco tedesco*, trans. E. Filippini (Torino: Einaudi, 1971). The page references refer to the Italian edition; the translation is mine.

100. Ibid., 250.

101. Ibid., 202.

102. Ibid., 220. Cf. M. De Certeau, *La fable mystique* (Paris: Gallimard, 1982).

103. Benjamin, *Trauerspiels*, 191.

104. Ibid., 219.

105. Ibid., 240, 246.

106. Kateb Yacine, *Nedjma* (Paris: Seuil, 1956), 174. "He filled the pipe and began again, slowly, distinctly, his eyes fixed on the foot of the Rock: 'Not the remains of the Romans. Not that kind of ruins, where the soul of the multitudes has only time to waste away, engraving their farewell in the rock, but the ruins watermarked from all time, the ruins steeped in the blood of our veins, the ruins we carry in secret, without ever finding the place or the time suitable for seeing them: the inestimable ruins of the present'" (*Nedjma*, trans. R. Howard [Charlottesville: University of Virginia Press, 1991], 232).

107. J. L. Borges, "The Circular Ruins," in *Labyrinths: Selected Stories and Other Writings*, ed. D. A. Yates and J. E. Irby (New York: New Directions, 1962–64), 50.

108. *Aqallâl* is a genre of oral poetry popular among the people of the qṣûr. Singing is accompanied by drums and by clapping.

109. *Ighrem* in Berber means qṣar, "village" or "fortified village." Thus these names mean the "village of Ugjgal," etc. (Cf. part 2, "Ḥasab and Nasab.") *Iger* means "garden," "cultivated plot."

110. The two poems I am quoting here are oral compositions in the genre of

rasma from the Wâd Draʿ region. (See "Impasse of the Angels" for a discussion of this poetry.) "She burned me with her foreign tongue" is an old poem, which I recorded from the late Sheikh Abdallah of Birshât. I owe the text of "We have fallen under the rule of a Stranger" to the poet Mohammed El Agidi in Zagora. This poem is a historical *qaṣida* from the turn of the century, and it is today sung by several oral poets in the Draʿ. The quotations below are also from this poem.

111. See Massignon, "Le temps dans la pensée Islamique," in *Opera minora,* for a philosophical discussion of the factor of discontinuity and break (*rupture*) as constitutive of what Massignon views as a generalized perception of temporality in Islam.

112. For the "Arab-Muslim acculturation" at the Norman court of Palermo, see R. Ettinghausen, *Arab Painting* (Geneva: Albert Skira, 1977). For a discussion of the hybrid cultural milieu of the Sicilian and other European courts at the beginning at the time of the Crusades, see M. Rodinson, *La fascination de l'Islam* (Paris: Maspero, 1980). For biographical information, see the article on al-Idrîsî in *The Encyclopedia of Islam,* ed. B. Lewis et al., vol. 3 (London: Brill, 1979); R. Dozy and M. De Goeje, *Description de l'Afrique et de l'Espagne par Edrisi* (Leiden, 1866).

113. Al-Idrîsî, *Kitab nuzhat al-mushtâq fî 'ikhtirâq al-âfâq,* the book of diversions for those who have a passion for peregrinations in faraway regions.

114. There are a number of versions of al-Idrîsî's map. Besides the planisphere, or global representation of the world, there is usually a map for each section of the seven climates, which was used to accompany and illustrate the narrative text. The version I use was published by K. Miller in *Mappae arabicae:* "Charta Rogeriana: Wiederhegestellt und herausgegeben" (Stuttgart: Konrad Miller, 1926).

115. Al-Idrîsî, *Kitâb nuzhat al-mushtâq,* trans. P. Jaubert, *Géographie d'Edrisi* (Paris, 1836), 349–50; my translation from the French.

116. "A proverb, one might say, is a ruin which stands on the site of an old story and in which a moral twines about a happening like ivy around a wall" (W. Benjamin, "The Storyteller," in *Illuminations,* ed. H. Arendt, trans. H. Zohn [New York: Schocken Books, 1969], 108).

117. Ayt Ḥaddiddu is a Tamazight-speaking (Berber) group from the High Atlas Mountains, as is Ayt ʿAṭṭa.

118. The idiom of "breaking"—*l-hers*—is central in the social memory of the Draʿ. In historical recollection it is the way violent invasions and razings are referred to. The famous alliteration by which the massacre of the village of Teyrsut is reckoned in the social memory is *ḥît thersat Tayrsût,* "when Teyrsut broke up" (cf. Si Lḥhussein's narrative). *L-hers* is also the technical term for "fracture" in the language of traditional bonesetting; and the idiom *Ayt Fulân therrsu,* "the family of so-and-so was broken," speaks of a major crisis, which may be social, political, or moral, or may refer to the loss of property and wealth.

119. *Arḥabi,* "the widening," or "the courtyard," is the open space now located at the center of the qṣar. See part 1, "Topology of a City."

120. Note how memory is spatialized. The space of the village, its alleys, its houses, like the space of the gardens, with its irrigation canals, is a theater for recollection.

121. Pulling out the poles is a magical act: a family/house is a *rasm,* symbolized by an utâd, a pole or stake dug in the ground—originally a tent pole—a fixed refer-

ence point. (Cf. the discussion about the utâd in part 2, "Ḥasab and Nasab.") The metal utâd in the wall are symbolically like all utâd, stakes; people hang tools and clothes from them. The first day after a wedding the female relatives of the bride come to the house of the groom, where the bride has just moved, and *key-rasmûha*, "settle her in." They hammer the utâd into the walls, and expose her possessions in a public display. To pull out the stakes from the walls means divorce. It expresses the wish to destroy the family of the husband.

122. A *gerruj* is an old water jug with the head and the handle cut off; only the round belly of the jug is left. It is used to store grains, and it is treated in discourse as a not very noble object. It is viewed as feminine, or rather as an image of a castrated masculinity. The two masculine parts of the water jug (*gulla*), are in fact the head (*râs l-gulla*) and the handle (*l-idd*), both missing in the *gerruj*. The play on the image of the headless water jug in the story, therefore, is doubly interesting. The *gerruj* is a mutilated jug—the ruined remains of a *gulla*. The sterile woman is told to fill it with feces—the remains of the body. Issues of castration, pollution, contamination, fermentation, death, and life are raised by the story, which recalls the narrative of Adam and Ḥawwa, and the origin of the mortal world from excrement (cf. part 2).

123. I. Calvino, "Leggerezza" (Lightness), in *Lezioni Americane* (Milan: Garzanti, 1988).

124. "To see her," writes J. P. Vernant of Medusa, "one has to enter the field of her *fascinum* at the risk of losing himself," and continues: "Le monstrueux dont nous parlons a ceci de characteristique qu'on le peut aborder que de face, dans un affrontement direct de la Puissance qui exige, pour qu'on la voie, qu'on entre dans la champ de sa fascination, avec le risque de s'y perdre. Voir la Gorgone c'est la regarder dans les yeux et, par le croisement des regards, cesser d'être soi meme, d'être vivant, pour devenir, comme elle, Puissance de mort. Dévisager Gorgo c'est, dans son oeil, perdre la vue, se transformer en pierre, aveugle et opaque" (*La mort dans les yeux: Figures de l'Autre dans la Grèce ancienne* [Paris: Hachette, 1985]).

125. In "Leggerezza" Calvino discusses the myth of Medusa as an allegory of the craft of writing. After killing Medusa, he says, Perseus carries her head around in a bag; he does not repudiate the monsters of his world; so does, or should do, the writer.

126. The technique Si Lḥassan calls *l-istinzâl*, "the descent" or "the bringing down," and which is generally known in southern Morocco under this name, is referred to in other regions as *l-maḥalla*, "the occupation," after the name of the sultan's army. In magical texts—such as those cited by Si Lḥassan—the technique is designated as *istiḥaḍâr al-jinn*, "the summoning or presentment of the jinn." A version of this chapter on the *istinzâl* was presented at the Séminaire du Symbolique, Institut Universitaire de la Recherche Scientifique, Rabat, May 1991. For a theoretical discussion of a related therapeutic technique, see S. Pandolfo, "Rapt de la voix," *Awal Cahiers d'Études Berbères*, no. 15 (1997): 31–50.

127. *Aders* (Tashelḥit) in Moroccan Arabic is called *dâḥis*. It is a much feared illness, a gangrene—often of the hand—which usually begins from a small cut, a thorn in a finger or the like, and spreads rapidly through the body until, people say, it reaches the heart and causes death. *Aders* is often suspected to be of magical origin. Like other illnesses of magical origin, it is said to "thin the blood," turn it into a

yellowish water, and draw the life (rûḥ) out of the person. Si Lḥassan's brother was killed by a gangrene of the hand in the space of four days.

128. Mohamad al-Tlamsânî al-Maghribî, *Sirr al-asrâr fî istiḥaḥâr al-jinni* (Secret of secrets concerning the presentment/summoning of the jinn).

129. J. L. Borges, "Averroe's Search," in *Labyrinths*, 154.

130. M. Blanchot, *L'espace littéraire* (Paris: Seuil, 1955), 358.

131. Benjamin, "Storyteller," 91.

132. *Qisma*, root *qsm*, means "partition," and in this context is the technical legal name of inheritance documents in which the estate of the father is divided among the children.

133. *T'alalut* is a Berber word meaning "hallway," "narrow path," and in the vocabulary of built space it means a "compound alley." It is related to the Arabic *'alawa*, "to be high, elevated." This is probably because these hallway-streets have very high ceilings.

134. "The possessed woman raises a double-edged question. On the one hand, it involves the possibility of acceding to the speech of the other, which is effectively the problem facing historians: what can we apprehend from the discourse of an absent being? How can we interpret documents bound to an insurmountable death, that is to say, to another period of time, and to an 'ineffable' experience always approached from an outside evaluation? On the other hand, there is the study of the alteration of language through possession" (M. De Certeau, *The Writing of History*, trans. T. Conley [New York: Columbia, 1988], 244).

135. A. Kilito, *L'auteur et ses doubles: Essai sur la culture arabe classique* (Paris: Seuil, 1985), 17. Kilito'a analysis of classical Arabic poetry emphasizes the centrality of the factors of "forgetting," "ruin," "absence," "loss," "scattered remains," as both the motivational drive of poetical inspiration and the structural principle of its composition, the making of its *ars poetica*. The condition of the classical Arab poet, a "melancholic archeologist," writes Kilito, is by definition that of a man contemplating "un campement en ruine," the remains of a former settlement. For ruin and forgetting are the necessary ingredients of his poetical craft. Bearer of a word that exists and can be heard only in the framework of repetition, "le poéte a pour tâche de dessiner sur un dessin, d'écrire sur de l'écriture à demi éffacée. . . . Face à une écriture en ruine, il faut bien que le poète y mette du sien pour qu'un nouveau campement voie le jour" (21). (The task of the poet is to draw over a drawing, to write over a text half-effaced. Confronted with writing in ruin, the poet must add something of his own for a new settlement to be born [my translation].)

136. Ibn Khaldûn, *Muqaddima*, 3:376–77. For a discussion of the motif of *al-aṭlâl* (or *al-ṭulûl*, "the remains or traces," "an abandoned settlement") in the classical *qaṣida*, see J. E. Bencheikh, *Poétique arabe* (Paris: Gallimard, 1975); Kilito, *L'auteur et ses doubles;* A. Hamori, *The Art of Medieval Arabic Literature* (Princeton: Princeton University Press, 1974). "It can be safely said that the *aṭlâl* motif is the most dramatic among the various *nasîb*-themes [introductory section of the *qaṣida*]—such as the description of parting, or a dream-visit by the lady's phantom—in that it contrasts the irreversible time of human experience with the recurrences possible in nature. . . . In the *aṭlâl* scene time present has no effective contents to speak of. The past has a specific burden; the present is indeterminate except by reference to a memory. The speaker arrives at a desolate but familiar spot; we are not told what

business led him there . . . in this way, the emptiness at the conclusion of the affair is given a depth of time. . . . The *aṭlâl* are the point where the temporal and spatial coordinates meet" (Hamori, *Art of Medieval Arabic Literature,* 17–19).

137. In his book *Morte e pianto rituale* (Milan: Boringhieri, 1958), Ernesto De Martino calls this condition of derealization "crisi di cordoglio" (crisis of mourning) or "crisi della presenza" (crisis of presence). De Martino borrows the expression "crisis of presence" from Sartre.

138. In writing about the uncanniness of the photographic image (and images in general), Roland Barthes calls "intractable reality" this being-absent manifested as presence (*Camera Lucida: Reflections on Photography,* trans. R. Howard [New York: Noonday Press, 1981], originally published as *La chambre claire* [Paris: Seuil, 1980]).

139. The poem that follows belongs to a different genre of oral poetry, called *rekba* (see below). Here I am just considering its content thematically: the image of the "broken wings," and of *l-hûl* as a paralysis of the imaginary.

140. *Biya deggêt l-maʿlûm,* which, following the explication of poets, I translated as "I am love-struck," literally means "in me are strikes of the well known."

141. I am glossing the colloquial use, especially in oral poetry. But also in literary Arabic, *al-hawl,* from the root *hwl* (to frighten, terrify, scare, appall, horrify, strike with terror), means terror, fright, shock, horror, dismay, and, interestingly, power (*Hans Wehr Dictionary of Modern Written Arabic*).

142. As does instead the little Ernst of the Freudian tale in *Beyond the Pleasure Principle.* Reacting to the experience of his mother's daily absence, Freud's Ernst inscribes that trauma into a game and reenacts it symbolically. He puts her absence dialectically at work into a language, and manages to master it. The game is "the Fort-Da" (gone/there). The boy throws a wooden reel under the bed, to later make it reappear by pulling the string that he holds in his hand. Freud explains: "At the outset he was in a passive situation—he was overpowered by the experience; but, by repeating it, unpleasurable though it was, as a game, he took on an active part. These efforts might be put down to an instinct for mastery" (Freud, *Beyond the Pleasure Principle,* 15). Freud's interpretation, however, is questioned by the development of his own text on repetition compulsion and the death instinct (cf. Derrida, "To Speculate—on Freud," in *The Postcard* [Chicago: University of Chicago Press, 1987]), where a certain "adialectical" quality of death is exposed which exceeds the possibility of symbolic mastery and is inscribed in the work of symbolization itself.

143. The different genres of poetry I am discussing here are not specific to the qṣar, but to a number of surrounding villages inhabited by (only) Arabic-speaking people: the Roḥâ Arabs, a sedentary group that still keeps a vivid memory of the values and the narratives of Arab nomadic culture, and the Awlâd Yaḥya Arabs, also sedentary, but among whom are still found some seminomadic groups. Even though the sedentary people of the qṣar and other kin villages (inhabited by Ḥarâr/Ḥarâtîn populations) have their own poetry, and until recently each qṣar had its organized performance group (*l-ʿawam* or *l-ʿâmma*) lead by a sheikh, poetry as such does not occupy such a central and encompassing place in the imagination of the qṣar dwellers, where reflection around themes of loss, life, and death is rather found in the historical narratives. The people of the qṣar look upon the neighboring Arabs as "the poets" and are impressed by their mastery of poetic language, a vocabulary that is sometimes opaque to them and in itself more hermetic than the poetic vocabulary

with which they are familiar. Yet the two traditions are in close contact, for marriages between the Arab villages and the qṣar have become extremely common.

144. Borges, "Circular Ruins," 50.

145. *Kelmât taʿt lâlâ: kelmât* (more commonly *klâm*) is the plural of *kelma,* "word." In the poetic vocabulary of this region a "word" is a poem, of a variable number of "stanzas" (*byût,* sing. *bît*), depending on the genre. In the genre sung by Belqasem, a "word" has always three verses, each verse (*bît*) composed of two halves. *Lâlâ* is the colloquial name for a genre called *rekba* (see below), from the modulation at the beginning of each sung poem, "le le le . . . le."

146. Cf. *Storia della musica,* a cura della società italiana di musicologia, vol. 1, G. Comotti, *La musica nella cultura greca e romana,* and vol. 2, G. Cattin, *Il medioevo* (Torino: EDT, 1979).

147. From the classical root *ghyẓ,* which in colloquial speech is pronounced *ḍ.* In the glossing of poets (who don't know how to write), it merges with the root *ghḍḍ,* which from a constellation of words indicating freshness, tenderness, and so forth, is used in poetry to connote femininity (*l-ghîḍât* means "the girls"). But the sense of fury and overflowing is by far the dominant one, so that sometimes poets say the *l-gûl kayṭlaʿ ʿala l-ḥîḍ u ʿala l-fîḍ,* where *l-fîḍ* is "the flood."

148. *ʿAllgû b-nunâtu,* literally "bound up in *n* letters," for in Arabic script the letter *n* is shaped like a horseshoe (ن).

149. *Dergûh tnaya,* literally "the Pairs hide him." The Pairs are the mountain passes. The gender reference of these poems is almost always in the masculine, because the masculine "hides" the feminine (like the mountain passes hide the object of longing). To respect this convention, I leave in the masculine the reference when it is masculine in the Arabic.

150. *Jâḥat l-ʿqel qbel ijîh ṣûm,* "the mind was flooded before fasting age," means that he was in love before even reaching puberty and the age of reason (which in Islam correspond to the age when an adolescent starts fasting in the month of Ramadan). In other words, he lost his reason before even having it.

151. *L-meftûm* (passive participle of *faṭama,* "to wean"), is the weaned, the child weaned from the mother's breast—a paradigmatic image of separation and loss. The poem plays with the similarity of sound between *l-meftûm* and *l-meftûn,* passive participle of *fatana* (from which the noun *l-fitna* derives), which would designate here the person who is madly in love.

152. Cauterization surgery, *l-kîy,* is still widely practiced in the region, and the memory of kiyyât is marked in the body of most. For a scholarly treatise on this technique, see Abû al-Qâsim (Albucasis), *On Surgery and Instruments,* ed. and trans. M. S. Spink and G. L. Lewis, bilingual edition (London: Wellcome Institute of the History of Medicine, 1973).

153. *L-klâm,* plural of *l-kelma,* can be translated as both "words" and "speech, discourse." But inasmuch as in this context it is understood as the plural of *kelma* in the sense of "poem," I prefer the literal translation "words." In the context of poetry *l-klâm* (or *l-klamât*) is equivalent to *l-gûl,* "the saying," which is poetry.

154. For a discussion of ritual repetition in the genre and formulaic structure of the classical qaṣida, see Hamori, *The Art of Medieval Arabic Literature,* "The Poet as Hero," "The Poet as Ritual Clown," "Two Views of Time."

155. W. Benjamin, "Agesilaus Santander," in G. Scholem, "Walter Benjamin and

His Angel," reprinted in *On Walter Benjamin: Critical Essays and Recollections*, ed. G. Smith (Cambridge: MIT Press, 1988).

156. M. Blanchot, *L'arrêt de mort* (Paris: Gallimard, 1948).

157. S. Freud, "Mourning and Melancholia" (1917), trans. J. Riviere, in *General Psychological Theory: Papers on Metapsychology*, ed. P. Rieff (New York: Macmillan, 1963). Quotes below are from pp. 165–66, 174.

158. I wish to express my gratitude to the poets who have patiently helped me interpret and explain their poems and the craft of poetry, in particular, Mohammed Ben Hammou, Mohammed El Agidi, Sheikh Mohammed Bû Lwyda, and Sheikh Abdallah of Birshât. Sheikh Mohammed and Sheikh Abdallah have since died. I dedicate this chapter to the memory of Sheikh Mohammed.

159. When used in the sense of poem, poetic composition, I will translate the term *kelma* (or *kalîma*) as "Word," capitalized.

160. *L-hijâ'* is from the verb *hajâ*, root *hjw*, which in classical Arabic means "to satirize" and "to compose defamatory poems." In Sheikh Moḥammed's technical vocabulary, and in general in the poetic use of the Dra', *l-hijâ'* carries a much stronger sense of a speech that wounds, effective speech, which is thrown like gunfire and "touches" (*mess*) the body of its recipient. Sheikh Moḥammed distinguishes between *klâm dyâl l-hijâ'*, "the words of the *hijâ*," words that hurt, and *klâm dyâl l-lûma*, "words of blame," insult or satire. The latter are unpleasant, but do not "touch" their addressee: "they are like shooting gunfire without bullets," he says.

161. For a suggestive approach to the study of poetic imagery in classical Arab poetry and rhetorics, see K. Abu Deeb, *Al-Jurjânî's Theory of Poetic Imagery* (Warminster, England: Aris and Phillips, 1979). Abu Deeb discusses al-Jurjânî's theory of *naẓm*, "construction" (tenth century), which he views as the central concept of his theoretical works on poetics. Not unlike Sheikh Moḥammed's use of the notions of *naḥû*, "grammar," and *tarâkîb*, "structure" or "construction," along with the concept of "black words," al-Jurjânî's concept of naẓm is based on a semiotic approach to poetic composition, in which what counts is not the meaning or content of a particular figure, but its value in a poetic configuration of form-content, what he calls *sûrat al-ma'na*, the "image of the meaning." In this configuration, "the whole that is created is a structure based on inner relations, on the interaction of the created elements."

"When someone wants to judge the distinction or lack of distinction of any species [or form of activity], he must base his judgement entirely on such characteristics and aspects that are inherent in the very essence of this [form of activity]. . . . And it is known that the nature of discourse (*kalâm*) is the same as that of image-making and silver-work, whereas the nature of the content (*ma'nâ*) which is being conveyed is that of the material upon which image-making and silver-work are carried out, such as silver or gold, when a ring or bracelet is made of them. As it is absurd for you, if you want to judge the making of a ring . . . to consider the silver or gold in which the picture is worked, so is absurd, if you want to discover where the distinction and high quality of discourse lie, to examine only its meaning. . . . Similarly, if we prefer one line of poetry to another because of its meaning, we will not be preferring it as poetry and expression (*kalâm*)" (al-Jurjânî, cited in Abu Deeb, *Al-Jurjânî's Theory of Poetic Imagery*, 51–52).

162. Al-Jurjânî, cited in Abu Deeb, *Al-Jurjânî's Theory of Poetic Imagery*, 52.

163. Literally "the hole" or "the unfathomable," from *ghârâ,* root *ghwr.* The theory of "names" is a theory of metaphor.

164. In classical Arab treatises of poetics a similar argument about metaphorical meanings and veiled words is developed in terms of the image of the shell, which hides the "other meaning" within it and is inaccessible to most (A. Kilito, "Sur le métalangage métaphorique des poéticiens arabes," *Poétique* 38 [1979]: 172): "Il n'est pas donné au premier venu d'accéder au *maʿnâ* second, qui ne se livre pas directement à la connaissance. . . . Pour retirer la perle, il faut auparavant briser la coquille qui l'emprisonne. . . . On en arrive alors à l'idée du 'voile' jeté sur le *maʿnâ* second, voile qu'il faut amoureusement 'déchirer.' Le plaisir sera à la mesure de la difficulté vaincue lors de cette quête du sens." (It is not for the first comer to gain access to the other *maʿnâ,* which withdraws from direct knowledge. To take the pearl, one must first break the shell where this is captured. And we get to the idea of the "veil" cast over the "other" meaning, a veil that must be lovingly "torn." The pleasure attained will be relative to the difficulty overcome in this quest of sense [my translation].) I would like to thank Abdelfattah Kilito for mentioning the classical model of the "pearl" in a dialogue with the theory of "black words" and the model of the "staircase" proposed by the oral poets from the Draʿ.

165. I am thinking here of the debates in classical Arabic poetics between the supporters of the "doctrine of words" (*lafẓ*), stating that the value of a poetic composition has to do with the beauty of the lexicon and the choice of individual words and their sounds, and the supporters of the theory of construction (structure), naẓm, arguing that the value of a composition depends on the internal harmony of the whole, and the way its organization of form and content is a poetic transfiguration of the real. See ibid. Sheikh Moḥammed's approach is somewhere between the two positions.

166. "Si la parole ne se répétait pas, elle disparaîtrait" (Ibn Rashîq, an eleventh-century scholar of poetics, cited and translated from Arabic by Kilito, *L'auteur et ses doubles,* 19).

167. W. Benjamin, "The Work of Art in the Age of Mechanical Reproduction," in *Illuminations,* ed. H. Arendt, trans. H. Zohn (New York: Schocken Books, 1969). These reflections on poetry could be read in counterpoint with Benjamin's argument.

168. A. Kilito, *L'auteur et ses doubles,* 21, my translation. Kilito cites this text from Ibn al-Manẓûr, *Akhbâr Abî Nuwâs,* and from A. Trabulsi, *La critique poétique des Arabes jusqu'au 5me siècle de l'hégire* (Damas, 1955).

169. Kilito, *L'auteur et ses doubles,* 20, 22, my translation.

170. For a discussion of the concept and practice of *ṭbaʿ,* see Bencheikh, *Poétique arabe,* chap. 4, "Les modes de la création."

171. A classical theme in the history of Arabic poetics is the debate between the advocates of poetic talent solely understood as "true inspiration" and "natural disposition," an immediacy expressed by the term *ṭbaʿ;* and those poets and rhetoricians who argued on the side of *ṣinâʿa,* "composition," "technique or craft." Jamel Eddine Bencheikh (*Poétique arabe*) reflects extensively on this debate, arguing for the side of *ṣinâʿa* and for the position of classical scholars of poetics such as Ibn Rashîq, Ibn Qutayba, and Ibn Khaldûn. In questioning the ideology of authenticity and immediate inspiration, from the point of view of poetry as a praxis, Bencheikh stresses the role of memory and technique: "A well trained memory, accustomed to the repeti-

tion of innumerable verses, the habit of using images whose proliferation must not hide the kinship . . . Such brilliant exercises are the result of an acquired automatism" (80, my translation).

In Bencheikh's view it is Ibn Khaldûn who best captured the dialectics of repetition and creation, improvisation and learned technique with the notion of *uslûb*, the aquired mental "form"—or style—which functions as a "mold" from which poets renew their compositions. In his critique of the theme of revelation and of the poet's creation "in trance," however—"une production dont sa conscience ne saurait être maitresse" (a production that his consciousness could not master and author, 77)—Bencheikh overemphasizes in my view the demiurgic role of the artist's consciousness and agency, and the individuality of his (her) subjective creation. If *la parole poétique*, poetic speech as individual utterance, is always the result of multiple repetitions and of "other voices" half audible in watermark, if, as in the case reported by Kilito, the poet must memorize and forget a library of other poems in order to be able to compose, then the poetic utterance is never fully one's own, always plural and hybrid; and the speaker is always spoken, somewhat, by a *parole* originating elsewhere.

172. "The fugue stops at the point where the three first themes, which are unrelated to the basic theme, are combined with each other. . . . It is perfectly possible to combine these three themes with the themes of the whole cycle. . . . The third theme begins with the notes F-flat, A-C-B: B-A-C-H; it is surprising that the composer had not used this musical signature before since he must have been quite conscious of it. . . . Was this superstition? Mystical fear? Was the use of the notes B-A-C-H linked here with the monumental book called *The Art of the Fugue* or even that of the composer's entire work?" (H. Eppstein, "Die Kunst der Fugue," program notes for the compact disk *Die Kunst der Fugue*, recorded by Hesperion 20, Astrée-Auvidis).

173. For a historical and stylistic discussion of the classical poetic genre of the qaṣida, see Bencheikh, *Poétique arabe;* Hamori, *The Art of Medieval Arabic Literature;* Ibn Khaldûn, *Muqaddima*, vol. 3.

174. *R-rîḥ*, air, breath, or wind, is formed from the same root as *r-rûḥ*, the "breath of life" or "spirit." The rîḥ could be understood as a sort of spirit of the poem, somewhere between the rîḥ wind that moves it, and the rûḥ spirit that holds it together and keeps it alive.

175. Discontinuity does not prevent the poem from having a "bodily" integrity of its own. Writing about connection and disconnection in the context of the classic qaṣida (a genre characterized by the independence of the individual verse and the coded succession of themes—from erotic love to the praise of a prince, the description of a caravan and the lament on ruins), Bencheikh argues for continuity, but in the musical sense. Elaborating on Ibn Khaldûn's considerations on verse, he writes of the poem as a "continuous suite," stitched together by the interlacing of language, and by a certain *à venir du discours*, which announces, through the verses, something to come, something that remains unresolved in the verses: "For Ibn Khaldun a poem is a continuous suite, an ensemble within which the verse is inserted. The verse is not just the vehicle of a meaning, a message delivered at once: it foretells a discursive advent. In that furrow which is a register, or even more precisely a theme, motifs are brought together, mixed or enchained, which only language intertwines and joins. Movement does not derive from a logical succession of thoughts; it resides

in the flow of speech [*verbe*], which captures in a succession the adjoining enunciations. The Arab verse is not independent because it has no connection with the verse that follows it, but because it can be disconnected from it without being mutilated" (*Poétique arabe*, 151, my translation).

176. In *Poétique arabe* Bencheikh introduces the issue of the human body as measure by citing a remark by Ibn al-Athîr: "Each verse is sufficient to itself [*qâ'im bi-dâtihi*]. . . . Given that the time of breathing cannot exceed the time [*durée*] of the hemistichs of a single verse . . . the enunciation must be interrupted." In other words, Bencheikh comments, the length of the verse corresponds to the length of an average breath; and "it is precisely measured by the breath [*souffle*] that allows a person to pronounce it." Married to the breath by way of the meter, the verse "searches its rhythms in the body of the poet" (*Poétique arabe*, 151).

177. Historically, this poem speaks of the Great Fitna of the Draʿ valley in the period immediately preceeding the arrival of the French. Loss and destruction are mourned from the point of view of the Roḥâ Arabs, who at that point in time were opposed to the French and to the Glâwî. Reference to the Drawâ as enemies—the sedentary population of the qṣûr, Ḥarâr and Ḥarâtîn—is because the Drawâ (in the eyes of the Arabs) were allied with the Glâwî; yet, more precisely, they were under the Glâwî's jug.

178. *Tamdet* (Tashelḥit Berber), "pond" or "swamp." In the vocabulary of the house it is the built pond where the waste waters of the house gather and then disperse underground.

179. J. Genet, *L'atelier d'Alberto Giacometti* (Paris: Arbalete, 1954), 29–30, 44.

180. J. Genet, "The Studio of Alberto Giacometti," in *The Selected Writings of Jean Genet*, trans. E. White (Hopewell, NJ: Ecco Press, 1993), 318, 328, translation slightly modified.

EPILOGUE

1. "May God grant you endurance" is the formula that is repeated to people in mourning after the first moment of loss.

2. In the houses there are only dry toilets, where the feces are collected under a hole and then, mixed with straw and other waste materials, are made into an organic compost. Only in the washing room of the mosque, because of the running water from the well, the fecal material is liquid and black, like that of a city sewer.

Acknowledgments

This book belongs to those—in the qṣar and in the Draʿ valley—who actively participated in its making. Without their intellectual and affective investment it would never have been written.

The friendship with Hadda (Ahmed Chebli) shaped the text and my life. His input is visible throughout.

Brahim Dagdid participated in the work through the years, welcomed me as a member of his household, sat with me through many of the conversations in the book, contributed to the interpretation-transcription of tapes, and came to the United States in 1987 to help me revise the written rendition of oral texts. Most chapters were discussed with him at one time or another.

Khadija Soqa is the interlocutor and friend who remains, nine years after her death, a haunting presence in my work. Abdellah Dagdid, Mina Lhussein, Zohra Dagdid, Lalla Fatima, and the late Si Lhussein shared with me stories, recollections, and thoughts.

L-Hajj l-Madani Tazgert was until his death in 1995 a passionate teller of stories. I owe to him many of the historical accounts of the period preceding the French conquest of the Draʿ valley. Fatima Miloud is the Shahrazad of many nights and days. She opened her oral library of tales and guided me through the feminine knowledge of bodies, processes, and spaces. A dear friend over the years, Fatima Lhussein is the muqaddema who introduced me to the ritual life of the qṣar. Mina Moha, Tatta Mohammed, and Tama Hadda gave me lessons on weaving and shared the fun and the burden of daily life.

I owe to Mohammed Ben Hammou the encounter with the errant seed of the poetical word. Nights spent at poetical sessions, days at analyzing poems on my tape recorder. Thanks also to Ahmed Ben Hammou, Lalla Shto, Dawya, and their children, who are now grown up; and to the young men of

Zawyât Tafrust, who welcomed my presence at their performances, recited and explained poems for me, and made possible many wonderful nights.

The work on poetry would not have been possible without the patient teachings of Sheikh Mohammed Bû Lwyda, who made his art accessible for me. His recent death was a loss. The late Sheikh Abdallah passed on to me his oral repertory of old *rasma* poems ("She burned me with her foreign tongue" is from him). Mohammed El Agidi—a poet who writes—helped me with the interpretation and the transcription of many difficult passages. It is in his voice that I first recorded "Tell me Sunken Well." In addition, I am grateful for permission to reprint a number of poems by Antonin Artaud. "Ci-Gît," "La recherche de la fécalité," and "L'exécration père-mère" in "Dossier d'Artaud le Mômo" originally appeared in *Oeuvres complètes* (Paris: Gallimard, 1956), vols. 12 and 13, © Editions Gallimard, reprinted by permission of Editions Gallimard. "Here Lies" (the translation of "Ci-Gît") and "The Pursuit of Fecality" (the translation of "La recherche de la fécalité") originally appeared in *Antonin Artaud: Selected Writings,* trans. H. Weaver (New York: Farrar, Straus & Giroux, 1976); translation copyright © 1976, reprinted by permission of Farrar, Straus & Giroux.

With scholarly generosity and intellectual curiosity, Si Mohammed u Brahim Debbah engaged with me over the years in an ongoing conversation on dreaming, mystical knowledge and, recently, psychoanalysis. L-Hajj Lhassan Kuwway and the late Faqir Mohammed introduced me to the medical arts of bone setting and cauterization surgery.

Throughout the work and after, Mohammed Chahid has been an invaluable friend and a challenging critical counterpoint. Hassan u Baba's awareness of power relations has been for me a constant reminder of the political implications of any historical work on memory.

Mohammed Toumi is the author of the map of the qṣar. Without his invaluable gift this work would not have been the same. Finally, I am grateful to those who gave me access to their family collections of written documents, and participated in long and exciting document-reading sessions.

The district authorities in the province of Ouarzazat and in the *cercle* of Zagora, and the Office Régionale de Mise en Valeur Agricole gave me crucial help at the outset of the research and throughout. The research from which this book originated was sponsored in 1984–86 by a fellowship from the Social Science Research Council, a Wenner-Gren Foundation grant, and a grant from the National Science Foundation. Further research trips were partly funded by a Rockefeller postdoctoral fellowship at the Center for Cultural Studies, Rice University, and by the University of California, Berkeley.

In Morocco, the United States, and France, friends and fellow scholars have generously discussed with me over the years the work that led to this book;

have helped, encouraged, disagreed, offered comparative insight or an engaged listening. Some read and criticized a version, or several versions, of this text. In different ways, all contributed to its shaping, and I thank them.

Abdelhaï Diouri, Timothy Mitchell, and Vincent Crapanzano have been, at different stages, influential interlocutors. They marked the questioning that runs through the work. Hildred Geertz and Gananath Obeyesekere passed on to me their interpretive sensibility and sense of respect. Jeanne Favret-Saada challenged me to write as a subject. Abdelfattah Kilito offered precious comparative insight on classical poetics, and shared a preoccupation with discourses of contradiction and diversity. Ahmed Toufiq invited me as a fellow at the Institut des études africaines in Rabat, offered a forum of debate, and provided orientation in the field of Sufi Islam. Michael Fischer and João Guilherme Biehl read closely versions of the manuscript and offered perceptive and constructive criticism. The ongoing dialogue with Paul Rabinow enriched and invigorated the last rewriting of the text. With a vigilant critical gaze, Mariane Ferme provided affective and intellectual support. Alan Dundes had faith in what he called a "Fellinian ethnography." Brinkley Messick participated in the inception of the work, offered encouragement and advice, and help in the work with documentary sources. Cosmopolitan intellectual companions, Jalal Toufic shared an interest in the Arab aesthetic of representation, Françoise Vergès in postcolonial visions.

Writer Cecile Pineda generously read the entire manuscript twice, offered enormous support and precious literary advice. With poetic sensibility and care, Katy Lederer edited the manuscript and made it better. Mustapha Kamal helped me establish the system of Arabic transcription, edited Arabic citations throughout the text, and revised the translations of poetry. Joann Hoy skillfully and patiently copyedited the manuscript for the University of Chicago Press. Natasha Schüll read closely the final version of the manuscript and composed the index. Artist Mohamed Bennani offered one of his paintings as the cover of the book.

I am also grateful to Halima Farhat, Abdelkebir Khatibi, Lila Abu-Lughod, Abdellah Hammoudi, Uday Mehta, Mario Biagioli, George Marcus, Steven Tyler, Nadine Tanio, Lawrence Rosen, Abdelahad Sebti, and Hakima Lebbar, each of whom provided insightful comments along the way.

I owe special debts to David Brent of the University of Chicago Press, the editor and friend who encouraged and defended this text, and made its publication possible; to my mother, Maria Nives Riccio; to my father, Arturo Pandolfo, who found, perhaps, in the voices from the qṣar, echoes from his forgotten childhood; and to Mohammed Hamdouni Alami, Fouch, interlocutor, critic, friend, and husband, who made my life, and this book, better.

index